N. YORK HARPER & BROTHERS 1848

HISTORY

OF

THE GIRONDISTS;

OR,

Personal Memoirs of the Patriots

OF

THE FRENCH REVOLUTION

FROM UNPUBLISHED SOURCES

BY

ALPHONSE DE LAMARTINE

Author of "Travels in the Holy Land," etc.

IN THREE VOLUMES.

VOL. I.

TRANSLATED BY H. T. RYDE.

NEW YORK:

HARPER & BROTHERS, PUBLISHERS

329 & 331 PEARL STREET

FRANKLIN SQUARE.

1868.

ADVERTISEMENT.

We have not thought it necessary to preface this recital by any introduction of the preceding epochs of the Revolution.

We have not re-produced, with the minute elaboration of an annalist, the numerous parliamentary and military details of all the events of these forty months. Two or three times we have, in order to group men and circumstances in masses, made unimportant anachronisms.

We have written after having scrupulously investigated facts and characters: we do not ask to be credited on our mere word only. Although we have not encumbered our work with notes, quotations, and documentary testimony, we have not made one assertion unauthorized by authentic memoirs, by unpublished manuscripts, by autograph letters, which the families of the most conspicuous persons have confided to our care, or by oral and well-confirmed statements gathered from the lips of the last survivors of this great epoch.

If some errors in fact or judgment have, notwithstanding, escaped us, we shall be ready to acknowledge them and repair them in sequent editions, when the proofs have been transmitted to us. We shall not reply one by one to such denials and contradictions as this book may give rise to; it might be a tedious and unprofitable paper-war in the newspapers. But we will make notes of every observation, and reply *en masse*, by our proofs and tests, after a certain lapse of time. We seek the truth only, and should blush to make our work a calumny of the dead.

As to the title of this book, we have only assumed it, as being unable to find any other which can so well define this recital, which has none of the pretensions of history, and therefore should not affect its gravity. It is an intermediate labor between history and memoirs. Events do not herein occupy so much space as men and ideas. It is full of private details, and details are the physiognomy of characters, and by them they engrave themselves on the imagination.

Great writers have already written the records of this memorable epoch, and others still to follow will write them also. It would be an injustice to compare us with them. They have produced, or will produce, the history of an age. We have produced nothing more than a "study" of a group of men and a few months of the Revolution.

A. L.

Paris, March 1, 1847.

CONTENTS.

BOOK I.

BOOK II.

BOOK III.

BOOK IV.

BOOK V.

BOOK VI.

BOOK VII.

BOOK VIII.

BOOK IX.

BOOK X.

BOOK XI.

BOOK XII.

BOOK XIII.

BOOK XIV.

BOOK XV.

BOOK XVI.

HISTORY OF THE GIRONDISTS.

BOOK I.

I.

INTRODUCTION.

I NOW undertake to write the history of a small party of men who, cast by Providence into the very centre of the greatest drama of modern times, comprise in themselves the ideas, the passions, the faults, the virtues of their epoch, and whose life and political acts forming, as we may say, the nucleus of the French Revolution, perished by the same blow which crushed the destinies of their country.

This history, full of blood and tears, is full also of instruction for the people. Never, perhaps, were so many tragical events crowded into so short a space of time, never was the mysterious connection which exists between deeds and their consequences developed with greater rapidity. Never did weaknesses more quickly engender faults,—faults crimes,—crimes punishment. That retributive justice which God has implanted in our very acts, as a conscience more sacred than the fatalism of the ancients,* never manifested itself more unequivocally; never was the law of morality illustrated by a more ample testimony, or avenged more mercilessly. Thus the simple recital of these two years is the most luminous commentary of the whole Revolution; and blood, spilled like water, not only shrieks in accents of terror and pity, but gives, indeed, a lesson and an example to mankind. It is in this spirit I would indite this work. The impartiality of history is not that of a mirror, which merely reflects objects, it should be that of a judge who sees, listens,

* See an elegant exposition of this idea in Schlegel's Dramatic Literature (Standard Library Edition, page 67.)

and decides. Annals are not history; in order to deserve that appellation it requires a conviction; for it becomes, in after times, *that* of the human race.

Recital animated by the imagination, weighed and judged by wisdom,—such is history as the ancients understood it; and of history conceived and produced in such a spirit, I would, under the Divine guidance, leave a fragment to my country.

II.

HISTORY OF THE GIRONDISTS.

MIRABEAU had just died. The instinct of the people led them to press around the house of his tribune, as if to demand inspiration even from his coffin; but had Mirabeau been still living, he could no longer have given it; his star had paled its fires before that of the Revolution; hurried to the verge of an unavoidable precipice by the very chariot he himself had set in motion, it was in vain that he clung to the tribune. The last memorial he addressed to the king, which the Iron Chest has surrendered to us, together with the secret of his venality, testify the failure and dejection of his mind. His counsels are versatile, incoherent, and almost childish:—now he will arrest the Revolution with a grain of sand—now he places the salvation of the Monarchy in a proclamation of the crown and a regal ceremony which shall revive the popularity of the king,—and now he is desirous of buying the acclamations of the tribune, and believes the nation, like him, to be purchasable at a price. The pettiness of his means of safety are in contrast with the vast increase of perils; there is a vagueness in every idea; we see that he is impelled by the very passions he has excited, and that unable any longer to guide or control them, he betrays, whilst he is yet unable to crush, them. The prime agitator is now but the alarmed courtier seeking shelter beneath the throne, and though still stuttering out terrible words in behalf of the nation and liberty, which are in the part set down for him, has already in his soul all the paltriness and the thoughts of vanity which are proper to a court. We pity genius when we behold it struggling with impossibility. Mirabeau was the most potent man of his time; but the greatest individual contending with an enraged element appears but a madman. A fall is only majestic when accompanied by virtue.

Poets say that clouds assume the form of the countries over which they have passed, and moulding themselves upon the valleys, plains, or mountains, acquire their shapes and move with them over the skies. This resembles certain men, whose genius being as it were acquisitive, models itself upon the epoch in which it lives, and assumes all the individuality of the nation to which it belongs. Mirabeau was a man of this class: he did not invent the Revolution, but was its manifestation. But for him it might perhaps have remained in a state of idea and tendency. He was born, and it took in him the form, the passion, the language which make a multitude say when they see a thing—There it is.

He was born a gentleman and of ancient lineage, refugee and established in Provence, but of Italian origin: the progenitors were Tuscan. The family was one of those whom Florence had cast from her bosom in the stormy excesses of her liberty, and for which Dante reproaches his country in such bitter strains for her exiles and persecutions. The blood of Machiavel and the earthquake genius of the Italian republics were characteristics of all the individuals of this race. The proportions of their souls exceed the height of their destiny: vices, passions, virtues are all in excess. The women are all angelic or perverse, the men sublime or depraved, and their language even is as emphatic and lofty as their aspirations. There is in their most familiar correspondence the color and tone of the heroic tongues of Italy.

The ancestors of Mirabeau speak of their domestic affairs as Plutarch of the quarrels of Marius and Sylla, of Cæsar and Pompey. We perceive the great men descending to trifling matters. Mirabeau inspired this domestic majesty and virility in his very cradle. I dwell on these details, which may seem foreign to this history, but explain it. The source of genius is often in ancestry, and the blood of descent is sometimes the prophecy of destiny.

III.

Mirabeau's education was as rough and rude as the hand of his father, who was styled the *friend of man*, but whose restless spirit and selfish vanity rendered him the persecutor of his wife and the tyrant of all his family. The only virtue he was taught was honor, for by that name in those days they dignified that ceremonious demeanor which was too frequently but the show of probity and the elegance of vice.

Entering the army at an early age, he acquired nothing of military habits except a love of licentiousness and play. The hand of his father was constantly extended not to aid him in rising, but to depress him still lower under the consequences of his errors: his youth was passed in the prisons of the state; his passions, becoming envenomed by solitude, and his intellect being rendered more acute by contact with the irons of his dungeon, where his mind lost that modesty which rarely survives the infamy of precocious punishments.

Released from jail, in order, by his father's command, to attempt to form a marriage beset with difficulties with Mademoiselle De Marignan, a rich heiress of one of the greatest families of Provence, he displayed, like a wrestler, all kinds of stratagems and daring schemes of policy in the small theatre of Aix. Cunning, seduction, courage, he used every resource of his nature to succeed, and he succeeded; but he was hardly married, before fresh persecutions beset him, and the stronghold of Pontarlier gaped to enclose him. A love, which his *Lettres à Sophie* has rendered immortal, opened its gates and freed him. He carried off Madame de Monier from her aged husband. The lovers, happy for some months, took refuge in Holland; they were seized there, separated and shut up, the one in a convent and the other in the dungeon of Vincennes. Love, which, like fire in the veins of the earth, is always detected in some crevice of man's destiny, lighted up in a single and ardent blaze all Mirabeau's passions. In his vengeance it was outraged love that he appeased; in liberty, it was love which he sought and which delivered him; in study, it was love which still illustrated his path. Entering obscure into his cell, he quitted it a writer, orator, statesman, but perverted—ripe for anything, even to sell himself, in order to buy fortune and celebrity. The drama of life was conceived in his head, he wanted but the stage, and that time was preparing for him. During the few short years which elapsed for him between his leaving the keep of Vincennes and the tribune of the National Assembly, he employed himself with polemic labors, which would have weighed down another man, but which only kept him in health. The Bank of Saint Charles, the Institutions of Holland, the books on Prussia, the skirmish with Beaumarchais, his style and character, his lengthened pleadings on questions of warfare, the balance of European power, finance, those biting invectives, that war of words with the ministers or men of the hour, resembled the Roman forum in the days of Clodius and Cicero. We discern the men of antiquity in even his most modern controversies. We may fancy that we hear the first roarings of those popular tumults which were so soon to burst forth, and which his voice was destined to control. At the first election of Aix, rejected with contempt by the *noblesse,* he cast himself into the arms of the people, certain of making the balance incline to the side on which he should cast the weight of his daring and his genius. Marseilles contended with Aix for the great plebeian; his two elections, the discourses he then delivered, the addresses he drew up, the energy he employed, commanded the attention of all France. His sonorous phrases became the proverbs of the Revolution; comparing himself, in his lofty language, to the men of antiquity, he placed himself already in the public estimation in the elevated position he aspired to reach. Men became accustomed to identify him with the names he cited; he made a loud noise in order to prepare minds for great commotions; he announced himself proudly to the nation in that sublime apostrophe in his address to the Marseillais: "When the last of the Gracchi expired, he flung dust towards heaven, and from this dust sprung Marius! Marius, less great for having exterminated the Cimbri than for having prostrated in Rome the aristocracy of the nobility."

From the moment of his entry into the National Assembly he filled it: he was the whole people. His gestures were commands; his movements *coups d'état.* He placed himself on a level with the throne, and the nobility felt itself subdued by a power emanating from its own body. The clergy, which is the people, and desires to reconcile the democracy with the church, lends him its influence, in order to destroy the double aristocracy of the nobility and bishops.

All that had been built by antiquity and cemented by ages fell in a few months. Mirabeau alone preserved his presence of mind in the midst of this ruin. His character of tribune ceases, that of the statesman begins, and in this he is even greater than in the other. There, when all else creep and crawl, he acts with firmness, advancing boldly. The Revolution in his brain is no longer a momentary idea—it is a settled plan. The philosophy of the eighteenth century, moderated by the prudence of policy, flows easily, and modelled from his lips. His eloquence, imperative as the law, is now the talent of giving force to reason. His language lights and inspires everything; and though almost alone at this moment, he has the courage to remain alone. He braves envy, hatred, murmurs, supported by the strong feeling of his superiority. He dismisses with disdain the passions which have hitherto beset him. He will no longer serve them when his cause no longer needs them. He speaks to men now only in the name of his genius. This title is enough to cause obedience to him. His power is based on the ascent which truth finds in all minds, and his strength again reverts to him. He contests with all parties, and rises superior to one and all. All hate him because he commands; and all seek him because he can serve or destroy them. He does not give himself up to any one, but negotiates with each: he lays down calmly on the tumultuous element of this assembly, the basis of the reformed constitution: legislation, finance, diplomacy, war, religion, political economy, balances of power, every question he approaches and solves, not as an Utopian, but as a politician. The solution he gives is always the precise mean between the theoretical and the practical. He places reason on a level with manners, and the institutions of the land in consonance with its habits. He desires a throne to support the democracy, liberty in the Chambers, and in the will of the nation, one and irresistible in the government. The characteristic of his genius, so well defined, so ill understood, was less audacity than justness. Beneath the grandeur of his expression is always to be found unfailing good sense. His very vices could not repress the clearness, the sincerity of his understanding. At the foot of the tribune he was a man devoid of shame or virtue: in the tribune he was an honest man. Abandoned to private debauchery, bought over by foreign powers, sold to the court in order to satisfy his lavish expenditure, he preserved, amidst all this infamous traffic of his powers, the incorruptibility of his genius. Of all the qualities of a great man of his age, he was only wanting in honesty. The people were not his devotees, but his instruments,—his own glory was the god of his idolatry; his faith was posterity; his conscience existed but in his thought; the fanaticism of his idea was quite human; the chilling materialism of his age had crushed in his heart the expansion, force, and craving for imperishable things. His dying words were "sprinkle me with perfumes, crown me with flowers, that I may thus enter upon eternal sleep." He was especially of his time, and his course bears no impress of infinity. Neither his character, his acts, nor his thoughts have the brand of a mortality. If he had believed in God, he might have died a martyr, but he would have left behind him the religion of reason and the reign of democracy. Mirabeau, in a word, was the reason of the people; and that is not yet the faith of humanity!

IV.

Grand displays cast a veil of universal mourning over the secret sentiments which his death inspired to all parties. Whilst the various belfries tolled his knell, and minute guns were fired: whilst, in a ceremony that had assembled two hundred thousand spectators, they awarded to a citizen the funeral obsequies of a monarch; whilst the Pantheon, to which they conveyed his remains, seemed scarcely a monument worthy of such ashes,—what was passing in the depths of men's hearts?

The king, who held Mirabeau's eloquence in pay, the queen, with whom he had nocturnal conferences, regretted him, perhaps, as the last means of safety: yet still he inspired them with more terror than confidence; and the humiliation of a crowned head demanding succor from a subject must have felt comforted at the removal of that destroying power which itself fell before the throne did. The court was avenged by death for the affronts it had undergone. He was to the nobility merely an apostate from his order. The climax of its shame must have been to be one day raised by him who had abased it. The National Assembly had grown weary of his superiority; the Duc d'Orleans felt that a word from this man would unfold and crush his premature aspirations; M. de La Fayette, the hero of the *bourgeoisie,* must have been in dread of the orator of the people. Between the dictator of the city and the dictator of the tribune there must have been a secret jealousy. Mirabeau, who had never assailed M. de La Fayette in his discourses, had often in conversation allowed words to escape with respect to his rival which print themselves as they fall on a man. Mirabeau the less, and then M. de La Fayette appeared the greater, and it was the same with all the orators of the Assembly. There was no longer any rival, but there were many envious. His eloquence, though popular in its style, was that of a patrician. His democracy was delivered from a lofty position, and comprised none of that covetousness and hate which excite the vilest passions of the human heart, and which see in the good done for the people nothing but an insult to the nobility. His popular sentiments were in some sort but the liberality of his genius. The vast expansiveness of his mighty soul had no resemblance with the paltry impulses of demagogues. In acquiring rights for the people he seemed as though he bestowed them. He was a volunteer of democracy. He recalled by his part, and his bearing, to those democrats behind him, that from the time of the Gracchi to his own, the tribunes who most served the people had sprung from the ranks of the patricians. His talent, unequalled for philosophy of thought, for depth of reflection, and loftiness of expression, was another kind of aristocracy, which could never be pardoned him. Nature placed him in the foremost rank; and death only created a space around him for secondary minds. They all endeavored to acquire his position, and all endeavored in vain. The tears they shed upon his coffin were hypocritical. The people only wept in all sincerity, because the people were too strong to be jealous, and they, far from reproaching Mirabeau with his birth, loved in him that nobility as though it were a spoil they had carried of from the aristocracy. Moreover, the nation, disturbed at seeing its institutions crumbling away one by one, and dreading a total destruction, felt instinctively that the genius of a great man was the last stronghold left to them. This genius quenched, it saw only darkness and precipices before the monarchy. The Jacobins alone rejoiced loudly, for it was only he who could outweigh them.

It was on the 6th of April, 1791, that the National Assembly resumed its sittings. Mirabeau's place, left vacant, reminded each gazer of the impossibility of again filling it; consternation was impressed on every countenance in the tribunes, and a profound silence pervaded the meeting. M. de Talleyrand announced to the Assembly a posthumous address of Mirabeau. They would hear him though dead. The weakened echo of his voice seemed to return to his country from the depths of the vaults of the Pantheon. The reading was mournful. Parties were burning to measure their strength free from any counterpoise. Impatience and anxiety were paramount, and the struggle was imminent. The arbitrator who controlled them was no more.

V.

Before we depict the state of these parties, let us throw a rapid glance over the commencement of the Revolution, the progress it had made, and the principal leaders who were about to attempt directing it in the way they desired to see it advance.

It was hardly two years since opinion had opened the breaches against the monarchy, yet it had already accomplished immense results. The weak and vacillating spirit of the government had convoked the Assembly of Notables, whilst public spirit had placed its grasp on power and convoked the States General. The States General being established, the nation had felt its omnipotence, and from this feeling to a legal insurrection there was but a word; that word Mirabeau had uttered. The National Assembly had constituted itself in front of, and higher than, the throne itself. The prodigious popularity of M. Necker was exhausted by concessions, and utterly vanished when he no longer had any of the spoils of monarchy to cast before the people. Minister of a monarch in retirement, his own had been utter defeat. His last step conducted him out of the kingdom. The disarmed king had remained the hostage of the ancient *régime* in the hands of the nation. The declaration of the rights of man and citizen, the sole metaphysical act of the Revolution to this time, had given it a social and universal signification. This declaration had been much jeered; it certainly contained some errors, and confused in terms the state of nature and the state of society; but it was, notwithstanding, the very essence of the new dogma.

VI.

There are objects in nature, the forms of which can only be accurately ascertained when contemplated afar off. Too near, as well as too far off, prevents a correct view. Thus it is with great events. The hand of God is visible in human things, but this hand itself has a shadow which conceals what it accomplishes. All that could then be seen of the French Revolution announced all that was great in this world, the advent of a new idea in human kind, the democratic idea, and afterwards the democratic government.

This idea was an emanation of Christianity. Christianity finding men in serfage and degraded all over the earth, had arisen on the fall of the Roman Empire, like a mighty ven geance, though under the aspect of a resignation. It had proclaimed the three words which 2000 years afterwards were re-echoed by French philosophy—liberty, equality, fraternity—amongst mankind. But it had for a time hidden this idea in the recesses of the Christian heart. As yet too weak to attack civil laws, it had said to the powers—"I leave you still for a short space of time possession of the political world, confining myself to the moral world. Continue if you can to enchain, class, keep in bondage, degrade the people, I am engaged in the emancipation of souls. I shall occupy 2000 years, perchance, in renewing men's minds before I become apparent in human institutions. But the day will come when my doctrines will escape from the temple, and will enter into the councils of the people; on that day the social world will be renewed."

This day had now arrived; it had been prepared by an age of philosophy, sceptical in appearance but in reality replete with belief. The scepticism of the 18th century only affected exterior forms, and the supernatural dogmata of Christianity, whilst it adopted with enthusiasm, morality and the social sense. What Christianity called revelation, philosophy called reason. The words were different, the meaning identical. The emancipation of individuals, of castes, of people, were alike derived from it. Only the ancient world had been enfranchised in the name of Christ, whilst the modern world was freed in the name of the rights which every human creature has received from the hand of God; and from both flowed the enfranchisement of God or nature. The political philosophy of the Revolution could not have invented a word more true, more complete, more divine than Christianity, to reveal itself to Europe, and it had adopted the dogma and the word of *fraternity*. Only the French Revolution attacked the form of this ruling religion; because it was incrusted in the forms of government, monarchical, theocratic, or aristocratic, which they sought to destroy. It is the explanation of that apparent contradiction of the mind of the 18th century, which borrowed all from Christianity in policy, and denied, whilst it despoiled, it. There was at one and the same time a violent attraction and a violent repulsion in the two doctrines. They recognized whilst they struggled against each other, and yearned to recognize each other even more completely when the contest was terminated by the triumph of liberty.

Three things were then evident to reflecting minds from and after the month of April, 1791; the one, that the march of the revolutionary movement advanced from step to step to the complete restoration of all the rights of suffering humanity—from those of the people by their government, to those of citizens by castes, and of the workman by the citizen; thus it assailed tyranny, privilege, inequality, selfishness, not only on the throne, but in the civil law; in the administration, in the legal distribution of property, in the conditions of industry, labor, family, and in all the relations of man with man, and man with woman: the second,—that this philosophic and social movement of democracy would seek its natural form in a form of government analogous to its principle, and its nature; that is to say, representing the sovereignty of the people; republic with one or two heads; and, finally, that the social and political emancipation would involve in it the intellectual and religious emancipation of the human mind; that the liberty of thought, of speaking and acting, should not pause before the liberty of belief; that the idea of God confined in the sanctuaries, should shine forth pouring into each free conscience the light of liberty itself; that this light, a revelation for some, and reason for others, would spread more and more with truth and justice, which emanate from God to overspread the earth.

VII.

Human thought, like God, makes the world in its own image.

Thought was revived by a philosophical age.

It had to transform the social world.

The French Revolution was therefore in its essence a sublime and impassioned spirituality. It had a divine and universal ideal. This is the reason why its passion spread beyond the frontiers of France. Those who limit, mutilate it. It was the accession of three moral sovereignties:

The sovereignty of right over force;

The sovereignty of intelligence over prejudices;

The sovereignty of people over governments.

Revolution in rights; equality.

Revolution in ideas; reasoning substituted for authority.

Revolution in facts; the reign of the people.

A Gospel of social rights.

A Gospel of duties, a charter of humanity.

France declared itself the apostle of this creed. In this war of ideas France had allies everywhere, and even on thrones themselves.

VIII.

There are epochs in the history of the human race, when the decayed branches fall from the tree of humanity; and when institutions grown old and exhausted, sink and leave space for fresh institutions full of sap, which renew the youth and recast the ideas of a people. Antiquity is replete with this transformation, of which we only catch a glimpse in the relics of history. Each decadence of effete ideas carries with it an old world, and gives its name to a new order of civilization. The East, China, Egypt, Greece, Rome, have seen these ruins and these renewals. The West experienced them when the Druidical theocracy gave way to the gods and government of the Romans. Byzantium, Rome, and the Empire effected them rapidly, and as it were instinctively by themselves when, wearied with, and blushing at, polytheism, they rose at the voice of Constantine against their gods, and swept away, like an angry tempest, those temples, those ideas and forms of worship, to which the people still clung, but which the superior portion of human thought had already abandoned. The civilization of Constantine and Charlemange grew old in its turn, and the beliefs which for eighteen centuries had supported altars and thrones, menaced the religious world, as well as the political world, with a catastrophe which rarely leaves power standing when faith is staggered. Monarchical Europe was the handiwork of catholicism; politics were fashioned after the image of the Church; authority was founded on a mystery. Rights came to it from on high, and power, like faith, was reputed divine. The obedience of the people was consecrated to it, and from that very reason inquiry was a blasphemy, and servitude a virtue. The spirit of philosophy, which had silently revolted against this for three centuries, as a doctrine which the scandals, tyrannies, and crimes of the two powers belied daily, refused any longer to recognize a divine title in those authorities which deny reason and subjugate a people. So long as catholicism had been the sole legal doctrine in Europe, these murmuring revolts of mind had not overset empires. They had been punished by the hands of rulers. Dungeons, punishments, inquisitions, fire, and faggot, had intimidated reason, and preserved erect the twofold dogma on which the two governments reposed.

But printing, that unceasing outpouring of the human mind, was to the people a second revelation. Employed at first exclusively for the Church, for the propagation of ruling ideas, it had begun to sap them. The dogmata of temporal power, and spiritual power, incessantly assailed by these floods of light, could not be long without being shaken, first in the human mind and afterwards in things, to the very foundations. *Guttemberg*, without knowing it, was the mechanist of the New World. In creating the communication of ideas, he had assured the independence of reason. Every letter of this alphabet which left his fingers, contained in it more power than the armies of kings, and the thunders of pontiffs. It was mind which he furnished with language. These two powers were the mistresses of man, as they were hereafter of mankind. The intellectual world was born of a material invention, and it had grown rapidly. The reformed religion was one of its early offspring.

The empire of catholic Christianity had undergone extensive dismemberments. Switzerland, a part of Germany, Holland, England, whole provinces of France, had been drawn away from the centre of religious authority, and passed over to the doctrine of free examination. Divine authority attacked and contested in catholicism, the authority of the throne remained at the mercy of the people. Philosophy, more-potent than sedition, approached it more and more near, with less respect, less fear. History had actually written of the weaknesses and crimes of kings. Public writers had dared to comment upon it, and the people to draw conclusions. Social institutions had been weighed by their real value for humanity. Minds the most devoted to power had spoken to sovereigns of duties, and to people of rights. The holy boldness of Christianity had been heard even in the consecrated pulpit, in the presence of Louis XIV. Bossuet, that sacerdotal genius of the ancient synagogue, had mingled his proud adulations to Louis XIV. with some of those austere warnings which console persons for their abasement. Fénélon, that evangelical and tender genius, of the new law, had written his instructions to princes, and his Telemachus, in the palace of the king, and in the cabinet of an heir to the throne. The political philosophy of Christianity, that insurrection of justice in favor of the weak, had glided from the lips of Louis XIV. into the ear of his grandson. Fénélon educated another revolution in the Duke of Burgundy. This the king perceived when too late, and expelled the divine seduction from his palace. But the revolutionary policy was born there; there the people read the pages of the holy archbishop: Versailles was destined to be, thanks to Louis XIV. and Fénélon, at once the palace of despotism and the cradle of the Revolution. Montesquieu had sounded the institutions, and analyzed the laws of all people. By classing governments, he had compared them, by comparing, he passed judgment on them; and this judgment brought out, in its bold relief, and contrast, on every page, right and force, privilege and equality, tyranny and liberty.

Jean Jacques Rousseau, less ingenious, but more eloquent, had studied politics, not in the laws, but in nature. A free but oppressed and suffering mind, the palpitation of his noble heart had made every heart beat that had been ulcerated by the odious inequality of social conditions. It was the revolt of the ideal against the real. He had been the tribune of nature, the Gracchus of philosophy—He had not produced the history of institutions, only its vision—but that vision descended from heaven and returned thither. There was to be seen the design of God and the excess of his love—but there was not enough seen of the infirmity of men. It was the Utopia of government; but by this Rousseau led further astray. To impel the people to passion there must be some slight illusion mingled with the truth; reality alone was too chilling to fanaticize the human mind; it is only roused to enthusiasm by things something out of nature. What is termed the ideal is the attraction and force of religions, which always aspire higher than they mount; this is how fanaticism is produced, that delirium of virtue. Rousseau was the ideal of politics, as Fénélon was the ideal of Christianity.

Voltaire had the genius of criticism, that power of raillery which withers all it overthrows. He had made human nature laugh at itself, had felled it low in order to raise it, had laid bare before it all errors, prejudices, iniquities, and crimes of ignorance; he had urged it to rebellion against consecrated ideas, not by the ideal but by sheer contempt. Destiny gave him eighty years of existence, that he might slowly decompose the decayed age; he had the time to combat against time, and when he fell he was the conqueror. His disciples filled courts, academies, and saloons; those of Rousseau grew splenetic and visionary amongst the lower orders of society. The one had been the fortunate and elegant advocate of the aristocracy, the other was the secret consoler and beloved avenger of the democracy. His book was the book of all oppressed and tender souls. Unhappy and devotee himself, he had placed God by the side of the people; his doctrines sanctified the mind, whilst they led the heart to rebellion. There was vengeance in his very accent, but there was piety also. Voltaire's followers would have overturned altars, those of Rousseau would have raised them. The one could have done without virtues, and made arrangements with thrones; the other had absolute need of a God, and could only have founded republics.

Their numerous disciples progressed with their missions, and possessed all the organs of public thought. From the seat of geometry to the consecrated pulpit, the philosophy of the 18th century invaded or altered everything. D'Alembert, Diderot, Raynal, Buffon, Condorcet, Bernardin Saint Pierre, Helvetius, Saint Lambert, La Harpe, were the church of the new era. One sole thought animated these diverse minds—the renovation of human ideas. Arithmetic, science, history, economy, politics, the stage, morals, poetry, all served as the vehicle of modern philosophy; it ran in all the veins of the times; it had enlisted every genius, it spoke every language. Chance or Providence had decided that this period, which elsewhere was almost barren, should be the age of France. From the end of the reign of Louis XIV. to the commencement of the reign of Louis XVI., nature had been prodigal of men to France. This brilliancy continued by so many geniuses of the first order, from Corneille to Voltaire, from Bossuet to Rousseau, from Fénélon to Bernardin Saint Pierre, had accustomed the people to look on this side. The focus of the ideas of the world shed thence its brilliancy. The moral authority of the human mind was no longer at Rome. The stir, light, direction, were from Paris; the European mind was French. There was, and there always will be, in the French genius something more potent than its potency, more luminous than its splendor; and that is its warmth, its penetrating power of communicating the attraction which it has, and which it inspires to Europe.

The genius of the Spain of Charles V. is high and adventurous, that of Germany is profound and severe, that of England skilful and proud, that of France is attractive,—it is in that it has its force. Easily seduced itself, it easily seduces other people. The other great individualities of the world of nations have only their genius. France for a second genius has its heart, and is prodigal in its thoughts, in its writings, as well as in its national acts. When Providence wills that one desire shall fire the world, it is first kindled in a Frenchman's soul. This communicative quality of the character of this race—this French attraction, as yet unaltered by the ambition of conquest,—was then the precursory mark of the age. It seems that a providential instinct turned all the attraction of Europe towards this point, as if motion and light could only emanate thence. The only real echoing point of the Continent was Paris. There the smallest things made great noise, literature was the vehicle of French influence; there intellectual monarchy had its books, its theatre, its writings even before it had its heroes.

Conquering by its intelligence, its printing-presses were its army.

IX.

The parties who divided the country after the death of Mirabeau were thus distributed; out of the Assembly, the Court, and the Jacobins; in the Assembly the right side and the left side, and between these two extreme parties—the one fanatic by its innovations, the other fanatic from its resistance—there was an intermediate party, consisting of the men of substance and peace belonging to both these parties. Their views moderate, and wavering between revolution and conservatism, desired that the one should conquer without violence, and the other concede without vindictiveness. These were the philosophers of the Revolution,—but it was not the hour for philosophy, it was the hour of victory; the two ideas required champions, not judges; they crushed men in their encounter. Let us enumerate the principal chiefs of the contending parties, and make them known before we bring them into action.

King Louis XVI. was then only thirty-seven years of age; his features resembled those of his race, rendered somewhat heavy by the German blood of his mother, a princess of the house of Saxony. Fine blue eyes, very wide open, and clear rather than dazzling, a round and retreating forehead, a Roman nose, the nostrils flaccid and large, and somewhat destroying the energy of the aquiline profile, a mouth smiling and gracious in expression, lips thick, but well shaped, a fine skin, fresh and high-colored in tint, though rather loose; of short stature, stout frame, timid carriage, irregular walk, and when not moving, a restlessness of body in shifting first one foot and then the other without advancing—a habit contracted either from that impatience common to princes compelled to undergo long audiences, or else the outward token of the constant wavering of an undecided mind. In his person there was an expression of *bonhommie* more vulgar than royal, which at the first glance inspired as much derision as veneration, and on which his enemies seized with contemptuous perversity, in order to show to the people in the features of their ruler the visible and personal sign of those vices they sought to destroy in royalty—in the *tout ensemble* some resemblance to the imperial physiognomy of the later Cæsars at the period of the fall of things and races,—the mildness of Antoninus, with the vast obesity of Vitellius;—this was precisely the man.

X.

This young prince had been educated in complete solitude at the court of Louis XV. The atmosphere which had infected the age had not touched his heir. Whilst Louis XV had changed his court into a place of ill-fame, his grandson, educated in a corner of the palace of Meudon by pious and enlightened masters, grew up in respect for his rank, in awe of the throne, and in a real love for the people whom he was one day to be called upon to govern. The soul of Fénélon seemed to have traversed two generations of kings in the palace where he had brought up the Duke of Burgundy, in order to inspire the education of his descendant. What was nearest the crowned vice upon the throne was perhaps the most pure of anything in France. If the age had not been as dissolute as the king, it would have directed his love in that direction. He had reached that point of corruption in which purity appears ridiculous, and modesty was treated with contempt.

Married at twenty years of age to a daughter of Maria Theresa of Austria, the young prince had continued until his accession to the throne in his life of domestic retirement.

study, and isolation. Europe was slumbering in a disgraceful peace. War, that exercise of princes, could not thus form him by contact with men and the custom of command Fields of battle, which are the theatre of great actors of his stamp, had not brought him under the observation of his people. No *prestige*, except the circumstance of birth, clung to him. His sole popularity was derived from the disgust inspired by his grandfather. He occasionally had the esteem of his people, but never their favor. Upright and well-informed, he called to him sterling honesty and clear intelligence in the person of Turgot. But with the philosophic sentiment of the necessity of reforms, the prince had not the feeling of a reformer; he had neither the genius nor the boldness; nor had his ministers more than himself. They raised all questions without settling any, accumulated storms, without giving them any impulse, and the tempests were doomed to be eventually directed against themselves. From M. de Maurepas to M. Turgot, from M. Turgot to M. de Calonne, from M. de Calonne to M. Necker, from M. Necker to M. de Malesherbes, he floated from an honest man to an *intriguant*, from a philosopher to a banker, whilst the spirit of system and charlatanism ill supplied the spirit of government. God, who had given many men of notoriety during this reign, had refused it a statesman; all was promise and deception. The court clamored, impatience seized on the nation, and violent convulsions followed. The Assembly of Notables, States General, National Assembly, had all burst in the hands of royalty; a revolution emanated from his good intentions more fierce and more irritable than if it had been the consequence of his vices. At the time when the king had this revolution before him in the National Assembly, he had not in his councils one man, not only capable of resisting but even of comprehending it. Men really strong prefer in such moments to be rather the popular ministers of the nation than the bucklers of the king.

XI.

M. de Montmorin was devoted to the king, but had no credit with the nation. The ministry had neither the initiative nor opposition; the initiative was in the hands of the Jacobins, and the executive power with the mob. The king without an organ, without privilege, without force, had merely the odious responsibility of anarchy. He was the butt against which all parties directed the hate or rage of the people. He had the privilege of every accusation· whilst from the tribune Mirabeau, Barnave, Pétion, Lameth, and Robespierre, eloquently threatened the throne; infamous pamphlets, factious journals painted the king in the colors of a tyrant who was brutalized by wine, who lent himself to every caprice of an abandoned woman, and who conspired in the recesses of his palace with the enemies of the nation. In the sinister feeling of his coming fall, the stoical virtue of this prince sufficed for the calming of his conscience, but was not adequate to his resolutions. On leaving the council of his ministers, where he loyally accomplished the constitutional conditions of his character, he sought, sometimes in the friendship of his devoted servants, sometimes from the very persons of his enemies, admitted by stealth to his confidence, the most important inspirations. Counsels succeeded to counsels, and contradicted one another in the royal ear, as their results contradicted each other in their operations. His enemies suggested concessions, promising him a popularity which escaped their hands just as they were about to insure it to him. The court counselled the resistance which it had only in its dreams; the queen the courage she felt in her soul; intriguants, corruption, the timid, flight; and in turns, and almost at the same time, he tried all these expedients: not one was efficacious; the time for useful resolutions had passed,—the crisis was without remedy. It was necessary to choose between life and the throne. In endeavoring to preserve the two, it was written that he should lose both.

When we place ourselves in imagination in the position of Louis XVI., and ask what could have saved him? we reply disheartened—nothing. There are circumstances which enfold all a man's movements in such a snare, that, whatever direction he may take, he falls into the fatality of his faults or his virtues. This was the dilemma of Louis XVI. All the unpopularity of royalty in France, all the faults of preceding administrations, all the vices of kings, all the shame of courts, all the griefs of the people, were as it were accumulated on his head, and marked his innocent brow for the expiation of many ages. Epochs have their sacrifices as well as their religions. When they desire to recast an institution which no longer suits them, they pile upon the individual who personifies this institution all the odium and all the condemnation of the institution itself,—they make of this man a victim whom they sacrifice to the time. Louis XVI. was this innocent sacrifice, overwhelmed with all the iniquities of thrones, and destined to be immolated as a chastisement for royalty. Such was the king.

XII.

The queen seemed to be created by nature to contrast with the king, and to attract forever the interest and pity of ages to one of those state dramas, which are incomplete unless the miseries and misfortunes of a woman mingle in them. Daughter of Maria Theresa, she had commenced her life in the storms of the Austrian monarchy. She was one of the children whom the Empress held by the hand when she presented herself as a supplicant before her faithful Hungarians, and the troops exclaimed, "We will die for our king, Maria Theresa." Her daughter, too, had the heart of a king. On her arrival in France, her beauty had dazzled the whole kingdom,—a beauty then in all its splendor. The two children whom she had given to the throne, far from impairing her good looks, added to the attractions of her person that character of maternal majesty which so well becomes the mother of a nation. The presentiment of her misfortunes, the recollection of the tragic scenes of Versailles, the uneasiness of each day somewhat diminished her youthful freshness. She was tall, slim, and graceful,—a real daughter of Tyrol. Her naturally majestic carriage in no way impaired the grace of her movements; her neck rising elegantly and distinctly from her shoulders gave expression to every attitude. The woman was perceptible beneath the queen, the tenderness of heart was not lost in the elevation of her destiny. Her light-brown hair was long and silky; her forehead, high and rather projecting, was united to her temples by those fine curves which give so much delicacy and expression to that seat of thought or the soul in women; her eyes of that clear blue which recall the skies of the North or the waters of the Danube; an aquiline nose, with nostrils open and slightly projecting, where emotions palpitate and courage is evidenced; a large mouth, brilliant teeth, Austrian lips, that is, projecting and well-defined; an oval countenance, animated, varying, impassioned, and the *ensemble* of these features replete with that expression impossible to describe which emanates from the look, the shades, the reflections of the face, which encompasses it with an iris like that of the warm and tinted vapor which bathes objects in full sunlight—the extreme loveliness which the ideal conveys, and which by giving it life increases its attraction. With all these charms, a soul yearning to attach itself, a heart easily moved, but yet earnest in desire to fix itself; a pensive and intelligent smile, with nothing of vacuity in it, nothing of preference or mere acquaintanceship in it, because it felt itself worthy of friendships. Such was Marie-Antoinette as a woman.

XIII.

It was enough to form the happiness of a man and the ornament of a court; to inspire a wavering monarch and be the safeguard of a state under trying circumstances, something more is requisite. The genius of government is required, and the queen had it not. Nothing could have prepared her for the regulation of the disordered elements which were about her; misfortune had given her no time for reflection. Hailed with enthusiasm by a perverse court and an ardent nation, she must have believed in the eternity of such sentiments. She was lulled to sleep in the dissipations of the Trianon. She had heard the first threatenings of the tempest without believing in its dangers: she had trusted in the love she inspired, and which she felt in her own heart. The court had become exacting, the nation hostile. The instrument of the intrigues of the court on the heart of the king, she had at first favored and then opposed all reforms which prevented or delayed the crisis that arose. Her policy was but infatuation; her system but the perpetual abandonment of herself to every partisan who promised her the king's safety. The Comte D'Artois, a youthful prince, chivalrous in etiquette, had much influence with her: he relied greatly on the noblesse; made frequent references to his sword. He laughed at the crises: he disdained this war of words, caballed against ministers, and treated passing events with levity. The queen, intoxicated with the adulation of those around her, urged the king to recall the next day what he had conceded on the previous evening. Her hand was felt in all the transactions of the government: her apartments were the focus of a perpetual conspiracy against the government; the nation detected it, and ultimately detested her.

Her name became for the people the phantom of all counter-revolution. We are apt to calumniate what we fear. She was depicted under the features of a Messalina. The most infamous pamphlets were in circulation; the most scandalous anecdotes were credited. She may be accused of tenderness, but never of depravity. Lovely, young, and adored, if her heart did not remain insensible, her innermost feelings, innocent perhaps, never gave just ground for open scandal. History has its modesty, and we will not violate it.

XIV.

On the days of the 5th and 6th of October the queen perceived (too late) the enmity of the people; her heart must have been full of vengeance. Emigration commenced, and she viewed it favorably. All her friends were at Coblentz: she was believed to be in close connection with them, and this belief was true. Stories of an Austrian committee were busily spread amongst the people. The queen was accused of conspiring for the destruction of the nation, who at every moment demanded her head. A people in revolt must have some one to hate, and they handed over to her the queen. Her name was the theme of their songs of rage. One woman was the enemy of a whole nation, and her pride disdained to undeceive them. She inclosed herself in her resentment and her terror. Imprisoned in the palace of the Tuileries, she could not put her head out of window without provoking an outrage and hearing insult. Every noise in the city made her apprehensive of an insurrection. Her days were melancholy, her nights disturbed: she underwent hourly agony for two years, and that anguish was magnified in her heart by her love for her two children, and her disquietude for the king. Her court was forsaken; she saw none but the shadows of authority; the ministers forced on her by M. de La Fayette, before whom she was compelled to mask her countenance in smiles. Her apartments were watched by spies in the guise of servants. It was necessary to mislead them, in order to have interviews with the few friends who remained to her. Private staircases, dark corridors, were the means by which at night her secret counsellors obtained access to her. These meetings resembled conspiracies; she left them every time with a different train of ideas, which she communicated to the king, whose behavior thus acquired the incoherence of a woman persecuted and distressed. Measures of resistance, bribing the Assembly, an entire surrender of the constitution, attempts by force, an assumption of royal dignity, repentance, weakness, terror, and flight,—all were discussed, planned, decided on, prepared and abandoned, on the same day. Women, so sublime in their devotion, are seldom capable of the continuous firmness of mind—the imperturbability requisite for a political plan. Their politics are in their heart, their passions trench so closely on their reason. Of all the virtues which a throne requires they have but courage; often heroes, they are never statesmen. The queen was another example of this: she did the king incredible mischief. With a mind infinitely superior, with more soul, more character than he, her superiority only served to inspire him with mischievous counsels. She was at once the charm of his misfortunes and the genius of his destruction; she conducted him step by step to the scaffold, but she ascended it with him.

XV.

The right side in the National Assembly consisted of men, the natural opponents of the movement, the nobility and higher clergy. All, however, were not of the same rank nor the same title. Seditions are found amongst the lower rank, revolutions in the higher. Seditions are but the angry workings of the people—revolutions are the ideas of the epoch. Ideas begin in the head of the nation. The French Revolution was a generous thought of the aristocracy. This thought fell into the hands of the people, who framed of it a weapon against the *noblesse*, the throne, and religion. The philosophy of the saloons became revolt in the streets: nevertheless all the great houses of the kingdom had given apostles to the first dogmata of the Revolution: the States General, the ancient theatre of the importance and triumphs of the higher nobility, had tempted the ambition of their heirs, and they had marched in the van of the reformers. *Esprit de corps* could not restrain them when the question of uniting with the Tiers Etat had been invoked. The Montmorencies, Noailles, La Rochefoucaulds, Clermont Tonnerres, Lally Tollendals, Virieux, d'Aiguillons, Lauzans, Montesquieus, Lameths, Mirabeaus, the Duc d' Orleans, first prince of the blood, the Count de Provence, brother of the king, king himself afterwards as Louis XVIII., had given an impulse to the boldest innovations. They had each borrowed their momentary popularity from principles easier to enunciate than restrain, and that popularity had nearly forsaken them all. So soon as these theorists of speculative revolution saw that they were carried away in the torrent, they attempted to ascend the stream from whose source they had started; some again surrounded the throne, others had emigrated after the days of the 5th and 6th of October. Others, more firm, remained in their places in the National Assembly; they fought without a hope, but still defended a fallen cause, gloriously resolute to maintain at least a monarchical power, and abandoning to the people, without a struggle, the spoils of the nobility and the church. Amongst these are Cazalès, the Abbé Maury, Malouet, and Clermont Tonnerre; they were the distinguished orators of this expiring party.

Clermont Tonnerre and Malouet were rather statesmen than orators; their cautious and reflective language weighed only on the reason; they sought for the mean between liberty and monarchy, and believed they had found it in the system of the Two Houses of English Legislature. The *modérés* of the two parties listened to them respectfully; like all half parties and half talents, they excited neither hatred nor anger; but events did not listen to them, but thrusting them aside, advanced towards results that were utterly absolute. Maury and Cazalès, less philosophic, were the two champions of the right side; different in character, their oratorical powers were much on a par. Maury represented the clergy, of which body he was a member; Cazalès, the *noblesse*, to whom he belonged. The one, Maury, early trained to struggles of polemical theology, had sharpened and polished in the pulpit the eloquence he was to bring into the tribune. Sprung from the lowest ranks of the people, he only belonged to the *ancien régime* by his garb, and defended religion and the monarchy as two texts, imposed upon him as themes for discourses. His conviction was the part he played; any other appointed character would have suited equally well; yet he sustained with unflinching courage and admirable consistency that which had been "set down for him."

Devoted from his youth to serious studies, endowed with abundant flow of words, striking and vivid in his language, his harangues were perfect treatises on the subjects he discussed. The only rival of Mirabeau, he needed but a cause more natural and more sterling to have become his equal; but sophistry could not deck abuses in colors more specious than those with which Maury invested the *ancien régime*.

Historical erudition and sacred learning supplied him with

ample sources of argument. The boldness of his character and language inspired words which even avenge a defeat, and his fine countenance, his sonorous voice, his commanding gesture, the defiance and good temper with which he braved the tribunes, frequently drew down the applauses of his enemies. The people, who recognized his invincible strength, were amused at his impotent opposition. Maury was to them as one of those gladiators whom they like to see fight, although well knowing that they must perish in the strife. One thing was wanting to the Abbé Maury,—weight to his eloquence; neither his birth, his faith, nor his life inspired respect in those who listened. The actor was visible in the man, the advocate in the cause, the orator and his language were not identified. Strip the Abbé Maury of the habit of his order, and he might have changed sides without a struggle, and have taken his seat amongst the innovators. Such orators grace a party, they never save it.

XVI.

Cazalès was one of those men who are themselves ignorant of their own powers until the hour arrives when circumstances call forth their genius, and assign to them a duty. An obscure officer in the ranks of the army, chance, which cast him into the tribune, revealed the orator. He did not inquire which side he should defend; noble, the *noblesse;* royalist, the king; a subject, the throne. His position made his creed; he bore in the Assembly the character and qualities of his uniform. Language to him was only another sword, and in all the spirit of chivalry, he devoted it to the cause of monarchy. Indolent and ill-educated, his natural good sense supplied the place of study. His monarchical faith was by no means fanaticism of the past: it admitted the modifications conceded by the king himself, and which were compatible with the inviolability of the throne and the working of the executive power. From Mirabeau to him the difference of the first principle was not wide apart, only one decried it as an aristocrat, and the other as a democrat. The one flung himself headlong into the midst of the people, the other attached himself to the steps of the throne. The characteristic of Cazalès' eloquence was that of a desperate cause. He protested more than he discussed and opposed to the triumphs of violence on the *côté gauche,* his ironic defiance, his bursts of bitter indignation, which for the moment acquired admiration, but never led to victory. To him the *noblesse* owed that it fell with glory; the throne, with majesty: and his eloquence attained something that was heroic.

Behind these two men there was only a party, soured by ill-fortune, discouraged by its isolation from the nation, odious to the people, useless to the throne, feeding on vain illusions, and only preserving of its fallen power the resentment of injuries, and that insolence which was perpetually provoking fresh humiliations. The hopes of this party were entirely sustained by their reliance on the armed intervention of foreign powers. Louis XVI. was in their eyes a prisoner king, whom Europe would come and deliver from his thraldom. With them, patriotism and honor were at Coblentz. Overcome by numbers, without skilful leaders who understood how to gain immortal names by timely retreats; with no strength to contend against the spirit of the age and refusing to move with it, the *côté droit* could only call for vengeance, its political power was now confined to an imprecation.

The left side lost at one blow its leader and controller; in Mirabeau the national man had ceased to exist, and only the men of party remained, and they were Barnave and the two Lameths. These men humbled, rebuked, before the ascendency of Mirabeau, had attempted, long before his death, to balance the sovereignty of his genius by the exaggeration of their doctrines and harangues. Mirabeau was but the apostle—they would fain have been the faction-leaders of the time. Jealous of his influence, they would have crushed his talents beneath the superiority of their popularity. Mediocrity thinks to equal genius by outraging reason. A diminution of thirty or forty votes had taken place in the left side. This was the work of Barnave and the Lameths. The club of the friends of the constitution become the Jacobin Club, responded to them from without. The popular agitation excited by them was restrained by Mirabeau, who rallied against them the left, the centre, and the intelligent members of the right side. They conspired, they caballed, they fomented divisions in opinion all the more that they had not control in the Assembly.

Mirabeau was dead, and now the field was open to them. The Lameths—courtiers, educated by the kindness of the royal family, overwhelmed by the favors and pensions of the king, had the conspicuous defection of Mirabeau without having the excuse of his wrongs against the monarchy: this defection was one of their titles to popular favor. Clever men, they carried with them into the national cause the conduct of courts in which they had been brought up: still their love of the Revolution was disinterested and sincere. Their eminent talents did not equal their ambition. Crushed by Mirabeau, they stirred up against him all those whom the shadow of that great man eclipsed in common with themselves. They sought for a rival to oppose to him, and found only men who envied him. Barnave presented himself, and they surrounded him, applauded him, intoxicated him with his self-importance. They persuaded him for a moment that phrases were politics, and that a rhetorician was a statesman.

Mirabeau was great enough not to fear, and just enough not to despise him. Barnave, a young barrister of Dauphiné, had made his *début* with much effect in the struggles between the parliament and the throne which had agitated his province, and displayed on small theatres the eloquence of men of the bar. Sent at thirty years of age to the States General, with Mounier his patron and master, he had soon quitted Mounier and the monarchical party, and made himself conspicuous amongst the democratic division. A word of sinister import which escaped not from his heart, but from his lips, weighed on his conscience with remorse. "Is then the blood that flows so pure?" he exclaimed at the first murder of the Revolution. This phrase had branded him on the brow with the mark of a ringleader of faction. Barnave was not this, or only as much so as was necessary for the success of his discourses; nothing in him was extreme but the orator: the man was by no means so, neither was he at all cruel. Studious, but without imagination; copious, but without warmth, his intellect was mediocre, his mind honest, his will variable, his heart in the right place. His talent, which they affected to compare with Mirabeau's, was nothing more than a power of skilfully rivetting public attention. His habit of pleading gave him, with its power of extempore speaking, an apparent superiority which vanished before reflection. Mirabeau's enemies had created him a pedestal on their hatred, and magnified his importance to make the comparison closer. When reduced to his actual stature, it was easy to recognize the distance that existed between the man of the nation, and the man of the bar.

Barnave had the misfortune to be the great man of a mediocre party, and the hero of an envious faction: he deserved a better destiny, which he subsequently acquired.

XVII.

Still deeper in the shade, and behind the chief of the National Assembly, a man almost unknown began to move, agitated by uneasy thoughts which seemed to forbid him to be silent and unmoved; he spoke on all occasions, and attacked all speakers indifferently, including Mirabeau himself. Driven from the tribune, he ascended it next day: overwhelmed with sarcasm, coughed down, disowned by all parties, lost amongst the eminent champions who fixed public attention, he was incessantly beaten but never dispirited. It might have been said, that an inward and prophetic genius revealed to him the vanity of all talent, and the omnipotence of a firm will and unwearied patience, and that an inward voice said to him, "These men who despise thee are thine; all the changes of this Revolution, which now will not deign to look upon thee, will eventually terminate in thee, for thou hast placed thyself in the way like the inevitable excess, in which all impulse ends."

This man was Robespierre.

There are abysses that we dare not sound, and characters we desire not to fathom, for fear of finding in them too great darkness, too much horror; but history, which has the unfliching eye of time, must not be chilled by these terrors, she must understand whilst she undertakes to recount Maximilien Robespierre was born at Arras, of a poor family, honest and respectable; his father, who died in Germany, was of English origin. This may explain the shade of Puritanism in his character. The bishop of Arras had defrayed the cost of his education. Young Maximilien had distinguished himself on leaving college, by a studious life, and austere manners. Literature and the bar shared his time. The philosophy of Jean Jacques Rousseau had made a profound impression on his understanding; the philosophy, falling upon an active imagination, had not remained a dead letter; it had become in him a leading principle, a faith, a fanaticism. In the strong mind of a sectarian, all conviction becomes a thing apart. Robespierre was the Luther of politics: and in obscurity he brooded over the confused thoughts of a renovation of the social world, and the religious world, as a dream which unavailingly beset his youth, when the

Revolution came to offer him what destiny always offers to those who watch her progress, opportunity. He seized on it. He was named deputy of the third estate in the States-General. Alone perhaps among all these men who opened at Versailles the first scene of this vast drama, he foresaw the termination; like the soul, whose seat in the human frame philosophers have not discovered, the thought of an entire people sometimes concentrates itself in the individual, the least known in the great mass. We should not despise any, for the finger of Destiny marks in the soul and not upon the brow. Robespierre had nothing: neither birth, nor genius nor exterior which should point him out to men's notice. There was nothing conspicuous about him; his limited talent had only shone at the bar or in provincial academies; a few verbal harangues filled with a tame and almost rustic philosophy, some bits of cold and affected poetry, had vainly displayed his name in the insignificance of the literary productions of the day: he was more than unknown, he was mediocre and contemned. His features presented nothing which could attract attention, when gazing round in a large assembly: there was no sign in visible characters of this power which was all within; he was the last word of the Revolution, but no one could read him.

Robespierre's figure was small, his limbs feeble and angular, his step irresolute, his attitudes affected, his gestures destitute of harmony or grace; his voice, rather shrill, aimed at oratorical inflexions, but only produced fatigue and monotony; his forehead was good, but small and extremely projecting above the temples, as if the mass and embarrassed movement of his thoughts had enlarged it by their efforts; his eyes, much covered by their lids and very sharp at the extremities, were deeply buried in the cavities of their orbits; they gave out a soft blue hue, but it was vague and unfixed, like a steel reflector on which a light glances; his nose straight and small was very wide at the nostrils, which were high and too expanded; his mouth was large, his lips thin and disagreeably contracted at each corner; his chin small and pointed, his complexion yellow and livid, like that of an invalid or a man worn out by vigils and meditations. The habitual expression of this visage was that of superficial serenity on a serious mind, and a smile wavering betwixt sarcasm and condescension. There was softness, but of a sinister character. The prevailing characteristic of this countenance was the prodigious and continual tension of brow, eyes, mouth, and all the facial muscles; in regarding him it was perceptible that the whole of his features, like the labor of his mind, converged incessantly on a single point with such power that there was no waste of will in his temperament, and he appeared to foresee all he desired to accomplish, as though he had already the reality before his eyes. Such then was the man destined to absorb in himself all those men, and make them his victims after he had used them as his instruments. He was of no party, but of all parties which in their turn served his ideal of the Revolution. In this his power consisted, for parties paused, but he never did. He placed this ideal as an end to reach in every revolutionary movement, and advanced towards it with those who sought to attain it; then, this goal reached, he placed it still further off, and again marched forward with other men, continually advancing without ever deviating, ever pausing, ever retreating. The Revolution, decimated in its progress, must one day or other inevitably arrive at a last stage, and he desired it should end in himself. He was the entire incorporation of the Revolution,—principles, thoughts, passions, impulses. Thus incorporating himself wholly with it, he compelled it one day to incorporate itself in him—that day was a distant one.

XVIII.

Robespierre, who had often struggled against Mirabeau with Duport, the Lameths, and Barnave, began to separate himself from them as soon as they appeared to predominate in the Assembly. He formed, with Pétion and some others of small note, a small band of opposition, radically democratic, who encouraged the Jacobins without, and menaced Barnave and the Lameths whenever they ventured to pause. Pétion and Robespierre in the Assembly, Brissot and Danton at the Jacobin Club, formed the nucleus of the new party which was destined to accelerate the movement and speedily to convert it into convulsions and catastrophes.

Pétion was a popular Lafayette: popularity was his aim, and he acquired it earlier than Robespierre. A barrister without talent but upright, he had imbibed no more of philosophy than the Social Contract; young, good-looking and a patriot, he was destined to become one of those complaisant idols of whom the people make what they please except a man; his credit in the streets and amongst the Jacobins gave him a certain amount of authority in the Assembly, where he was listened to as the significant echo of the will out of doors. Robespierre affected to respect him.

XIX.

The constitution was completed, the regal power was but a mere name, the king was but the executive of the orders of the national representation, his ministers only responsible hostages in the hands of the Assembly. The vices of this constitution were evident before it was entirely finished. Voted in the rage of parties, it was not a constitution, it was a vengeance of the people against the monarchy, the throne only existing as the substitute of a unique power, which was everywhere instituted, but which no one yet dared to name. The people, parties, trembled lest on removing the throne they should behold an abyss in which the nation would be ingulfed: it was thus tacitly agreed to respect its forms, though they daily despoiled and insulted the unfortunate monarch whom they kept chained to it.

Things were at that point where they have no possible termination except in a catastrophe. The army, without discipline, added but another element to the popular ferment: forsaken by its officers who emigrated in masses, the subalterns seized upon democracy and propagated it in their ranks. Affiliated in every garrison with the Jacobin Club, they received from it their orders, and made of their troops soldiers of anarchy, accomplices of faction. The people, to whom they had cast as a prey the feudal rights of the nobility and the tithes of the clergy, feared to have wrested from it what it held with disquietude, and saw in every direction plots which it anticipated by crimes. The sudden burst of liberty, for which it was not prepared, agitated without strengthening it: it evinced all the vices of enfranchised men without having got the virtues of the free man. The whole of France was but one vast sedition: anarchy swayed the state, and in order that it might be, as it were, self-governed, it had created its government in as many clubs as there were large municipalities in the kingdom. The dominant club was that of the Jacobins: this club was the centralization of anarchy. So soon as a powerful and high passioned will moves a nation, their common impulse brings men together; individuality ceases, and the legal or illegal association organizes the public prejudice. Popular societies thus have birth. At the first menaces of the court against the States-General, certain Breton deputies had a meeting at Versailles, and formed a society to detect the plots of the court and assure the triumphs of liberty; its founders were Siéyès, Chapelier, Barnave, and Lameth. After the 5th and 6th of October, the Breton Club, transported to Paris in the train of the National Assembly, had there assumed the more forcible name of "Society of the Friends of the Constitution." It held its sittings in the old convent of the Jacobins Saint Honoré, not far from the Manège, where the National Assembly sat. The deputies, who had founded it at the beginning for themselves, now opened their doors to journalists, revolutionary writers, and finally to all citizens. The presentation by two of its members, and an open scrutiny as to the moral character of the person proposed, were the sole conditions of admission: the public was admitted to the sittings by inspectors, who examined the admission card. A set of rules, an office, a president, a corresponding committee, secretaries, an order of the day, a tribune, and orators, gave to these meetings all the forms of deliberative assemblies: they were assemblies of the people only without elections and responsibility; feeling alone gave them authority: instead of framing laws they formed opinion.

The sittings took place in the evening, so that the people should not be prevented from attending in consequence of their daily labor: the acts of the National Assembly, the events of the moment, the examination of social questions, frequently accusations against the king, ministers, the *côté droit*, were the texts of the debates. Of all the passions of the people, their hatred was the most flattered; they made it suspicious in order to subject it. Convinced that all was conspiring against it,—king, queen, court, ministers authorities, foreign powers,—it threw itself headlong into the arms of its defenders. The most eloquent in its eyes was he who inspired it with most dread—it had a parching thirst for denunciations, and they were lavished on it with prodigal hand. It was thus that Barnave, the Lameths, then Danton, Marat, Brissot, Camille, Desmoulins, Pétion, Robespierre, had acquired their authority over the people. These names had increased in reputation as the anger of the people grew hotter; they cherished their wrath in order to retain their greatness. The nightly sittings of the Jacobins and the Cordeliers frequently stifled the echo of the sittings of the

National Assembly: the minority, beaten at the Manège, came to protest, accuse, threaten at the Jacobins.

Mirabeau himself, accused by Lameth on the subject of the law of emigration, came a few days before his death to listen face to face to the invectives of his denouncer, and had not disdained to justify himself. The clubs were the exterior strength, where the factious of the Assembly gave the support of their names in order to intimidate the national representation. The national representation had only the laws; the club had the people, sedition, and even the army.

XX.

This expression of public opinion, thus organized into a permanent association at every point in the empire, gave an electric shock which nothing could resist. A motion made in Paris was echoed from club to club to the extremest provinces. The same spark lighted at once the same passion in millions of souls. All the societies corresponded with one another and with the mother society. The impulse was communicated and the response was felt every day. It was the government of factions infolding in their nets the government of the law; but the law was mute and invisible, whilst faction was erect and eloquent. Let us imagine one of these sittings, at which the citizens, already agitated by the stormy air of the period, took their places at the close of day in one of those naves recently devoted to another worship. Some candles brought by the affiliated, scarcely lighted up the gloomy place; naked walls, wooden benches, a tribune instead of an altar. Around this tribune some favôred orators pressed in order to speak. A crowd of citizens of all classes, of all costumes, rich, poor, soldiers, workpeople; women, to create excitement, enthusiasm, tenderness, tears whenever they enter; children, whom they raise in their arms as if to make them inspire, with their earliest breath, the feelings of an irritated people: a gloomy silence interrupted by shouts, applause, or hisses, just as the speaker is loved or hated: then inflammatory discourses shaking to the very centre by phrases of magical effect, the passions of this mob new to all the effects of eloquence. The enthusiasm real in some, feigned in others; stirring propositions, patriotic gifts, civic crowns, busts of leading republicans paraded round, symbols of superstition and aristocracy burnt, songs loudly vociferated by demagogues in chorus at the opening of each sitting. What people, even in a time of tranquillity, could have resisted the pulsations of this fever, whose throbbings were daily renewed from the end of 1790 in every city in the kingdom? It was the rule of fanaticism preceding the reign of terror.

Thus was the Jacobin Club organized.

XXI.

The club of the Cordeliers, which is sometimes confounded with that of the Jacobins, even surpassed it in turbulence and demagogism. Marat and Danton ruled there.

The moderate constitutional party had also attempted its clubs, but passion is wanting to defensive societies: it is only the offensive that groups in factions; and thus the former expired of themselves until the establishment of the Club of Feuillants. The people drove away with a shower of stones the first meeting of the deputies, at M. De Clermont Tonnerre's. Barnave reproached his colleagues in the tribune, and devoted them to public execration with the same voice which had raised and rallied the *Friends of the Constitution.* Liberty was as yet but a partial arm, which was unblushingly broken in the hands of an opponent.

What remained to the king thus pressed between an Assembly, which had usurped all the executive functions, and those factious clubs, which usurped to themselves all the rights of representation? Placed without adequate strength between two rival powers, he was only there to receive the blows of each in the struggle, and to be cast as a daily sacrifice to popularity by the National Assembly; one power alone still maintained the shadow of the throne and exterior order, the national guard of Paris. But the national guard, which as a neutral force, whose only law was in public opinion, and was wavering itself between factions and the monarchy, might very well maintain safety in a public place, was unable to serve as a strong and independent support to political power. It was itself of the people; every serious intervention against the will of the people, appeared to it as sacrilege. It was a body of municipal police; it could never again be the army of the throne or the constitution; it was born of itself on the day after the 14th of July on the steps of the Hôtel de Ville, and it received no orders but from the municipality. The municipality had assigned M. de La Fayette as its head—nor could it have chosen better: an honest people, directed by its instinct, could not have selected a man who would represent it more faithfully.

XXII.

The Marquis de La Fayette was a patrician, possessor of an immense fortune, and allied, through his wife, daughter of the Duc d'Ayen, with the greatest families of the court. Born at Chavaignac in Auvergne on the 6th of September, 1757, married at sixteen years of age, a precocious instinct of renown drove him in 1777 from his own country. It was at the period of the war of Independence in America, the name of Washington resounded throughout the two continents. A youth dreamed the same destiny for himself in the delights of the effeminate court of Louis XV. That youth was La Fayette. He privately fitted out two vessels with arms and provisions, and arrived at Boston. Washington hailed him as he would have hailed the open succor of France. It was France without its flag. La Fayette and the young officers who followed him assured him of the secret wishes of a great people for the independence of the new world. The American general employed M. de La Fayette in this long war, the least of whose skirmishes assumed in traversing the seas the importance of a great battle. The American war, more remarkable for its results than its campaigns, was more fitted to form republicans than warriors. M. de La Fayette joined in it with heroism and devotion: he acquired the friendship of Washington. A French name was written by him on the baptismal register of a transatlantic nation. This name came back to France like the echo of liberty and glory. That popularity which seizes on all that is brilliant, was accorded to La Fayette on his return to his native land, and quite intoxicated the young hero. Opinion adopted him, the opera applauded him, actresses crowned him; the queen smiled upon him, the king created him a general; Franklin made him a citizen, and national enthusiasm elevated him into its idol. This excess of public estimation decided his life. La Fayette found this popularity so sweet that he could not consent to lose it. Applause, however, is by no means glory, and subsequently he deserved that which he acquired. He gave to democracy that of which it was worthy, honesty.

On the 14th of July, M. de La Fayette was ready for elevation on the shields of the *bourgeoisie* of Paris. A *fron-*

deur of the court, a revolutionist of high family, an aristocrat by birth, a democrat in principles, radiant with military renown acquired beyond seas, he united in his own person many qualities for rallying around him a civic militia, and for becoming the natural chief of an army of citizens. His American glory shone forth brilliantly in Paris. Distance increases every reputation—his was immense; it comprised and eclipsed all; Necker, Mirabeau, the Duc d'Orleans, the three most popular men in Paris,—all

Paled their ineffectual fires

before La Fayette, whose name was the nation's for three years. Supreme arbiter, he carried into the Assembly his authority as commandant of the national guard; his authority, as an influential member of the Assembly. Of these two conjoined titles he made a real dictatorship of opinion. As an orator he was but of slight consideration; his gentle style, though witty and keen, had nothing of that firm and electric manner which strikes the senses, makes the heart vibrate and communicates its vigor and effects to all who listen. Elegant as the language of a drawing-room, and overwhelmed in the mazes of diplomatic intrigues, he spoke of liberty in court phrases. The only parliamentary act of M. La Fayette was a proclamation of the *rights of man,* which was adopted by the National Assembly. This decalogue of free men, formed in the forests of America, contained more metaphysical phrases than sound policy. It applied as ill to an old society as the nudity of the savage to the complicated wants of civilized man: but it had the merit of placing man bare for the moment, and, by showing him what he was, and what he was not, of setting him on the discovery of the real value of his duties and his rights. It was the cry of the revolt of nature against all tyrannies. This cry was destined to crumble into dust an old world used up in servitude, and to produce another new and breathing. It was to La Fayette's honor that he first proposed it.

The federation of 1790 was the apogee of M. de La Fayette: on that day he surpassed both king and assembly. The nation armed and reflective was there in person, and he commanded it; he could have done everything and attempted nothing: the misfortune of that man was in his situation. A man of transition, his life passed between two ideas; if he had

had but one he could have been master of the destinies of his country. The monarchy or the republic were alike in his hand; he had but to open it wide, he only half opened it, and it was only a semi-liberty that issued from it. In inspiring his country with a desire for a republic, he defended a constitution and a throne. His principles and his conduct were in opposition; he was honest, and yet seemed to betray; whilst he struggled with regret from duty to the monarchy, his heart was in the republic. Protector of the throne, he was at the same time its bugbear. One life can only be devoted to one cause. Monarchy and republicanism had the same esteem, the same wrongs in his mind, and he served for and against both. He died without having seen either of them triumphant, but he died virtuous and popular. He had, besides his private virtues, a public virtue, which will ever be a pardon to his faults, and immortality to his name; he had before all, more than all, and after all, the feeling, constancy, and moderation of the Revolution.

Such was the man and such the army on which reposed the executive power, the safety of Paris, the constitutional throne, and the life of the king.

XXIII.

Thus on the 1st of June, 1791, were parties situated, such the men and things in the midst of which the irresistible spirit of a vast social renovation advanced with occult and continuous impulse. What but contention, anarchy, crime, and death, could emanate from such elements! No party had the reason, no mind had the genius, no soul had the virtue, no arm had the energy, to control this chaos, and extract from it justice, truth, and strength. Things will only produce what they contain. Louis XVI. was upright and devoted to well doing, but he had not understood, from the very first symptoms of the Revolution, that there was only one part for the leader of a people, and that was to place himself in the van of the newly-born idea, to forbear any struggle for the past, and thus to combine in his own person the twofold power of chief of the nation, and chief of a party. The character of moderation is only possible on the condition of having already acquired the unreserved confidence of the party whom it is desired to control. Henri IV. assumed this character, but it was *after* victory; had he attempted it *before* Ivry, he would have lost not only the kingdom of France, but also of Navarre.

The court was venal, selfish, corrupt; it only defended in the king's person the sources of its vanities,—profitable exactions. The clergy, with Christian virtues, had no public virtues: a state within a state, its life was apart from the life of the nation; its ecclesiastical establishment seemed to be wholly independent of the monarchical establishment. It had only rallied round the monarchy, on the day it had beheld its own fortune compromised; and then it had appealed to the faith of the people, in order to preserve its wealth; but the people now only saw in the monks mendicants, and in the bishops extortioners. The nobility, effeminate by lengthened peace, emigrated in masses, abandoning their king to his besetting perils, and fully trusting in the prompt and decisive intervention of foreign powers. The third estate, jealous and envious, fiercely demanded their place and their rights amongst the privileged castes; its justice appeared hatred. The Assembly comprised in its bosom all these weaknesses, all this egotism, all these vices. Mirabeau was venal, Barnave jealous, Robespierre fanatic, the Jacobin Club bloodthirsty, the National Guard selfish, La Fayette a waverer, the government a nullity. No one desired the Revolution but for his own purpose, and according to his own scheme; and it must have been wrecked on these shoals a hundred times, if there were not in human crises something even stronger than the men who appear to guide them—the will of the event itself.

The Revolution in all its comprehensive bearings was not understood at that period by any one except, perchance, Robespierre and the thorough-going democrats. The king viewed it only as a vast reform, the Duc d'Orleans as a great faction, Mirabeau but in its political point of view, La Fayette only in its constitutional aspect, the Jacobins as a vengeance, the mob as the abasing of the higher orders, the nation as a display of patriotism. None ventured as yet to contemplate its ultimate consummation.

All was thus blind, except the Revolution itself. The virtue of the Revolution was in the idea which forced these men on to accomplish it, and not in those who actually accomplished it; all its instruments were vitiated, corrupt, or personal; but the idea was pure, incorruptible, divine. The vices, passions, selfishness of men were inevitably doomed to produce in the coming crises those shocks, those violences, those perversities, and those crimes which are to human passions what consequences are to principles.

If each of the parties or men, mixed up from the first day with these great events, had taken their virtue, instead of their impulses as the rule of their actions, all these disasters which eventually crushed them, would have been saved to them and to their country. If the king had been firm and sagacious, if the clergy had been free from a longing for things temporal, and if the aristocracy had been good; if the people had been moderate, if Mirabeau had been honest, if La Fayette had been decided, if Robespierre had been humane, the Revolution would have progressed, majestic and calm as a heavenly thought, through France, and thence through Europe; it would have been installed like a philosophy in facts, in laws, and in creeds. But it was otherwise decreed. The holiest, most just and virtuous thought, when it passes through the medium of imperfect humanity, comes out in rags and in blood. Those very persons who conceived it, no longer recognize, disavow it. Yet it is not permitted, even to crime, to degrade the truth, that survives all, even its victims. The blood which sullies men does not stain its idea; and despite the selfishness which debases it, the infamies which trammel it, the crimes which pollute it, the blood-stained Revolution purifies itself, feels its own worth, triumphs, and will triumph.

BOOK II.

I.

The National Assembly, wearied with two years of existence, relaxed in its legislative movement: from the moment when it had nothing more to destroy, it really was at a loss what to do. The Jacobins took umbrage at it, its popularity was disappearing, the press inveighed against it, the clubs insulted it; the worn-out tool by which the people had acquired conquest, it felt the people were about to snap it asunder if it did not dissolve of its own accord. Its sittings were inanimate, and it was completing the constitution as a task inflicted on it, but at which it was discouraged before completion. It had no belief in the duration of that which it proclaimed imperishable. The lofty voices which had shaken France so long were now no more, or were silent from indifference. Maury, Cazalès, Clermont Tonnerre seemed careless of continuing a conflict in which honor was saved, and in which victory was henceforth impossible. From time to time, indeed, some burst of passion between parties interrupted the usual monotony of these theoretical discussions. Such was the struggle of the 10th of June between Cazalès and Robespierre with respect to the disbanding the officers of the army. "What is it," exclaimed Robespierre, "that the committees propose to us? to trust to the oaths, to the honor of officers, to defend a constitution which they detest! Of what honor do they talk to us? What is that honor more than virtue and love of country? I take credit to myself for not believing in such honor."

Cazalès himself arose indignantly. "I could not listen tamely to such calumniating language," he exclaimed. At these words violent murmurs arose on the left, and cries (order! to the Abbaye! to the Abbaye!) burst forth from the ranks of the revolution: "What," said the royalist orator, "is it not enough to have restrained my indignation on hearing two thousand citizens thus accused, who in all moments of peril have presented an example of most heroic patience! I have listened to the previous speaker, because I am, and I assert it, a partisan of the most unlimited declaration of opinions; but it is beyond human endurance for me to conceal the contempt I feel for such diatribes. If you adopt the disbanding proposed you will no longer have an army, our frontiers will be delivered up to foreign invasion, and the interior to excesses and the pillage of an infuriated soldiery." These energetic words were the funeral oration of the old army, the project of the committee was adopted.

The discussion on the abolition of the punishment of death presented to Adrien Duport an opportunity to pronounce in favor of the abolition one of those orations which survive time, and which protest, in the name of reason and philosophy, against the blindness and atrocity of criminal legislation. He demonstrated with the most profound logic that society, by reserving to itself the right of homicide, justifies it to a certain extent in the murderer; and that the means most efficacious for preventing murder and making it infamous was to evince its own horror of the crime. Robespierre, was subsequently who fated to allow of unlimited immolation, demanded that society should be disarmed of the power of putting to death. If the prejudices of jurists had not prevailed over the wholesome doctrines of moral philosophy, who can say how much blood might not have been spared in France.

But these discussions, confined to the interior of the Manège, occupied less public attention than the fierce controversies of the periodical press. Journalism, that universal and daily *forum* of the people's passions, had expanded with the progress of liberty. All ardent minds had eagerly embraced it, Mirabeau himself having set the example when he descended from the tribune. He wrote his letters to his constituents in the *Courrier de Provence.* Camille Desmoulins, a young man of great talent but weak reasoning powers, threw into his lucubrations for the press the feverish tumult of his thoughts. Brissot, Gorsas, Carra, Prudhomme, Fréron, Danton, Fauchet, Condorcet, edited democratic journals: they began by demanding the abolition of royalty, "the greatest scourge," said the *Revolutions de Paris,* "which has ever dishonored the human species." Marat seemed to have concentrated in himself all the evil passions which ferment in a society in a state of decomposition: he constituted himself the permanent representative of popular hate. By pretending this, he kept it up, writing all the while with bitterness and ferocity. He became a cynic in order the more intimately to know the masses. He assumed the language of the lowest reprobates. Like the elder Brutus, he feigned idiocy, but it was not to save his country, it was to urge it to the uttermost bounds of madness, and then control it by its very insanity. All his pamphlets, echoes of the Jacobins and Cordeliers, daily excited the uneasiness, suspicions, and terrors of the people.

"Citizens," said he, "watch closely around this palace: the inviolable asylum of all plots against the nation, there a perverse queen lords it over an imbecile king and rears the cubs of tyranny. Lawless priests there consecrate the arms of insurrection against the people. They prepare the Saint Bartholomew of patriots. The genius of Austria is there, hidden in the committees over which Antoinette presides; they correspond with foreigners, and by concealed means forward to them the gold and arms of France, so that the tyrants who are assembling in arms on your frontier may find you famished and disarmed. The emigrants—d'Artois and Condé—there receive instructions of the coming vengeance of despotism. A guard of Swiss stipendiaries is not enough for the liberticide schemes of the Capets. Every night the good citizens who watch around this den see the ancient nobility entering stealthily and concealing arms beneath their clothes. Can knights of the poniard be anything but the enrolled assassins of the people? What is La Fayette doing, —is he a dupe or an accomplice? Why does he leave free the avenue of the palace, which is only opened for vengeance or flight? Why do we leave the Revolution incomplete, and also leave in the hands of our crowned enemy, still in the midst of us, the time to overcome and destroy it? Do you not see that specie is disappearing and assignats are discredited? What means the assemblings on your frontier of emigrants and armed bodies, who are advancing to inclose you in a circle of iron? What are your ministers doing? Why is not the property of emigrants confiscated, their houses burnt, their heads set at a price? In whose hands are arms? In the hands of traitors. Who command your troops? traitors! Who hold the keys of your strong places? traitors, traitors, traitors, everywhere traitors; and in this palace of treason, the king of traitors! the inviolable traitor, the king! They tell you that he loves the constitution,—humbug! he comes to the Assembly,—humbug; the better he conceals his flight. Watch! watch! a great blow is preparing, is ready to burst; if you do not prevent it by a counter-blow more sudden, more terrible, the people and liberty are annihilated."

These declarations were not wholly void of foundation. The king, honest and good, did not conspire against his people, the queen did not think of selling to the House of Austria the crown of her husband and her son. If the constitution now completed had been able to restore order to the country and security to the throne, no sacrifice of power would have been felt by Louis XVI.: never did prince find more innate in his character the conditions of his moderation: that passive resignation, which is the character of constitutional sovereigns, was his virtue. He neither desired to reconquer nor to avenge himself. All he desired was, that his sincerity should be appreciated by the people, order re-established within and power without; that the Assembly, receding from the encroachments it had made on the executive power, should raise the constitution, correct its errors, and restore to royalty that power indispensable for the weal of the kingdom.

The queen herself, although of a mind more powerful and absolute, was convinced by necessity, and joined the king in his intentions; but the king, who had not two wills, had nevertheless two administrations, and two policies, one in France with his constitutional ministers, and another without with his brothers, and his agents with other powers. Baron de Breteuil, and M. de Calonne, rivals in intrigue, spake and diplomatized in his name. The king disowned them, sometimes with, and sometimes without, sincerity, in his official letters to ambassadors. This was not hypocrisy, it was weakness; a captive king, who speaks aloud to his jailers, and in whispers to his friends, is excusable. These two languages not always agreeing, gave to Louis XVI. the appearance of dis loyalty and treason: he did not betray, he hesitated.

His brothers, and especially the Comte d'Artois, did vio lence from without to his wishes, interpreting his silence ac cording to their own desires. This young prince went from court to court to solicit in his brother's name the coalition of the monarchical powers against principles which already threatened every throne. Received graciously at Florence by the Emperor of Austria, Leopold, the queen's brother, he obtained a few days afterwards at Mantua, the promise of a force of 35,000 men. The King of Prussia, and Spain, the King of Sardinia, Naples, and Switzerland, guaranteed equal forces. Louis XVI. sometimes entertained the hope of an European intervention as a means of intimidating the Assembly, and compelling it to a reconciliation with him; at other times he repulsed it as a crime. The state of his mind in this respect depended on the state of the kingdom; his understanding followed the flux and reflux of interior events. If a good decree, a cordial reconciliation with the Assembly, a return of popular applause came to console his sorrows, he resumed his hopes, and wrote to his agents to break up the hostile gatherings at Coblentz. If a new *emeute* disturbed the palace—if the Assembly degraded the royal power by some indignity or some outrage—he again began to despair of the Constitution, and to fortify himself against it. The incoherence of his thoughts was rather the fault of his situation than his own; but it compromised his cause equally within and without. Every thought which is not at unity destroys itself. The thought of the king, although right in the main, was too fluctuating not to vary with events, but those events had but one direction—the destruction of the monarchy.

II.

Nevertheless, in the midst of these vacillations of the royal will, it is impossible for history to misunderstand that from the month of November, 1790, the king vaguely meditated a plan of escape from Paris in collusion with the emperor. Louis XVI. had obtained from this prince the promise of sending a body of troops on the French frontier at the moment when he should desire it; but had the king the intention of quitting the kingdom and returning at the head of a foreign force, or simply to assemble round his person a portion of his own army in some point of the frontier, and there to treat with the Assembly? This latter is the more probable hypothesis.

Louis XVI. had read much history, especially the history of England. Like all unfortunate men, he sought, in the misfortunes of dethroned princes, analogies with his own unhappy position. The portrait of Charles I., by Van Dyck, was constantly before his eyes in his closet in the Tuileries; his history continually open on his table. He had been struck by two circumstances; that James II. had lost his throne because he had left his kingdom, and that Charles I. had been beheaded for having made war against his parliament and his people. These reflections had inspired him with an instinctive repugnance against the idea of leaving France, or of casting himself into the arms of the army. In order to compel his decision one way or the other in favor of one of these two extreme parties, his freedom of mind was completely oppressed by the imminence of his present perils, and the dread which beset the château of the Tuileries night and day had penetrated the very soul of the king and queen.

The atrocious threats which assailed them whenever they showed themselves at the windows of their residence, the insults of the press, the vociferations of the Jacobins, the riots and murders which multiplied in the capital and the provinces, the violent obstacles which had been opposed to their departure from St. Cloud, and then the recollections of the daggers which had even pierced the queen's bed on the evening of the 5th to the 6th of October, made their life one continued scene of alarms. They began to comprehend that the insatiate Revolution was irritated even by the concessions they had made; that the blind fury of factions which had not paused before royalty surrounded by its guards, would not hesitate before the illusory inviolability decreed by a constitution; and that their lives, those of their children, and those of the royal family which remained, had no longer any assurance of safety but in flight.

Flight was therefore resolved upon, and was frequently discussed before the time when the king decided upon it. Mirabeau himself, bought by the court, had proposed it in his mysterious interviews with the queen. One of his plans presented to the king was, to escape from Paris, take refuge in the midst of a camp, or in a frontier town, and there treat with the baffled Assembly. Mirabeau remaining in Paris, and again possessing himself of the public mind, would lead matters, as he declared, to accommodation, and a voluntary restoration of the royal authority. Mirabeau had carried these hopes away with him into the tomb. The king himself, in his secret correspondence, testified his repugnance to intrusting his fate into the hands of the ringleader of the factions. Another cause of uneasiness troubled the king's mind, and gave the queen great anxiety; they were not ignorant that it was a question without, either at Coblentz or in the councils of Leopold and the King of Prussia, to declare the throne of France virtually vacant, by default of the king's liberty, and to nominate as regent one of the emigrant princes, in order that he might call around him with a show of legality all his loyal subjects, and give to foreign troops an incontestible right of intervention. A throne even in fragments will not admit of participation.

An uneasy jealousy still prevailed in the midst of so many other alarms even in this palace, where sedition had already effected so many breaches. "M. le Comte d'Artois will then become a hero," said the queen ironically, who at one time was excessively fond of this young prince, but now hated him. The king, on his part, feared that moral forfeiture with which he was menaced, under pretence of delivering the monarchy. He knew not which to fear the most, his friends or his enemies. Flight only, to the centre of a faithful army, could remove him from both these perils; but flight was also a peril. If he succeeded, civil war might spring up, and the king had a horror of blood spilled in his defence; if it did not succeed, it would be imputed to him as a crime, and then who could say where the national fury would stop? Forfeiture, captivity, death, might be the consequence of the slightest accident, or least indiscretion. He was about to suspend by a slender thread his throne, his liberty, his life, and the lives a thousand times more dear to him—those of his wife, his two children, and his sister.

His tormenting reflections were long and terrible, lasting for eight months, during which time he had no confidants but the queen, Madame Elizabeth, a few faithful servants within the palace, and the Marquis de Bouillé without.

III.

The Marquis de Bouillé, cousin of M. de La Fayette, was of a character totally different to that of the hero of Paris. Severe and stern soldier, attached to the monarchy by principle, to the king by an almost religious devotion, his respect for his sovereign's orders had alone prevented him from emigrating; he was one of the few general officers popular amongst the soldiers who had remained faithful to their duty amidst the storms and tempests of the last two years, and who, without openly declaring for or against these innovations, had yet striven to preserve that force which outlives, and not unfrequently supplies, the deficiency of all others,—the force of discipline. He had served with great distinction in America, in the colonies in India, and the authority of his character and name had not as yet lost their influence over the soldiery; the heroic repression of the famous outbreak amongst the troops at Nancy in the preceding August had greatly contributed to strengthen this authority; and he alone of all the French generals had re-obtained the supreme command, and had crushed insubordination. The Assembly, alarmed in the midst of its triumphs by the seditions amongst the troops, had passed a vote of thanks to him as the saviour of his country. La Fayette, who commanded the citizens, feared only this rival who commanded regiments, he therefore watched and flattered M. de Bouillé. He constantly proposed to him a coalition of their forces, of which they would be the commanders-in-chief, and by thus acting in concert secure at once the revolution and the monarchy. M. de Bouillé, who doubted the loyalty of La Fayette, replied with a cold and sarcastic civility, that but ill concealed his suspicions. These two characters were incompatible,—the one was the representative of modern patriotism, the other of ancient honor: they could not harmonize.

The Marquis de Bouillé commanded the troops of Loraine, Alsace, Franche-Comté, and Champagne, and his government extended from Switzerland to the Sambre. He had no less than ninety battalions of foot, and a hundred and four squadrons of cavalry under his orders. Out of this number the general could only rely upon twenty battalions of German troops and a few cavalry regiments; the remainder were in favor of the Revolution: and the influence of the clubs had spread amongst them the spirit of insubordination and hatred for the king; the regiments obeyed the municipalities rath than their generals.

IV.

Since the month of February, 1791, the king, who had the most entire confidence in M. de Bouillé, had written to this general that he wished him to make overtures to Mirabeau, and through the intervention of the Count de Lamarck, a foreign nobleman, the intimate and confidential friend of Mirabeau. "Although these persons are not over estimable," said the king in his letter, "and although I have paid Mirabeau very dearly, I yet think he has it in his power to serve me. Hear all he has to say, without putting yourself too much in his hands." The Count de Lamarck arrived soon after at Metz. He mentioned to M. de Bouillé the object of his mission, confessed to him that the king had recently given Mirabeau 600,000f. (24,000*l.*), and that he also allowed him 50,000f. a month. He then revealed to him the plan of his counter-revolutionary conspiracy, the first act of which was to be an address to Paris and the Departments, demanding the liberty of the king. Everything in this scheme depended upon the rhetoric of Mirabeau. Carried away by his own eloquence, the salaried orator was ignorant that words, though all-powerful to excite, are yet impotent to appease; they urge nations forward, but nothing but the bayonet can arrest them. M. de Bouillé, a veteran soldier, smiled at these chimerical projects of the citizen orator; but he did not, however, discourage him in his plans, and promised him his assistance: he wrote to the king to repay largely the desertion of Mirabeau; "A clever scoundrel," said he, "who perhaps has it in his power to repair through cupidity the mischief he has done through revenge;" and to mistrust La Fayette, "A chimerical enthusiast, intoxicated with popularity, who might become the chief of a party, but never the support of a monarchy."

After the death of Mirabeau, the king adhered to the project with some modification; he wrote in cipher to the

Marquis de Bouillé at the end of April, to inform him that he should leave Paris almost immediately with his family in one carriage, which he had ordered to be built secretly and expressly for this purpose; and he also desired him to establish a line of posts from Châlons to Montmédy, the frontier town he had fixed upon. The nearest road from Paris to Montmédy was through Rheims; but the king having been crowned there dreaded recognition. He therefore determined, in spite of M. de Bouillé's reiterated advice, to pass through Varennes. The chief inconvenience of this road was, that there were no relays of post-horses, and it would be therefore necessary to send relays thither under different pretexts; the arrival of these relays would naturally create suspicion amongst the inhabitants of the small towns. The presence of detachments along a road not usually frequented by troops was likewise dangerous, and M. de Bouillé was anxious to dissuade the king from taking this road. He pointed out to him in his answer, that if the detachments were strong they would excite the alarm and vigilance of the municipal authorities, and if they were weak they would be unable to afford him protection: he also entreated him not to travel in a berlin made expressly for him, and conspicuous by its form, but to make use of two English carriages, then much in vogue, and better fitted for such a purpose; he, moreover, dwelt on the necessity of taking with him some man of firmness and energy to advise and assist him in the unforeseen accidents that might happen on his journey; he mentioned as the fittest person the Marquis d'Agoult, major in the French guards; and he lastly besought the king to request the Emperor to make a threatening movement of the Austrian troops on the frontier near Montmédy, in order that the disquietude and alarm of the population might serve as a pretext to justify the movements of the different detachments and the presence of the different corps of cavalry in the vicinity of the town.

The king agreed to this, and also to take with him the Marquis d'Agoult; to the rest he positively refused to accede. A few days prior to his departure he sent a million in assignats (£40,000) to M. de Bouillé, to furnish the rations and forage, as well as to pay the faithful troops who were destined to favor his flight. These arrangements made, the Marquis de Bouillé dispatched a trusty officer of his staff, M. de Guoguelas, with instructions to make a minute and accurate survey of the road and country between Châlons and Montmédy, and to deliver an exact report to the king. This officer saw the king, and brought back his orders to M. de Bouillé.

In the meantime M. de Bouillé held himself in readiness to execute all that had been agreed upon; he had sent to a distance the disaffected troops, and concentrated the twelve foreign battalions on which he could rely. A train of sixteen pieces of artillery was sent towards Montmédy. The regiment of *Royal Allemand* arrived at Stenay, a squadron of hussars was at Dun, another at Varennes; two squadrons of dragoons were to be at Clermont on the day the king would pass through; they were commanded by Count Charles de Damas, a bold and dashing officer, who had instructions to send forward a detachment to Sainte Menehould, and fifty hussars, detached from Varennes, were to march to Pont Sommeville between Châlons and Sainte Menehould, under pretence of securing the safe passage of a large sum of money sent from Paris to pay the troops. Thus once through Châlons the king's carriage would be surrounded at each relay by tried and faithful followers. The commanding officers of these detachments had instructions to approach the window of the carriage whilst they changed horses, and to receive any orders the king might think proper to issue. In case his majesty wished to pursue his journey without being recognized, these officers were to content themselves with ascertaining that no obstacle existed to bar the road. If it was his pleasure to be escorted, then they would mount their men and escort him. Nothing could be better devised, and the most inviolable secrecy enveloped all.

The 27th of May the king wrote that he should set out the 19th of the next month between twelve and one at night; that he should leave Paris in a hired carriage, and at Bondy, the first stage out of Paris, he should take his berlin; that one of his body-guard, who was to serve as courier, would await him at Bondy; that in case the king did not arrive before two, it was because he had been arrested on his way; the courier would then proceed alone to Pont Sommeville to inform M. de Bouillé the scheme had failed, and to warn the general, and those of his officers engaged in the plot, to provide for their own safety.

V.

After the receipt of these last orders, M. de Bouillé dispatched the Duke de Choiseul to Paris, with orders to await the king's instructions, and to precede his departure by twelve hours. M. de Choiseul was to desire his servants to be at Varennes on the 18th with his own horses, which would draw the king's carriage; the spot where the horses were placed was to be clearly explained to the king, in order that they might be changed without any loss of time. On his return M. de Choiseul had instructions to take the command of the hussars posted at Pont Sommeville, to await the king, to escort him with his hussars as far as Sainte Menehould, and to station his troopers there, with positive orders to allow no one to pass on the road from Paris to Verdun, and from Paris to Varennes, for four and twenty hours after the king's arrival. M. de Choiseul received from M. de Bouillé orders signed by the king himself, enjoining him, as well as all the other commanding officers of the detachments, to employ force, should it be necessary, to rescue his majesty if the populace attempted to lay violent hands on him. In case the carriage was stopped at Lyons, M. de Choiseul was to give instant information to the general to assemble all the detachments, and march to the king's rescue. He received six hundred louis in gold, to distribute amongst the soldiers, and thus insure their fidelity, when the king arrived and made himself known to them.

M. de Guoguelas left at the same for Paris, to reconnoitre the roads a second time, passing by Stenay, Dun, Varennes, and Sainte Menehould, and to explain clearly to the king the topography of the country; he was also to bring back the latest orders for M. de Bouillé, and to return to Montmédy by another route. The Marquis de Bouillé left Metz himself, under pretence of visiting the fortresses under his command, and drew near Montmédy. The 15th he was at Longwy, where he received a message from the king, informing him that they had put off their journey for four and twenty hours, in consequence of the necessity of concealing the preparations of their departure from a femme de chambre of the queen, a fanatical democrat, who was fully capable of betraying them, and whose duties only terminated on the 19th. His majesty added that the Marquis d'Agoult would not accompany him, because Madame de Tourzel, the governess of the royal children, had claimed the privileges of her post, and wished to accompany them.

This delay rendered necessary counter-orders of the most fatal nature; all the arrangements as to time and place were thus thrown out. The detachments were forced to remain at places they were only to have marched through, and the relays stationed on the road might be withdrawn. However, the Marquis de Bouillé remedied all these evils as far as was in his power; sent modified orders to the commanders of the detachments, and advanced in person the 20th to Stenay, which was garrisoned by the Royal Allemand regiment, on whose fidelity he could rely. The 21st he assembled the generals under his orders, informed them that the king would pass in the course of the night by Stenay, and would be at Montmédy the next evening; he ordered General Klinglin to prepare under the guns of the fortress a camp of twelve battalions and twenty-four squadrons; the king was to reside in a chateau behind the camp: this chateau would thus serve as head-quarters, and the king's position would be at once more secure and more dignified surrounded by his army. The generals did not hesitate for an instant. M. de Bouillé left General de Hoffelizze at Stenay with the Royal Allemand regiment, with orders to saddle the horses at night fall, to mount at daybreak, and to send at ten o'clock at night a detachment of fifty troopers between Stenay and Dun, to await the king and escort him to Stenay.

At night M. de Choiseul quitted Stenay with several officers on horseback, and advanced to the very gate of Dun, but he would not enter lest his presence might in any way work on the people. There he awaited, in silence and obscurity, the courier who was to precede the carriages by an hour. The destiny of the monarchy, the throne of a dynasty, the lives of the royal family, king, queen, princess, children, all weighed down his spirit and lay heavily on his heart. The night seemed interminable, yet it passed without the sound of horses' feet announcing to the group who so anxiously awaited the intelligence, that the king of France was saved or lost.

VI.

What passed at the Tuileries during these decisive hours? the secret of the projected flight had been carefully confined to the king, the queen, the princess Elizabeth, two or three faithful attendants, and the Count de Fersen, a **Swedish** gentleman who had the care of the exterior arrangements confided to him. Some vague rumors, like presentiments of coming events, had, it is true, been bruited amongst the people for some days past, but these rumors originated rather in the state of popular excitement than any actual disclosures of the intended departure. These reports, however, which were constantly transmitted to M. de La Fayette and his staff, occasioned a stricter *surveillance* round the palace and the king's apartments. Since the 5th and 6th of October the household guards had been disbanded; the companies of the body-guard, every soldier of whom was a gentleman, and whose honor, descent, ancient traditions, and party feeling assured their fidelity, existed no longer; that respectful vigilance that rendered their service a matter of duty with them, had given place to the jealous watchfulness of the national guard, who were rather spies on the king than guardians of the monarchy. The Swiss guards still, it is true, surrounded the Tuileries, but they only occupied the exterior posts; the interior of the Tuileries, the staircases, the communications between the apartments, were guarded by the national guards. M. de La Fayette was constantly going to and fro, his officers at night were at every issue, and they had secret orders not to allow even the king to quit the palace after midnight. To this official vigilance was now joined the secret and close *espionage* of the numerous domestics of the palace, amongst whom revolutionary feeling had crept in to encourage treachery, and sanction ingratitude: amongst them, as amongst their superiors, betrayal was termed virtue, and treason, patriotism. Within the walls of the palace of his fathers the king could alone count on the queen, his sisters, and a few nobles still faithful in his misfortunes, and even whose gestures were duly reported to M. de La Fayette. This general had driven by violence from the Tuileries many of the faithful gentlemen who had come to strengthen the guard, on the day of the *emeute* at Vincennes. The king had witnessed, with tears in his eyes, his most faithful adherents ignominiously driven from his palace and exposed by his official protector to the insults and outrages of the populace. Thus the royal family could hope to find no one disposed to aid their escape without the palace walls.

VII.

The Count de Fersen was the principal agent and confidant of this hazardous enterprise. Young, handsome, and accomplished, he had been admitted during the happy years of Marie Antoinette's life to the parties and fêtes of Trianon. It was said, that a chivalrous admiration, to which respect alone prevented his giving the name of love, had bound him to the queen. And now this admiration had been changed into the most passionate devotion to her in misfortune. The queen perceived this, and when she reflected to whom she could confide the safety of the king and her children, she thought of M. de Fersen—he instantly quitted Stockholm, saw the king and queen, and undertook to prepare for the flight the carriages, which were to meet them at Bondy. His position as a foreigner favored his plans, and he combined them with a skill only equalled by his fidelity. Three soldiers of the body-guard, MM. de Valorg, de Moustier, et de Maldan, were taken into his confidence, and the parts they were to play were fully explained to them; they were to disguise themselves as servants, mount behind the carriages, and protect the royal family at all risks. The names of three obscure gentlemen effaced that day the names of the courtiers. Should they be discovered, their fate was sealed; but in the hope of aiding the escape of their king, they courageously offered themselves a sacrifice to the popular fury.

VIII.

The queen had for many months entertained the project of escape. Since the month of March she had commissioned one of her waiting-maids to procure her from Brussels a complete wardrobe for Madame and the Dauphin; she had sent most of her valuables to her sister, the Archduchess Christina, the regent of the Low Countries, under pretence of making her a present; her diamonds had been intrusted to her hair-dresser, Leonard, who had started before herself with the Duke de Choiseul. These slight indications of a projected flight had not entirely escaped the vigilance of a waiting-maid; this woman had noticed that whispered conversations were carried on; she had seen desks opened on the table, and empty jewel-boxes lying about; she denounced these facts to M. de Gouvion, M. de La Fayette's *aide-de-camp,* whose mistress she was, and M. de Gouvion reported all again to the mayor of Paris and his general. But these denunciations had been so often made, and by so many different persons, and had so often proved false, that now but little importance was attached to them. However, in consequence of the revelations of this woman, a stricter watch than usual was kept round the chateau. M. de Gouvion detained several officers of the national guard under various pretexts in the palace, he placed them at the different doors, and he himself, with five *chefs-de-bataillon*, passed part of the night at the door of the apartment formerly occupied by the Duke de Villequier, which had been specially pointed out to him. He had been told (which was the case) that there existed a secret communication from the queen's cabinet to the apartment of the former captain of the guard; and that the king, who it is well known was an expert locksmith, had made false keys that opened all the doors; at last these reports (that went the round of all the clubs) transformed every patriot on that night into the king's jailer.. We read with surprise in the journal of Camille Desmoulins of the 20th of June, 1791:—"The evening passed most tranquilly at Paris; I returned at eleven o'clock from the Jacobin's Club with Danton and several other patriots; we only met a single patrol all the way. Paris appeared to me that night so deserted, that I could not help remarking it. One of us, Fréron, who had in his pocket a letter warning him that the king would escape that night, wished to observe the chateau; he saw M. de La Fayette enter it at eleven."

A little further on Camille Desmoulins relates the restless fears of the people on the fatal night. "The night," says he "on which the family of the Capets escaped, Busebi, a perruke-maker in the Rue de Bourbon, called on Hucher a baker and Sapeur in the Bataillon of the Théatins, to communicate his fears on what he had just learnt relative to the king's projected flight. They instantly aroused their neighbors, to the number of thirty, and went to La Fayette to inform him of the fact, and to summon him to take instant measures to prevent it. M. de La Fayette laughed, and advised them to go home. In order to avoid being stopped by the patrols, they asked for the pass-word, which he gave them. Armed with this they hastened to the Tuileries, where nothing was visible except several hackney coachmen drinking round one of the small shops near the wicket gate of the Carrousel. They inspected all the courts until they came to the door of the Manége without perceiving anything suspicious, but at their return they were surprised to find that every hackney coach had disappeared, which made them conjecture that these coaches had been used by some of the attendants of this unworthy (*indigne*) family."

It is too evident from the state of agitation of the public mind and the severity of the king's captivity, how difficult it must have been. However, either owing to the connivance of some of the national guards who had on that day demanded the custody of the interior posts, and who winking at this infraction of the orders,—to the skilful management of the Count de Fersen,—or that Providence afforded a last ray of hope and safety to those whom she was so soon about to overwhelm with misfortunes, all the watchfulness of the guardians was in vain, and the Revolution suffered its prey for some time to escape.

IX.

The king and queen received, as was their custom at their *coucher*, those persons who were in the habit of paying their respects to them at that time, nor did they dismiss their servants any earlier than was their wont. But no sooner were they alone than they again dressed themselves in plain travelling dress adapted to their supposed station. They met Madame Elizabeth and their children, in the queen's room, and thence they passed by a secret communication into the apartment of the Duke de Villequier, first gentleman of the bed-chamber, and left the palace at intervals, in order that the attention of the sentinels in the court might not be attracted by the appearance of groups of persons at that late hour; owing to the bustle of the servants and workpeople leaving the chateau, and which M. de Fersen had no doubt taken care should on that evening be greater than usual, they arrived, without having been recognized, at the Carrousel. The queen leaned on the arm of one of the bodyguard, and led Madame Royale by the hand. As she crossed the Carrousel she met M. La Fayette with one or two officers of his staff proceeding to the Tuileries, in order to satisfy himself that the measures ordered in consequence of the revelations made that day had been strictly complied with. She shuddered as she recognized the man who in her eyes was the representative of insurrection and captivity, but in escaping him she fancied she had escaped the whole nation.

and smiled as she thought of his appearance the next day when he could no longer produce his prisoners to the people. Madame Elizabeth also held the arm of one of the guards, and followed them at some distance, whilst the king, who had insisted upon being the last, held the Dauphin (who was in his seventh year) by the hand. The Count de Fersen, disguised as a coachman, walked a little ahead of the king to show him the way. The meeting place of the royal family was on the Quai des Théatins, where two hackney coaches awaited them; the queen's waiting women, and the Marquise de Tourzel had preceded them.

Amidst the confusion of so dangerous and complicated a flight, the queen and her guide crossed the Pont Royal and entered the Rue de Bac, but instantly perceiving their error, with hasty and faltering steps they retraced their road. The king and his son, obliged to traverse the darkest and least frequented streets to arrive at the rendezvous, were delayed half an hour, which seemed to his wife and sister an age. At last they arrived, sprang into the coach, the Count de Fersen seized the reins and drove the royal family to Bondy, the first stage between Paris and Châlons: there they found, ready harnessed for the journey, a berlin and a small travelling carriage; the queen's women and one of the disguised body-guard got into the smaller carriage, whilst the king, the queen, and the Dauphin, Madame Royale, Madame Elizabeth, and the Marquise de Tourville, took their places in the berlin; one of the body-guard sat on the box, and the other behind; Count de Fersen kissed the hands of the king and queen, and returned to Paris, from whence he went the same night to Brussels, by another road, in order to rejoin the royal family at a later period. At the same hour Monsieur the king's brother, Count de Provence, left the Luxembourg palace, and arrived safely at Brussels.

X.

The king's carriage rolled on the road to Châlons, and relays of eight horses were ordered at each post-house: this number of horses, the remarkable size and build of the berlin, the number of travellers who occupied the interior, the three body-guards, whose livery formed a strange contrast to their physiognomy and martial appearance, the Bourbonian features of Louis XVI. seated in a corner of the carriage, and which was totally out of character with the *rôle* of valet de chambre the king had taken on himself,—all these circumstances were calculated to excite distrust and suspicion, and to compromise the safety of the royal family. But their passport removed all objections,—it was perfectly formal, and in these terms: "*De par le roi. Mandons de laisser passer Madame la Baronne de Korf, se rendant à Franckfort avec ses deux enfants, une femme de chambre, un valet de chambre, et trois domestiques.*" And lower down, "*La Ministre des Affaires étrangeres,* MONTMORIN."

This foreign name, the title of German Baroness, the proverbial wealth of the bankers of Frankfort, to whom the people were accustomed to attribute everything that was singular and bizarre, had been most admirably combined by the Count de Fersen, to account for anything strange or remarkable in the appearance of the royal equipages; nothing, however, excited attention, and they arrived without interruption at Montmirail, a little town between Meaux and Châlons: there some necessary repairs to the berlin detained them an hour; this delay, during which the king's flight might be discovered, and couriers dispatched to give information to all the country, threw them into the greatest alarm.

However the carriage was soon repaired, and they once more started on their journey, ignorant that this hour's delay would ultimately cost the lives of four out of five persons who composed the royal family.

They were full of security and confidence; the success with which they had escaped from the palace, the manner in which they had left Paris, the punctuality with which the relays were furnished, the loneliness of the roads, the absence of anything like suspicion or vigilance in the towns they had passed through, the dangers they had left behind them, the security they were so fast approaching, each turn of the wheel bringing them nearer M. de Bouillé and his faithful troops; the beauty of the scene and the time, doubly beautiful to their eyes, that for two years had looked on nought save the seditious mob that daily filled the courts of the Tuileries, or the glittering bayonets of the armed populace beneath their windows,—all this seemed to them as if Providence had at last taken pity on them, that the fervent and touching prayers of the babes that slept in their arms, and of the angelic Madame Elizabeth had at last vanquished the fate that had so long pursued them.

It was under the influence of these happy feelings that they entered Châlons, the only large town through which they had to pass, at half-past three in the afternoon. A few idlers gathered round the carriage whilst the horses were being changed; the king somewhat imprudently put his head out of the window, and was recognized by the post-master; but this worthy man felt that his sovereign's life was in his hands, and without manifesting the least surprise, he helped to put to the horses, and ordered the postilions to drive on; he alone of this people was free from the blood of his king. The carriage passed the gates of Châlons, the king, the queen, and Madame Elizabeth exclaimed, with one voice, "We are saved." Châlons once passed, the king's security no longer depended on chance, but on prudence and force. The first relay was at Pont Sommeville. It will be remembered, that in obedience to the orders of M. de Bouillé, M. de Choiseul and M. de Guoguelas, at the head of a detachment of fifty hussars, were to meet the king and follow in his rear, and besides, as soon as the king's carriage appeared, to send off a hussar to warn the troops at Sainte Menehould and at Clermont of the vicinity of the royal family. The king felt thus certain of meeting faithful and armed friends; but he found no one. M. de Choiseul, M. de Guoguelas, and the fifty hussars had left half an hour before. The populace seemed disturbed and restless; they looked suspiciously at the travellers, and whispered from time to time in a low voice with each other. However, no one ventured to oppose their departure, and the king arrived at half-past seven at Sainte Menehould; at this season of the year, it was still broad daylight; and alarmed at having passed two of the relays without meeting the friends he expected, the king by a natural impulse put his head out of the window, in order to seek amidst the crowd for some friend, some officer posted there to explain to him the reason of the absence of the detachments: that action caused his ruin. The son of the post-master, Drouet, recognized the king, whom he had never seen, by his likeness to the effigy on the coins in circulation.

Nevertheless as the horses were harnessed, and the town occupied by a troop of dragoons, who could force a passage, the young man did not venture to attempt to detain the carriages at this spot.

XI.

The officer commanding the detachment of dragoons in

the town, was also, under pretence of walking on the Grand Place, on the watch for the royal carriages, which he recognized instantly, by the description of them with which he was furnished. He ordered his soldiers to mount and follow the king; but the national guards of Sainte Menehould, amongst whom the rumor of the likeness between the travellers and the royal family had been rapidly circulated, surrounded the barracks, closed the stables, and opposed by force the departure of the soldiers. During this rapid and instinctive movement of the people, the postmaster's son saddled his best horse, and galloped as fast as possible to Varennes, in order to arrive before the carriages, inform the municipal authorities of his suspicions, and arouse the patroles to arrest the monarch. Whilst this man, who bore the king's fate, galloped on the road to Varennes, the king himself, unconscious of danger, pursued his journey towards the same town. Drouet was certain to arrive before the king; for the road from Sainte Menehould to Varennes forms a considerable angle, and passes through Clermont, where a relay of horses was stationed; whilst the direct road, accessible only to horsemen, avoids Clermont, runs in a straight line to Varennes, and thus lessens the distance between this town and Menehould by four leagues. Drouet had thus two hours before him, and danger far outstripped safety. Yet by a strange coincidence death followed Drouet also, and threatened without his being aware of it, the life of him who in his turn (and without *his* knowledge) threatened the life of his sovereign.

A quarter-master (maréchal des logis) of the dragoons shut up in the barracks at Sainte Menehould, had alone found means to mount his horse, and escape the vigilance of the people. He had learnt from his commanding officer of Drouet's precipitate departure, and, suspecting the cause, he followed him on the road to Varennes, resolved to overtake and kill him; he kept within sight of him, but always at a distance in order that he might not arouse his suspicions, and with the intention of overtaking and killing him at a favorable opportunity, and at a retired spot. But Drouet, who had repeatedly looked round to ascertain whether he were pursued, had conjectured his intentions; and, being a native of the country, and knowing every path, he struck into some bye roads, and at last under cover of a wood he escaped from the dragoon and pursued his way to Varennes.

On his arrival at Clermont the king was recognized by Count Charles de Damas, who awaited his arrival at the head of two squadrons. Without opposing the departure of the carriages, the municipal authorities, whose suspicions had been in some measure aroused by the presence of the troops, ordered the dragoons not to quit the town, and they obeyed these orders. The Count de Damas alone, with a corporal and three dragoons found means to leave the town, and galloped towards Varennes at some distance from the king, a too feeble or too tardy succor. The royal family shut up in their berlin—and seeing that no opposition was offered to their journey, was unacquainted with these sinister occurrences. It was half-past eleven at night, when the carriages arrived at the first houses of the little town of Varennes; all were or appeared to be asleep; all was silent and deserted. It will be remembered, that Varennes not being on the direct line from Châlons to Montmédy, the king would not find horses there. It had been arranged between himself and M. de Bouillé, that the horses of M. de Choiseul should be stationed beforehand in a spot agreed upon in Varennes, and should conduct the carriages to Dun and Stenay, where M. de Bouillé awaited them. It will also be borne in mind that in compliance with the instructions of M. de Bouillé, M. de Choiseul and M. de Guoguelas, who, with the detachment of fifty hussars, were to await the king at Pont Sommeville, and then follow in his rear, had not awaited him nor followed him. Instead of reaching Varennes at the same time as the king, these officers on leaving Pont Sommeville had taken a road that avoids Sainte Menehould, and thus materially lengthens the distance between Pont Sommeville and Varennes. Their object in this was to avoid Sainte Menehould, in which the passage of the hussars had created some excitement the day previous. The consequence was, that neither M. de Guoguelas, nor M. de Choiseul, these two guides and confidants of the king's flight, were at Varennes on his arrival, nor did they reach there until an hour after. The carriages had stopped at the entrance of Varennes. The king, surprised to meet neither M. de Choiseul nor M. de Guoguelas, neither escort nor relays, hoped that the cracking of the postilions' whips would procure them fresh horses to continue their journey. The three body-guards went from door to door, to inquire where the horses had been placed, but could obtain no information.

XII.

The little town of Varennes is formed into two divisions, the upper and lower town, separated by a river and bridge. M. Guoguelas had stationed the fresh horses in the lower town on the other side of the bridge; the measure was in itself prudent, because the carriages would cross the bridge at full speed, and also, because in case of popular tumult, the changing horses and departure would be more easy when the bridge was once crossed; but the king should have been, but was not, informed of it. The king and queen, greatly alarmed, left the carriage, and wandered about in the deserted streets of the upper town for half an hour, seeking for the relays. In vain did they knock at the doors of the houses in which lights were burning, they could not hear of them. At last they returned in despair to the carriages, from which the postilions, wearied with waiting, threatened to unharness the horses: by dint of bribes and promises, however, they persuaded them to remount and continue their road: the carriages again were in motion, and the travellers reassured themselves that this was nothing but a misunderstanding, and that in a few moments they should be in the camp of M. de Bouillé. They traversed the upper town without any difficulty, all was buried in the most perfect tranquillity,—a few men alone are on the watch, and they are silent and concealed.

Between the upper and lower town is a tower at the entrance of the bridge that divides them; this tower is supported by a massive and gloomy arch, which carriages are compelled to traverse with the greatest care, and in which the least obstacle stops them; a relic of the feudal system in which the nobles captured the serfs, and in which, by a strange retribution, the people were destined to capture the monarchy. The carriages had hardly entered this dark arch than the horses, frightened at a cart that was overturned, stopped, and five or six armed men seizing their heads, ordered the travellers to alight and exhibit their passports at the Municipality. The man who thus gave orders to his sovereign was Drouet: scarcely had he arrived at Sainte Menehould than he hastened to arouse the young *patriotes* of the town, to communicate to them his conjectures and his apprehensions. Uncertain as to how far their suspicions were correct, or wishing to reserve for themselves the glory of arresting the king of France, they had neither warned the authorities nor aroused the populace. The plot awakened their patriotism; they felt that they represented the whole of the nation.

At this sudden apparition, at these shouts, and the aspect of the naked swords and bayonets, the body-guard seized their arms and awaited the king's orders; but the king forbade them to force the passage; the horses were turned round, and the carriages, escorted by Drouet and his companions, stopped before the door of a grocer named Sausse, who was at the same time Procureur Syndic of Varennes. There the king and his family were obliged to alight, in order that their passports might be examined, and the truth of the people's suspicions ascertained. At the same instant the friends of Drouet rushed into the town, knocked at the doors, mounted the belfry, and rang the alarm-bell. The affrighted inhabitants awoke, the national guards of the town and the adjacent villages hastened one after another to M. Sausse's door; others went to the quarters of the troops, to gain them over to their interest, or to disarm them. In vain did the king deny his rank—his features and those of the queen betrayed them. He at last discovered himself to the mayor and the municipal officers, and taking M. de Sausse's hand, "Yes," said he, "I am your king, and in your hands I place my destiny, and that of my wife, of my sister, and of my children; our lives, the fate of the empire, the peace of the kingdom, the safety of the constitution even, depends upon you. Suffer me to continue my journey; I have no design of leaving the country; I am going in the midst of a part of the army, and in a French town, to regain my real liberty, of which the factions at Paris deprive me, and from thence make terms with the Assembly, who, like myself, are held in subjection through fear. I am not about to destroy, but to save and secure the constitution; if you detain me, the constitution, I myself, France, all are lost. I conjure you as a father, as a husband, as a man, as a citizen, leave the road free to us; in an hour we shall be saved, and with us France is saved; and if you guard in your hearts that fidelity your words profess for him who was your master, I order you as your king."

XIII.

The men, touched by these words, respectful even in their violence, hesitated, and seemed touched. It is evident, by the expression of their features, by their tears, that they are wavering between their pity for so terrible a reverse of fortune and their conscience as patriots. The sight of their king, who pressed their hands in his, of their queen, by turns suppliant and majestic, who strives by despair or entreaties to wring from them permission to depart, unmanned them. They would have yielded had they consulted the dictates of their heart alone; but they began to fear for themselves the responsibility of their indulgence; the people will demand from them their king, the nation its chief. Egotism hardened their hearts; the wife of M. Sausse, with whom her husband repeatedly exchanged glances, and in whose breast the queen hoped to find pity and compassion, was the least moved of any. Whilst the king harangued the municipal authorities, the queen, seated with her children on her lap between two bales of goods in the shop, showed her infants to Madame Sausse. "You are a mother, madame," said the queen; "you are a wife; the fate of a wife and mother is in your hands—think what I must suffer for these children, for my husband. At one word from you I shall owe them to you; the queen of France will owe you more than her kingdom, more than life." "Madame," returned the grocer's wife unmoved, with that petty common sense of minds in which calculation stifles generosity, "I wish it was in my power to serve you; you are thinking of the king; I am thinking of M. Sausse. It is a wife's duty to think of her husband." All hope is lost when no pity can be found in a woman's heart. The queen, indignant and hurt, retired with Madame Elizabeth and the children into two rooms at the top of the house, and there she burst into tears. The king, surrounded by municipal officers and national guard, relinquished all hope of softening them. He repeatedly mounted the wooden staircase of the wretched shop; he went from the queen to his sister, from his sister to his children; that which he had been unable to obtain from pity, he hoped to obtain from time and compulsion. He could not believe that these men, who still showed something like feeling, and manifested so much respect for him, would persist in their determination of detaining him, and awaiting the orders of the Assembly. At all events he felt certain that before the return of the couriers from Paris he should be rescued by the forces of M. de Bouillé, by which he knew he was surrounded without the knowledge of the people. He was only astonished that these succors should delay their appearance so long. Hour after hour chimed, the night wore away, and yet they came not.

XIV.

The officer who commanded the squadron of hussars stationed at Varennes by M. de Bouillé, was not entirely acquainted with the plan of action, or its nature; he had merely been told that a large sum in gold would pass through, and that it would be his duty to escort it. No courier preceded the king's carriage, no messenger had arrived from Sainte Menehould to warn him to assemble his troopers; MM. de Choiseul and de Guoguelas, who were to be at Varennes before the king's arrival, and communicate to this officer the last secret orders relative to his duty, were not there; thus the officer was left with nothing but his own conjectures to guide him. Two other officers, who were informed by M. de Bouillé of the real facts, had been sent by the general to Varennes, but they remained in the lower town at the same inn where the horses of M. de Choiseul had been stationed; they were totally ignorant of all that was passing in the upper town; they awaited, in compliance with their orders, the arrival of M. de Choiseul, and were only aroused by the sound of the alarm-bell.

M. de Choiseul and M. de Guoguelas, with Count Charles de Damas, and his three faithful dragoons, galloped towards Varennes, having with the greatest difficulty escaped the insurrection of the squadrons at Clermont. On their arrival at the gates of the town, three-quarters of an hour after the king's arrest, they were recognized and stopped by the national guard, who, before they would allow the little troop to enter, compelled them to dismount. They demanded to see the king, and this they were permitted to do. The king, however, forbade them to use any violence, as he expected every instant the arrival of M. de Bouillé's superior force. M. de Guoguelas, however, left the house; and seeing the hussars intermingled with the crowd that filled the streets, wished to make trial of their fidelity. "Hussars," exclaimed he imprudently, "are you for the nation or the king?" "*Vive la nation!*" replied the soldiers; "we are, and always shall be, in her favor." The people applauded this declaration; and a sergeant of the national guard headed them, whilst their commanding officer succeeded in making his escape, and hastened to join the two officers, who, together with M. de Choiseul's horses, had been stationed in the lower town, and they all three quitted Varennes, and hastened to inform their general at Dun.

These officers had been fired upon, when, learning the royal carriages had been stopped, they endeavored to gain access to the king. The whole night passed in these different occurrences. Already had the national guards of the neighboring villages arrived at Varennes; barricades were erected between the upper and lower town; and the authorities sent off expresses to warn the inhabitants of Metz and Verdun, and to demand that troops and cannon might be instantly sent, to prevent the king being rescued by the approaching troops of M. de Bouillé.

The king, the queen, Madame Elizabeth, and the children, lay down for a short time, dressed as they were, in the rooms at M. Sausse's, amidst the threatening murmurs of the people and the noise of footsteps, that at each instant increased beneath their window. Such was the state of affairs at Varennes at seven o'clock in the morning. The queen had not slept; all her feelings as a wife, a mother, a queen—rage, terror, despair,—waged so terrible a conflict in her mind, that her hair, which had been auburn on the previous evening, was in the morning white as snow.

XV.

At Paris the most profound mystery had covered the king's departure. M. de La Fayette, who had twice been to the Tuileries, to assure himself with his own eyes that his orders had been strictly obeyed, quitted it at midnight, perfectly convinced that its walls would securely guard the people's hostages. It was only at seven o'clock in the morning of the 21st of June, that the servants of the chateau, on entering the apartments of the king and queen, found the beds undisturbed and the rooms deserted, and spread the alarm amongst the palace guard. The fugitive family had thus ten or twelve hours' start of any attempt that could be made to pursue them; and even supposing it could be ascertained which road they had taken, they could be only stopped by couriers, and the body-guard who accompanied the king would arrest the couriers without difficulty. Moreover, no attempt could be made to oppose their flight by force before they had reached the town in which were stationed the detachments of M. de Bouillé.

All Paris was in the greatest confusion. The report flew from the chateau, and spread like wildfire into the neighboring *quartiers*, and from thence into the faubourgs. The words, "The king has escaped," were in everybody's mouth; yet no one could believe it. Crowds flocked to the chateau, to assure themselves of the fact—they questioned the guards—inveighed against the traitors—every one believed that some conspiracy was on the point of breaking out. The name of M. de La Fayette, coupled with invectives, was on every tongue. "Is he a fool—is he a confederate? how is it possible that so many of the royal family could have passed the gates—the guards—without connivance?" The doors were forced open, to enable the people to visit the royal apartments. Divided between stupor and insult, they avenged themselves on inanimate objects, for the long respect with which these dwellings of kings had inspired them—and they passed from awe to derision. A portrait of the king was taken from the bed-chamber and hung up at the gate of the chateau, as an article of furniture for sale. A fruit woman took possession of the queen's bed, to sell her cherries in, saying, "It is to-day the nation's turn to take their ease."

A cap of the queen's was placed on the head of a young girl, but she exclaimed it would sully her forehead, and trampled it under foot with indignation and contempt. They entered the school-room of the young dauphin—there the people were touched, and respected the books, the maps, the toys of the baby king. The streets and public squares were crowded with people; the national guards assembled; the drums beat to arms; the alarm-gun thundered every minute. Men armed with pikes, and wearing the *bonnet rouge*, reappeared, and eclipsed the uniforms. Santerre, the brewer and agitator of the faubourgs, alone led a band of 2000 pikes. The people's indignation began to prevail over their terror, and showed itself in satirical outcrys and injurious actions against royalty. On the Place de la Grève, the bust of Louis XVI., placed beneath the fatal lantern, that had been the instrument of the first crimes of the Revolution, was mutilated. "When," exclaimed the demagogues, "will the people execute justice for themselves upon all these kings of bronze and marble—shameful monuments of their slavery and their idolatry?" The statues of the king were torn from the shops; some broke them into pieces, others merely tied a bandage over the eyes, to signify the blindness attributed to the king. The names of king, queen, Bourbon, were effaced from all the signs. The Palais Royal lost its name, and was now called Palais d'Orléans. The clubs, hastily convoked, rang with the most frantic motions; that of the Cordeliers decreed that the National Assembly had devoted France to slavery, by declaring the crown hereditary; they demanded that the name of the king should be forever abolished, and that the kingdom should be constituted into a republic. Danton gave it its audacity, and Marat its madness.

The most singular reports were in circulation, and contradicted each other at every moment. According to one, the king had taken the road to Metz, to another, the royal family had escaped by a drain. Camille Desmoulins excited the people's mirth as the most insulting mark of their contempt. The walls of the Tuileries were placarded with offers of a small reward to any one who would bring back the noxious or unclean animals that had escaped from it. In the garden, in the open air, the most extravagant proposals were made. "People," said one of these orators, mounting on a chair, "it will be unfortunate, should this perfidious king be brought back to us,—what should we do with him? He would come to us like Thersites to pour forth those big tears, of which Homer tells us; and we should be moved with pity. If he returns, I propose that he be exposed for three days to public derision, with the red handkerchief on his head, and that he be then conducted from stage to stage to the frontier, and that he be then kicked out of the kingdom."

Frèron caused his papers to be sold amongst the groups. "He is gone," said one of them, "this imbecile king, this perjured monarch. She is gone, this wretched queen, who, to the lasciviousness of Messalina, unites the insatiable thirst of blood that devoured Medea. Execrable woman, evil genius of France, thou wast the leader, the soul of this conspiracy." The people repeating these words, circulated from street to street these odious accusations, which fomented their hate, and envenomed their alarm.

XVI.

It was only at ten o'clock that three cannon shots proclaimed (by order of the municipal and departmental authorities) the event of the night to the people. The National

Assembly had already met; the president informed it that M. Bailly, the mayor of Paris, was come to acquaint them that the king and his family had been carried off during the night from the Tuileries by some enemies of the nation; the Assembly, who were already individually aware of this fact, listened to the communication with imposing gravity. It seemed as though at this moment the critical juncture of public affairs gave them a majestic calmness, and that all the wisdom of the great nation was concentrated in its representatives—one feeling alone dictated every act, every thought, every resolution,—to preserve and defend the constitution, even although the king was absent, and the royalty virtually dead. To take temporary possession of the regency of the kingdom, to summon the ministers, to send couriers on every road, to arrest all individuals leaving the kingdom; to visit the arsenal, to supply arms, to send the generals to their posts, and to garrison the frontiers,—all this was the work of an instant; there was no "right," no "left," no "centre;" the "left" comprised all. The Assembly was informed that one of the aides-de-camp of M. de La Fayette, sent by him on his own responsibility, and previous to any orders from the Assembly, was in the power of the people, who accused M. de La Fayette and his staff of treason; and messengers were sent to free him.

The aide-de-camp entered the chamber and announced the object of his mission; the Assembly gave a second order, sanctioning that of M. de La Fayette, and he departed. Barnave, who perceived in the popular irritation against La Fayette a fresh peril, hastened to mount the tribune; and although up to that period he had been opposed to the popular general, he yet generously, or adroitly, defended him against the suspicions of the people, who were ready to abandon him. It was said that for some days past Lameth and Barnave, in succeeding Mirabeau in the Assembly, felt, like himself, the necessity of some secret intelligence with this remnant of the monarchy. Much was said of secret relations between Barnave and the king, of a planned flight, of concealed measures; but these rumors, accredited by La Fayette himself in his memoirs, had not then burst forth; and even at this present period they are doubtful. "The object which ought to occupy us," said Barnave, "is to re-establish the confidence in him to whom it belongs. There is a man against whom popular movement would fain create distrust, that I firmly believe is undeserved: let us throw ourselves between this distrust and the people. We must have a concentrated, a central force, an arm to act, when we have but one single head to reflect. M. de La Fayette, since the commencement of the revolution, has evinced the opinions and the conduct of a good citizen. It is absolutely necessary that he should retain his credit with the nation. Force is necessary at Paris, but tranquillity is equally so. It is you, who must direct this force."

These words of Barnave were voted to be the text of the proclamation. At this moment information was brought that M. de Cazalès, the orator of the *côté droit*, was in the hands of the people, and exposed to the greatest danger at the Tuileries.

Six commissioners were appointed to go to his succor, and they conducted him to the chamber. He mounted the tribune, irritated at once against the people, from whose violence he had just escaped, and against the king, who had abandoned his partisans without giving them any timely information.

"I have narrowly escaped being torn in pieces by the people," cried he; "and thus without the assistance of the national guard, who displayed so much attachment for me ——." At these words which indicated the pretension to personal popularity lurking in the mind of the royalist orator, the Assembly gave marked signs of disapprobation, and the *côté gauche* murmured loudly. "I do not speak for myself," returned Cazalès, "but for the common interest. I will willingly sacrifice my petty existence, and this sacrifice has long ago been made; but it is important to the whole empire that your sittings be undisturbed by any popular tumult in the critical state of affairs at present, and in consequence I second all the measures for preserving order and tranquillity that have just been proposed." At length, on the motion of several members, the Assembly decided, that in the king's absence, all power should be vested in themselves, and that their decrees should be immediately put in execution by the ministers without any further sanction or acceptance. The Assembly seized on the dictatorship with a prompt and firm grasp, and declared themselves permanent.

XVII.

Whilst the Assembly, by the rights alike of prudence and

necessity, seized on the supreme power, M. de La Fayette cast himself with calm audacity amidst the people, to grasp again, at the peril of his life, the confidence that he had lost. The first impulse of the people would naturally be to massacre the perfidious general, who had answered for the safe custody of the king with his life, and had yet suffered him to escape. La Fayette saw his peril, and, by braving, averted the tempest. One of the first to learn the king's flight, from his officers, he hurried to the Tuileries, where he found the mayor of Paris, Bailly, and the president of the Assembly, Beauharnais. Bailly and Beauharnais lamented the number of hours that must be lost in the pursuit before the Assembly could be convoked, and the decrees executed. "Is it your opinion," asked La Fayette, "that the arrest of the king and the royal family is absolutely essential to the public safety, and can alone preserve us from civil war?" "No doubt can be entertained of that," returned the mayor and the president. "Well then," returned La Fayette, "I take on myself all the responsibility of this arrest;" and he instantly wrote an order to all the national guards and citizens to arrest the king. This was also a dictatorship, and the most personal of all dictatorships, that a single man, taking the place of the Assembly, and the whole nation, thus assumed. He, on his private authority and the right of his civic foresight, struck at the liberty and perhaps the life of the lawful ruler of the nation. This order led Louis XVI. to the scaffold, for it restored to the people the victim who had escaped their clutches. "Fortunately for him," he writes in his Memoirs, after the atrocities committed on these august victims, "fortunately for him, their arrest was not owing to his orders, but to the accident of being recognized by a postmaster, and to their ill arrangements." Thus the citizen ordered that which the man trembled to see fulfilled; and tardy sensibility protested against patriotism.

Quitting the Tuileries, La Fayette went to the Hôtel de Ville, on horseback. The quays were crowded with persons whose anger vented itself in reproaches against him, which he supported with the utmost apparent serenity. On his arrival at the Place de Grève, almost unattended, he found the Duke d'Aumont, one of his officers, in the hands of the populace, who were on the point of massacring him; and he instantly mingled with the crowd, who were astonished at his audacity, and rescued the Duke d'Aumont. He thus recovered by courage the dominion, which he would have lost (and with it his life) had he hesitated.

"Why do you complain?" he asked of the crowd. "Does not every citizen gain twenty sous by the suppression of the civil list? If you call the flight of the king a misfortune, by what name would you then denominate a counter-revolution that would deprive you of liberty?" He again quitted the Hôtel de Ville with an escort, and directed his steps with more confidence towards the Assembly. As he entered the chamber, Camus, near whom he seated himself, rose indignantly: "No uniforms here," cried he; "in this place we should behold neither arms nor uniforms." Several members of the left side rose with Camus, exclaiming to La Fayette, "Quit the chamber!" and dismissing with a gesture the intimidated general. Other members, friends of La Fayette, collected around him, and sought to silence the threatening vociferations of Camus. M. de La Fayette at last obtained a hearing at the bar. After uttering a few common places about liberty and the people, he proposed that M. de Gouvion, his second in command, to whom the guard of the Tuileries had been intrusted, should be examined by the Assembly. "I will answer for this officer," said he; "and take upon myself the responsibility." M. de Gouvion was heard, and affirmed that all the outlets from the palace had been strictly guarded, and that the king could not have escaped by any of the doors. This statement was confirmed by M. Bailly, the mayor of Paris. The intendant of the civil list, M. de Laporte, appeared, to present to the Assembly the manifesto the king had left for his people. He was asked, "How did you receive it?" "The king," replied M. de Laporte, "had left it sealed, with a letter for me." "Read this letter," said a member. "No, no," exclaimed the Assembly, "it is a confidential letter, we have no right to read it." They equally refused to unseal a letter for the queen that had been left on her table. The generosity of the nation, even in this moment, predominated over their irritation.

The king's manifesto was read amidst much laughter and loud murmurs.

"Frenchmen," said the king in this address to his people, "so long as I hoped to behold public happiness and tranquillity restored by the measures concerted by myself and the Assembly, no sacrifice was too great; calumnies, insult, injury, even the loss of liberty,—I have suffered all without a murmur. But now that I behold the kingdom destroyed, property violated, personal safety compromised, anarchy in every part of my dominions, I feel it my duty to lay before my subjects the motives of my conduct. In the month of July, 1789, I did not fear to trust myself amongst the inhabitants of Paris. On the 5th and 6th of October, although outraged in my own palace, and a witness of the impunity with which all sorts of crimes were committed, I would not quit France, lest I should be the cause of civil war. I came to reside in the Tuileries, deprived of almost the necessaries of life; my body-guard was torn from me, and many of these faithful gentlemen were massacred under my very eyes. The most shameful calumnies have been heaped upon the faithful and devoted wife, who participates in my affection for the people, and who has generously taken her share of all the sacrifices I have made for them. Convocation of the States-General, double representation granted to the third estate (*le tiers état*), reunion of the orders, sacrifice of the 20th of June,—I have done all this for the nation; and all these sacrifices have been lost, misinterpreted, turned against me. I have been detained as a prisoner in my own palace; instead of guards, jailers have been imposed on me. I have been rendered responsible for a government that has been torn from my grasp. Though charged to preserve the dignity of France in relation to foreign powers, I have been deprived of the right of declaring peace or war. Your constitution is a perpetual contradiction between the titles with which it invests me, and the functions it denies me. I am only the responsible chief of anarchy, and the seditious power of the clubs wrests from you the power you have wrested from me. Frenchmen, was this the result you looked for from your regeneration? Your attachment to your king was wont to be reckoned amongst your virtues; this attachment is now changed into hatred, and homage into insult. From M. Necker down to the lowest of the rabble, every one has been king except the king himself. Threats have been held out of depriving the king even of this empty title, and of shutting up the queen in a convent. In the nights of October, when it was proposed to the Assembly to go and protect the king by its presence, they declared it was beneath their dignity to do so. The king's aunts have been arrested, when from religious motives they wished to journey to Rome. My conscience has been equally outraged; even my religious principles have been constrained: when after my illness I wished to go to St. Cloud, to complete my convalescence, it was feared that I was going to this residence to perform my pious duties with priests who had not taken the oaths; my horses were unharnessed, and I was compelled by force to return to the Tuileries. M. de La Fayette himself could not insure obedience to the law, or the respect due to the king. I have been forced to send away the very priests of my chapels, and even the adviser of my conscience. In such a situation, all that is left me is to appeal to the justice and affection of my people, to take refuge from the attacks of the factions and the oppression of the Assembly and the clubs, in a town of my kingdom, and to resolve there, in perfect freedom, on the modifications the constitution requires; of the restoration of our holy religion; of the strengthening of the royal power, and the consolidation of true liberty."

The Assembly, who had several times interrupted the reading of this manifesto by bursts of laughter or murmurs of indignation, proceeded with disdain to the order of the day, and received the oaths of the generals employed at Paris. Numerous deputations* from Paris and the neighboring departments came successively to the bar to assure the Assembly that it would ever be considered as the rallying point by all good citizens.

The same evening the clubs of the Cordeliers and the Jacobins caused the motions for the king's dethronement to be placarded about. The club of the Cordeliers declared in one of its placards that every citizen who belonged to it had sworn individually to poniard the tyrants. Marat, one of its members, published and distributed in Paris an incendiary proclamation. "People," said he, "behold the loyalty, the honor, the religion of kings. Remember Henry III. and the Duke de Guise: at the same table as his enemy did Henry receive the sacrament, and swear on the same altar eternal friendship; scarcely had he quitted the temple than he distributed poniards to his followers, summoned the duke to his cabinet, and there beheld him fall pierced with wounds. Trust then to the oaths of princes! On the morning of the 19th, Louis XVI. laughed at his oath, and enjoyed beforehand the alarm his flight would cause you. The Austrian woman has seduced La Fayette last night. Louis XVI., disguised in a priest's robe, fled with the dauphin, his wife, his brother, and all the family. He now laughs at the folly of the Parisians, and ere long he will swim in their blood. Citizens, this escape has been long prepared by the traitors of the National Assembly. You are on the brink of ruin; hasten to provide for your safety. Instantly choose a dictator; let your choice fall on the citizen who has up to the present displayed most zeal, activity, and intelligence; and do all he bids you do to strike at your foes; this is the time to lop off the heads of Bailly, La Fayette, all the scoundrels of the staff, all the traitors of the Assembly. A tribune, a military tribune, or you are lost without hope. At present I have done all that was in the power of man to save you. If you neglect this last piece of advice, I have no more to say to you, and take my farewell of you forever. Louis XVI., at the head of his satellites, will besiege you in Paris, and the friend of the people will have a burning pile (*four ardent*) for his tomb, but his last sigh shall be for his country, for liberty, and for you."

XVIII.

The members of the constitutional party felt it their duty to attend the sitting of the Jacobins on the 22d, in order to moderate its ardor. Barnave, Siéyès, and La Fayette also appeared there, and took the oath of fidelity to the nation. Camille Desmoulins thus relates the results of this sitting:

"Whilst the National Assembly was decreeing, decreeing, decreeing, the people were acting. I went to the Jacobins, and on the Quai Voltaire I met La Fayette. Barnave's words had begun to turn the current of popular opinion, and some voices cried, 'Vive La Fayette.' He had reviewed the battalions on the quay. Convinced of the necessity of rallying round a chief, I yielded to the impulse that drew me towards the white horse. 'Monsieur de La Fayette,' said I to him in the midst of the crowd, 'for more than a year I have constantly spoken ill of you, this is the moment to convict me of falsehood. Prove that I am a calumniator, render me execrable, cover me with infamy, and save the state.' I spoke with the utmost warmth, while he pressed my hand. 'I have always recognized you as a good citizen,' returned he; 'you will see that you have been deceived: our common oath is to live free, or to die—all goes well—there's but one feeling amongst the National Assembly—the common danger has united all parties.' 'But why,' I inquired, 'does your Assembly affect to speak of the carrying off (*enlèvement*) of the king in all its decrees, when the king himself writes that he escaped of his own free will? what baseness, or what treason, in the Assembly to employ such language, when surrounded by three millions of bayonets.' 'The word *carrying off* is a mistake in dictation, that the Assembly will correct,' replied La Fayette; then he added, 'This conduct of the king is infamous.' La Fayette repeated this several times, and shook me heartily by the hand. I left him, reflecting that possibly the vast field that the king's flight opened to his ambition, might bring him back to the party of the people. I arrived at the Jacobins, striving to believe the sincerity of his demonstrations, of his patriotism, and friendship; and to persuade myself of this, which, in spite of all my efforts, escaped by a thousand recollections, and a thousand issues."

When Camille Desmoulins entered Robespierre was in the tribune: the immense credit that this young orator's perseverance and incorruptibility had gained him with the people, made his hearers crowd around him.

"I am not one of those," said he, "who term this event a disaster; this day would be the most glorious of the Revolution, did you but know how to turn it to your advantage. The king has chosen to quit his post at the moment of our most deadly perils, both at home and abroad. The Assembly has lost its credit; all men's minds are excited by the approaching elections. The emigrés are at Coblentz. The emperor and the king of Sweden are at Brussels; our harvests are ripe to feed their troops; but three millions of men are under arms in France, and this league of Europe may easily be vanquished. I fear neither Leopold, nor the king of Sweden. That which alone terrifies me, seems to reassure all others. It is the fact that since this morning all our enemies affect to use the same language as ourselves. All men are united, and in appearance wear the same aspect. It is impossible that all can feel the same joy at the flight of a king who possessed a revenue of forty millions of francs, and who distributed all the offices of state amongst his adherents and our enemies; there are traitors, then, among us; there is a secret understanding between the fugitive king and these traitors who have remained at Paris. Read the king's manifesto, and the whole plot will be there unveiled. The king, the emperor, the king of Sweden, d'Artois, Condé, all the fugitives, all these brigands, are about to march against us. A paternal manifesto will appear, in which the king will talk of his love of peace, and even of liberty; whilst at the same time the traitors in the capital and the departments will represent you, on their part, as the leaders of the civil war. Thus the Revolution will be stifled in the embraces of hypocritical despotism and intimidated moderatism.

"Look already at the Assembly: in twenty decrees the king's flight is termed carrying off by force (*enlèvement*). To whom does it intrust the safety of the people? To a minister of foreign affairs, under the inspection of a diplomatic committee. Who is the minister? A traitor whom I have unceasingly denounced to you, the persecutor of the patriot soldiers, the upholder of the aristocrat officers. What is the committee? A committee of traitors, composed of all our enemies beneath the garb of patriots. And the minister for foreign affairs, who is he? A traitor, a Montmorin, who but a short month ago declared a perfidious *adoration* of the constitution. And Delissart, who is he? A traitor, to whom Necker has bequeathed his mantle to cover his plots and conspiracies.

"Do you not see the coalition of these men with the king, and the king with the European league? That will crush us! In an instant you will see all the men of 1789—mayor, general, ministers, orators,—enter this room. How can you escape Antony?" continued he, alluding to La Fayette. "Antony commands the legions that are about to avenge Cæsar; and Octavius, Cæsar's nephew, commands the legions of the republic.

"How can the republic hope to avoid destruction? We are continually told of the necessity of uniting ourselves; but when Antony encamped at the side of Lepidus, and all the foes to freedom were united to those who termed themselves its defenders, nought remained for Brutus and Cassius, save to die.

"It is to this point that this feigned unanimity, this perfidious reconciliation of patriots, tends. Yes, this is the fate prepared for you. I know that by daring to unveil these conspiracies I sharpen a thousand daggers against my own life. I know the fate that awaits me; but if, when almost unknown in the National Assembly, I, amongst the earliest apostles of liberty, sacrificed my life to the cause of truth, of humanity, of my country; to-day, when I have been so amply repaid for this sacrifice, by such marks of universal goodwill, consideration, and regard, I shall look at death as a mercy, if it prevents my witnessing such misfortunes. I have tried the Assembly, let them in their turn try me."

XIX.

These words so artfully combined, and calculated to fill every breast with suspicion, were hailed like the last speech of a martyr for liberty. All eyes were suffused with tears. "We will die with you," cried Camille Desmoulins, extending his arms towards Robespierre, as though he would fain embrace him. His excitable and changeable spirit was borne away by the breath of each new enthusiastic impulse. He passed from the arms of La Fayette into those of Robespierre like a courtezan. Eight hundred persons rose *en masse;* and by their attitudes, their gestures, their spontaneous and unanimous inspiration, offered one of those most imposing tableaux, that prove how great is the effect of oratory, passion, and circumstance over an assembled people. After they had all individually sworn to defend Robespierre's life, they were informed of the arrival of the ministers and members of the Assembly who had belonged to the club in '89, and who in this perilous state of their country, had come to fraternize with the Jacobins.

"Monsieur le President," cried Danton, "if the traitors venture to present themselves, I undertake solemnly either that my head shall fall on the scaffold, or to prove that their heads should roll at the feet of the nation they have betrayed."

The deputies entered: Danton, recognizing La Fayette amongst them, mounted the tribunal, and addressing the general, said:—"It is my turn to speak, and I will speak as though I were writing a history for the use of future ages. How do you dare, M. de La Fayette, to join the friends of the constitution; you, who are a friend and partisan of the system of the two chambers invented by the priest Siéyès, a system destructive of the constitution and liberty? Did you not yourself tell me that the project of M. Mounier was too execrable for any one to venture to reproduce it, but that it was possible to cause an equivalent to it to be accepted by the Assembly? I dare you to deny this fact—that damns you. How comes it that the king in his proclamation uses the same language as yourself? How have you dared to infringe an order of the day on the circulation of the pamphlets of the defenders of the people, whilst you grant the protection of your bayonets to cowardly writers, the destroyers of the constitution? Why did you bring back prisoners, and as it were in triumph, the inhabitants of the Faubourg

St. Antoine, who wished to destroy the last stronghold of tyranny at Vincennes? Why, on the evening of this expedition to Vincennes, did you protect in the Tuileries assassins armed with poniards to favor the king's escape? Explain to me by what chance, on the 21st June, the Tuileries was guarded by the company of the grenadiers of the Rue de l'Oratoire, that you had punished on the 18th of April for having opposed the king's departure? Let us not deceive ourselves: the king's flight is only the result of a plot; there has been a secret understanding, and you, M. de La Fayette, who lately staked your head for the king's safety, do you by appearing in this assembly seek your own condemnation? The people must have vengeance; they are wearied of being thus alternately braved or deceived. If my voice is unheard here, if our weak indulgence for the enemies of our country continually endanger it, I appeal to posterity, and leave it to them to judge between us."

M. de La Fayette, thus attacked, made no reply to these strong appeals; he merely said that he had come to join the Assembly, because it was there that all good citizens should hasten in perilous times; and he then left the place. The Assembly having issued a decree next day calling on the general to appear and justify himself, he wrote that he would do so at a future period; he however never did so. But the motions of Robespierre and Danton did not in the least injure his influence over the national guard. Danton on that day displayed the greatest audacity. M. de La Fayette had the proofs of the orator's venality in his possession—he had received from M. de Montmorin 100,000 francs. Danton knew that M. de La Fayette was well aware of this transaction; but he also knew that La Fayette could not accuse him without naming M. de Montmorin, and without also accusing himself of participation in this shameful traffic, that supplied the funds of the civil list. This double secret kept them mutually in check, and obliged the orator and general to maintain a degree of reserve that lessened the fury of the contest. Lameth replied to Danton, and spoke in favor of concord. The violent resolutions proposed by Robespierre and Danton had no weight that day at the Jacobins' Club. The peril that threatened them taught the people wisdom, and their instinct forbade their dividing their force before that which was unknown.

XX.

The same evening the National Assembly discussed and adopted an address to the French nation, in these terms :—

"A great crime has been committed. The king and his family have been *carried off*, (the continuance of this pretended *enlèvement* of the king excited loud murmurs,) but your representatives will triumph over all these obstacles. France wishes to be free, and she shall be; the Revolution will not retrograde. We have saved the law by resolving that our decrees shall be the law. We have saved the nation by sending to the army reinforcements of 300,000 men. We have saved public peace by placing it under the safeguard of the zeal and patriotism of the armed citizens. In this position we await our enemies. In a manifesto dictated to the king by those who had offered violence to his affection for his people, you are accused—the constitution is accused—the law of impunity of the 6th of October is accused. The nation is more just, for she does not accuse the king of the crimes of his ancestors. (Applause.)

"But the king swore on the 14th of July to protect this constitution; he has therefore consented to perjure himself. The changes made in the constitution of the kingdom are laid to the charge of the *soidisant* factious. A few factious? that is not sufficient; we are 26,000,000 of factious. (Loud applause.) We have re-constructed the power, we have preserved the monarchy, because we believe it useful to France. We have doubtless reformed it, but it was to save it from its abuses and its excesses; we have granted a yearly sum of 50,000,000 of francs to maintain the legitimate splendor of the throne. We have reserved to ourselves the right of declaring war, because we would not that the blood of the people should belong to the ministers. Frenchmen! all is organized, every man is at his post. The Assembly watches over all. You have nought to fear save from yourselves, should your just emotion lead you to commit any violence or disorders. The people who seek to be free should remain unmoved in great crises.

"Behold Paris, and imitate the example of the capital. All goes on as usual; the tyrants will be deceived. Before they can bend France beneath their yoke, the whole nation must be annihilated. Should despotism venture to attempt it, it will be vanquished; or even though it triumph, it will triumph over nought save ruins!" (Loud and unanimous applause followed the conclusion of the address.)

The sitting which had been suspended during an hour, re-opened at half-past nine. Much agitation prevailed in the chamber, and the words *He is arrested! He is arrested!* ran along the benches, and from the benches to the tribune. The president announced that he had just received a packet containing several letters which he would read; at the same time recommending them to abstain from any marks of approbation or disapprobation. He then opened the packet amidst a profound silence, and read the letters of the municipal authorities at Varennes and of St. Menehould brought by M. Mangin, surgeon, at Varennes. The Assembly then nominated three commissioners out of the members to bring the king back to Paris. These three commissioners were Barnave, Pétion, and Latour-Maubourg, and they instantly started off to fulfil their mission. Let us now for a brief space leave Paris a prey to all the different emotions of surprise, joy, and indignation excited by the flight and arrest of the king.

XXI.

The night at Varennes had been passed by the king, the queen, and the people in alternate feelings of hope and terror. Whilst the children, fatigued with a long day's journey, and the heat of the weather, slept soundly, the king and queen, guarded by the municipal guards of Varennes, discussed, in a low voice, the danger of their position, their pious sister, Madame Elizabeth, prayed by their side; her kingdom was, indeed, "in heaven." Nothing had induced her to remain at the court, from which she was estranged, alike by her piety and her renouncement of all worldly pleasure, but her affection for her brother, and she had shared only the sorrows and sufferings of the throne.

The prisoners were far from despairing yet; they had no doubt that M. de Bouillé, warned by one of the officers whom he had stationed on the road, would march all night to their assistance; and they attributed his delay to the necessity of collecting a sufficient force to overpower the numerous troops of national guards whom the sound of the tocsin had summoned to Varennes. But at each instant they expected to see him appear, and the least movement of the populace, the slightest clash of arms in the streets, seemed to announce his arrival; the courier dispatched to Paris by the authorities of Varennes to receive the orders of the Assembly, only left at three o'clock in the morning. He could not reach Paris in less than twenty hours, and would require as much more for his return; and the Assembly would require, at least three or four hours more to deliberate; thus M. de Bouillé must have forty-eight hours' start of any orders from Paris.

Moreover, in what state would Paris be? what would have happened there at the unexpected announcement of the king's departure? Had not terror or repentance taken possession of every mind; would not anarchy have destroyed the feeble barriers that an anarchical assembly might have opposed to it? Would not the cry of treason have been the first signal of alarm? La Fayette have been torn to pieces as a traitor, and the national guard disbanded? Would not the well intentioned and loyal citizens have again obtained the mastery over the factious and turbulent in the confusion and terror that would prevail? Who would give orders? who would execute them?

The nation trembling, and in disorder, would fall perhaps at the feet of its king. Such were the chimeras, the last fond hopes of this unfortunate family, and on which they sustained their courage, during this fatal night, in the small and suffocating room into which they were all crowded.

The king had been allowed to communicate with several officers: M. de Guoguelas, M. de Damas, M. de Choiseul had seen him. The procureur syndic, and the municipal officers of Varennes, showed both respect and pity for their king even in the execution of what they believed to be their duty. The people do not pass at once from respect to outrage. There is a moment of indecision in every sacrilegious act, in which they seem yet to reverence that which they are about to destroy. The authorities of Varennes and M. Sausse, although believing they were the saviours of the nation, were yet far from wishing to offend the king, and guarded him as much as their sovereign as their captive. This did not escape the king's notice; he flattered himself that at the first demand made by M. de Bouillé, respect would prevail over patriotism, and that he would be set at liberty, and he expressed this belief to his officers.

One of them, M. Derlons, who commanded the squadron of hussars stationed at Dun, between Varennes and Stenay, had been informed of the king's arrest at two o'clock in the morning by the commander of the detachment at Varennes: having escaped this town, M. Derlons, without awaiting any orders from the general, and anticipating them, he ordered his hussars to mount, and galloped to Varennes, determined to rescue the king by force. On his arrival at the gates of that town, he found them barricaded and defended by a numerous body of national guards, who refused to allow the hussars to enter the town. M. Derlons dismounted, and leaving his men outside, demanded to see the king, which was consented to. His aim was to inform the king that M. de Bouillé was about to march thither at the head of the royal Allemand regiment, and also to assure himself, if it was impossible for his squadron to force the obstacles, to break down the barricades in the upper town, and carry off the king. The barricades appeared to him impregnable to cavalry, he therefore gained admittance to the king, and asked him what were his orders. "Tell M. de Bouillé," returned the king, "that I am a prisoner, and can give no orders. I much fear he can do no more for me, but I pray him to do all he can." M. Derlons, who was an Alsatian, and spoke German, wished to say a few words in that language to the queen, in order that no person present might understand what passed. "Speak French, sir," said the queen, "we are overheard." M. Derlons said no more, but withdrew in despair; but he remained with his troops at the gates of Varennes, awaiting the arrival of the superior forces of M. de Bouillé.

XXII.

The aide-de-camp of M. de La Fayette, M. Romeuf, dispatched by that general, and bearer of the order of the Assembly, arrived at Varennes at half-past seven. The queen, who knew him personally, reproached him in the most pathetic manner with the odious mission with which his general had charged him. M. Romeuf sought in vain to calm her indignation, by every mark of respect and devotion compatible with the rigor of his orders. The queen then changing from invectives to tears, gave a free vent to her grief. M. Romeuf having laid the order of the Assembly on the Dauphin's bed, the queen seized the paper, threw it on the ground, and trampled it under her feet, exclaiming that such a paper would sully her son's bed. "In the name of your safety, of your glory, madam," said the young officer, master your grief; would you suffer any one but myself to witness such a fit of despair?"

The preparations for their departure were hastened, through fear, lest the troops of M. de Bouillé might march on the town, or cut them off. The king used every means in his power to delay them, for each minute gained gave them a fresh hope of safety, and disputed them one by one. At the moment they were entering the carriage, one of the queen's women feigned a sudden and alarming illness. The queen refused to start without her, and only yielded at last to threats of force, and the shouts of the impatient populace. She would suffer no one to touch her son, but carried him herself to the carriage; and the royal cortége, escorted by three or four thousand national guards, moved slowly towards Paris.

XXIII.

What was M. de Bouillé doing during this long and agonizing night the king passed at Varennes! He had, as we have already seen, passed the night at the gates of Dun, two leagues from Varennes, awaiting the couriers who were to inform him of the king's approach. At four in the morning, fearing to be discovered, and having seen no one, he regained Stenay, in order to be nearer his troops, in case any accident had happened to the king. At half-past four he was at the gates of Stenay, when the two officers whom he had left there the previous evening, and the commanding officer of the squadron that had abandoned him, arrived and informed him that the king had been arrested since eleven o'clock at night. Stupefied and astonished at being informed so late, he instantly ordered the royal Allemand regiment, which was at Stenay, to mount and follow him. The colonel of this regiment had received the previous evening orders to keep the horses saddled. This order had not been executed, and the regiment lost three-quarters of an hour, in spite of the repeated messages of M. de Bouillé, who sent his own son to the barracks. The general was powerless without this regiment, and no sooner were they outside the town than M. de Bouillé endeavored to ascertain its disposition towards the king. "Your king," said he "who was hastening hither to dwell amongst you, has been stopped by the inhabitants of Varennes, within a few leagues. Will you let him remain a prisoner, exposed to every insult at the hands of the national guards? Here are his orders: he awaits you; he counts every moment. Let us march to Varennes. Let us hasten to deliver him, and restore him to the nation and liberty."

Loud acclamations followed this speech. M. de Bouillé distributed 500 or 600 louis amongst the soldiers, and the regiment marched forward.

Stenay is at least nine leagues from Varennes, and the road very hilly and bad. M. de Bouillé, however, used all possible dispatch, and at a little distance from Varennes he met the advanced guard of the regiment, halted at the entrance of a little wood, defended by a body of the national guard. M. de Bouillé ordered them to charge, and putting himself at the head of the troop, arrived at Varennes at a quarter to nine, closely followed by the regiment. Whilst reconnoitering the town, previous to an attack, he observed a troop of hussars, who appeared also to watch the town. It was the squadron from Dun, commanded by M. Derlons, who had passed the night here, awaiting reinforcements. M. Derlons hastened to inform the general that the king had left the town more than an hour and a half; he added, the bridge was broken, the streets barricaded; that the hussars of Clermont and Varennes had fraternized with the people, and the commanders of the detachments, MM. de Choiseul, de Damas, and de Guoguelas, were prisoners. M. de Bouillé, baffled, but not discouraged, resolved to follow the king, and rescue him from the hands of the national guard. He dispatched officers to find a ford by which they could pass the river; but, unfortunately, although one existed, they were unable to find it.

Whilst thus engaged, he learnt that the garrisons of Metz and Verdun were advancing with a train of artillery to the aid of the people. The country was swarming with troops and national guards. The troops began to show symptoms of hesitation; the horses fatigued by nine leagues over a bad road, could not sustain the speed necessary to overtake the king at Sainte Menehould. All energy deserted them with hope. The regiment turned round, and M de Bouillé led them back in silence to Stenay: thence, followed only by a few of the officers most implicated, he gained Luxembourg, and passed the frontier amidst a shower of balls and [illegible]ing for death more than he shunned the punishment.

XXIV.

The royal carriages, however, rolled rapidly along the road to Châlons, attended by the national guard, who relieved each other in order to escort them on; the whole population lined the road on either side, to gaze upon a king brought back in triumph by the nation that believed itself betrayed. The pikes and bayonets of the national guards could scarcely force them a passage through this dense throng, that at each instant grew more and more numerous, and who were never weary of uttering cries of derision and menace, accompanied by the most furious gestures.

The carriages pursued their journey amidst a torrent of abuse, and the clamor of the people recommenced at every turn of the wheel. It was a Calvary of sixty leagues, every step of which was a torture. One gentleman, M. de Dampierre, an old man, accustomed all his life to venerate the king, having advanced towards the carriage to show some marks of respectful compassion to his master, was instantly massacred before their eyes, and the royal family narrowly escaped passing over his bleeding corpse. Fidelity was the only unpardonable crime amongst this band of savages. The king and queen, who had already made the sacrifice of their lives, had summoned all their dignity and courage, in order to die worthily. Passive courage was Louis XVI.'s virtue, as though Heaven, who destined him to suffer martyrdom, had gifted him with heroic endurance, that cannot resist, but can die. The queen found in her blood and her pride sufficient hatred for the people, to return with inward scorn the insults with which they profaned her. Madame Elizabeth prayed mentally for divine assistance; and the two children wondered at the hatred of the people they had been taught to love, and whom they now saw only a prey to the most violent fury. The august family would never have reached Paris alive, had not the commissioners of the Assembly, who by their presence overawed the people, arrived in time to subdue and control this growing sedition.

The commissioners met the carriages between Dormans and Epernay, and read to the king and people the order of the Assembly, giving them the absolute command of the troops and national guards along the line; and which enjoined them to watch not only over the king's security, but also to maintain the respect due to royalty, represented in his person. Barnave and Pétion hastened to enter the king's carriage, to share his danger, and shield him with their bodies. They succeeded in preserving him from death, but not from outrage. The fury of the people, kept aloof from the carriages, found vent farther off; and all persons suspected of feeling the least sympathy were brutally ill-treated.

An ecclesiastic having approached the berlin, and exhibited some traces of respect and sorrow on his features, was seized by the people, thrown under the horses' feet, and was on the point of being massacred before the queen's eyes, when Barnave, with a noble impulse, leant out of the carriage. "Frenchmen," exclaimed he, "will you, a nation of brave men, become a people of murderers?" Madame Elizabeth, struck with admiration at his courageous interference, and fearing lest he might spring out, and be in his turn torn to pieces by the people, held him by his coat whilst he addressed the mob. From this moment the pious princess, the queen, and the king himself conceived a secret esteem for Barnave. A generous heart amidst so many cruel ones, inspired them with a species of confidence in the young *député*. They had known him only as a leader of faction, and by his voice heard amidst all their misfortunes; and they were astonished to find a respectful protector in the man whom they had hitherto looked upon as an insolent foe.

Barnave's features were marked, yet attractive and open; his manners polished, his language elegant; his bearing saddened by the aspect of so much beauty, so much majesty, and so great a reverse of fortune. The king in the intervals of calm and silence frequently spoke to him, and discoursed of the events of the day. Barnave replied, with the tone of a man devoted to liberty, but faithful still to the throne; and who in his plans of regeneration, never separated the nation from the throne. Full of attention to the queen, Madame Elizabeth, and the royal children, he strove by every means in his power to hide from them the perils and humiliations of the journey. Constrained, no doubt, by the presence of his rough colleague, Pétion, if he did not openly avow the feeling of pity, admiration, and respect which had conquered him during the journey, he showed it in his actions, and a tacit treaty was concluded by looks. The royal family felt that amidst this wreck of all their hopes they had yet gained Barnave. All his subsequent conduct justified the confidence of the queen. Audacious, when opposed to tyranny, he was powerless against weakness, beauty, and misfortune; and this lost him his life, but rendered his memory glorious. Until then he had been only eloquent; he now showed that he possessed sensibility. Pétion, on the contrary, remained cold as a sectarian, and rude as a *parvenu;* he affected a brusque familiarity with the royal family, eating in the queen's presence, and throwing the rind of fruit out of the window, at the risk of striking the king's face. When Madame Elizabeth poured him out some wine, he raised his glass without thanking her to show that he had enough. Louis XVI. having asked him if he was in favor of the system of the two chambers, or for the republic—"I should be in favor of a republic," returned Pétion, "if I thought my country sufficiently ripe for this form of government." The king, offended, made no reply, and did not once speak until they arrived at Paris.

The commissioners had written from Dormans to the Assembly, to inform them what road the king would take, and at what day and hour he would arrive. The approach to Paris offered increasing danger, owing to the numbers and fury of the populace through which the king had to pass. The Assembly redoubled its energy and precaution to assure the inviolability of the king's person. The people, too, recovered the sentiment of their own dignity before this great success fate granted them: they would not dishonor their own triumph. Thousands of placards were stuck on the walls—"*Whoever applauds the king shall be beaten; whoever insults him shall be hung.*" The king had slept at Meaux, and the commissioners advised the Assembly to sit permanently, in order to be in readiness for any unforeseen event that might take place on the king's arrival at Paris; and the Assembly, consequently, did not dissolve. The hero of the day, the author of the king's arrest, Drouet, son of the postmaster of Sainte Menehould, appeared before it, and gave the following evidence:—"I have served in Condé's regiment of dragoons, and my comrade, Guillaume, in the Queen's dragoons. The 21st of June, at seven in the evening, two carriages and eleven horses arrived at Sainte Menehould, and I recognized the king and queen; but, fearful of being deceived, I resolved to ascertain the truth of this by arriving at Varennes, by a bye-road, before the carriages. It was eleven o'clock, and quite dark, when I reached Varennes; the carriages arrived also, and were delayed by a dispute between the couriers and the postilions, who refused to go any further. I said to my comrade, 'Guillaume, are you a good patriot?' 'Do not doubt it,' replied he. 'Well, then, the king is here; let us arrest him.' We overturned a cart, filled with goods, under the arch of the bridge; and when the carriage arrived, demanded their passports. 'We are in a hurry, gentlemen,' said the queen. However, we insisted, and made them alight at the house of the procureur of the district; then, of his own accord, Louis XVI. said to us, 'Behold your king—your queen—and my children! Treat us with that respect that Frenchmen have always shown to their king.' We, however, detained him; the national guards hastened to the town, and the hussars espoused our cause; and after having done our duty, we returned home, amidst the acclamations of our fellow-citizens, and to-day come to offer the homage of our services to the National Assembly."

Drouet and Guillaume were loudly applauded after this speech.

The Assembly then decreed that immediately after the arrival of Louis XVI. at the Tuileries, a guard should be given him, under the orders of La Fayette, who should be responsible for his security. Malouet was the only one who ventured to remonstrate against this captivity. "It at once destroyed inviolability and the constitution; the legislative and executive powers are now united." Alexandre Lameth opposed Malouet's motion, and declared that it was the duty of the Assembly to assume and retain, until the completion of the constitution, a dictatorship, forced upon it by the state of affairs, but that the monarchy being the form of government necessary to the concentration of the forces of so great a nation, the Assembly would immediately afterwards resume a division of powers, and return to the forms of a monarchy.

XXV.

At this moment the captive king entered Paris. It was on the 25th of June, at seven o'clock in the evening. From Meaux to the suburbs of Paris, the crowd thickened in every place as the king passed. The passions of the city, the Assembly, the press, and the clubs worked more intensely, and even closer in this population of the environs of Paris. These passions, written on every countenance, were repressed by their very violence. Indignation and contempt controlled their rage. Insult escaped them only in under tones; the populace was sinister, and not furious. Thousands of glances darted death into the windows of the carriages, but not one tongue uttered a threat.

This calmness of hatred did not escape the king; the day was burning hot. A scorching sun, reflected by the pavement and the bayonets, was almost suffocating in the berlin, where ten persons were squeezed together. Volumes of dust raised by the trampling of two or three hundred thousand spectators, was the only veil which from time to time covered the humiliation of the king and queen from the triumph of the people. The sweat of the horses, the feverish breath of this multitude compact and excited, made the atmosphere dense and fetid. The travellers panted for breath, the foreheads of the two children were bathed in perspiration. The queen, trembling for them, let down one of the windows of the carriage quickly, and addressing the crowd in an appeal to their compassion, "See, gentlemen," she exclaimed, "in what a state my poor children are—one is choking!" "We will choke you in another fashion," replied these ferocious men in an under tone.

From time to time violent attempts of the mob broke through the line, pushed aside the horses, and men reaching the doors mounted on the steps. Merciless ruffians, looking in silence on the king, the queen, and the dauphin, seemed calculating on final crimes, and feeding on the degradation of royalty. Bodies of *gendarmerie* restored order from time to time. The procession resumed its way in the midst of the clashing of sabres, and the cries of men trampled under the horses' hoofs. La Fayette, who feared attempts and surprises in the streets of Paris, desired General Damas, the commandant of the escort, not to traverse the city. He placed troops in deep lines on the boulevard from the barrier De l'Etoile to the Tuileries. The national guard bordered this line. The Swiss guards were also drawn up, but their flags no longer lowered before their master. No military honor was paid to the supreme head of the army. The national guards, resting on their arms, did not salute them, but saw the *cortége* pass by in an attitude of force, indifference, and contempt.

XXVI.

The carriages entered in the garden of the Tuileries by the turning bridge. La Fayette, on horseback at the head of his staff, had gone to meet the procession, and now headed it.

During his absence an immense crowd had filled the garden, the terraces, and obstructed the gate of the chateau. The escort had the greatest difficulty in forcing its way through this tumultuous mass. They made every man keep his hat on. M. de Guillermy, a member of the Assembly, alone remained uncovered, in spite of the threats and insults which this mark of respect brought down upon him. It was then that the queen, perceiving M. de La Fayette, and fearing for her faithful body-guard sitting in the carriage, and threatened by the people, exclaimed, "Monsieur de La Fayette, save the *gardes du corps*."

The royal family descended from the carriage at the end of the terrace. La Fayette received them from the hands of Barnave and Pétion. The children were carried in the arms of the national guard. One of the members of the left side of the Assembly, the Vicomte de Noailles, approached the queen with eagerness, and offered his arm. The queen indignantly rejected it, and cast a look of contempt at the offer of protection from an enemy, then perceiving a deputy of the right, demanded his arm. So much degradation might depress, but could not overcome her. The dignity of the empire displayed itself unabated in the gesture and the heart of the woman.

The prolonged clamors of the crowd at the entrance of the king at the Tuileries announced to the Assembly its triumph. The excitement suspended the sitting for nearly half an hour. A deputy, rushing into the meeting, exclaimed that three *gardes du corps* were in the hands of the people, who would rend them in pieces. Twenty *commissaires* went out at the moment to rescue them. They entered some minutes afterwards. The riot had been appeased by them. They stated that they had seen Pétion protecting with his person the door of the king's carriage. Barnave entered, mounted the tribune, covered as he was with the dust of his journey, and said, "We have fulfilled our mission to the honor of France and the Assembly; we have assured the public tranquillity and the safety of the king. The king has declared to us that he had no intention of passing the boundaries of the kingdom. (Murmurs.) We advanced rapidly as far as Meaux, in order to avoid the pursuit of M. de Bouillé's troops. The national guards and the troops have done their duty. The king is at the Tuileries."

Pétion added, in order to flatter public opinion, that when the carriage stopped some persons had attempted to lay hands on the *gardes du corps* that he himself had been seized by the collar and dragged from his place by the carriage-door, but that this movement by the people was legal in its intention, and had no other object than to enforce the execution of the law which had ordered the arrest of the accomplices of the court. It was decreed that information should be drawn up by the tribunal of the *arrondissement* of the Tuileries concerning the king's flight, and that three commissioners appointed by the Assembly should receive the declarations of the king and queen. "What means this obsequious exception?" exclaimed Robespierre. "Do you fear to degrade royalty by handing over the king and queen to ordinary tribunals? A citizen, a *citoyenne*, any man, any dignity, how elevated soever, can never be degraded by the law." Buzot supported this opinion; Duport opposed it. Respect prevailed over outrage. The commissioners named were Tronchet, Dandré, and Duport.

XXVII.

Once more in his own apartments, Louis XVI. measured with a glance the depth of his fall. La Fayette presented himself with all the demeanor of regret and respect, but with the reality of command. "Your majesty," said he to the king, "knows my attachment for your royal person, but at the same time you are not ignorant that if you separated yourself from the cause of the people, I should side with the people." "That is true," replied the king. "You follow your principles—this is a party matter, and I tell you frankly, that until lately I had believed you had surrounded me by a turbulent faction of persons of your own way of thinking in order to mislead me, but that yours was not the real opinion of France. I have learnt during my journey that I was deceived, and that this was the general wish." "Has your majesty any orders to give me?" replied La Fayette. "It seems to me," retorted the king with a smile, "that I am more at your orders than you are at mine."

The queen allowed the bitterness of her ill-restrained resentment to display itself. She wished to force on M. de La Fayette the keys of her caskets, which were in the carriages: he refused. She insisted; and when he was firm in his refusal, she placed them in his hat with her own hands. "Your majesty will have the goodness to take them back," said M. de La Fayette, "for I shall not touch them." "Well, then," answered the queen, "I shall find persons less delicate than you." The king entered his closet, wrote several letters, and gave them to a footman, who presented them to M. de La Fayette for inspection. The general appeared indignant that he should be deemed capable of such an unworthy office as acting the spy over the king's acts; he was desirous that the thraldom of the monarch should at least preserve the outward appearance of liberty.

The service of the chateau went on as usual; but La Fayette gave the pass-word without first receiving it from the king. The iron gates of the courts and gardens were locked. The royal family submitted to La Fayette the list of persons whom they desired to receive. Sentinels were placed at every door, in every passage, in the corridors between the chambers of the king and queen. The doors of these chambers were constantly kept open—even the queen's bed was inspected. Every place, the most sacred, was suspected; female modesty was in no wise respected. The gestures, looks, and words of the king, and queen—all were watched, spied, and noted. They were obliged to manage by stealth some secret interviews. An officer of the guard passed twenty-four hours at a time at the end of a dark corridor, which was placed behind the apartment of the queen's —a single lamp lighted it, like the vault of a dungeon. This post, detested by the officers on service, was sought after by the devotion of some of them; they affected zeal, in order to cloak their respect. Saint Prix, a celebrated actor of the Theatre Français, frequently accepted this post,—he favored the hasty interviews of the king, his wife, and sister.

In the evening one of the queen's women moved her bed between that of her mistress and the open door of the apartment, that she might thus conceal her from the eyes of the sentinels. One night the commandant of the guard, who watched between the two doors, seeing that this womon was asleep, and the queen was awake, ventured to approach the couch of his royal mistress, and gave her in a low tone some information and advice as to her situation. This conversation aroused the sleeping attendant, who, alarmed at seeing a man in uniform close to the royal bed, was about to call aloud, when the queen desired her to be silent, saying, "Do not alarm yourself; this is a good Frenchman, who is mistaken as to the intentions of the king and myself, but whose conversation betokens a sincere attachment to his master."

Providence thus made some of their persecutors to convey

some consolation to the victims. The king, so resigned, so unmoved, was bowed for a moment beneath the weight of so many troubles—so much humiliation. Such was his mental occupation, that he remained for ten days without exchanging a word with one of his family. His last struggle with misfortune seemed to have exhausted his strength. He felt himself vanquished, and desired, it would almost seem, to die by anticipation. The queen, throwing herself at his feet, and presenting to him his children, forced him to break this mournful silence. "Let us," she exclaimed, "preserve all our fortitude, in order to sustain this long struggle with fortune. If our destruction be inevitable, there is still left to us the choice of how we will perish; let us perish as sovereigns, and do not let us wait without resistance, and without vengeance, until they come and strangle us on the very floor of our own apartments!" The queen had the heart of a hero; Louis XVI. had the soul of a sage; but the genius which combines wisdom with valor was wanting to both: the one knew how to struggle—the other knew how to submit—neither knew how to reign.

XXVIII.

The effect of this flight, had it succeeded, would have wholly changed the aspect of the Revolution. Instead of having in the king, captive in Paris, an instrument and a victim, the Revolution would have had in an emancipated king, an enemy or a mediator; instead of being an anarchy, she would have had a civil war; instead of having massacres, she would have gained victories; she would have triumphed by arms, and not by executions.

Never did the fate of so many men and so many ideas depend so plainly on a chance! And yet this was not a chance. Drouet was the means of the king's destruction: if he had not recognized the monarch from his resemblance with his portrait on the assignats—if he had not rode with all speed, and reached Varennes before the carriages, in two hours more the king and his family must have been saved. Drouet, this obscure son of a post-master, sauntering and idle that evening before the door of a cottage, decided the fate of a monarchy. He took the advice of no one but himself—he set off, saying, "I will arrest the king." But Drouet would not have had this decisive impulse, if, at this moment, as it were, he had not personified in himself all the agitation and all the suspicions of the people. It was the fanaticism of his country which impelled him, unknown to himself, to Varennes, and which urged him to sacrifice a whole family of fugitives to what he believed to be the safety of the nation.

He had not received instructions from any one; he took upon himself alone the arrest and the death that ensued. His devotion to his country was cruel; his silence and commiseration would have drawn down minor calamities.

As to the king himself, this flight was in him a fault if not a crime: it was too soon or too late. Too late—for the king had already too far sanctioned the Revolution, to turn suddenly against it without appearing to betray his people and give himself the lie; too soon—for the constitution which the National Assembly was drawing up was not yet completed, the government was not yet pronounced powerless; and the foes of the king and his family were not yet so decidedly menaced that the care of his safety as a man should surpass his duties as a king. In case of success, Louis XVI. had none but foreign forces to recover his kingdom; in case of arrest, he found only a prison in his palace. On which side soever we view it, flight was fatal—it was the road to shame or to the scaffold. There is but one route by which to flee a throne and not to die—abdication. On his return from Varennes, the king should have abdicated. The Revolution would have adopted his son, and have educated him in its own image. He did not abdicate—he consented to accept the pardon of his people; he swore to execute a constitution from which he had fled. He was a king in a state of amnesty. Europe beheld in him but a fugitive from his throne led back to his punishment, the nation but a traitor, and the Revolution but a plaything.

BOOK III.

I.

THERE is for a people, as for individuals, an instinct of conservation which warns and "gives them pause," even under the impulses of the most blind passions, before the dangers into which they are about to fling themselves headlong. They seem suddenly to recede at the aspect of this abyss, into which but now they were hastening precipitately. The intermissions of human passions are short and fugitive, but they give time to events, returns to wisdom, and opportunities to statesmen. These are moments in which they seize the hesitating and intimidated spirit of the people, in order to make them create a reaction against their own excesses, and to lead them back by the very revulsion of the passions that have already urged them too far. The day after the 25th of June, 1791, France experienced one of those throes of repentance which save a people. There was only the statesman wanting.

Never had the National Assembly presented a spectacle so imposing and so calm as during the five days which had succeeded the king's departure. It would appear as though it felt the weight of the whole empire resting on it, and it sustained its attitude in order to bear it with dignity. It accepted the power without desiring either to usurp or to retain it. It covered with a respectful fiction the king's desertion—called the flight a carrying off, and sought for the guilty around the throne—regarding the throne itself as inviolable. The man disappeared, for it, in Louis XVI. :—in the irresponsible chief of the state. These three months may be considered as an interregnum, during which public reason was her sole constitution. There was no longer a king, for he was a captive, and his sanction was taken from him: there was no longer law, for the constitution was incomplete: there was no longer a minister, for the executive power was suspended; and yet the kingdom was standing erect, was acting, organizing, defending itself, preserving itself—and what is still more marvellous, controlled itself. It held in reserve in a palace the principal machinery of the constitution,—Royalty; and the day when the work is accomplished, it puts the king in his place, and says to him. "Be free and reign."

II.

One thing only dishonors this majestic interregnum of the nation—the temporary captivity of the king and his family. But we must remember that the nation had the right to say to its chief; "If thou wilt reign over us, thou shalt not quit the kingdom, thou shalt not convey the royalty of France amongst our enemies." And as to the forms of that captivity in the Tuileries, we must remember too that the National Assembly had not prescribed them,—that in fact it had risen with indignation at the word imprisonment,—that it had commanded a political resistance and nothing more, and that the severity and odium of the precautionary measures used were occasioned by the zealous responsibility of the national guard, more than to the irreverence of the Assembly. La Fayette guarded, in the person of the king, the dynasty, its proper head, and the constitution—a hostage against the republic and royalty at the same time. *Maire du palais,* he intimidated by the presence of a weak and degraded monarch, the discouraged royalists and the restrained republicans. Louis XVI. was his pledge.

Barnave and the Lameths had within the Assembly the attitude of La Fayette without. They required the king, in order to defend themselves from their enemies. So long as there was a man (Mirabeau) between the throne and themselves, they had played with the republic and sapped the throne in order to crush a rival. But Mirabeau dead and the throne shaken, they felt themselves weak against the very impulse they had given. They sustained, therefore, this wreck of monarchy in order to be sustained in their turn. Founders of the Jacobins, they trembled before their own handiwork:—they took refuge in the constitution which they themselves had dilapidated, and passed from the character of destructives to that of statesmen. But for the first part there is only violence needed; for the second genius is required. Barnave had talent only. He had something more, however—he had a heart, and he was a good man. The first excesses of his language were in him but the excitements of the tribune; he was desirous of tasting the popular applause, and it was showered upon him beyond his real merit. Hereafter it was not with Mirabeau he was about to measure his strength; it was with the Revolution in all its force. Jealousy took from him the pedestal which it had lent, and he was about to appear as he really was.

III.

But a sentiment more noble than that of his personal safety impelled Barnave to side with the monarchical party. His heart had passed before his ambition to the side of weakness, beauty, and misfortune. Nothing is more dangerous than for a sensitive man to know those against whom he contends. Hatred against the cause shrinks before the feeling for the persons. We become partial unwittingly. Sensibility disarms the understanding, and we soften instead of reasoning, whilst the sensitiveness of a commiserating man soon usurps the place of his opinion.

It was thus that Barnave's mind was worked upon, after the return from Varennes. The interest he had conceived for the queen had converted this young republican into a royalist. Barnave had only previously known this princess through a cloud of prejudice, amid which parties enshroud those whom they wish to have detested. A sudden communication caused this conventional atmosphere to dissipate, and he adored, when close, what he had calumniated at a distance. The very character which fortune had cast for him in the destiny of this woman had something unexpected and romantic, capable of dazzling his lofty imagination, and deeply affecting his generous disposition. Young, obscure, unknown but a few months before, and now celebrated, popular, and powerful—thrown in the name of a sovereign assembly between the people and the king—he became the protector of those whose enemy he had been. Royal and suppliant hands met his plebeian touch! He who opposed the popular royalty of talent and eloquence to the royalty of the blood of the Bourbons! He covered with his body the life of those who had been his masters. His very devotion was a triumph; the object of that devotion was in his queen. That queen was young, handsome, majestic; but brought to the level of ordinary humanity by her alarm for her husband and his children. Her tearful eyes besought their safety from Barnave's eyes. He was the leading orator in that Assembly which held the fate of the monarch in his house. He was the favorite of that people whom he controlled by a gesture, and whose fury he averted during the long journey between the throne and death. The queen had placed her son, the young dauphin, between his knees. Barnave's fingers had played with the fair hair of the child. The king, the queen, Madame Elizabeth, had distinguished, with tact, Barnave from the inflexible and brutal Pétion. They had conversed with him as to their situation: they complained of having been deceived as to the nature of the public mind in France. They unveiled their repentance and constitutional inclinations. These conversations, marred in the carriage by the presence of the other commissioner and the eyes of the people, had been stealthily and more intimately renewed in the meetings which the royal family nightly held. Mysterious political correspondences and secret interviews in the Tuileries were contrived. Barnave, the inflexible partisan, reached Paris a devoted man. The nocturnal conference of Mirabeau with the queen, in the park of Saint Cloud, was ambitioned by his rival; but Mirabeau sold, Barnave gave, himself. Heaps of gold bought the man of genius; a glance seduced the man of sentiment.

IV.

Barnave had found Duport and the Lameths, his friends, in the most monarchical moods, but from other motives than his own. This triumvirate was in terms of good understanding at the Tuileries. Lameths and Duport saw the king. Barnave, who at first dared not venture to visit the chateau, subsequently went there secretly. The utmost precaution and concealment attended these interviews. The king and queen sometimes awaited the youthful orator in a small apartment on the *entre sol* of the palace, with a key in their hand, so as to open the door the moment his footsteps were heard. When these meetings were utterly impossible, Barnave wrote to the queen. He reckoned greatly on the strength of his party in the Assembly, because he measured the power of their opinions by the talent with which they expressed them. The queen did not feel a similar confidence. "Take courage, madame," wrote Barnave; "it is true our banner is torn, but the word *Constitution* is still legible thereon. This word will recover all its pristine force and *prestige*, if the king will rally to it sincerely. The friends of this constitution, retrieving past errors, may still raise and maintain it firmly. The Jacobins alarm public reason; the emigrants threaten our nationality. Do not fear the Jacobins—put no trust in the emigrants. Throw yourself into the national party which now exists. Did not Henry IV. ascend the throne of a Catholic nation at the head of a Protestant party?"

The queen with all sincerity adopted this tardy counsel, and arranged with Barnave all her measures, and all her foreign correspondence. She neither said nor did anything which could thwart the plans he had conceived for the restoration of royal authority. "A feeling of legitimate pride," said the queen when speaking of him, "a feeling which I am far from blaming in a young man of talent born in the obscure ranks of the third estate, has made him desire a revolution which should smooth the way to fame and influence. But his heart is loyal, and if ever power is again in our hands, Barnave's pardon is already written on our hearts." Madame Elizabeth partook of this regard of the king and queen for Barnave. Defeated at all points, they had ended by believing that the only persons capable of restoring the monarchy were those who had destroyed it. This was a fatal superstition. They were induced to adore that power of the Revolution which they could not bend.

V.

The first acts of the king were too much imbued with the inspirations of Barnave and the Lameths for the royal dignity. He addressed to the commissioners of the Assembly charged with interrogating him as to the circumstances of the 21st of June, a reply, the bad faith of which called for the smile rather than the indulgence of his enemies.

"Introduced into the king's chamber and alone with him," said the commissioners of the Assembly, "the king made to us the following declaration:—The motives of my departure were the insults and outrages I underwent on the 18th of April, when I wished to go to St. Cloud. These insults remained unpunished, and I thereupon believed that there was neither safety nor decorum in my staying any longer in Paris. Unable to quit publicly, I resolved to depart in the night, and without attendants; my intention was never to leave the kingdom. I had no concert with foreign powers, nor with the princes of my family who have emigrated. My residence would have been at Montmédy, a place I had chosen because it is well fortified, and that being close to the frontier, I was more ready to oppose every kind of invasion. I have learnt during my journey that public opinion was decided in favor of the constitution, and so soon as I learnt the general wish I have not hesitated, as I never have hesitated, to make the sacrifice of what concerns myself for the public good."

"The king," added the queen, in her declaration, "desiring to depart with his children, I declare that nothing in nature could prevent my following him. I have sufficiently proved, during two years, and under the most painful circumstances, that I will never separate from him."

Not content with this inquiry into the motives and circumstances of the king's flight, public opinion, much irritated, demanded that the hand of the nation should be extended even to the paternal authority, and that the Assembly should appoint a governor for the dauphin. Eighty names, for the most part of obscure persons, were found in the division which was openly taken. They were hailed with shouts of general derision. This outrage to the king and father was spared him. The governor subsequently named by Louis XVI., M. de Fleurieu, never entered upon his duties. The governor of the heir to an empire was the jailer of a prison of malefactors.

The Marquis de Bouillé addressed from Luxembourg a threatening letter to the Assembly, in order to turn from the king all popular indignation, and to assume to himself the projection and execution of the king's departure. "If," he added, "one hair of the head of Louis XVI. fall to the ground, not one stone of Paris shall remain upon another. I know the roads, and will guide the foreign armies thither." A laugh followed these words. The Assembly was sufficiently wise not to require the advice of M. de Bouillé, and strong enough to despise the threats of a proscribed man.

M. de Cazalès sent in his resignation, in order to *to go and fight* (*aller combattre*). The most prominent members of the right side, amongst whom were Maury, Montlozier, the abbé Montesquieu, the abbé de Pradt, Virieu, &c. &c., to the number of two hundred and ninety, took a pernicious resolution, which, by removing all counterpoise from the extreme party of the Revolution, precipitated the fall of, and destroyed, the king, under the pretext of a sacred respect for royalty. They remained in the Assembly, but they annulled their power, and would only be considered as a living protest against the violation of the royal liberty and authority. The Assembly refused to hear the reading of their protest, which was itself a violation of their elective power; and they then published it and circulated it profusely all over the kingdom. "The decrees of the Assembly," they said, "have wholly absorbed the royal power. The seal of state is on the president's table; the king's sanction is annihilated. The king's name is erased from the oath which is taken from the law. The commissioners convey the orders of the committees direct to the armies. The king is a captive; a provisional republic occupies the interregnum. Far be it from us to concur in such acts; we would not even consent to be witnesses of it, if we had not still the duty of watching over the preservation of the king. Excepting this sole interest, we shall impose on ourselves the most absolute silence. This silence will be the only expression of our constant opposition to all your acts."

These words were the abdication of an entire party, for any party that protests abdicates. On this day there was emigration in the Assembly. This mistaken fidelity, which deplored instead of combating, obtained the applause of the nobility and clergy; it merited the utmost contempt of politicians. Abandoning, in their struggle against the Jacobins, Barnave and the monarchical constitutionalists, it gave the victory to Robespierre, and by assuring the majority to his proposition for the non re-election of the members of the National Assembly to the Legislative Assembly, it sanctioned the convention. The royalists took away the weight of one great opinion from the balance, which consequently then leaned towards the disorders that ensued, and which in their progress carried off the head of the king and their own heads. A great opinion never lays down its arms with impunity for its country.

VI.

The Jacobins perceived this great error, and rejoiced at it. On seeing so large a body of the supporters of the constitutional monarchy withdraw from the contest voluntarily, they at once foresaw what they might dare, and they dared it. Their sittings became more significant in proportion as those of the Assembly grew more dull and impotent. The words of "forfeiture" and "republic" were heard there for the first time. Retracted at first, they were afterwards again pronounced: uttered at first like blasphemies, they were not long in being familiar as principles. Parties did not at first know what they themselves desired—they learnt it from success. The daring broached distempered ideas; if repulsed, the sagacious disavowed them—if caught up, the leaders resumed them. In conflicts of opinions *reconnaissances* are employed, as they are in the campaigns of armies. The Jacobins were the advanced guard of the Revolution, who measured the opposing obstacles of the monarchical feeling.

The club of Cordeliers sent to the Jacobins a copy of a proposed address to the National Assembly, in which the annihilation of royalty was openly demanded.

"We are *free and without a king*," said the Cordeliers, "as the day after the taking of the Bastille; it is only for us to decide whether or no we shall name another. We are of opinion that the nation should do everything by itself, or by agents removable by her. We think, that the more important an employ, the more temporary should be its tenure. We think that royalty, and especially hereditary royalty, is incompatible with liberty; we anticipate the crowd of opponents such a declaration will create, but has not the declaration of rights produced as many? In leaving his post the king virtually abdicated,—let us profit by the occasion and our right—let us swear that France is a republic."

This address, read to the club of Jacobins on the 22d, at first excited universal indignation. On the 23d, Danton mounted the tribune, demanded the positive forfeiture of the throne (*la déchéance*), and the nomination of a council of regency. "Your king," he said, "is an idiot, or a criminal. It would be a horrid spectacle to present to the world, if, having the option of declaring a king criminal or idiotic, you did not prefer the latter alternative."

On the 27th, Girey Dupré, a young writer who awaited the Gironde, mooted the judgment of Louis XVI. "We can punish a perjured king, and we ought;" such was the text of his discourse. Brissot opened the question as Pétion had done at the preceding sitting, "*Can a perjured king be brought to trial* (*jugé*)?"

"Why," asked Brissot, "should we divide ourselves into dangerous denominations? we are all of one opinion. What do they want who are here hostile to the republicans? They detest the turbulent assemblies of Athens and Rome; they fear the division of France into isolated federations. They only want the representative constitution, and they are right. What do they want who boast of the name of republicans? They fear, they abhor equally, the turbulent assemblies of Rome and Athens, and equally dread a federated republic. They desire a representative constitution—nothing more, nothing less—and thus, we all concur. The head of the executive power has betrayed his oath,—must we bring him to judgment? This is the only point on which we differ. Inviolability will else be impunity to all crimes, an encouragement for all treason—common sense demands that the punishment should follow the offence. I do not see an inviolable man governing the people, but a *God* and 25,000,000 of *brutes!* If the king had on his return entered France at the head of foreign forces, if he had ravaged our fairest provinces, and if, checked in his career, you had made him prisoner, what would you then have done with him? Would you have allowed his inviolability to have saved him? Foreign powers are held up before you as a threat; do not fear them; Europe in arms is impotent against a people who will be free."

In the National Assembly Muguer, in the name of the joint committees, brought up the report on the king's flight; he maintained the inviolability of Louis XVI. and the accusation of his accomplices. ROBESPIERRE opposed the inviolability; he avoided all show of anger in his language, and was careful to veil all his conclusions beneath the cover of mildness and humanity. "I will not pause to inquire," he said, "whether the king fled voluntarily, of his own act, or if from the extremity of the frontiers a citizen carried him off by his advice: I will not inquire either, whether this flight is a conspiracy against the public liberty. I shall speak of the king as of an imaginary sovereign, and of inviolability as a principle." After having combated the principle of inviolability by the same arguments which Girey, Dupré and Brissot had applied, Robespierre thus concluded. "The measures you propose cannot but dishonor you; if you adopt them, I demand to declare myself the advocate of all the accused. I will be the defender of the three *gardes du corps*, the dauphine's governess, even of Monsieur de Bouilié. By the principles of your committees, there is no crime; yet, invariably, where there is no crime there can be no accomplices. Gentlemen, if it be a weakness to spare a culprit, to visit the weaker culprit when the greater one escapes, is cowardice—injustice. You must pass sentence on all the guilty alike, or pronounce a general pardon."

Gregoire supported the accusation party. Salles defended the recommendation of the committee.

Barnave at length spoke, and in support of Salles' opinion. He said: "The French nation has just undergone a violent shock; but if we are to believe all the auguries which are delivered, this recent event, like all others which have preceded it, will only serve to advance the period, to confirm the solidity of the revolution we have effected. I will not dilate on the advantages of monarchical government·

you have proved your conviction by establishing it in your country: I will only say that every government, to be good, should comprise within itself the principles of its stability; for otherwise, instead of prosperity there would be before us only the perspective of a series of changes. Some men, whose motives I shall not impugn, seeking for examples to adduce, have found, in America, a people occupying a vast territory with a scanty population, nowhere surrounded by very powerful neighbors, having forests for their boundaries, and having for customs the feelings of a new race, and who are wholly ignorant of those factitious passions and impulses which effect revolutions of government. They have seen a republican government established in that land, and have thence drawn the conclusion that a similar government was suitable for us. These men are the same who at this moment are contesting the inviolability of the king. But, if it be true that in our territory there is a vast population spread, —if it be true that there are amongst them a multitude of men exclusively given up to those intellectual speculations which excite ambition and the love of fame,—if it be true that around us powerful neighbors compel us to form but one compact body in order to resist them,—if it be true that all these circumstances are irresistible, and are wholly independent of ourselves, it is undeniable that the sole existing remedy lies in a monarchical government. When a country is populous and extensive, there are—and all political experience proves it—but two modes of assuring to it a solid and permanent existence. Either you must organize those parts separately;—you must place in each section of the empire a portion of the government, and thus you will maintain security at the expense of unity, strength, and all the advantages which result from a great and homogeneous association:—or else you will be forced to centralize an unchangeable power, which, never renewed by the law, presenting incessantly obstacles to ambition, resists with advantage the shocks, rivalries, and rapid vibrations of an immense population, agitated by all the passions engendered by long established society. These facts decide our position. We can only be strong through a federative government, which no one here has the madness to propose, or by a monarchical government, such as you have established, that is to say, by confiding the reins of the executive power to a family having the right of hereditary succession. You have intrusted to an inviolable king the exclusive function of naming the agents of his power, but you have made those agents responsible. To be independent the king must be inviolable: do not let us set aside this axiom. We have never failed to observe this as regards individuals, let us regard it as respects the monarch. Our principles, the constitution, the law, declare that he has not forfeited (*qu'il n'est pas déchu*): thus, then, we have to choose between our attachment to the constitution and our resentment against an individual. Yes, I demand at this moment from him amongst you all, who may have conceived against the head of the executive power prejudices however strong, and resentment however deep; I ask at his hands whether he is more irritated against the king than he is attached to the laws of his country? I would say to those who rage so furiously against an individual who has done wrong,—I would say, Then you would be at his feet if you were content with him? (Loud and lengthened applause.) Those who would thus sacrifice the constitution to their anger against one man, seem to me too much inclined to sacrifice liberty from their enthusiasm for some other man; and since thev love a republic, it is indeed, the moment to say to them, What, would you wish a republic in such a nation? How is it you do not fear that the same variableness of the people, which to-day manifests itself by hatred, may on another day be displayed by enthusiasm in favor of some great man? Enthusiasm even more dangerous than hatred: for the French nation, you know, understands better how to love than to hate. I neither fear the attacks of foreign nations nor of emigrants: I have already said so; but I now repeat it with the more truth, as I fear the continuation of uneasiness and agitation, which will not cease to exist and affect us until the Revolution be wholly and pacifically concluded. We need fear no mischief from without; but vast injury is done to us from within, when we are disturbed by painful ideas—when chimerical dangers, excited around us, create with the people some consistency and some credit for the men who use them as a means of unceasing agitation. Immense damage is done to us when that revolutionary impetus, which has destroyed everything there was to destroy, and which has urged us to the point where we must at last pause, is perpetuated. If the Revolution advance one step further it cannot do so without danger. In the line of liberty, the first act which can follow is the annihilation of royalty; in the line of equality, the first act which must follow is an attempt on all property. Revolutions are not effected with metaphysical maxims—there must be an actual tangible prey to offer to the multitude that is led astray. It is time, therefore, to end the Revolution. It ought to stop at the moment when the nation is free, and when all Frenchmen are equal. If it continue in trouble, it is dishonored, and we with it; yes, all the world ought to agree that the common interest is involved in the close of the Revolution. Those who have lost ought to perceive that it is impossible to make it retrograde. Those who fashioned it must see that it is at its consummation. Kings themselves—if from time to time profound truths can penetrate to the councils of kings—if occasionally the prejudices which surround them will permit the sound views of a great and philosophical policy to reach them—kings themselves must learn that there is for them a wide difference between the example of a great reform in the government and that of the abolition of royalty: that if we pause here, where we are, they are still kings! but be their conduct what it may, let the fault come from them and not from us. Regenerators of the empire! follow straightly your undeviating line; you have been courageous and potent—be to-day wise and moderate. In this will consist the glorious termination of your efforts. Then, again returning to your domestic hearths, you will obtain from all, if not blessings, at least the silence of calumny." This address, the most eloquent ever delivered by Barnave, carried the report in the affirmative; and for several days checked all attempts at republic and forfeiture in the clubs of the Cordeliers and Jacobins. The king's inviolability was consecrated in fact as well as in principle. M. de Bouillé, his accomplices and adherents, were sent for trial to the high national court of Orleans.

VII.

Whilst these men, exclusively political, each measuring the advance of the Revolution, step by step, with their eyes, desired courageously to stop it, or check their own views, the Revolution was continually progressing. Its own thought was too vast for any head of public man, orator, or statesman to contain. Its breath was too powerful for any one breast to respire it solely. Its end was too comprehensive to be included in any of the successive views that the ambition of certain factions, or the theories of certain statesmen could propound. Barnave, the Lameths, and La Fayette, like Mirabeau and Necker, endeavored, in vain, to oppose to it the power and influence they had derived from it. It was destined, before it was appeased or relaxed in its onward career, to frustrate many other systems, make many other breasts pant in vain, and outstrip a multitude of other aims.

Independent of the national assemblies it had given to itself as a government, and in which were, for the most part, concentrated the political instruments of its impulse, it had also given birth to two levers, still more potent and terrible to move and sweep away these political bodies when they attempted to check her when she chose to advance. These two levers were the press and the clubs. The clubs and the press were, to the legal assemblies, what free air is to confined air. Whilst the air of these assemblies became vitiated, and exhausted itself in the circle of the established government, the air of journalism and popular societies was impregnated and incessantly stirred by an inexhaustible principle of vitality and movement. The stagnation within was fully credited, but the current was without.

The press, in the half century which had preceded the Revolution, had been the echo, well organized and calm, of the thoughts of sages and reformers. From the time when the Revolution burst forth, it had become the turbulent and frequently cynical echo of the popular excitement.

It had itself transformed the modes of communicating ideas; it no longer produced books—it had not the time: at first it expended itself in pamphlets, and subsequently in a multitude of flying and diurnal sheets, which, published at a low price amongst the people, or gratuitously placarded in the public thoroughfares, incited the multitude to read and discuss them. The treasury of the national thought, whose pieces of gold were too pure, or too bulky, for the use of the populace, it had, if we may be allowed the expression, converted into a multitude of smaller coins, struck with the impress of the passions of the hour, and often tarnished with the foulest oxides. Journalism, like an irresistible element of the life of a people in revolution, had made its own place, without listening to the law which had been made to restrain it.

Mirabeau, who required that his speeches should echo throughout the departments, had given birth to this speaking trumpet of the Revolution, (despite the orders in council) in his *Letters to my Constituents*, and in the *Courrier de Pro-*

vence. At the opening of the States General, and at the taking of the Bastille, other journals had appeared. At each new insurrection there was a fresh inundation of newspapers. The leading organs of public agitation were then the *Revolution of Paris,* edited by Loustalot; a weekly paper with a circulation of 200,000 copies; the feeling of the man may be seen in the motto of his paper: "The great appear great to us only because we are on our knees—let us rise!" The *Discours de la Lanterne aux Parisiens,* subsequently called the *Revolutions de France et de Brabant,* was the production of Camille Desmoulins. This young student, who became suddenly a political character on a chair in the garden of the Palais Royal, on the first outbreak of the month of July, 1789, preserved in his style, which was frequently very brilliant, something of his early character. It was the sarcastic genius of Voltaire descended from the saloon to the pavement. No man in himself ever personified the people better than did Camille Desmoulins. He was the mob with his turbulent and unexpected movements, his variableness, his unconnectedness, his rages interrupted by laughter, or suddenly sinking into sympathy and sorrow for the very victims he immolated. A man, at the same time so ardent and so trifling, so trivial and so inspired, so indecisive between blood and tears, so ready to crush what he had just deified with enthusiasm, must have the more empire over a people in revolt, in proportion as he resembled them. His character was his nature. He not only aped the people, he was the people himself. His newspapers cried in the public streets, and their sarcasm, bandied from mouth to mouth, has not been swept away with the other impurities of the day. He remains, and will remain, a Menippus, the satirist stained with blood. It was the popular chorus which led the people to their most important movements, and which was frequently stifled by the whistling of the cord of the street lamp, or in the hatchet-stroke of the guillotine. Camille Desmoulins was the remorseless offspring of the Revolution, —Marot was its fury; he had the clumsy tumblings of the brute in his thought, and its gnashing of teeth in his style. His journal (*L'Ami du Peuple*), the People's Friend, smelt of blood in every line.

VIII.

Marat was born in Switzerland. A writer without talent

a *savant* without reputation, with a desire for fame without having received from society or nature the means of acquiring either, he revenged himself on all that was great not only in society but in nature. Genius was as hateful to him as aristocracy. Wherever he saw anything elevated or striking, he hunted it down as though it were a deadly enemy. He would have levelled creation. Equality was his mania, because superiority was his martyrdom; he loved the Revolution because it brought down all to his level; he loved it even to blood, because blood washed out the stain of his long-during obscurity; he made himself a public denouncer by the popular title; he knew that denouncement is flattery to all who tremble, and the people are always trembling. A real prophet of demagogism, inspired by insanity, he gave his nightly dreams to daily conspiracies. The Seid of the people, he interested it by his self-devotion to its interests. He affected mystery like all oracles. He lived in obscurity, and only went out at night; he only communicated with his fellows with the most sinistrous precautions. A subterranean cell was his residence, and there he took refuge safe from poniard and poison. His journal affected the imagination like something supernatural. Marat was wrapped in real fanaticism. The confidence reposed in him nearly amounted to worship. The fumes of the blood he incessantly demanded had mounted to his brain. He was the delirium of the Revolution, himself a living delirium!

IX.

Brissot, as yet obscure, wrote *Le Patriote Français*. A politician, and aspiring to leading parts, he only excited revolutionary passions in proportion as he hoped one day to govern by them. At first a constitutionalist and friend of Necker and Mirabeau, a hireling before he became a *doctrinaire*, he saw in the people only a sovereign more suitable to his own ambition. The republic was his rising sun; he approached it as to his own fortune, but with prudence, and frequently looking behind him to see if opinion followed his traces.

Condorcet, an aristocrat by genius, although an aristocrat by birth, became a democrat from philosophy. His passion was the transformation of human reason. He wrote *La Chronique de Paris*.

Carra, an obscure demagogue, had created for himself a name of fear in the *Annales Patriotiques*. Fréron, in the

Orateur du Peuple, rivalled Marat. Fauchet, in the *Bouche de Fer*, elevated democracy to a level with religious philosophy. The "last not least," Laclos, an officer of artillery author of an obscene novel, and the confidant of the Duc D'Orleans, edited the *Journal des Jacobins*, and stirred up through France the flame of ideas and words of which the focus was in the clubs.

All these men used their utmost efforts to impel the people beyond the limits which Barnave had prescribed to the event of the 21st June. They desired to avail themselves of the instant when the throne was left empty to obliterate it from the constitution. They overwhelmed the king with insults and objurgations, in order that the Assembly might not dare to replace at the head of their institutions a prince whom they had vilified. They clamored for interrogatory, sentence, forfeiture, abdication, imprisonment, and hoped to degrade royalty forever by degrading the king. The republic saw its hour for the first moment, and trembled to allow it to escape. All these hands at once urged men's minds towards a decisive movement. Articles in the journals provoked motions, motions petitions, and petitions riots. The altar of the country in the Champ-de-Mars, which remained erected for a new federation, was the place which was already pointed out for the assemblies of the people. It was the *Mons Aventinus*, whither it was to retire, and whence it was to dictate to a timid and corrupt senate.

"No more king,—let us be republicans," wrote Brissot in the *Patriote*. "Such is the cry at the Palais Royal, and it does not gain ground fast enough; it would seem as though it were blasphemy. This repugnance for assuming the name of the condition in which the state *actually is* is very extraordinary in the eyes of philosophy." "No king! no protector! no regent! Let us have done with man-eaters of every sort and kind," re-echoed the *Bouche de Fer*. "Let the eighty-three departments enter into a federation, and declare that they will no longer endure tyrants, monarchs, or protectors. Their shade is as fatal to the people as that of the Bohonupas is deadly to all that lives. If we nominate a regent we shall soon fight for the choice of a master. Let us only contend for liberty."

Provoked by this reference to the regency, which appeared to point to him, the Duc d'Orleans wrote to the journals that he was ready to serve his country by land or by sea; but in respect to any question of regency, he from that moment renounced, and forever, any pretensions to that title which the constitution might give him. "After having made so many sacrifices to the cause of the people," he said, "I am no longer in a condition to quit my position as a simple citizen. Ambition in me would be an inexcusable inconsistency."

Already discredited by all parties, this prince, henceforth incapable of serving the throne, was equally incapable of serving the republic. Odious to the royalists, put aside by the demagogues, suspected by the constitutionalists, there only remained to him the stoical attitude in which he took refuge. He had abdicated his rank, abdicated his own faction; he had abdicated the favor of the people. His life was all that remained to him.

At the same moment Camille Desmoulins was thus satirically apostrophizing La Fayette, the first idol of the Revolution:—"Liberator of two worlds, flower of Janissaries, phœnix of Alguazils-major, Don Quixotte of Capet and the two chambers, constellation of the white horse,* my voice is too weak to raise itself above the clamor of your thirty thousand spies, and as many more your satellites, above the noise of your four hundred drums, and your cannons loaded with grape. I had until now misrepresented your—more than—royal highness through the allusions of Barnave, Lameth, and Duport. It was after them that I denounced you to the eighty-three departments as an ambitious man who only cared for parade, a slave of the court similar to those marshals of the league to whom revolt had given the *bâton*, and who, looking upon themselves as bastards, were desirous of becoming legitimate; but all of a sudden you embrace each other, and proclaim yourselves mutually fathers of your country! You say to the nation, 'Confide in us; we are the Cincinnati, the Washingtons, the Aristides.' Which of these two testimonies are we to believe? Foolish people! The Parisians are like those Athenians to whom Demosthenes said, 'Shall you always resemble those athletes who, struck in one place cover it with their hand,—struck in another place they place their hand there, and thus always occupied with the blows they receive, do not know either how to strike or defend themselves!' They are beginning to doubt whether Louis XVI. could be perjured since he is at Varennes. I think I see the same great eyes open when they

* La Fayette rode a favorite white horse on public occasions during this period.—H. T. R.

shall see La Fayette open the gates of the capital to despotism and aristocracy. May I be deceived in my conjectures, for I am going from Paris, as Camillus my patron departed from an ungrateful country, wishing it every kind of prosperity I have no occasion to have been an emperor like Diocletian to know that the fine lettuces of Salernum, which are far superior to the empire of the East, are quite equal to the gay scarf which a municipal authority wears, and the uneasiness with which a Jacobin journalist returns to his home in the evening, fearing always lest he should fall into an ambuscade of the cut-throats of the general. For me it was not to establish two chambers that I first mounted the tri-color cockade!"

X.

Such was the general tone of the press, such the exhaustless laughter which this young man diffused, like the Aristophanes of an irritated people. He accustomed it to revile men, majesty, misfortune, and worth. The day came when he required for himself and for the young and lovely woman whom he adored, that pity which he had destroyed in the people. He found, in his turn, only the brutal derision of the multitude, and he himself then became sad and sorry for the first and last time.

The people, all whose political idea is from the senses, could not at all comprehend why the statesmen of the Assembly should impose upon them a fugitive king, out of respect for abstract royalty. The moderation of Barnave and Lameth seemed to them full of suspicion; and cries of treason were uttered at all their meetings. The decree of the Assembly was the signal for increased ferment, which developed from and after the 13th of July, in zealous meetings, imprecations, and threats. Large bodies of workmen, leaving their work, congregated in the public places and demanded bread of the municipal authorities. The commune, in order to appease them, voted for distributions and supplies. Bailly, the mayor of Paris, harangued them, and gave them extraordinary work. They went to it for a moment, and then quitted it, being speedily attracted by the mob becoming dense and uttering cries of hunger.

The crowd betook itself from the Hôtel-de-Ville to the Jacobins, from the Jacobins to the National Assembly, clamorous for the forfeiture of the crown, and the republic. This popular gathering had no other leader than the uneasiness that excited it. A spontaneous and unanimous instinct assured it that the Assembly would be found wanting at the hour of great resolutions. This mob desired to compel it again to seize the opportunity. Its will was the more potent as it was wholly impossible to trace it to its source—no chief gave it any visible impetus. It advanced of itself, spake of itself, and wrote with its own hand in the streets—on the corner stone—its threatening petitions.

The first that the people presented to the Assembly, on the 14th, and which was escorted by 4000 petitioners, was signed "*The People.*" The 14th of July and the 6th of October had taught it its name. The Assembly, firm and unmoved, passed to the order of the day.

On quitting the Assembly, the crowd went to the Champ-de-Mars, where it signed, in greater numbers, a second petition in still more imperative terms. "Intrusted with the representation of a free people, will you destroy the work we have perfected? Will you replace liberty by a reign of tyranny? If, indeed, it were so, learn that the French people, which has acquired its rights, will not again lose them."

On quitting the Champ-de-Mars, the people thronged round the Tuileries, the Assembly, and the Palais Royal. Of their own accord they shut up the theatres, and proclaimed the suspension of all public entertainments, until justice should be done to them. That evening 4000 persons went to the Jacobins, as though to identify in the agitators who met there the real assembly of the people. The chiefs in whom they reposed confidence were there: the tribune was occupied by a member who was denouncing to the meeting a citizen for having made a remark injurious to Robespierre; the accused was justifying himself, and they drove him tumultuously from the chamber. At this moment Robespierre appeared, and begged them to pardon the citizen who had insulted him. His generous intercession was hailed with applause, and enthusiasm for Robespierre was at its height. "Sacred vaults of the Jacobins," were the words of an address from the departments; "you guarantee to us Robespierre and Danton, these two oracles of patriotism." Laclos proposed a petition to be sent into the departments, and covered with ten millions of signatures. A member opposes this proposition, from love of order and peace. Danton rises,—"And I, too, love peace, but not the peace of slavery. If we have energy, let us show it. Let those who do not feel courage to rise and beard tyranny refrain from signing our petition: we want no better proof by which to understand each other. Here it is to our hand."

Robespierre next spoke, and demonstrated to the people that Barnave and the Lameths were playing the same game as Mirabeau. "They concert with our enemies, and then they call us factious!" More timid than Laclos and Danton, he did not give any opinion as to the petition. A man of calculation rather than of passion, he foresaw that the disorderly movement would split against the organized resistance of the *bourgeoisie*. He reserved to himself the power of falling back upon the legality of the question, and kept on terms with the Assembly. Laclos pressed his motion, and the people carried it. At midnight they separated, after having agreed to meet the next day in the Champ-de-Mars, there to sign the petition.

The day following was lost to sedition, by disputes between the clubs as to the terms of the petition. The Republicans negotiated with La Fayette, to whom they offered the presidency of an American government. Robespierre and Danton, who detested La Fayette—Laclos, who urged on the Duc d'Orleans, concerted together, and impeded the impulse given by the Cordeliers subservient to Danton. The Assembly watchful, Bailly on his guard, La Fayette resolute, watched in unison for the repression of all outbreak. On the 16th the Assembly summoned to its bar the municipality and its officers, to make it responsible for the public peace. It drew up an address to the French people, in order to rally them around the constitution. Bailly, the same evening, issued a proclamation against the agitators. The fluctuating Jacobins themselves declared their submission to the decrees of the Assembly. At the moment when the struggle was expected, the leaders of the projected movement were invisible. The night was spent in military preparations against the meeting on the morrow.

XI.

On the 17th, very early in the morning, the people, without leaders, began to collect in the Champ-de-Mars, and surround the altar of the country, raised in the centre of the large square of the confederation. A strange and melancholy chance opened the scenes of murder on this day.

When the multitude is excited, everything becomes the occasion of crime. A young painter, who, before the hour of meeting, was copying the patriotic inscriptions engraved in front of the altar, heard a slight noise at his feet: astonished, he looked around him and saw the point of a gimlet, with which some men, concealed under the steps of the altar, were piercing the planks of the pedestal. He hastened to the nearest guard-house, and returned with some soldiers. They lifted up one of the steps and found beneath two invalids, who had got under the altar in the night, with no other design, as they declared, than a childish and obscene curiosity. The report instantly spread that the altar of the country was undermined, in order to blow up the people; that a barrel of gunpowder had been discovered beside the conspirators; that the invalids, surprised in the preliminaries to their criminal design, were well known satellites of the aristocracy; that they had confessed their deadly design, and the amount of reward promised on the success of their wickedness. The mob mustered, and raging with fury, surrounded the guard-house of the Gros-Caillou. The two invalids underwent an interrogatory. The moment when they left the guard-house, to be conveyed to the Hôtel-de-Ville, the populace rushed upon them, tore them from the soldiers who were escorting them, rent them in pieces, and their heads, placed on the tops of pikes, were carried by a band of ferocious children to the environs of the Palais Royal.

XII.

The news of these murders, confusedly spread and variously interpreted in the city, in the Assembly, among various groups, excited various feelings, according as it was viewed as a crime of the people or a crime of its enemies. The truth was only made apparent long after. The agitation increased from the indignation of some and the suspicions of others. Bailly, duly informed, sent three commissaries and a battalion. Other commissaries traversed the quarters of the capital, reading to the people the proclamation of the magistrates and the address of the National Assembly.

The ground of the Bastille was occupied by the national guard and the patriotic societies, which were to go thence to the field of the Federation. Danton, Camille Desmoulins, Fréron, Brissot, and the principal ringleaders of the people had disappeared; some said in order to concert insurrectional measures, at Legendre's house in the country; others, in order to escape the responsibilities of the day. The former version was the more generally accredited, from Robespierre's known hatred to Danton, to whom Saint Just said in his accusation—"Mirabeau, who meditated a change of dynasty, appreciated the force of thy audacity, and laid hands upon it. Thou didst startle him from the laws of stern principle; we heard nothing more of thee until the massacres of the Champ-de-Mars. Thou didst support that false measure of the people, and the proposition of the law, which had no other object than to serve for a pretext for unfolding the red banner, and an attempt at tyranny. The patriots, not initiated in this treachery, had opposed thy perfidious advice. Thou wast named in conjunction with Brissot to draw up this petition. You both escaped the prey of La Fayette, who caused the slaughter of ten thousand patriots. Brissot remained calmly in Paris, and thou didst hasten to Arcis-sur-Aube, to pass some agreeable days. Can one fancy thy tranquil joys—thou being one of the drawers up of this petition, whilst those who signed the document were loaded with irons, or weltering in their blood? You were then—thou and Brissot—objects for the gratitude of tyranny; because, assuredly, you could not be the objects of its detestation!"

Camille Desmoulins thus justifies the absence of Danton, himself, and Fréron, by asserting that Danton had fled from proscription and assassination to the house of his father-in-law, at Fontenay, on the previous night, and was tracked thither by a band of La Fayette's spies; and that Fréron, whilst crossing the Pont Neuf, had been assailed, trampled under foot, and wounded by fourteen hired ruffians; whilst Camille himself, marked for the dagger, only escaped by a mistake in his description. History has not put any faith in these pretended assassinations of La Fayette.

Camille, invisible all day, repaired in the evening to the Jacobins.

XIII.

In the meanwhile the crowd began to congregate in vast masses in the Champ-de-Mars—agitated, but inoffensive—the national guard, every battalion of whom La Fayette had ordered out, were under arms. One of the detachments which had arrived that morning in the Champ-de-Mars, with a train of artillery, withdrew by the quays, in order that the appearance of an armed force might not irritate the people. At twelve o'clock the crowd assembled round the "altar of the country" (*autel de la patrie*), not seeing the commissioners of the Jacobin club, who had promised to bring the petition to be signed, of their own accord chose four commissioners of their number to draw up one. One of the commissioners took the pen, the citizens crowded round him, and he wrote as follows:—

"On the altar of the country, July 13, in the year III. Representatives of the people, your labors are drawing to a close. A great crime has been committed; Louis flies, and has unworthily abandoned his post—the empire is on the verge of ruin—he has been arrested, and has been brought back to Paris, where the people demand that he be tried. You declare he shall be king. This is not the wish of the people, and the decree is therefore annulled. He has been carried off by the two hundred and ninety-two *aristocrates*, who have themselves declared that they have no longer a voice in the National Assembly. It is annulled because it is in opposition to the voice of the people, your sovereign. Repeal your decree: the king has abdicated by his crime: receive his abdication; convoke a fresh constitutive power; point out the criminal, and organize a new executive power."

This petition was laid on the altar of the country, and quires of paper, placed at the four corners of the altar, received six thousand autographs.

This petition is still preserved in the archives of the Municipality, and bears on it the indelible imprint of the hand of the people. It is the medal of the Revolution struck on the spot in the fused metal of popular agitation. Here and there on it are to be traced those sinister names that for the first time emerged from obscurity. These names are like the hieroglyphics of the ancient monuments. The acts of men now famous, who signed names then unknown and obscure, give to these signatures a retrospective signification, and the eye dwells with curiosity on these characters that seem to contain in a few marks the mystery of a long life—the whole horror of an epoch. Here is the name of *Chaumette, then a medical student, Rue Mazarine, No.* 9. There *Maillard*, the president of the fearful massacres of September. Further on, *Hébert;* underneath it, *Hanriot*, Inspector Warden of the condemned prisoners (*Général des*

Suppliciés) during the reign of terror. The small and scrawled signature of Hébert, who was afterwards the "*Père* Duchesne," or le Peuple en colère, is like a spider that extends its arms to seize its prey. Santerre has signed lower down: this is the last name of note, the rest are alone those of the populace. It is easy to discern how many a hasty and tremulous hand has traced the witness of its fury or ignorance on this document. Many were even unable to write. A circle of ink with a cross in the centre marks their anonymous adhesion to the petition. Some female names are to be seen, and numerous names of children are discernible, from the inaccuracy of their hand, guided by another: poor babes, who professed the opinions of their parents, without comprehending them; and who signed the attestation of the passions of the people, ere their infant tongues could utter a manly sound.

XIV.

The municipal body had been informed at two o'clock of the murders committed at the Champ-de-Mars, and of the insults offered to the body of national guards sent to disperse the mob. M. de La Fayette himself, who headed this detachment, had been struck by several stones hurled at him by the populace. It was even reported that a man in the uniform of the national guard had fired a pistol at him, and that he had generously pardoned and released this man, who had been seized by the escort. This popular report cast a halo of heroism around M. de La Fayette, and animated anew the national guard, who were devoted to him. At this recital Bailly did not hesitate to proclaim martial law, and to unfurl the red flag, the last resource against sedition. On their side, the mob, alarmed at the aspect of the red flag floating from the windows of the Hôtel-de-Ville, dispatched twelve of their number as a deputation to the municipality. These commissioners with difficulty made their way to the audience-hall, through a forest of bayonets, and demanded that three citizens who had been arrested should be given up to them. No attention was paid to them, however, and the resolution of employing force was adopted. The mayor and authorities descended the steps of the Hôtel-de-Ville, uttering threats of their intentions. At the sight of Bailly preceded by the red flag a cry of enthusiasm burst from the ranks, and the national guards clashed the butts of their muskets loudly against the stones. The public force, indignant with the clubs, was in a state of that nervous excitement that occasionally takes possession of large bodies as well as individuals.

La Fayette, Bailly, and the municipal authorities commenced their march preceded by the red flag, and followed by 10,000 national guards, the paid battalions of grenadiers of this army of citizens formed the advanced guard. An immense concourse of people followed by a natural impulse this mass of bayonets that slowly descended the quays and the rue du Gros-Caillou, towards the Champ-de-Mars. During this march, the people congregated around the altar of the country since the morning continued to sign the petition in peace. They were aware that the troops were called out, but did not believe any violence was intended; their calm and lawful method of proceeding, and the impunity of their sedition for two years, made them believe in a perpetual impunity, and they looked on the red flag merely as a fresh law to be despised.

On his arrival at the glacis of the Champ-de-Mars, La Fayette divided his forces into three columns; the first debouched by the avenue of the Ecole Militaire, the second and third by the two successive openings that intersect the glacis between the Ecole Militaire and the Seine. Bailly, La Fayette, and the municipal body with the red flag, marched at the head of the first column. The *pas de charge* beaten by 400 drums, and the rolling of the cannon over the stones, announced the arrival of the national army. These sounds drowned for an instant the hollow murmurs and the shrill cries of 50,000 men, women, and children, who filled the centre of the Champ-de-Mars, or crowded on the glacis. At the moment when Bailly debouched between the glacis, the populace, who from the top of the bank looked down on the mayor, the bayonets, and the artillery, burst into threatening shouts and furious outcries against the national guard. "*Down with the red flag! Shame to Bailly! Death to La Fayette!*" The people in the Champ-de-Mars responded to these cries with unanimous imprecations. Lumps of wet mud, the only arms at hand, were cast at the national guard, and struck La Fayette's horse, the red flag, and Bailly himself; and it is even said that several pistol shots were fired from a distance; this however was by no means proved,—the people had no intention of resisting, they wished only to intimidate. Bailly summoned them to disperse legally, to which they replied by shouts of derision; and he then, with the grave dignity of his office, and the mute sorrow that formed part of his character, ordered them to be dispersed by force. La Fayette first ordered the guard to fire in the air; but the people, encouraged by this vain demonstration, formed into line before the national guard, who then fired a discharge that killed and wounded 600 persons, the republicans say 10,000. At the same moment the ranks opened, the cavalry charged, and the artillerymen prepared to open their fire; which, on this dense mass of people, would have taken fearful effect. La Fayette, unable to restrain his soldiers by his voice, placed himself before the cannon's mouth, and by this heroic act saved the lives of thousands. In an instant the Champ-de-Mars was cleared, and nought remained on it save the dead bodies of women, and children, trampled under foot, or flying before the cavalry; and a few intrepid men on the steps of the altar of their country, who, amidst a murderous fire and at the cannon's mouth, collected, in order to preserve them, the sheets of the petition, as proofs of the wishes, or bloody pledges of the future vengeance, of the people, and they only retired when they had obtained them.

The columns of the national guard, and particularly the cavalry, pursued the fugitives into the neighboring fields, and made two hundred prisoners. Not a man was killed on the side of the national guard; the loss of the people is unknown. The one side diminished it, in order to extenuate the odium of an execution without resistance; the others augmented it in order to rouse the people's resentment. At night, which was already fast approaching, the bodies were cast into the Seine. Opinions were divided as to the nature and details of this execution, some terming it a crime, and others a painful duty; but this day of unresisting butchery still retains the name given it by the people, *The Massacre of the Champ-de-Mars.*

XV.

The national guard, headed by La Fayette, marched victorious, but mournful, again into Paris: it was visible by their demeanor that they hesitated between self-congratulation and shame, as though undecided on the justice of what they done. Amidst a few approving acclamations that saluted them on their passage, they heard smothered imprecations;

and the words *murderers* and *vengeance* were substituted for *patriotism* and *obedience to the law.* They passed with a gloomy air beneath the windows of that Assembly they had so lately protected; still more sadly and more silently beneath the windows of the palace of that monarchy, whose cause rather than whose king, they had just defended. Bailly, calm and glacial as the law—La Fayette, resolute and stern as a system, knew not how to awake any feeling beyond that of imperious duty. They furled the red flag, stained with the first drops of blood; and dispersed battalion after battalion, in the dark streets of Paris, more like gensd'armes after an execution, than an army returning from a victory.

Such was this "*Day of the Champ-de-Mars,*" which gave a reign of three months to the Assembly, by which they did not profit; which intimidated the clubs for a few days, but which did not restore to the monarchy or to the public tranquillity the blood it had cost. La Fayette had on this day the destiny of the monarchy and the republic in his hands: he merely re-established order.

XVI.

The next morning Bailly appeared before the Assembly to report to them the triumph of the law. He displayed the heartfelt sorrow of his mind, and the masculine energy that formed part of his duty.

"The conspiracy had been formed," said he; "it was necessary to employ force, and severe punishment has overtaken the crime." The president approved, in the name of the Assembly, of the mayor's conduct, and Barnave thanked the national guard in cold and weak language, whilst his praises seemed near akin to excuses. The enthusiasm of the victors had already subsided, and Pétion perceiving this, rose and said a few words concerning a *projet de décret* that had just been proposed, against those who should assemble the people in numbers. These words, in the mouth of Pétion, who was well known to be the friend of Brissot and the conspirators, were at first received with sarcastic cries by the *côté droit,* and then with loud applause from the *côté gauche* and the tribunes. The victory of the Champ-de-Mars was already contested in the Assembly, and the clubs re-opened that evening. Robespierre, Brissot, Danton, Camille Desmoulins, and Marat, who had for some days past disappeared, now took fresh courage, for the hesitation of their enemies reassured them,—by constantly attacking a power that was contented to remain on the defensive, they could not fail to weary it out, and thus, from accused they transformed themselves into accusers. Their papers, abandoned for a short time, became more malignant from their temporary panic, and heaped ridicule and odium on Bailly and La Fayette. They aroused the people to vengeance by displaying unceasingly before their eyes the blood of the Champ-de-Mars. The red flag became the emblem of the government and the winding-sheet of liberty. The conspirators figured as victims, and constantly kept popular excitement on the rack, by imaginary stories of the most odious persecutions.

XVII.

"See," wrote Desmoulins, "see how the furious satellites of La Fayette rush from their barracks, or rather from their taverns,—see, they assemble and load their arms with ball, in the presence of the people, whilst the battalions of *aristocrates* mutually excite each other to the massacre. It is chiefly in the eyes of the cavalry that you behold the love of blood aroused by the double influence of wine and vengeance. It was against women and babes that this army of butchers chiefly directed their fury. The altar of the country is strewn with dead bodies,—it is thus that La Fayette has dyed his hands in the gore of citizens: those hands which, in my eyes, will ever appear to reek with this innocent blood—this very spot where he had raised them to heaven to swear to defend them. From this moment, the most worthy citizens are proscribed; they are arrested in their beds, their papers are seized, their presses broken, and lists of the names of those proscribed are signed; the *modérés* sign these lists, and then display them. 'Society must be purged,' is their cry, 'of such men as *Brissot, Carra, Pétion, Bonneville, Fréron, Danton,* and *Camille.*' Danton and I found safety in flight alone from our assassins. The patriots are timid factions." "And," added *Fréron,* "there are men to be found, who venture to justify these cowardly murders—these informations—these *lettres de cachet*—these seizures of papers—these confiscations of presses. The red flag floats for a week from the balcony of the Hôtel-de-Ville, like as in times of old, the banners torn from the grasp of the dying foeman floated from the arched roof of our temples." In another part he says, "Marat's presses have been seized—the name of the author should have sufficed to protect the typographer. The press is sacred, as sacred as the cradle of the first-born, which even the officers of the law have orders to respect. The silence of the tomb reigns in the city, the public places are deserted, and the theatres re-echo alone with servile applause of royalism, that triumphs alike on the stage and in our streets. You were impatient, Bailly, and you treacherous, La Fayette, to employ that terrible weapon, martial law, so dangerous, so difficult to be wielded. No, no, nought can ever efface the indelible stain of the blood of your brethren, that has spurted over your scarfs and your uniforms. It has sunk even to your heart—it is a slow poison that will consume ye all."

Whilst the revolutionary press thus infused the spirit of resentment into the people, the clubs, reassured by the indolence of the Assembly, and by the scrupulous legality of La Fayette, suffered but slightly the effects of this body blow of the victory of the Champ-de-Mars. A schism took place in the assembly of the Jacobins between the intolerant members and its first founders, Barnave, Duport, and the two Lameths. This schism took its rise in the great question of the non-re-eligibility of the members of the National Assembly for the Legislative Assembly which was so soon to succeed. The pure Jacobins, together with Robespierre, wished that the National Assembly should abdicate, *en masse*, and voluntarily sentence themselves to a political ostracism, in order to make room for men of newer ideas and more imbued with the spirit of the time. The moderate and constitutional Jacobins looked upon this abdication as equally fatal to the monarch, as it dealt a mortal blow to their ambition, for they wished to seize on the direction of the power they had just created; they deemed themselves alone competent to control the movement that they had excited, and they sought to rule in the name of those laws of which they were the framers. Robespierre, on the contrary, who felt his own weakness in an assembly composed of the same elements, wished these elements to be excluded from the new assembly; he himself suffered by the law that he laid down for his colleagues; but with scarcely a rival to dispute his authority at the Jacobins, they formed his assembly. His instinct or calculation told him that the Jacobins must have supreme sway in a newly formed assembly composed of men whose very names were unknown to the nation. One of the faction himself, it was enough for him that the factions reigned; and the tool he possessed in the Jacobins, and his immense popularity, gave him the positive assurance that he should rule the factions.

This question, at the time of the events of the Champ-de-Mars, agitated, and already tended to dissolve the Jacobins. The rival club of the Feuillants, composed almost entirely of constitutionalists and members of the National Assembly, had a more legal and monarchical appearance. The irritation caused by the popular excesses, and their hatred for Robespierre and Brissot, induced the ancient founders of the club to join the Feuillants. The Jacobins trembled lest the empire of the factions should escape them, and that division should weaken them. "It is the court," said Camille Desmoulins, the friend of Robespierre, "it is the court that foments this schism amongst us, and has invented this perfidious stratagem to destroy the popular party. It knows the two Lameths, La Fayette, Barnave, Duport, and the others who first figured in the Jacobin assembly. 'What,' the court asked itself, 'is the aim of all these men?' their aim was to be elevated to rank and station, by the voice of the people, and by the gales of popularity, of command of the ministers, of gold: what they needed was court favor to serve as the sails of their ambition; and, wanting these sails, they use the oars of the people. Let us prove to Lameth and Barnave that they will not be re-elected, that they cannot fill any important place before four years have passed away. They will be indignant, and return to our party. I saw Alexandre and Theodore Lameth the evening of the day on which Robespierre's motion of the non-re-eligibility was carried. The Lameths were then patriots, but the next day they were no longer the same. 'It is impossible to submit to this,' said they,—'in concert with Duport—we must quit France.' What! shall those who have been the architects of the constitution undergo the mortification of witnessing the downfall of the edifice they have reared, by this approaching system of legislation? We shall be condemned to hear from the galleries of the Assembly, some fool in the tribune attack our wisest enactments, which we are denied the power of defending. Would to Heaven! that they would quit France. Is it not enough to cause us to despise both the Assembly and the people of Paris, when we see that the clue of this is, that the supreme control was on the point of eluding the grasp of Lameth and La Fayette, and that Duport and Barnave would not be again elected."

Pétion, alarmed at these symptoms of discord, addressed the tribune of the Jacobins in conciliatory terms—"You are lost," said he, "should the members of the Assembly quit your party, and betake themselves *en masse* to the Feuillants. The empire of public opinion is deserting you; and these countless affiliated societies, imbued with your spirit, will sever the bonds of fraternity, and unite them to you. Forestall the designs of your enemies. Publish an address to the affiliated societies, and re-assure them of your constitutional intentions; tell them that you have been belied to them, and that you are no promoters of faction. Tell them that far from wishing to disturb public tranquillity, your sole design is to avert those troubles entailed on you by the king's departure. Tell them that we submit to the rapid and imposing influence of opinion, and that respect for the Assembly, fidelity to the constitution, devotion to the cause of your country and of liberty, form your principles." This address, dictated by the hypocrisy of fear, was adopted and sent to all the societies in the kingdom. This measure was followed by a remodelling of the Jacobins; the primitive nucleus alone was suffered to remain, which re-organized the rest by the ballot over which Pétion presided.

On their side the Feuillants wrote to the patriotic societies of the provinces, and for a brief space there was an interregnum of the factions; but the societies of the provinces speedily declared *en masse*, and with an almost unanimous and revolutionary enthusiasm, in favor of the Jacobins.

"Free and sincere union with our brothers in Paris:" such was the rallying cry of the clubs. Six hundred clubs sent in their adherence to the Jacobins; eighteen alone declared for the Feuillants. The factions felt the importance of unity as fully as the nation, and the schism of opinion was stifled by the enthusiasm for the grandeur of their work. Pétion, in a letter to his constituents which made a great sensation, spoke of these fruitless attempts at dissension amongst the patriots, and denounced those who dissented from it. "I tremble for my country," said he; "the *modérés* are meditating the reform of the constitution already; and to place again in the king's hands the power the people have scarcely acquired. My mind is overwhelmed by these gloomy reflections, and I despond. I am ready to quit the post you have confided to me. Oh, my country, be but thou saved, and I shall breathe my last sigh in peace!"

Such were Pétion's words, and from that hour he became the idol of the people. He possessed neither the abilities nor the audacity of Robespierre; but he had hypocrisy, that shameless veil of doubtful positions. The people believed him to be sincere, and his speeches had the same influence over them as his reputation.

XVIII.

The coalition which he denounced to the people was true. Barnave had an understanding with the court. Malouet, an eloquent and able member of the right, had an understanding with Barnave: a plan for modifying the constitution had been concerted between these two men—yesterday foes, to-day allies. The moment was come for uniting in one general measure all these scattered laws valid during a revolution of thirty months. In separating, on this review of the acts of the Assembly, what was integral from that which was not, the occasion must arise for a revision of every act of the constitution. It was, therefore, the moment to profit (in order to amend them in a sense more monarchical), by the reaction produced by La Fayette's victory. What impulse and anger had too violently taken from the prerogatives of the crown, reason and reflection could restore to it. The same men who had placed the executive power in the hands of the Assembly, hoped to be able to withdraw it from them. They believed they could effect everything by their eloquence and popularity. Like all who are descending the tide of a revolution, they thought they were able to ascend the stream with equal ease. They did not see that their strength, of which they were so proud, was not in themselves, but in the current which bore them along. Events were about to teach them that there is no opposing passions to which concession has been once made. The strength of a statesman is his power. One concession, how slight soever, to factions, is an irrevocable engagement with them: when once we consent to become their instrument, we may be made their idol and their victim, never their master. Barnave was doomed to learn this when too late; and the Girondists were to learn it after him. The plan was thus arranged:—Malouet was to ascend the tribune, and in a vehement but well-reasoned discourse was to attack all the errors of the constitution; he was to demonstrate that if these vices were not amended by the Assembly before the constitution itself should be presented to the king and the people to swear to, it would be anarchy registered by an oath. The three hundred members of the *côté droit* were to support the charges of their spokesman by vehement plaudits. Barnave was then to demand a reply, and in a discourse, apparently much excited, was to have vindicated the constitution from the invectives of Malouet, at the same time conceding that as this constitution was suddenly produced by the enthusiastic ardor of the Revolution, and under the impulse of desperately contending circumstances, there might be some imperfections in a certain portion of the construction; that the grave consideration and wisdom of the Assembly might remedy these errors before it dissolved; and that, amongst other ameliorations which might be applied to this work, they might retouch two or three articles in which the power assigned to the executive authority and the legislative authority had been ill defined, so as to restore to the executive power the independence and scope indispensable to their existence. The friends of Barnave, Lameth, and Duport, as well as all the members of the left, would have clamorously supported the speaker, except Robespierre, Pétion, Buzot, and the republicans. A commission would have been instantly named for the special revision of the articles alluded to. This commission would have made its report before the end of the meeting of the chambers; and the three hundred votes of Malouet, united to the constitutional votes of Barnave, would have assured to the monarchical amendments the majority which was to restore royalty.

XIX.

But the members of the right refused to give their unanimous concurrence to this plan. "To amend the constitution was to sanction revolt. To unite themselves with the factious, was to become factious themselves. To restore royalty by the hands of a Barnave, was to degrade the king even to gratitude towards a member of a faction. Their hopes had not fallen so low that it was thus they had but the option of accepting a character in a comedy of startled revolutionists. Their hopes were not in any amelioration of present ill, but in its progress towards worse. The very excess of disorder would punish disorder itself. The king was at the Tuileries, but royalty was not there—it was at Coblentz, it was on all the thrones of Europe. Monarchies were all in connection; they knew very well how to restore the French monarchy without the fellowship of those who had overturned it."

Thus reasoned the members of the right. Feelings and resentments closed their ears to the counsels of moderation and wisdom, and the monarchy was not less systematically pushed towards its catastrophe by the hand of its friends than that of its enemies. The plan was abortive.

Whilst the captive king kept up a twofold understanding with his emigrant brothers to learn the strength and inclination of foreign powers, and with Barnave to attempt the conquest of the Assembly, the Assembly itself lost its power; and the spirit of the Revolution, quitting the place in which it had no longer any hopes, went to excite the clubs and municipalities, and bestow its energies on the elections. The Assembly had committed the fault of declaring its members not re-eligible for the new legislature. This act of renunciation of itself, which resembled the heroism of disinterestedness, was in reality the sacrifice of the country; it was the ostracism of superior power, and an assurance of triumph to mediocrity. A nation how rich soever in genius and virtue, never possesses more than a definite number of great citizens. Nature is chary of superiority. The social conditions necessary to form a public man are rarely in combination. Intelligence, clear-sightedness, virtue, character, independence, leisure, fortune, consideration already acquired, and devotion,—all this is seldom united in one individual. An entire society is not decapitated with impunity. Nations are like their soil: after having pared off the vegetable earth, we find only the sand beneath, and that is unproductive. The Constituent Assembly had forgotten this truth, or rather its abdication had assumed the form of a vengeance. The royalist party had voted the non-re-eligibility, in order that the Revolution, thus eluding Barnave's grasp, should fall into the clutch of the demagogues. The republican party had voted in order to annihilate the constitutionalists. The constitutionalists voted in order to chastise the ingratitude of the people, and to make themselves regretted by the unworthy spectacle which they expected their successors would present. It was a vote of contending passions, all evil, and which could only produce a loss to all parties. The king alone was averse from this measure. He perceived repentance in the National Assembly—he was in communication with its leading members—he had the key to many consciences. A new nation, unknown and impatient, was about to present it before him in a new Assembly. The reports of the press, the clubs, and places of popular bruit told him, but too plainly, on what men the excited people would bestow their confidence He preferred known, exhausted opponents, men partly gained over, to new and ardent enemies who would surpass in exactions those they replaced. To them there only remained his throne to overthrow,—to him there was left to yield but his life.

XX.

The principal names discussed in the public newspapers in Paris, were those of Condorcet, Brissot, Danton;—in the departments those of Vergniaud, Gaudet, Isnard, Louvet,—who were afterwards Girondists; and those of Thuriot, Merlin, Carnot, Couthon, Danton, Saint Just, who subsequently united with Robespierre, were, by turns, his instruments or his victims. Condorcet was a philosopher, as intrepid in his actions as bold in his speculations. His political creed was a consequence of his philosophy. He believed in the divinity of reason, and in the omnipotence of the human understanding, with liberty as its handmaid. Heaven, the abode of all ideal perfections, and in which man places his most beautiful dreams, was limited by Condorcet to earth: his science was his virtue; the human mind his deity. The intellect impregnated by science, and multiplied by time, it appeared to him must triumph necessarily over all the resistance of matter, must lay bare all the creative powers of nature, and renew the face of creation. He had made of this system a line of politics, whose first idea was to adore the future and abhor the past. He had the cool fanaticism of logic, and the reflective anger of conviction. A pupil of Voltaire, D'Alembert, and Helvetius, he, like Bailly, was of that intermediate generation by which philosophy was imbodied with the Revolution. More ambitious than Bailly, he had not his impassibility. Aristocrat by birth, he, like Mirabeau, had passed over to the camp of the people. Hated by the court, he hated it as do all renegades. He had become one of the people, in order to convert the people into the army of philosophy. He wanted of the republic no more than was sufficient to overturn its prejudices. Ideas once become victorious,—he would willingly have confided it to the control of a constitutional monarchy. He was rather a man for dispute than a man of anarchy. Aristocrats always carry with them, into the popular party, the desire of order and command. They would fain

"Ride in the whirlwind and direct the storm."

Real anarchists are those who are impatient of having always obeyed, and feel themselves impotent to command. Condorcet had edited the *Chronique de Paris* from 1789. It was a journal of constitutional doctrines, but in which the throbbings of anger were perceivable beneath the cool and polished hand of the philosopher. Had Condorcet been endowed with warmth and command of language, he might have been the Mirabeau of another assembly. He had his earnestness and constancy, but had not the resounding and energetic tone which made his own soul and feelings felt by another. The club of electors of Paris, who met at La Sainte Chapelle, elected Condorcet to the chamber. The same club returned Danton.

XXI.

Danton, whom the Revolution had found an obscure barrister at the Châtelet, had increased with it in influence. He had already that celebrity which the multitude easily assigns to him whom it sees everywhere, and always listens to. He was one of those men who seem born of the stir of revolutions, and which float on its surface until it swallows them up. All in him was like the mass—athletic, rude, coarse. He pleased them because he resembled them. His eloquence was like the loud clamor of the mob. His brief and decisive phrases had the martial curtness of command. His irresistible gestures gave impulse to his plebeian auditories. Ambition was his whole line of politics. Devoid of honor, principles, or morality, he only loved democracy because it was exciting. It was his element, and he plunged into it. He sought there not so much command as that voluptuous sensuality which man finds in the rapid movement which bears him away with it. He was intoxicated with the revolutionary vertigo as a man becomes drunken with wine; yet he bore his intoxication well. He had that superiority of calmness in the confusion he created, which enabled him to control it: preserving *sang froid* in his excitement and his temper, even in a moment of passion, he jested with the clubs in their stormiest moods. A burst of laughter interrupted bitterest imprecations; and he amused the people even whilst he impelled them to the uttermost pitch of fury. Satisfied with his two-fold ascendency, he did not care to respect it himself, and neither spoke to it of principles nor of virtue, but solely of force. Himself, he adored force, and force only. His sole genius was contempt for honesty; and he esteemed himself above all the world, because he had trampled under foot all scruples. Everything was to him a means. He was a statesman of materialism, playing the popular game, with no end but the terrible game itself, with no stake but his life, and with no responsibility beyond nonentity. Such a man must be profoundly indifferent either to despotism or to liberty. His contempt of the people must incline him rather to the side of tyranny. When we can detect nothing divine in men, the better part to play is to make use of them. We can only serve well that which we respect. He was only with the people because he was of the people, and thus the people ought to triumph. He would have betrayed it, as he served it, unscrupulously. The court well knew the tariff of his conscience. He threatened it in order to make it desirous of buying him; he only opened his mouth in order to have it stuffed with gold. His most revolutionary movements were but the marked prices at which he was purchasable. His hand was in every intrigue, and his honesty was not checked by any offer of corruption. He was bought daily, and next morning was again for sale. Mirabeau, La Fayette, Montmorin, M. de Laporte, the intendant of the civil list, the Duc d'Orleans, the king himself, all knew his price. Money had flowed with him from all sources, even the most impure, without remaining with him. Any other individual would have felt shame before men and parties who had the secret of his dishonor; but he only was not ashamed, and looked them in the face without a blush. His was the quietude of vice.* He was the focus of all those men who seek in events nothing but fortune and impunity. But others had only the baseness of crime—Danton's vices partook of the heroic—his intellect was all but genius. He had upon him

* "Infamous and contented."—*Junius.*

the bright flash of circumstances, but it was as sinister as his face. Immorality, which was the infirmity of his mind, was in his eyes the essence of his ambition; he cultivated it in himself as the element of future greatness. He pitied anybody who respected anything. Such a man had of necessity a vast ascendency over the bad passions of the multitude. He kept them in continual agitation, and always boiling on the surface ready to flow into any torrent, even if it were of blood.

XXII.

Brissot de Warville was another of these popular candidates for the representation. As this individual was the root of the Girondist party, the first apostle and first martyr of the republic, we ought to know him. Brissot was the son of a pastrycook at Chartres, and had received his education in that city with Pétion, his fellow countryman. An adventurer in literature, he had begun by assuming the name of *Warville,* which concealed his own. It is a plebeian nobility not to blush at one's father's name. Brissot had not done so. He began by furtively appropriating one of the titles of that aristocracy of races against which he was about to raise equality. Like Rousseau in everything but his genius, he sought his fortune hither and thither, and descended even lower than he into misery and intrigue, before he acquired celebrity. Dispositions became weakened and stained by such a struggle with the difficulties of life in the dregs of great corrupted cities. Rousseau had paraded his indigence and his reveries in the bosom of nature; and as its consideration calms and purifies everything he quitted it a philosopher. Brissot had dragged his misery and vanity into the heart of Paris and of London, and into those haunts of infamy in which adventurers and pampleteers drag on a filthy existence: he left them an intriguer. Yet in the very midst of these vices which had rendered his honesty dubious, and name bespotted, he nurtured in the depths of his soul three virtues capable of again elevating him—an unshaken love for a young girl, whom he married in spite of his family, a love of occupation, and a courage against the difficulties of life, which he had afterwards to display in the face of death. His philosophy was identical with Rousseau's. He believed in God. He had faith in liberty, truth, and virtue. He had in his soul that unqualified devotion towards the human species which is the charity of philosophers. He detested society, for in it there was no place awarded to him; but what he hated with unmitigated hate was the state of society; its prejudices—its falsehoods. He would have recast it, less for himself than for the benefit of mankind. He would have consented to be crushed beneath its ruins, provided those ruins were to give place to his ideal plan of the government of reason. Brissot was one of those mercenary scribes who write for those who pay best. He had written on all subjects, for every minister; especially Turgot. Criminal laws, political economy, diplomacy, literature, philosophy, even libels,—his pen was at the hire of the first comer. Seeking the support of celebrated and influential men, he had adulated all from Voltaire and Franklin down to Marat. Known to Madame de Genlis, he had, through her, some acquaintance with the Duc d'Orleans. Sent to London by the minister on one of those missions which are nameless, he there became connected with the editor of the *Courrier de l'Europe*, a French journal, printed in London, and the boldness of whose style was offensive at the court of the Tuileries. He engaged himself to Swinton, the proprietor of this newspaper, and edited it in a manner favorable to the views of Vergennes. He knew at Swinton's several writers, amongst others one Morande. These libellers, outcasts of society, frequently then become the refuse of the pen, and live at the same time on the disgraces of vice and in the pay of spies. Their collision infected Brissot. He was or appeared to be sometimes their accomplice. Hideous blotches thus stain his life, and were cruelly revived by his enemies, when the time came in which he was compelled to appeal to public esteem.

Returning to France at the first symptoms of the Revolution, he watched its successive phases, with the ambition of an impatient man, and with the indecision of one not knowing what part to take. He was frequently wrong. He compromised himself by his devotion, too early displayed, towards certain men who had seemed to him for a moment to be all-powerful, especially towards La Fayette. Editor of the *Patriote Français*, he had occasionally put forth revolutionary feelers, and flattered the future by going even faster than the factions themselves. He had even been disowned by Robespierre. "Whilst I content myself," said Robespierre, referring to him, "with defending the principles of liberty, without opening any other question, what are you doing,

Brissot and Condorcet? Known until now by your great moderation and your connection with La Fayette, for a long time followers of the aristocratic club of '89, you suddenly blazon forth the word Republic. You issue a journal entitled the *Republican*! Then minds become in a ferment. The mere word Republic throws division amongst patriots, and affords to our enemies a pretext which they seek for announcing that there exists in France a party which conspires against the monarchy and the constitution. Under this title we are persecuted, and peaceable citizens are sacrificed on the altars of their country! At this name we are transformed into factions, and the Revolution is made to recede, perhaps, half a century. It was at the same moment that Brissot came to the Jacobins, where he had never before appeared, to propose a republic of which the simplest rules of prudence had forbidden us to speak in the National Assembly. By what fatality did Brissot find himself there? I would fain discover no craft in his conduct; I would prefer detecting only imprudence and folly. But now that his connection with La Fayette and Narbonne are no longer a mystery—now that he no longer dissimulates his schemes of dangerous innovations, let him clearly understand that the nation will at once and effectually break through all the plots framed during so many years by pitiful intriguers."

So spake Robespierre, jealous by anticipation, and yet just, on Brissot's presenting himself as a candidate. The Revolution rejected him, the Counter-revolution repudiated him no less. Brissot's old allies in London, especially Morande, returned to Paris under cover of the troublous times, revealed to the Parisians in the *Argus*, and in placards, the secret intrigues and the disgraceful literary career of their former associate. They quoted actual letters, in which Brissot had lied unblushingly as to his name, the condition of his family, and his father's fortune, in order to acquire Swinton's confidence, to gain credit, and make dupes in England. The proofs were damning. A considerable sum had been extorted from a man named Desforges, under pretence of erecting an institution in London, and this sum had been expended by Brissot on himself. This was but a trifle: Brissot, on quitting England, had left in the hands of this Desforges twenty-four letters, which but too plainly established his participation in the infamous trade of libels carried on by his allies. It was proved to demonstration that Brissot had connived at the sending into France, and the propagation of, odious pamphlets by Morande. The journals hostile to his election seized on these scandalous facts, and held them up to public obloquy. He was, besides, accused of having extracted from the funds of the district of the *Filles-Saint-Thomas*, of which he was president, a sum for his own purse, long forgotten. His defence was labored and obscure; yet it was held by the club of the Rue de la Michodière sufficient proof of his innocence and integrity. Some journals, solely occupied with the political bearing of his life, took up his defence, and made loud complaints against his calumny. Manuel, his friend, who edited a vile journal, wrote thus, to console him:—"These ordures of calumny, spread abroad at the moment of scrutiny, always end by leaving a dirty stain on those who scatter them. But it is allowing a triumph to the enemies of the people, to repulse thus a man who fearlessly attacks them. They give me votes, in spite of my drivellings, and my love of the bottle. Leave 'Père Duchesne'* alone, and let us nominate Brissot; he is a better man than I am."

Marat, in his *Ami du Peuple,* wrote thus ambiguously of Brissot:—"Brissot," says the Friend of the People, "was never, in my eyes, a thorough-going patriot. Either from ambition or baseness, he has up to this time betrayed the duties of a good citizen. Why has he been so tardy in leaving a system of hypocrisy? Poor Brissot, thou art the victim of a court valet, of a base hypocrite!—why lend thy paw to La Fayette? Why, thou must expect to experience the fate of all men of indecision. Thou hast displeased everybody; thou canst never make thy way. If thou hast one atom of proper feeling left, hasten, and scratch out thy name from the list of candidates for the approaching general election."

Thus appeared on the scene for the first time, in the midst of the hootings of both parties, this man, who attempted in vain to escape from the general contempt accumulated on his name from the faults of his youth, in order to enter on the gravity of his political career—a mingled character, half intrigue, half virtue. Brissot, destined to serve as the centre of a rallying point to the party of the *Gironde,* had, by anti

* "Père Duchesne" was one of the most virulent, gross and blood thirsty productions of the Revolution. It was edited by Manuel and Hébert. Its success and profit were so great, that it had many imitators It was rather a pamphlet than a newspaper, the price fifty sous a month. H. T. R.

cipation in his character, all there was in after days, of destiny in his party, of intrigue and patriotism, of faction and martyrdom. The other marked candidates in Paris, were, Pastoret, a man of the South, prudent and skilful as a Southron, steering ably betwixt parties, giving sufficient guarantee to the Revolution to be accepted by it, enough devotion to the court to retain its secret confidence; borne hither and thither by the alternating favors of the two opinions, like a man who seeks fortune for his talent in the Revolution, but never looking for it beyond the limits of the just and honorable. Lacepede, Cerutti, Hérault de Séchelles, and Gouvion, La Fayette's aide-de-camp. The elections of the department occupied but little attention. The National Assembly had exhausted the country of its characters and its talents; the ostracism it had exercised had imposed on France but secondary ability. There was but little enthusiasm for untried men: the public eyes were only fixed on the names about to disappear. A country cannot contain a twofold renown: that of France was departing with the members of the dissolved Assembly—another France was about to rise.

BOOK IV.

I.

At this juncture the germ of a new opinion began to display itself in the south, and Bordeaux felt its full influence. The department of the Gironde had given birth to a new political party in the twelve citizens who formed its deputies. This department, far removed from the *centre*, was at no distant period to seize on the empire alike of opinion and of eloquence. The names (obscure and unknown up to this period,) of *Ducos, Guadet, Lafond-Ladebat, Grangeneuve, Gensonné, Vergniaud*, were about to rise into notice and renown with the storms and the disasters of their country; they were the men who were destined to give that impulse to the Revolution that had hitherto remained in doubt and indecision, before which it still trembled with apprehension, and which was to precipitate it into a republic. Why was this impulse fated to have birth in the department of the Gironde and not in Paris? Nought but conjectures can be offered on this subject; and yet perhaps the republican spirit was more likely to manifest itself at Bordeaux than at Paris, where the presence and influence of a court had for ages past enervated the independence of character, and enfeebled the austerity of principle that form the basis of patriotism and liberty. The states of Languedoc, and the habits that necessarily result from the administration of a province governed by itself, could not fail to predispose the inclination of the Gironde in favor of an elective and federative government. Bordeaux was a parliamentary country; the parliaments had everywhere encouraged the spirit of resistance, and had often created a factious feeling against the king. Bordeaux was a commercial city, and commerce, which requires liberty through interest, at last desires it through a love of freedom. Bordeaux was the great commercial link between America and France, and their constant intercourse with America had communicated to the Gironde their love for free institutions. Moreover Bordeaux was more exposed to the enlightening influence of the sun of philosophy than the centre of France. Philosophy had germed there ere it arose in Paris, for Bordeaux was the birthplace of Montaigne and Montesquieu, those two great republicans of the French school. The one had deeply investigated the religious dogmata, the other the political institutions; and the president Dupaty had long after awakened there enthusiasm for the new system of philosophy. Bordeaux, in addition, was a country where the traditions of liberty and the *Roman Forum* had been perpetuated in the bar. A certain leaven of antiquity animated each heart, and lent vigor to every tongue, and the town was still more republican by eloquence than by opinion; though there was something of Latin emphasis in their patriotism. It was in the birthplace of Montaigne and Montesquieu that the republic was to take its origin.

II.

The period of the elections was the signal for a still more obstinate attack from the public press. The papers were insufficient: men sold pamphlets in the streets, and the "*Journaux affiches*" were invented, which were placarded against the walls of Paris, and around which groups of people were constantly collected. Wandering orators, inspired or hired by the different parties, took their stand there and commented aloud on these impassioned productions:—Loustalot, in the *Revolutions de Paris*, founded by Prudhomme, and continued alternately by Chaumette and Fabre d'Eglantine; Marat, in the *Publiciste* and the *Ami du Peuple;* Brissot, in the *Patriote Française;* Gorsas, in the *Courrier de Versailles;* Condorcet, in the *Chronique de Paris;* Cérutti, in the *Feuille Villageoise;* Camille Desmoulins, in the *Discours de la Lanterne,* and the *Revolutions de Brabant*, Fréron, in the *Orateur du Peuple;* Hébert and Manuel, in the *Père Duchesne;* Carra, in the *Annales Patriotiques;* Fleydel, in the *Observateur;* Laclos, in the *Journal des Jacobins;* Fauchet, in the *Bouche de Fer;* Royon, in the *Ami du Roi;* Champcenetz-Rivarol, in the *Actes des Apôtres;* Suleau and André Chénier, in several *royaliste* or *modérée* papers,—excited and disputed dominion over the minds of the people. It was the ancient tribune transported to the dwelling of each citizen, and adapting its language to the comprehension of all men, even the most illiterate. Anger, suspicion, hatred, envy, fanaticism, credulity, invective, thirst of blood, sudden panics, madness and reflection, treason and fidelity, eloquence and folly, had each their organ in this concert of every passion and feeling in which the city revelled each night. All toil was at an end; the only labor in their eyes was to watch the throne, to frustrate the real or fancied plots of the aristocracy, and to save their country. The hoarse bawling of the venders of the public journals, the patriotic chants of the Jacobins as they quitted their clubs, the tumultuous assemblies, the convocations to the patriotic ceremonies, fallacious fears as to the failure of provisions—kept the population of the city and faubourgs in a perpetual state of excitement, which suffered no one to remain inactive; indifference would have been considered treason; and it was necessary to feign enthusiasm in order to be in accordance with public opinion. Each fresh event quickened this feverish excitement, which the press constantly instilled into the veins of the people. Its language already bordered on delirium, and borrowed from the population even their proverbs, their love of trifles, their obscenity, their brutality, and even their oaths, with which the articles were interlarded, as though to impress more forcibly its hatred on the ear of its foes. Danton, Hébert, and Marat were the first to adopt this tone, these gestures, and these exclamations of the populace, as though to flatter them by imitating their vices. Robespierre never condescended to this, and never sought to obtain ascendency over the people by pandering to their brutality, but by appealing to their reason; and the fanatical tone of his speeches possessed at least that decency that attends great ideas—he ruled by respect, and scorned to captivate them by familiarity. The more he gained the confidence of the lower classes, the more did he affect the philosophical tone and austere demeanor of the statesman. It was plainly perceptible in his most radical propositions, that however he might wish to renew social order he would not corrupt its elements, and that in his eyes to emancipate the people was not to degrade them.

III.

It was at this period that the Assembly ordered the removal of Voltaire's remains to the Pantheon; philosophy thus avenged itself on the anathemas that had been thundered forth, even against the ashes of the great innovator. The body of Voltaire, on his death, in Paris, A.D. 1778, had been furtively removed by his nephew at night, and interred in the church of the abbey of Sellières in Champagne; and when the nation sold this abbey, the cities of Troyes and Romilly mutually contended for the honor of possessing the bones of the greatest man of the age. The city of Paris, where he had breathed his last, now claimed its privilege as the capital of France, and addressed a petition to the National Assembly, praying that Voltaire's body might be brought back to Paris and interred in the Pantheon, that cathedral of philosophy. The Assembly eagerly hailed the idea of this homage, that traced liberty back to its original source. "The people owe their freedom to him," said Regnault de Saint Jean d'Angély; "for by enlightening them, he gave them power; nations are enthralled by ignorance alone, and when the torch of reason displays to them the ignominy of bearing these chains, they blush to wear them, and snap them asunder."

On the 11th of July, the departmental and municipal authorities went in state to the barrier of Charenton, to receive the mortal remains of Voltaire, which were placed on the ancient site of the Bastille, like a conqueror on his trophies; his coffin was exposed to public gaze, and a pedestal was formed for it of stones torn from the foundations of this ancient stronghold of tyranny; and thus Voltaire when dead, triumphed over those stones which had triumphed over and confined him when living. On one of the blocks was the inscription, "*Receive on this spot, where despotism once fettered thee, the honors decreed to thee by thy country.*"

IV.

The next day when the rays of a brilliant sun had dissipated the mists of the night, an immense concourse of people followed the car that bore Voltaire to the Pantheon. This car was drawn by twelve white horses, harnessed four abreast; their manes plaited with flowers and golden tassels, and the reins held by men dressed in antique costumes, like those depicted on the medals of ancient triumphs. On the car was a funeral couch, extended on which was a statue of the philosopher, crowned with a wreath. The National Assembly, the departmental and municipal bodies, the constituted authorities, the magistrates, and the army, surrounded, preceded, and followed the sarcophagus. The boulevards, the streets, the public places, the windows, the roofs of houses, even the trees, were crowded with spectators; and the suppressed murmurs of vanquished intolerance could not restrain this feeling of enthusiasm. Every eye was riveted on the car; for the new school of ideas felt that it was the proof of their victory that was passing before them, and that philosophy remained mistress of the field of battle.

The details of this ceremony were magnificent; and in spite of its profane and theatrical trappings, the features of every man that followed the car wore the expression of joy, arising from an intellectual triumph. A large body of cavalry, who seemed to have now offered their arms at the shrine of intelligence, opened the march. Then followed the muffled drums, to whose notes were added the roar of the artillery that formed a part of the cortège. The scholars of the colleges of Paris, the patriotic societies, the battalions of the national guard, the workmen of the different public journals, the persons employed to demolish the foundations of the Bastille, some bearing a portable press, which struck off different inscriptions in honor of Voltaire as the procession moved on; others carrying the chains, the collars and bolts, and bullets found in the dungeons and arsenals of the state prisons; and lastly, busts of Voltaire, Rousseau, and Mirabeau, marched between the troops and the populace. On a litter was displayed the *procès-verbal* of the electors of '89, that *hegyra* of the insurrection. On another stand, the citizens of the Faubourg Saint Antoine exhibited a plan in relief of the Bastille, the flag of the donjon, and a young girl, in the costume of an Amazon, who had fought at the siege of this fortress. Here and there, pikes surmounted with the Phrygian cap of liberty arose above the crowd, and on one of them was a scroll bearing the inscription, "*From this steel sprung Liberty!*"

All the actors and actresses of the theatres of Paris followed the statue of him who for sixty years had inspired them; the titles of his principal works were inscribed on the sides of a pyramid that represented his immortality. His statue, formed of gold and crowned with laurel, was borne on the shoulders of citizens wearing the costumes of the nations and the times whose manners and customs he had depicted; and the seventy volumes of his works were contained in a casket, also of gold. The members of the learned bodies, and of the principal academies of the kingdom surrounded this ark of philosophy. Numerous bands of music, some marching with the troops, others stationed along the road of the procession, saluted the car as it passed with loud bursts of harmony, and filled the air with the enthusiastic strains of liberty. The procession stopped before the principal theatres, a hymn was sung in honor of his genius, and the car then resumed its march. On their arrival at the quai that bears his name, the car stopped before the house of M. de Villette, where Voltaire had breathed his last, and where his heart was preserved. Evergreen shrubs, garlands of leaves, and wreaths of roses decorated the front of the house, which bore the inscription, "*His fame is everywhere, and his heart is here.*" Young girls dressed in white, and wreaths of flowers on their heads, covered the steps of an amphitheatre erected before the house. Madame de Villette, to whom Voltaire had been a second father, in all the splendor of her beauty, and the pathos of her tears, advanced and placed the noblest of all his wreaths, the wreath of filial affection, on the head of the great philosopher.

At this moment the crowd burst into one of the hymns of the poet Chenier, who, up to his death, most of all men cherished the memory of Voltaire. Madame de Villette and the young girls of the amphitheatre descended into the street, now strewed with flowers, and walked before the car. The Theâtre Français, then situated in the Faubourg St. Germain, had erected a triumphal arch on its peristyle. On each pillar a medallion was fixed, bearing in letters of gilt bronze the title of the principal dramas of the poet; on the pedestal of the statue erected before the door of the theatre was written, "*He wrote Irène at eighty-three years; at seventeen he wrote Œdipus.*"

The immense procession did not arrive at the Pantheon until ten o'clock at night, for the day had not been sufficiently long for this triumph. The coffin of Voltaire was deposited between those of Descartes and Mirabeau,—the spot predestined for this intermediary genius between philosophy and policy, between the design and the execution. This apotheosis of modern philosophy, amidst the great events that agitated the public mind, was a convincing proof that the Revolution comprehended its own aim, and that it sought to be the inauguration of those two principles represented by these cold ashes—Intelligence and Liberty. It was intelligence that triumphantly entered the city of Louis XIV. over the ruins of the prejudices of birth. It was philosophy taking possession of the city and the temple of Sainte Geneviève. The remains of two schools, of two ages, and two creeds were about to strive for the mastery even in the tomb. Philosophy who, up to this hour, had timidly shrunk from the contest, now revealed her latest inspiration—that of transferring the veneration of the age from one great man to another.

V.

Voltaire, the sceptical genius of France in modern ages, combined in himself the double passion of this people at such a period—the passion of destruction, and the desire of innovation, hatred of prejudices and love of knowledge: he was destined to be the standard-bearer of destruction; his genius, although not the most elevated, yet the most comprehensive in France, has hitherto been only judged by fanatics or his enemies. Impiety deified his very vices; superstition anathematized his very virtues; in a word, despotism, when it again seized on the reins of government in France, felt that to reinstate tyranny it would be necessary first to unseat Voltaire from his high position in the national opinion. Napoleon, during fifteen years, paid writers who degrade, vilify, and deny the genius of Voltaire; he hated his name, as *might* must ever hate *intellect*; and so long as men yet cherished the memory of Voltaire, so long he felt his position was not secure, for tyranny stands as much in need of prejudice to sustain it as falsehood of uncertainty and darkness; the restored church could no longer suffer his glory to shine with so great a lustre; she had the right to hate Voltaire, not to deny his genius.

If we judge of men by what they have *done*, then Voltaire is incontestably the greatest writer of modern Europe. No one has caused, through the powerful influence of his genius alone, and the perseverance of his will, so great a commotior in the minds of men; his pen aroused a world, and has shaken a far mightier empire than that of Charlemagne, the European empire of a theocracy. His genius was not *force* but *light*. Heaven had destined him not to destroy but to illuminate, and wherever he trod light followed him, for reason (which is *light*) had destined him to be first her poet, then her apostle, and lastly her idol.

VI.

Voltaire was born a plebeian in an obscure street of old Paris.* Whilst Louis XIV. and Bossuet reigned in all the pomp of absolute power and Catholicism at Versailles, the child of the people, the Moses of incredulity, grew up amidst them: the secrets of destiny seem thus to sport with men, and are alone suspected when they have exploded. The throne and the altar had attained their culminating point in France. The Duc d'Orleans, as regent, governed during an interregnum,—one vice in the room of another, weakness instead of pride. This life was easy and agreeable, and corruption avenged itself for the monacal austerity of the last years of Madame de Mainténon and Letellier. Voltaire, alike precocious by audacity as by talent, began already to sport with those weapons of the mind of which he was destined, after years, to make so terrible a use. The regent, all unsuspicious of danger, suffered him to continue, and repressed, for form's sake alone, some of the most audacious of his outbreaks, at which he laughed even whilst he punished them. The incredulity of the age took its rise in debauchery and not in examination, and the independence of thought was rather a *libertinage* of manners, than a conclusion arising from reflection. There was vice

* It has been generally understood that Voltaire was born at Châtenay, *near* Paris, in February, 1694.—H. T. R.

in irreligion, and of this Voltaire always savored. His mission began by a contempt and derision of holy things, which, even though doomed to destruction, should be touched with respect. From thence arose that mockery, that irony, that cynicism too often on the lips, and in the heart, of the apostle of reason; his visit to England gave assurance and gravity to his incredulity, for in France he had only known libertines, in London he knew philosophers; he became passionately attached to eternal reason, as we are all eager after what is new, and he felt the enthusiasm of the discovery. In so active a nature as the French, this enthusiasm and this hatred could not remain in mere speculation as in the mind of a native of the north. Scarcely was he himself persuaded, than he wished in his turn to persuade others; his whole life became a multiplied action, tending to one end, the abolition of theocracy, and the establishment of religious toleration and liberty. He toiled at this with all the powers with which God had gifted him; he even employed falsehood (*ruse*), aspersion, cynicism, and immorality; he used even those arms that respect for God and man denies to the wise; he employed his virtue, his honor, his renown to aid in this overthrow; and his apostleship of reason had too often the appearance of a profanation of piety; he ravaged the temple instead of protecting it.

From the day when he resolved upon this war against Christianity, he sought for allies also opposed to it. His intimacy with the king of Prussia, Frederic II., had this sole inducement. He desired the support of thrones against the priesthood. Frederic, who partook of his philosophy, and pushed it still further, even to atheism and the contempt of mankind, was the Dionysius of this modern Plato. Louis XV., whose interest it was to keep up a good understanding with Prussia, dared not to show his anger against a man whom the king considered as his friend. Voltaire, thus protected by a sceptre, redoubled his audacity. He put thrones on one side, whilst he affected to make their interests mutual with his own, by pretending to emancipate them from the domination of Rome. He handed over to kings the civil liberty of the people, provided that they would aid him in acquiring the liberty of consciences. He even affected—perhaps he felt—respect for the absolute power of kings. He pushed that respect so far as even to worship their weaknesses. He palliated the infamous vices of the great Frederic, and brought philosophy on its knees before the mistresses of Louis XV. Like the courtezan of Thebes, who built one of the pyramids of Egypt from the fruits of her debaucheries, Voltaire did not blush at any prostitution of genius, provided that the wages of his servility enabled him to purchase enemies against Christ. He enrolled them by millions throughout Europe, and especially in France. Kings were reminded of the middle ages, and of the thrones outraged by the popes. They did not see, without umbrage and secret hate, the clergy as powerful as themselves with the people, and who under the name of cardinals, almoners, bishops or confessors, spied, or dictated its creeds even to courts themselves. The parliaments, that civil clergy, a body redoubtable to sovereigns themselves, detested the mass of the clergy, although they protected its faith and its decrees. The nobility, warlike, corrupted, and ignorant, leaned entirely to the unbelief which freed it from all morality. Finally, the *bourgeoisie*, well-informed or learned, prefaced the emancipation of the third estate by the insurrection of the new condition of ideas.

Such were the elements of the revolution in religious matters. Voltaire laid hold of them at the precise moment, with that *coup d'œil* of strong instinct which sees clearer than genius itself. To an age, young, fickle, and unreflecting, he did not present reason under the form of an austere philosophy, but beneath the guise of a facile freedom of ideas, and a scoffing irony. He would not have succeeded in making his age think, he did succeed in making it smile. He never attacked it in front, nor with his face uncovered, in order that he might not set the laws in array against him; and to avoid the fate of Servetius, he, the modern Æsop, attacked under imaginary names the tyranny which he wished to destroy. He concealed his hate in history, the drama, light poetry, romance, and even in jests. His genius was a perpetual allusion, comprehending all his age, but impossible to be seized on by his enemies. He struck, but his hand was concealed. Yet the struggle of a man against a priesthood, an individual against an institution, a life against eighteen centuries, was by no means destitue of courage.

VII.

There is an incalculable power of conviction and devotion of idea, in the daring of one against all. To brave at once, with no other power than individual reason, with no other support than conscience, human consideration, that cowardice of the mind, masked under respect for error; to dare the hatred of earth and the anathema of heaven, is the heroism of the writer. Voltaire was not a martyr in his body, but he consented to be one in his name, and devoted it during his life and after his death. He condemned his own ashes to be thrown to the winds, and not to have either an asylum or a tomb. He resigned himself even to lengthened exile in exchange for the liberty of a free combat. He isolated himself voluntarily from men, in order that their too close contact might not interfere with his thoughts.

At eighty years of age, feeble, and feeling his death nearly approaching, he several times made his preparations hastily in order to go and struggle still, and die at a distance from the roof of his old age. The unwearied activity of his mind was never checked for a moment. He carried his gayety even to genius, and under that pleasantry of his whole life we may perceive a grave power of perseverance and conviction. Such was the character of this great man. The enlightened serenity of his mind concealed the depth of its workings: under the joke and laugh his constancy of purpose was hardly sufficiently recognized. He suffered all with a laugh, and was willing to endure all, even in absence from his native land, in his lost friendships, in his refused fame, in his blighted name, in his memory accursed. He took all—bore all—for the sake of the triumph of the independence of human reason. Devotion does not change its worth in changing its cause, and this was his virtue in the eyes of posterity. He was not the truth, but he was its precursor, and walked in advance of it.

One thing was wanting to him—the love of a God. He saw him in mind, and he detested those phantoms which ages of darkness had taken for him, and adored in his stead. He rent away with rage those clouds which prevent the divine idea from beaming purely on mankind; but his weakness was rather hatred against error, than faith in the Divinity. The sentiment of religion, that sublime *résumé* of human thought; that reason, which, enlightened by enthusiasm, mounts to God as a flame, and unites itself with him in the unity of the creation with the Creator, of the ray with the focus—this, Voltaire never felt in his soul. Thence sprung the results of his philosophy; it created neither morals, nor worship, nor charity; it only decomposed—destroyed. Negative, cold, corrosive, sneering, it operated like poison—it froze—it killed—it never gave life. Thus, it never produced—even against the errors it assailed, which were but the human alloy of a divine idea—the whole effect it should have elicited. It made sceptics, instead of believers. The theocratic reaction was prompt and universal, as it ought to have been. Impiety clears the soul of its consecrated errors, but does not fill the heart of man. Impiety alone will never ruin a human worship; a faith destroyed must be replaced by a faith. It is not given to irreligion to destroy a religion on earth. There is but a religion more enlightened which can really triumph over a religion fallen into contempt, by replacing it. The earth cannot remain without an altar, and God alone is strong enough against God.

VIII.

It was on the 5th of August, 1791, the first anniversary of the famous night of the 4th of August, 1790, when feudality crumbled to atoms, that the National Assembly commenced the revision of the constitution. It was a solemn and imposing act, was this comprehensive *coup d'œil* cast by legislators at the end of their career, over the ruins they had scattered, and the foundations they had laid in their course. But how different at this moment was the disposition of their mind from what they felt in commencing this mighty work! They had begun it with an enthusiasm of the ideal, they now contemplated it with the misgivings and the sadness of reality. The National Assembly was opened amidst the acclamations of a people unanimous in their hopes, and was about to close amidst the clamorous recriminations of all parties.

The king was captive, the princes emigrants, the clergy at feud, the nobility in flight, the people seditious; Necker's popularity had vanished, Mirabeau was dead, Maury silenced, Cazalès, Lally, Mounier, had deserted from their work. Two years had carried off more men and things than a generation removes in ordinary times. The great voices of '89, inspired with philosophy and vast hopes, no longer resounded beneath those vaults. The foremost ranks had fallen. The men of second order were now to contend in their stead. Intimidated, discouraged, repentant, they had neither the spirit to yield to the impulse of the people nor the power to resist it. Barnave had recovered his virtue in his sensibility; but virtue which comes late is like the experience which follows the act, and only enables us to measure the extent of our errors. In revolutions there is no repentance—there is only expiation. Barnave, who might have saved the monarchy, had he only united with Mirabeau, was just commencing his expiatory sentence. Robespierre was to Barnave what Barnave had been to Mirabeau; but Robespierre, more powerful than Barnave, instead of acting on the impulse of a passion as fluctuating as jealousy, acted under the influence of a fixed idea, and an unalterable theory. Robespierre had the whole people at his back.

IX.

From the opening of the sittings Barnave attempted to consolidate around the constitution the opinions so fiercely shaken by Robespierre and his friends. He did it with a caution which bespoke but too well the weakness of his position, notwithstanding the boldness of his language. "The labors of your committee of the constitution are assailed," he said. "There exist against our work but two kinds of opposition. Those who, up to the present time, have constantly shown themselves inimical to the Revolution—the enemies of equality, who hate our constitution because it is the condemnation of their aristocracy. Yet there is another class hostile also, and I will divide it into two distinct species. One of these is the men who, in the opinion of their own conscience, give the preference to another government which they disguise more or less in their language, and seek to deprive our monarchical government of all the strength which can retard the advent of a republic. I declare that these persons I shall not attack. Whosoever has a pure political opinion has a right to communicate it; but we have another class of foes. They are the foes of all government. If this class betrays its opposition, it is not because it prefers the republic to the monarchy, democracy to aristocracy, it is because all that concentrates the political machine, all that is order, all that places in his right position the honest man and the rogue, the candid man and the calumniator, is contrary and hateful to its system." (Long and loud applause from the majority on the left.) "Yes, gentlemen," continued Barnave, "such is the party which has the most strongly opposed our labors. They have sought fresh sources of revolution because the revolution as defined by us escaped them. These are the men who, changing the name of things, by uttering sentiments apparently patriotic, in the stead of sentiments of honor, probity, purity—by sitting even in the most august places with a mask of virtue, have believed that they would impose upon public opinion, and have coalesced with certain writers. (The plaudits here redoubled, and all eyes were turned towards Robespierre and Brissot.) If we desire to see our constitution carried out, if you desire that the nation, after having owed to you its hopes of liberty,—for as yet it is but hope, (Murmurs of dissent,)—shall owe to you reality, prosperity, happiness, peace, let us endeavor to simplify it, by giving to the government—by which I mean all the powers established by this constitution—the amount of simultaneous strength requisite to move the social machine, and to preserve to the nation the liberty you have conferred upon it. If the welfare of your country is dear to you, take care what you are about to do. Above all, let us discard injurious mistrust, which can serve none but our enemies, when they would believe that this National Assembly, this constant majority, at once bold and sagacious, which has so much cast upon it since the king's departure, is ready to disappear before the divisions so skilfully fomented by perfidious imputations. (Loud cheering.) You will see renewed, do not doubt this, the disorders, the convulsions of which you are weary, and to which the completion of the Revolution ought also to be a completion. You will see renewed without hopes, projects, temptations which we openly brave because we feel our strength and are united—because we know that so long as we are united they will not be attempted; and if extravagant ideas should dare to try them, it would always result in their shame. But the attempts would succeed, and on the success of them they might with some semblance rely, if we were once divided amongst ourselves, not knowing in whom we might believe. We suspect each other of different plans when we have but the same idea—of contrary feelings, when every one of us has in his heart the testimony of his colleague's purity, during two years of labor performed together—during consecutive proofs of courage—during sacrifices which nothing can compensate but the approving voice of conscience."

Here Barnave's voice was lost in the applauses of the majority, and the Assembly, electrified, seemed for the moment unanimous in its monarchical feeling.

X.

At the sitting of the 25th of August, the Assembly discussed the article of the constitution which declared that the members of the royal family could not exercise the rights of citizens. The Duc d'Orleans ascended the tribune to protest against this article, and declared, in the midst of applauses and murmurs, that if it were adopted, there remained to him the right of choosing between the title of a French citizen and his eventual right to the throne; and that, in that case, he should renounce the throne. Sillery, the friend and confidant of this prince, spoke after him, and combated with much eloquence the conclusions of the committee. This discourse, full of allusions to the position of the Duc d'Orleans, impossible to be misunderstood, was the only act of direct ambition attempted by the Orleans party. Sillery begun by boldly replying to Barnave:—"Let me be allowed," he exclaimed, "to lament over the deplorable abuse which some orators make of their talents. What strange language! It is attempted to make you believe that you have here men of faction and anarchy—enemies of order, as if order could only exist by satisfying the ambition of certain individuals! It is proposed to you to grant to all individuals of the royal family the title of prince, and to deprive them of the rights of a citizen? What incoherence, and what ingratitude! You declare the title of French citizen to be the most admirable of titles, and you propose to exchange it for the title of prince, which you have suppressed, as contrary to equality! Have not the relatives of the king, who still remain in Paris, constantly displayed the purest patriotism? What services have they not rendered to the public cause by their example and their sacrifices! Have they not themselves abjured all their titles for one only—that of citizen? and yet you propose to despoil them of it! When you suppressed the title of prince, what happened? The fugitive princes formed a league against the country; the others ranged themselves with you. If to-day the title of prince is re-established, we concede to the enemies of our country all they covet; we deprive the patriotic relatives of the king of all they esteem! I see the triumph and the recompence on the side of the conspiring princes; I see the punishment of all sacrifices on the side of the popular princes. It is said to be dangerous to admit the members of the royal family into the legislative body. This hypothesis would then be established, that every individual of the royal family must be for the future a corrupt courtier or factious partisan! However, is it not possible to suppose that there are patriots amongst them? Is it those you would thus brand? You condemn the relatives of a king to hate the constitution and conspire against a form of government which does not leave them the choice between the character of courtiers or that of conspirators. See, on the other hand, what may accrue if the love of country inspire them! Cast your eyes on one of the branches of that race, whom it is proposed to you to exile. Scarcely out of his childhood, he had the happiness of saving the life of three citizens, at the peril of his own. The city of Vendôme decreed to him a civic crown. Unhappy child! is that indeed the last which thy race shall obtain?"

The applause which constantly interrupted, and for a long time followed this discourse, after the orator had concluded, proved that the idea of a revolutionary dynasty already tempted some imaginations, and that if there existed no faction of Orleans, at least it was not without a leader. Robespierre, who no less detested a dynastic faction than the monarchy itself, saw with terror this symptom of a new power which appeared in the distant horizon. "I remark," he replied, "that there is too much reference to individuals, and not enough to the national interest. It is not true that we seek to degrade the relations of the king: there is no design to place them beneath other citizens—we wish to separate them from the people by an honorable distinction. What is the use of seeking titles for them? The relatives of the king will be simply the relatives of the king. The splendor of the throne is not derived from such vain denominations of rank. We cannot declare with impunity that there exists in France any particular family above another: it would be a nobility by itself. The family would remain in the midst of us, like the indestructible root of that nobility which we have destroyed—it would be the germ of a new aristocracy." Violent murmurs hailed these remarks of Robespierre. He was obliged to break off and apologize. "I see," he said in conclusion, "that we are no longer allowed to utter here, without reproach, opinions which our adversaries amongst the first have maintained in this assembly."

XI.

The whole difficulty of the situation was in the question whether or not, that constitution once completed, the nation would recognize in the constitution the right to revise and alter itself. It was on this occasion that Malouet, although abandoned by his party, and hopeless, endeavored, single-handed, the restoration of the royal authority. His discourse, worthy of the genius of Mirabeau, was a bill of terrible accusation against the excesses of the people, and the inconsistencies of the Assembly. Its moderation heightened its effect—the man of integrity was seen beneath the orator, and the statesman in the legislator. Something of the serene and stoical soul of Cato breathed in his words; but political eloquence is rather in the people who listen, than in the man who speaks. The voice is nothing without the reverberation that multiplies its echo. Malouet, deserted by his party, left by Barnave who listened with dismay, only spoke from his conscience; he fought no longer for victory, he only struggled for principle. Thus did he speak:—

"It is proposed to you to determine the epoch, and the conditions of the use of a new constituent power; it is proposed to you to undergo twenty-five years of disorder and anarchy before you have the right to amend. Remark, in the first place, under what circumstances it is proposed to you to impose silence on the appeals of the nation as to the new laws; it is when you have not as yet heard the opinion of those whose instincts and passions these new laws favor, when all contending passions are subdued by terror or by force; it is when France is no longer expounded but through the organ of her clubs. When it has been a question of suspending the exercise of the royal authority itself, what has been the language addressed to you from this tribune? You have been told '*we should have begun the Revolution from thence; but we were not aware of our strength.*' Thus it only remains for your successors to measure their strength in order to attempt fresh enterprises. Such, in effect, is the danger of making a violent revolution and a free constitution march side by side. The one is only produced in tumultuous periods, and by passions and weapons; the other is only established by amicable arrangements between old interests and new. (Laughter, murmurs, and 'that is the point.') We do not count voices, we do not discuss opinions, to make a revolution. A revolution is a storm during which we must furl our sails, or we sink. But after the tempest, those who have been beaten by it, as well as those who have not suffered, enjoy in common the serenity of the sky. All becomes calm, and the horizon is cleared. Thus after a revolution, the constitution, if it be good, rallies all its citizens. There should not be one man in the kingdom who incurs danger of his life in expressing his free views of the constitution. Without this security there is no free will, no expression of opinion, no liberty; there will be only a predominant power, a tyranny popular or otherwise, until you have separated the constitution from the workings of the revolution. Behold all these principles of justice, morality, and liberty which you have laid down, hailed with joy, and oaths renewed, but violated immediately with unprecedented audacity and rage. It is at a moment when the holiest or the freest of constitutions has been proclaimed that the most infamous attempts against liberty, against property,—nay, what do I say?—against humanity and conscience, are multiplied and perpetuated! Does not this contrast alarm you? I will tell you wherefore. Yourselves deceived as to the mechanism of political society, you have sought its regeneration without reflecting on its dissolution; you have considered as an obstacle to your plans the discontent of some, and as a means the enthusiasm of others. Only desirous to overcome obstacles, you have overturned principles, and taught the people to brave everything. You have taken the passions of the people for auxiliaries. It is to raise an edifice by sapping the foundations. I repeat to you then, there is no free and durable constitution out of despotism but that which terminates a revolution, and which is proposed, accepted, and executed, by forms, calm, free, and totally different from the forms of the Revolution. All we do, all we seek for with excitement before we reach this point of repose, whether we obey the people or are obeyed by them; whether we would flatter, deceive, or serve them, is but the work of folly,—madness. I demand, therefore, that the constitution be peaceably and freely accepted by the majority of the nation and by the king. (Violent murmurs.) I know we call the national will, all that we know of proposed addresses, of assent, of oaths, agitations, menaces, and violence. (Loud expressions of angry dissent.) Yes, we must close the Revolution, by beginning to destroy every tendency to violate it. Your committees of inquiry, laws respecting emigrants, persecutions of priests, despotic imprisonments, criminal proceedings against persons accused without proofs, the fanaticism and domination of clubs; but this is not all, license has gone to such unbounded extent,—the dregs of the nation ferment so tumultuously :—(Loud bursts of indignation.) Do we then pretend to be the first nation which has no dregs? The fearful insubordination of troops, religious disturbances, the discontents of the colonies, which already sound so ominously in our ports,—if the Revolution does not stop here and give place to the constitution; if order be not re-established at once, and on all points, the shattered state will be long agitated by the convulsions of anarchy. Do you remember the history of the Greeks, where a first revolution not terminated produced so many others during a period of only half a century? Do you remember that Europe has her eyes fixed on your weakness and agitations, and whilst she will respect you if you are free within the limits of order, she will surely profit by your disorders, if you only know how to weaken yourself and alarm her by your anarchy?"

Malouet demanded, therefore, that the constitution should be submitted to the judgment of the people, and to the free acceptance of the king.

XII.

This magnificent harangue only sounded as the voice of remorse in the bosom of the Assembly. It was listened to with impatience, and then forgotten with all speed. M. de La Fayette opposed, in a short speech, the proposition of M. Dandré, who desired to adjourn for thirty years the revision of the constitution. The Assembly neither adopted the advice of Dandré nor of La Fayette, but contented itself with inviting the nation not to make use for twenty-five years of its right to modify the constitution. "Behold us, then," said Robespierre, "arrived at the end of our long and painful career: it only remains for us to give it stability and duration. Why are we asked to submit to the acceptance of the king? The fate of the constitution is independent of the will of Louis XVI. I do not doubt he will accept it with delight. An empire for patrimony, all the attributes of the executive power, forty millions for his personal pleasures,—such is our offer! Do not let us wait, before we offer it, until he be away from the capital and environed by ill advisers. Let us offer it to him in Paris

Let us say to him, Behold the most powerful throne in the universe—will you accept it? Suspected gatherings, the system of weakening your frontiers, threats of your enemies without, manœuvres of your enemies within,—all warns you to hasten the establishment of an order of things which assures and fortifies the citizens. If we deliberate, when we should swear, if our constitution may be again attacked, after having been already twice assailed, what remains for us to do? Either to resume our arms or our fetters. We have been empowered," he added, looking towards the seats of Barnave and the Lameths, "to constitute the nation, and not to raise the fortunes of certain individuals, in order to favor the coalition of court intriguers, and to assure to them the price of their complaisance or their treason."

XIII.

The constitutional act was presented to the king on the 3d of September, 1791. Thouret reported to the National Assembly in these words the result of the solemn interview between the conquered will of the monarch and the victorious will of his people:—"At nine o'clock in the evening our deputation quitted this chamber, proceeding to the chateau escorted by a guard of honor, consisting of various detachments of the national guard and *gendarmerie*. It was invariably accompanied by the applauses of the people. It was received in the council-chamber, where the king was attended by his ministers and a great number of his servants. I said to the king, 'Sire, the representatives of the nation come to present to your majesty the constitutional act, which consecrates the indefeasible rights of the French people—which gives to the throne its true dignity, and regenerates the government of the empire.' The king received the constitutional act, and thus replied: 'I receive the constitution presented to me by the National Assembly. I will convey to it my resolution after the shortest possible delay which the examination of so important an act must require. I have resolved on remaining in Paris. I will give orders to the commandant of the national Parisian guard for the duties of my guard.' The king, during the whole time, presented an aspect of satisfaction; and from all we saw and heard we anticipate that the completion of the constitution will be also the termination of the Revolution." The Assembly and the tribunes applauded several times. It was one of those days of public hope, when faction retreats into the shade, to allow the serenity of good citizens to shine forth.

La Fayette removed the degrading *consignes*, which made the Tuileries a jail to the royal family. The king ceased to be the hostage of the nation, in order to become its ostensible head. He gave some days to the apparent examination which he was supposed to bestow upon the Constitution. On the 13th he addressed to the Assembly, by the minister of justice, a message concerted with Barnave, thus conceived:—"I have examined the constitutional act. I accept it, and will have it carried into execution. I ought to make known the motives of my resolution. From the commencement of my reign I have desired the reform of abuses, and in all my acts I have taken for rule public opinion. I have conceived the project of assuring the happiness of the people on permanent bases, and of subjecting my own authority to settled rules. From these intentions I have never varied. I have favored the establishment of trials of your work before it was even finished. I have done so in all sincerity; and, if the disorders which have attended almost every epoch of the Revolution have frequently affected my heart, I hoped that the law would resume its force, and that on reaching the term of your labors, every day would restore to it that respect without which the people can have no liberty, and a king no happiness. I have long entertained that hope; and my resolution has only changed at the moment when I could hope no longer. Remember the moment when I quitted Paris: disorder was at its height—the licence of the press and the insolence of parties knew no bounds. Then, I avow, if you had offered to me the constitution, I should not have thought it my duty to accept it.

"All has changed. You have manifested the desire to re-establish order; you have revised many of the articles; the will of the people is no longer doubtful to me, and therefore I accept the constitution under better auspices. I freely renounce the co-operation I had claimed in this work, and I declare that when I have renounced it no other but myself has any right to claim it. Unquestionably I still see certain points in the constitution in which more perfection might be attained; but I agree to allow experience to be the judge. When I shall have fairly and loyally put in action the powers of government confided to me no reproach can be addressed to me, and the nation will make itself known by the means which the constitution has reserved to it. (Applause.) Let those who are restrained by the fear of persecutions and troubles out of their country return to it in safety. In order to extinguish hatreds let us content to a mutual forgetfulness of the past. (The tribunes and the left renewed their acclamations.) Let the accusations and the prosecutions which have sprung solely from the events of the constitution, be obliterated in a general reconciliation. I do not refer to those which have been caused by an attachment to me. Can you see any guilt in them? As to those who from excess, in which I can see personal insult, have drawn on themselves the visitation of the laws, I prove with respect to them that I am the king of all the French. I will swear to the constitution in the very place where it was drawn up, and I will present myself to-morrow at noon to the National Assembly."

The Assembly adopted unanimously, on the proposition of La Fayette, the general amnesty demanded by the king. A numerous deputation went to carry to him this resolution. The queen was present. "My wife and children, who are here," said the king to the deputation, "share my sentiments." The queen, who desired to reconcile herself to public opinion, advanced, and said, "Here are my children; we all agree to participate in the sentiments of the king." These words reported to the Assembly, prepared all hearts for the pardon which royalty was about to implore. Next day the king went to the Assembly; he wore no decoration but the cross of Saint Louis, from deference to a recent decree suppressing the other orders of chivalry. He took his place beside the president, the Assembly all standing.

"I come," said the king, "to consecrate solemnly here the acceptance I have given to the constitutional act. I swear to be faithful to the nation and the law, and to employ all the power delegated to me for maintaining the constitution, and carrying its decrees into effect. May this great and memorable epoch be that of the re-establishment of peace, and become the gage of the happiness of the people, and the prosperity of the empire." The unanimous applauses of the chamber, and the tribunes ardent for liberty, but kindly disposed towards the king, demonstrated that the nation entered with enthusiasm into this conquest of the constitution.

"Old abuses," replied the president, "which had for a long time triumphed over the good intentions of the best of kings, oppressed France. The National Assembly has re-established the basis of public prosperity. What it has desired the nation has willed. Your majesty no longer desires in vain the happiness of Frenchmen. The National Assembly has nothing more to wish, now that on this day in its presence you consummate the constitution by accepting it. The attachment of Frenchmen decrees to you the crown, and what assures it to you is the need that so great a nation must always have of an hereditary power. How sublime, sire, will be in the annals of history this regeneration, which gives citizens to France, to Frenchmen a country, to the king a fresh title of greatness and glory, and a new source of happiness !"

The king then withdrew, being accompanied to the Tuileries by the entire Assembly; the procession with difficulty making its way through the immense throng of people which rent the air with acclamations of joy. Military music and repeated salvos of artillery taught France that the nation and the king, the throne and liberty, were reconciled in the constitution, and that after three years of struggles, agitations, and shocks, the day of concord had dawned. These acclamations of the people in Paris spread throughout the empire. France had some days of delirium. The hopes which softened men's hearts, brought back their old feelings for its king. The prince and his family were incessantly called to the windows of their palace to receive the applause of the crowds. They sought to make them feel how sweet is the love of a people.

The proclamation of the constitution on the 18th had the character of a religious fête. The Champ-de-Mars was covered with battalions of the national guard. Bailly, mayor of Paris, the municipal authorities, the department, public functionaries, and all the people betook themselves thither. One hundred and one cannon shots hailed the reading of the constitutional act, made to the nation from the top of the altar of the country. One cry of *Vive la Nation!* uttered by 300,000 voices, was the acceptation by the people. The citizens embraced, as members of one family. Balloons, bearing patriotic inscriptions, rose in the evening in the Champs Elysées, as if to bear to the skies the testimony of the joy of a regenerated people. Those who went up in them threw out copies of the book of the constitution. The night was splendid with illuminations. Garlands of flames, running from tree to tree, formed, from the Arc de l'Etoile to the Tuileries, a sparkling avenue, crowded with the population of Paris. At intervals, orchestras filled with musicians sounded forth the pealing notes of glory and public joy. M. de La Fayette rode on horseback at the head of his staff. His presence seemed to place the oaths of the people and the king under the guard of the armed citizens. The king, the queen, and their children appeared in their carriage at eleven o'clock in the evening. The immense crowd that surrounded them as if in one popular embrace, —the cries of *Vive le Roi! Vive la Reine! Vive le Dauphin!*—hats flung in the air, the gestures of enthusiasm and respect, made for them a triumph on the very spot over which they had passed two months previously in the midst of the outrages of the multitude, and deep murmuring of the excited populace. The nation seemed desirous of redeeming these threatening days, and to prove to the king how easy it was to appease the people, and how sweet to it was the reign of liberty! The national acceptance of the laws of the Constituent Assembly was the counterproof of its work. It had not the legality, but it had really the value, of an individual acceptance by primary assemblies. It proved that the will of the public mind was satisfied. The nation voted by acclamation, what the wisdom of its Assembly had voted on reflection. Nothing but security was wanting to the public feeling. It seemed as if it desired to intoxicate itself by the delirium of its happiness; and that it compensated, by the very excess of its manifestations of joy, for what it lacked in solidity and duration.

The king sincerely participated in this general joyous feeling. Placed between the recollections of all he had suffered for three years, and the lowering storms he foresaw in the future, he endeavored to delude himself, and to feel persuaded of his good fortune. He said to himself, that perhaps he had mistaken the popular opinion; and that having at least surrendered himself unconditionally to the mercy of his people—that people would respect in him his own power and his own will: he swore in his honest and good heart fidelity to the constitution and love to the nation he really loved.

The queen herself returned to the palace with more national thoughts: she said to the king, "They are no longer the same people;" and, taking her son in her arms, she presented him to the crowd who thronged the terrace of the chateau, and seemed thus to invest herself in the eyes of the people with the innocence of age and the interest of maternity.

The king gave, some days afterwards, a fête to the people of Paris, and distributed abundant alms to the indigent. He desired that even the miserable should have his day of content, at the commencement of that erà of joy, which his reconciliation with his people promised to his reign. The *Te Deum* was sung in the cathedral of Paris, as on a day of victory, to bless the cradle of the French constitution. On the 30th of September, the king closed the Constituent Assembly. Before he entered the chamber, Bailly, in the name of the municipality; Pastoret, in the name of the departments, congratulated the Assembly on the conclusion of its work:—"Legislators," said Bailly, "you have been armed with the greatest power that men can require. To-morrow you will be nothing. It is not, therefore interest or flattery which praises you—it is your works. We announce to you the benedictions of posterity, which commence for you from to-day!" "Liberty," said Pastoret, "had fled beyond the seas, or taken refuge in the mountains,—you have raised her fallen throne. Despotism had effaced every page of the book of nature; you have re-established the decalogue of freemen!"

XIV.

The king, surrounded by his ministers, entered the Assembly at three o'clock: lengthened cries of *Vive le roi* for a moment checked his speaking. "Gentlemen," said Louis XVI., "after the completion of the constitution, you have resolved on to-day terminating your labors. It would have been desirable, perhaps, that your session should have been prolonged, in order that you, yourselves, should prove your work. But you have wished, no doubt, to mark by this the difference which should exist between the functions of a constituent body and ordinary legislators. I will exercise all the power you have confided to me in assuring to the constitution the respect and obedience due to it. For you, gentlemen, who, during a long and painful career, have evinced an indefatigable zeal in your labors, there remains a last duty to fulfil when you are scattered over the face of the empire; it is to enlighten your fellow-citizens as to the spirit of the laws you have made; to purify and unite opinions by the example you will give to the love of order and submission to the laws. Be, on your return to your homes, the interpreters of my sentiments to your fellow-citizens; tell them that the king will always be their first and most faithful friend—that he desires to be loved by them, and can only be happy with them and by them."

The president replied to the king:—"The National Assembly having arrived at the termination of its career, enjoys, at this moment the first fruit of its labors. Convinced that the government best suited to France is that which reconciles the respected prerogatives of the throne with the inalienable rights of the people, it has given to the state a constitution which equally guarantees royalty and liberty. Our successors, charged with the onerous burden of the safety of the empire, will not misunderstand their rights, nor the limits of the constitution: and you, sire, you have almost completed everything—by accepting the Constitution, you have consummated the Revolution."

The king departed amidst loud acclamations. It appeared that the National Assembly was in haste to lay down the responsibility of events which it no longer felt itself capable of controlling. "The National Assembly declares," says Target, its president, "that its mission is finished, and that, at this moment, it terminates its sittings."

The people, who crowded round the Manège, and saw with pain the Revolution abdicated into the hands of the king, insulted, as it recognized them, the members of the Right—even Barnave. They experienced even on the first day the ingratitude they had so often fomented. They separated in sorrow and in discouragement.

When Robespierre and Pétion went out, the people crowned them with oaken chaplets, and took the horses off their carriage in order to drag them home in triumph. The power of these two men already proved the weakness of the constitution, and presaged its fall. An amnestied king returned powerless to his palace. Timid legislators abdicated in trouble. Two triumphant tribunes were elevated by the people. In this was all the future. The Constituent Assembly, begun in an insurrection of principles, ended as a sedition. Was it the error of those principles—was it the fault of the Constituent Assembly? We will examine the question at the end of the last book of this volume, in casting a retrospect over the acts of the Constituent Assembly; till then we will delay this judgment, in order not to interfere with the progress of the recital.

BOOK V.

I.

WHILST an instant's breathing time was permitted to France between two convulsive efforts, and the Revolution as yet knew not whether it should maintain the constitution it had gained, or employ it as a weapon to obtain a republic, Europe began to rouse itself; egotistical and improvident, she merely beheld in the first movement in France a comedy played at Paris on the stage of the States General and the Constituent Assembly—between popular genius, represented by Mirabeau, and the vanquished genius of the aristocracy, personified in Lous XVI. and the clergy. This grand spectacle had been in the eyes of the sovereigns and their ministers merely the continuation of the struggle (in which they had taken so much interest, and showed so much secret favor) between Voltaire and Jean Jacques Rousseau on one side, and the old aristocratical and religious system on the other. To them the Revolution was the philosophy of the eighteenth century, which had migrated from the *salons* into the public streets, and from books to speeches. This earthquake in the moral world, and these shocks at Paris, the presages of some unknown change in European destinies, attracted far more than they affrighted them. They had not as yet learned that institutions are but ideas, and that those ideas, when overthrown, involve in their fall thrones and nations. Whatsoever the spirit of God wills, that also do all mankind will, and are to accomplish, unperceived even by themselves. Europe bestowed attention, time, and astonishment on the commencement of the French Revolution, and that was all it needed to bring it to maturity. The spark not having been extinguished at its outbreak, was fated to kindle and consume everything before it. The moral and political state of Europe was eminently favorable to the contagion of new ideas. Time, men, and things, all lay at the mercy of France.

II.

A long period of peace had softened the minds, and deadened those hereditary hatreds that oppose the communication of feelings and the similarity of ideas between different nations. Europe, since the treaty of Westphalia, had become a republic of perfectly balanced powers, where the general equilibrium of power resulting from each formed a counterpoise to the other. One glance sufficed to show the solidity and unity of this European *building*, every beam of which, opposing an equal resistance to the others, afforded an equal support by the pressure of all the states.

Germany was a confederation presided over by Austria, the emperors were the chiefs only of this ancient feudalism of kings, dukes, and electors. The house of Austria was more powerful through itself and its vast possessions than through the imperial dignity. The two crowns of Hungary and Bohemia, the Tyrol, Italy, and the Low Countries, gave it an ascendency, which the genius of Richelieu had been able to fetter, but not to destroy. Powerful to resist, but not to impel, Austria was more fitted to *sustain* than to *act*; her force lies in her situation and immobility, for she is like a block in the middle of Germany,—her power is in her *weight*; she is the pivot of the balance of European power. But the federative diet weakened and enervated its designs by those secret influences all federations naturally possess. Two new states, unperceived until the time of Louis XIV., had recently risen, out of reach of the power, and the long rivalry of the houses of Bourbon and Austria: the one in the north of Germany, Prussia; the other in the east, Russia. The policy of England had encouraged the rise of these two infant powers, in order to form the elements of political combinations that would admit of her interests obtaining a firm footing.

III.

A hundred years had hardly elapsed since an emperor of Austria had conferred the title of king on a margrave of Prussia, a subordinate sovereign of two millions of men, and yet Prussia already balanced in Germany the influence of the house of Austria. The Machiavelian genius of Frederic the Great had become the genius of Prussia. His monarchy, composed of territories acquired by victory, required war to strengthen itself, still more of agitation and intrigue to legitimize itself. Prussia was in a ferment of dissolution amidst the German states. Scarcely had it risen into existence, than it abdicated all German feeling by leaguing with England and Russia; and England, always on the watch to widen these breaches, had used Prussia as her lever in Germany. Russia, whose twofold ambition already had designs on Asia on the one hand, on Europe on the other, had made it an advanced guard on the west, and used it as an advanced camp on the borders of the Rhine. Thus Prussia was the point of the Russian sword in the very heart of France. Military power was everything; its government was only discipline, its people only an army. As for its ideas, its policy was to place itself at the head of the Protestant states, and offer protection, assistance, and revenge to all those whose interest or whose ambition was threatened by the house of Austria. Thus by its nature Prussia was a revolutionary power.

Russia, to whom nature had assigned a sterile yet immense place on the globe, the ninth part of the habitable world, and a population of forty millions of men, all compelled by the savage genius of Peter the Great to unite themselves into one nation, seemed yet to waver between two roads, one of which led to Germany, the other to the Ottoman empire. Catherine II. governed it: a woman endowed with wondrous beauty, passion, genius, and crime—such are necessary in the ruler of a barbarous nation, in order to add the *prestige* of adoration to the terror inspired by the sceptre. Each step she took in Asia awakened an echo of surprise and admiration in Europe, and for her was revived the name of Semiramis. Austria, Prussia, and France, intimidated by her fame, applauded her victories over the Turks, and her conquests in the Black Sea, without apparently comprehending that she weighed down the European power, and that once mistress of Poland and Constantinople, nothing then would prevent her from carrying out her designs on Germany, and extending her arm over all the West.

IV.

England, humiliated in her maritime pride by the brilliant rivalry of the French fleet in the Indian Seas, irritated by the assistance given by France to aid America in her struggle for independence, had secretly allied herself in 1788 with Prussia and Holland, to counterbalance the effect of the alliance of France with Austria, and to intimidate Russia in her invasion of Turkey. England at this moment relied on the genius of one man, Mr. Pitt, the greatest statesman of the age, son of Lord Chatham, the only political orator of modern ages who equalled (if he did not surpass) Demosthenes. Mr. Pitt, in a manner born in the council of kings, and brought up at the tribune of his country, at the age of twenty-three was launched in political life. At this age, when other men have scarcely emerged from childhood, he was already the most eminent of all that aristocracy that confided their cause to him as the most worthy to uphold it, and when almost a boy he acquired the government of his country from the admiration excited by his talents, and held it almost without interruption up to his death by his enlightened views of policy, and the energy of his resolution. He showed the House of Commons what a great statesman, supported by the opinion of the nation, can dare to attempt and accomplish, with the consent (and sometimes against it) of a parliament. He was the despot of the constitution, if we may link together those two words that can alone express his lawful omnipotence. The struggle against the French Revolution was the continual act of his twenty-five years of ministerial life; he became the antagonist of France, and died vanquished.

And yet it was not the Revolution that he hated, it was France, and in France it was not liberty he hated, for at heart he loved freedom; it was the destruction of this balance of Europe that, once destroyed, left England isolated in its ocean. At this moment, England, hostile towards America, at war with India, a coolness existing between itself and Spain, secretly hating Russia, had on the Continent nothing but Prussia and the Stadtholder; and observation and temporization became a necessary part of its policy.

V.

Spain, enervated by the reign of Philip III. and Ferdinand VI., had recovered some degree of internal vitality and external dignity during the long reign of Charles III.; Campomanes, Florida Blanca, the Comte d'Aranda, his ministers, had struggled against superstition, that second nature of the Spaniards. A *coup de'état,* meditated in silence, and executed like a conspiracy by the court, had driven out of the kingdom the Jesuits, who reigned under the name of the kings. The family agreement between Louis XV. and Charles III., in 1761, had guaranteed the thrones, and all the possessions of the different branches of the house of

Bourbon. But this political compact had been unable to guarantee this many-branched dynasty against the decay of its root, and that degeneracy that gives effeminate and weak princes as successors to mighty kings. The Bourbons became satraps at Naples, and in Spain crowned monks, and the very palace of the Escurial had assumed the appearance and the gloom of a monastery.

The *monachal* system devoured Spain, and yet this unfortunate country adored the evil that destroyed it. After having been subject to the caliphs, Spain became the conquest of the popes; and their authority reigned paramount there under every costume; whilst theocracy made its last efforts there. Never had the sacerdotal system more completely swayed a nation, and never had a nation been reduced to a more abject state of degradation. The Inquisition was its government,—the *auto-da-fés* its triumphs,—bull-fights and processions its only diversions. Had the inquisitorial reign lasted a few years more, this people would have been no longer reckoned amongst the civilized inhabitants of Europe.

Charles III. had trembled at each new effort he made to emancipate his government; his good intentions had all been frustrated and checked, and he had been forced to sacrifice his ministers to the vengeance of superstition. Florida Blanca and d'Aranda died in exile, to which they had been condemned for the crime of having served their country. The weak Charles IV. had mounted the throne and reigned for several years, guided by a faithless wife, a confessor, and a favorite. The loves of Godoy and the queen formed the whole of the Spanish policy, and to the fortune of the favorite all the rest of the empire was sacrificed. What mattered it that the fleet rotted in the unfinished ports of Charles III.—that Spanish America asserted its independence,—that Italy bent beneath the yoke of Austria—that the house of Bourbon combated in vain in France the progress of a new system—that the Inquisition and the monks cast a gloom over and devoured the whole of the peninsula,—all this was nothing to the court, provided the queen were but loved and Godoy great. The palace of Aranjuez was like the walled tomb of Spain, into which the active spirit that now agitated Europe could no longer penetrate.

VI.

The state of Italy was yet worse; for it was severed into pieces that, unlike the snake, were unable to re-unite. Naples was under the severe sway of Spain, and the yoke of Austria pressed on Milan and Lombardy. Rome was nought but the capital of an idea—her people had disappeared, and she had now become the modern Ephesus, at which each cabinet sought an oracle favorable to its own cause, and paid for this purpose the members of the sacred college. Although the centre of all diplomatic intrigue, and the spot where all worldly ambition humbled itself but to increase its power, —although this court could shake Europe to its foundations, it was yet unable to govern it. The elective aristocracy, cardinals chosen by powers at variance with each other; the elective monarchy, a pope whose qualifications were old age and feebleness, and who was only crowned on condition of a speedy decease: such was the *temporal* government of the Roman states. This government combined in itself all the weakness of anarchy, and all the vices of despotism. It had produced its inevitable result, the servitude of the state, the poverty of the government and the misery of the population; Rome was no longer anything but the great Catholic municipality, and her government nought save a republic of diplomatists. Rome possessed a temple enriched with the offerings of the Christian world, a sovereign and ambassadors, but neither population, treasure, nor army. It was the venerated shadow of that universal monarchy to which the popes had pretended in the golden age of Catholicism, and of which they had preserved only the capital and the court.

VII.

Venice drew near its fall, but the silence and mystery of its government concealed even from the Venetians the decrepitude of the state. The government was an aristocratic sovereignty, founded on the corruption of the people and treachery, for the master sinew of the government was *espionage;* its *prestige,* mystery; its power, the torture. It lived on terror and voluptuousness; its police was a system of secret confession, of each against the other. Its cells, termed the *Piombi,* or *Leads,* and which were entered at night by the *Bridge of Sighs,* were a hell that closed on the captive never to re-open. The wealth of the East flowed in on Venice from the fall of the Lower Empire. She became the refuge of Greek civilization, and the Constantinople of the Adriatic; and the arts had emigrated thither from Byzance, with commerce. Its marvellous palaces, washed by the waves, were crowded together on a narrow spot of ground, so that the city was like a vessel at anchor, on board which a people driven from the land have taken refuge with all their treasures. She was thus impregnable, but could not exercise the least influence over Italy.

VIII.

Genoa, a more popular and more turbulent republic, subsisted only by her fleet and her commerce. Hemmed in between barren mountains and a gulf without a shore, it was only a port peopled by sailors. The marble palaces, built one above the other on the rocky banks, looked down on the sea, their sole territory. The portraits of the doges and the statue of Andreà Doria constantly reminded the Genoese that from the waves had proceeded their riches and their renown, and that *there* alone they could hope to look for them. Its ramparts were impregnable, its arsenals full; and thus Genoa formed the stronghold of armed commerce.

The immense country of Tuscany, governed and rendered illustrious by the *Médici,* those Pericles of Italy, was learned, agricultural, industrious, but unwarlike. The house of Austria ruled it by its archdukes, and these princes of the north, transported to the palaces of the Pitti or the Cômo, contracted the mild and elegant manners of the Tuscans; and the climate and serenity of the hills of Florence softened there even tyranny, and these princes became voluptuaries or sages. Florence, the city of Leo X., of philosophy, and the arts, had transformed even religion. Catholicism, so ascetic in Spain, so gloomy in the north, so austere and literal in France, so popular at Rome, had become at Florence, under the *Médici* and the Grecian philosophers, a species of luminous and Platonic theory, whose dogmata were only sacred symbols, and whose pomps were only pleasures that overpowered the mind and the senses. The churches at Florence were more museums of Christ than his sanctuaries; the colonies of all the arts and trades of Greece had emigrated, on the entry of Mahomet II. into Constantinople, to Florence, and there they had prospered; and a new Athens, enriched like the ancient with temples, porticoes, and statues, beautified the banks of the Arno.

Leopold, the philosopher prince, awaited there, busied in learning the art of governing men and putting in practice new theories of political economy, the moment to mount the imperial throne of Austria, where his destiny was not to leave him long. He was the Germanicus of Germany, and philosophy could alone display him to the world, after having lent him for a few years to Italy.

Piedmont, whose frontiers reached to the heart of France by the Alpine valleys, and on the other side the walls of Genoa and the Austrian possessions on the Po, was governed by the house of Savoy, one of the most ancient of the royal lines in Europe. This military monarchy had its intrenched camp, rather than its capital in Turin. The plains it occupied in Italy had been, and were destined to be, the field of battle for Austria and France; and her positions were the keys of Italy.

This population, accustomed to war, was necessarily constantly under arms to defend itself, or to unite with that one of the two powers whose rivalry could alone assure its independence. Thus, military disposition was its strength; its weakness lay in having half its possessions in Italy, half in France. The whole of Savoy is French in language, descent, and manners; and at any great commotion Savoy must detach itself from Italy, and fall on this side of its own accord. The Alps are too essential a frontier to two people to belong to only one; for if their south side looks to Italy, their north looks to France. The snow, the sun, and the torrents have thus willed this division of the Alps between two nations. Policy does not long prevail against nature, and the house of Savoy was not sufficiently powerful to preserve the neutrality of the valleys of the Alps and the roads of Italy; and though it increase in power in Italy, yet it must be worsted in a struggle against France. The court of Turin was doubly allied to the house of France by the marriage of the Comte d'Artois, and the Comte de Provence, brothers of Louis XVI., with two princesses of the house of Savoy. The clergy had more influence at this court than at any other in Italy; and hated instinctively all revolutions, because they threatened its political influence. From religious feeling—from family feeling—from political feeling, Savoy was destined to become the first scene of conspiracy against the French Revolution.

IX.

There was yet another in the north, and that was Sweden but there it was neither a superstitious attachment to Catholicism, nor family feeling, nor even national interest, that excited the hostility of a king against the Revolution; it was a more noble sentiment—the disinterested glory of combating for the cause of kings; and, above all, for a queen whose beauty and whose misfortunes had won the heart of Gustavus III., in which blazed the last spark of that chivalrous feeling that vowed to avenge the cause of ladies, to assist the oppressed, and succor the right. Extinguished in the south, it burnt, for the last time, in the north, and in the breast of a king. Gustavus III. had in his policy something of the adventurous genius of Charles XII., for the Sweden of the race of Wasa is the land of heroes. Heroism, when disproportioned to genius and its resources, resembles folly: there was a mixture of heroism and folly in the projects of Gustavus against France; and yet this folly was noble, as its cause—and great, as his own courage. Fortune had accustomed Gustavus to desperate and bold enterprises; and success had taught him to believe nothing impossible. Twice he had made a revolution in his kingdom, twice he had striven single-handed against the gigantic power of Russia, and had he been seconded by Prussia, Austria, and Turkey, Russia would have found a rampart against her in the north. The first time, abandoned by his troops, in his tent by his revolted generals, he had escaped, and alone, made an appeal to his brave Dalecarlians. His eloquence, and his magnanimous bearing had caused a new army to spring from the earth. He had punished traitors, rallied cowards, concluded the war, and returned triumphant to Stockholm, borne on the shoulders of his people, wrought up to a pitch of enthusiasm. The second time, seeing his country torn by the anarchical predominance of the nobility, he had resolved, in the depths of his own palace, on the overthrow of the constitution. United in feeling with the *bourgeoisie* and the people, he had led on his troops, sword in hand; imprisoned the senate in its chamber; dethroned the nobility, and acquired for royalty the prerogatives it required in order to defend and govern the country. In three days, and before one drop of blood had been shed, Sweden under his sword had become a monarchy. Gustavus's confidence in his own boldness was confirmed. The monarchical feeling in him was strengthened by all the hatred which he bore to the privileges of the orders he had overturned. The cause of the king was identified with his own.

He had embraced with enthusiasm that of Louis XVI. Peace, which he had concluded with Russia, allowed him to direct his attention and his forces towards France. His military genius dreamed of a triumphant expedition to the banks of the Seine. It was there that he desired to acquire glory. He had visited Paris in his youth; under the name of the Count de Haga he had partaken of the hospitalities of Versailles. Marie Antoinette, then in the brilliancy of her youth and beauty, now appeared humiliated, and a captive in the hands of a pitiless people. To deliver this woman, restore the throne, to make himself at once feared and blessed by this capital, seemed to him one of those adventures formerly sought by crowned chevaliers. His finances alone opposed the execution of this bold design. He negotiated a loan with the Court of Spain, attached to him the French emigrants renowned for their military talents, requested plans from the Marquis de Bouillé, and solicited the courts of St. Petersburg and Berlin to unite with him in this crusade of kings. He asked of England nothing but neutrality. Russia encouraged him; Austria temporized; Spain trembled; England looked on. Each new shock of the Revolution at Paris found Europe undecided and always behindhand in counsels and resolutions. Monarchical Europe, hesitating and divided, did not know what it had to fear, nor what it ought to do.

Such was the political situation of cabinets with respect to France. But as to ideas, the feelings of the people were different.

The movement of intelligence and philosophy at Paris was responded to by the agitation of the rest of Europe, and especially in America. Spain, under M. d'Aranda, was become alive to the general feeling; the Jesuits had disappeared; the Inquisition had extinguished its fires; the Spanish nobility blushed for the sacred theocracy of its monks. Voltaire had correspondents at Cadiz and at Madrid. The forbidden produce of our ideas was favored even by those whose charge was to exclude it. Our books crossed the snows of the Pyrenees. Fanaticism, tracked by the light to its last den, felt Spain escaping from it. The excess of a tyranny long undergone, prepared ardent minds for the excess of liberty.

In Italy, and even at Rome, the sombre Catholicism of the middle age was lighted up by the reflections of time. It played even with the dangerous arms which philosophy was about to turn against it. It seemed to consider itself as a weakened institution, which ought to have its long duration pardoned in consequence of its complaisance towards princes and the age. Benedict XIV. (Lambertini) received from Voltaire the dedication of "Mahomet." The Cardinals *Passionei* and *Quirini*, in their correspondence with Ferney,*—Rome, in its bulls, preached tolerance for dissenters, and obedience to princes. The pope disavowed and reformed the company of Jesus: he soothed the spirit of the age. Clement XIV. (Ganganelli) shortly after secularized the Jesuits, confiscated their possessions, and imprisoned their superior, Ricci, in the castle of Saint Angelo, the Bastille of papacy. Severe only towards exaggerated zealots, he enchanted the Christian world by the evangelical sweetness, the grace of his understanding, and the poignancy of his wit; but pleasantry is the first step to the profanation of dogmata. The crowd of strangers and English whom his affability attracted to Italy and retained at Rome, caused, with the circulation of gold and science, the inflowing of scepticism and indifference, which destroy creeds before they sap institutions.

Naples, under a corrupt court, left fanaticism to the populace. Florence, under a philosophical prince, was an experimental colony of modern doctrines. The poet Alfieri, that Tyrtæus of Italian liberty, produced there his revolutionary dramas, and there sowed his maxims against the twofold tyranny of popes and kings in every theatre in Italy

Milan, beneath the Austrian flag, had within its walls a republic of poets and philosophers. Beccaria wrote there more daringly than Montesquieu. His work on "Crimes and Punishments" was a bill of accusation of all the laws of his native country. *Parini, Monte, Cesarotti, Pindemonte, Ugo Foscolo*, gay, serious, and heroic poets, then satirized the absurdities of their tyrants, the baseness of their fellow-countrymen, or sang, in patriotic odes, the virtues of their ancestors, and the approaching deliverance of their country.

Turin alone, attached to the house of Saxony, was silent, and proscribed Alfieri.

In England, the mind a long time free, had produced

* Voltaire's residence in Switzerland, where he lived nearly twenty years.—H. T. R.

sound morals. The aristocracy felt itself sufficiently strong never to become persecuting. Worship was there as independent as conscience. The dominant religion was a political institution, which, whilst it bound the citizen, left the believer to his free will. The government itself was popular, only the people consisted of none but its leading citizens. The House of Commons more resembled a senate of nobles than a democratic forum; but this parliament was an open and resounding chamber, where they discussed openly in face of the throne, as in the face of all Europe, the most comprehensive measures of the government. Royalty, honored in form, whilst in fact it is excluded and powerless, merely presides over these debates, and adds order to victory; it was, in reality, nothing more than a perpetual consulate of this Britannic senate. The voices of the leading orators, who contested the rule of the nation, echoed thence, through and out of Europe. Liberty finds its level in the social world, like the waves in the common bed of the ocean. One nation is not free with impunity—one people is not in bondage with impunity—all finally compares and equalizes itself.

X.

England had been intellectually the model of nations, and the envy of the reflecting universe. Nature and its institutions had conferred upon it men worthy of its laws. Lord Chatham, sometimes leading the opposition, sometimes at the head of the government, had expanded the space of parliament to the proportions of his own character and his own language. Never did the manly liberty of a citizen before a throne—never did the legal authority of a prime minister before a people, display themselves in such a voice to assembled citizens. He was a public man in all the greatness of the phrase—the soul of a nation personified in an individual—the inspiration of the nation in the heart of a patrician. His oratory had something as grand as action—it was the heroic in language. The echo of Lord Chatham's discourses were heard—felt on the Continent. The stormy scenes of the Westminster elections* shook to the very depths the feelings of the people, and that love of turbulence which slumbers in every multitude, and which it so often mistakes for the symptoms of true liberty. These words of counter-

* Qu. Middlesex in 1769?—H. T. R.

poise to royal power, to ministerial responsibility, to laws in operation, to the power of the people, explained at the present by a constitution—explained in the past by the accusation of Strafford, the tomb of Sidney, on the scaffold of a king, had resounded like old recollections and strange novelties.

The English drama had the whole world for audience. The great actors for the moment were Pitt, the controller of these storms, the intrepid organ of the throne, of order, and the laws of his country; Fox, the precursory tribune of the French Revolution, who propagated the doctrines by connecting them with the revolutions of England, in order to sanctify them in the eyes of the English; Burke, the philosophical orator, every one of whose orations was a treatise, then the Cicero of the opposition party, and who was so speedily to turn against the excesses of the French Revolution, and curse the new faith in the first victim immolated by the people; and lastly, Sheridan, an eloquent debauchee, liked by the populace for his levity and his vices, seducing his country instead of elevating it. The warmth of the debates on the American war, and the Indian war, gave a more powerful interest to the storms of the English parliament.

The independence of America, effected by a newly-born people, the republican maxims on which this new continent founded its government, the reputation attached to the fresh names, which distance increased more than their victories,—Washington, Franklin, La Fayette, the heroes of public imagination; those dreams of ancient simplicity, of primitive manners, of liberty at once heroic and pastoral, which the fashion and illusion of the moment had transported from the other side of the Atlantic,—all contributed to fascinate the spirit of the Continent, and nourish in the mind of the people contempt for their own institutions, and fanaticism for a social renovation.

Holland was the workshop of innovators; it was there that, sheltered by a complete toleration of religious dogmata, by an almost republican liberty, and by an authorized system of contraband, all that could not be uttered in Paris, in Italy, in Spain, in Germany, was printed. Since Descartes, independent philosophy had selected Holland for its asylum: Boyle had there rendered scepticism popular: it was the land sacred to insurrection against all the abuses of power, and had subsequently become the seat of conspiracy against kings. Every one who had a suspicious idea to promulgate, an attack to make, a name to conceal, went to borrow the presses of Holland. Voltaire, Jean Jacques Rousseau, Diderot, Helvetius, Mirabeau himself, had gone there to naturalize their writings in this land of publicity. The mask of concealment which these writers assumed in Amsterdam deceived no one, but it effected their security. All the crimes of thought were there inviolable; it was at the same time the asylum and the arsenal of new ideas. An active and vast trade in books made a speculation of the overthrow of religion and thrones. The prodigious demand for prohibited works which were thus circulated in the world, proved sufficiently the increasing alteration of ancient beliefs in the mind of the people.

XI.

In Germany, the country of phlegm and patience, minds apparently so slow shared with serious and concentrated ardor in the general movement of mind in Europe. Free thought there assumed the form of an universal conspiracy. It was enveloped in mystery. Learned and formal Germany liked to give even to its insurrection the appearances of science and tradition. The Egyptian initiations, mystic ceremonies of the middle age, were imitated by the adepts of new ideas. Men thought as they conspired. Philosophy moved veiled in symbols; and that veil was torn away only in secret societies, from which the profane were excluded. The *prestiges* of the imagination, so powerful in the ideal and dreamy nature of Germany, served as a bait to the newly arisen truths.

The great Frederic had made his court the centre of religious incredulity. Sheltered by his power altogether military, contempt for Christianity and of monarchical institutions was freely propagated. Moral force was nothing to this materialist prince. Bayonets were in his eyes the right of princes; insurrection the right of the people; victories or defeats the public right. His constant run of good fortune was the accomplice of his immorality. He had received the recompence of every one of his vices, because his vices were great. Dying, he had bequeathed his perverse genius to Berlin. It was the corrupting city of Germany. Military men educated in the school of Frederic, academies modelled after the genius of Voltaire, colonies of Jews enriched by war, and the French refugees, peopled Berlin and formed the public mind. This mind, full of levity, sceptic, impertinent and sneering, intimidated the rest of Germany. The weakened spirit of that land may be dated from the period of Frederic II. He was the corrupter of the empire—he conquered Germany in the French spirit—he was a hero of a falling destiny.

Berlin continued it after his death; great men always bequeath the impulse of their spirit to their country. The reign of Frederic had at least one happy result: religious tolerance arose in Germany from the very contempt in which Frederic had held religious creeds. Under the wing of this toleration the spirit of philosophy had organized occult associations, after the image of freemasonry. The German princes were initiated. It was thought an act of superior mind to penetrate into those shadows, which, in reality, included nothing beyond some general principles of humanity and virtue, with no direct application to civil institutions. Frederic in his youth had been initiated himself, at Brunswick, by Major Bielfeld; the emperor Joseph II., the most bold innovator of his time, had also desired to undergo these proofs at Vienna, under the tutelage of the baron de Born, the chief of the freemasons in Austria. These societies, which had no religious tendency in England, because there liberty conspired openly in parliament and in the press, had a wholly different sense on the Continent. They were the secret council-chambers of independent thought: the thought, escaping from books, passed into action. Between the initiated and established institutions, the war was concealed, but the more deadly.

The hidden agents of these societies had evidently for aim the creation of a government of the opinion of the human race, in opposition to the governments of prejudice. They desired to reform religious, political, and civil society, beginning by the most refined classes. These lodges were the catacombs of a new worship. The sect of *illuminés* founded and guided by Weishaupt, was spreading in Germany in conjunction with the *freemasons* and the *rosicrucians*. The *theosophists* in their turn produced the symbols of supernatural perfection, and enrolled all susceptible minds and ardent imaginations around dogmata full of love and infinity. The theosophists, the Swedenborgians, disciples of the sublime but obscure Swedenborg, the Saint Martin of Germany, pretended to complete the Gospel, and to transform humanity by overcoming death and the senses. All these dogmata were mingled in an equal contempt for existing institutions in one same aspiration for the renewal of the mind and things. All were democratic in their last conclusion, for all were inspired by a love of mankind without distinction of classes.

Affiliations were multiplied *ad infinitum.* Prejudice, as it always occurs when zeal is ardent, was added fraudulently to truth, as if error or falsehood were the inevitable alloy of truth, and even the virtues of the human mind; they called up past ages, summoned spectres, and the dead were heard to speak. They played upon the plastic imagination of princes, by rapid transition from terror to enthusiasm. The knowledge of the phantasmagoria, then but little known, served as an auxiliary in these deceptions. On the death of Frederic II., his successor submitted to such tests, and was worked upon by wonders. Kings conspired against thrones. The princes of Gotha gave Weishaupt an asylum. Augustus of Saxony, prince Ferdinand of Brunswick, the prince of Neuvied, even the coadjutor of the ecclesiastical principalities on the banks of the Rhine, those of Mayence, Worms, and Constance, signalized themselves by their ardor for the mystic doctrines of freemasonry or the illuminati. Cagliostro was astounding Strasburgh—Cardinal de Rohan ruined himself, and bent before his voice. Like at the fall of great empires—like at the cradle of great things—these signs appeared everywhere. The most infallible was the general convulsion of human ideas. When a creed is crumbling to atoms, all mankind trembles.

The lofty geniuses of Germany and Italy were already singing the new era to their offspring; Göethe the sceptic poet, Schiller the republican poet, Klopstock the sacred poet, intoxicated with their strophes the universities and theatres; each shock of the events of Paris had its *contre coup* and sonorous echo, multiplied by these writers on the borders of the Rhine. Poetry is the remembrance and anticipation of things: what it celebrates is not yet dead, and what it sings already hath existence. Poetry sang everywhere the unformed but impassioned hopes of the people. It is a sure augury—it is full of enthusiasm, for its voice is heard on all sides; science, poetry, history, philosophy, the stage, mysticism, the arts, the genius of Europe under every form, had passed over to the Revolution: not one name of a man of reputation in all Europe could be cited who remained attached to the party of the past. The past was overcome, because the mind of the human race had withdrawn from it

—when the spirit hath flown life is extinct. None but mediocrities remain under the shelter of old forms and institutions. There was a general mirage in the horizon of the future; and, whether the small saw therein their safety, or the great an abyss, all went headlong towards the novelty.

XII.

Such was the tendency of minds in Europe, when the princes, brothers of Louis XVI., and the emigrant gentlemen, spread themselves over Savoy, Switzerland, Italy, and Germany, to demand succor and vengeance from powers and principalities against the Revolution. Never, from the first great emigrations of ancient people, fleeing from the Roman invasions, had been seen such a movement of terror and perturbation as this, which cast forth from the territory all the clergy and all the aristocracy of a nation. An immense vacuum was created in France: first, in the steps of the throne itself; next, in the court, in châteaux, in ecclesiastical dignities; and finally, in the ranks of the army. Officers, all noble, emigrated in masses; the navy followed somewhat later, the example of the army, which also abandoned the flag. It was not that the clergy, the nobility, the land and sea officers were more pressed upon by the stir of revolutionary ideas which had agitated the nation in 1789; on the contrary, the movement commenced by them. Philosophy had in the first place enlightened the apex of the nation. The thought of the age was especially in the higher classes; but those classes who sought a reform by no means desired a disorganization. When they had seen the moral agitation of ideas transform itself into an insurrection of the people, they had trembled. The reins of government violently snatched from the king by Mirabeau and La Fayette, at the Tennis court; the attempts of the 5th and 6th of October; privileges suppressed without compensation, titles abolished, the aristocracy handed over to execration, to pillage, to fire, and even to murder, in the provinces; religion deposed, and compelled to nationalize itself by a constitutional oath; and finally the king's flight, his imprisonment in his palace, the threats of death vomited forth by the patriotic press, or the tribunes of popular clubs, against all aristocracy, the triumphant riots in the provinces, the defection of the French guard in Paris, the revolt of the Swiss of Châteauvieux at Nancy the excesses of the soldiery, mutinous and unpunished, a

Caen, Brest, and everywhere, had changed into horror and hatred the favorable feeling of the noblesse for the progress of opinion. It saw that the first act of the people was to degrade superior authority. The *esprit de caste* impelled the nobility to emigrate, the *esprit de corps* similarly influenced the officers, and the *esprit de cour* made it shameful to remain on a soil stained with so many outrages to royalty. The women, who then formed public opinion in France, and whose tender and easily excited imagination is soon transferred to the side of their victims, all sided with the throne and the aristocracy. They despised those who would not go and seek their avengers in foreign lands. Young men departed at their desire; those who did not, dared not show themselves. They sent them distaffs, as a token of their cowardice!

But it was not shame alone that led the officers and the nobles to join the ranks of the army, it was also the appearance of a duty; for the last virtue that was left to the French nobility was a religious fidelity to the throne; their honor, their second and almost only religion, was to die for their king, and any design against the throne, in their belief, was a design against heaven. Chivalry, that code of aristocratic feeling, had preserved and disseminated this noble prejudice throughout Europe; and, to the nobility, the king represented their country. This feeling, eclipsed for a while by the debaucheries of the regency, the scandalous vices of Louis XV., and the bold maxims of Rousseau's philosophy, was awakened in the heart of the gentlemen at the spectacle of the degradation and danger of the king and queen. In their eyes, the Assembly was nothing but a band of revolutionary subjects, who detained their sovereign a prisoner. The most voluntary acts of the king were suspected by them, and beneath his constitutional speeches, they imagined they discovered another and a contrary meaning; and the very ministers of Louis XVI. were believed to be nothing but his jailers. A secret understanding existed between these gentlemen and the king, and counsels were held in secluded apartments of the Tuileries, at which the king alternately encouraged and forbade his friends to emigrate. And his orders, varied at each day, and each fresh occurrence, were sometimes constitutional and patriotic when he hoped to re-establish and moderate the constitution at home; at other times, despairing and blamable when it seemed to him that the security of the queen and his children could only proceed from another country. Whilst he addressed official letters through his minister for foreign affairs to his brothers, and the Prince de Condé, to recall them, and point out to them their duty as citizens, the Baron de Breteuil, his confidential agent to the Foreign Powers, transmitted to the king of Prussia letters that revealed the secret thoughts of the king. The following letter to the king of Prussia, found in the archives of the chancellorship of Berlin, dated December 3rd, 1790, leaves no doubt of this double diplomacy of the unfortunate monarch. Louis XVI. wrote:—

"Monsieur mon Frère,

"I have learnt from M. de Moustier how great an interest your majesty has displayed, not only for my person but for the welfare of my kingdom, and your majesty's determination to prove this interest, whenever it can be for the good of my people, has deeply touched me; and I confidently claim the fulfilment of it, at this moment, when, in spite of my having accepted the new constitution, the factious portion of my subjects openly manifest their intention of destroying the remainder of the monarchy. I have addressed the emperor, the empress of Russia, and the kings of Spain and Sweden, and I have suggested to them the idea of a congress of the principal powers of Europe, *supported by an armed force,* as the best measure to check the progress of faction here, to afford the means of establishing a better order of things, and preventing the evil that devours this country from seizing on the other states of Europe. I trust that your majesty will approve my ideas, *and maintain the strictest secrecy respecting the step I have taken in this matter,* as you will feel that the critical position in which I am placed at present compels me to use the greatest circumspection. It is for this reason that the Baron de Breteuil is alone acquainted with my secret, and through him your majesty can transmit me whatever you may think fit."

XIII.

This letter, added to that addressed by Louis XVI. to M. de Bouillé, informing him that his brother-in-law the emperor Leopold was about to march a body of troops on Longwi, in order to afford a pretext for the concentration of the French troops on that frontier, and thus favor his flight from Paris, are irrefragable proofs of the counter-revolutionary understanding existing between the king and the foreign powers, no less than between the king and the leaders of the emigrés. The memoirs of the emigrés are full of proofs of this fact; and nature even attests them, for the cause of the king, the aristocracy, and the religious institutions was identical. The emperor Leopold was the brother of the queen of France; the dangers of the king were the dangers of all the other princes; for the example of the triumph of one people was contagious to all nations. The emigrés were the friends of the monarchy, and the defenders of kings; had they not exchanged a word more on the subject, they would have been united by the same feelings, the same interests. But in addition to this, they had preconcerted communication with each other, and the suspicions of the people were no empty chimeras, but the presentiment of the plots of their enemies.

The conspiracy of the court with all the courts and aristocracies abroad, with all the aristocracies of the emigrés, with their relations, of the king with his brothers, had no need of being carried on in writing. Louis XVI. himself, the most really revolutionary of all the monarchs who have occupied the throne, had no thought of treachery to the people or to the revolution, when he implored the armed succor of the other powers. This idea of an appeal to foreign forces, or even the emigrated forces, was not his real desire; for he dreaded the intervention of the enemies of France, he disapproved of emigration, and he was not without a feeling of offence at his brothers intriguing abroad, sometimes in his name, but often against his wishes. He shrank from the idea of passing in the eyes of Europe for a prince in leading-strings, whose ambitious brothers seized upon his rights in adopting his cause, and stipulated for his interests without his intervention. At Coblentz a regency was openly spoken of, and bestowed on the Comte de Provence, the brother of Louis XVI.; and this regency, that had devolved on a prince of the blood by emigration, whilst the king maintained a struggle at Paris, greatly humiliated Louis XVI. and the queen. This usurpation of their rights, although clothed in the dress of devotion and tenderness, was even more bitter to them than the outrages of the Assembly and the people. We always dread most that which is nearest to us, and the triumph of the emigration only promised them a throne disputed by the regent who had restored it. This gratitude appeared to them a disgrace, and they knew not whether they had most to hope or to apprehend from the emigrés.

The queen, in her conversations with her friends, spoke of them with more bitterness than confidence. The king loudly complained of the disobedience of his brothers, and dissuaded from flight all those who demanded his advice; but his advice was as changeable as events; like all men balancing between hope and fear, he alternately bent and stood erect beneath the pressure of circumstances. His acts were culpable, but not his intentions; it was not the king who conspired, but the man, the husband, the father, who sought by foreign aid to insure the safety of his wife and children; and he alone became criminal when all seemed desperate. The "tangled thread" of negotiation was incessantly broken off and renewed: that which was resolved yesterday was to-morrow disavowed; and the secret negotiators of these plots, armed with credentials and powers which had been recalled, yet continued to employ them, in spite of the king's orders, to carry on in his name those plans of which he disapproved. The Prince de Condé, the Comte de Provence, and the Comte d'Artois had each his separate line of policy and court, and abused the king's name in order to increase his own credit and interest. Hence arises the difficulty, to those who write the history of that period, of tracing the hand of the king in all these conspiracies, carried on in his name, and to pronounce either his entire innocence or his palpable treachery He did not betray his country, or sell his subjects; but he did not observe his oaths to the constitution or his country An upright man, but a persecuted king, he believed that oaths, extorted by violence and eluded through fear, were no perjuries; and he broke each day some of those to which he had bound himself, under the belief, doubtless, that the excesses of the people freed him from his oath. Educated with all the prejudices of personal sovereignty, he sought with sincerity amidst this chaos of parties, who disputed with each other the empire, to find the nation; and failing to discover the object of his search, he fancied he had the right to find it in his own person. His crime, if there be any in his actions, was less the crime of his heart than the crime of his birth, his situation, and his misfortunes.

XIV.

The Baron de Breteuil, an old minister and ambassador

a man incapable of making the least concession, and ever counselling strong and forcible measures, had quitted France at the commencement of the year 1790, the king's secret plenipotentiary to all the other powers. He alone was, to all intents, and for all purposes, the sole minister of Louis XVI. He was, moreover, absolute minister; for once invested with the confidence and unlimited power of the king, who could not revoke, without betraying the existence of his occult diplomacy, he was in a position to make any use of it and to interpret at will the intentions of Louis XVI. to his own views. The Baron de Breteuil did abuse it; not, as it is said, from personal ambition, but from excess of zeal for the welfare and dignity of his master. His negotiations with Catherine, Gustavus, Frederic, and Leopold were a constant incitement to a crusade against the Revolution of France.

The Count de Provence (afterwards Louis XVIII.), and the Count d'Artois (afterwards Charles X.), after several visits to the different courts of the South and North, had met at Coblentz, where Louis Venceslas, elector of Treves, their maternal uncle, received them with a more kind than politic welcome. Coblentz became the *Paris* of Germany, the focus of the counter-revolutionary conspiracy, the head-quarters of all the French nobles assembled round their natural leaders, the two brothers of the captive king. Whilst they held there their wandering court, and formed the first links of the coalition of Pilnitz, the Prince de Condé, who, from inclination and descent, was of a more military disposition, formed the army of the Princes, consisting of eight or ten thousand officers, and no soldiers, and thus it was the head of the army severed from the trunk. Names renowned in history's annals, fervent devotion, youthful ardor, heroic bravery, fidelity, the conviction of success,—nothing was wanting to this army at Coblentz save an understanding with their country and time. Had the French *noblesse* but employed one half of the virtues and efforts they made to subdue the Revolution, in regulating it, the Revolution, although it changed the laws, would not have changed the monarchy. But it is useless to expect that institutions can comprehend the means that transform them. The king, the nobility, and the priests could not understand a revolution that threatened to destroy the noblesse, the clergy, and the throne. A contest became unavoidable; they had not space for the struggle in France, and they took their stand on a foreign soil.

XV.

Whilst the army of the princes thus increased in strength at Coblentz, the counter-revolutionary diplomacy was on the eve of the first great result it had been enabled to obtain in the actual state of Europe. The conferences of Pilnitz had opened, and the Count de Provence had sent the Baron Roll from Coblentz to the king of Prussia, to demand in the name of Louis XVI. the assistance of his troops to aid in the re-establishment of order in France. The king of Prussia, before deciding, wished to learn the state of France from a man whose military talents and devoted attachment to the monarchy had gained him the confidence of the foreign courts,—the Marquis de Bouillé. He fixed the Château de Pilnitz as the meeting place, and requested him to bring a plan of operation for the foreign armies on the different French frontiers; and on the 24th of August Frederic William, accompanied by his son, his principal generals, and his ministers, arrived at the Château de Pilnitz, the summer residence of the court of Saxony, where he had been preceded by the emperor.

The Archduke Francis, afterwards the emperor Francis II., the Maréchal de Lascy, the Baron de Spielman, and a numerous train of courtiers, attended the emperor. The two sovereigns, the rivals of Germany, seemed for a time to have laid aside their rivalry to occupy themselves solely with the safety of the thrones of Europe; this fraternity of the great family of monarchs prevailed over every other feeling, and they treated each other more like brothers than sovereigns, whilst the elector of Saxony, their entertainer, enlivened the conference by a succession of splendid fêtes.

In the midst of a banquet the unexpected arrival of the Count d'Artois at Dresden was announced, and the king of Prussia requested permission from the emperor for the French prince to appear. The emperor consented, but previous to admitting him to their official conferences the two monarchs had a secret interview, at which two of their most confidential agents only were present. The emperor inclined to peace, the inertness of the Germanic body weighed down his resolve, for he felt the difficulty of communicating to this vassal federation of the empire the unity and energy necessary to attack France in the full enthusiasm of her Revolution. The generals, and even the Maréchal de Lascy himself, hesitated before frontiers reputed to be impregnable, whilst the emperor was apprehensive for the Low Countries and Italy. The French maxims had passed the Rhine, and might explode in the German states at the moment when the princes and people were called upon to take arms against France, and the diet of the people might prove more powerful than the diet of the kings. Dilatory measures would have the same intimidating effect on the revolutionary genius, without presenting the same dangers to Germany; and would it not be more prudent to form a general league of all the European powers to surround France with a circle of bayonets, and summon the triumphant party to restore liberty to the king, dignity to the throne, and security to the Continent? "Should the French nation refuse," added the emperor, "*then* we will threaten her in a manifesto, with a general invasion, and should it become necessary, we will crush her beneath the irresistible weight of the united forces of all Europe." Such were the counsels of that temporizing genius of empires that awaits necessity without ever forestalling, and would fain be assured of everything without the least risk.

XVI.

The king of Prussia, more impatient and more threatening, confessed to the emperor that he had no faith in the effect of these threats. "Prudence," said he, "is a feeble defence against audacity, and the defensive is but a timid position to assume in the face of the Revolution. We must attack it in its infancy; for to give time to the French principles, is to give them strength. To treat with the popular insurrection, is to prove to them that we fear, and are disposed to form a compact with them. We must surprise France in the very act of anarchy, and publish a manifesto to Europe when the armies have crossed the frontiers and success has given authority to our declaration."

The emperor appeared moved; he, however, insisted on the dangers to which a sudden invasion would inevitably expose Louis XVI., he showed the letters of this prince, and intimated that the Marquis de Noailles and M. de Montmorin —the one French ambassador at Vienna, the other minister for Foreign Affairs at Paris, who were both devoted to the king—held out hopes to the court of Vienna of the speedy re-establishment of order and monarchical modifications of the constitution in France; and he demanded the right of suspending his decision until the month of September, although in the meanwhile military preparations should be made by both powers. The scene was changed the next morning by the Count d'Artois. This young prince had received from the hand of nature all the exterior qualifications of a chevalier: he spoke to the sovereigns in the name of the thrones; to the emperor in the name of an outraged and dethroned sister. The whole emigration, with its misfortunes, its nobility, its valor, its illusions, seemed personified in him. The Marquis de Bouillé and M. de Calonne, the genius of war and the genius of intrigue, had followed him to these conferences. He obtained several audiences of the two sovereigns, he inveighed with respect and energy against the temporizing system of the emperor, and violently roused the Germanic sluggishness. The emperor and the king of Prussia authorized the Baron de Spielman for Austria, the Baron de Bischofswerden for Prussia, and M. de Calonne for France, to meet the same evening, and draw up a declaration for the signature of the monarchs.

The Baron de Spielman, under the immediate dictation of the emperor, drew up the document. M. de Calonne in vain combated, in the name of the Count d'Artois, the hesitation that disconcerted the impatience of the emigrés. The next day, on their return from a visit to Dresden, the two sovereigns, the Count d'Artois, M. de Calonne, the Maréchal de Lascy, and the two negotiators, met in the emperor's apartment, where the declaration was read and discussed, every sentence weighed, and some expressions modified; and at the proposal of M. de Calonne, and the entreaties of the Count d'Artois, the emperor and the king of Prussia consented to the insertion of the last phrase, that threatened the Revolution with war.

Subjoined is the document that was the date of a war of twenty-two years' duration.

"The emperor and the king of Prussia, having listened to the wishes and representations of *Monsieur* and *Monsieur le Compte d'Artois*, declare conjointly that they look upon the present position of the king of France as an object of common interest to all the sovereigns of Europe. They trust that this interest cannot fail to be acknowledged by all the powers whose assistance is claimed; and that, in consequence, they will not refuse to employ, conjointly with the emperor and the king of Prussia, the most efficacious means, proportioned to their forces, for enabling the king of France to strengthen with the most perfect liberty the bases of a monarchical government, equally conformable to the rights of sovereigns and the welfare of the French nation. Then, and in that case, their aforesaid majesties are resolved to act promptly and in concert with the forces requisite to attain the end proposed and agreed on. In the meantime they will issue all needful orders to their troops to hold themselves in a state of readiness."

This declaration, at once timid and threatening, was evidently too much for peace, too little for war; for such words encourage the Revolution, without crushing it. They at once showed the impatience of the emigrés, the resolution of the king of Prussia, the hesitation of the powers, the temporizing policy of the emperor. It was a concession to force and weakness, to peace and war; the whole state of Europe was there unveiled, for it was the declaration of the uncertainty and anarchy of its councils.

XVII.

After this imprudent and useless act, the two sovereigns separated. Leopold to go and be crowned at Prague, and the king of Prussia returning to Berlin, began to put his army on a war footing. The emigrants, triumphing in the engagement they had entered into, increased in numbers. The courts of Europe, with the exception of England, sent in equivocal adhesions to the courts of Berlin and Vienna. The noise of the declaration of Pilnitz burst forth, and died away in Paris in the midst of the fêtes in honor of the acceptance of the constitution.

However, Leopold, after the conferences at Pilnitz, was more earnest than ever in his attempts to find excuses for peace. The Prince de Kaunitz, his minister, feared all violent shocks, which might derange the old diplomatic mechanism, whose workings he so well knew. Louis XVI. sent the Count de Fersen secretly to him, in order to disclose his real motives in accepting the constitution, and to entreat him not to provoke, by any preparation of arms, the bad feelings of the Revolution, which seemed to be quieted by its triumph.

The emigrant princes, on the contrary, filled all courts with the words uttered in favor of their cause in the declaration of Pilnitz. They wrote a letter to Louis XVI., in which they protested against the oath of the king to the constitution, forced, as they declared, from his weakness and his captivity. The king of Prussia, on receiving the circular of the French cabinet, in which the acceptance of the constitution was notified, exclaimed, "I see the peace of Europe assured!" The courts of Vienna and Berlin feigned to believe that all was concluded in France by the mutual concessions of the king and the Assembly. They made up their minds to see the throne of Louis XVI. abased, provided that the Revolution would consent to allow itself to be controlled by the throne.

Russia, Sweden, Spain, and Sardinia were not so easily appeased. Catherine II. and Gustavus III., the one from a proud feeling of her power, and the other from a generous devotion to the cause of kings, arranged together, to send 40,000 Russians and Swedes to the aid of the monarchy. This army, paid by a subsidy of 15,000,000f. of Spain, and commanded by Gustavus in person, was to land upon the coast of France, and march upon Paris, whilst the forces of the empire crossed the Rhine.

These bold plans of the two northern courts were displeasing to Leopold and the king of Prussia. They reproached Catherine with not keeping her promises, and making peace with the Turks. Could the emperor march his troops on the Rhine whilst the battles of the Russians and Ottomans continued on the Danube and threatened the remoter provinces of his empire? Catherine and Gustavus nevertheless did not abate in their open protection to the emigration party. These two sovereigns accredited ministers plenipotentiary to the French princes at Coblentz. This was declaring the forfeiture of Louis XVI., and even the forfeiture of France. It was recognizing that the government of the kingdom was no longer at Paris, but at Coblentz. Moreover, they contracted a treaty of alliance, offensive and defensive, between Sweden and Russia, in the common interest of the re-establishment of the monarchy.

Louis XVI. then earnestly desiring the disarming, sent to Coblentz the Baron Vioménil and the Chevalier de Coigny, to command his brothers and the Prince de Condé to disarm and disperse the emigrants. They received his orders as coming from a captive, and disobeyed without even sending him a reply. Prussia and the empire showed more deference to the king's intentions. These two courts disbanded the army collected by the princes, and ordered to be punished in their states all insults offered to the tricolor cockade; but at the very moment when the emperor thus gave evidence of his desire to maintain peace, war was about to involve him in spite of himself. What human wisdom sometimes refuses to the greatest causes, it sees itself compelled to accord to the smallest. Such was Leopold's situation. He had refused war to the great interests of the monarchy, and the strong feelings of the family which asked it from him, and yet was about to grant it to the insignificant interests of certain princes of the empire, whose possessions were in Alsace and Lorraine, and whose personal rights were violated by the new French constitution. He had refused succor to his sister, and was about to accord it to his vassals. The influence of the diet, and his duties as head of the empire, led him on to steps to which his personal feelings would never have urged him. By his letter of 3d December, 1791, he announced to the cabinet of the Tuileries the formal resolution on his part "of giving aid to the princes holding lands in France, if he did not obtain their perfect restoration to all the rights which belonged to them by treaty."

XVIII.

This threatening letter, secretly communicated in Paris, (before it was officially sent,) by the French ambassador in Vienna, was received by the king with much alarm, and with joy by certain of his ministers, and the political party of the Assembly. War cuts through everything. They hailed it as a solution to the difficulties which they felt were crushing them. When there is no longer any hope in the regular order of events, there is in what is unknown. War appeared to these adventurous spirits a necessary diversion to the universal ferment; a career to the Revolution; a means for the king again to seize on power by acquiring the support of the army. They hoped to change the fanaticism of liberty into the fanaticism of glory, and to deceive the spirit of the age by intoxicating it with conquests instead of satisfying it with institutions.

The Girondist deputies were of this party. Brissot was their inspiration. Flattered by the title of statesmen, which they already assumed from vanity, and which was used towards them with irony, they were desirous to justify their pretensions by a bold stroke, which would change the scene, and disconcert, at the same time, the king, the people, and Europe. They had studied Machiavel, and considered the disdain of the just as a proof of genius. They little heeded the blood of the people, provided that it cemented their ambition.

The Jacobin party, with the exception of Robespierre, clamored loudly for war: his fanaticism deceived him as to his weakness. War was to these men an armed apostleship, which was about to propagate their social philosophy over the universe. The first cannon shot fired in the name of the rights of man would shake thrones to their centre. Then there was finally a third party which hoped for war, that of the constitutional *modérés*, which flattered itself that it would restore sound energy to the executive power, by the necessity of concentrating the military authority in the hands of the king at the moment when the nationality should be menaced. All extremity of war places the dictatorship in the hands of the party which makes it; and they hoped, on behalf of the king, and of themselves, for this dictatorship of necessity.

XIX.

A young, but already influential, female had lent to this latter party the *prestige* of her youth, her genius and her enthusiasm—it was Madame de Stäel. Necker's daughter, she had inspired politics from her birth. Her mother's *salon* had been the *cœnaculum* of the philosophy of the 18th century. Voltaire, Rousseau, Buffon, D'Alembert, Diderot, Raynal, Bernardin de Saint Pierre, Condorcet had played with this child, and fostered her earliest ideas. Her cradle was that of the Revolution. Her father's popularity had played about her lips, and left there an inextinguishable thirst for fame. She sought it in the storms of the populace, in calumny, and death. Her genius was great, her soul pure, her heart deeply impassioned. A man in her energy, a woman in her tenderness, that the ideal of her ambition should be satisfied, it was necessary for her to associate in the same character genius, glory, and love.

Nature, education, and fortune rendered possible this triple dream of a woman, a philosopher, and a hero. Born in a republic, educated in a court, daughter of a minister, wife of an ambassador, belonging by birth to the people, to the literary world by talent, to the aristocracy by rank, the three elements of the Revolution mingled or contended in her. Her genius was like the antique chorus, in which all the great voices of the drama unite in one tumultuous concord. A deep thinker by inspiration, a tribune by eloquence, a woman in attraction, her beauty, unseen by the million, required intellect to be admired, and admiration to be felt. Hers was not the beauty of form and features, but visible inspiration and the manifestation of passionate impulse. Attitude, gesture, tone of voice, look—all obeyed her mind, and created her brilliancy. Her black eyes, flashing with fire, gave out from beneath their long lids as much tenderness as pride. Her look, so often lost in space, was followed by those who knew her, as if it were possible to find with her the inspiration she sought. That gaze, open, yet profound as her understanding, had as much serenity as penetration. We felt that the light of her genius was only the reverberation of a mine of tenderness of heart. Thus there was a secret love in all the admiration she excited; and she, in admiration, cared only for love. Love with her was but enlightened admiration.

Events rapidly ripened; ideas and things were crowded into her life: she had no infancy. At twenty-two years of age she had maturity of thought with the grace and softness of youth. She wrote like Rousseau, and spoke like Mirabeau. Capable of bold conceptions and complicated designs, she could contain in her bosom at the same time a lofty idea and a deep feeling. Like the women of old Rome who agitated the republic by the impulses of their hearts, or who exalted or depressed the empire with their love, she sought to mingle her feelings with her politics, and desired that the elevation of her genius should elevate him she loved. Her sex precluded her from that open action which public position, the tribune, or the army only accord to men in public governments; and thus she compulsorily remained unseen in the events she guided. To be the hidden destiny of some great man, to act through and by him, to grow with his greatness, be eminent in his name, was the sole ambition permitted to her—an ambition tender and devoted, which seduces a woman whilst it suffices to her disinterested genius. She could only be the mind and inspiration of some political man; she sought such a one, and in her delusion believed she had found him.

XX.

There was then in Paris a young general officer of illustrious race, excessively handsome, and with a mind full of attraction, varied in its powers and brilliant in its display. Although he bore the name of one of the most distinguished families at court, there was a cloud over his birth. Royal blood ran in his veins, and his features recalled those of Louis XV. The affection of Mesdames the aunts of Louis XVI. for this youth, educated under their eyes, attached to their persons, and who rose by their influence to the highest employments in the court and army, gave credit to many mysterious rumors.

This young man was the Count Louis de Narbonne. Sprung from this origin, brought up in this court, a courtier by birth; spoiled by the hands of these females, only remarkable for his good looks, his levities and his hasty wit; it was not to be expected that such a person was imbued with that ardent faith which casts a man headlong into the centre of revolutions, or the stoical energy which produces and controls them. He saw in the people only a sovereign, more exacting and more capricious than any others, towards whom it was necessary to display more skill to seduce, more policy to manage them. He believed himself sufficiently plastic for the task, and resolved to attempt it. Without a lofty imagination, he yet had ambition and courage, and he viewed the position of affairs as a drama, similar to the Fronde,* in which skilful actors could enlarge their hopes in proportion to the facts, and direct the catastrophe. He had not sufficient penetration to see, that in a revolution there is but one serious actor—enthusiasm; and he had none. He stammered out the words of a revolutionary tongue—he assumed the costume, but had not the spirit of the times.

The contrast of this nature and of this part, this court favorite casting himself into the crowd to serve the nation, this aristocratic elegance, masked in patriotism of the tribune, pleased public opinion for the moment. They applauded

* This appellation is given to a period of French history extending from 1643 to 1655. By some it is styled an attempt to establish a balanced constitution in the state,—by others, the last essay of expiring feudality. The *frondeur* leaders were the Duc de Beaufort, Cardinal de Retz, Prince de Conti, Duc de Bouillon, Mareschaux Turenne and de la Motte. On the side of their opponents, called *Mazarins*, were the Cardinal Mazarin himself, the Prince de Condé, Maréchal de Grammont, and the Duc de Chatillon, while the Duc d' Orleans, a vacillating man, wavered between the two parties. The successes of the rival powers were alternate for a long time; eventually the *frondeurs* were defeated, and De Retz escaping into Lorraine, Mazarin returned to Paris triumphant in February, 1653.—H. T. R.

this transformation as a difficulty overcome. The people was flattered by having great lords with it. It was a testimony of its power. It felt itself king, by seeing courtiers bowing to it, and excused their rank by reason of their complaisance.

Madame de Stäel was seduced as much by the heart as the intellect of M. de Narbonne. Her masculine and sensitive imagination invested the young soldier with all she desired to find in him. He was but a brilliant, active, high-couraged man; she pictured him a politician and a hero. She magnified him with all the endowments of her dreams, in order to bring him up to her ideal standard. She found patrons for him; surrounded him with a *prestige;* created a name for him, marked him out a course. She made him the living type of her politics. To disdain the court, gain over the people, command the army, intimidate Europe, carry away the Assembly by his eloquence, to struggle for liberty, to save the nation, and become, by his popularity alone, the arbiter between the throne and the people, to reconcile them by a constitution, at once liberal and monarchical; such was the perspective that she opened for herself and M. de Narbonne.

She but awakened his ambition, yet he believed himself capable of the destinies which she dreamed of for him. The drama of the constitution was concentrated in these two minds, and their conspiracy was for some time the entire policy of Europe.

Madame de Stäel, M. de Narbonne, and the constitutional party were for war; but theirs was to be a partial and not a desperate war which, shaking nationality to its foundations would carry away the throne and throw France into a Republic. They contrived by their influence to renew all the personal staff of the diplomacy, exclusively devoted to the emigrants or the king. They filled foreign courts with their adherents. M. de Marbois was sent to the Diet of Ratisbon, M. Barthélemy to Switzerland, M. de Talleyrand to London, M. de Ségur to Berlin. The mission of M. de Talleyrand was to endeavor to fraternize the aristocratic principle of the English constitution with the democratic principle of the French constitution, which they believed they could effect and control by an Upper Chamber. They hoped to interest the statesmen of Great Britain in a Revolution, imitated from their own, which, after having convulsed the people, was now becoming moulded in the hands of an intelligent aristocracy. This mission would be easy, if the Revolution were in regular train for some months in Paris. French ideas were popular in London. The opposition was revolutionary. Fox and Burke, then friends, were most earnest in their desire for the liberty of the Continent.* We must render this justice to England, that the moral and popular principle concealed in the foundation of its constitution, has never stultified itself by combating the efforts of other nations to acquire a free government. It has everywhere accorded the liberty similar to its own.

XXI.

The mission of M. de Ségur at Berlin was more delicate. Its object was to detach the king of Prussia from his alliance with the emperor Leopold, whose coronation was not yet known, and to persuade the cabinet of Berlin into an alliance with revolutionary France. This alliance held out to Prussia with its security on the Rhine the ascendency of the new-sprung ideas in Germany: it was a Machiavelian idea, which would smile at the agitating spirit of the great Frederic, who had made of Prussia the corrosive influence (*la puissance corrosive*) of the empire.

These two words—seduce and corrupt—were all M. de Ségur's instructions. The king of Prussia had favorites and mistresses. Mirabeau had written in 1786, "There can be at Berlin no secrets for the ambassador of France, unless money and skill be wanting; the country is poor and avaricious, and there is no state secret which may not be purchased with three thousand louis." M. de Ségur imbued with these ideas, made it his first object to buy over the two favorites. The one was daughter of Elie Enka, who was a musician in the chapel of the late king. Handsome and witty, she had at twelve years of age attracted the notice of the king, then prince royal, and he had, at that early age, as in anticipation of his amour, bestowed on her all the care and all the cost of a royal education. She had travelled in

* If M. de Lamartine would convey the idea that Burke was a partisan of the French Revolution, we must combat the assertion by a reference to dates. Talleyrand was ambassador in England in 1792. In October, 1791, Burke's "Reflections on the Revolution in France" appeared, to which Tom Paine's "Rights of Man" was one of the replies, and Sir James Mackintosh's "Vindiciæ" another; and previously, in 1789 and 1790, Burke had condemned the tendencies of the Revolution and the conduct of the Revolutionists.—H. T. R.

France and in England, and knew all the European laguages she had polished her natural genius by contact with the lettered men and artists of Germany. A feigned marriage with Rietz, valet de chambre of the king, was the pretext for her residence at court, and gave her the opportunity for surrounding herself with the leading men in politics and literature in the city of Berlin. Spoiled by the precocity of her fortune, yet careless as to its retention, she had allowed two rivals to dispute the king's heart. One, the young Countess d'Ingenheim, had just died in the flower of her youth; the other, the Countess d'Ashkof, had borne the king two children, and flattered herself, in vain, with having extricated him from the empire of Madame Rietz.

The Baron de Roll, in the name of the Count d'Artois, and the Viscount de Caraman, in the name of Louis XVI., had possessed themselves of all the avenues to this cabinet. The Count de Goltz, ambassador from Prussia to Paris, had informed his court of the object of M. de Ségur's mission. The report ran amongst well-informed persons that this envoy carried with him several millions (francs), destined to pay the weakness or the treason of the Berlin cabinet.

A copy of the secret instructions of M. de Ségur reached Berlin two hours before him, which revealed to the king the whole plan of seduction and venality that the agent of France was to practise on his favorites and mistresses, whose character, ambition, rivalries, weaknesses, true or feigned, the means of acting by them on the mind of the king, were all and severally noted down with the security of confidence. There was a tariff for all consciences,—a price for every treachery. The favorite aide-de-camp of the king, Rischofwerder, then very powerful, was to be assailed by irresistible offers, and in case his connivance should be revealed, a splendid establishment in France was to guarantee him against any eventuality.

These instructions fell into the very hands of those whose fidelity was thus priced, and they gave them to the king with all the innocence of individuals shamefully calumniated. The king blushed for himself at the empire over his politics thus ascribed to love and intrigue. He was indignant at the fidelity of his subjects being thus assailed: all negotiation was nipped in the bud before the arrival of the negotiator. M. de Ségur was received with coldness and all the irony of contempt. Frederic William affected never to mention him in his circle, and asked aloud before him, of the envoy of the elector of Mayence, news of the Prince de Condé: the envoy replied that this prince was approaching the frontiers of France with his army. "He is right," said the king, "for he is on the point of entering there." M. de Ségur, accustomed, from his long residence and his familiar footing at the court of Catherine, to take love for the intermediary of his affairs, induced, it is said, the Countess d'Ashkof and Prince Henry of Prussia to join the peace party. This success was but a snare for his negotiation. The king, arranging with the emperor, affected for some time to lean towards France, to complain of the exactions of emigration, and to make much of the ambassador; who, thus cajoled, sent the warmest assurances to the French cabinet as to the intentions of Prussia. But the sudden disgrace of the Countess d'Ashkof and the offer of alliance with France insultingly repulsed, threw at once light and confusion into the plots of M. de Ségur: he demanded his recall. The humiliation of seeing his talents played with, the hopes of his party annihilated, the prospect of his country's misfortunes, and Europe in flames, had, it was reported, urged his sadness to despair. The report ran that he had attempted his life. This imputed suicide was but a brain fever occasioned by the anguish of a proud mind deeply wounded.

XXII.

The same party attempted, and at nearly the same time, to acquire for France a sovereign whose renown weighed as heavily as a throne in the opinion of Europe. This was the Duke of Brunswick, a pupil of the great Frederic, the presumed heir of his military fame and inspiration, and proclaimed, by anticipation, by the public voice, generalissimo, in the coming war against France. To carry off from the emperor and the king of Prussia the chief of their armies, was to deprive Germany of confidence and of victory.

The name of the Duke of Brunswick was a prestige which invested Germany with a feeling of terror and inviolability. Madame de Staël and her party attempted it. This secret negotiation was concerted amongst Madame de Staël, M. de Narbonne, M. de La Fayette, and M. de Talleyrand. M. de Custine, son of the general of that name, was chosen to convey to the Duke of Brunswick the wishes of the constitutional party. The young negotiator was well prepared for his mission: witty, attractive, clever, an intense admirer of

Prussian tactics and the Duke of Brunswick, from whom he had had lessons in Berlin, he inspired confidence into this prince beforehand. He offered to him the rank of generalissimo of the French armies, an allowance of three millions of francs, and an establishment in France equivalent to his possessions and rank in the empire. The letter bearing these offers was signed by the minister of war and Louis XVI. himself.

M. de Custine set out from France in the month of January; on his arrival he handed his letter to the duke. Four days elapsed before an interview was accorded to him. On the fifth day the duke admitted him to a personal and private interview. He expressed to M. de Custine with military frankness his pride and gratitude that the price attached to his merits by France must inspire in him: "But," he added, "my blood is German and my honor Prussia's; my ambition is satisfied with being the second person in this monarchy, which has adopted me. I would not exchange for an adventurous glory on the shifting stage of revolutions, the high and firm position which my birth, my duty, and some reputation already acquired have secured for me in my native land."

After this conversation, M. de Custine, finding the prince immovable, disclosed his ultimatum, and held before his eyes the dazzling chance of the crown of France, if it fell from the brow of Louis XVI. into the hands of a conquering general. The duke appeared overwhelmed, and dismissed M. de Custine without depriving him of all hope of his accepting such an offer. But shortly afterwards, the duke, from duplicity, repentance, or prudence, replied by a formal refusal to both these propositions. He addressed his reply to Louis XVI., and not to his minister; and this unhappy king thus learnt the last word of the constitutional party, and how frail was the tenure on his brow of a crown which was already offered perspectively to the ambition of a foe!

BOOK VI.

I.

Such were the mutally threatening dispositions of France and Europe at the moment when the Constituted Assembly, after having proclaimed its principles, left to others to defend and apply them; like the legislator who retires into private life, thence to watch the effect and the working of his laws. The great idea of France abdicated, if we may use the expression, with the Constituted Assembly; and the government fell from its high position into the hands of the inexperience or the impulses of a new people. From the 29th of September to the 1st of October, there seemed to be a new reign: the Legislative Assembly found themselves on that day face to face with a king who, destitute of authority, ruled over a people destitute of moderation. They felt on their first sitting the oscillation of a power without a counterpoise, that seeks to balance itself by its own wisdom, and changing from insult to repentance, wounds itself with the weapon that has been placed in its grasp.

II.

An immense crowd had attended the first sittings; the exterior aspect of the Assembly had entirely changed; almost all the white heads had disappeared, and it seemed as though France had beceme young again in the course of a night. The expression of the physiognomies, the gestures, the attire of the members of the Assembly were no longer the same; that pride of the French noblesse, visible alike in the look and bearing; that dignity of the clergy and the magistrates; that austere gravity of the deputies of the *Tiers état* had suddenly given place to the representatives of a new people, whose confusion and turbulence announced rather the invasion of power than the custom and the possession of supreme power. Many members were remarkable for their youth; and when the president, by virtue of his age, summoned all the deputies who had not yet attained their twenty-sixth year, in order to form the provisional *bureau*, sixty young men presented themselves, and disputed the office of secretary to the Assembly. This youth of the representatives of the nation alarmed some, whilst it rejoiced others; for if, on the one hand, such a representation did not possess that mature calmness and that authority of age that the ancient legislators sought in the council of the people; on the other, this sudden return to youth of the representatives of the nation, seemed a symptom of the regeneration of all the established institutions. It was visible to everybody that this new generation had discarded all the traditions and prejudices of the old order of things; and its very age was a guarantee opposite to established rule, and which required that every statesman should by his age give pledges for the past, whilst from these were required guarantees for the future. Their inexperience was made a merit, their youth an oath. Old men are needed in times of tranquillity, young ones in times of revolutions.

Scarcely was the Assembly constituted, than the twofold feeling that was destined to dispute and contest every act—the monarchical and republican feeling—commenced upon a frivolous pretext, a struggle, puerile in appearance, serious in reality, and in which each party in the course of two days was alternately the conqueror and the conquered. The deputation that had waited on the king to announce to him the constitution of the Assembly, reported the result of its mission through the medium of the *député* Ducastel, the president of this deputation. "We deliberated," said he, "as to what form of words we should make use of in addressing his majesty, as we feared to wound the national dignity or the royal dignity, and we agreed to use these terms:—'Sire, the Assembly is formed, and has deputed us to inform your majesty.' We proceeded to the Tuileries; the minister of justice announced to us that the king could not receive us before to-day at one o'clock. We, however, thought that the public safety required that we should be instantly admitted to the king's presence, and we therefore persisted. The king then informed us he would give us audience at nine o'clock, at which hour we again presented ourselves. At four paces distance from the king I saluted him, and addressed him in the terms agreed upon; he inquired the names of my colleagues, and I replied, 'I do not know them;' we were about to withdraw, when he recalled us, saying, 'I cannot see you before Friday.'"

An ill-repressed agitation, which had hitherto pervaded the ranks of the Assembly, now broke forth at these last words. "I demand," cried a deputy, "that this title of

Majesty be no longer employed." "I demand," added another, "that this title of Sire be abolished; it is only an abbreviation of Seigneur, which recognizes a sovereignty in the man to whom it is given." "I demand," said the deputy Bequet, "that we be no longer treated as automata, obliged to sit down or stand, just as it pleases the king to rise or to sit down." Couthon made his voice heard for the first time, and his first speech was a threat against royalty. "There is no other majesty here," said he, "than that of the law and the people. Let us leave the king no other title than that of King of the French. Let this scandalous chair be removed, the gilded seat brought for his use the last time he appeared in this chamber, if he really is anxious to fill the simple place of the president of a great people. Let an equality exist between us as regards ceremony: when he is uncovered and standing, let us stand and uncover our heads; when he is covered and seated, let us sit and wear our hats." "The people," said Chabot, "has sent you here to maintain its dignity; will you permit the king to say, 'I will come at three o'clock,' as if you were unable to adjourn the Assembly without awaiting him?"

It was decreed that every member should have the right to sit covered in the king's presence. "This decree," observed Garrau de Coulon, "is calculated to create a degree of confusion in the Assembly; this privilege, given indiscriminately, would enable some to display pride, and others flattery." "So much the better," said a voice; "if there are any flatterers, we shall know them." It was also decreed that there should be only two chairs, placed in a line, one for the king, the other for the president; and lastly, that the king should have no other title than that of King of the French.

III.

These decrees humiliated the king, spread consternation amongst the constitutional party, and agitated the people. All had hoped that harmony would be established between the powers, and yet this understanding was destroyed at the outset, and the constitution tottered at its first step. This deprivation of the titles of royalty seemed a greater humiliation than the deprivation of the absolute power. Had we alone kept our king to expose him to the insults and derision of the people's representatives? how will a nation that does not respect its hereditary chief, respect its elected representatives? and is it by such outrages that liberty hopes to render herself acceptable to the throne? Or, is it by infusing similar feelings of resentment in the breast of the king, that he will be induced to protect the constitution, and to aid the maintenance of the rights of the people? If the executive power be a necessary reality, we must respect it, even in the king; if it be but a shadow, still should we respect and honor it. The ministerial council assembled, and the king declared that he was not forced by the new constitution to expose the monarchical dignity represented in his person to the outrages of the Assembly, and that he would order the ministers to preside at the opening of the legislative body.

This rumor created a re-action in Paris in favor of the king. The Assembly, as yet undecided, felt the blow; and that the popularity it sought was fast disappearing. "What has been the result of the decree of yesterday?" said the deputy Vosgien, at the opening of the sitting of the 6th of October. "Fresh hopes for the enemies of the public welfare, agitation of the people, depreciation of our credit, general disquietude. Let us pay to the hereditary representative of the people the respect that is his due. Do not let him believe that he is destined to be the mockery and the plaything of each fresh legislation; it is time for the constitution to cast anchor, and fix itself with firmness and stability."

Vergniaud, the hitherto unknown orator of the Gironde, displayed in his opening speech that audacious yet undecided character that was the type of his policy. His speeches were uncertain as his mind; he spoke in favor of one party, and voted for the other. "We all appear to agree," said he, "that if this decree concerns our internal regulations, it should be instantly put into execution; and it is evident to me that the decree does concern our internal regulations, for there can be no connection of authority between the legislative body and the king. It is merely a question of those marks of respect which are demanded to be shown to the royal dignity. I know not why the titles of Sire and Majesty, which recal feudality, should be restored; for the king ought to glory in the title of King of the French. I ask you, whether the king demanded a decree to regulate the etiquette of his household when he received your deputation? However, to speak my opinion without reserve, I think that if the king, as a mark of respect to the Assembly rises and uncovers his head, the Assembly, as a mark of respect to the king, should imitate his example."

Hérault de Séchelles demanded the repeal of the decree, and Champion, deputy of the Jura, reproached his colleagues for employing their meetings in such puerile debates. "I do not fear that the people will worship a gilded chair," said he, "but I dread a struggle between the two powers. You will not permit that the words *sire* and *majesty* be used, you will not even permit us to applaud the king; as if it were possible to forbid the people from manifesting their gratitude when the king has merited it. Do not let us dishonor ourselves, gentlemen, by a culpable ingratitude towards the National Assembly, who has retained these marks of respect for the king. The founders of liberty were not slaves; and previous to fixing the prerogatives of royalty, they established the rights of the people. It is the nation that is honored in the person of its hereditary representative. It is the nation who, after having created royalty, has invested it with a splendor that remounts to the source from whence it sprung, and gives it a double lustre."

Ducastel, the president of the deputation sent to the king, spoke on the same side, but having inadvertently used the expression *sovereign,* in speaking of the king, and that the legislative power was vested in the Assembly and the king, this blasphemy and involuntary heresy raised a terrible storm in the chamber. Every word of this nature seemed to them to threaten a counter-revolution; for they were still so near despotism, that they feared at each step again to fall into its toils. The people was a slave, freed but yesterday, and who still trembled at the clank of his chains. However, the offensive decree was repealed, and this retraction was rapturously hailed by the royalists and the national guard. The constitutionalists saw in it the augury of renewed harmony between the ruling powers of the state; the king saw in it the triumph of a fidelity that had been deadened, but which blazed forth again on the least appearance of outrage to his person.

They were all deceived: it was but a movement of generosity, succeeding one of brutality; the hesitation of a nation that dares not, at one stroke, destroy the idol before which it has so long bowed the knee.

The royalists, however, attacked this return to moderation in their journals. "See," they cried, "how contemptible is this revolution—how conscious of its own weakness! This feeling of its own feebleness is a defeat already anticipated; see in two days how often it has given itself the lie. The authority that concedes is lost unless it possess the art of masking its retreat, of retreating by slow and imperceptible steps, and of causing its laws to be rather forgotten than repealed. Obedience arises from two causes, respect and fear. And both have been alike snapped asunder by the sudden and violent retrograde movement of the Assembly; for how can we respect or dread that power that trembles at its own audacity? The Assembly has abdicated by not completing that which it had dared to commence: the revolution that does not advance, retreats; and the king has conquered without striking a blow."

On their side the revolutionary party assembled that evening at the Jacobins, deplored their defeat, accused every one, and mutually recriminated on each other. "See," said their orators, "what underhand work has been accomplished in one night; what a triumph of corruption and fraud! The members of the former Assembly have mixed with the new members in the chamber, and have infused into the ears of their successors those concessions that have ruined them. After the sitting of that evening they mingled with the groups in the Palais Royal, spread alarm around, hinted of a second flight of the king, prognosticated trouble and anarchy, and made the people of Paris, who prefer their own private interests to the public weal, fear the utter destruction of confidence and the depression of the public credit. Can this venal race resist such arguments?"

All the real feelings of Paris were infused the next day into the attitude and discourses of the Assembly. "At the opening of the sitting," says a Jacobin, "I took my place amongst the deputies who were discussing the best means to obtain the repeal of the decree. I remarked that the decree having been carried the previous evening almost unanimously, it appeared impracticable to reckon upon so sudden and so scandalous a change of opinion. 'We are sure of the majority,' was their reply. I quitted my seat and took another, where precisely the same conversation passed. I then took refuge in that part of the chamber that had been so long the sanctuary of patriotism: there I heard the same arguments, the same apostasy. All had been purchased in the course of the night, and the best proof that this work of corruption had been accomplished before the deliberation is, that all the orators who spoke against the decree had their speeches ready written. Whence arises this surprise of the patriots? Because the well-intentioned members of the Assembly do not know each other; they have not met or reckoned their numbers here. It is true that you have opened your doors to receive them: they have entered this room to examine your countenance and ascertain your forces; but they are not as yet associated and knit together; nor have they acquired, by frequent visits here, and by listening to your discourses, that confidence and patriotism that form the great and good citizen."

The people, who sighed for repose after so many exciting scenes, destitute of work, money, and food, and intimidated by the approach of a severe winter, saw with indifference the attempt and the retraction of the Assembly, and suffered the deputies who had supported the decree to be insulted with impunity. Goupilleau, Couthon, Basire, Chabot, were threatened in the very Assembly by the officers of the national guard. "Beware!" said these soldiers of the people, bought over to the cause of the throne; "we will not suffer the Revolution to advance another step. We know you—we will watch you—you shall be hewed to pieces by our bayonets." These deputies, seconded by Barrère, came to the Jacobins' club, to denounce these outrages; but no effect was produced, and they gained nothing save expression of sterile indignation.

IV.

The king, re-assured by this state of public feeling, proceeded, on the 7th, to the Assembly, where his appearance was the signal for unanimous acclamations. Some applauded *the king*, others applauded the constitution, in the person of the king. It inspired with real fanaticism that mass that judges of things by words alone, and believes all that the law proclaims sacred to be imperishable. Not content with crying *Vive le Roi*, they cried also *Vive sa Majesté;* and the acclamations of one part of the people thus avenged themselves on the offences of the others, and revered those titles that a decree had striven to efface. They even applauded the restoration of the royal chair beside that of the president, and it seemed to the royalists that this chair was a throne on which the people replaced the monarchy. The king addressed them, standing and bareheaded; his speech re-assured their minds and touched their hearts; and if he lacked the language of enthusiasm, he had at least the accent of sincerity. "In order," said he, "that our labors may produce the beneficial results we have a right to expect, it is necessary that a constant harmony and an unalterable confidence should exist between the king and the legislative body. The enemies of our repose will seek every opportunity to spread disunion amongst us, but let the love of our country ally us, the public interest render us inseparable. Thus, public power will unfold itself without opposition, and the administration be harassed by no vain fears. The property and the opinions of every man shall be protected, and no excuse will remain for any one to live away from a country where the laws are in force, and the rights of all respected." This allusion to the emigrés, and this indirect appeal to the king's brothers, caused a sensation of joy and hope to pervade the ranks of the Assembly.

The president Pastoret, a moderate constitutionalist, beloved alike by the king and the people, because, with the doctrines of power, he possessed the acuteness of the diplomatist and the language of the constitution, replied,—"Sire, your presence in this assembly is a fresh oath you take of fidelity to your country: the rights of the people were forgotten and all power confused. A constitution is born, and with it the liberty of France. As a citizen, it is your duty to cherish—as a king, to strengthen and defend it. Far from shaking your power, it has confirmed it, and has given you friends in those who formerly were styled your subjects. You said a few days ago in this temple of our country, that you have need of being beloved by all Frenchmen, and we also have need of being beloved by you. The constitution has rendered you the greatest monarch in the world; your attachment to it will place your majesty amongst those kings most beloved by the people. Strong by our union, we shall soon feel its salutary effects. To purify the legislation, support public credit, and crush anarchy,—such is our duty, such our wishes. Such are yours, sire; and the blessing of the French nation will be the recompence."

This day awakened hope once more in the hearts of the king and queen. They believed they had again found their subjects; and the people believed that they had again found their king. All recollections of what had passed at Varennes seemed buried in oblivion; aud popularity had one of those sudden blasts that drive away the clouds in the sky for a short space, and deceive even those who have learnt to mistrust them. The royal family wished to enjoy it, and to let Madame and the dauphin profit by it; for these two infants knew nothing of the people save their fury; they had alone seen the nation through the bayonets of the 6th of October,—the rags of the *émeute*,—of the dust of the return from Varennes; the king wished they should now see them in a state of tranquillity and affection for him, for he taught his son to love the people, and not to avenge their offences towards him. In the pangs he had suffered, the most bitter was rather the ingratitude of the nation, than his own personal humiliations; for, to be misconstrued by the nation, was, in his eyes, far more painful than to be persecuted by them. One moment of justice on the part of public opinion made him forget two years of outrage. He went that evening to the Théâtre Italien with the queen, Madame Elizabeth, and his children. The hopes to which the events of the day had given rise—his words of that morning—the expression of confidence and affection on his features—the beauty of the two princesses—the infantine grace of his children, produced on the spectators one of those impressions, where pity vies with respect, and enthusiasm softens the heart into veneration.

The theatre rang with applause mingled with sobs; every eye was fixed on the royal box, as though in mute reparation for so many insults offered to the king and his family. The populace can never resist the sight of children, there are so many mothers in every crowd; the dauphin, a lovely child, seated on the lap of his mother, and absorbed in the play, repeated the gestures of the actors to his mother as though to explain the piece to her. This careless tranquillity of innocence between the two storms—this childish sport at the foot of a throne, so soon to become a scaffold—this expansion of the heart of the queen, that had been so long closed to joy and security, filled every eye with tears, not excepting the king himself.

There are moments in every revolution when the most furious and enraged populace becomes gentle and compassionate; it is when it suffers nature and not policy to sway it; and instead of being a people, it becomes a man. Paris had such an instant: it was of short duration.

V.

The Assembly was very anxious to re-acquire the public

feeling of which a momentary weakness had dispossessed it. It already blushed at its moderation for a day, and was anxious to cast fresh jealousies between the throne and the nation. A numerous party in the chamber was desirous of pushing matters to extremities, and to tighten the cord of the present posture of affairs until it snapped. For this purpose the party required agitation; tranquillity by no means suited its designs. It had ambitious desires as vast as its talents, ardent as its youth, impatient as its thirst for advancement. The Constituent Assembly, composed of reflective men of eminence in the state, and in the social hierarchy, had but the ambition of advancing the ideas of liberty and fame; the new Assembly had that of tumult, fortune, and power. Formed of obscure, poor and unknown men, it aspired to the acquisition of all in which it was deficient.

This latter party, of which Brissot was the journalist, Pétion the popular member, Vergniaud the genius, the party of the Girondists the body, entered on the scene with the boldness and unity of a conspiracy. It was the *bourgeoisie* triumphant, envious, turbulent, eloquent, the aristocracy of talent, desiring to acquire and control by itself alone liberty, power, and the people. The Assembly was made up of unequal portions of three elements; the constitutionalists, who formed the aristocratic liberty and moderate monarchy party; the Girondists, the party of the movement, sustained until the Revolution fell into their hands; the Jacobins, the party of the people, and of philosophy in action; the first arrangement and transition, the second boldness and intrigue, the third fanaticism and devotion. Of these last two parties the Jacobin was not the most hostile to the king. The aristocracy and the clergy destroyed, that party had no repugnance to the throne; it possessed in a high degree the instinct of the unity of power; it was not the Jacobins who first demanded war, and who first uttered the word republic, but it was the first who uttered and often repeated the word *dictatorship*. The word *republic* appertained to Brissot and the Girondists. If the Girondists, on their coming into the Assembly, had united with the constitutional party in order to save the constitution by moderate measures, and the Revolution by not urging it into war, they would have saved their party and controlled the throne. The honesty in which their leader was deficient was also wanting in their conduct —they were all intrigue. They made themselves the agitators in an Assembly of which they might have been the statesmen. They had not confidence in the republic, but feigned it. In revolutions sincere characters are the only skilful characters. It is glorious to die the victim of a faith, it is pitiful to die the dupe of one's ambition.

VI.

Three causes of uneasiness agitated men's minds at the moment when the Assembly opened its sittings—the clergy, emigration, and impending war.

The Constituent Assembly had committed a gross error in stopping at a half measure in reforming the clergy in France. Mirabeau himself had been weak on this question. The Revolution was at the bottom only the legitimate rising of political liberty against despotism, and of religious liberty against the legal domination of Catholicism, because a political institution. The constitution had emancipated the citizens, and it was necessary to emancipate the faithful, and to claim consciences for the state, in order to restore them to themselves, to individual reason, and to God. This is what philosophy desired, which is only the rational expression of the mind's impulses.

The philosophers of the Constituent Assembly receded before the difficulties of this labor. Instead of an emancipation, they made a compact with the power of the clergy, the dreaded influences of the court of Rome, and the inveterate habits of the people. They contented themselves with relaxing the chain which bound the state to the church. Their duty was to have snapped it asunder. The throne was chained to the altar, they desired to chain the altar to the throne. It was only displacing tyranny,—oppressing conscience by law instead of oppressing the law by conscience.

The civil constitution of the clergy was the expression of this reciprocal false position. The clergy was deprived of these endowments in landed estates, which decimated property and population in France. They deprived it of its benefices, its abbeys, and its tithes—the altar's feudality. It received in lieu an endowment in salaries levied on the taxes. As the condition of this arrangement, which gave to the working clergy an existence, influence, and a powerful body of ministers of worship paid by the state, they required the clergy to take the oath of the constitution. This constitution comprised articles which affected the spiritual supremacy and administrative privileges of the court of Rome. Catholicism became alarmed and protested; consciences were disturbed. The Revolution, until then exclusively political, became schism in the eyes of a portion of the clergy and the faithful. Amongst the bishops and the priests, some took the civil oath, which was the guarantee of their existence; others refused, or, after having taken it, retracted. This gave rise to trouble in many minds, agitation in consciences, division in the temples. The great majority of parishes had two ministers,—the one a constitutional priest, salaried and protected by the government, the other refractory, refusing the oath, deprived of his income, driven from the church, and raising altar opposing altar in some clandestine chapel, or in the open field. These two ministers of the same worship excommunicated each other, the one in the name of the constitution, and the other in the name of the pope and of the church. The population was also divided according to the greater or lesser degree of revolutionary spirit prevailing in the province. In cities and the more enlightened districts the constitutional worship was exercised almost without dispute. In the open country and the less civilized departments, the priest who had not taken the oath became a consecrated tribune, who at the foot of the altar, or in the elevation of the pulpit, agitated the people and inspired it, in all the horror of a constitutional and schismatic priesthood, with hatred of the government which protected it. This was not actually persecution or civil war, but the sure prelude to both.

The king had signed with repugnance and even constraint the civil constitution of the clergy: but he had done so only as king, and reserving to himself his liberty and the faith of his conscience. He was Christian and Catholic in all the simplicity of the Gospel, and in all the humility of obedience to the church. The reproaches he had received from Rome for having ratified by his weakness the schism in France, wounded his conscience and distracted his mind. He had never ceased to negotiate officially or secretly with the pope, in order to obtain from the head of the church either an indulgent concession to the necessities of religion in France, or prudent temporizing. It was on these terms only that he could restore peace to his mind. Inexorable Rome had only granted him its pity. Fulminating bulls were in circulation by the hands of nonjuring priests, cast at the heads of the population, and only stopping at the foot of the throne. The king trembled, to see them burst one day on his own head.

On the other hand, he felt that the nation of which he was the legitimate head, would never forgive him for sacrificing it to his religious scruples. Placed thus between the menaces of Heaven and the threats of his own people, he procrastinated with all his might the denunciations of Rome and the votes of the Assembly. The Constitutional Assembly understood this anxiety of the king's feelings and the dangers of persecution. It had given time to the king, and displayed forbearance to men's consciences: it had not intermeddled with the faith of the simple believer, but left each at liberty to pray with the priest of his choice. The king had been the first to avail himself of this liberty, and had not thrown open the chapel of the Tuileries to the constitutional worship. The choice of his confessor sufficiently indicated the choice of his conscience. The man in him protested against the political necessities which oppressed the monarch. The Girondists wished to compel him to declare himself. If he yielded to them he infringed upon his dignity: if he resisted, he lost the remaining shreds of his popularity. To compel him to decide was a great point for the Girondists.

The public feeling served their designs. Religious troubles began to assume a political character. In ancient Brittany the conforming priests became objects of the people's horror, and they fled from contact with them. The nonjuring priests all retained their flocks. On Sundays large bodies of many thousand souls were seen to follow their ancient pastors, and go to chapels situated two or three leagues from any dwelling, or in concealed hermitages, sanctuaries which had never been stained by the ceremonies of a constitutional worship. At Caen blood had even flowed in the very cathedral, where the nonjuring priest disputed the altar with the conforming pastor. The same disorders threatened to spread over all parts of the kingdom: everywhere were to be seen two pastors and a divided flock. Resentment, which already displayed itself in insult, of necessity soon arrived at bloodshed. The one half of the people, disturbed in its faith, reverted to the aristocracy out of love for its worship. The Assembly must thus alienate the popular element, which it had so recently caused to triumph over royalty. It was highly necessary to provide against this unexpected peril.

There were only two means of extinguishing this flame at its source: either by freedom of conscience, stoutly maintained by the executive power, or persecution of the ministers of the ancient faith. The undecided Assembly wavered between these two parties. On a report of Gallois and Gensonné, sent as commissioners into the departments of the west, to investigate the causes of the agitation and the feelings of the people, the discussion commenced. Fauchet, a conforming priest and celebrated preacher, subsequently constitutional bishop of Calvados, opened the debate. He was one of those men who, beneath an ecclesiastical garb, conceal the heart of a philosopher. Reformers from feeling, priests by the state, sensible of the wide discrepancy between their opinions and their character, a national religion, a revolutionary Christianity was the sole means remaining to them to reconcile their interest and their policy: their faith, wholly academic, was only a religious convenience. They desired to transform Catholicism insensibly into a moral code, of which the dogma was now but a symbol, which, in the people's eyes, comprised sacred truths; and which, gradually stripped of holy fictions, would allow the human understanding to glide insensibly into a symbolic deism, whose temple should be flesh, and whose Christ should be hardly more than Plato rendered a divinity. Fauchet had the daring mind of a sectarian and the intrepidity of a man of resolution.

VII.

"We are accused of a desire to persecute. It is calumny. No persecution. Fanaticism is greedy of it, real religion repulses it, philosophy holds it in horror. Let us beware of imprisoning the nonjurors; of exiling, even of displacing them. Let them think, say, write all they please against us We will oppose our thoughts to their thoughts; our truths to their errors; our charity to their hatred. Time will do the rest. But in awaiting its infallible triumph we must find an efficacious and prompt mode of hindering them from prevailing over weak minds, and propagating ideas of a counter-revolution. A counter-revolution! This is not a religion gentlemen! Fanaticism is not compatible with liberty. Look else at these ministers—they would have swum in the blood of patriots. This is their own expression. Compared with these priests, atheists are angels. (Applause.) However, I repeat, let us tolerate them, but do not let us pay them. Let us not pay them to rend our country in pieces. It is to this measure only that we should confine ourselves. Let us suppress all salary from the national treasury to the nonjuring priests. Nothing is due to them but in their clerical capacity. What service do they render? They invoke ruin on our laws; and they say they follow their consciences! Must we pay consciences which push them to the extremity of crime against their country? The nation supports them: is not that enough? They appeal to the article of the constitution which says, 'The salaries of the ministers of Catholic worship form a portion of the national debt.' Are they ministers of the Catholic worship? Does the state recognize any other Catholicity than its own? If they would attempt any other it is open to them and their sectarians! The nation allows all sorts of worship, but only pays one. And what a saving for the nation to be freed from thirty millions (of francs), which she pays annually to her most implacable enemies! (Bravo.) Why have we this phalanx of priests, who have abjured their ministry? these legions of canons and monks; these cohorts of abbés, friars, and beneficed clergy of all sorts, who were not remarkable otherwise except for their pretensions, inutility, intrigues and licentious life; and are only so to-day by their vindictive interference, their schemes, their unwearied hatred of the Revolution? Why should we pay this army of dependents from the funds of the nation? What do they do? They preach emigration, they send coin from the realm, they foment conspiracies against us from within and without. Go, say they to the nobility, and combine your attacks with the foreigner; let blood flow in streams, provided that we recover our privileges! This is their church! If hell had one on earth it is thus that it would speak. Who shall say we ought to endow it?"

Tourné, the constitutional bishop of Bourges, replied to the Abbé Fauchet as Fénélon would have answered Bossuet. He proved that, in the mouth of his adversary, toleration was fanatical and cruel. "You have proposed to you violent remedies for the evils which anger can only envenom; it is a sentence of starvation which is demanded of you against our nonjuring brethren. Simple religious errors should be strangers to the legislator. The priests are not guilty—they are only led astray. When the eye of the law falls on these errors of the conscience, it envenoms them. The best means of curing them is not to see them. To punish by the pangs of hunger simple and venial errors, would be an opprobrium to legislation—a horror in morals. The legislator leaves to God the care of avenging his own glory, if he believe it violated by an indecorous worship. Would you, in the name of tolerance, again create an inquisition which would not have, like the other, the excuse of fanaticism? What, gentlemen, would you transform into arbitrary proscribers the founders of liberty? You will judge, you will exile, you will imprison, *en masse*, men amongst whom, if there are some guilty, there are still more innocent! Crimes are no longer individual, and guilt would be decreed by category; but were they all and all equally guilty, could you have the cruelty to strike, at the same time, this multitude of heads; when under similar circumstances the most cruel despots would be content with decimating them? What then have you to do? One thing only: to be consistent, and found practical liberty and the peaceable co-existence of different worships on the basis of tolerance. Why do not our brethren of the priesthood enjoy the power of worshipping beside us the same God—whilst in our cities, where we refuse them the right of celebrating our holy mysteries, we allow heathens to celebrate the mysteries of Iris and Osiris? Mahometans to invoke their prophet? the rabbin to make his burnt-offerings? To what extent, I ask, shall such strange tolerance be permissible? to what extent, I ask also, will you push despotism and persecution? When the law shall have regulated the civil arts, births, marriage, burial, with religious ceremonies, by which Christians consecrate them; when the law will permit the same sacrifice on two altars, with what consistency can it forbid the virtue of the same sacraments? These temples, it will be repeated, are the council-chambers of the factious. True, if they be rendered clandestine, as the persecutors would make them; but if these temples be open and free, the eye of the law will penetrate there and everywhere else: it will be no longer religious worship, it will be crime they will watch and detect—and what do you fear? Time is with you; this class of the nonjurors will be extinct, and never renewed. A worship supported by individuals, and not by the state, constantly tends to weaken itself; at least, the factious, who are in their commencement animated by the divinity of their faith, gradually become reconciled, and identify themselves with the general freedom. Look at Germany—look at Virginia—where opposite creeds mutually borrow the same sanctuaries, and where different sects fraternize in the same patriotism. This is what we should tend to; these are the principles which ought gradually to implant themselves widely amongst a people: light ought to be the great precursor of the law. Let us leave to despotism to prepare its slaves for its commands by ignorance."

VIII.

Ducos, a young and generous-hearted Girondist, with whom enthusiasm for the honest carried him beyond the policy of his party, moved for the printing of this speech. His voice was drowned amidst the applause and murmurs which followed—a testimony of the indecision and impartiality of men's minds. Fauchet replied at the next sitting, and pointed out the connection between civil troubles and religious quarrels. "The priests," he said, "are of unreasonable tyranny, which still maintains its hold on consciences by the ill-broken thread of its power. It is a faction 'scotched, not killed'—it is the most dangerous of factions."

Gensonné spoke like a statesman, and counselled toleration towards conscientious priests, and the repulsion by force of law of the turbulent clergy. During this discussion, couriers daily arriving from the country, brought news of fresh disorders. Everywhere the constitutional priests were insulted, driven away, massacred at the foot of the altars. The country churches, closed by order of the National Assembly, were burst open by axes, the nonjuring priests returned to them, urged by the fanaticism of the people. Three cities were besieged and on the point of being burnt down by the country people. The threatened civil war seemed the prelude to the counter-revolution. "See," exclaimed Isnard, "whither the toleration and impunity you have preached, conduct you!"

Isnard, deputy of Provence, was the son of a perfumer of Grasse. His father had educated him for a literary life, and not for business. He had studied politics in the antiquities of Greece and Rome. He had in his mind the idea of one of the Gracchi; he had his courage in his soul and his tone in his voice. Still very young, his eloquence was as fervent as his blood; his language was but the fire of his passion, colored by a southern imagination; his words poured forth like the rapid bursts of impatience. He was the revolutionary impetus personified. The Assembly followed him breathless, and with him arrived at fury before it attained conviction. His discourses were magnificent odes, which elevated discussion to lyric poetry, and enthusiasm to convulsion; his action bespoke the tripod rather than the tribune. He was the Danton of the Gironde, as Vergniaud was to become its Mirabeau.

IX.

It was his maiden speech in the Assembly. "Yes," he said, "look at the point to which impunity conducts us! It is always the source of great crimes, and is now the sole cause of the disorganized state into which society is plunged. The plans of toleration proposed to you are very well for tranquil times; but can we tolerate those who will neither tolerate the constitution nor the laws? Will it be when French blood has at last stained the waves of the sea, that you will become sensible of the dangers of indulgence? It is time that everything is submitted to the will of the nation; that tiaras, diadems, and censers should yield to the sceptre of the laws. The facts you have just heard are but the prelude of what is about to occur in the rest of the kingdom. Consider the circumstances of these troubles, and you will see that they have the effect of a disorganized system contemporary with the constitution. This system was born there! (the orator pointed to the right) it is sanctioned at the court of Rome. It is but a real fanaticism we have to unmask—it is but hypocrisy! The priests are the privileged brawlers, who ought to be punished by penalties more severe than mere private individuals. Religion is an all-powerful weapon. 'The priest,' says Montesquieu, 'takes the man from the cradle, and accompanies him to the tomb;' is it then astonishing that he should have so much control over the mind of the people, and that it is requisite to make laws, in order that under a pretence of religion it should not trouble the public peace? What should be the nature of such a law? I maintain that one only can be efficacious, and that is banishment from the realm. (The tribunes hailed this with loud applause.) Do you not see that it is necessary to separate the factious priest from the people whom he misleads, and send away these plague-spotted men to the lazarettos of Italy and Rome? I am told that the measure is too severe. What!—you are then blind and mute at all that occurs! Are you then ignorant that a priest can effect more mischief than all your enemies? I am answered,

'Ah! you should not persecute.' My answer is, that to punish is not to persecute. I answer thus to those who repeat what I heard retorted here on the Abbé Maury, that nothing is more dangerous than to make martyrs. This danger only exists when you have to strike fanatics in earnest, or men really pious, who believe the scaffold to be the nearest footstool to heaven. This is not the present case; for if there be priests who earnestly reject the constitution, they will not give any trouble to public order. Those who really trouble it, are men who only weep over religion in order to recover their lost privileges; those who should be punished without pity; and be assured that you will not thereby augment the strength of the emigrants: for we know that the priest is cowardly—as cowardly as vindictive—that he knows no other weapon but superstition; and that, accustomed to combat in the mysterious arena of confession, he is a nullity in every other battle-field. The thunders of Rome will fall harmless on the bucklers of liberty. The foes to your regeneration will never grow weary; no, they will never grow weary of crimes, so long as you leave them the means! You must overcome them, or be overcome by them; and whosoever sees not this is blind. Open the page of history; you will see the English sustaining for fifty years a disastrous war, in order to maintain their revolution. You will see in Holland seas of blood flowing in the war against Philip of Spain. When in our times, the Philadelphians would be free, have we not also seen war in the two hemispheres? You have been witnesses of the recent outbreaks in Brabant, and do you believe that your Revolution, which has snatched the sceptre from despotism, and from aristocracy its privileges, from nobility its pride, from the clergy its fanaticism—a Revolution which has dried up so many golden sources from the grasp of the priesthood, torn so many frocks, crushed so many theories—do you believe that such a Revolution will absolve you? No—no!—this Revolution will have a *dénouement*, and I say—and with no intention of provocation—that we must advance boldly towards this *dénouement*. The more you delay, the more difficult and blood-stained will be that triumph!" (Violent murmurs.)

"But do you not see," resumed Isnard, "that all counter-revolutionists are obstinate, and leave you no other part than that of vanquishing them? It is better to have to contend against them, while the citizens are still up and stirring, and well remember the perils they have encountered, than to allow patriotism to grow cold! Is it not true that already we are no longer what we were in the first year of liberty. (Some of the chamber applaud, whilst others disapprove.) If fanaticism had then raised its head, the law would have been subjected! Your policy should be to compel victory to declare itself; drive your enemies to extremities, and you will have them return to you from fear, or you will subdue them by the sword. Under important circumstances, prudence is a weakness. It is especially with respect to rebels that you should be decisive and severe; they should be hewn down as they rise. If time be permitted to them to have meetings and earnest partisans, then they spread over the empire like an irresistible torrent. It is thus that despotism acts, and it was thus that one individual kept beneath his yoke a whole nation. If Louis XVI. had employed this great means whilst the Revolution was but yet in its cradle, we should not now be here! This rigor, the vice of a despot, is the virtue of a nation. Legislators, who shrink from such extreme means, are cowards—criminals: for when the public liberty is assailed, to pardon is to share the crime. (Great applause.)

"Such rigor might perchance cost an effusion of blood? I know it! But if you do not make use of it, will not more blood flow? Is not civil war a still greater misfortune? Cut off the gangrened member to save the whole frame.* Indulgence is the snare into which you are tempted. You will find yourselves abandoned by the nation for not having dared to sustain, nor known how to defend it. Your enemies will hate you no less. Your friends will lose confidence in you. The law is my God: I have no other—the public good, that is my worship! You have already struck the emigrants—again a decree against the refractory priests, and you will have gained over ten millions of arms! My decree would be comprised in two words: compel every Frenchman, priest or not, to take the civil oath, and ordain that every man who will not sign shall be deprived of all salary or pension. Sound policy would decree that every one who does not sign the contract should leave the kingdom. What proofs against the priests do we require? If there be but a complaint lodged against the priest by the citizen with whom he lives, let him be at once expelled! As to those against

* ——— immedicabile vulnus
Ense recidendum, ne pars sincera trahatur.

whom the penal code shall pronounce punishment more severe than exile, there is but one sentence left: *Death.*"

X.

This oration, which pushed patriotism even to impiety and made of the public safety an implacable deity, to which even the innocent were to be sacrificed, excited a frantic enthusiasm in the ranks of the Girondist party, a bitter indignation amongst the moderate party. "To propose the printing of such a speech," said Lecos, a constitutional bishop, "is to propose the printing of a code of atheism. It is impossible that a society can exist, if it have not an immutable morality derived from the idea of a God." Derisive sneers and murmurings hailed this religious protest. The decree against the priests, presented by François de Neufchâteau, and adopted by the legislative committee, was couched in these terms:—"Every ecclesiastic not taking the oaths is required to present himself before the expiration of the week at his municipality, and there take the civil oath.

"Those who shall refuse are not entitled in future to receive any allowance or pension from the public treasury.

"Every year there shall be an aggregate made of those pensions which the priests have forfeited, and this sum shall be divided amongst the eighty-three departments, to be employed in charitable works, and in giving succor to the indigent.

"These priests shall be, moreover, from their simple refusal of the oath, reputed as suspected of rebellion and specially *surveillés.*

"They may in consequence thereof be sent from their domicile, and another be assigned to them.

"If they refuse to change their domicile when called upon to do so, they shall be imprisoned.

"The churches employed for the paid worship of the state, cannot be devoted to any other service. Citizens may hire other churches or chapels, and exercise their worship therein. But this permission is forbidden to nonjuring priests suspected of revolt."

XI.

This decree, which created more fanaticism than it repressed, and which accorded freedom of worship not as a right but as a favor, saddened the heart of the faithful; and the revolt in La Vendée, and persecution everywhere, followed. Suspended as a fearful weapon over the conscience of the king, it was sent for his assent.

The Girondists were delighted at thus keeping the wretched monarch between their law and his own faith—schismatic if he recognized the decree, and a traitor to the nation if he refused it. Conquerors in this victory, they advanced towards another.

After having forced the king to strike at the religion of his conscience, they wished to force him to deal a blow at the nobility and his own brothers. They renewed the question of the emigrants. The king and his ministers had anticipated them. Immediately after the acceptance of the constitution, Louis XVI. had formally renounced all conspiracy, interior or exterior, in order to recover his power. The omnipotence of opinion had convinced him of the vanity of all the plans submitted to him for crushing it. The momentary tranquillity of spirits after so many shocks, the reception he had met with in the Assembly, the Champ-de-Mars, in the theatre,—the freedom and honors restored to him in his palace, had persuaded him that, if the constitution had some fanatics, royalty had no implacable enemies in his kingdom. He believed the constitution easy of execution in many of its provisions, and impracticable in others. The government which they imposed on him seemed to him as a philosophical experiment which they desired to make with their king. He only forgot one thing, and that is, the experiments of a people are catastrophes. A king who accepts the terms of a government which are impossible, accepts his own overthrow by anticipation. A well-considered and voluntary abdication is more regal than that daily abdicacation which is undergone in the degradation of power. A king saves, if not his life, at least his dignity. It is more suitable to majesty royal to descend by its own will, than to be cast down headlong. From the moment when the king is king no longer, the throne becomes the last place in the kingdom.

Be this as it may, the king frankly declared to his ministers his intention of legally executing the constitution, and of associating himself unreservedly and without guile to the will and destiny of the nation. The queen herself, by one of those sudden and inexplicable changes in the heart of woman, threw herself, with the trust of despair, into the party of the constitution. "Courage," she said to M. Bertrand de Molleville, minister and confidant of the king: "Courage! I hope with patience, firmness, and perseverance, that all is not lost."

The minister of marine, Bertrand de Molleville, wrote, by the king's orders, to the commandants of the ports a letter, signed by the king:—"I am informed," he said, in this circular, "that emigrations in the navy are fast increasing. How is it that the officers of a service always so dear to me, and which has invariably given me proofs of its attachment, are so mistaken at what is due to their country, to me, and to themselves! This extreme step would have seemed to me less surprising some time since, when anarchy was at its height, and when its termination was unseen; but now, when the nation desires to return to order and submission to the laws, is it possible that generous and faithful sailors can think of separating from their king? Tell them to remain where their country calls them. The precise execution of the constitution is to-day the surest means of appreciating its advantages, and of ascertaining what is wanting to make it perfect. It is your king who desires you to remain at your posts as he remains at his. You would have considered it a crime to resist his orders, you will not refuse his prayers."

He wrote to general officers, and to commandants of the land forces:—"In accepting the constitution, I have promised to maintain it within, and defend it against enemies without; this solemn act should banish all uncertainty. The law and the king are henceforth identified. The enemy of the law becomes that of the king. I cannot consider those sincerely devoted to my person who abandon their country at the moment when it has the greatest need of their services. Those only are attached to me who follow my example and unite with me for the public weal, and remain inseparable from the destiny of the empire!"

Finally, he ordered M. de Lessart, the minister for foreign affairs, to publish the following proclamation, addressed to the French emigrants:—"The king," thus it ran, "informed that a great number of French emigrants are withdrawing to foreign lands, cannot see without much grief such an emigration. Although the law permits to all citizens a free power to quit the kingdom, the king is anxious to enlighten them as to their duties, and the distress they are preparing for themselves. If they think, by such means, to give me a proof of their affection, let them be undeceived; my real friends are those who unite with me in order to put the laws in execution, and re-establish order and peace in the kingdom. When I accepted the constitution, I was desirous of putting an end to civil discord—I believed that all Frenchmen would second my intentions. However, it is at this moment that emigration is increasing: some depart because of the disturbances which have threatened their lives and property. Ought we not to pardon the circumstances? Have not I too my sorrows? And when I forget mine, can any one remember his perils? How can order be again established if those interested in it abandon it by abandoning themselves? Return, then, to the bosom of your country: come and give to the laws the support of good citizens. Think of the grief your obstinacy will give to the king's heart; they would be the most painful he could experience."

The Assembly was not blinded by these manifestations; it saw beneath a secret design of escaping from the severest measures; it was desirous of compelling the king to carry them out, and let us add, the nation and the public safety also required it.

XII.

Mirabeau had treated the question of the emigration of the Constituent Assembly rather as a philosopher than a statesman. He had disputed with the legislator the right of making laws against emigration: he was mistaken. Whenever a theory is in contradiction to the welfare of society it is because that theory is false, for society is the supreme truth.

Unquestionably in ordinary times, man is not imprisoned by nature, and ought not to be by the law, within the frontiers of his native land; and, with this view, the laws against emigration should only be exceptional laws. But, because exceptional, are these laws therefore unjust? Evidently not. The public danger has its peculiar laws, as necessary and as just as laws made in a time of security. A state of war is not a state of peace. You shut your frontiers to strangers in war time; you may close them to your citizens. A city is legally put in a state of siege during a sedition. We can put the nation in a state of siege in case of external danger co-existent with internal conspiracy. By what absurd abuse of liberty can a state be constrained to tolerate on a foreign soil gatherings of citizens armed against itself, which it would not tolerate in its own land? And if these gatherings should be culpable without, why should the state be interdicted from shutting up those roads which lead emigrants to these gatherings? A nation defends itself from its foreign enemies by arms, from its internal foes by its laws. To act otherwise would be to consecrate without the country the inviolability of conspiracies which were punished within: it would be to proclaim the legality of civil war, provided it was mixed up with foreign war, and that sedition was covered by treason. Such maxims ruin a whole people's nationality, in order to protect abuse of liberty by certain citizens. The Constituent Assembly was so wrong as to sanction such. Had it proclaimed from the beginning the laws repressive of emigration in troubled times, during revolutions, or on the eve of war, it would have proclaimed a national truth, and prevented one of the great dangers and principal causes of the excesses of the Revolution. The question now was no longer to be treated with reason, but by vindictive feelings. The imprudence of the Constituent Assembly had left this dangerous weapon in the hands of parties who were about to turn it against the king.

XIII.

Brissot, the inspirer of the Gironde, the dogmatic statesman of a party which needed ideas and a leader, ascended the tribune in the midst of anticipated plaudits, which betokened his importance in the new Assembly. His voice was for war, as the most efficacious of laws.

"If," said he, "it be really desired to check the tide of emigration, we must more particularly punish the more elevated offenders, who establish in foreign lands a centre of counter-revolution. We should distinguish three classes of emigrants; the brothers of the king, unworthy of belonging to him,—the public functionaries, deserting their posts and deluding citizens,—and finally, the simple citizens, who follow example from imitation, weakness, or fear. You owe hate and banishment to the first, pity and indulgence to the others. How can the citizens fear you, when the impunity of their chiefs insures their own? Have you then two scales of weights and measures? What can the emigrants think, when they see a prince, after having squandered 40,000,000 (of francs) in ten years, still receive from the National Assembly more millions, in order to provide for his extravagance and pay his debts?

"Divide the interests of the rebellious by alarming the prime criminals. Patriots are still amused by paltry palliatives against emigration; the partisans of the court have thus trifled with the credulity of the people, and you have seen even Mirabeau deriding those laws, and telling you they would never be put into execution, because a king would not himself become the accuser of his own family. Three years without success, a wandering and unhappy life, their intrigues frustrated, their conspiracies overthrown, all these defeats have not cured the emigrants; their hearts were corrupted from the cradle. Would you check this revolt? then strike the blow on the other side of the Rhine: it is not in France. It was by such decided steps that the English prevented James II. from impeding the establishment of their liberty. They did not amuse themselves with framing petty laws against emigration, but demanded that foreign princes should drive the English princes from their dominions. (Applause.) The necessity of this measure was seen here from the first. Ministers will talk to you of considerations of state, family reasons; these considerations, these weaknesses cover a crime against liberty. The king of a free people has no family. Again, I counsel you attack the leaders only; let it no longer be said, 'These malcontents are then very strong; these 25,000,000 of men must then be very weak thus to consider them.'

"It is to foreign powers especially that you should address your demands and your menaces. It is time to show to Europe what you are, and to demand of it an account of the outrages you have received from it. I say it is necessary to compel those powers to reply to us, one of two things; either they will render homage to our constitution, or they will declare against it. In the first place, you have not to balance, it is necessary that you should assail the powers that dare to threaten you. In the last century when Portugal and Spain lent an asylum to James II., England attacked both. Have no fears—the image of liberty, like the head of Medusa, will affright the armies of our enemies; they fear to be abandoned by their soldiers, and that is why they prefer the line of expectation, and an armed mediation. The English constitution and an aristocratic liberty will be the basis of the reforms they will propose to you, but you will be unworthy of all liberty if you accept yours at the hands of your enemies. The English people love your Revolution; the emperor fears the force of your arms: as to this empress of Russia, whose aversion to the French constitution is well known, and who in some degree resembles Elizabeth, she cannot hope for success more brilliant than had Elizabeth against Holland. It is with difficulty that slaves are subjugated fifteen hundred leagues off; they cannot enslave free men at this distance. I will not condescend to speak of other princes; they are not worthy of being included in the number of your serious enemies. I believe then that France ought to elevate its hopes and its attitude. Unquestionably you have declared to Europe that you will not attempt any more conquests, but you have a right to say to it, 'Choose between certain rebels and a nation.'"

XIV.

This discourse, although in several parts very contradictory, proved that Brissot had the intention of playing three parts in one, and of captivating at once the three parties in the Assembly. In his philosophical principles he affected the tone of a moderator, and repeated the axioms of Mirabeau against the laws relative to expatriation; in his attack on the princes he included the king, and held him up to the people as an object of suspicion; and lastly, in his denunciation of the diplomacy of the ministers, he urged them to a war *à l'outrance,* and displayed in this measure the energy of a patriot and the foresight of a statesman; for in case war should be the result, he did not conceal from himself the jealousy of the nation against the court, and he knew that the first act of open war would be to declare the king a traitor to his country.

This speech placed Brissot at the head of the conspirators of the Assembly; he brought to the young and untried party of the Gironde his reputation as a public writer, and a man who had had ten years' experience of the factions; the audacity of his policy flattered their impatience, and the austerity of his language made them believe in the depth of his designs. Condorcet, the friend of Brissot, and, like him, devoured by insatiable and unscrupulous ambition, mounting the tribune, merely commented on the preceding discourse, and concluded, like Brissot, by summoning the powers to pronounce for or against the constitution, and demanded the renewal of the *corps diplomatique.*

This discourse was visibly concerted, and it was evident that a party, already formed, took possession of the tribune, and was about to arrogate to itself the dominion of the Assembly. Brissot was its conspirator, Condorcet its philosopher, Vergniaud its orator. Vergniaud mounted the tribune, with all the *prestige* of his marvellous eloquence, the fame of which had long preceded him. The eager looks of the Assembly, the silence that prevailed, announced in him one of the great actors of the revolutionary drama, who only appear on the stage to win themselves popularity, to intoxcate themselves with applause, and—to die

XV.

Vergniaud, born at Limoges, and an advocate at the bar of Bordeaux, was now in his thirty-third year, for the revolutionary movement had seized on and borne him along with its currents when very young. His dignified, calm, and unaffected features announced the conviction of his power. Facility, that agreeable concomitant of genius, had rendered alike pliable his talents, his character, and even the position he assumed. A certain *nonchalance* announced that he easily laid aside these faculties from the conviction of his ability to recover all his forces at the moment when he should require them. His brow was contemplative, his look composed, his mouth serious and somewhat sad; the deep inspiration of antiquity was mingled in his physiognomy with the smiles and the carelessness of youth. At the foot of the tribune he was loved with familiarity; as he ascended it each man was surprised to find that he inspired him with admiration and respect; but at the first words that fell from the speaker's lips they felt the immense distance between the man and the orator. He was an instrument of enthusiasm, whose value and whose place was in his inspiration. This inspiration, heightened by the deep musical tones of his voice, and an extraordinary power of language, had drunk in deep draughts at the purest sources of antiquity; his sentences had all the images and harmony of poesy, and if he had not been the orator of a democracy he would have been its philosopher and its poet. His genius, devoted to the people, yet forbade him to descend to the language of the people, even to flatter them. All his passions were noble as his words, and he adored the Revolution as a sublime philosophy destined to ennoble the nation without immolating on its altars other victims than prejudices and tyranny. He had doctrines, and no hatreds; the thirst of glory, and not of ambition,—nay, power itself was, in his eyes, too real, too vulgar a thing for him to aim at, and he disdained it for himself, and alone sought it for his ideas. Glory and posthumous fame were his objects alone; he mounted the tribune to behold them, and he beheld them later from the scaffold; and he plunged into the future, young, handsome, immortal in the annals of France, with all his enthusiasm, and some few stains, already effaced in his generous blood. Such was the man whom nature had given to the Girondists as their chief. He disdained the office, although he possessed all the qualities and the views, of a statesman; too careless to be the leader of a party, too great to be second to any one. Such was Vergniaud,—more illustrious than useful to his friends; he would not lead, but immortalized, them.

We will describe this great man more in detail at the period when his talent places him in a more conspicuous situation. "Are there circumstances," said he, "in which the natural rights of man can permit a nation to adopt any measure against emigrations?" Vergniaud spoke against those pretended natural rights, and recognized, above all individual rights, the right of society, which comprises and dominates over all, just as the whole predominates over a portion: he compared political liberty to the right of a citizen to do what he pleases, provided he do nothing injurious to his country; but there he stops. Man can, no doubt, materially use this right to abdicate the country in which he was born and to which he belongs, as the limb belongs to the body, but this abdication is treason; for it severs the union between the nation and himself, and the nation no longer owes him or his property any protection. After having on this principle destroyed the puerile distinction between the functionary and the mere emigrant, he proved that society falls into decay if she refuse herself the right of retaining those who forsake her in her hour of danger and difficulty. When she gave him all the universe for his country, she refused him that which gave him birth. But what will be the consequence if this emigrant, ceasing to play merely the part of a cowardly fugitive, becomes a foe, and, assembling with his fellow-traitors, surrounds the nation with a band of conspirators? What, shall attack be permitted to the émigrés, and good citizens forbidden to defend themselves?

XVI.

"But," continued he, "is France in this situation that she ought to fear from these men, who are about to excite all the ancient hatreds of the foreign courts against us? No; we shall soon see these proud mendicants, who are now receiving the roubles of Catherine and the millions of Holland, expiate in shame and misery the crimes their pride has entailed on them. Moreover these kings hesitate to attack us; they know that, to the spirit of philosophy that has infused into us the breath of liberty, there are no Pyrenees; they dread that the foot of their soldiers should touch a soil that blazes with this holy flame; they tremble, lest on the day of battle the patriots of every country should recognize each other, and two armies ready to combat be converted into a band of brethren, united against their tyrants. But should it be necessary to appeal to arms, we well remember that a thousand Greeks, combating for liberty, trampled on a million of Persians.

"We are told 'the émigrés have no evil designs against their country; it is only a temporary absence: where are the legal proofs of what you assert? when you produce them it will be time enough to punish the guilty.' Oh you who use such language, why were you not in the Roman senate when Cicero denounced Catiline? You would have asked him for the legal proof. I can picture his astonishment to myself: whilst he sought for proofs Rome would have been sacked, and you and Catiline have reigned over a heap of ruins. Legal proofs! And have you calculated the blood they will cost you to obtain? Now let us forestall our enemies, by adopting rigorous measures; let us rid the nation of this swarm of insects, greedy of its blood,—by whom it is pursued and tormented. But what should these measures be? In the first place seize on the property of the absentees. This is but a petty measure, you will say. What matter its importance or its insignificancy, so that it be just? As for the officers who have deserted, the *Code pénal* prescribes their fate—death and infamy. The French princes are even more culpable; and the summons to return to their country, which it is proposed to address to them, is neither sufficient for your honor nor your safety. Their attempts are openly made; either they must tremble before you, or you must tremble before them; you must choose. Men talk of the profound grief this will cause the king: Brutus immolated his guilty offspring at the shrine of his country, but the heart of Louis XVI. shall not be put to so severe a trial. If these princes, alike bad brothers and citizens, refuse to obey, let him turn to the hearts of the French nation, and they will amply repay his losses." (Loud applause.)

Pastoret, who spoke after Vergniaud, quoted the saying of Montesquieu, "*There is a time when it is necessary to cast a veil over the statue of Liberty, as we conceal the statues of the gods.*" To be ever on the watch, and to fear nothing, should be the maxim of every free people. He concluded by proposing repressive, but moderate and gradual measures, against the absentees.

XVII.

Isnard declared that the measures proposed until then were satisfactory to prudence, but not to justice, and the vengeance which an outraged nation owed to itself; and he thus continued :—

"If I am allowed to speak the truth, I shall. say, that if we do not punish all these heads of the rebellion, it is not that we do not know, at the bottom of our hearts, that they are guilty, but because they are princes; and, although we have destroyed the nobility and distinctions of blood, these vain phantoms still affect our minds. Ah! it is time that this great level of equality, which has passed over France, should at length take its full effect. Then only will they believe in our equality. You should fear by this evidence of impunity that you may urge the people to excesses. The anger of the people is but too often the sequel to the silence of the laws. The law should enter the palaces of the great, as well as in the hovel of the poor, and as inexorable as death, when it falls upon the guilty, should make no distinction between ranks and titles. They try to lull you to sleep. I tell you that the nation should watch incessantly. Despotism and aristocracy do not sleep; and if nations doze but for a moment, they awake in fetters. If the fire of heaven was in the power of men, it should be darted at those who attempt the liberties of the people: thus, the people never pardon conspirators against their liberties. When the Gauls scaled the walls of the capitol, Manlius awoke, hastened to the breach, and saved the republic That same Manlius, subsequently accused of conspiring against public liberty, was cited before the tribunes. He presented bracelets, javelins, twelve civic crowns, thirty spoils torn from conquered enemies, and his breast scarred with cicatrices; he reminded them that he had saved Rome, and yet the sole reply was to cast him headlong from the same rock whence he had precipitated the Gauls. These, sirs, were a free people.

"And we, since the day we acquired our liberty, have not ceased to pardon our patricians their conspiracies, have not ceased to recompense their crimes by sending them chariots of gold: as for me, if I voted such gifts, I should die of remorse. The people contemplate and judge us, and on their sentence depends the destiny of our labors. Cowards, we lose the public confidence; firm, our enemies would be disconcerted. Do not then sully the sanctity of the oath, by making it pause in deference before mouths thirsting for our blood. Our enemies will swear with one hand, whilst with the other they will sharpen their swords against us."

Each violent sentence in this harangue excited in the Assembly and the tribunes those displays of public feeling which found expression in loud applause. It was felt that, for the future, the only line of policy would be in the anger of the nation; that the time for philosophy in the tribune was passed, and that the Assembly would not be slow in throwing aside principles in order to take up arms.

The Girondists, who did not wish that Isnard should have gone so far, felt that it was necessary to follow him whithersoever popularity should lead him. In vain did Condorcet defend his proposition for a delay of the decree. The Assembly, in a report brought up by Ducastel, adopted the decree of its legislative committee. The principal clauses were, that the French, assembled on the other side of the frontiers, should be, from that moment, declared actuated by conspiracy towards France; that they should be declared actual conspirators, if they did not return before the 1st of January, 1792, and as such punished with death; that the French princes, brothers of the king, should be punishable with death, like other emigrants, if they did not obey the summons thus sent to them; that, for the present, their revenues should be sequestrated; and, finally, that those military and naval officers who abandoned their posts without leave, or their resignation being accepted, should be considered as deserters, and punished with death.

XVIII

These two decrees struck terror to the heart of the king, and consternation to his council. The constitution gave him the right of suspending them by the royal *veto;* but to suspend the effects of the national indignation against the armed enemies of the Revolution, was to invoke it on his own head. The Girondists artfully fomented these elements of discord between the Assembly and the king. They impatiently awaited until the refusal to sanction the decrees should urge irritation to its height, and force the king to fly or place himself in their hands.

The most monarchical spirit of the Constituent Assembly still reigned in the Directory of the department of Paris. Desmeuniers, Baumetz, Talleyrand-Perigord, Larochefoucauld, were the principal members. They drew up an address to the king, entreating him to refuse his sanction to the decree against the nonjuring priests. This address, in which the Legislative Assembly was treated with much disdain, breathes the true spirit of government as regards religious matters. It is comprised in the axiom which is or ought to be the code of all consciences, "Since no religion is a law, let no religion be a crime!"

A young writer whose name, already celebrated, was to be hereafter consecrated by martyrdom, André Chénier, considering the question in the highest strain of philosophy, published on the same subject a letter worthy of posterity. It is the property of genius not to allow its views to be obscured by the prejudices of the moment. Its gaze is too lofty for vulgar errors to deprive it of the ever-during light of truth. It has by anticipation in its decisions the impartiality of the future.

"All those," says André Chénier, "who have preserved the liberty of their reason, and in whom patriotism is not a violent desire for rule, see with much pain that the dissensions of the priests have of necessity occupied the first sittings of the Assembly. It is true that the public mind is enlightened on this point, on which even the Constituent Assembly itself is deceived. It has pretended to form a civil code of religion, that is to say, it had the idea of creating one priesthood after having destroyed another. Of what consequence is it that one religion differs from another? Is it for the National Assembly to re-unite the divided sects, and weigh all their differences? Are politicians theologians?

We shall only be delivered from the influence of these men when the National Assembly shall have maintained for each the perfect liberty of following or inventing whatsoever religion may please it; when every one shall pay for the worship he prefers to adopt, and pays for no other; and when the impartiality of tribunals, in such cases, shall punish alike the persecutors or the seditious of all forms of worship: and the members of the National Assembly say also, that all the French people are not yet sufficiently ripe for this doctrine. We must reply to them,—this may be, but it is for you to ripen us by your words, your acts, your laws! Priests do not trouble states when states do not trouble them. Let us remember that eighteen centuries have seen all the Christian sects, torn and bleeding from theological absurdities and sacerdotal hatreds, always terminate by arming themselves with popular power."

This letter passed over the heads of the parties who disputed the conscience of the people; but the petition of the Directory of Paris, which demanded the *veto* of the king against the decrees of the Assembly, produced violent opposition petitions. For the first time, Legendre, a butcher of Paris, appeared at the bar of the Assembly, where he vociferated in oratorical strain the imprecations of the people against the enemies of the nation and crowned traitors. Legendre decked his trivial ideas in high-sounding language. From this junction of vulgar ideas with the ambitious expressions of the tribune sprung that strange language in which the fragments of thought are mingled with the tinsel of words, and thus the popular eloquence of the period resembles the ill-combined display at an extravagant *parvenu*. The populace was proud at robbing the aristocracy of its language, even to turn it against them; but whilst it filched, it soiled it. "Representatives," said Legendre, "bid the eagle of victory and fame to soar over your heads and ours; say to the ministers, We love the people,—let your punishment begin: the tyrants must die!"

XIX.

Camille Desmoulins, the Aristophanes of the Revolution, then borrowed the sonorous voice of the Abbé Fauchet, in order to make himself heard. Camille Desmoulins was the Voltaire of the streets; he struck on the chord of passion by his sarcasms. "Representatives," said he, "the applauses of the people are its civil list: the inviolabililty of the king is a thing most infinitely just, for he ought, by nature, to be always in opposition to the general will and our interest. One does not voluntarily fall from so great a height. Let us take example from God, whose *commandments are never impossible;* let us not require from the *ci-devant* sovereign an *impossible love* of the national sovereignty is it not very natural that he should give his *veto* to the best decrees? But let the magistrates of the people—let the Directory of Paris—let the same men, who, four months since, in the Champ-de-Mars, fired upon the citizens who were signing a petition against one decree, inundate the empire with a petition, which is evidently but the first page of a vast register of counter-revolution, a subscription to civil war, sent by them for signature to all the fanatics, all the idiots, all the slaves, all the robbers of the eighty-three departments, at the head of which are the exemplary names of the members of the Directory of Paris—fathers of their country! There is in this such a complication of ingratitude and fraud, prevarication and perverseness, philosophical hypocrisy and perfidious moderation, that on the instant we rally round the decrees and around yourselves. Continue faithful, mandatories, and if they obstinately persist in not permitting you to save the nation, well, then, we will save it ourselves! For at last the power of the royal *veto* will have a term, and the taking of the Bastille is not prevented by a *veto*.

"For a long while we have been in possession of the civism of our Directory, when we saw it in an incendiary proclamation, not only again open the evangelical pulpits to the priests, but the seditious tribunes to conspirators in surplices! Their address is a manifesto tending to degrade the constitutional powers: it is a collective petition—it is an incentive to civil war, and the overthrow of the constitution. Assuredly we are no admirers of the representative government, of which we think with J. J. Rousseau; and if we like certain articles but little, still less do we like civil war. So many grounds of accusation! The crime of these men is settled. Strike, then! If the head sleeps, shall the arm act? Raise not that arm again; do not rouse the national club only to crush insects. A Varnier or De Lâtre! Did Cato and Cicero accuse Cethegus or Catiline? It is the leaders we should assail. Strike at the head."

The strain of irony and boldness, less applauded by the clapping of hands than by shouts of laughter, delighted the tribunes. They voted the sending of the *procès verbal* of the meeting into every department. It was legislatively elevating a pamphlet to the dignity of a public act, and to distribute ready-made insult to the citizens, that they might have a supply to vent against public authority. The king trembled before the pamphleteer; he felt from this first treatment of his baffled prerogative that the constitution would crumble in his hands each time that he dared to make use of it.

The next day the constitutional party in greater force at the meeting recalled the sending of this pamphlet to the departments. Brissot was angry in his journal, the *Patriote Français*. It was there and at the Jacobins more than in the tribune, that he gave instructions to his party, and allowed the idea of a republic to escape him. Brissot had not the properties of an orator: his dogged spirit, sectarian and arbitrary, was fitter for conspiracy than action: the ardor of his mind was excessive, but concentrated. He shed neither those lights nor those flames which kindle enthusiasm—that explosion of ideas. It was the lamp of the Gironde party; it was neither its beacon nor its torch.

XX.

The Jacobins, weakened for a time by the great number of their members elected to the Legislative Assembly, remained for a brief space without a fixed course to pursue, like an army disbanded after victory. The club of the Feuillants, composed of the remains of the constitutional party in the Constituted Assembly, strove to resume the ascendency over the mind of the people. Barnave, Lameth, and Duport were the leaders of this party. Fearful of the people, and convinced that an Assembly without anything to counterbalance it would inevitably absorb the poor remnant of the monarchy, this party wished to have two chambers and an equally poised constitution. Barnave, whose repentance had led him to join this party, remained at Paris, and had secret interviews with Louis XVI.; but his counsels, like those of Mirabeau in his latter days, were but vain regrets, for the Revolution was beyond their power to control, and no longer obeyed them. They yet, however, maintained some influence over the constituted bodies of Paris, and the resolutions of the king, who could not bring himself to believe that these men, who yesterday were so powerful against it, were to-day destitute of influence; and they formed his last hope against the new enemies he saw in the Girondists.

The national guard, the directory of the department of Paris! the mayor of Paris himself, Bailly, and all that party in the nation who wished to maintain order, still supported them—theirs was the party of repentance and terror. M. de La Fayette, Madame de Stäel, and M. de Narbonne, had a secret understanding with the Feuillants, and a part of the press was on their side. These papers sought to render M. de Narbonne popular, and to obtain for him the post of minister of war. The Girondist papers already excited the anger of the people against this party. Brissot sowed the seeds of calumny and suspicion: he denounced them to the hatred of the nation. "Number them—name them," said he; "their names denounce them; they are the relics of the dethroned aristocracy, who would fain resuscitate a constitutional nobility, establish a second legislative chamber and a senate of nobles, and who implore, in order to gain their ends, the armed intervention of the powers. They have sold themselves to the Château de Tuileries, and sell there a great portion of the members of the Assembly; they have amongst them neither men of genius nor men of resolution; their talent is but treason, their genius but intrigue."

It was thus that the Girondists and the Jacobins, though at this moment beaten, prepared those enmities against the Feuillants that, at no remote period, were destined to disperse the club. Whilst the Girondists followed this course, the royalists continually urged the people to excesses through the medium of their papers, in order, as they said, to find a remedy for the evil in the evil itself. Thus they encouraged the Jacobins against the Feuillants, and heaped ridicule and insult on those leaders of the constitutional party who sought to save a remnant of the monarchy; for that which they detested most was the success of the Revolution. Their doctrine of absolute power was less humiliatingly contradicted in their eyes by the overthrow of the empire and throne, than in the constitutional monarchy that preserved at once the king and liberty. Since the aristocracy lost the possession of the supreme power, its sole ambition—its only aim—was to see it fall into the hands of those most unworthy to hold it. Incapable of again rising by its own force, it sought to find in disorder the means of so doing; and from the first day of the Revolution to the last, this party had no other instinct, and it was thus that it ruined itself whilst it ruined the monarchy. It carried the hatred of the Revolution even to posterity; and though they did not take an active part in the crimes of the Revolution, yet their best wishes were with it. Every fresh excess of the people gave a new ray of hope to its enemies: such is the policy of despair, blind and criminal as herself.

XXI.

An example of this at this moment occurred. La Fayette resigned the command of the national guard into the hands of the council general of the commune. At this meeting blazed the last faint spark of popular favor. After he quitted the chamber a deliberation was held as to what mark of gratitude and regard the city of Paris should offer him. The general addressed a farewell letter to the civic force, and affected to believe that the formation of the constitution was the era of the Revolution, and reduced him, like Washington, to the rank of a simple citizen of a free country. "The time of revolution," said he, in this letter, "has given place to a regular organization, owing to the liberty and prosperity it assures us. I feel it is now my duty to my country to return unreservedly into her hands all the force and influence with which I was intrusted for her defence during the tempests that convulsed her—such is my only ambition. Beware how you believe," added he, in conclusion, "that every species of despotism is extinct!" And he then proceeded to point out some of those perils and excesses into which liberty might fall at her first outset.

This letter was received by the national guard with an enthusiasm rather feigned than sincere. They wished to strike a last blow against the factious by adhering to the principles of their general, and voted to him a sword forged from the bolts of the Bastille, and a marble statue of Washington. La Fayette hastened to enjoy this premature triumph, and resigned the dictatorship at the moment when a dictatorship was most necessary to his country. On his retirement to his estates in Auvergne, he received the deputation of the national guard, who brought him the *procès verbal* of the debate. "You behold me once more amidst the scenes where I was born," said he; "I shall not again quit them, save to defend and confirm our new-formed liberty should it be menaced."

The different opinions of parties followed him in his retirement. "Now," said the *Journal de la Revolution,* "that the hero of two worlds has played out his part at Paris, we are curious to know if the ex-general has done more harm than good to the Revolution. In order to solve the problem, let us examine his acts. We shall first see that the founder of American liberty does not dare comply with the wishes of the people in Europe, until he had asked permission from the monarch. We shall see that he grew pale at the sight of the Parisian army on its road to Versailles—alike deceiving the people and the king; to the one he said, 'I deliver the king into your power,' to the other, 'I bring you my army.' We should have seen him return to Paris, dragging in his train those brave citizens who were alone guilty of having sought to destroy the keep of Vincennes as they had destroyed the Bastille, their hands bound behind their backs. We see him on the morrow of the *journeé des poignards,* touch the hands of those whom he had denounced to public indignation the yesterday. And now we behold him quit the cause of liberty, by a decree which he himself had secretly solicited, and disappear for a moment in Auvergne to re-appear on our frontiers. Yet he has done us some service, let us acknowledge it. We owe to him to have accustomed our national guards to go through the civic and religious ceremonies; to bear the fatigue of the morning drill in the Champs Elysées; to take patriotic oaths and to give suppers. Let us then bid him adieu! La Fayette, to consummate the greatest revolution that a nation ever attempted, we required a leader, whose mind was on an equality with so great an event. We accepted you; the pliability of your features, your studied orations, your premeditated axioms—all those productions of art that nature disavows, seemed suspicious to the more clear-sighted patriots. The boldest of them followed you, tore the mask from your visage, and cried—Citizens, this hero is but a courtier, this sage but an impostor. Now, thanks to you, the Revolution can no longer bite, you have cut the lion's claws; the people is more formidable to its conductors; they have reassumed the whip and spur, and you fly. Let civic crowns strew your paths, though we remain; but where shall we find a Brutus?"

XXII.

Bailly, mayor of Paris, withdrew at the same time, abandoned by that party of whom he had been the idol, and whose victim he began to be; but his philosophic mind rated more highly the good done to the people than its favor, and more ambitious of being useful than of governing it, he already testified that heroic contempt for the calumnies of his enemies he afterwards displayed for death.

His voice was, however, lost in the tumult of the approaching municipal elections; two men already disputed the dignity of mayor of Paris, for in proportion as the royal authority declined, and that of the constitution was absorbed in the troubles of the kingdom, the mayor of Paris would become the real dictator of the capital.

These two men were La Fayette and Pétion. La Fayette supported by the constitutionalists and the national guard, Pétion by the Girondists and the Jacobins. The royalist party, by pronouncing for or against one of them, would decide the election. The king had no longer the influence of the government, which he had suffered to escape from his grasp, but he still possessed the occult powers of corruption over the leaders of the different parties. A portion of the twenty-five millions of francs (1000,000*l.*) was applied by M. de Laporte, the intendant de la liste civile, and by MM. Bertrand de Molleville and Montmorin, his ministers, in purchasing votes at the elections, motions at the clubs, applause or hisses in the Assembly. These subsidies, which had commenced with Mirabeau, now descended to the lowest dregs of the factions; they bribed the royalist press, and found their way into the hands of the orators and writers apparently most inveterate against the court; and many false manœuvres, to which the people were urged, arose from no other source. There was a ministry of corruption, over which perfidy presided. Many obtained from this source, under pretence of aiding the court, the power of moderating or betraying the people; then fearing lest their treachery should be discovered, they hid it by a second betrayal, and turned against the king his own motions. Danton was of this number. Sometimes, through motives of charity or peace, the king gave a monthly sum to be distributed amongst the national guard, and the *quartiers* in which insurrection was most to be apprehended. M. de La Fayette, and Pétion himself, often drew money from this source. Thus the king could, by employing those means, insure the election, and by joining the constitutionalist party determine the choice of Paris in favor of M. de La Fayette. M. de La Fayette was one of the first originators of this revo lution which humbled the throne; his name was associated with every humiliation of the court, with all the resentment of the queen, all the terrors of the king; he had been first their dread, then their protector, and, lastly, their guardian: could he be now their hope? Would not this post of mayor of Paris, this vast, civil, and popular dignity, after this long-armed dictatorship in the capital, be to La Fayette but a second stepping-stone that would raise him higher than the throne, and cast the king and constitution into the shade? This man, with his theoretically liberal ideas, was well-intentioned, and wished rather to dominate than to reign; but could any reliance be placed on these good intentions that had been so often overcome? Was it not full of these good intentions that he had usurped the command of the civic force—captured the Bastille with the insurgent Gardes Françaises—marched to Versailles at the head of the populace of Paris—suffered the château to be forced on the 6th of October—arrested the royal family at Varennes, and retained the king a prisoner in his own palace? Would he now resist should the people again command him? Would he abandon the *rôle* of the French Washington when he had half fulfilled it? The human heart is so constituted that we rather prefer to cast ourselves into the power of those who would destroy us than seek safety from those who humiliate us. La Fayette humiliated the king, and more especially the queen.

A respectful independence was the habitual expression of La Fayette's countenance in the presence of Marie Antoinette. There was perceptible in the general's attitude, it was to be seen in his words, distinguishable in his accent, beneath the cold and polished forms of the courtier, the inflexibility of the citizen. The queen preferred the factions. She thus plainly spoke to her confidents. "M. de La Fayette," she said, "will not be the mayor of Paris in order that he may the sooner become the *maire du Palais*. Pétion is a Jacobin, a republican; but he is a fool, incapable of ever becoming the leader of a party: he would be a nullity as *maire*, and, besides, the very interest he knows we should take in his nomination might bind him to the king."

Pétion was the son of a *procureur* at Chartres, and a townsman of Brissot; was brought up in the same way as he,—in the same studies, same philosophy, same hatreds. They were two men of the same mind. The Revolution, which had been the ideal of their youth, had called them on the scene the same day, but to play very different parts. Brissot, the scribe, political adventurer, journalist, was the man of theory; Pétion, the practical man. He had in his countenance, in his character, and his talents, that solemn mediocrity which is of the multitude, and charms it; at least he was a sincere man, a virtue which the people appreciate beyond all others in those who are concerned in public affairs. Called by his fellow-citizens to the National Assembly, he acquired there a name rather from his efforts than his success. The fortunate compeer of Robespierre, and then his friend, they had formed by themselves that popular party, scarcely visible at the beginning, which professed pure democracy and the philosophy of J. J. Rousseau; whilst Cazalès, Mirabeau, and Maury, the nobility, clergy, and *bourgeoisie,* alone disputed the government. The despotism of a class appeared to Robespierre and Pétion as odious as the despotism of a king. The triumph of the *tiers état* was of little consequence, so long as the people, that is to say, all human kind, in its widest acceptation, did not prevail. They had given themselves as a task, not victory to one class over another, but the victory and organization of a divine and absolute principle—humanity. This was their weakness in the first days of the Revolution, and subsequently, their strength. Pétion was beginning to gather in its harvest.

He had gradually, by his doctrines and his speeches, insinuated himself into the confidence of the people of Paris; he connected himself with literary men by the cultivation of his mind; with the Orleans party by his intimacy with Madame de Genlis, the favorite of the prince, and governess to his children. He was spoken of in one place as a sage, who sought to imbody philosophy in the constitution; in another as a sagacious conspirator, who desired to sap the throne, or to place upon it the Duc D'Orleans, imbodying the interests and dynasty of the people. This twofold reputation was equally advantageous to him. Honest men believed him to be an honest man,—malcontents to be a malcontent: the court disdained to fear him; it saw in him only an innocent Utopian, and had for him that contemptuous indulgence which aristocrats have invariably for men of political creed; besides, Pétion ridded it of La Fayette. To change its foe was to give it breathing time.

These three elements of success gave Pétion an immense majority; he was nominated mayor of Paris by more than 6,000 votes. La Fayette had but 3,000. He might at this moment, from the depth of his retreat, have fairly measured by these figures the decline of his popularity. La Fayette represented the city, Pétion the nation. The armed *bourgeoisie* quitted public affairs with the one, and the people assumed them with the other. The Revolution marked with a proper name the fresh step she had made.

Pétion, scarcely elected, went in triumph to the Jacobins, and was thus carried in the arms of patriots into the tribune. Old Dusault, who occupied it at the moment, stammered out a few words, interrupted by his sobs, in honor of his pupil. "I look on M..Pétion," said he, "as my son; it is very bold no doubt." Pétion, overcome, embraced the old man with ardor; the tribunes applauded and wept.

The other nominations were made in the same spirit. Manuel* was named *procureur de la commune*;—Danton, his deputy, which was his first step in popularity; he did not owe it, like Pétion, to the public esteem, but to his own intriguing. He was appointed in spite of his reputation. The people are apt to excuse the vices they find useful.

The nomination of Pétion to the office of *maire* of Paris gave the Girondists a constant *point d'appui* in the capital. Paris, as well as the Assembly, escaped from the king's hands. The work of the Constituent Assembly crumbled away in three months. The wheels gave way before they were set in motion. All presaged an approaching collision between the executive power and the power of the Assembly. Whence arose this sudden decomposition? It is now the moment for throwing a glance over this labor of the Constituent Assembly and its framers.

BOOK VII.

I.

THE Constituent Assembly had abdicated in a storm.

This assembly had consisted of the most imposing body of men that had ever represented, not only France, but the human race. It was in fact the œcumenical council of modern

* Co-editor with Hébert of the disgusting "Père Duchesne."—H. T. R.

reason and philosophy. Nature seemed to have created expressly, and the different orders of society to have reserved for this work, the geniuses, characters, and even vices most requisite to give to this focus of the lights of the age the greatness, *éclat*, and movement of a fire destined to consume the remnants of an old society, and to illumine a new one. There were sages, like Bailly and Mounier; thinkers, like Siéyès; factious partisans, like Barnave; statesmen like Talleyrand; men, epochs, like Mirabeau, and men, principles, like Robespierre. Each cause was personified by what most distinguished each party. The very victims were illustrious. Cazalès, Malouet, Maury, sounded forth in bursts of grief and eloquence the successive falls of the throne, the aristocracy, and the clergy. This active centre of the thoughts of a century, was sustained during the whole time by the storm of perpetual political conflict. Whilst they were deliberating within, the people were acting without, and struck at the doors. These twenty-six months of consultations were one uninterrupted sedition. Scarcely had one institution crumbled to pieces in the tribune, than the nation swept it away to clear the space for another institution. The anger of the people was only its impatience of obstacles, its madness was only the excitement of its reason. Even in its fury it was always a truth that agitated it. The tribunes only blinded, by dazzling it. The unique characteristic of this Assembly was that passion for the ideal which it always felt itself irresistibly urged on to accomplish. An act of perpetual faith in reason and justice: a holy passion for the good and right, which possessed it, and made it devote itself to its work; like the statuary who seeing the fire in the furnace, where he was casting his bronze, on the point of being extinguished, threw his furniture, his children's bed, and even his house into the flame, preferring rather that all should perish than that his work should be lost.

Thus it is that the Revolution has become a date in the human mind, and not merely an event in the history of the people. The men of the Constituent Assembly were not Frenchmen, they were universal men. We mistake, we vilify them when we consider them only as priests, aristocrats, plebeians, faithful subjects, malcontents or demagogues. They were, and they felt themselves to be, better than that, —workmen of God; called by him to restore social reason, and found right and justice throughout the universe. None of them, except those who opposed the Revolution, limited the extent of its thought to the boundaries of France. The declaration of the Rights of Man proves this. It was the decalogue of the human race in all languages. The modern Revolution called the Gentiles, as well as the Jews, to partake of the light and reign of Fraternity.

II.

Thus, not one of its apostles who did not proclaim peace amongst nations. Mirabeau, La Fayette, Robespierre himself erased war from the symbol which they presented to the nation. It was the malcontent and ambitious who subsequently demanded it, and not the leading Revolutionists. When war burst out the Revolution had degenerated. The Constituent Assembly took care not to place on the frontiers of France the boundaries of its truths, and to limit the sympathizing soul of the French Revolution to a narrow patriotism. The globe was the country of its dogmata. France was only the workshop; it worked for all other people. Respectful of, or indifferent to, the question of national territories, from the first moment it forbade conquest. It only reserved to itself the property, or rather the invention of universal truths which it brought to light. As vast as humanity, it had not the selfishness to isolate itself. It desired to give, and not to deprive. It sought to spread itself by right, and not by force. Essentially spiritual, it sought no other empire for France than the voluntary empire which imitation by the human mind conferred upon it.

Its work was prodigious, its means a nullity; all that enthusiasm can inspire, the Assembly undertook and perfected, without a king, without a military leader, without a dictator, without an army, without any other strength than deep conviction. Alone, in the midst of an amazed people, with a disbanded army, an emigrating aristocracy, a despoiled clergy, a conspiring court, a seditious city, hostile Europe—it did what it designed. Such is the will, such the real power of a people—and such is truth, the irresistible auxiliary of the men who agitate themselves for God. If ever inspiration was visible in the prophet or ancient legislator, it may be asserted that the Constituent Assembly had two years of sustained inspiration. France was the inspired of civilization.

III.

Let us examine its work. The principle of power was entirely displaced; royalty had ended by believing that it was the exclusive depositary of power. It had demanded of religion to consummate this robbery in the eyes of the people, by telling them that tyranny came from God, and was responsible to God only. The long heirship of throned races had made it believed that there was a right of reigning in the blood of crowned families. Government instead of being a function had become a possession; the king master instead of being chief. This misplaced principle displaced everything. The people became a nation, the king a crowned magistrate. Feudality, subaltern royalty, assumed the rank of actual property. The clergy, which had had institutions and inviolable property, was now only a body paid by the state for a sacred service. It was from this only one step to receiving a voluntary salary for an individual service. The magistracy ceased to be hereditary. They left it its unremovability to conform its independence. It was an exception to the principle of offices when a dismissal was possible, a semi-sovereignty of justice—but it was one step towards the truth. The legislative power was distinct from the executive power. The nation in an assembly freely chosen, declared its will, and the heredtiary and irresponsible king executed it. Such was the whole mechanism of the Constitution—a people—a king—a minister. But the king irresponsible, and consequently passive, was evidently a concession to custom, the respectful fiction of suppressed royalty.

IV.

He was no longer will; for to will is to do. He was not a functionary; for the functionary acts and replies. The king did not reply. He was but a majestic inutility in the constitution. The functions destroyed, they left the functionary. He had but one attribute, the *suspensive veto*, which consisted of his right to suspend, for three years, the execution of the Assembly's decrees. He was an obstacle; legal, but impotent for the wishes of the nation. It was evident that the Constituent Assembly, perfectly convinced of the superfluity of the throne in a national government, had only placed a king at the summit of its institutions to check ambition, and that the kingdom should not be called a republic.

The only part of such a king was to prevent the truth from appearing, and to make a show in the eyes of a people accustomed to a sceptre. This fiction, or this nullity cost the people 30,000,000 (of francs) a year in the civil list, a court, continual jealousies, and the interminable corruption practised by the court on the organs of the nation. This was the real vice of the constitution of 1791: it was not consistent. Royalty embarrassed the constitution; and all that embarrasses injures. The motive of this inconsistency was less an error of its reason than a respectful piety for an ancient prejudice, and a generous tenderness towards a race which had long worn the crown. If the race of the Bourbons had been extinct in the month of September, 1791, certainly the Constituent Assembly would not have invented a king.

V.

However, the royalty of '91, very little different from the royalty of to-day, could work for a century, as well as a day. The error of all historians is to attribute to the vices of the constitution the brief duration of the work of the Constituent Assembly. In the first place, the work of the Constituent Assembly was not principally to perpetuate this wheelwork of useless royalty, placed out of complaisance to the people's eyes, in machinery which did not regulate it. The work of the Constituent Assembly was the regeneration of ideas and government, the displacing of power, the restoration of right, the abolition of all subjugation even of the mind, the freedom of consciences, the formation of an administration; and this work lasts, and will endure as long as the name of France. The vice of the institution of 1791 was not in any one particular point. It has not perished because the *veto* of the king was suspensive instead of absolute; it has not perished, because the right of peace or war was taken from the king, and reserved to the nation; it has not perished, because it did not place the legislative power in one chamber only instead of in two: these asserted vices are to be found in many other constitutions, which still endure. The diminution of the royal power was not the main danger to royalty in '91; it was rather its salvation, if it could have been saved.

VI.

The more power was given to the king, and action to the monarchical principle, the quicker the king and the principle would have fallen; for the greater would have been the distrust and hatred against him. Two chambers, instead of one, would not have preserved anything. Such divisions of power would have no value, but in proportion as they are sacred. They are only sacred in proportion as they are the representatives of real existing force in the nation. Would a revolution which had not paused before the iron gates of the Château of Versailles have respected the metaphysical distinction of power of two kinds!

Besides, where were, and where would be now, the constitutive elements of two chambers, in a nation whose entire revolution is but a convulsion towards unity? If the second chamber be democratic and temporary, it is but a twofold democracy with but one common impulse. It can only serve to retard the common impulse, or destroy the unity of the public will. If it be hereditary and aristocratic, it supposes an aristocracy pre-existent in, and acknowledged by, the state. Where was this aristocracy in 1791? Where is it now? A modern historian says, "In the nobility, in the presence of social inequalities." But the Revolution was made against the nobility, and in order to level social hereditary inequalities. It was to ask of the Revolution itself to make a counter-revolution. Besides, these pretended divisions of power are always fictions; power is never really divided. It is always here or there, in reality and in its integrity,—it is not to be divided. It is like the will, it is *one* or it is not. If there be two chambers, it is in one of the two; the other complies or is dissolved. If there be one chamber and a king, it is in the king or the chamber. In the king, if he subjugates the Assembly by force, or if he buys it by corruption; in the chamber if it agitates the public mind, and intimidates the court and the army by the power of its language, and the superiority of its opinions. Those who do not see this have no eyes. In this *soi-disant* balance of power there is always a controlling weight: equilibrium is a chimera. If it did exist, it would produce mere immobility.

VII.

The Constituent Assembly had then done a good work; wise, and as durable as are the institutions of a people in travail, in an age of transition. The constitution of '91 had written all the truths of the times, and reduced all human reason to its epoch. All was true in its work except royalty, which had but one wrong, which was making the monarchy the depository of its code.

We have seen that this very fault was an excess of virtue. It receded before the deposing from the throne the family of its kings; it had the superstition of the past without having its faith, and desired to reconcile the republic and the monarchy. It was a virtue in its intentions; it was a mistake in its results; for it is an error in politics to attempt the impossible. Lous XVI. was the only man in the nation to whom the constituent royalty could not be confided, since it was he from whom the absolute monarchy had just been snatched: the constitution was a shared royalty, and but a few days previously, and he had possessed it entire. With any other person this royalty would have been a gift, for him alone it was an insult. If Louis XVI. had been capable of this abnegation of supreme power which makes disinterested heroes (and he was one), the deposed party, of which he was the natural head, was not like him; we may expect an act of sublime disinterestedness from a virtuous man, never from a party *en masse.* Party is never magnanimous; they never abdicate, they are extirpated. Heroic acts come from the heart, and party has no heart; they have only interests and ambition. A body is a thing of unvarying selfishness.

Clergy, nobility, court, magistracy, all abuses, all falsehoods, all contumelies, every injustice of a monarchy, are personified, in spite of Louis XVI., in the king. Degraded with him, they must desire to rise with him. The nation, which well perceived this fatal connection between the king and the counter-revolution, could not confide in the king, however it might venerate the man; it saw, in him, of necessity, the accomplice of every conspiracy against itself. The *parvenus* of liberty are as thinskinned as the *parvenus* of fortune. Jealousies must arise, suspicions would produce insults, insults resentments, resentments factions, factions shocks and overthrows; the momentary enthusiasm of the people, the sincere concessions of the king, avert nothing. The situations were false on both sides.

If there were in the Constituent Assembly more statesmen than philosophers, it must have perceived that an intermediate state was impossible, under the guardianship of a half-dethroned king. We do not confide to the vanquished the care and management of the conquests. To act as she acts, was to drive the king, without redemption, to treason or the scaffold. An absolute party is the only safe party in great crises. The tact consists in knowing when to have recourse to extreme measures at the critical minute. We say it unhesitatingly—history will hereafter say as we do. Then came a moment when the Constituent Assembly had the right to choose between the monarchy and the republic, and when she had to choose the republic. There was the safety of the Revolution and its legitimacy. In wanting resolution it failed in prudence.

VIII.

But, they say with Barnave, France is monarchical by its geography as by its character, and the contest arises in minds directly between the monarchy and the republic. Let us make ourselves understood:—

Geography is of no party; Rome and Carthage had no frontiers; Genoa and Venice had no territories. It is not the soil which determines the nature of the constitutions of people, it is time. The geographical objection of Barnave fell to the ground a year afterwards, before the prodigies in France in 1792. It proved that if a republic fails in unity and centralization, it is unable to defend a continental nationality. Waves and mountains are the frontiers of the weak—men are the frontiers of a people. Let us then have done with geography. It is not geometricians but statesmen who form social constitutions.

Nations have two great interests which reveal to them the form they should take, according to the hour of the national life which they have attained—the instinct of their conservation, and the instinct of their growth. To act, or be idle, to walk, or sit down, are two acts wholly different, which compel men to assume attitudes wholly diverse. It is the same with nations. The monarchy or the republic correspond exactly amongst a people to the necessities of these two opposite conditions of society—repose or action. We here understand two words; these two words, repose and action, in their most absolute acceptation; for there is repose in republics, as there is action in monarchies.

Is it a question of preservation, of reproduction, of development in that kind of slow and insensible growth which people have like vast vegetables? Is it a question of keeping in harmony with the European balance; of preserving its laws and manners; of maintaining its traditions, perpetuating opinions and worship, of guaranteeing properties and right conduct, of preventing troubles, agitation, factions? The monarchy is evidently more proper for this than any other state of society. It protects in lower classes that security which it desires for its own elevated condition. It is order in essence and selfishness: order is its life—tradition its dogma, the nation is its heritage, religion its ally, aristocracies are its barrier against the invasions of the people. It must preserve all this or perish. It is the government of prudence, because it is also that of great responsibility. An empire is the stake of a monarch—the throne is everywhere a guarantee of immobility. When we are placed on high we fear every shake, for we have but to lose or to fall.

When then a nation is placed in a sufficing territory, with settled laws, fixed interests, sacred creeds, its worship in full force, its social classes graduated, its administration organized, it is monarchical in spite of seas, rivers, or mountains. It abdicates and empowers the monarchy to foresee, to will, to act for it. It is the most perfect of governments for such functions. It calls itself by the two names of society itself; *unity* and *hereditary right.*

IX.

If a people, on the contrary, is at one of those epochs when it is necessary to act with all the intensity of its strength in order to operate within and without one of those organic transformations which are as necessary to people as is a current to waves or explosion to compressed powers—a republic is the obligatory and fated form of a nation at such a moment.

For a sudden, irresistible, convulsive action of the social body, the arm and will of all is needed: the people become a mob, and rush headlong to danger. It can alone suffice to its own danger. What other arm but that of the whole people could stir what it has to stir?—displace what it has to displace?—instal what it desires to found? The monarch would break his sceptre into fragments on it. There must be a lever capable of raising thirty millions of wills—this lever the nation alone possesses. It is in itself the moving power, the fulcrum and the lever.

X.

We cannot ask of the law to act against the law, of tradition to act against tradition, of established order to act against established order. It would be to require strength from weakness, life from suicide; and, besides, we should ask in vain of the monarchical power to accomplish these changes, in which very often all perish, and the king foremost. Such a course would be the contradiction to the monarchy: how could it attempt it?

To ask a king to destroy the empire of a religion which consecrates him; to despoil of their riches a clergy who has them by the same divine title as that by which he has tenure of his kingdom; to degrade an aristocracy which is the first step of his throne; to throw down social hierarchies of which he is the head and crown; to undermine laws of which he is the highest,—is to ask of the vaults of an edifice to sap the foundation. The king could not do so, and would not. In thus overthrowing all that serves him for support, he feels that he would be rendered wholly destitute. He would be playing with his throne and dynasty. He is responsible for his race. He is prudent by nature, and a temporizer from necessity. He must soothe, please, manage, and be on terms with all constituted interests. He is the king of the worship, aristocracy, laws, manners, abuses, and falsehoods of the empire. Even the vices of the constitution form a portion of his strength. To threaten them is to destroy himself. He may hate them: he dares not to attack them.

XI.

A republic alone can suffice for such crises; nations know this, and cling to it as their sole hope of preservation. The will of the people becomes the ruling power. It drives from its presence the timid, seeks the bold and the determined, summons all men to aid in the great work, makes trial of, employs, and combines the force, the devotion, the heroism of every man. It is the populace that holds the helm of the vessel, on which the most prompt, or the most firm seizes, until it is again torn from him by a stronger hand. But every one governs in the common name. Private consideration, timidity of situation, difference of rank, all disappears. No one is responsible—to-day he rises to power—to-morrow he descends to exile or the scaffold—there is no *morrow*, all is *to-day*—resistance is crushed by the irresistible power of movement. All bends—all yields before the people. The resentments of castes—the abolished forms of worship—the decimation of property—the extirpated abuses—the humiliated aristocracies—all are lost in the thundering sound of the overthrow of ancient ideas and things. On whom can we demand revenge? The nation answers for all to all, and no man has aught to require from it. It does not survive itself, it braves recrimination and vengeance—it is absolute as an element—anonymous, as fatality—it completes its work, and when that is ended, says, "Let us rest; and let us assume monarchy."

XII.

Such a plan of action is the republic—the only one that befits the trying period of transformation. It is the government of passion, the government of crises, the government of revolutions. So long as revolutions are unfinished, so long does the instinct of the people urge them to a republic; for they feel that every other hand is too feeble to give that onward and violent impulse necessary to the Revolution. The people (and they act wisely), will not trust an irresponsible, perpetual, and hereditary power to fulfil the commands of the epochs of creation—they will perform them themselves. Their dictatorship appears to them indispensable to save the nation; and what is a dictatorship but a republic? It cannot resign its power until every crisis be over, and the great work of revolution completed and consolidated. Then it can again resume the monarchy, and say, "Reign in the name of the ideas I have given thee!"

XIII.

The Constituent Assembly was then blind and weak, not to create a republic as the natural instrument of the Revolution. Mirabeau, Bailly, La Fayette, Siéyès, Barnave, Talleyrand, and Lameth acted in this respect like philosophers, and not great politicians, as events have amply proved. They believed the Revolution finished as soon as it was written, and the monarchy converted as soon as it had sworn to preserve the constitution. The Revolution was but begun and the oath of royalty to the Revolution as futile as the oath of the Revolution to royalty. These two elements could not mingle until after an interval of an age—this interval was the republic. A nation does not change in a day, or in fifty years, from revolutionary excitements to monarchical repose. It is because we forgot it at the hour when we should have remembered it, that the crisis was so terrible, and that we yet feel its effects. If the Revolution, which perpetually follows itself, had had its own natural and fitting government, the republic—this republic would have been less tumultuous and less perturbed than the five attempts we made for a monarchy. The nature of the age in which we live protests against the traditional forms of power: at an epoch of movement—a government of movement—such is the law.

XIV.

The national Assembly, it is said, had not the right to act thus; for it had sworn allegiance to the monarchy and recognized Louis XVI., and could not dethrone him without a crime. The objection is puerile, if it originates in minds who do not believe in the possession of the people by dynasties. The Assembly at its outset had proclaimed the inalienable right of the people; and the lawfulness of necessary insurrection, and the oath of the Tennis Court (*Serment du Jeu de Paume*), were nought but an oath of disobedience to the king and of fidelity to the nation. The Assembly had afterwards proclaimed Louis XVI. king of the French. If they possessed the power of proclaiming him king, they also possessed that of proclaiming him a simple citizen. Forfeiture for the national utility, and that of the human race, was evidently one of its principles, and yet how did it act? It leaves Louis XVI. king, or makes him king, not through respect for that institution, but out of respect for his person, and pity for so great a downfall. Such was the truth; it feared sacrilege, and fell into anarchy. It was clement, noble, and generous. Louis XVI. had deserved well from his people; who well can dare to censure so magnanimous a condescension? Before the king's departure for Varennes, the absolute right of the nation was but an abstract fiction, the *summum jus* of the Assembly. The royalty of Louis XVI. was respectable and respected, once again it was established.

XV.

But a moment arrived, and this moment was when the king fled his kingdom, protesting against the will of the nation, and sought the assistance of the army, and the intervention of foreign powers, when the Assembly legitimately possessed the rigorous right of disposing of the power, thus abandoned or betrayed. Three courses were open: to declare the downfall of the monarchy, and proclaim a republican revolution; the temporary suspension of the royalty, and govern in its name during its moral eclipse; and, lastly, to restore the monarchy.

The Assembly chose the worst alternative of the three. It feared to be harsh, and was cruel; for by retaining the supreme rank for the king, it condemned him to the torture of the hatred and contempt of the people; it crowned him with suspicions and outrages; and nailed him to the throne, in order that the throne might prove the instrument of his torture and his death.

Of the two other courses, the first was the most logical, to proclaim the downfall of the monarchy and the formation of a republic.

The republic, had it been properly established by the Assembly, would have been far different from the republic traitorously and atrociously extorted nine months after by the insurrection of the 10th of August. It would have doubtless suffered the commotion, inseparable from the birth of a new order of things. It would not have escaped the disorders of nature in a country where everything was done by first impulse, and impassioned by the magnitude of its perils. But it would have originated in law and not in sedition—in right, and not in violence—in deliberation, and not in insurrection. This alone could have changed the sinister conditions of its birth and its future fate; it might become an agitating power, but it would remain pure and unsullied.

Only reflect for a moment how entirely its legal and premeditated proclamation would have altered the course of events. The 10th of August would not have taken place—the perfidy and tyranny of the commune of Paris—the massacre of the guards—the assault on the palace—the flight of the king to the Assembly—the outrages heaped on him there—and his imprisonment in the temple—would have never occurred.

The republic would not have killed a king, a queen, an innocent babe, and a virtuous princess; it would not have had the massacres of September, those St. Bartholomews of the people—that have left an indelible stain on the whole robes of liberty. It would not have been baptized in the blood of three hundred thousand human beings—it would not have armed the revolutionary tribunal with the axe of the people, with which it immolated a generation to make way for an idea,—it would not have had the 31st of May. The Girondists arriving at the supreme power, unsullied by crime, would have possessed more force with which to combat the demagogues; and the republic calmly and deliberately instituted, would have intimidated Europe far more than an *émeute* legitimized by bloodshed and assassination. War might have been avoided, or, if it was inevitable, have been more unanimous and more triumphant; our generals would not have been massacred by their soldiers amidst cries of treason. The spirit of the people would have combated with us, and the horror of our days of August, September, and January would not have alienated from our standards the nations attracted thither by our doctrines. Thus a single change in the origin of the republic changed the fate of the Revolution.

XVI.

But if this vigorous resolution was yet repugnant to the feelings of France, and if the Assembly had feared they had given birth to a republic prematurely, the third course was yet open, to proclaim the temporary cessation of royalty during ten years, and govern in a republican form in its name until the constitution was firmly and securely established. This course would have saved all the respect due to royalty; the life of the king—the life of the royal family—the rights of the people—the purity of the Revolution—it was at once firm and calm, efficacious and legitimate. It was such a dictatorship as the people had instinctively figured in the critical times of their existence. But instead of a short, fugitive, disturbed, and ambitious dictatorship of one man, it was the dictatorship of the nation, governing itself through its National Assembly. The nation might have respectfully laid by royalty during ten years, in order itself to carry out a work above the power of the king. This accomplished, resentment extinguished, habits formed, the laws in operation, the frontiers protected, the clergy secularized, the aristocracy humbled, the dictatorship could terminate. The king or his dynasty could ascend without danger a throne from which all danger was now averted. This veritable republic would have thus resumed the name of a constitutional monarchy, without changing anything, and the statue of royalty would have been replaced on its pedestal when the base had been consolidated. Such would have been the consulate of the people, far superior to that consulate of a man who was to finish by ravaging Europe, and by the double usurpation of a throne and a revolution.

Or, if at the expiration of this national dictatorship, the nation, well governed and guided, found it dangerous or useless to re-establish the throne, what prevented it from saying, I now assume as a definitive government that which I assumed as a dictatorship: I proclaim the French republic as the only government befitting the excitement and energy of a regenerative epoch; for the republic is a dictatorship perpetuated and constituted by the people. What avails a throne? I remain erect: it is the attitude of a people in travail!

In a word, the Constituent Assembly, whose light illumined the globe—whose audacity in two years transformed an empire, had but one fault, that of coming to a close. It should have perpetuated itself: it abdicated. A nation that abdicates after a reign of two years, and on heaps of ruins, bequeaths the sceptre to anarchy. The king *could* reign no longer, the nation *would not.* Thus faction reigned, and the Revolution perished; not because it had gone too far, but because it had not been sufficiently bold. So true is it that the timidity of nations is not less disastrous than the weakness of kings; and that a people who knows not how to seize and guard all that which pertains to it, falls at once into tyranny and anarchy. The Assembly dared to do everything save to reign: the Reign of the Revolution was nought but a republic: and the Assembly left this name to factions, and this form to terror. Such was its fault—it expiated it: and the expiation is not yet ended for France.

BOOK VIII.

I.

Whilst the king, isolated at the summit of the constitution, sought support, sometimes by hazardous negotiations with foreigners, sometimes by rash attempts at corruption in the capital, a body, some Girondists and other Jacobins, but as yet confounded under the common denomination of patriots, began to unite and form the nucleus of a great republican idea: they were Pétion, Robespierre, Brissot, Buzot, Vergniaud, Guadet, Gensonné, Carra, Louvet, Ducos, Fonfrède, Duperret, Sillery-Genlis, and many others, whose names have scarcely emerged from obscurity. The home of a young woman, daughter of an engraver of the Quai des Orfévres, was the meeting place of this union. It was there that the two great parties of the *Gironde* and the *Montagne* assembled, united, separated, and after having acquired power, and overturned the monarchy in company, tore the bosom of their country with their dissensions, and destroyed liberty whilst they destroyed each other. It was neither ambition, nor fortune, nor celebrity which had successively attracted these men to this woman's residence, then without credit, name, or comforts: it was conformity of opinion; it was that devoted worship which chosen spirits like to render in secret as in public to a new truth which promises happiness to mankind; it was the invisible attraction of a common faith, that communion of the first neophytes in the religion of philosophy, where the necessity for souls to unite before they associate by deeds, is felt. So long as the thoughts common to political men have not reached that point where they become fruitful, and are organized by contact, nothing is accomplished. Revolutions are ideas, and it is this communion which creates parties.

The ardent and pure mind of a female was worthy of becoming the focus to which converged all the rays of the new truth, in order to become prolific in the warmth of the heart, and to light the pile of old institutions. Men have the spirit of truth, women only its passion. There must be love in the essence of all creations; it would seem as though truth, like nature, has two sexes. There is invariably a woman at the beginning of all great undertakings; one was requisite to the principle of the French Revolution.* We may say that philosophy found this woman in Madame Roland.

The historian, led away by the movement of the events which he retraces, should pause in the presence of this serious and touching figure, as passengers stopped to contemplate her sublime features and white dress on the tumbril which conveyed thousands of victims to death. To understand her we must trace her career from the *atelier* of her father to the scaffold. It is in a woman's heart that the germ of virtue lies; it is almost always in private life that the secret of public life is reposed.

II.

Young, lovely, radiant with genius, recently married to a man of serious mind, who was touching on old age, and but recently mother of her first child, Madame Roland was born in that intermediary condition in which families scarcely emancipated from manual labor are, it may be said, amphibious between the laborer and the tradesman, and retain in their manners the virtues and simplicity of the people, whilst they already participate in the lights of society. The period in which aristocracies fall is that in which nations regenerate. The sap of the people is there. In this was born Jean Jacques Rousseau, the virile type of Madame Roland. A portrait of her when a child represents a young girl in her father's workshop, holding in one hand a book, and in the other an engraving tool. This picture is the symbolic definition of the social condition in which Madame Roland was born, and the precise moment between the labor of her hands and her mind.

Her father, Gratien Phlippon, was an engraver and painter in enamel. He joined to these two professions that of a trade in diamonds and jewels. He was a man always aspiring higher than his abilities allowed, and a restless speculator, who incessantly destroyed his modest fortune in his efforts to extend it in proportion to his ambitious yearnings. He adored his daughter, and could not, for her sake, content himself with the perspective of the workshop. He gave her an education of the highest degree, and nature had conferred upon her a heart for the most elevated destinies. We need not say what dreams, misery, and misfortunes men

* "Dux fœmina facti."—VIRG.

with such characters invariably bring upon their honest families.

The young girl grew up in this atmosphere of luxuriant imagination and actual wretchedness. Endowed with a premature judgment, she early detected these domestic miseries, and took refuge in the good sense of her mother from the illusions of her father and her own presentiments of the future.

Marguerite Bimont (her mother's name) had brought her husband a calm beauty, and a mind very superior to her destiny, but angelic piety and resignation armed her equally against ambition and despair. The mother of seven children, who had all died in the birth, she concentrated in her only child all the love of her soul. Yet this very love guarded her from any weakness in the education of her daughter. She preserved the nice balance of her heart and her mind; of her imagination and her reason. The mould in which she formed this youthful mind was graceful; but it was of brass. It might have been said that she foresaw the destinies of her child, and infused into the mind of the young girl that masculine spirit which forms heroes and inspires martyrs.

Nature lent herself admirably to the task, and had endowed her pupil with an understanding even superior to her dazzling beauty. This beauty of her earlier years, of which she has herself traced the principal features with infinite ingenuousness in the more sprightly pages of her memoirs, was far from having gained the energy, the melancholy, and the majesty which she subsequently acquired from repressed love, high thought, and misfortune.

A tall and supple figure, flat shoulders, a prominent bust, raised by a free and strong respiration, a modest and most becoming demeanor, that carriage of the neck which bespeaks intrepidity, black and soft hair, blue eyes, which appeared brown in the depth of their reflection, a look which like her soul passed rapidly from tenderness to energy, the nose of a Grecian statue, a rather large mouth, opened by a smile as well as speech, splendid teeth, a turned and well-rounded chin gave to the oval of her features that voluptuous and feminine grace without which even beauty does not elicit love, a skin marbled with the animation of life, and veined by blood which the least impression sent mounting to her cheeks, a tone of voice which borrowed its vibrations from the deepest fibres of her heart, and which was deeply modulated to its finest movements (a precious gift, for the tone of voice, which is the channel of emotion in a woman, is the medium of persuasion in the orator, and by both these titles nature owed her the charm of voice, and had bestowed it on her freely.) Such at eighteen years of age was the portrait of this young girl, whom obscurity long kept in the shade, as if to prepare for life or death a soul more strong, and a victim more perfect.

III.

Her understanding lightened this beauteous frame-work with a precocious and flashing intelligence, which was already inspiration. She acquired, as it were, the most difficult accomplishments even from looking into their very elements. What is taught to her age and sex was not sufficient for her. The masculine education of men was a want and sport to her. Her powerful mind had need of all the means of thought for its due exercise. Theology, history, philosophy, music, painting, dancing, the exact sciences, chemistry, foreign tongues and learned languages, she learned all and desired more. She herself formed her ideas from all the rays which the obscurity of her condition allowed to penetrate into the laboratory of her father. She even secreted the books which the young apprentices brought and forgot for her in the workshop. Jean Jacques Rousseau, Voltaire, Montesquieu, and the English philosophers, fell into her hands; but her real food was Plutarch.

"I shall never forget," she said, "the Lent of 1763, during which I every day carried that book to church, instead of the book of prayers: it was from this moment that I date the impressions and ideas which made me republican, when I had never formed a thought on the subject." After Plutarch, Fénélon made the deepest impression upon her. Tasso and the poets followed. Heroism, virtue, and love were destined to pour from their three vases at once into the soul of a woman destined to this triple palpitation of grand impressions.

In the midst of this fire in her soul her reason remained calm, and her purity spotless. She scarcely owns to the slightest and fugitive emotions of the heart and senses. "When, as I read behind the screen which closed up my chamber from my father's apartment," she writes, "my breathing was at all loud, I felt a burning blush overspread my cheek, and my altered voice would have betrayed my agitation. I was Eucharis to Telemachus, and Herminia to Tancred. Yet, transformed as I was into them, I never thought myself of becoming anything to anybody. I made no reflection that individually affected me; I sought nothing around me: it was a dream without awaking. Yet I remember having beheld with with much agitation a young painter named Taboral, who called on my father occasionally. He was about twenty years of age, with a sweet voice, intelligent countenance, and blushed like a girl. When I heard him in the *atelier*, I had always a pencil or something to look after; but as his presence embarrassed as much as it pleased me, I went away quicker than I entered, with a palpitating heart, a tremor that made me run and hide myself in my little room."

Although her mother was very pious, she did not forbid her daughter from reading. She wished to inspire her with religion, and not enforce it upon her. Full of good sense and toleration, she left her with confidence to her reason, and sought neither to repress nor dry up the sap which would hereafter produce its fruit in her heart. A servile, not voluntary religion, appeared to her degradation and slavery which God could not accept as a tribute worthy of him. The pensive mind of her daughter naturally tended towards the great objects of eternal happiness or misery, and she was sure, at an earlier age than any other, to plunge deeply into their mysteries. The reign of sentiment began in her through the love of God. The sublime delirium of her pious contemplations embellished and preserved the first years of her youth, composed the rest by her philosophy, and seemed as if it must preserve her forever from the tempests of passion. Her devotion was ardent; it took the tints of her soul, and she aspired to the cloister, and dreamed of martyrdom. Entering a convent, she found there propitious moments, surrendering her thoughts to mysticism and her heart to first friendships. The monotonous regularity of this life gently soothed the activity of her meditations. In the hours of relaxation she did not play with her companions, but retired beneath some tree to read and muse. As sensitive as Rousseau to the beauty of foliage, the rustling of the grass, the odor of the herbs, she admired the hand of God, and kissed it in his works. Overflowing with gratitude and inward delight, she went to adore him at church. There the sonorous organ's lengthened peal, uniting with the voices of the youthful nuns, completed the excess of her ecstacy. The Catholic religion has every mysterious fascination for the senses, and pleasure for the imagination. A novice took the veil during her residence in the convent. Her presentation at the entrance, her white veil, her crown of roses, the sweet and soothing hymns which directed her from earth to heaven, the mortuary cloth cast over her youthful and buried beauty, and over her palpitating heart, made the young artist shudder, and overwhelmed her with tears. Her destiny opened to her the image of great sacrifices, and she felt within herself by anticipation all the courage and the suffering.

IV.

The charm and custom of these religious feelings were never effaced from her mind. Philosophy, which soon became her worship, dissipated her faith, but left the impression it had created. She could not assist at the ceremonies of a worship whose mysteries her reason had repudiated, without feeling their attraction and respect. The sight of weak men united to adore and pray to the Father of the human race affected her sensibly. The music raised her to the skies. She quitted these Christian temples happier and better; so much are the recollections of infancy reflected and prolonged even in the most troubled existence.

This impassioned taste for infinity and pious sentiment continued their influences over her after her return to her father's house. "My father's house had not," she writes, "the solitary tranquillity of the convent, still plenty of air, and a wide space on the roof of our house near the *Pont Neuf*, were before my dreamy and romantic imagination. How many times from my window, which looked northward, have I contemplated with emotions the vast deserts of heaven, its glorious azure vault, so splendidly framed from the blue dawn of morning, behind the *Pont-du-Change*, until the golden sunset, when the glorious purple faded away behind the trees of the Champs Elysées and the houses of Chaillot. I did not fail thus to employ some moments at the close of a fine day; and quiet tears frequently stole deliciously from my eyes, whilst my heart, throbbing with an inexpressible sentiment, happy thus to beat, and grateful to exist, offered to the Being of beings a homage pure and worthy of him."

Alas! when she wrote these lines, she no longer saw but

in her mind that narrow strip of the heaven of Paris, and the remembrance of those glorious evenings only illumined with a fugitive gleam the walls of her dungeon.

V.

But she was then happy, between her aunt Angelique and her mother, in what she calls the beautiful quarter of the Isle Saint Louis. On these straight quays, on this tranquil bank, she took the air on summer evenings, watching the graceful course of the river, and the distant landscape. In the morning she traversed these quays with holy zeal, in order to go to church, and that she might not meet in this lone road anything to distract her attention. Her father, who liked her lofty studies, and was intoxicated at his daughter's success, was still desirous of initiating her in his own craft, and made her begin to engrave. She learned to handle the *burin*, and succeeded in this as in everything else. As yet she did not derive any salary from it; but at the fête of her grandfather and grandmother, she presented to them as her offering, sometimes a head which she had applied herself to execute for this express purpose, sometimes a small brass plate, highly polished, on which she had engraved emblems or flowers; and they in return gave her ornaments or something for her toilette, for which she confesses always to have been anxious.

This taste, natural to her age and sex, did not, however, distract her from the more humble domestic duties. She was not ashamed, after appearing on Sundays at church, or walking out, elegantly dressed, to put on during the week a cotton gown, and go to market with her mother. She used even to go out to shops in their neighborhood to buy parsley or salad, which had been forgotten. Although she felt herself somewhat humiliated by these domestic cares, which brought her down from the eminence of her Plutarch, and her visionary wanderings, she combined so much grace, and so much natural dignity, that the fruit-woman used to take pleasure in serving her before her other customers; and the first comers took no offence at this preference. This young girl, this future Héloïse of the eighteenth century, who read serious books, who expounded the circles of the celestial globe, handled the pencil and *burin*, and in whose soul aspiring thoughts and impassioned feelings already found space, was often called into the kitchen to prepare the vege tables for dinner. This mixture of serious shades, elegant research, and domestic occupations, ordered and sensibly mingled by her mother's sagacity, seemed to prepare her already for the vicissitudes of fortune, and in after days helped her to support them. It was Rousseau at Charmettes piling up the woodstack of Madame de Warens with the hand which was to write the *Contrat Social,* or Philopœmen chopping his wood.

VI.

From the retirement of such secluded life, she sometimes perceived the higher world which shone above her. The lights which displayed to her this great world offended, more than they dazzled, her sight. The pride of this aristocratic society, which saw without valuing her, weighed on her sensitive mind—a society in which her position was not assigned to her, seemed badly framed. It was less envy than justice that revolted in her. Superior beings have their places marked out by nature, and everything that keeps them from occupying them, seems to them an usurpation. They find society frequently the reverse of nature, and take their revenge by despising it: from this arises the hatred of genius against power. Genius dreams of an order of things, in which the ranks should be marked out by nature and virtue; whilst in reality they are almost always derived from birth—that blind allotment of fate. There are few great minds which do not feel in their earliest progress the persecution of fortune, and who do not begin by an internal revolt against society. They are only quieted by their own discouragement. Some are resigned from a more lofty feeling to the place which God assigns to them. To put up with the world humbly is still more beautiful than to control it. This is the very acme of virtue. Religion leads to it in a day; philosophy only conducts to it by a lengthened life, misery, or death. These are days when the most elevated place in the world is a scaffold.

VII.

The young maiden once conducted by her grandmother to an aristocratic house, of which her humble parents were *free,* was deeply hurt at the tone of condescending superiority with which her grandmother and herself were treated. "My pride took alarm," she writes, "my blood boiled more than usual, and I blushed violently. I no longer inquired of myself why this lady was seated on a sofa, and my grandmother on a low stool; but my feelings led to such reflection, and I saw the end of the visit with satisfaction as if a weight was taken off my mind."

Another time she was taken to pass eight days at Versailles, in the palace of that king and queen whose throne she was one day to sap. Lodged in the attics with one of the female domestics of the Château, she was a close observer of this royal luxury, which she believed was paid for by the misery of the people, and that grandeur of things founded on the servility of courtiers. The lavishly spread tables, the walks, the play, presentations—all passed before her eyes in the pomp and vanity of the world. These ceremonious details of power were repugnant to her mind, which fed on philosophy, truth, liberty, and the virtue of the olden time. The obscure names, the humble attire, of the relatives who took her to see all this, only procured for her mere passing looks and a few words, which meant more protection than favor. The feeling that her youth, beauty, and merit, were unperceived by this crowd, who only adored favor or etiquette, oppressed her mind. The philosophy, natural pride, imagination, and fixedness of her soul were all wounded during this sojourn. "I preferred," she says, "the statues in the gardens to the personages of the palace." And her mother inquiring if she were pleased with her visit—"Yes," was her reply, "if it be soon ended; for else, in a few more days I shall so much detest all the persons I see, that I should not know what to do with my hatred." "What harm have they done you?" inquired her mother. "To make me feel injustice, and look upon absurdity." As she contemplated these splendors of the despotism of Louis XIV., which were drooping into corruption, she thought of Athens, but forgot the death of Socrates, the exile of Aristides, the condemnation of Phocion. "I did not then foresee," she writes, in melancholy mood, as she pens these lines—"that destiny reserved me to be the witness of crimes such as those of which they were the victims, and to participate in the glory of their martyrs, after having professed their principles."

Thus, the imagination, character, and studies of this girl prepared her, unknown to herself, for the republic. Her religion alone, then so powerful over her, restrained her within the bounds of that resignation which submits the thoughts to the will of God. But philosophy became her creed, and this creed formed a portion of her politics. The emancipation of the people united itself in her mind with the emancipation of ideas. She believed, by overturning thrones, that she was working for man; and, by overthrowing altars, that she was laboring for God. Such is the confession which she herself made of her change.

VIII.

However, the young girl had already attracted many suitors for her hand. Her father wished to marry her in the class to which he himself belonged. He loved, esteemed commerce, because he considered it the source of wealth. His daughter despised it because it was, in her eyes, the source of avarice and the food of cupidity. Men in this condition of life were repugnant to her. She desired in a husband ideas and feelings sympathizing with her own. Her ideal was a soul and not a fortune. "Brought up from my infancy in connection with the great men of all ages, familiar with lofty ideas and illustrious examples—had I lived with Plato, with all the philosophers, all the poets, all the politicians of antiquity, merely to unite myself with a shopkeeper, who would neither appreciate nor feel anything as I did?"

She who wrote these lines was at that moment demanded in marriage of her parents by a rich butcher of the neighborhood. She refused every offer. "I will not descend from the world of my noble chimeras," she replied to the incessant remonstrances of her father; "what I want is not a position but a mind. I will die single rather than prostitute my own mind in a union with a being with whom I have no sympathies."

Deprived of her mother by an early death, alone in the house of a father where disorder was the consequence of a second *amour*, melancholy gained possession of her mind, though it did not overcome it. She became more collected and reserved, in order to strengthen her feelings against isolation and misfortune. The perusal of the *Héloïse* of Rousseau, which was lent to her about that time, made on her heart the same impression that Plutarch had made on her mind. Plutarch had shown her liberty; Rousseau made her dream of happiness: the one fortified, the other weakened her. She found the earnest desire of pouring forth her feelings.

Melancholy was her rigid muse. She began to write, in order to console herself in the nurture of her own thoughts. Without any intention of becoming an authoress, she acquired by these solitary trials that eloquence with which she subsequently animated her friends.

IX.

Thus gradually ripened this patient and resolute mind, working on towards its destiny, when she believed she had found the man of the olden time of whom she had so long dreamed. This man was Roland de la Platière.

He was introduced to her by one of her early friends, married at Amiens, where Roland then carried on the functions of inspector of manufactures. "You will receive this letter," wrote her friend, "by the hand of the philosopher of whom I have spoken to you already, M. Roland, an enlightened man, of antique manners; without reproach, except for his passion for the ancients, his contempt of his age, and his too high estimation of his own virtue. This portrait," she adds, "was just and well depicted. I saw a man nearly fifty years of age, tall, careless in his attitude, with that kind of awkwardness which a solitary life always produces; but his manners were easy and winning, and without possessing the elegance of the world, they united the politeness of the well-bred man to the seriousness of the philosopher. He was very thin, with a complexion much tanned; his brow, already covered by very little hair, and very broad, did not detract from his regular but unattractive features. He had, however, a pleasing smile, and his features an animated play, which gave them a totally different appearance when he was excited in speaking or listening. His voice was manly, his mode of speech brief, like a man with shortened breath; his conversation, full of matter, because his head was full of ideas, occupied the mind more than it flattered the ear. His language was sometimes striking, but harsh and inharmonious. This charm of the voice is a gift very rare, and most powerful over the senses," she adds, "and does not merely depend on the quality of the sound, but equally upon that delicate sensibility which varies the expression by modifying the accent." This is enough to assure us that Roland had not this charming gift.

X.

Roland, born of an honest tradesman's family, which had held magisterial offices and asserted claims to nobility, was the youngest of five brothers, and intended for the church. To avoid this destiny, which disgusted him, he fled from his father's roof at nineteen, and went to Nantes. Procuring a situation with a ship-builder, he was about to embark for India in trade, when an illness at the moment he was to embark prevented him. One of his relations, a superintendent of a factory, received him at Rouen, and gave him a situation in his office. This house, animated by the spirit of Turgot, made experiments in the details of its business with all the sciences, and by political economy with the loftiest problems of governments. It was peopled by philosophers, amongst whom Roland distinguished himself, and the government sent him to Italy to watch the progress of commerce there.

He left his young friend with reluctance, and forwarded to her regularly scientific letters, intended as notes to the work which he proposed to write on Italy—letters in which the sentiment that displayed itself beneath science, more resembled the studies of a philosopher than the conversations of a lover.

On his return she saw in him a friend. His age, gravity, manners, laborious habits, made her consider him as a sage who existed solely on his reason. In the union they contemplated, and which less resembled love, than the ancient associations of the days of Socrates and Plato—the one sought a disciple rather than a wife, and the other married a master rather than a husband. M. Roland returned to Amiens, and thence wrote to the father to demand his daughter's hand, which was bluntly denied to him. He feared in Roland, whose austerity displeased him, a censor for himself, and a tyrant for his child. Informed of her father's refusal, she grew indignant, and went to a convent destitute of everything. There she lived on the coarsest food, prepared by her own hands. She plunged into deep study, and strengthened her heart against adversity. *She revenged herself by deserving the happiness of a lot which was not accorded to her.* In the evening she visited her friends; in the day an hour's walk in a garden surrounded with high walls. That feeling of strength which steels against fate—that melancholy which softens the soul, and feeds it on its own sensibility,—helped her to pass long winter months in her voluntary captivity.

A feeling of internal bitterness, however, poisoned even this sacrifice. She said to herself that this sensibility was not recompensed. She had flattered herself that M. Roland, on learning of her resolution and retreat, would hasten to take her from this convent and unite their destinies. Time passed on. Roland came not, and scarcely wrote. At the end of six months he arrived, and was again deeply enamored on seeing his beloved behind a grating. He resolved on offering her his hand, which she accepted. However, so much calculation, hesitation, and coldness had dissipated the little illusion which the young captive had left, and reduced her feelings to deep esteem. She devoted rather than gave herself. It appeared to her sublime to immolate herself for the happiness of a worthy man; and she consummated this sacrifice with all the seriousness of reason and without a grain of heartfelt enthusiasm. Her marriage was to her an act of virtue, which she performed, not because it was agreeable to her, but because she deemed it sublime.

The pupil of Jean Jacques Rousseau is seen again at this decisive moment of her existence. The marriage of Madame Roland is a palpable imitation of that of Héloïse with M. de Volmar. But the bitterness of reality was not slow in developing itself beneath the heroism of her devotion. "By dint," she herself says, "of occupying myself with the happiness of the man with whom I was associated, I felt that something was wanting to my own. I have not for a moment ceased to see in my husband one of the most estimable persons that exists, and to whom it was an honor to me to belong; but I often felt that similarity was wanting between us,—that the ascendency of a dominating temper, united to that of twenty years more of age, made one of these superiorities too much. If we lived in solitude I had sometimes very painful hours to pass: if we went into the world, I was liked by persons, some one of whom I was fearful might affect me too closely. I plunged into my husband's occupations, became his copying clerk, corrected his proofs, and fulfilled the task with an unrepining humility, which contrasted strongly with a spirit as free and tried as mine. But this humility proceeded from my heart: I respected my husband so much, that I always liked to suppose that he was superior to myself. I had such a dread of seeing a shade over his countenance, he was so tenacious of his own opinions, that it was a long time before

I ventured to contradict him. To this labor I joined that of my house; and observing that his delicate health could not endure every kind of diet, I always prepared his meals with my own hands. I remained with him four years at Amiens, and became there a mother and nurse. We worked together at the *Encyclopédie Nouvelle,* in which the articles relative to commerce had been confided to him. We only quitted this occupation for our walks in the vicinity of the town."

Roland, dictatorial and exacting, had insisted from the beginning of their marriage, that his wife should refrain from seeing her young and attached friends whom she had loved in the convent, and who lived at Amiens. He dreaded the least participation of affection. His prudence outstepped the bounds of reason. To an union as solemn as marriage, the pleasure of friendship was necessary. This tyranny of an exclusive feeling was not compensated by love. Roland demanded everything from his wife's compliance. If there was no faltering in her conduct, still she felt these sacrifices, and joyed over the accomplishment of her duties as the stoic enjoys his sufferings.

XI.

After some years passed at Amiens, Roland was promoted to the same duties at Lyons, his native place. In winter he dwelt in the town, and the rest of the year was passed in the country in his paternal home, where his mother still lived, a respectable old woman, but meddlesome and overbearing in her household. Madame Roland, in all the flower of youth, beauty, and genius, thus found herself tormented and beset by a domineering mother-in-law, a rough brother-in-law, and an exacting husband. The most passionate love could scarcely have been proof against so trying and painful a position. To soothe her she had the consciousness of discharging her duties, her occupation, her philosophy, and her child. It was sufficing, and eventually transformed this gloomy retreat into the abode of harmony and peace. We love to follow her into that solitude, when her mind was becoming tempered for her struggle, as we go to seek at Charmettes the still fresh and sparkling source of the life and genius of Jean Jacques Rousseau.

XII.

At the foot of the mountains of Beaujolais, in the large basin of the Sâone, in face of the Alps, there is a series of small hills scattered like the sea sands, which the patient vine-dresser has planted with vines, and which form amongst themselves, at their base, oblique valleys, narrow and sinuous ravines, interspersed with small verdant meads. These meadows have each their thread of water, which filters down from the mountains: willows, weeping birch, and poplars, show the course and conceal the bed of the streams. The sides and tops of these hills only bear above the lowly vines a few wild peach trees, which do not shade the grapes and large walnut trees in the orchards near the houses. On the declivity of one of these sandy protuberances was *La Platière,* the paternal inheritance of M. Roland, a low farm-house, with regular windows, covered with a roof of red tiles nearly flat; the eaves of this roof project a little beyond the wall, in order to protect the windows from the rain of winter and the summer's sun. The walls, straight and wholly unornamented, were covered with a coating of white plaister, which time had soiled and cracked. The vestibule was reached by ascending five stone steps, surmounted by a rustic balustrade of rusty iron. A yard surrounded by out-houses, where the harvest was gathered in, presses for the vintage, cellars for the wine, and a dove-cote, abutted on the house. Behind was levelled a small kitchen-garden, whose beds were bordered with box, pinks, and fruit trees, pruned close down to the ground. An arbor was formed at the extremity of each walk. A little further on was an orchard, where the trees inclining in a thousand attitudes, cast a degree of shade over an acre of cropped grass; then a large inclosure of low vines, cut in right lines by small green sward paths. Such is this spot. The gaze is turned from the gloomy and lowering horizon to the mountains of Beaujeu, spotted on their sides by black pines, and severed by large inclined meadows, where the oxen of Charolais fatten, and to the valley of the Sâone, that immense ocean of verdure, here and there topped by high steeples. The belt of the higher Alps, covered with snow, and the apex of Mont Blanc, which overhangs the whole, frame this extensive landscape. There is in this something of the vastness of the infinite sea: and if on its bounded side it may inspire recollection and resignation, in its open part it seems to solicit thought to expand, and to convey the soul to far off hopes and to the eminences of imagination.

Such was, for five years, the bounded horizon of this young woman. It was there that she plunged into the plenitude of that nature of which, in her infancy, she had so frequently dreamed, and in which she had perceived only some small bits of sky, and some confused perspectives of royal forests, from the height of her window over the roofs of Paris. It was there that her simple tastes and loving soul found nutriment and scope for her sensibility.

Her life was there divided between household cares, the improvement of her mind, and active charity—that cultivator of the heart. Adored by the peasants, whose protectress she was, she applied to the consolation of their miseries the little to spare which a rigid economy left to her, and to the cure of their maladies the knowledge she had acquired in medicine. She was fetched from three and four leagues' distance to visit a sick person. On Sunday the steps of her court-yard were covered with invalids, who came to seek relief, or convalescents, who came to bring her proofs of their gratitude; baskets of chestnuts, goats' milk cheeses, or apples from their orchards. She was delighted at finding the country people grateful and sensible of kindness. She had drawn her own picture of the people residing in the vicinity of large cities. The burning of châteaux, during the outbreak and massacres of September, taught her subsequently that these seas of men, then so calm, have tempests more terrible than those of the ocean, and that society requires institutions, just as the waves require a bed, and strength is as indispensable as justice to the government of a people.

XIII.

The hour of the Revolution of '89 had struck, and came upon her in the bosom of this retreat. Intoxicated with philosophy, passionately devoted to the ideal of humanity, an adorer of antique liberty, she became on fire at the first spark of this focus of new ideas;—she believed with all her faith, that this revolution, like a child born without a mother's sufferings, must regenerate the human race, destroy the misery of the working classes, for whom she felt the deepest sympathy, and renew the face of the earth. Even the piety of great souls has its imagination. The generous illusion of France at this epoch was equal to the work which

France had to accomplish. If she had not dared to hope so much, she would have dared nothing: her faith was her strength.

From this day, Madame Roland felt a fire kindled within her which was never to be quenched but in her blood. All the love which lay slumbering in her soul was converted into enthusiasm and devotion for the human race. Her sensibility deceived—too ardent, unquestionably, for one man—spread over a nation. She adored the Revolution like a lover. She communicated this flame to her husband and to all her friends. All her repressed feelings were poured forth in her opinions; she avenged herself on her destiny, which refused her individual happiness, by sacrificing herself for the happiness of others. Happy and beloved, she would have been but a woman; unhappy and isolated, she became the leader of a party.

XIV.

The opinions of M. and Madame Roland excited against them all the commercial aristocracy of Lyons, an honest, right-minded city, but one of money, where all becomes a calculation, and where ideas have the weight and immobility of interests. Ideas have an irresistible current, which attract even the most stagnant populations; Lyons was led on and overwhelmed by the opinions of the epoch. M. Roland was raised to the municipality at the first election, and spoke out with all the earnestness of his principles, and the energy inspired by his wife. Feared by the timid, adored by the eager, his name, at first a byword, became a rallying point;—public favor recompensed him for the insults of the rich. He was deputed to Paris by the municipal council, there to defend the commercial interests of Lyons, in the committees of the Constituent Assembly.

The connection of Roland with philosophers and economists who formed the practical party of philosophy, his necessary intercourse with influential members of the Assembly, his literary tastes, and, above all, the attraction and natural temptation which drew and retained eminent men around a young, eloquent, and impassioned woman, soon made the *salon* of Madame Roland an ardent, though not as yet noted, focus of the Revolution. The names which were found there reveal, from the first days, extreme opinions. For these opinions, the constitution of 1791 was only a halt.

It was on the 20th February, 1791, that Madame Roland

returned to that Paris which she had quitted five years before, a young girl, unknown and nameless, and whither she came as a flame to animate an entire party, found a republic, reign for a moment, and—die! She had in her mind a confused presentiment of this destiny. Genius and Will know their strength—they feel before others and prophesy their mission. Madame Roland had beforehand seemed carried on by hers to the heart of action. She hastened on the day after her arrival to the sittings of the Assembly. She saw the powerful Mirabeau, the dazzling Cazalès, the daring Maury, the crafty Lameth, the impassive Barnave. She remarked with annoyance and intense hate, in the attitude and language of the right side, that superiority conferred by the habit of command and confidence in the respect of the million; on the left side, she saw the inferiority of manners, and the insolence that mingles with low breeding. And thus did the antique aristocracy survive in blood, and avenge itself, even after its defeat on the democracy, which envied, whilst it beat it to the earth. Equality is written in the laws long before it is established in races. Nature is an aristocrat, and it requires a long use of independence to give to a republican people the noble attitude and polished dignity of the citizen. Even in revolutions, the *parvenu* of liberty is long seen in the vanquisher. Woman's tact is very sensitive to these nice shades. Madame Roland understood them, but, so far from allowing herself to be seduced by this superiority of aristocracy, she was but the more indignant, and felt her hatred redoubled against a party which it was possible to overcome but impossible to humble.

XV.

It was at this period that she and her husband united with some of the most ardent amongst the apostles of popular ideas. It was not they who, as yet, were foremost in the favor of the people, and the *éclat* of talent,—it was they who appeared to it, to love the Revolution for the Revolution itself, and to devote themselves, with sublime disinterestedness, not to the success of their fortune, but to the progress of humanity. Brissot was one of the first. M. and Madame Roland had been, for a long time, in correspondence with him on matters of public economy, and the more important problems of liberty. Their ideas had fraternized and expanded together. They were united beforehand by all the fibres of their revolutionary hearts, but, as yet, did not know it. Brissot, whose adventurous life, and unwearied contentions were allied to the youth of Mirabeau, had already acquired a name in journalism and the clubs. Madame Roland awaited him with respect; she was curious to judge if his features resembled the physiognomy of his mind. She believed that nature revealed herself by all forms, and that the understanding and virtue modelled the external senses of men just as the statuary impresses on the clay the outward forms of his conception. The first appearance undeceived, without discouraging her in her admiration of Brissot. He wanted that dignity of aspect, and that gravity of character which seem like a reflection of the dignity, life, and seriousness of his doctrines. There was something in the man political, which recalled the pamphleteer. His levity shocked her; even his gayety seemed to her a profanation of the grave ideas of which he was the organ. The Revolution, which gave passion to his style, did not throw any passion into his countenance. She did not find in him enough hatred against the enemies of the people. The mobile mind of Brissot did not appear to have sufficient consistency for a feeling of devotion. His activity, directed upon all matters, gave him the appearance of a novice in ideas rather than an apostle. They called him an intriguer.

Brissot brought Pétion, his fellow-student and friend. Pétion, already member of the Constituent Assembly, and whose harangues in two or three cases had excited interest. Brissot was reputed to have inspired these orations. Buzot and Robespierre, both members of the same Assembly, were introduced there. Buzot, whose pensive beauty, intrepidity, and eloquence, were destined hereafter to agitate the heart and soften the imagination of Madame Roland; and Robespierre, whose disquiet mind and fanatic hatred cast him henceforward into all meetings where conspiracies were formed in the name of the people. Some others, too, came, whose names will subsequently appear in the annals of this period. Brissot, Pétion, Buzot, Robespierre, agreed to meet four evenings in each week in the *salon* of Madame Roland.

XVI.

The motive of these meetings was to confer secretly as to the weakness of the Constituent Assembly, on the plots laid by the aristocracy to fetter the Revolution, and on the impulse necessary to impress on the lukewarm opinions, in order to consolidate the triumph. They chose the house of Madame Roland, because this house was situated in a quarter equidistant from the homes of all the members who were to assemble there. As in the conspiracy of Harmodius, it was a woman who held the torch to light the conspirators.

Madame Roland thus found herself cast, from the first, in the midst of the movement party. Her invisible hand touched the first threads of the still entangled plot which was to disclose such great events. This part, the only one that could be assigned to her sex, equally flattered her woman's pride and passion for politics. She went through it with that modesty which would have been in her a *chef d'œuvre* of skill if it had not been a natural endowment. Seated out of the circle near a work-table, she worked or wrote letters, listening all the time with apparent indifference to the discussions of her friends. Frequently tempted to take a share in the conversation, she bit her lips in order to check her desire. Her soul of energy and action was inspired with secret contempt for the tedious and verbose debates which led to nothing. Action was expended in words, and the hour passed away taking with it the opportunity which never returns.

The conquests of the National Assembly soon enervated the conquerors. The leaders of this Assembly retreated from their own handiwork, and covenanted with the aristocracy and the throne to grant the king the revision of the constitution in a more monarchical spirit. The deputies who met at Madame Roland's lost heart and dispersed, until, at length, there only remained that small knot of unshaken men who attached themselves to principles regardless of their success, and who are attached to desperate causes with the more fervor in proportion as fortune seems to forsake them. Of this number were Buzot, Pétion, and Robespierre.

XVII.

History must have a sinister curiosity in ascertaining the first impression made on Madame Roland, by the man who, warmed at her hearth, and then conspiring with her, was one day to overthrow the power of his friends, immolate them *en masse*, and send her to the scaffold. No repulsive feeling seems, at this period, to have warned her that in conspiring to advance Robespierre's fortune, she conspired for her own death. If she have any vague fear, that fear is instantly cloaked by a pity which is akin to contempt. Robespierre appeared to her an honest man; she forgave him his evil tongue and affected utterance. Robespierre, like all men with one idea, appeared overcome with *ennui*. Still she had remarked that he was always deeply attentive at these committees, that he never spoke freely, listened to all other opinions before he delivered his own, and then never took the pains to explain his motives. Like men of imperious temper, his conviction was to him always a sufficing reason. The next day he entered the tribune, and profiting, for his reputation's sake, by the confidential discussions to which he had listened on the previous evening, he anticipated the hour of action agreed upon with his allies, and thus divulged the plan concerted. When blamed for this at Madame Roland's, he made but slight excuse. This wilfulness was attributed to his youth, and the impatience of his *amour-propre*. Madame Roland, persuaded that this young man was passionately attached to liberty, took his reserve for timidity, and these petty treasons for independence. The common cause was a cover for all. Partiality transforms the most sinister tokens into favor or indulgence. "He defends his principles," said she, "with warmth and pertinacity—he has the courage to stand up singly in their defence at the time when the number of the people's champions is vastly reduced. The court hates him, therefore we should like him. I esteem Robespierre for this, and show him that I do; and then too, though he is not very attentive at the evening meetings, he comes occasionally and asks me to give him a dinner. I was much struck with the affright with which he was agitated on the day of the king's flight to Varennes. He said the same evening at Pétion's that the Royal Family had not taken such a step without preparing in Paris a Saint Bartholomew for the patriots, and that he expected to die before he was twenty-four hours older. Pétion, Buzot, Roland, on the contrary, said that this flight of the king's was his abdication, that it was necessary to profit by it in order to prepare men's minds for the republic. Robespierre, sneering and biting his nails, as usual, asked what a republic was."

It was on this day that the plan of a journal, called the *Republican*, was arranged between Brissot, Condorcet, Dumont of Geneva, and Duchâtelet. We thus see that the idea of a republic was born in the cradle of the Girondists before it emanated from Robespierre, and that the 10th of August was no chance, but a plot.

At the same epoch, Madame Roland had given way, in order to save Robespierre's life, to one of those impulses which reveal a courageous friendship, and leave their traces even in the memory of the ungrateful. After the massacre of the Champ-de-Mars, accused of having conspired with the originators of the petition of forfeiture, and threatened with vengeance by the National Guard, Robespierre was obliged to conceal himself. Madame Roland, accompanied by her husband, went at 11 o'clock at night to his retreat in the Marais, to offer him a safer asylum in their own house. He had already quitted his domicile. Madame Roland then went to their common friend Buzot, and entreated him to go to the Feuillants, where he still retained influence, and with all speed to exculpate Robespierre before any act of accusation was issued against him.

Buzot hesitated for a moment, then replied,—"I will do all in my power to save this unfortunate young man, although I am far from partaking the opinion of many respecting him. He thinks too much of himself to love liberty; but he serves it, and that is enough for me. I shall be there to defend him." Thus, three of Robespierre's subsequent victims combined that night, and unknown to him, for the safety of the man by whom they were eventually to die. Destiny is a mystery whence spring the most remarkable coincidences, and which tend no less to offer snares to men through their virtues than their crimes. Death is everywhere: but, whatever the fate may be, virtue alone never repents. Beneath the dungeons of the Conciergerie Madame Roland remembered that night with satisfaction. If Robespierre recalled it in his power, this memory must have fallen colder on his heart than the axe of the headsman.

BOOK IX.

I.

After the dispersion of the Constituent Assembly, the mission of M. and Madame Roland having terminated, they quitted Paris. This woman, who had just left the centre of faction and business, returned to La Platière to resume the cares of her rustic household, and the pruning of her vines. But she had quaffed of the intoxicating cup of the Revolution. The movement in which she had participated for a moment impelled her still, though at a distance. She carried on a correspondence with Robespierre and Buzot; political and formal with Robespierre, pathetic and tender with Buzot. Her mind, her soul, her heart, all recalled it. Then took place between herself and her husband a deliberation, apparently impartial, in order to decide whether they should bury themselves in the country, or should return to Paris. But the ambition of the one, and the ardent desire of the other, had decided, unknown to, and before, either. The most trifling pretext was sufficient for their impatience. In the month of December they were again installed in Paris.

It was the period when all their friends arrived. Pétion had just been elected *maire*, and was creating a republic in the *commune*. Robespierre, excluded from the Legislative Assembly by the law which forbade the re-election of the members of the Constituent Assembly, found a tribune in the Jacobins. Brissot assumed Buzot's place in the new Assembly, and his reputation, as a public writer and statesman, brought around him and his doctrines the young Girondists, who had arrived from their department, with the ardor of their age, and the impulse of a second revolutionary tide. They cast themselves, on their arrival, into the places which Robespierre, Buzot, Laclos, Danton, and Brissot had marked out for them.

Roland, the friend of all these men, but in the background, and concealed in their shadow, had one of those peculiar reputations, the more potent over opinion, as it made but little display: it was spoken of as though an antique virtue, beneath the simple appearance of a rustic: he was the Siéyès of his party. Beneath his taciturnity his deep thought was assured, and in his mystery the oracle was accredited. The brilliancy and genius of his wife attracted all eyes towards him: his very mediocrity, the only power that has the virtue of neutralizing envy, was of service to him. As no one feared him, everybody thrust him forward—Pétion as a cover for himself—Robespierre to undermine him—Brissot to put his own villanous reputation under the shelter of proverbial probity—Buzot, Vergniaud, Louvet, Gensonné, and the Girondists, from respect for his science, and the attraction towards Madame Roland; even the court, from confidence in his honesty and contempt for his influence. This man advanced to power without any effort on his own part, borne onwards by the favor of a party, by the *prestige* which the unknown has over opinion, by the disdain of his opponents and the genius of his wife.

II.

The king had for some time hoped that the wrath of the Revolution would be softened down by its triumph. Those violent acts, those stormy oscillations between insolence and repentance, which had marked the inauguration of the Assembly, had painfully undeceived him. His astonished ministry already trembled before so much audacity, and in the council avowed their incompetency. The king was desirous of retaining men who had given him such proofs of devotion to his person. Some of them, confidants or accomplices, served the king and queen, either by keeping up communications with the emigrants or by their intrigues in the interior.

M. de Montmorin, an able man, but unequal to the difficulties of the crisis, had retired. The two principal men of the ministry were M. de Lessart for Foreign Affairs; M. Bertrand de Molleville in the Marine Department. M. de Lessart, placed by his position between the armed emigrants, the impatient Assembly, undecided Europe, and the inculpated king, could not fail to fall under his own good intentions. His plan was to avoid war in his own country by temporizing and negotiations—to suspend the hostile demonstration of foreign power: to present to the intimidated Assembly the king, as sole arbiter and negotiator of peace between his people and the foreigner; and he trusted thus to adjourn the final collisions between the Assembly and the throne, and to re-establish the regular authority of the king by preserving peace. The personal arrangements of the emperor Leopold aided him in his plans; he had only to contend against the fatality which urges men and things to their *dénouement*. The Girondists, and Brissot especially, overwhelmed him with accusations, inasmuch as he was the man who could most retard their triumph. By sacrificing him they could sacrifice a whole system: their press and their harangues pointed him out to the fury of the people;—the partisans of war marked him down as their victim. He was no traitor—but with them to negotiate was to betray. The king, who knew he was irreproachable and confided all his plans to him, refused to sacrifice him to his enemies, and thus accumulated resentments against the minister. As to M. de Molleville, he was a secret enemy of the constitution. He advised the king to play the hypocrite, acting in the letter, and thus to destroy the spirit of the law,--advancing by subterranean ways to a violent catastrophe,—when according to him the monarchical cause must come out victorious. Confiding in the power of intrigue more than in the influence of opinion, seeking everywhere traitors to the popular cause, paying spies, bargaining for consciences, believing in no one's incorruptibility, keeping up secret intelligence with the most violent demagogues, paying in hard money for the most incendiary propositions under the idea of making the Revolution unpopular from its very excesses, and filling the tribunes of the Assembly with his agents in order to choke down with their hootings, or render effective by their applause, the discourses of certain orators, and thus to feign in the tribunes a false people and a false opinion; men of small means in great matters presuming that it is possible to deceive a nation as if it were an individual. The king, to whom he was devoted, liked him as the depositary of his troubles, the confidant of his relations with foreign powers, and the skilful mediator of his negotiation with all parties. M. de Molleville thus kept himself in well-managed balance between his favor with the king, and his intrigues with the revolutionary party. He spoke the language of the constitution well—he had the secret of many consciences bought and paid for.

It was between these two men that the king, in order to comply with popular opinion, called M. de Narbonne to the ministry of war. Madame de Stäel and the constitutional party sought the aid of the Girondists. Condorcet was the mediator between the two parties. Madame de Condorcet, an exceedingly lovely woman, united with Madame de Stäel in enthusiasm for the young minister. The one lent him the brilliancy of her genius, the other the influence of her beauty. These two females appeared to fuse their feelings in one common devotion for the man honored by their preference. Rivalry was sacrificed at the shrine of ambition.

III.

The point of union of the Girondist party with the con

stitutional party, in that combination of which M. de Narbonne's elevation was the guarantee, was the thirst of both parties for war. The constitutional party desired it, in order to divert internal anarchy, and dispel those fermentations of agitation which threatened the throne. The Girondist party desired it in order to push men's minds to extremities. It hoped that the dangers of the country would give it strength enough to shake the throne and produce the republican régime.

It was under these auspices that M. de Narbonne took office. He also was desirous of war; not to overthrow the throne in whose shadow he was born, but to dazzle and shake the nation, to hazard fortune by desperate casts, and to replace at the head of the people under the arms of the high military aristocracy of the country, La Fayette, Biron, Rochambeau, the Lameths, Dillon, Custines, and himself. If victory favored the French flag, the victorious army, under constituent chiefs, would control the Jacobins, strengthen the reformed monarchy, and maintain the establishment of the two chambers; if France was destined to reverses, unquestionably the throne and aristocracy must fall, but better to fall nobly in a national contest of France against her enemies, than to tremble perpetually and to perish at last in a riot by the pikes of the Jacobins. This was the adventurous and chivalrous policy which pleased the young men by its heroism, and the women by its *prestige*. It betokened the high courage of France. M. de Narbonne personified it in the council. His colleagues, MM. de Lessart and Bertrand de Molleville, saw in him the total overthrow of all their plans. The king, as usual, was all indecision; one step forward and one backwards; surprised by the event in his hesitation, and thus unable to resist a shock, or himself to give any impulse.

Besides these official councillors, certain constituents not in the Assembly, especially the Lameths, Duport, and Barnave, were consulted by the king. Barnave had remained in Paris some months after the dissolution of the Constituent Assembly. He redeemed by sincere devotion to the monarchy the blows he had previously dealt upon it. He had measured with an eye of judgment, the rapid declivity down which the love of popular favor had impelled him. Like Mirabeau, he wished to pause when it was too late. Henceforth, remaining on the brink of events, he was besieged with terror and remorse. If his intrepid heart did not tremble for himself, the sympathy he experienced for the queen and royal family urged him to give the king advice which had but one fault,—it was impossible now to follow it.

These consultations, held at Adrien Duport's, the friend of Barnave and the oracle of the party, only served to embarrass the mind of the king with another element of hesitation. La Fayette and his friends also added their imperious counsel. La Fayette could not believe that he was supplanted. The national guard, which yet remained attached to him, still credited his omnipotence,—all these men and all these parties lent M. de Narbonne secret support. A courtier in the eyes of the court, an aristocrat in the eyes of the nobility, a soldier in the eyes of the army, one of the people in the eyes of the people, irresistible in the eyes of the women, he was the minister of public hope. The Girondists alone had an *arrière-pensée* in their apparent favor towards him. They elevated him to make his fall the more conspicuous: M. de Narbonne was to them but the hand which prepared the way for their advent.

IV.

Scarcely had he taken his place in the cabinet, than this young minister displayed all the activity, frankness, and grace of his character in the discussion of affairs, and his intercourse with the Assembly. He employed the system of confidence, and surprised the Assembly by his *abandon*, and these austere and suspicious men, who had hitherto seen nothing but deceit in the language of ministers, now yielded to the charm of his speeches. He addressed them, not in the official and cold language of diplomacy, but in the open and cordial tone of a patriot. He brought the dignity of his office to the tribune; he generously assumed all responsibility, and he professed the most cherished principles of the people with a sincerity that precluded the possibility of suspicion. He openly disclosed his projects, and the energy of his mind communicated itself to those men who were the most difficult to be won over. The nation too saw with delight an *aristocrate* so well adapt himself to their costume, their principles, and their passions. The ardor of his patriotism did not suffer the impulse, that confounded in him the king and the people, to slacken; and in the course of his short administration he did wonders of activity. He visited and put in a state of defence all the fortified places; raised an army, harangued the troops; arrested the emigration of the nobility, in the name of the common danger; nominated the generals, and summoned La Fayette, Rochambeau, and Luckner. A patriotic sentiment, of which he was the soul, pervaded France; by rendering the throne the centre of the national defence, he rendered the king again popular for a short time, and in the enthusiasm felt for their country, all parties became reconciled. His eloquence was rapid, brilliant, and sonorous as the clash and din of arms. This expansion of his heart was a part of his character; he bared his breast to the eyes of his adversaries, and by this confidence won them to his side.

The first day of his appointment to office, instead of announcing his nomination by a letter to the president, as was customary with the other ministers, he proceeded to the Assembly, and mounted the tribune. "I come to offer you," said he, "the profoundest respect for the authority with which the people have invested you; from attachment for the constitution, to which I have sworn; a courageous love for liberty and equality—yes, for equality, which has no longer any opponents, but which should nevertheless possess no less energetic supporters." Two days afterwards he gained the entire confidence of the Assembly, when speaking of the responsibility of the ministers. "I accept," cried he, "the definition of the situation of ministers just made, that tells us responsibility is death. Spare no threats, no dangers. Load us with personal fetters, but afford us the means of aiding the constitution to progress. For my own part, I embrace this opportunity of entreating the members of this Assembly to inform me of everything which they deem useful to the welfare of the nation, during my administration. Our interests, our enemies are the same; and it is not the letter of the constitution only that we should seek to enforce, but the spirit; we must not seek merely to acquit ourselves, but to succeed. You will see that the minister is convinced that there is no hope for liberty unless it proceed through you and from you: cease then for awhile to mistrust us, condemn us afterwards if we have merited it; but first give us with confidence the means of serving you."

Such words as these touched even the most prejudiced, and it was unanimously voted that the speech should be printed, and sent to all the departments. In order to cement the reconciliation of the king and the nation, M. de Narbonne went to the committees of the Assembly, communicated to them his plans, discussed his measures, and won over all to his resolutions. This government in common was the spirit of the constitution; the other ministers saw in this the abasement of the executive power and an abdication of royalty, whilst M. de Narbonne saw in it the sole means of winning back public feeling to the king. Opinion had dethroned the royalty; it was to opinion that he looked to strengthen it, and therefore he made himself the minister of public opinion.

At the moment when the emperor sent to the king a communication threatening the frontiers, and the king personally informed the Assembly of the energetic measures he had adopted, M. de Narbonne, re-entering the Assembly after the king's departure, mounted the tribune. "I am on the eve of quitting Paris," said he, "in order to visit our frontiers; not that I believe the mistrust felt by the soldiers for their officers has any foundation, but because I hope to dissipate them by addressing all in the name of their king and their country. I will say to the officers, that ancient prejudices and an affection for their king carried to an excess for a time, may have excused their conduct, but that the word treason is unknown amongst nations of honorable men. To the soldiers, your officers who remain at the head of the army are bound by their oath and their honor to the Revolution. The safety of the state depends on the discipline of the army. I confide my post to the minister of foreign affairs, and such is my confidence, such should be the confidence of the nation in his patriotism, that I take on myself the responsibility of all the orders that he may give in my name." M. de Narbonne displayed on this occasion as much skill as magnanimity; he felt that he had sufficient credit with the nation to cover the unpopularity of his colleague, M. de Lessart, already denounced by the Girondists, and thus placed himself between them and their victim. The Assembly was carried away by his enthusiasm; he obtained 20,000,000 of francs for the preparations for war, and the grade of marshal of France for the aged Luckner. The press and the clubs themselves applauded him, for the general eagerness for war swept away all before it, even the resentments of faction.

One man alone of the Jacobins resisted the influence of this enthusiasm: this man was Robespierre. Up to this time Robespierre had been merely a discusser of ideas, a subaltern agitator, indefatigable and intrepid, but eclipsed by other and greater names. From this day he became a statesman; he felt his own mental strength; he based this strength on a principle, and alone and unaided ventured to cope with the truth. He devoted himself without regarding even the number of his adversaries, and by exercising he doubled his force.

All the cabinets of the princes threatened by the Revolution still debated the question of peace or war. It was discussed alike in the councils of Louis XVI., in the meetings of parties in the Assembly, at the Jacobins, and in the public journals. The moment was decisive, for it was evident that the negotiation between the emperor Leopold and France on the subject of the reception of emigrants in the states dependent on the empire was fast drawing to a close, and that before long the emperor would have given satisfaction to France by dispersing these bodies of emigrés, or that France would declare war against him, and by this declaration draw on herself the hostilities of all her enemies at the same time. France thus would defy them all.

We have already seen that the Statesmen, and Revolutionists, Constitutionalists, and Girondists, Aristocrats, and Jacobins, were all in favor of war. War was, in the eyes of all, an appeal to destiny, and the impatient spirit of France wished that it would pronounce at once, either by victory or defeat. Victory seemed to France the sole issue by which she could extricate herself from her difficulties at home, and even defeat did not terrify her. She believed in the necessity of war, and defied even death. Robespierre thought otherwise, and it is for that reason that he was Robespierre.

He clearly comprehended two things; the first, that war was a gratuitous crime against the people; the second, that a war, even though successful, would ruin the cause of democracy. Robespierre looked on the Revolution as the rigorous application of the principles of philosophy to society. A passionate and devoted pupil of Jean Jacques Rousseau, the *Contrat Social* was his gospel; war, made with the blood of the people, was in the eyes of this philosopher—what it must ever be in the eyes of the wise—wholesale slaughter to gratify the ambition of a few, glorious only when it is defensive. Robespierre did not consider France placed in such a position as to render it absolutely necessary for her safety that the human vein should be opened.

whence would flow such torrents of blood. Imbued with a firm conviction of the omnipotence of the new ideas on which he nourished faith and fanaticism within a heart closed against intrigue, he did not fear that a few fugitive princes, destitute of credit, and some thousand aristocratic emigrés, would impose laws or conditions on a nation whose first struggle for liberty had shaken the throne, the nobility, and the clergy. Neither did he think that the disunited and wavering powers of Europe would venture to declare war against a nation that proclaimed peace so long as we did not attack them. But should the European cabinets be sufficiently mad to attempt this new crusade against human reason, then Robespierre fully believed they would be defeated, for he knew that there lies invincible force in the justice of a cause—that right doubles the energy of a nation, that despair often supplies the want of weapons, and that God and men were for the people.

He thought, moreover, that if it was the duty of France to propagate the advantages and the light of reason and liberty, the natural and peaceful extension of the French Revolution in the world would prove far more infallible than our arms, —that the Revolution should be a doctrine and not a universal monarchy realized by the sword, and that the patriotism of nations should not coalesce against his dogmata. Their strength was in their minds, for in his eyes the power of the Revolution lay in its enlightenment. But he understood more: he understood that an offensive war would inevitably ruin the Revolution, and annihilate that premature republic of which the Girondists had already spoken to him, but which he himself could not as yet define. Should the war be unfortunate, thought he, Europe will crush without difficulty beneath the tread of its armies the earliest germs of this new government, to the truth of which perhaps a few martyrs might testify, but which would find no soil from whence to spring anew. If fortunate, military feeling, the invariable companion of aristocratic feeling, honor, that religion that binds the soldier to the throne; discipline, that despotism of glory, would usurp the place of those stern virtues to which the exercise of the constitution would have accustomed the people,—then they would forgive everything, even despotism, in those who had saved them. The gratitude of a nation to those who have led its children to victory is a pitfall in which the people will ever be ensnared,—nay, they even offer their necks to the yoke; civil virtues must ever fade before the brilliancy of military exploits. Either the army would return to surround the ancient royalty with all its strength, and France would have her Monk, or the army would crown the most successful of its generals, and liberty would have her Cromwell. In either case the Revolution escaped from the people, and lay at the mercy of the soldiery, and thus to save it from war was to save it from a snare. These reflections decided him; as yet he meditated no violence; he but saw into the future, and read it aright. This was the original cause of his rupture with the Girondists; their justice was but policy, and war appeared to them politic. Just or unjust, they wished for it as a means of destruction to the throne, of aggrandizement for themselves. Posterity must decide, if in this great quarrel the first blame lies on the side of the democrat, or the ambitious Girondists. This fierce contest, destined to terminate in the death of both parties, began on the 12th of December at a meeting of the Jacobin Club.

V.

"I have meditated during six months, and even from the first day of the Revolution," said Brissot, the leader of the Gironde, "to what party I should give my support. It is by the force of reason, and by considering facts, that I have come to the conviction that a people, who, after ten centuries of slavery, have reconquered liberty, have need of war. War is necessary to consolidate liberty, and to purge the constitution from all taint of despotism. War is necessary to drive from amongst us those men whose example might corrupt us. You have the power of chastising the rebels, and intimidating the world; have the courage to do so. The emigrés persist in their rebellion, the sovereigns persist in supporting them. Can we hesitate to attack them? Our honor, our public credit, the necessity of strengthening our revolution, all make it imperative on us. France would be dishonored, did she tamely suffer the insolence and revolt of a few factions, and outrages that a despot would not bear for a fortnight. How shall we be looked upon? No! we must avenge ourselves, or become the opprobrium of all the other nations. We must avenge ourselves by destroying these herds of *brigands*, or consent to behold faction, conspiracy, and rebellion perpetuated, and the insolence of the aristocrats greater than ever. They rely on the army at

Coblentz,—in that they put their trust. If you would at one blow destroy the aristocracy, destroy Coblentz, and the chief of the nation will be compelled to reign, according to the Constitution, with us and through us."

These words, pronounced by the statesman of the Gironde, awakened an echo in the breast of every man, from the Jacobin Club to the extremity of the country. The vehement applause of the tribunes was merely the expression of that impatience to know the final decision that pervaded all parties. Robespierre needed iron nerve and determination to confront his friends, his enemies, and public opinion; and yet he sustained this struggle of a single idea against all this passion for weeks. Great convictions are indefatigable; and Robespierre, by his own unaided exertions, balanced all France during a month. His very enemies spoke with respect of his firmness, and those who had not the courage to follow him, yet would have been ashamed not to esteem him. His eloquence, which had been dry, verbose, and dialectic, now became more elegant and more imposing. The public journals printed his speeches. "You, O people, who do not possess the means of procuring the speeches of Robespierre, I promise them to you," said the *Orateur du Peuple*, the Jacobin paper. "Preserve carefully the numbers that contain these speeches; they are masterpieces of eloquence, that should be preserved in every family, in order to teach future generations that Robespierre existed for the public good and the preservation of liberty."

After having exhausted every argument that philosophy, policy, and patriotism could suggest against an offensive war, commenced by the Gironde, and secretly fomented by the ministers, and carried on by the generals most suspected by the people, he mounted the tribune for the last time, against Brissot, on the night of the 13th January, and declared his conviction against war, in a speech as admirable as it was pathetic.

VI.

"Yes, I am vanquished; I yield to you," cried he, in a broken voice; "I also demand war. What do I say?—I demand a war, more terrible, more implacable than you demand. I do not demand it as an act of prudence, an act of reason, an act of policy, but as the resource of despair. I demand it on one condition, which doubtless you have anticipated,—for I do not think that the advocates of war have sought to deceive us. I demand it deadly—I demand it heroic—I demand it such as the genius of Liberty would declare against all despotism—such as the people of the Revolution, under their own leaders, would render it; not such as intriguing cowards would have it, or as the ambitious and traitorous ministers and generals would carry it on.

"Frenchmen, heroes of the 14th of July, who, without guide or leader, yet acquired your liberty, come forth, and let us form that army which you tell us is destined to conquer the universe. But where is the general, who, imperturbable defender of the rights of the people, and born with a hatred to tyrants, has never breathed the poisonous air of the courts, and whose virtue is attested by the hatred and disgrace of the court; this general, whose hands, guiltless of our blood, are worthy to bear before us the banner of freedom; where is he, this new Cato, this third Brutus, this unknown hero? let him appear and disclose himself, he shall be our leader. But where is he? Where are these soldiers of the 14th of July, who laid down, in the presence of the people, the arms furnished them by despotism. Soldiers of Châteauvieux, where are you? Come and direct our efforts. Alas! it is easier to rob death of its prey than despotism of its victims. Citizens! Conquerors of the Bastille, come! Liberty summons you, and assigns you the honor of the first rank! They are mute. Misery, ingratitude, and the hatred of the aristocracy, have dispersed them. And you, citizens, immolated at the Champ-de-Mars, in the very act of a patriotic confederation, you will not be with us. Ah, what crime had these females, these massacred babes committed? Good God! how many victims, and all amongst the people—all amongst the patriots, whilst the powerful conspirators live and triumph. Rally round us, at least you national guards, who have especially devoted yourselves to the defence of our frontiers in this war with which a perfidious court threatens us. Come—but how?—you are not yet armed. During two whole years you have demanded arms, and yet have them not. What do I say? You have been refused even uniforms, and condemned to wander from department to department, objects of contempt to the minister, and of derision to the patricians, who receive you only to enjoy the spectacle of your distress. No matter; come, we will combat naked like the American savages.

"But shall we await the orders of the war office to destroy

thrones? Shall we await the signal of the court? Shall we be commanded by these patricians, these eternal favorites of despotism, in this war against aristocrats and kings? No—let us march forward alone; let us be our own leaders. But see, the orators of war stop me! Here is Monsieur Brissot, who tells me that Monsieur le Comte de Narbonne must conduct this affair; that we must march under the orders of Monsieur le Marquis de La Fayette; that the executive power alone possesses the right of leading the nation to victory and freedom. Ah, citizens, this word has dispelled all the charm! Adieu, victory, and the independence of the people; if the sceptres of Europe ever be broken, it will not be by such hands. Spain will continue for some time the degraded slave of superstition and royalism. Leopold will continue the tyrant of Germany and Italy, and we shall not speedily behold Catos or Ciceros replace the pope and the cardinals in the conclave. I declare openly, that war, as I understand the term—war, such as I have proposed, is impracticable. And if it be the war of the court, of the ministers, of the patricians who affect patriotism, that we must accept—oh, then, far from believing in the freedom of the world, I despair of your liberty. The wisest course left us is to defend it against the perfidy of those enemies at home who lull you with these heroic illusions.

"I continue calmly and sorrowfully. I have proved that liberty possesses no more deadly foe than war; I have proved that war, advised by men already objects of suspicion, was, in the hands of the executive power, nought save a means of annihilating the constitution, only the end of a plot against the Revolution. Thus to favor these plans of war, under what pretext soever, is to associate ourselves with these treasonable plots against the Revolution. All the patriotism in the world, all the pretended political commonplaces, cannot change the nature of things. To inculcate, like M. Brissot and his friends, confidence in the executive power, and to call down public favor on the generals, is to disarm the Revolution of its last hope—the vigilance and energy of the nation. In the horrible position in which despotism, intrigue, treason, and the general blindness have placed us, I consult alone my head and my heart. I respect nothing, save my country; I obey nought, save truth. I know that some patriots blame the frankness with which I present this discouraging future of our situation. I do not conceal my fault from myself. Is not the truth already sufficiently guilty because it is the truth? Ah! so that our slumbers be light, what matter, though we be awakened by the clash of chains?—and in the quietude of slavery let us no longer disturb the repose of these fortunate patriots. No, but let them know that we can measure with a firm eye and steady heart the depths of the abyss. Let us adopt the device of the palatine of Posnania—'*I prefer the storms of liberty to the serenity of slavery.*'

"If the moment of emancipation be not yet arrived, at least we should have the patience to await it. If this generation was but destined to struggle in the quicksand of vice, into which despotism had plunged it; if the theatre of our revolution was destined but to present to the eyes of the universe a struggle between perfidy and weakness, egotism and ambition;—the rising generation would commence the task of purifying this earth, so sullied by vice. It would bring, not the peace of despotism or the sterile agitations of intrigue, but fire and sword, to lay low the thrones and exterminate the oppressors. O more fortunate posterity, thou art not stranger to us! It is for thee that we brave the storms and the intrigues of tyranny. Often discouraged by the obstacles that environ us, we feel the necessity of struggling for thee. Thou shalt complete our work. Retain on thy memory the names of the martyrs of liberty." The sentiments of Rousseau were to be traced in these words.

VII.

Louvet, one of the friends of Brissot, felt their power, and mounted the tribune in order to move the man who alone arrested the progress of the Gironde. "Robespierre," said he, apostrophizing him directly; "Robespierre—you alone keep the public mind in suspense—doubtless this excess of glory was reserved for you. Your speeches belong to posterity, and posterity will come to judge between you and me. But you will mar a great responsibility by persisting in your opinions; you are accountable to your cotemporaries, and even to future generations—yes, posterity will judge between us, unworthy as I may be of it. It will say, a man appeared in the Constituent Assembly—inaccessible to all passions, one of the most faithful defenders of the people—it was impossible not to esteem and cherish his virtues, not to admire his courage—he was adored by the people, whom he had constantly served, and he was worthy of it. A precipice opens. Fatigued by too much labor, this man imagined he saw peril where there was none, and did not see it where it really was. A man of no note was present, entirely occupied with the present moment, aided by other citizens—he perceived the danger, and could not remain silent. He went to Robespierre, and sought to make him touch it with his finger. Robespierre turned away his eyes, and withdrew his hand; the stranger persisted, and saved his country."

Robespierre smiled with disdain and incredulity at these words. The suppliant gestures of Louvet, and the adjurations of the tribunes found him the next morning firm and unmoved. Brissot resumed the debate on war;—"I implore Monsieur Robespierre," said he, in conclusion, "to terminate so unworthy a struggle, which profits alone the enemies of the public welfare." "My surprise was extreme," cried Robespierre, "at seeing this morning, in the journal edited by M. Brissot, the most pompous eulogium on M. de La Fayette." "I declare," replied Brissot, "that I am utterly ignorant of the insertion of this letter in '*Le Patriote Français*.'" "So much the better," returned Robespierre. "I am delighted to find that M. Brissot is not a party to any such apologies." Their words became as bitter as their hearts, and hate became more perceptible at every reply. The aged Dusaulx interfered, made a touching appeal to the patriots, and entreated them to embrace. They complied. "I have now fulfilled a duty of fraternity, and satisfied my heart," cried Robespierre. "I have yet a more sacred debt to pay my country. All personal regard must give place to the sacred interests of liberty and humanity. I can easily reconcile them here with the regard and respect I have promised to those who serve them; I have embraced M. Brissot, but I persist in opposing him: let our peace repose only on the basis of patriotism and virtue." Robespierre, by his very isolation, proved his force, and obtained fresh influence over the minds of the waverers. The papers began to side with him. Marat heaped invectives on Brissot; Camille Desmoulins, in his pamphlets, exposed the shameful association of Brissot, in London, with Morande, the dishonored libelist. Danton himself, the orator of success, fearing to be deceived by fortune, hesitated between the Girondists and Robespierre. He remained silent for a long time, and then made a speech full of high-sounding words, beneath which was visible the hesitation of his convictions, and the embarrassment of his mind.

BOOK X.

I.

Whilst this was passing at the Jacobins, and the journals —those echoes of the clubs—excited in the people the same anxiety and the same hesitation, the underhand diplomacy of the cabinet of the Tuileries, and the emperor Leopold, who sought in vain to postpone the termination, were about to behold all their schemes thwarted by the impatience of the Gironde and the death of Leopold. This philosophic prince was destined to bear away with him all desire of reconciliation and every hope of peace, for he alone restrained Germany. M. de Narbonne thwarted by public demonstrations the secret negotiations of his colleague M. de Lessart, who strove to temporize, and to refer all the differences of France and Europe to a congress.

The diplomatic committee of the Assembly, urged by Narbonne, and composed of Girondists, proposed decisive resolutions. This committee, established by the Assembly, and influenced by the ideas of Mirabeau, called the ministers to account for everything that occurred: out of the kingdom diplomacy was thus unmasked—the negotiations broken off—all combination rendered impossible, for the cabinets of Europe were continually cited before the tribune of Paris. The Girondists, the actual leaders of this committee, possessed neither the skill nor the prudence necessary to handle without breaking the fine threads of diplomacy. A speech was in their eyes far more meritorious than a negotiation; and they cared not that their words should re-echo in foreign cabinets, provided they sounded well in the chamber or the tribune. Moreover, they were desirous of war, and looked on themselves as statesmen, because at one stroke they had disturbed the peace of Europe. Ignorant of politics, they yet deemed themselves masters of it, because they were unscrupulous; and because they affected the indifference of Machiavel, they deemed they possessed his depth.

The emperor Leopold, by a proclamation, on the 21st of December, furnished the Assembly with a pretext for an outbreak. "The sovereigns united," said the emperor, "for the maintenance of public tranquillity and the honor and safety of the crowns." These words excited the minds of all to know what could be their meaning; they asked each other how the emperor, the brother-in-law, and ally of Louis XVI., could speak to him for the first time of the sovereigns acting in concert? and against what, if not against the Revolution? And how could the ministers and ambassadors of the Revolution have been ignorant of its existence? Why had they concealed from the nation their knowledge, if they had known it? There was, then, a double diplomacy, each striving to outwit the other. The Austrian Alliance was, then, no dream of faction; there was either incompetence or treason in official diplomacy, perhaps both. A projected congress was spoken of—could it have any other object than that of imposing modifications on the constitution of France?—And all felt indignant at the idea of ceding even one tittle of the constitution to the demand of monarchical Europe.

II.

It was whilst the public mind was thus agitated that the diplomatic committee presented, through the Girondist Gensonné, its report on the existing state of affairs with the emperor. Gensonné, an advocate of Bordeaux, elected to the Legislative Assembly on the same day as Guadet and Vergniaud, his friends and countrymen, composed, with these deputies, that triumvirate of talent, opinion, and eloquence, afterwards termed the Gironde. An obstinate and dialectic style of oratory, bitter and keen irony, were the characteristics of the talents of the Gironde; it did not carry away by its eloquence, it constrained; and its revolutionary passions were strong, yet under the control of reason.

Before entering the Assembly, he had been sent as a commissioner with Dumouriez, afterwards so celebrated, to study the state of the popular feeling in the department of the west, and to propose measures likely to tend to the pacification of these countries, then distracted by religious differences. His clear and enlightened report had been in favor of tolerance and liberty—those two topics of all consciences. He was then, in common with the other Girondists, resolved to carry out the Revolution to its extreme and definite form—a republic, without, however, too soon destroying the constitutional throne, provided the constitution was in the hands of his party.

The intimate friend of the Minister Narbonne, his calumniators accused him of having sold himself to him. Nothing however, bears out this suspicion; for if the soul of the Girondists was not free from ambition and intrigue, their hands at least were pure from corruption.

Gensonné, in his report in the name of the diplomatic committee, asked two questions; first, what was our political situation with regard to the emperor; secondly, should his last *office* be regarded as an act of hostility; and in this case was it advisable to accelerate this inevitable rupture by commencing the attack.

"Our situation with regard to the emperor," replied he to himself, "is, that the French interests are sacrificed to the house of Austria; our finances and our armies wasted in her service—our alliances broken, and what mark of reciprocity do we receive? The Revolution insulted; our cockade profaned; the emigrés permitted to congregate in the states dependent on Austria; and lastly, the avowal of the coalition of the powers against us. When from the heart of Luxembourg our princes threaten us with an invasion, and boast of the support of the other powers, Austria remains silent, and thus tacitly sanctions the threats of our enemies. It is true she affects from time to time to blame the hostile demonstrations against France, but this was but a hypocritical peace. The white cockade and the counter-revolutionary uniform are openly worn in her states, whilst our national colors are proscribed. When the king threatened the elector of Trèves that he would march into his territories and disperse the emigrés by force, the emperor ordered General Bender to advance to the assistance of the elector of Trèves. This is but a slight matter; in the report drawn up at Pilnitz, the emperor declares, in concert with the king of Prussia, that the two powers would consider the steps to be taken, with regard to France, by the other European courts; and that should war ensue, they would mutually assist each other. Thus it is manifest that the emperor had violated the treaty of 1756, by contracting alliances without the knowledge of France; and that he has made himself the promoter and pivot of an anti-French system. What can be his aim but to intimidate and subdue us, in order to bring us to accept a congress, and the introduction of shameful modifications in our new institutions?

"Perhaps," added Gensonné, "this idea has germinated in France? Perhaps secret information induces the emperor to hope that peace may be maintained on such conditions. He is deceived: it is not at the moment when the flame of liberty is first kindled in a nation of twenty-four millions, that Frenchmen would consent to a capitulation, to which they would prefer death. Such is our situation, that war, which in other times would be a scourge to the human race, would now be useful to the public welfare. This salutary crisis would elevate the people to the level of their destiny; it would restore to them their pristine energy—it would re-establish our finances, and stifle the germ of intestine dissension. In a similar situation Frederic the Great broke the league formed against him by the court of Vienna, by forestalling it. Your committee propose that the preparations for war be accelerated. A congress would be a disgrace—war is necessary—public opinion wishes for it—and public safety demands it."

The committee concluded, by demanding clear and satisfactory explanations from the emperor; and that in case these explanations should not be given before the 10th of February, this refusal to reply should be considered as an act of hostility.

III.

Scarcely was the report terminated than Guadet, who presided that day at the Assembly, mounted the tribune, and began to comment on the report of his friend and colleague. Guadet, born at Saint Emelion, near Bordeaux, already celebrated as an advocate before the age at which men have generally made themselves a reputation, impatiently expected by the political tribunes, had at last arrived at the Legislative Assembly. A disciple of Brissot, less profound, but equally courageous and more eloquent than his master, he was intimately connected with Gensonné, Vergniaud, to whom he was bound by being of the same age, the same passions, and the same country; endowed with an undaunted and energetic mind, and winning powers of oratory, equally fitted to resist the movement of a popular assembly, or to precipitate them to a termination; all these natural advantages were heightened by one of those southern casts of face and feature that serve so well to illustrate the working of the mind within.

"A congress has just been spoken of," said he; "what, then, is this conspiracy formed against us? How long shall we suffer ourselves to be fatigued by these manœuvres—to be outraged by these hopes? Have those who have planned them, well weighed this? The bare idea of the possibility of a capitulation of liberty might hurry into crime those malcontents who cherish the hope; and these are the crimes we should crush in the bud. Let us teach these princes that the nation is resolved to preserve its constitution pure and unchanged, or to perish with it. In one word, let us mark out the place for these traitors, and let that place be the scaffold. I propose that the decree pass at this instant; That the nation regards as infamous, as traitors to their country, and as guilty of *leze-majesté*, every agent of the executive power, every Frenchman (several voices, 'every *legislator*'), who shall take part, directly or indirectly, at this congress, whose object is to obtain modifications in the constitution, or a mediation between France and the rebels."

At these words the Assembly rose as if by common consent. Every hand was raised in the attitude of men ready to take a solemn oath; the tribunes and the chamber confounded their applause, and the decree was passed.

M. de Lessart, whom the gesture and the allusion of Gaudet seemed to have already designated as the victim to the suspicions of the people, could not remain silent under the weight of these terrible allusions. "Mention has been made," said he, "of the political agents of the executive power: I declare that I know nothing which can authorize us to suspect their fidelity. For my own part, I will repeat the declaration of my colleagues in the ministry, and adopt it for my own—the constitution or death."

Whilst Gensonné and Guadet aroused the Assembly by this preconcerted scene, Vergniaud aroused the crowd by the copy of an address to the French people, which had been spread abroad for the last few days amongst the masses. The Girondists remembered the effect produced two years previously by the proposed address to the king to dismiss the troops.

"Frenchmen," said Vergniaud, "war threatens your frontiers; conspiracies against liberty are rife. Your armies are assembling: mighty movements agitate the empire. Seditious priests prepare in the confessional, and even in the pulpit, a rising against the constitution; martial law becomes essential. Thus it appeared to us just. But we only succeeded in brandishing the thunderbolts for a moment before the eyes of the rebels—the king has refused to sanction our decrees; the German princes make their territories a stronghold for the conspirators against us. They favor the plots of the emigrés, and furnish them with an asylum, arms, horses, and provisions. Can patience endure this without becoming guilty of suicide? Doubtless you have renounced the desire of conquest; but you have not promised to suffer insolent provocation. You have shaken off the yoke of tyrants; surely, then, you will not bow the knee to foreign despots? Beware! you are surrounded by snares; traitors seek to reduce you through disgust or fatigue to a state of languor that enervates your courage; and soon perhaps they will strive to lead it astray. They seek to separate you from us; they pursue a system of calumny against the National Assembly to criminate the Revolution in your eyes. Oh, beware of these excessive terrors! Repulse indignantly these impostors, who, whilst they affect a hypocritical zeal for the constitution, yet unceasingly speak of the *monarchy*. The *monarchy* is to them the counter-revolution. The *monarchy* is the *nobility;* the counter-revolution—that is taxation, the feudal system, the Bastille, chains, and executions, to punish the sublime impulses of liberty. Foreign satellites in the interior of the state—bankruptcy, ingulfiing with your *assignats* your private fortunes and the national wealth —the fury of fanaticism, of vengeance, murder, rapine, conflagration, despotism, and slaughter, contending, in rivers of blood and over the heaps of dead, for the mastery of your unhappy country. Nobility—that is, two classes of men, one for greatness, the other for poverty; one for tyranny, the other for slavery. Nobility; ah! the very word is an insult to the human race.

"And yet it is to insure the success of this conspiracy against you that all Europe is in arms.—You must annihilate these guilty hopes by a solemn declaration. Yes, the representatives of France, free, and deeply attached to the constitution, will be buried beneath her ruins, rather than suffer a capitulation unworthy of them to be wrung from them. Rally yourselves, take courage! In vain do they strive to excite the nations against you, they will only excite the princes, for the hearts of the people are with you, and you embrace their cause by defending your own. Hate war: it is the greatest crime of mankind, and the most fearful scourge of humanity; but since it is forced on you, follow the course of your destiny. Who can foresee how far will extend the punishment of those tyrants who have forced you to take arms ?" Thus, these three statesmen joined their voices to impel the nation to war.

IV.

The last words of Vergniaud gave the people a tolerably clear prospect of a universal republic. Nor were the constitutionalists less eager in directing the ideas of the nation towards war. M. de Narbonne, on his return from his hasty journey, presented a most encouraging report to the Assembly, of the state of the fortified towns. He praised every one. He presented to the country the young Mathieu de Montmorency, one of the most illustrious names of France, and whose character was even more noble than his name, as the representative of the aristocracy devoting itself to liberty. He declared that the army, in its attachment to its country, did not separate the king from the Assembly. He praised the commanders of the troops, nominated Rochambeau general-in-chief of the army of the north, Berthier at Metz, Biron at Lisle, Luckner and La Fayette on the Rhine. He spoke of plans for the campaign, concerted between the king and these officers; he enumerated the national guards, ready to serve as a second line to the active army, and solicited that they should be promptly armed; he described these volunteers, as giving the army the most imposing of all characters —that of national feeling; he vouched for the officers, who had sworn fidelity to the constitution, and exonerated from the charge of treason those who had not done so; he encouraged the Assembly to mistrust those that hesitated. "Mistrust," said he, "is, in these stormy times, the most natural, but the most dangerous feeling; confidence wins men's hearts, and it is important that the people should show they have friends only." He ended by announcing that the active force of the army was 110,000 foot, and 20,000 cavalry, ready to take the field.

This report, praised by Brissot in his journal, and by the Girondists in the Assembly, afforded no longer any pretext for delaying the war. France felt that her strength was equal to her indignation, and she could be restrained no longer. The increasing unpopularity of the king augmented the popular excitement. Twice had he already arrested, by his royal *veto*, the energetic measures of the Assembly—the decree against the emigrés, and the decree against the priests who had not taken the oath. These two *vetoes*, the one dic tated by his honor, the other by his conscience, were two terrible weapons, placed in his hand by the constitution, yet which he could not wield without wounding himself. The Girondists revenged themselves for this resistance by compelling him to make war on the princes, who were his brothers, and the emperor, whom they believed to be his accomplice.

The pamphleteers and the Jacobin journalists constantly spoke of these two *vetoes* as acts of treason. The disturbances in Vendée were attributed to a secret understanding between the king and the rebellious clergy. In vain did the department of Paris, composed of men who respected the conscience of others, such as M. de Talleyrand, M. de la Rochefoucauld, and M. de Beaumetz, present to the king a petition in which the true principles of liberty protested against the revolutionary inquisition: counter-petitions poured in from the departments.

V.

Camille Desmoulins, the Voltaire of the clubs, lent to the petition of the citizens of Paris that insolent raillery, which made the success of his talent.

"Worthy representatives," ran the petition,* "applauses are the civil list of the people, therefore do not reject ours. To collect the homages of good citizens, and the insults of the bad, is, to a National Assembly, to have combined all suffrages. The king has put his *veto* to your decree against the emigrants, a decree equally worthy of the majesty of the Roman people and the clemency of the French people. We do not complain of this act of the king, because we remember the maxim of the great politician Machiavel, which we beg of you to meditate upon profoundly—*It is against nature to fall voluntarily from such a height.* Penetrated with this truth, we do not then require from the king an impossible love for the constitution, nor do we find fault that he is opposed to your best decisions. But let public functionaries foresee the royal veto, and declare their rebellion against your decree, against the priests; let them carry off public opinion; let these men be precisely the same who caused to be shot in the Champ-de-Mars the citizens who were signing a petition against a decree which was not yet decided upon; let them inundate the empire with copies of

* This extract has been given before at p. 238 - *Translator.*

this petition, which is nothing more than the first leaf of a great counter-revolutionary register and a subscription for civil war sent for signature to all the fanatics, all the idiots, all permanent slaves. Fathers of the country! there is here such complicated ingratitude and abuse of confidence, of contradiction and chicanery, of prevarication and treason, that profoundly indignant at so much wickedness concealed beneath the cloak of philosophy and hypocritical civism, we say to you—Your decree has saved the country, and if they are obstinate in refusing you permission to save the country, well, the nation will save itself, for, after all, the power of a *veto* has a termination—a veto does not prevent the taking of the Bastille.

"You are told that the salary of the priests was a national debt. But when you only request the priests to declare that they will not be seditious—are not they who refuse this declaration already seditious in their hearts? And these seditious priests, who have never lent anything to the state —who are only creditors of the state in the name of benevolence—have they not a thousand times forfeited the donation through their ingratitude? Away, then, with these miserable sophisms, fathers of the country, and have no more doubt of the omnipotence of a free people. If liberty slumbers, how can the arm act? Do not raise this arm again, do not again lift the national club to crush insects. Did Cato and Cicero proceed against Cethegus or Catiline? It is the chiefs we should assail: strike at the head."

A scornful laugh echoed from the tribunes of the Assembly to the populace. The *procès-verbal* of this sitting was ordered to be sent to the eighty-three departments. Next day the Assembly reconsidered this, and negatived its vote of the previous evening; but publicity was still given to it, and it echoed through the provinces, carrying with it the disquietude, derision, and hatred attached to the *Royal Veto.* The constitution, handed over to ridicule and hooted in full assembly, had now become the plaything of the populace.

For many months the state of the kingdom resembled the state of Paris. All was uproar, confusion, denunciation, disturbance in the departments. Each courier brought his riots, seditions, petitions, outbreaks, and assassinations. The clubs established as many points of resistance to the constitution as there were communes in the empire. The civil war hatching in La Vendée burst out by massacres at Avignon.

VI.

This city and comtal, united to France by the recent decree of the Constituent Assembly, had remained from this period in an intermediary state between two dominations, so favorable to anarchy. The partisans of the papal government, and the partisans of the reunion with France, struggled there in alternations of hope and fear, which prolonged and envenomed their hate. The king, from a religious scruple, had for too long suspended the execution of the decree of reunion. Trembling to infringe upon the domain of the church, he deferred his decision, and his impolitic delays gave time for crimes.

France was represented in Avignon by mediators. The provisional authority of these mediators was supported by a detachment of troops of the line. The power, entirely municipal, was confided to the dictatorship of the municipality. The populace, excited and agitated, was divided into the French or revolutionary party, and the party opposed to the reunion by France and the Revolution. The fanaticism of religion with one, the fanaticism of liberty with the other, impelled the two parties even to crimes. The warmth of blood, the thirst of private vengeance, the heat of the climate, all added to civil passions. The violences of Italian republics were all to be seen in the manners of this Italian colony, of this branch establishment of Rome on the banks of the Rhone. The smaller states are, the more atrocious are their civil wars. There opposite opinions become personal hatreds; contests are but assassinations. Avignon commenced these wholesale assassinations by private murders.

On the 16th of October a gloomy agitation betrayed itself by the mobs of people collecting on various points, particularly consisting of persons enemies of the Revolution. The walls of the church were covered with placards, calling on the people to revolt against the provisional authority of the municipality. There were bruited about rumors of absurd miracles, which demanded in the name of Heaven vengeance for the assaults made against religion. A statue of the Virgin worshipped by the people in the church of the Cordeliers had blushed at the profanations of her temple. She had been seen to shed tears of indignation and grief. The people, educated under the papal government in such superstitious credulities had gone in a body to the Cordeliers to avenge the cause of their protectress. Animated by fanatical exhortations, confiding in the divine interposition, the mob, on quitting the Cordeliers, and increasing as it went, hurried to the ramparts, closed the doors, turned the cannon on the city, and then spread themselves through the streets, demanding with loud clamors the overthrow of the government. The unfortunate Lescuyer, notary of Avignon, secretary (*greffier*) of the municipality, more particularly pointed out to the fury of the mob, was dragged violently from his residence, and along the pavement to the altar of the Cordeliers, where he was murdered by sabre-strokes and blows from bludgeons, trampled under foot, his dead body outraged and cast as an expiatory victim at the feet of the offended statue. The national guard having dispatched a detachment with two pieces of cannon from the fort, drove back the infuriated populace, and picked from the pavement the naked and lifeless carcase of Lescuyer. The prisons of the city had been broken open, and the miscreants they contained came to offer their assistance for other murders. Horrible reprisals were feared, and yet the mediators, absent from the city, were asleep, or closed their eyes upon the actual danger. The understanding between the leaders of the Paris clubs and the rioters of Avignon became more fearfully intimate.

VII.

One of those sinister persons who seem to smell blood and presage crime, reached Avignon from Versailles: his name was Jourdan. He is not to be confounded with another revolutionist of the same name, born at Avignon. Sprung from the arid and calcined mountains of the south, where the very brutes are more ferocious; by turns, butcher, farrier, and smuggler, in the gorges which separate Savoy from France; a soldier, deserter, horse-jobber, and then a keeper of a low wine shop in the suburbs of Paris; he had wallowed in all the lowest vices of the dregs of a metropolis. The first murders committed by the people in the streets of Paris had disclosed his real character. It was not that of contest but of murder. He appeared after the carnage to mangle the victims, and render the assassination fouler. He was a butcher of men, and he boasted of it. It was he who had thrust his hands into the open breasts and plucked forth the hearts of Foulon and Berthier.* It was he who had cut off the head of the two *gardes-de-corps*, de Varicourt and des Huttes, at Versailles, on the 6th of October. It was he who, entering Paris, bearing the two heads at the end of a pike, reproached the people with being content with so little, and having made him go so far to cut off only two heads! He hoped for better things at Avignon, and went thither.

There was at Avignon a body of volunteers called the army of Vaucluse, formed of the dregs of that country, and commanded by one Patrix. This Patrix having been assassinated by his troop, whose excesses he desired to moderate, Jourdan was elevated to the command by the claims of sedition and wickedness. The soldiers, when reproached with their robberies and murders, similar to those of the *Gueux* of Belgium, and the *sans-culottes* of Paris, received the reproach as an honor, and called themselves the *brave brigands* of Avignon. Jourdan at the head of this band, ravaged and fired le Comtal, laid siege to Carpentras, was repulsed, lost five hundred men, and fell back upon Avignon, still shuddering at the murder of Lescuyer. He resolved on lending his arm and his troop to the vengeance of the French party. On the 30th of August Jourdan and his myrmidons closed the city-gates, dispersed through the streets, going to the houses noted as containing enemies to the Revolution, dragging out the inhabitants—men, women, aged persons, and children,—all without distinction of age, sex or innocence, and shut them up in the palace. When night came, the assassins broke down the doors, and murdered with iron crowbars these disarmed and supplicating victims. In vain did they shriek to the national guard for aid ; the city hears the massacre without daring to give any signs of animation. The daring of the crime chilled and paralyzed every citizen. The murderers preluded the death of the females by derision and insults which added shame to terror, and the agonies of modesty to the pangs of murder. When there were no more to be slain they mutilated the carcases, and swept the blood into the sewer of the palace. They dragged the mutilated

* Foulon was a contractor, who, odious to the populace, was compelled to fly from Paris, but being discovered, was brought back, and eventually murdered by the mob in July, 1789. Berthier was his son-in-law, and also incurring the displeasure of the people, was a few days later stabbed by a hundred bayonets whilst on his way to prison. H. T. R.

corses to La Glacière, walled them up, and the vengeance of the people was stamped upon them. Jourdan and his satellites offered the homage of this night to the French mediators and the National Assembly. The scoundrels of Paris admired—the Assembly shook with indignation, and considered this crime as an outrage: whilst the president fainted on reading the recital of this night at Avignon. The arrest of Jourdan and his accomplices was commanded. Jourdan fled from Avignon, pursued by the French; he dashed his horse into the river of the Sargue: caught in the middle of the river, by a soldier, he fired at him and missed. He was seized and bound, and punishment awarded him, but the Jacobins compelled the Girondists to agree to an amnesty for the crimes of Avignon. Jourdan making sure of impunity, and proud of his iniquities, went thither to be revenged on his denouncers.

The Assembly shuddered for a moment at the sight of this blood, and then hastily turned its eyes away. In its impatience to reign alone, it had not the time to display pity. There was, besides, between the Girondists and the Jacobins a contest for leadership, and a rivalry in going ahead of the Revolution which made each of the two factions afraid that the other should be in advance. Dead bodies did not make them pause, and tears shed for too long a time might have been taken for weakness.

VIII.

However, victims multiplied daily, and disasters followed disasters. The whole empire seemed ready to fall and crush its founders. San Domingo, the richest of the French colonies, was swimming in blood. France was punished for its egotism. The Constituent Assembly had proclaimed, in principle, the liberty of the blacks, but, in fact, slavery still existed. Two hundred thousand slaves served as human cattle to some thousands of colonists. They were bought and sold, and cut and maimed, as if they were inanimate objects. They were kept by speculation out of the civil law, and out of the religious law. Property, family, marriage, all was forbidden to them. Care was taken to degrade them below men, to preserve the right of treating them as brutes If some unions furtive, or favored by cupidity, were formed amongst them, the wife and children belonged to the master. They were sold separately, without any regard to the ties of nature, all the attachments with which God has formed the chain of human sympathies were rent asunder without commiseration.

This crime *en masse,* this systematic brutality, had its theorists and apologists; human faculties were denied to the blacks. They were classed as a race between the flesh and the spirit. Thus the infamous abuse of power, which was exercised over this inert and servile race, was called necessary guardianship. Tyrants have never wanted sophists: on the other hand, men of right feeling towards their fellows, who had, like Gregoire, Raynal, Barnave, Brissot, Condorcet, La Fayette, embraced the cause of humanity, and formed the "*Society of the Friends of the Blacks,*" had circulated their principles in the colonies, like a vengeance rather than as justice. These principles had burst forth without preparation, and unanticipated in colonial society, where truth had no organ but insurrection. Philosophy proclaims principles; politics administer them; the friends of the blacks were contented with proclaiming them. France had not had courage to dispossess and indemnify her colonists: she had acquired liberty for herself alone: she adjourned, as she still adjourns at the moment I write these lines, the reparation for the crime of slavery in her colonies: could she be astonished that slavery should seek to avenge herself, and that liberty, warmly proclaimed in Paris, should not become an insurrection at San Domingo? Every iniquity that a free society allows to subsist for the profit of the oppressor, is a sword with which she herself arms the oppressed. Right is the most dangerous of weapons; woe to him who leaves it to his enemies!

IX.

San Domingo proved this. Fifty thousand black slaves rose in one night at the instigation, and under the command, of the mulattoes, or men of color. The men of color, the intermediary race, springing from white colonists and black slaves, were not slaves, neither were they citizens. They were a kind of freedmen, with the defects and virtues of the two races; the pride of the whites, the degradation of the blacks; a fluctuating race who, by turning sometimes to the side of the slaves, sometimes to that of the masters, inevitably produced those terrible oscillations which inevitably superinduce the overthrow of society.

The mulattoes, who themselves possessed slaves, had begun by making common cause with the colonists, and by opposing the emancipation of the blacks more obstinately than even the whites themselves. The nearer they were to slavery, the more doggedly did they defend their share in tyranny. Man is thus made: none is more ready to abuse his right than he who, with difficulty, has acquired it; there are no tyrants worse than slaves, and no men prouder than *parvenus.*

The men of color had all the vices of *parvenus* of liberty. But when they perceived that the whites despised them as a mingled race, that the Revolution had not effaced the tinge of their skin, and the injurious prejudices which were attached to their color; when they in vain claimed for themselves the exercise of civil rights, which the colonists opposed, they passed with the impetuosity and levity of their conduct from one passion to another, from one party to the other, and made common cause with the oppressed race. Their habits of command, fortune, intelligence, energy, boldness, naturally pointed them out as the leaders of the blacks. They fraternized with them, they became popular amongst the blacks, from the very tinge of skin for which they had recently blushed, when in company with the whites. They secretly fomented the germs of insurrection at the nightly meetings of the slaves. They kept up a clandestine correspondence with the friends of the blacks in Paris. They spread widely in the huts, speeches and papers from Paris, which instructed the colonists in their duties and informed the slaves of their indefeasible rights. The rights of man, commented upon by vengeance, became the catechism of all dwellings.

The whites trembled; terror urged them to violence. The blood of the mulatto Ogé and his accomplices, shed by M. de Blanchelande, governor of San Domingo and the colonial council, sowed everywhere despair and conspiracy.

X.

Ogé, deputed to Paris by the men of color to assert their rights in the Constituent Assembly, bad become known to Brissot, Raynal, Grégoire, and was affiliated with them to the Society of the Friends of the Blacks. Passing thence into England, he became known to the admirable philanthropist, Clarkson. Clarkson and his friend at this time were pleading the cause of the emancipation of the negroes: they were the first apostles of that religion of humanity who believed that they could not raise their hands purely towards God, so long as those hands retained a link of that chain which holds a race of human beings in degradation and in slavery. The association with these men of worth expanded Ogé's mind. He had come to Europe only to defend the interest of the mulattoes; he now took up with warmth the more liberal and holy cause of all the blacks; he devoted himself to the liberty of all his brethren. He returned to France, and became very intimate with Barnave; he entreated the Constituent Assembly to apply the principles of liberty to the colonies, and not to make any exception to Divine law, by leaving the slaves to their masters; excited and irritated by the hesitation of the committee, who withdrew with one hand what it gave with the other, he declared that if justice could not suffice for their cause, he would appeal to force. Barnave had said, "*Perish the colonies rather than a principle!*" The men of the 14th of July had no right to condemn, in the heart of Ogé, that revolt which was their own title to independence. We may believe that the secret wishes of the friends of the blacks followed Ogé, who returned to San Domingo. He found there the rights of men of color and the principles of liberty of the blacks more denied and more profaned than ever. He raised the standard of insurrection, but with the forms and rights of legality. At the head of a body of two hundred men of color, he demanded the promulgation in the colonies of the decrees of the National Assembly, despotically delayed until that time. He wrote to the military commandant of the Cape, "We require the proclamation of the law which makes us free citizens. If you oppose this, we will repair to Leogane, we will nominate electors, and repel force by force. The pride of the colonists revolts at sitting beside us: was the pride of the nobility and clergy consulted when the equality of citizens was proclaimed in France?"

The government replied to this eloquent demand for liberty by sending a body of troops to disperse the persons assembled, and Ogé drove them back.

XI.

A larger body of troops being dispatched, they contrived, after a desperate resistance, to disperse the mulattoes. Ogé escaped, and found refuge in the Spanish part of the island. A price was set upon his head. M. de Blanchelande in his proclamations imputed it as a crime to him that he had claimed the rights of nature in the name of the Assembly, which had so loudly proclaimed the rights of the citizen They applied to the Spanish authorities to surrender this Spartacus, equally dangerous to the safety of the whites in both countries. Ogé was delivered up to the French by the Spaniards, and sent for trial to the Cape. His trial was protracted for two months, in order to afford time to cut asunder all the threads of the plot of independence, and intimidate his accomplices. The whites, in great excitement, complained of these delays, and demanded his head with loud vociferations. The judges condemned him to death for a crime which in the mother-country had constituted the glory of La Fayette and Mirabeau.

He underwent torture in his dungeon. The rights of his race, centred and persecuted in him, raised his soul above the torments of his executioners. "Give up all hope," he exclaimed, with unflinching daring; "give up all hope of extracting from me the name of even one of my accomplices. My accomplices are everywhere where the heart of man is raised against the oppressors of men." From that moment he pronounced but two words, which sounded like a remorse in the ears of his persecutors—*Liberty! Equality!* He walked composedly to his death; listened with indignation to the sentence which condemned him to the lingering and infamous death of the vilest criminals. "What!" he exclaimed; "do you confound me with criminals because I have desired to restore to my fellow-creatures the rights and titles of men which I feel in myself? Well! you have my blood, but an avenger will arise from it!" He died on the wheel, and his mutilated carcass was left on the highway. This heroic death reached even to the National Assembly, and gave rise to various opinions. "He deserved it," said Malouet; "Ogé was a criminal and an assassin." "If Ogé be guilty," replied Grégoire, "so are we all; if he who claimed liberty for his brothers perished justly on the scaffold, then all Frenchmen who resemble us should mount there also."

XII.

Ogé's blood bubbled silently in the hearts of all the mulatto race. They swore to avenge him. The blacks were an army all ready for the massacre; the signal was given to them by the men of color. In one night 60,000 slaves, armed with torches and their working tools, burnt down all their masters' houses in a circuit of six leagues round the Cape. The whites were murdered; women, children, old men—nothing escaped the long-repressed fury of the blacks. It was the annihilation of one race by the other. The bleeding heads of the whites, carried on the tops of sugar canes, were the standards which guided these hordes, not to combat, but to carnage. The outrages of so many centuries, committed by the whites on the blacks, were avenged in one night.. A rivalry of cruelty seemed to arise between the two colors. The negroes imitated the tortures so long used upon them, and invented new ones. If certain noble and faithful slaves placed themselves between their old masters and death, they were sacrificed together. Gratitude and pity are virtues which civil war never recognizes. Color was a sentence of death without exception of persons; the war was between the races, and no longer between men. The one must perish for the other to live! Since justice could not make itself understood by them, there was nothing but death left for them. Every gift of life to a white was a treason which would cost a black man's life. The negroes had no longer any pity; they were men no longer, they were no longer a people, but a destroying element which spread over the land, annihilating everything.

In a few hours eight hundred habitations, sugar and coffee stores, representing an immense capital, were destroyed. The mills, magazines, utensils, and even the very plant which reminded them of their servitude and their compulsory labor, were cast into the flames. The whole plain, as far as eye could reach, was covered with nothing but the smoke and the ashes of conflagration. The dead bodies of whites, piled in hideous trophies of heads and limbs, of men, women, and infants assassinated, alone marked the spot of the rich residences, where they were supreme on the previous night. It was the revenge of slavery: all tyranny has such fearful reverses.

Some whites, warned in time of the insurrection by the generous indiscretion of the blacks, or protected in their flight by the forests and the darkness, had taken refuge at the Cape Town; others, concealed with their wives and children in caves, were fed and attended to by attached slaves, at the peril of their lives. The army of blacks increased without the walls of the Cape Town, where they formed and disciplined a fortified camp. Guns and cannons arrived by the aid of invisible auxiliaries. Some accused the English, others the Spaniards, others, "the friends of the blacks," with being accomplices of this insurrection. The Spaniards, however, were at peace with France; the revolt of the blacks menaced them equally with ourselves. The English themselves possessed three times as many slaves as the French: the principle of the insurrection, excited by success, and spreading with them, would have ruined their establishments, and compromised the lives of their colonists. These suspicions were absurd; there was no one culpable but liberty itself, which is not to be repressed with impunity in a portion of the human race. It had accomplices in the very heart of the French themselves.

The weakness of the resolutions of the Assembly on the reception of this news proved this. M. Bertrand de Molleville, minister of marine, ordered the immediate departure of 6,000 men as reinforcement for the isle of San Domingo.

Brissot attacked these repressive measures in a discourse in which he did not hesitate to cast the odium of the crime on the victims, and to accuse the government of complicity with the aristocracy of the colonists.

"By what fatality does this news coincide with a moment when emigrations are redoubled? when the rebels assembled on our frontiers warn us of an approaching outbreak? when, in fact, the colonies threaten us, through an illegal deputation, with withdrawing from the rule of the mother-country? Has not this the appearance of a vast plan combined by treason?"

The repugnance of the friends of the blacks, numerous in the Assembly, to take energetic measures in favor of the colonists, the distance from the scene of action, which weakens pity, and then the interior movement which attracted into its sphere minds and things, soon effaced these impressions, and allowed the spirit of independence amongst the blacks to form and expand at San Domingo, which showed itself in the distance in the form of a poor old slave—Toussaint-L'Ouverture.

XIII.

The internal disorder multiplied at every point of the

empire. Religious liberty, which was the desire of the Constituent Assembly, and the most important conquest of the Revolution, could not be established without this struggle in face of a displaced worship, and a schism which spread far and wide amongst the people. The counter revolutionary party was allied everywhere with the clergy. They had the same enemies, and conspired against the same cause. The nonjuring priests had assumed the character of victims, and the interest of a portion of the people, especially in the country, attached to them. Persecution is so odious to the public feeling that its very appearance raises generous indignation against it. The human mind has an inclination to believe that justice is on the side of the proscribed. The priests were not as yet persecuted, but from the moment that they were no longer paramount they believed themselves humiliated. The ill-repressed irritation of the clergy had been more injurious to the Revolution than all the conspiracies of the emigrated aristocracy. Conscience is man's most sensitive point. A superstition attacked, or a faith disturbed in the mind of a people, is the fellest of conspiracies. It was by the hand of God, invisible in the hand of the priesthood, that the aristocracy roused La Vendée. Frequent and bloody symptoms already betrayed themselves in the west, and in Normandy, that concealed focus of religious war.

The most fearful of these symptoms burst out at Caen. The Abbé Fauchet was constitutional bishop of Calvados. The celebrity of his name, the elevated patriotism of his opinions, the *éclat* of his revolutionary renown, his eloquence, and his writings, disseminated widely in his diocese, were the causes of greater excitement throughout Calvados than elsewhere.

Fauchet, whose conformity of opinions, honesty of feelings for renovation, and even whose somewhat fanciful imagination, which were subsequently destined to associate him in acts, and even on the scaffold with the Girondists, was born at Dornes, in the ancient province of Nivernais. He embraced the Catholic faith, entered into the free community of the priests of Saint Roch, at Paris, and was for some time preceptor to the children of the Marquis de Choiseul, brother of the famous Duke de Choiseul, the last minister of the school of Richelieu and Mazarin. A remarkable talent for speaking gave him a distinguished reputation in the pulpit. He was appointed preacher to the king, abbé of

Montfort, and grand-vicaire of Bourges. He advanced rapidly towards the first dignities of the church; but his mind had imbibed the spirit of the times. He was not a destructive, but a reformer of the church, in whose bosom he was born. His work, entitled *De l'Eglise Nationale,* proves in him as much respect for the principles of the Christian faith as boldness of desire to change its discipline. This philosophic faith, which so closely resembles the Christian Platonism which was paramount in Italy under the Medici, and even in the palace of the popes themselves under Leo X., breathed throughout his sacred discourses. The clergy was alarmed at these lights of the age shining in the very sanctuary. The Abbé Fauchet was interdicted, and struck off the list of the king's preachers.

But the Revolution already opened other tribunes to him. It burst forth, and he rushed headlong into it, as imagination rushes towards hope. He fought for it from the day of its birth, and with every kind of weapon. He shook the people in the primary assemblies, and in the sections; he urged with voice and gesture the insurgent masses under the cannon of the Bastille. He was seen, sword in hand, to lead on the assailants. Thrice did he advance under fire of the cannon, at the head of the deputation which summoned the governor to spare the lives of the citizens, and to surrender.* He did not soil his revolutionary zeal with any blood or crime. He inflamed the mind of the people for liberty; but with him liberty was virtue; nature had endowed him with this twofold character. There were in his features the high-priest and the hero. His exterior pleased and attracted the populace. He was tall and slender, with a wide chest, oval countenance, black eyes, and his dark brown hair set off the paleness of his brow. His imposing but modest appearance inspired at the first glance favor and respect. His voice clear, impressive, and full-toned; his majestic carriage, his somewhat mystical style, commanded the reflection, as well as the admiration, of his auditors. Equally adapted to the popular tribune or the pulpit, electoral assemblies or cathedral were alike too circumscribed in limits for the crowds who flocked to hear him. It seemed as though he were a revolutionary saint—Bernard preaching political charity, or the crusade of reason.

His manners were neither severe nor hypocritical. He

* See Michelet's History of the French Revolution, vol. i. p. 154. *Standard Library.*

himself confessed that he loved with legitimate and pure affection Madame Carron, who followed him everywhere, even to the churches and clubs. "They calumniated me with respect to her," he said, "and I attached myself the more strongly to her, and yet I am pure. You have seen her, even more lovely in mind than face, and who, for the ten years I have known her, seems to me daily more worthy of being loved. She would lay down her life for me; I would resign my life for her; but I would never sacrifice my duty to her. In spite of the malignant libels of the aristocrats, I shall go every day at breakfast-time to taste the charms of the purest friendship in her society. She comes to hear me preach! Yes, no doubt of it: no one knows better than herself the sincerity with which I believe in the truths I profess. She comes to the assemblies of the Hôtel-de-Ville! Yes, no doubt of it: it is because she is convinced that patriotism is a second religion, that no hypocrisy is in my soul, and that my life is really devoted to God, to my country, and friendship."

"And you dare to assert that you are chaste," retorted the faithful and indignant priests, by the Abbé de Valmeron. "How absurd! Chaste, at the moment when you confess the most unpardonable inclinations; when you attract a woman from the bed of her husband—her duties as a mother—when you take about everywhere this infatuated female, attached to your footsteps, in order to display her ostentatiously to the public gaze! And who follow, sir! A troop of ruffians and abandoned women. Worthy pastor of this foul populace, which celebrates your pastoral visit by the only rejoicings that can give you pleasure—your progress is marked by every excess of rapine and debauchery." These bitter reproaches resounded in the provinces, and caused great excitement. The conforming and nonconforming priests were disputing the altars. A letter from the minister of the interior came to authorize the nonjuring priests to celebrate the holy sacrifice in the churches where they had previously done duty. Obedient to the law, the constitutional priests opened to them their chapels, supplied them with the ornaments necessary for divine worship; but the multitude, faithful to their ancient pastors, threatened and insulted the new clergy. Bloody struggles took place between the two creeds on the very threshold of God's house. On Friday, November the 4th, the former *cure* of the parish of Saint Jean, at Caen, came to perform the mass

The church was full of Catholics. This meeting offended the constitutionalists and excited the other party. The *Te Deum,* as a thanksgiving, was demanded and sung by the adherents of the ancient *curé,* who, encouraged by this success, announced to the faithful that he should come again the next day at the same hour to celebrate the sacrament. "Patience!" he added; "let us be prudent, and all will be well."

The municipality, informed of these circumstances, entreated the *curé* to abstain from celebrating the mass the next day, as he had announced; and he complied with their wishes. The multitude, not informed of this, filled the church, and clamored for the priest and the promised *Te Deum.* The gentry of the neighborhood, the aristocracy of Caen, the clients and numerous domestics of the leading families in the neighborhood, had arms under their clothes. They insulted the grenadiers; an officer of the national guard reprimanded them. "You come to seek what you shall get," replied the aristocrats: "we are the stronger, and will drive you from the church." At these words some young men rushed on the national guards to disarm them: a struggle ensued, bayonets glittered, pistol shots resounded in the cathedral, and they made a charge, sword in hand. Companies of chasseurs and grenadiers entered the church, cleared it, and followed the crowd, step by step, who fired again upon them when in the street. Some killed and others wounded, were the sad results of the day. Tranquillity seemed restored. Eighty-two persons were arrested, and on one of them was found a pretended plan of counter-revolution, the signal for which was to be given on the following Monday. These documents were forwarded to Paris. The nonjuring priests were suspended from the celebration of the holy mysteries in the churches of Caen until the decision of the National Assembly. The Assembly heard with indignation the recital of these troubles, occasioned by the enemies of the constitution, and the adherents of fanaticism and the aristocracy. "The only part we have to take," said Cambon, "is to convoke the high national court, and send the accused before it." They deferred pronouncing on this proposition until the moment when they should be in possession of all the papers relative to the troubles in Caen.

Gensonné detailed the particulars of similar disturbances in La Vendée: the mountains of the south, La Lozère, l'Herault, l'Ardèche, which were but ill repressed by the recent dispersion of the camp of Jalès, the first act of the counter-revolutionary army, were now greatly agitated by the two-fold impulse of their priests and gentry. The plains, furnished with streams, roads, towns, and easily kept down by the central force, submitted without resistance to the *contre-coups* of Paris. The mountains preserve their customs longer, and resist the influence of new ideas as to a conquest by armed strangers. It seems as though the appearance of these natural ramparts gave their inhabitants confidence in their strength, and a solid conviction of the unchangeableness of things, which prevents them from being so easily carried away by the rapid currents of alteration.

The mountaineers of these countries felt for their nobles that voluntary and traditional devotion which the Arabs have for their sheiks, and the Scots for the chieftains of their clans. This respect and this attachment form part of the national honor in these rural districts. Religion, more fervent in the south, was in the eyes of these people a sacred liberty, on which revolution made attempts in the name of political liberty. They preferred the liberty of conscience to the liberty as citizens. Under all these titles the new institutions were odious: faithful priests nourished this hatred, and sanctified it in the hearts of the peasantry, whilst the nobility kept up a royalism, which pity for the king's misfortunes and the royal family made more full of sympathy at the daily recital of fresh outrages.

Mende, a small village hidden at the bottom of deep valleys, half way between the plains of the south and those of the Lyonnais, was the centre of counter-revolutionary spirit. The *bourgeoisie* and the nobility, mingled together from the smallness of their fortunes, the familiarity of their manners, and the frequent unions of their families, did not entertain towards each other that intestine envy, hatred, and malice, which was favorable to the Revolution. There was neither pride in the one nor jealousy in the other: it was as it is in Spain, one single people, where nobility is only, if we may say so, but a right of first birth of the same blood. These people had, it is true, laid down their arms after the insurrection of the preceding year in the camp of Jalès: but hearts were far from being disarmed. These provinces watched with an attentive eye for the favorable moment in which they might rise *en masse* against Paris. The insults to the dignity of the king, and the violence done to religion by the Legislative Assembly, excited their minds even to fanaticism. They burst out again, as though involuntarily, on the occasion of a movement of troops across their valleys. The tricolored cockade, emblem of infidelity to God and the king, had entirely disappeared for several months in the town of Mende, and they put up the white cockade, as a *souvenir* and a hope of that order of things to which they were secretly devoted.

The directory of the department, consisting of men strangers to the country, resolved on having the emblem of the constitution respected, and applied for some troops of the line. This the municipality opposed, in a resolution addressed to the directory, and made an insurrectional appeal to the neighboring municipalities, and a kind of federation with them to resist together the sending of any troops into their districts. However, the troops sent from Lyons at the request of the directory approached; on their appearance, the municipality dissolved the ancient national guard, composed of a few friends of liberty, and formed a fresh national guard, of which the officers were chosen by itself, from amongst the gentry and most devoted royalists of the neighborhood. Armed with this force, the municipality compelled the directory of the department to supply them with arms and ammunition.

Such were the movements of the town of Mende, when the troops entered the place. The national guard under arms, replied to the cry of *Vive la nation*, uttered by the troops, by the cry of *Vive le roi*. Then they followed the soldiers to the principal square in the city, and there took, in presence of the defenders of the constitution, an oath to obey the king only, and to recognize no one but the king. After this audacious display, the national guard, in parties, paraded the town, insulting, braving the soldiers: swords were drawn, and blood flowed. The troops pursued made a stand, and took to their weapons. The municipality, having the directory in check, and holding it as hostage, compelled it to send the troops orders to withdraw to their quarters. The commandant of the forces obeyed. This victory emboldened the national guard; and during the night it compelled the directory to send the troops an order to leave the city and evacuate the department. The national guard, drawn up in a line of battle in the square of Mende, saw hourly its ranks increase by detachments of the neighboring municipalities, who came down from the mountains armed with fowling-pieces, scythes, and plough-shares The troops would have been massacred if they had not retired under cover of the night. They retreated from the city amidst victorious cries from the royalists. The following day was a series of fêtes, in which the royalists of the town and those of the city celebrated their common triumph, and fraternized together. They insulted all the emblems of the Revolution; hooted the constitution; plundered the hall of the Jacobins; burnt down the houses of the principal members of this hateful club—put some in prison. But their vengeance confined itself to outrage. The people, controlled by the gentlemen and the *curés*, spared the blood of their enemies.

XIV.

Whilst humiliated liberty was threatened by fanaticism in the south, it, in its turn, carried on the work of assassination in the north. Brest was the very focus of Jacobinism—the close proximity of La Vendée gave this city reason to apprehend the counter-revolution that constantly threatened them—the presence of the fleet, commanded by officers suspected of favoring the aristocratic part—a population greatly composed of strangers and sailors, accessible to corruption, and capable of being readily excited to crime—rendered this city more turbulent and more agitated than any other port in the kingdom. The clubs constantly strove to work on the sailors to mutiny against their officers, whilst the revolutionists mistrusted the navy, as that was far more independent of the people than the army, for the court could at a moment change the station of the fleet, and turn their cannon against the constitution, and the feeling of discipline, of aristocracy, and of the colonies, were all contrary to the new school of ideas; and for this reason the Jacobins had for some time striven to disorganize the fleet. The appointment of M. de Lajaille to the command of one of the vessels destined to carry assistance to San Domingo, caused an outbreak of the suspicions infused into the minds of the inhabitants of Brest, and of the officers of the navy. M. de Lajaille was designated by the clubs as a traitor to the nation, who was about to introduce the counter-revolutionary feeling in the colonies. Attacked at the moment he was about to embark, by a crowd of nearly three thousand persons, he was covered with wounds, stretched senseless on the ground, and would have been killed, but for the heroic devotion of a workman, who shielded him with his own body, and defended him until the arrival of the civic guard. M. de Lajaille was, however, to appease popular feeling, imprisoned: in vain did the king order the municipal authorities of Brest to set this innocent and valuable officer free; in vain did the minister of justice demand chastisement for this attempted murder, committed in broad daylight, in the presence of the whole town; in vain was a sabre and a gold medal voted to the courageous Lanvergent, who had saved de Lajaille; the dread of a more formidable outbreak assured the guilty of impunity, and detained the innocent in prison. On the eve of war the naval officers, threatened with mutiny on board their vessels, and assassination on shore, had as much to apprehend from their crews as from the enemy

XV.

The same discords were fomented in all the garrisons between the soldiers and the officers, and the insubordination of the troops was, in the eyes of the clubs, the chief virtue of the army. The people everywhere sided with the soldiers, and the officers were constantly disturbed by conspiracies and revolts in the regiments. The fortified towns were the theatres of military outbreaks, which invariably terminated in the impunity of the soldier, and the imprisonment or the forced emigration of the officers. The Assembly, the supreme and partial judge, always decided in favor of insubordination: unable to restrain the people, it flattered their excesses. Perpignan was a new proof of this.

In the night of the 6th of December, the officers of the regiment of Cambrésis, in garrison in this town, went in a body to M. de Chollet, the general who commanded the division, and urged him to retire into the citadel, as they had learnt that a conspiracy was formed in the regiment, which threatened alike his and their lives. M. de Chollet complied with their earnest request, whilst they went to the barracks, and ordered the men to follow them to the citadel. The soldiers replied that they would only obey M. Desbordes, their lieutenant-colonel, in whose patriotism they had the greatest confidence. M. Desbordes came, and read to the soldiers the order of the general; but the inflexion of his voice, the expression of his face, his glance, alike seemed to protest against the order which his duty as a soldier compelled him to communicate to them. The troops understood this mute appeal, and declared that they would not quit their quarters, because the municipal authorities had forbidden them: the national guard joined them and patrolled the streets: the officers shut themselves up in the citadel, and shots were fired from the ramparts. Lieutenant Colonel Desbordes, the national guard, the *gendarmerie,* and the regiments, stormed the citadel. The officers of the regiment of Cambrésis were imprisoned by their soldiers; one, however, escaped, and committed suicide on the frontiers of Spain. The unfortunate general, Chollet, victim of the violence of the officers and soldiers, was impeached with fifty officers, or inhabitants of Perpignan. They were ordered before the high national court of Orleans; and thus were fifty victims predestined to perish in the massacre at Versailles.

XVI.

Blood flowed everywhere. The clubs seduced the regiments; patriotic motions, denunciations against the generals, perfidious insinuations against the fidelity of the officers, were constantly instilled into the minds of the army by the people. The officer was a prey to terror, the soldier to mistrust. The premeditated plan of the Jacobins and Girondists was to destroy in concert this body that was yet attached to the king, deprive the nobility of their command, substitute plebeians for nobles as officers, and thus give the army to the nation. In the meantime they surrendered it to anarchy and sedition; but these two parties finding that the disorganization was not sufficiently rapid, wished to sum up in one act the systematic corruption of the army, the ruin of all military discipline, and the legal triumph of the insurrection.

We have already mentioned how prominent a part the Swiss regiment of Châteauvieux had taken in the famous insurrection of Nancy during the latter period of the existence of the Constituent Assembly. An army under M. de Bouillé had been necessary to repress the armed revolt of several regiments that threatened all France with the rule of the tyrannical soldiery. M. de Bouillé, at the head of a body of troops from Metz, and the battalions of the national guard, had surrounded Nancy, and after a desperate contest at the gates, and in the streets of the town, forced the rebels to lay down their arms. These vigorous measures for the restoration of order were applauded by all parties, and reflected equal glory on M. de Bouillé and disgrace on the soldiers. Switzerland, by virtue of her treaties with France, preserved her right of federal justice over the regiments of her nation, and this essentially military country had tried by court-martial the regiment of Châteauvieux. Twenty-four of the ringleaders had been condemned and executed in expiation of the blood they had shed, and the fidelity they had violated, the remainder had been decimated, and forty-one soldiers now were undergoing their sentence on board the galleys at Brest. The amnesty proclaimed by the king for the crimes committed during the civil troubles, when he accepted the constitution, could not be applied to these foreign soldiers, for the right to pardon belongs alone to those who have the right to punish.

Sentenced by the judgment of the Helvetian jurisdiction, neither the king nor the Assembly could invalidate the judgment, or annul its effects. The king had, at the entreaty of the Constituent Assembly, in vain attempted to obtain the pardon of these soldiers from the Swiss confederation.

These fruitless negotiations served the Jacobins and the National Assembly as food for accusation against M. de Montmorin. In vain did he justify himself by alleging the impossibility of obtaining such an amnesty from Switzerland, at a moment when this country, who had suffered from civil commotions, sought to restore order by the laws of Draco. "We shall be then the compulsory jailers of this ferocious people," cried Guadet and Collot d'Herbois. "France must then degrade herself so far as to punish in her very ports those heroes who have gained the people a triumph over the aristocratic officers, and shed their blood for the nation in stead of pouring it out in the cause of despotism."

Pastoret, an influential member of the moderate party and who was said to concert all his measures with the king, supported Guadet's motion, in order to give the king popularity by an act agreeable to the nation; and the freedom of the soldiers of Châteauvieux was voted by the Assembly. The king, having delayed his sanction for some time, in order not to wound the cantons by this violent usurpation of their rights over their own countrymen, afforded the Jacobins fresh ground for imprecation and invective against the court and the ministers. "The moment is come when one man must perish for the safety of all," cried Manuel, "and this man must be a minister; they all appear to me so guilty, that I firmly believe the Assembly would be free from crime did it cause them to draw lots for who should perish on the scaffold." "All, all," vociferated the tribunes. But at this very moment Collot d'Herbois mounted the tribune, and announced amidst loud applause, that the royal assent to the decree for their liberation had been given the previous evening, and that in a few days he should present to his brother deputies these victims of discipline.

The soldiers of Châteauvieux were in reality advancing to Paris, having been liberated from the galleys at Brest, and their march was one continued triumph, but Paris prepared for them a still more brilliant one through the exertions of the Jacobins. In vain did the Feuillants and the Constitutionalists energetically protest, through the mouth of André Chénier, the Tyrtæus of moderation and good sense, of Dupont de Nemours, and the poet Roucher, against the insolent oration of the assassins of the generous Désilles. Collot d'Herbois, Robespierre, the Jacobins, the Cordeliers, and the very commune of Paris clung to the idea of this triumph, which, according to them, would cover with opprobium the court and La Fayette. The feeble interposition of Pétion, who appeared as though he wished to moderate the scandal, served only to encourage it, for he of all men was most fitted to plunge the people into the last degreee of excess. His affected virtue served only to cloak violence, and to cover with a hypocritical appearance of legality the outbreaks he dared not punish; and had a representative of anarchy been sought to be placed at the head of the commune of Paris, it could have found no fitter type than Pétion. His paternal reprimands to the people were but promises of impunity. The public force always arrived too late to punish; excuse was always to be found for sedition, amnesty for crime. The people felt that their magistrate was their accomplice and their slave, and yet whilst they despised they loved him.

XVII.

"This *fête* that is preparing for these soldiers," wrote Chénier, "is attributed to enthusiasm. For my part, I confess I do not perceive this enthusiasm. I see a few men who create a degree of agitation, but the rest are alarmed or indifferent. We are told that the national honor is interested in this reparation,—I can scarcely comprehend this; for, either the national guards of Metz, who put down the revolt of Nancy, are enemies of the public weal, or the soldiers of Châteauvieux are assassins: there is no medium. How, then, is the honor of Paris interested in *fêting* the murderers of our brothers? Other profound politicians say, this *fête* will humiliate those who have sought to fetter the nation. What! in order to humiliate, according to their judgment, a bad government, it is necessary to invent extravagances capable of destroying every species of government—recompense rebellion against the laws—crown foreign satellites for having shot French citizens in an *émeute.* It is said, that in every place where this procession passes, the statues will be veiled:—Ah! they will do well to veil the whole city, if this hideous orgy takes place; but it is not alone the statues of despots that should be veiled, but the face of every good citizen. It will be the duty of every youth in the kingdom, of every national guard in the kingdom to assume mourning on the day when the murder of their brothers confers a title of glory on foreign and seditious soldiers; it is the eyes of the army that should be veiled, that they may not behold the reward of insubordination and revolt; it is the National Assembly—the king—the administrators—the country—that should veil their faces, in order that they may not become complaisant or silent witnesses of the outrages offered to the authorities and the country. The book of the law must be covered, when those who have torn and stained its pages by musket-balls and sabre-cuts receive the civic honors. Citizens of Paris, honest yet weak men, there is not one of you who, when he interrogates his own heart, does not feel how much the country—how much he its child—are insulted by these outrages offered to the laws,—to those who execute them, and those who are for them. Do you not blush that a handful of turbulent men, who appear numerous because they are united and make a noise, should constrain you to do their pleasure, by telling you it is your own, and by amusing your puerile curiosity by unworthy spectacles? In a city that respected itself, such a *fête* would find before it silence and solitude, the streets and public places abandoned, the houses shut up, the windows deserted, and the flight and scorn of the passers-by would tell history what share honest and well-disposed men took in this scandalous and bacchanalian procession."

XVIII.

Collot d'Herbois insulted André Chénier and Roucher in his reply. Roucher replied by a letter full of sarcasm, in which he reminded Collot d'Herbois of his falls on the stage and his misadventures as an actor. "This personage of comic romance," said he, "who has leapt from the trestles of Punch to the tribune of the Jacobins, rushes at me, as though to strike me with the oar the Swiss have brought him from the galleys."

Placards for or against the *fête* covered the walls of the Palais Royal, and were alternately torn down by groups of young men or Jacobins.

Dupont de Nemours, the friend and master of Mirabeau, laid aside his philosophical calm, to address a letter on the same subject to Pétion, in which his conscience, as an honest man, braved the popularity of the tribune. "When the danger is imminent, it is the duty of all honest men to warn the magistrates of it. More particularly, when the magistrates themselves create it. You told a falsehood when you asserted that these soldiers had aided the Revolution on the 14th of July, and that they had refused to combat against the people of Paris. It is untrue that the Swiss refused to combat against the people of Paris, and it is true that they assassinated the national guards of Nancy. You have the audacity to term those men patriots who dare command the legislative body to send a deputation to the *fête* prepared for these rebels; these are the men whom you adopt as your friends; it is with them that you dine at *la Rapée*, so that the general of the national guard is obliged to gallop about for two hours to receive your orders before he can find you, and you seek in vain to conceal your embarrassment by high-flown phrases. You seek in vain to conceal this banquet given to assassins beneath the pretext of a banquet in honor of liberty. But these subterfuges are no longer available; the moment is urgent, and you will no longer deceive the sections, the army, or the eighty-three departments. Those who rule you, as they would a child, have agreed to surrender Paris to ten thousand pikes, to whom the bar of the Assembly will be thrown open the day the national guard is disarmed; the men destined to bear them arrive every day, and Paris receives an accession of twelve or fifteen hundred bandits every twenty-four hours, and beg, until the day of pillage arrives, which they await as ravens await their prey

I have not told all;—generals are prepared for this hideous army. The friends of Jourdan, impatient to behold the man whom the amnesty had not delivered sufficiently soon, have broken open his prison at Avignon. Already, he has been received in triumph in several cities of the south, like the Swiss of the Châteauvieux, and will arrive at Paris to-morrow; Sunday he will be present at the *fête* with his companions—with the two Mainvielle—with Pegtavin;—with all those cold-blooded scoundrels who have killed in one night sixty-eight defenceless persons, and violated females before they murdered them. Catiline!—Cethegus!—march forward, the soldiers of Sylla are in the city, and the consul himself undertakes to disarm the Romans. The measure is full,—it overflows!"

Pétion strove miserably to justify himself in a letter in which his weakness and connivance revealed themselves beneath the multiplicity of excuses. At the same time Robespierre, mounting the tribune of the Jacobins, exclaimed, "You do not trace to their source the obstacles that oppose the expansion of the sentiments of the people. Against whom think you that you have to strive? Against the aristocracy?—No. Against the court?—No. Against a general who has long entertained great designs against the people. It is not the national guard that views these preparations with alarm; it is the genius of La Fayette that conspires in the staff; it is the genius of La Fayette that conspires in the directory of the department; it is the genius of La Fayette that perverts the minds of so many good citizens in the capital who would but for him be with us.

"La Fayette is the most dangerous of the enemies of liberty, because he wears the mask of patriotism; it is he who, after having wrought all the evil in his power in the Constituent Assembly, has affected to withdraw to his estates, and then comes to strive for this post of mayor of Paris, not to obtain it, but to refuse it, in order to affect disinterestedness; it is he who has been appointed to the command of the French armies, in order to turn them against the Revolution. The national guards of Metz were as innocent as those of Paris, they can be nothing but patriots; it is La Fayette who, through the medium of Bouillé, his relation and accomplice, has deceived them. How can we inscribe on the banners of this fête, *Bouillé is alone guilty?* Who sought to stifle the revolt at Nancy, and cover it with an impenetrable veil? Who demands crowns for the assassins of the soldiers of Châteauvieux? La Fayette. Who prevented me from speaking? La Fayette. Who are those who now dart such threatening glances at me? La Fayette and his accomplices." (Loud applause.)

XIX.

The preparations for this ceremony gave rise to a still more exciting drama at the National Assembly. At the opening of the sitting, a member demanded that the forty soldiers of Châteauvieux should be admitted to pay their respects to the legislative body. M. de Jaucourt opposed it: "If these soldiers," said he, "are only admitted to express their gratitude, I consent to their being admitted to the bar; but I demand that afterwards they be not allowed to remain during the debate." The speaker was interrupted by loud murmurs, and cries of *à bas! à bas!* from the tribunes. "An amnesty is neither a triumph nor a civic crown," continued he; "you cannot dishonor the names of the brave Désilles, or of those generous citizens who perished defending the laws against them; you cannot lacerate by this triumph the hearts of those among you who took part in the expedition of Nancy. Allow a soldier, who was ordered on this expedition with his regiment, to point out to you the effects this decision would have on the army. (The murmurs redouble.) The army will see in your conduct only an encouragement to insurrection; and these honors will lead the soldiers to believe that you look on these men, whom an amnesty has freed, not as men whose punishment was too severe, but as innocent victims." The tumult here became so great that M. de Jaucourt was forced to descend. But one of the members, who, it is evident to all, was almost overpowered by emotion, took his place. It was M. de Gouvion, a young officer, whose name was already gloriously inscribed in the early pages of the annals of our wars. He was clothed in deep black, and every feature of his face wore an expression of intense grief, which inspired the Assembly with involuntary interest, and the tumult was instantly changed into attention. His voice was tremulous and scarcely audible at first; it was evident that indignation as much as sorrow choked his utterance.

"Gentlemen," said he, "I had a brother, a good patriot, who, through the estimation in which he was held by his fellow citizens, had been successively elected commandant of the national guard, and member for the department. Ever ready to sacrifice himself for the revolution and the law, it was in the name of the revolution and the law that he was called upon to march to Nancy at the head of the brave national guards, and there he fell pierced by five bayonet-wounds, and by the hand of those who, ... I demand, if I am condemned to behold here the assassins of my brother." "Well, then, leave the chamber," cried a stern voice. The tribunes applauded this speech, more cruel and poignant than the thrust of a dagger. Indignation enabled M. de Gouvion to overcome his contempt. "Who is the dastard who hides himself in order to insult the grief of a brother?" cried he, glancing around to discover the speaker. "I will tell my name—'tis I," replied the deputy Choudieu, rising from his seat. Loud applause from the tribunes followed this insult of Choudieu's; it would seem as though this crowd had no longer any feeling, and that passion triumphed over nature. But M. de Gouvion was sustained by a sentiment stronger than popular fury—that of generous despair; he continued: "As a man, I applauded the clemency of the National Assembly when it burst the fetters of these unhappy soldiers who were misled." He was again interrupted, but continued: "The decrees of the Constituent Assembly, the orders of the king, the voice of their officers, the cries of their country, all were unavailing; without provocation on the part of the national guards of the two departments, they fired on Frenchmen, and my brother fell a victim to his obedience to the laws. No, I cannot remain silent, so long as the memory of the national guards is disgraced by the honors decreed to these men who murdered them."

Couthon, a young Jacobin, seated not far from Robespierre, from whose eyes he seemed to gain his secret inspirations, rose and replied to Gouvion, without insulting him. "Who is the slave of prejudices that would venture to dishonor men whom the law has absolved; who would not repress his personal grief in the interest and the triumph of liberty?' But Gouvion's voice touched that chord of justice and natural emotion that always vibrates beneath the insensibility of opinion. Twice did the Assembly, summoned by the president to vote for or against their admission to the debate, rise in an even number for and against this motion. And the secretaries, the judges of these decisions, hesitated to pronounce on which side the majority was; they at length, after two attempts, declared that the majority was in favor of the admission of the Swiss; but the minority protested, and the *appel nominal* was demanded. This pronounced a feeble majority that the Swiss should be admitted; and they instantly entered, amidst the applause of the tribunes, whilst the unfortunate Gouvion left the chamber by the opposite door, his forehead scarlet with indignation, and vowing never to set foot in that Assembly, where he was forced to behold and welcome the murderers of his brother. He instantly applied to the minister of war to join the army of the north, and fell there.

XX.

The soldiers were introduced, and Collot d'Herbois presented them to the admiring tribunes. The national guard of Versailles, who had followed them to the Assembly, defiled in the hall amidst the sound of drums, and cries of "*Vive la Nation!*" Groups of citizens and females of Paris, with tri-colored flags and pikes brandished over their heads, followed them; then the members of the popular societies of Paris presented to the president flags of honor given to the Swiss by the departments which these conquerors had just traversed. The men of the 14th of July, with Gouchon, the agitator of the faubourg St. Antoine, as their spokesman, announced that this faubourg had fabricated 10,000 pikes to defend their liberties and their country. This legitimate ovation, offered by the Girondists and Jacobins to undisciplined soldiers, authorized the people of Paris to decree to them the triumph of such an infamous proceeding (*le triomphe du scandale*).

It was no longer the people of liberty, but the people of anarchy; the day of the 15th of April combined all its emblems. Revolt armed against the laws, for instance, mutinous soldiers as conquerors; a colossal galley, an instrument of punishment and shame, crowned with flowers as an emblem; abandoned women and girls, collected from the lowest haunts of infamy, carrying and kissing the broken fetters of these galley-slaves; forty trophies, bearing the forty names of these Swiss; civic crowns on the names of these murderers of citizens; busts of Voltaire, Rousseau, Franklin, Sidney, the greatest philosophers and most virtuous patriots, mingled with the ignoble busts of these malefactors, and sullied by the contact; these soldiers themselves, astonished if not ashamed of their glory, advancing in the midst of a group of rebellious French guard, in all the glorification of the forsaking of flags and want of discipline; the march closed by a car imitating in its form the prow of a galley: in this car the statue of Liberty armed in anticipation with the bludgeon of September, and wearing the *bonnet rouge,* an emblem borrowed from Phrygia by some, from the galleys by others; the book of the Constitution carried processionally in this fête, as if to be present at the homage decreed to those who were armed against the laws; bands of male and female citizens, the pikes of the faubourg, the absence of the civic bayonets, fierce threats, theatrical music, demagogic hymns, derisive halts at the Bastille, the Hôtel-de-Ville, the Champ-de-Mars; at the altar of the country the vast and tumultuous rounds danced several times by chains of men and women round the triumphal galley, amidst the foul chorus of the air of the *Carmagnole;* embraces, more obscene than patriotic, between these women and the soldiers, who threw themselves into each others' arms; and in order to put the cope-stone on this debasement of the laws, Pétion the Maire of Paris, the magistrates of the people assisting personally at this fête, and sanctioning this insolent triumph over the laws by their weakness or their complicity. Such was this fête: a humiliating copy of the 14th of July, an infamous parody of an insurrection, which parodied a revolution!

France blushed; good citizens were alarmed; the national guard began to be afraid of pikes; the city to fear the faubourgs, and the army herein received the signal of the most entire disorganization.

The indignation of the constitutional party burst forth in ironical strophes in a hymn of André Chénier, in which that young poet avenged the laws, and marked himself out for the scaffold.

> "Salut divin triomphe! Entre dans nos murailles!
> Rends nous ces soldats, illustrés
> Par le sang de Désilles et par les funérailles
> De nos citoyens massacrés!"*

---

* "Hail mighty triumph!—enter these our walls!
Restore those soldiers, heroes of the day
When fell Désilles, pierced by their murderous balls,
And blood of citizens bedew'd the clay!"

BOOK XI.

I.

The echo of these triumphs of insubordination and murder was felt everywhere in the mutinous conduct of the troops, the disobedience of the national guard, and the risings of the populace; whilst at Paris they *fêted* the Swiss of Châteauvieux, the mob of Marseilles demanded with much violence that the Swiss regiment of *Ernst* should be expelled from the garrison at Aix, under pretext that they favored the aristocracy, and that the security of Provence was thereby menaced. On the refusal of this regiment to quit the city, the Marseillaise marched upon Aix as the Parisians had marched upon Versailles in the days of October. They by violence compelled the national guard to accompany them, who had been destined to repress them; they surrounded the regiment of Ernst with cannon, made them lay down their arms, and shamefully drove them before sedition. The national guard, a force essentially revolutionary, because it participates, like the people, in the opinions, feelings, and passions, which, as a civic guard, it ought to repress, followed in every direction, from weakness or example, the fickle impressions of the mob. How could men, just leaving clubs, where they had been listening to, applauding, and frequently exciting sedition in patriotic discourses,—how could they, changing their feelings and part at the door of popular societies, take arms against the seditious? Thus they remained spectators, when they were not accomplices of insurrections. The scarcity of colonial produce, the dearness of grain, the rigor of a hard winter, all contributed to disturb the people: the agitators turned all these misfortunes of the times into accusations and grounds of hatred against royalty.

II.

The government, powerless and disarmed, was rendered responsible for the severities of nature. Secret emissaries, armed bands, went amongst the towns and cities where markets were held, and there disseminated the most alarming reports, provoking the people to tax grain and flour, stigmatizing the corn-dealers as monopolists—the perfidious charge of monopoly being a sure sentence of death. The fear of being accused of starving the people checked every specula tion of business, and tended much more than actual want to the dearth of the markets. Nothing is so scarce as a commodity which is concealed. The corn-stores were crimes in the eyes of consumers of bread. The maire of Etampes, Simoneau, an honest man, and an intrepid magistrate, was one victim sacrificed to the people's suspicions. Etampes was one of the great markets that supplied Paris. It was therefore necessary for it to preserve the liberty of commerce and the supply of flour. A mob, composed of men and women of the adjacent villages, assembling at the sound of the tocsin, marched upon the city one market-day, preceded by drums, armed with guns and pitchforks, in order to carry off the grain by force from the proprietors, divide it amongst themselves, and to exterminate, as they declared, the monopolists, amongst whom sinister voices mingled in low tones the name of Simoneau. The national guard disappeared, a detachment of one hundred men of the eighteenth regiment of cavalry were at Etampes, and the sole force at the maire's disposal.

The officer answered for these soldiers *as for himself.* After long conversations with the seditious, to bring them back to reason and the law, Simoneau returned to the *maison commune,* ordered the red flag to be unfurled, proclaimed martial law, and then advanced upon the rebels, surrounded by the municipal body, and in the centre of the armed force; on reaching the square of the town, the crowd surrounded and cut off the detachment. The troopers left the maire exposed—not one drew his sword in his defence. In vain did he summon them, in the name of the law, and by the weapons they wore, to render aid to the magistrate against assassins—in vain did he seize the bridle of one of the horsemen near him, crying, "*Help, my friends.*"

Struck by blows of pitchforks and guns, at the moment when he appealed to the soldiery, he fell, shot, grasping in his hands the bridle of the cowardly trooper whom he was entreating: the fellow, in order to disengage himself, struck with the back of his sabre the arm of the maire already dead, and left his body to the insults of the people. The miscreants, remaining in possession of the carcass, brutally mangled the palpitating limbs, and deliberated together as to cutting off the head. The leaders made their followers defile, passing over the body of the maire, and trampling in his blood. Then they went away beating their drums, and went to get drunk in the suburbs; and the taking away the grain, the apparent motive of the riot, was neglected in the moment of triumph. There was no pillage—either the blood made the people forget their hunger, or their hunger was but the pretext for assassination.

III.

At the moment when all was thus crumbling to pieces round the throne, a man, celebrated by the vast part attributed to him in the common ruin, sought to reconcile himself with the king: this was Louis-Philippe Joseph, Duc d'Orleans, first prince of the blood. I pause for this man, before whom history has hitherto paused, without being able to discover the real place which should be assigned to him amongst the passing events. An enigma to himself, he remains an enigma for posterity. Was the real solution of this enigma ambition or patriotism, weakness or conspiracy? Let facts reply.

Public opinion has its prejudices. Struck by the immensity of the work it accomplishes; giddy, as it were, by the rapidity of the movement which urges things on, it cannot believe that a series of natural causes, combined by Providence with the rise of certain ideas in the human mind, and aided by the coincidence of the times, can of itself produce such vast commotions. It seeks, then, the supernatural—the wonderful,—fatality. It takes pleasure in imagining latent causes acting with mystery, and compelling with hidden hand men and events. It takes, in a word, every revolution for a conspiracy; and if it meets at starting, in the middle, or at the end of such crises some leading man, to whose interest these events may tend, it supposes itself the author, attributes to itself all the action of these revolutions, and all the scope of idea that accomplishes them; and, fortunate or unfortunate, innocent or guilty, claims for itself all the glory or demerit of the result. It renders its name divine or its memory accursed. Such, for fifty years, was the destiny of the Duc d'Orleans.

IV.

It is a historic tradition amongst people from the highest antiquity, that the throne wears out royal races, and that whilst the reigning branches grow enervated by the possession of empire, younger branches become stronger and greater, by nourishing the ambition of becoming more powerful, and inspiring more closely to the people an air less corrupt than that which pervades courts. Thus, whilst primogeniture gives power to the elder, the people confer popularity on the juniors.

This singularity of a handsomer and more popular family than the reigning family, increasing near the throne, and having a dangerous rivalry with the throne in the mind of the nation, had always existed in the house of Orleans, since the time of Louis XIV. If this equivocal situation gave to the princes of this family some virtues, it gave them also corresponding vices. More intelligent and more ambitious than the king's sons, they were also more restless. The very restraint in which the policy of the reigning house kept them, condemned their idea or their courage to inaction, and forced them to misapply, in irregularities or indolence, the faculties with which nature had endowed them, and the immense fortune for which they had no other occupation: too great for citizens, too dangerous at the head of armies or in affairs, they had no place either amongst the people or at court; and thus they assumed it in opinion.

The Regent, a very superior man, long kept down by the inferiority of his part, had been the most brilliant example of all the virtues and all the vices of the blood of Orleans. Since the Regent, the princes endowed, like himself, with natural wit and courage, had felt the glory of great actions in their early youth. They had then again fallen back into obscurity, pleasures or devotion, by the jealousy of the reigning house. At the first show of brilliancy attached to their name, it had been darkened. Guilty by their very merit, their name urged them on to glory: and as soon as they proved themselves deserving, it was forbidden to them. These princes were destined to transmit with their family honors that impatience of a change of government which allows them to be men.

Louis-Philippe Joseph, Duc d'Orleans, was born at the precise epoch, when his rank, fortune and character were to throw him into a current of new ideas, which his family passions called on him to favor, and into which, once drawn, it would be impossible for him to pause, except at the throne or the scaffold. He was twenty when the first symptoms of the Revolution manifested themselves.

He was handsome, like all his race. Slender figure, firm step, smiling countenance, piercing glance, limbs made supple by all bodily exercises, with a heart disposed to love, and a splendid horseman, that great accomplishment of princes; a condescension void of familiarity, a ready eloquence, unquestionable courage, liberal to the arts, even to extravagance; those faults which are only due to the luxuries of the age, all marked him out as a popular favorite. He took every advantage of it; and, perhaps, his early intoxication with it somewhat affected his natural good sense. The love of the people appeared to him a means of avenging himself for the contempt in which the court neglected him. In his mind he braved the king of Versailles, feeling himself king of Paris.

He had married a princess of a race as beloved by the people; the only daughter of the Duc de Penthièvre. Lovely, amiable, and virtuous, she brought to her husband as dowry, with the vast fortune of the Duc de Penthièvre, that amount of consideration and public esteem which belonged to her house. The first political act of the Duc d'Orleans was a bold resistance to the wishes of the court, at the period of the exile of the parliaments. Exiled himself in his château of *Villars-Cotterêts*, the esteem and interest of the people followed him. The applauses of France sweetened the disgrace of the court. He believed that he comprehended the part of a great citizen in a free country; he desired to do so. He forgot too easily, in the atmosphere of adulation which surrounded him, that a man is not a great citizen only to please the people, but to defend, serve, and frequently to resist them.

Returned to Paris, he was desirous of joining the *prestige* of glory of arms to the civic crowns, with which his name was already decorated. He solicited of the court the dignity of *grand-admiral* of France, the survivorship of which belonged to him, after the Duc de Penthièvre, his father-in-law. He was refused. He embarked as a volunteer on board the fleet, commanded by the Comte d'Orvilliers, and was at the battle of Ouessant on the 17th of July, 1778. The results of this fight, when victory remained without conquest, in consequence of a false manœuvre, were imputed to the weakness of the Duc d'Orleans, who wished to check the pursuit of the enemy. This dishonoring report, invented and disseminated by court hatred, soured the resentments of the young prince, but could not hide the brilliancy of his courage, which he displayed in caprices unworthy of his rank. At St. Cloud he sprang into the first balloon that carried aerial navigators into space. Calumny followed him even there, and a report was spread that he had burst the balloon with a thrust of his sword, in order to compel his companions to descend. Then arose between the court and himself a continual struggle of boldness on the one hand and slander on the other. The king treated him, however, with the indulgence which virtue testifies for youth's follies. The Comte d'Artois took him as the constant companion of his pleasures. The queen, who liked the Comte d'Artois, feared for him the contagion of the disorders and amours of the Duc d'Orleans. She hated equally in this young prince the favorite of the people of Paris and the corrupter of the Comte d'Artois. She made the king purchase the almost royal palace of St. Cloud, the favorite seat of the Duc d'Orleans. Infamous insinuations against him were incessantly transpiring from the half confidences of courtiers. He was accused of having induced courtezans to poison the blood of the Prince de Lamballe, his brother-in-law, and of having enervated him in debauches, in order that he might be the sole heir of the immense property of the house of Penthièvre. This crime was the pure invention of malice.

Thus persecuted by the animosity of the court, the Duc d'Orleans was more and more driven to retirement. In his frequent visits to England he formed a close intimacy with the Prince of Wales, heir to the throne, who took for his friends all the enemies of his father; playing with sedition, dishonored by debts, of scandalous life, prolonging beyond the usual term those excesses of princes—horses, pleasure of the table, gaming, women; abetting the intrigues of Fox, Sheridan and Burke, and prefacing his advent to royal power by all the audacity of a refractory son and a factious citizen.

The Duc d'Orleans thus tasted of the joys of liberty in a London life. He brought back to France habits of insolence against the court, a taste for popular disturbances, contempt for his own rank, familiarity with the multitude, a citizen's life in a palace, and that simple style of dress, which, by abandoning the uniform of the French nobility, and blending attire generally, soon destroyed all inequalities of costume amongst citizens.

Then given up entirely to the exclusive care of repairing his impaired fortune, the Duc d'Orleans constructed the

Palais Royal. He changed the noble and spacious gardens of his palace into a market of luxury, devoted by day to traffic, and by night to play and debauchery—a complete sink of iniquities, built in the heart of the capital—a work of cupidity which antique manners never could forgive this prince; and which, being gradually adopted like the forum by the indolence of the Parisian population, was destined to become the cradle of the Revolution. This Revolution was striding onwards. The prince awaited it in supineness, as if liberty of the world had been but one more mistress.

His well-known hatred against the court had naturally drawn into his acquaintance all who desired a change. The Palais Royal was the elegant centre of a conspiracy with open doors, for the reform of government: the philosophy of the age there encountered politics and literature: it was the palace of opinion. Buffon came there constantly to pass the latter evenings of his life. Rousseau there received at a distance the only worship which his proud sensitiveness would accept even from princes. Franklin and the American republicans; Gibbon and the orators of the English opposition, Grimm and the German philosophers, Diderot, Siéyès, Sillery, Laclos, Suard, Florian, Raynal, La Harpe, and all the thinkers or writers who anticipated the new mind, met there with celebrated artists and *savans*. Voltaire himself, proscribed from Versailles by the human respect of a court, which admired his genius, had arrived thither on his last journey. The prince presented to him his children, one of whom reigns to-day over France. The dying philosopher blessed them, as he did those of Franklin, in the name of reason and liberty.

V.

If the prince himself had not a love of literature and a highly refined mind, he had sufficiently cultivated his mind to appreciate perfectly the pleasures of the understanding; but the revolutionary feeling instinctively counselled him to surround himself with all the strength that might one day serve liberty. Early tired of the beauty and virtue of the Duchesse d'Orleans, he had conceived for a lovely, witty, insinuating woman a sentiment which did not enchain the caprices of his heart, but which controlled his inconsistency and directed his mind. This woman, then seducing and since celebrated, was the Comtesse de Sillery-Genlis, daughter of the Marquis Ducret de Saint Aubin, a gentleman oı Charolais, without fortune. Her mother, who was still young and handsome, had brought her to Paris, to the house of M. de la Popelinière, a celebrated financier, whose old age she had taken captive. She educated her daughter for that doubtful destiny which awaits women on whom nature has lavished beauty and mind, and to whom society has refused their right position—adventuresses in society, sometimes raised, sometimes degraded.

The first masters formed this child by all the arts of mind and hand—her mother directed her to ambition. The second-rate position of this mother at the house of her opulent protector, formed the child to the plasticity and adulation which her mother's domestic condition required and illustrated. At sixteen years of age her precocious beaty and musical talent caused her to be already sought in the *salons*. Her mother produced her there in the dubious publicity between the theatre and the world. An *artiste* for some, she was, with others, a well educated girl; all were attracted by her: old men forgot their age. Buffon called her "*ma fille.*" Her relationship with Madame de Montesson, widow of the Duc d'Orleans, gave her a footing in the house of the young prince. The Comte de Sillery-Genlis fell in love with her, and married her in spite of his family's opposition. Friend and confidant of the Duc d'Orleans, the Comte de Sillery obtained for his wife a place at the court of the Duchesse d'Orleans. Time and her ability did the rest.

The duke attached himself to her with the twofold power of admiration for her beauty and admiration of her superior understanding—the one empire confirmed the other. The complaints of the insulted duchess only made the duke more obstinate in his liking. He was governed, and desirous of having his feelings honored, he announced it openly, merely seeking to color it under the pretext of the education of his children. The Comtesse de Genlis followed at the same time the ambition of courts and the reputation of literature. She wrote with elegance those light works which amuse a woman's idle hours, whilst they lead their hearts astray into imaginary amours. Romances, which are to the west what opium is to the Orientals, waking day-dreams had become necessities and events for the *salons*. Madame de Genlis wrote in a graceful style, and clothed her characters and ideas with a certain affectation of austerity which gave a be comingness to love: she moreover affected an universal acquaintance with the sciences, which made her sex disappear before the pretensions of her mind, and which recalled in her person those women of Italy who profess philosophy with a veil over their countenances.

The Duc d'Orleans, an innovator in everything, believed he had found, in a woman, the Mentor for his sons. He nominated her governess of his children. The duchess, greatly annoyed, protested against this; the court laughed, and the people were amazed. Opinion, which yields to all who brave it, murmured, and then was silent. The future proved that the father was right: the pupils of this lady were not princes, but men. She attracted to the Palais Royal all the dictators of public opinion. The first club in France was thus held in the very apartments of a prince of the blood. Literature, concealed from without these meetings as the madness of the first Brutus concealed his vengeance. The duke was not, perhaps, a conspirator, but henceforth there was an Orleans party. Siéyès, the mystic oracle of the Revolution, who seemed to carry it on his pensive front, and brood over it in silence; the Duc de Lauzun, passing from the confidence of Trianon to the consultations of the Palais Royal; Laclos, a young officer of artillery, author of an obscene romance, capable at need of elevating romantic intrigue to a political conspiracy; Sillery, soured against his order, at enmity with the court, an ambitious malcontent, awaiting nothing but what the future might bring forth; and others more obscure, but not less active, and serving as unknown guides for descending from the *salons* of a prince into the depths of the people: some the head, others the arms, of the duke's ambition, attended these meetings. Perhaps they might be ignorant of the aim, but they placed themselves on the declivity, and allowed Fortune to do as she pleased. Fortune was a revolution. The wonderful, that marvel of the masses, which is to the imagination what calculation is to reason, was not wanting to the Orleans party. Prophecies, those popular presentiments of destiny, domestic prodigies, admitted by the interested credulity of numerous clients of this house, announced the throne shortly to one of these princes. These rumors were rife amongst the people, from themselves, or the skilful insinuations of the partisans of the house of Orleans. In the convocation of States-General, the duke had not hesitated to pronounce in favor of the most popular reforms. The instructions which he had drawn up for the electors of his dominions were the work of the Abbé Siéyès. The prince himself intrigued for the name and style of *Citoyen*. Elected deputy of the the noblesse of Paris at Crespy and at Villars-Cotterêts, he selected Crespy, because the electors of this bailiwick were the more patriotic. At the procession of the States-General he left his own place vacant amongst the princes, and walked in the midst of the deputies. This abdication of his dignity near the throne to assume the dignity of a citizen, procured him the applauses of the nation.

VI.

Public favor towards him was such, that had he been a Duc de Guise, and Louis XVI. a Henry III., the States-General would have finished, as did those of Blois, by an assassination or usurpation. Uniting with the *tiers état*, to obtain equality and the friendship of the nation against the nobility, he took the oath of the Tennis Court. He took his place behind Mirabeau, to disobey the king. Nominated president by the National Assembly, he refused this honor in order to remain a citizen. The day on which the dismissal of Necker betrayed the hostile projects of the court, and when the people of Paris named its leaders and defenders by acclamation, the name of the Duc d'Orleans was the first uttered. France took in the gardens of the palace the colors of his livery for a cockade. At the voice of Camille Desmoulins, who uttered the cry of alarm in the Palais Royal, the populace gathered, Legendre and Fréron led them; they placed the bust of the Duc d'Orleans beside that of Necker, covered them with black crape, and promenaded them, bareheaded themselves, in the presence of the silent citizens. Blood flowed; the dead body of one of the citizens who carried the busts, killed by the mob, serving as a standard to the people. The Duc d'Orleans was thus mixed up from his palace—his name and his image—with the first struggle and first murder of liberty. This was enough to make it believed that his hand moved all the threads of events. Whether from lack of boldness or ambition, he never assumed the appearance of the part which public opinion assigned to him. He did not then appear to push things beyond the conquest of a constitution for his country, and the character of a great patriot for himself. He respected or despised the throne. One or other of these feelings gave him importance in the eyes of history. All the world was of his party except himself.

Impartial men did honor to his moderation, the revolutionists imputed shame to his character. Mirabeau, who was seeking a pretender to personify the revolt, had had secret interviews with the Duc d'Orleans; had tested his ambition, to judge if it aspired to the throne. He had left him dissatisfied; he had even betrayed his dissatisfaction by angry phrases. Mirabeau required a conspirator; he had only found a patriot. What he despised in the Duc d'Orleans was not the meditation of a crime, but the refusal to be his accomplice. He had not anticipated such scruples; he revenged himself by terming this carelessness about the throne the cowardice of an ambitious man.

La Fayette instinctively hated in the Duc d'Orleans an influential rival. He accused the prince of fomenting troubles which he felt himself powerless to repress. It was asserted that the Duc d'Orleans and Mirabeau had been seen mingled with groups of men and women, and pointing to the château. Mirabeau defended himself by a smile of contempt. The Duc d'Orleans proved his innocence in a more serious manner. An assassination which should kill the king or queen would still leave the monarchy, the laws of the kingdom, and the princes inheritors of the throne. He could not mount to it, except over the dead bodies of five persons placed by nature between himself and his ambition. These steps of crime could only have incurred the execrations of the nation, and must have even wearied the assassins themselves. Besides, he proved by numerous and undeniable witnesses, that he had not gone to Versailles either on the 4th or 5th of October. Quitting Versailles on the 3rd, after the sitting of the National Assembly, he had returned to Paris. He had passed the day of the 4th in his palace and gardens at Mousseaux. On the 5th, he again was at Mousseaux; his cabriolet having broken down on the boulevard, he had gone on foot by the Champs Elysées. He had passed the day at Passy with his children and Madame de Genlis. He had supped at Mousseaux with some intimate friends, and slept again in Paris. It was not until the 6th, in the morning, that, informed of the events of the previous evening, he had gone to Versailles, and that his carriage had been stopped at the bridge of Sèvres, by the mob carrying the bleeding heads of the king's guard.* If this was not the conduct

* In Michelet's *History of the French Revolution*, published contem-

of a prince of the blood, who flies to the succor of his king and places himself at the foot of the throne, between the threatened sovereign and the people, neither was it that of an audacious usurper who tempts revolt by occasion, and at least presents to the people a completed crime.

The conduct of this prince was but that of one who looks to a contingent reversion: either that he would not receive the crown except by a fatality of events, and without thrusting forth his hand to fortune, or that he had more indifference than ambition for supreme power, or that he would not place his royalty as a check upon the way of liberty; that he sincerely desired a republic, and that the title of first citizen of a free nation appeared to him greater than that of king.

VII.

However, a short time after the days of the 5th and 6th October, La Fayette desired to break off the intimacy between the Duc d'Orleans and Mirabeau. He resolved at all risks to compel the prince to remove from the scene, and by an exercise of moral restraint or the fear of a state prosecution, to absent himself and go to London. He made the king and queen enter into his plans, by alarming them as to the prince's intrigues, and designating him as a competitor for the throne. La Fayette said one day to the queen, that this prince was the only man upon whom the suspicion of so lofty an ambition could fall. "Sir," replied the queen, with a look of incredulity, "is it necessary then to be a prince in order to pretend to the throne?" "At least, madame," replied the general, "I only know the Duc d'Orleans who aspires to it." La Fayette presumed too much on the prince's ambition.

VIII.

Mirabeau, discouraged at the hesitations and scruples of

poraneously with this work, the author acquits the Duc d'Orleans of any participation in the riots and bloodshed at Versailles, on the 4th and 5th of October; but says, page 280, "Depositions prove that he was seen everywhere between Paris and Versailles, but that he did nothing. Between eight and nine o'clock in the morning of the 6th, so soon after the massacre that the court of the castle was still stained with blood, he went and showed himself to the people, with an enormous cockade in his hat, laughing and flourishing a switch in his hand."—*Standard Library.*—H. T. R.

the Duc d'Orleans, and finding him above or below crime, cast him off like a despised accomplice of ambition, and tried to ally himself with La Fayette, who, possessed of the armed force, and who saw in Mirabeau the whole of the moral force, smiled at the idea of a duumvirate, which could assume to themselves empire. There were secret interviews at Paris and at Passy between these two rivals. La Fayette rejecting every idea of a usurpation profitable to the prince, declared to Mirabeau that he must renounce every conceived plot against the queen if he would come to an understanding with him. "Well, general," replied Mirabeau, "since you will have it so, let her live! A humbled queen may be fit for something, but a queen with her throat cut is only good as the subject of a bad tragedy!" This atrocious remark, which treated the bloodshed of a woman as a jest, was subsequently known by the queen, who however forgave Mirabeau, and did not allow it to interfere with her *liaisons* with the great orator. But the cold-blooded infamy must have found its way to her heart as an ominous warning of what she might fear hereafter.

La Fayette, sure of the consent of the king and queen, supported by the feelings of the national guard, who were growing weary of factions and the factious, ventured to assume quietly towards the prince the tone of a dictator, and to pronounce against him an arbitrary exile under the appearance of a mission freely accepted. He sent to request of the Duc d'Orleans a meeting at the Marquise de Coigny's, a noble intelligent lady attached to La Fayette, and in whose *salon* the Duc d'Orleans occasionally met him. After a conversation heard by the walls alone, but the result of which showed its tenor, and which Mirabeau, to whom it was communicated, termed *very imperious on the one side, and very resigned on the other*, it was agreed that the Duc d'Orleans should forthwith set out for London. The friends of the prince induced him to change his resolution that same night, and he sent La Fayette a note to this effect. La Fayette requested another interview, in which he called upon him to keep his word, enjoined him to depart in twenty-four hours, and then conducted him to the king. There the prince accepted the feigned mission, and promised to leave nothing neglected to expose in England the plots of the conspirators of the kingdom. "You are more interested than any one," said La Fayette, in the king's presence, "for no one is more compromised than yourself." Mirabeau, cognizant of this oppression of La Fayette and the court over the mind of the Duc d'Orleans, offered his services to the duke, and tempted him with the last offers of supreme power. The subject of his address to the Assembly was already prepared: he intended to denounce, as a conspiracy of despotism, this *coup d'état* against one citizen, in which the liberty of all citizens was attempted. "This violation of the inviolability of the representatives of the nation in the palpable exile of a prince of the blood; he was to point out La Fayette, making use of the royal hand to strike the rivals of his popularity, and to cover his own insolent dictatorship under the venerated sanction of the chief of the nation and the head of the family." Mirabeau had no doubt of the resentment of the Assembly against so odious an attempt, and promised the friends of the Duc d'Orleans one of those returns of opinion which raise a man to a higher elevation than that from which he has fallen. This language, backed by the entreaties of Laclos, Sillery, Lauzun, a second time shook the prince's resolution. He saw now disgrace in this voluntary exile, where at first he had only seen magnanimity. At the break of day he wrote that he declined the mission. La Fayette then sent for him to the minister for foreign affairs. There the prince, again overcome, wrote to the Assembly a letter, which destroyed beforehand all the denunciation of Mirabeau. "My enemies pretend," said the duke to La Fayette, "that you boast of having against me proofs of my share in the attempts of the 5th of October." "They are rather my enemies who say so," replied La Fayette: "if I had proofs against you I should already have arrested you. I have none, but I am seeking for them." The Duc d'Orleans went. Nine months had passed away since his return. The Constituent Assembly had left, without any other defence than anarchy, the constitution it had so lately voted. Disorder prevailed throughout the kingdom: the first acts of the Legislative Assembly announced the hesitation of a people which halts on a declivity, but is doomed to descend to the very bottom.

IX.

The Girondists, at the first step, going ahead of the Barnaves and Lameths, showed a disposition to push France, all unprepared, into a republic. The Duc d'Orleans, whose long residence in England had allowed him to reflect at a distance from the attractions of events and factions, felt his Bourbon blood rise within him. He did not cease to be a patriot, but he understood that the safety of the country on the brink of a war was not in the destruction of the executive power. Unquestionably pity for the king and queen awakened in a heart in which hatred had not stifled every generous feeling. He felt himself too much avenged by the days of the 5th and 6th October, by the humiliation of the king before the Assembly, by the daily insults of the populace under the windows of Marie Antoinette, and by the fearful nights of this family, whose palace was but a prison; and perhaps also he feared for himself the ingratitude of revolutions.

He had gone to England on compulsion, and had remained there under the idea, which was perfectly just, that his name might be used as a pretext for agitation in Paris. Laclos had gone to him in London from time to time to try again to tempt the exile's ambition, and make him ashamed of a deference for La Fayette, which France took to be cowardice. The prince's pride was roused at this, and he threatened to return; but the representations of M. de la Luzerne, minister of France in England, those of M. de Boinville, one of La Fayette's aides-de-camp, and his own reflections, had prevailed over the incitements of Laclos. Proof of this is found in a note of M. de la Luzerne's, found in an iron chest amongst the king's secret papers. "I attest," says M. de la Luzerne, "that I have presented to M. the Duc d'Orleans, M. de Boinville, aide-de-camp of M. de La Fayettte, that M. de Boinville declared to the Duc d'Orleans that they were very uneasy as to the troubles which might at this moment be excited in Paris by malcontents, who would not scruple to make use of his name to disturb the capital, and perhaps the kingdom; and he was urged on these grounds to protract the time of his departure. The Duc d'Orleans, unwilling in any way to afford plea or pretext for any disturbance of public tranquillity, consented to delay his return."

X.

He at last left England, and on his return made several fruitless attempts to be again employed in the navy. Whilst his mind was thus wavering, he received the intelligence, through M. Bertrand de Molleville, that the king had nominated him to the rank of admiral. The Duc d'Orleans went to thank that minister, and added that, "He was rejoiced at the honor the king conferred on him, as it would give him an opportunity of communicating to the king his real sentiments, which had been odiously calumniated. I am very unfortunate," continued he; "my name has been involved in all the crimes imputed to me, and I have been deemed guilty, because I disdained to justify myself; but time will show whether my conduct belies my words."

The air of frankness and good faith, and the significant tone with which the Duc d'Orleans uttered these words, struck the minister, who until then had been greatly prejudiced against his innocence. He inquired if his royal highness would consent to repeat these expressions to the king, as they would rejoice his majesty, and he feared that they might lose some of their force if repeated by himself. The duke eagerly embraced the idea of seeing the king, if the king would receive him, and expressed his intention of presenting himself at the château the next day. The king, informed of this by his minister, awaited the prince, and had a long and private conference with him.

A confidential document, written with the prince's own hand, and drawn up in order to justify his memory in the eyes of his children and his friends, informs us of what passed at this interview. "The ultra-democrats," said the Duc d'Orleans, "deemed that I wished to make France a republic; the ambitious, that I wished, by my popularity, to force the king to resign the administration of the kingdom into my hands; lastly, the virtuous and patriotic had the illusion of their own virtue concerning me, for they deemed that I sacrificed myself entirely to the public good. The one party deemed me worse than I was; the others, better. I have merely followed my nature, and that impelled me, above all, to liberty. I fancied I saw her image in the parliaments, which at least possessed her tone and forms, and I embraced this phantom of representative freedom. Thrice did I sacrifice myself for those parliaments; twice from a conviction on my part; the third, not to belie what I had previously done. I had been in England; I had there seen true liberty, and I doubted not that the States-General, and France also, wished to obtain freedom. Scarcely had I foreseen that France would possess citizens, than I wished to be one of these citizens myself, and I made unhesitatingly the sacrifice of all the rank and privileges that separated me from the nation: they cost me nothing; I aspired to be a deputy—I was one. I sided with the *tiers état*, not from factious feeling, but from justice. In my opinion, it was impossible to prevent the completion of the Revolution, although some persons around the king thought otherwise. The troops were assembled, and surrounded the National Assembly. Paris imagined it was threatened, and rose *en masse;* the Gardes Françaises, who lived amongst the people, followed the stream, and the report was circulated that I had bribed this regiment with my gold. I will frankly declare my opinion: if the Gardes Françaises had acted differently, I should in that case have deemed they had been bought over; for their hostility against the people of Paris would have been unnatural. My bust was carried with that of M. Necker on the 14th of July. Why? because this minister, on whom every public hope reposed, was the idol of the nation, and because my name was amongst the list of those deputies of the Assembly, who, it was said, were to have been arrested by the troops summoned to Versailles. Amidst all these events, so favorable to a factious man, what was my behavior? I withdrew from the eyes of the people; I did not flatter their excesses, but retired to my house at Mousseaux, where I passed the night; and the next morning I went, unattended, to the National Assembly at Versailles. At the fortunate moment when the king resolved to cast himself into the arms of the Assembly, I refused to form one of the deputation of members dispatched to Paris to announce these tidings to the capital, for I feared lest some of the homages which the city owed to the king alone might be paid to me. And such was again my conduct on the days of October; I again absented myself, not to add fresh fuel to the excitement of the people; and I only re-appeared when calm again prevailed. I was met at Sèvres by the bands of straggling assassins, who bore back the bleeding heads of the king's guards: these men stopped my carriage, and fired on the postillion. Thus I, who was the pretended leader of these men, narrowly escaped being their victim, and owed my safety to a body of the national guard, who escorted me to Versailles; and as I went to wait on the king I repressed the last murmurs of the people in the Cour des Ministres. I signed the decree which declared the Assembly inseparable from the person of the king. It was at this time that M. de La Fayette called on me, and informed me of the king's desire that I should quit Paris, in order to afford no pretext for popular tumult. Convinced now, that the Revolution was accomplished, and only fearing the troubles with which attempts might be made to fetter its onward progress, I unhesitatingly obeyed, only demanding the consent of the National Assembly to my departure ; this they granted, and I left Paris. The inhabitants of Boulogne, who had been worked upon by an intrigue which may be laid to my charge, but to which I was a stranger, since I would not yield to it, wished forcibly to detain me, and opposed my embarkation. I confess I was much touched, but I did not yield to this violent manifestation of public favor, and I myself persuaded them to return to their allegiance. Advantage has been taken of this voyage and my absence to impute to me, without refutation on my part, the most odious crimes. It was I who wished to force the king to fly with the Dauphin from Versailles,—but Versailles is not France; the king would have found his army and the nation when once he left this town, and the only result of my ambition would be civil war, and a military dictatorship given to the king. But the Count de Provence was alive; he was the natural heir to the throne thus abandoned. He was popular; he had, like myself, joined the commons,—thus I should only have labored for him. But the Count d'Artois was in safety in another country, his children were secure from my pretended murders, they were nearer the throne than myself. What a series of follies, absurdities, or useless crimes! The French nation, amidst the Revolution, have neither changed their character nor their sentiments. I fully believe that the Count d'Artois, whom I have myself loved, will prove this. I believe that, by drawing nearer to a monarch whom he loves, and by whom he is loved, and to a people to whose love his brilliant qualities give him so great a right, he will, when these troubles have ceased, enjoy this portion of his inheritance, the love which the most sensible and affectionate of nations has vowed to the descendants of Henri IV."

XI.

These excuses, mingled doubtless with expressions of repentance and tears, and heightened by those attitudes and gestures, more eloquent than words, that add so much pathos to solemn explanations, convinced the heart if not the mind of the king ; and he forgave—he excused, and he trusted. "I am of your opinion," said he to his minister, yet a prey to the emotion of this scene, "that the Duc d'Orleans really regrets his past errors, and that he will do all in his power to repair the evil he has done, and in which perhaps he has not had so great a share as we believed."

The prince left the king's apartments reconciled with himself, and more than ever resolved to withdraw himself from the factious party. It had cost him but little to sacrifice his ambition, for he had none; and his popularity of her own accord had quitted him for other men of inferior rank and station than his own, and he could only hope to find security, and an honorable refuge at the foot of the throne, to which he was alike guided by inclination and duty. Louis XVI. as a man had far more influence over him than as a king, but the adulation and resentment of the court ruined all.

The Sunday following this reconciliation, the Duc d'Orleans presented himself at the Tuileries to pay his respects to the king and queen. It was the day and hour of the *grandes receptions*, and crowds of courtiers thronged the courts, the staircases, the corridors, some hoping that fortune might yet be propitious; others, come from the provinces to the court of their unfortunate master, drawn thither by the double tie of misfortune and fidelity. At the sight of the Duc d'Orleans, whose reconciliation with the king had not as yet transpired, astonishment and horror appeared on every face, and an indignant murmur followed the announcement of his name. The crowd opened and shrank from him, as though his touch was odious to them. In vain did he seek one glance of respect or welcome amongst all these gloomy visages. As he approached the king's chamber, the courtiers and guards barred his entrance by turning their backs, and crowding together as if by accident, repulsed him; he entered the apartments of the queen, where the royal family's dinner was prepared. "Look to the dishes," cried voices, as though some public and well-known poisoner had been seen to enter. The indignant prince turned alternately pale and red, and imagined that these insults were offered him, at the instigation of the queen, and the order of the king. As he descended the stairs to quit the palace, fresh cries and outrages followed him; some even spat on his coat and head. A poniard stab would have been far less painful to bear than these withering marks of hatred and contempt. He had entered the palace appeased, he quitted it implacable; he felt that his only refuge against the court was in the last ranks of democracy, and he enrolled himself resolutely in them to find safety or vengeance.

The king and queen, who were soon informed of these insults, of which, however, they were entirely innocent, took no steps to make any reparation for them; possibly they were secretly flattered by the wrath of their adherents, and the humiliation of their enemy. The queen was too prodigal of her favor, and too hasty in her displeasure; the king did not want kindness, but grace; one word, such as Henri IV. knew so well how to employ, would have punished these insulters, and have brought the prince to his feet, yet he knew not how to say it; resentment brooded over her wrongs in silence, and destiny took its course.

XII.

The Duc d'Orleans severed himself on that day from the Girondists, to whom he was alone held by Pétion and Brissot, and passed over to the side of the Jacobins; he opened his palace to Danton and Barrère, and no longer followed any but the extreme party, which he adopted without hesitation in silence, even to the republic, to regicide, to death.

XIII.

However, the alarm with which the preparations of the emperor inspired the people, and the mischief excited by the speeches of the Girondists against the court and the ministers, agitated the capital more and more every day. At each fresh communication from M. de Lessart, minister of foreign affairs, the party of the Gironde raised a fresh cry of war and treason. Fauchet denounced the minister. Brissot exclaimed, "The mask has fallen,—our enemy is now known,—it is the emperor. The princes, who hold possessions in Alsace, whose cause he affects to espouse, are but the pretexts of his hate; and the *emigrês* themselves are but his instruments. Let us despise these *emigrés*: it is the duty of the high national court to execute justice on these mendicant princes. The electors of the empire are not worthy of your anger; fear causes them beforehand to prostrate themselves at your feet—a free people does not crush a fallen foe: strike at the head—this head is the emperor."

He communicated his own ardor to the Assemby; but Brissot, although a skilful politician, and the able counsellor of his party, did not possess that sonorous oratory that elevates an opinion to the level of the voice of a nation. Vergniaud alone was gifted with a soul, in which was combined all the passion and eloquence of a party; by meditating on the annals of the past, he elevated his mind to scenes that passed then analogous to those in which he was an actor, and communicated an importance and solemnity to every word. "Our revolution," said he at the same sitting, "has spread alarm amongst every throne, for it has given an example of the destruction of the despotism that sustains them. Kings hate our constitution because it renders men free, and because they would reign over slaves. This hate has been manifested on the part of the emperor by all the measures he has adopted, to disturb us or to strengthen our enemies, and encourage those Frenchmen who have rebelled against the laws of their country. We must not believe that this hate has ceased to exist, but it must cease to work. The genius of liberty watches over our frontiers, which are less defended by our troops and our national guards than by the enthusiasm of freedom. Liberty, since its birth, has been the object of a shameful and secret war, waged against it even in its very cradle. What is this war? Three armies of reptiles and venomous insects breed and creep in your own breast: one is composed of paid libellists and hired calumniators, who strive to arm the two powers against each other by inspiring them with mutual distrust; the other army, equally dangerous, is composed of seditious priests, who feel that their God is forsaking them, and that their power is crumbling away with their *pristige*, and who, to retain their empire, term vengeance religion, and crime virtue. The third is composed of greedy speculators and financiers, who can grow rich only on our ruin; national prosperity would be destruction to their egotistical speculations; and our death would be their life. They are like those beasts of prey, who wait the issue of the battle that they may batten and feast on the corpses of the slain. (Loud applause.)

"They know that the expenses of your preparations for defence are numerous; and they reckon upon the failure of the credit of the treasury, and the scarcity of specie; they reckon upon the weariness of those citizens who have abandoned their wives, their babes, to hasten to the frontiers, and who will abandon them, whilst millions, distributed at home, will arouse insurrections, in which the people, armed by madness, will themselves destroy their rights, whilst they imagine they are defending them; then the emperor will advance at the head of a powerful army to rivet your fetters. Such is the war that they make on you, and that they seek to make. (Loud applause.)

"The people has sworn to maintain the constitution, because in that lies its honor and its liberty; but if you suffer it to remain in a state of troubled immobility, that weakens its force and exhausts all our resources, will not the day of this exhaustion be the last of the constitution? The state in which we are kept is one of annihilation that may lead us to disgrace or to death. (Applause.) To arms, citizens! to arms, freemen! defend your liberty! assure the hope of that liberty to the whole human race, or you will not deserve even pity in your misfortunes. (Applause.) We have no other allies than the eternal justice, whose rights we defend; but is it forbidden us to seek others, and to interest those powers who, like ourselves are threatened by the rupture of the equilibrium in Europe? No, doubtless, let us declare to the emperor, that from this moment all treaties are broken. (Vehement applause.) The emperor has himself violated them; and if he does not attack us, it is because he is not yet prepared; but he is unmasked; felicitate yourselves upon this. The eyes of Europe are fixed upon you; show them what is really the National Assembly of France. If you display the dignity that befits the representatives of a great nation, you will gain esteem, applause, and assistance. If you evince weakness, if you do not avail yourselves of the occasion offered you by Providence, of freeing yourselves from a situation that fetters you, dread the degradation that is prepared for you by the hatred of Europe, of France, of your own time and of posterity. (Applause.) Do more; demand that your flag be respected beyond the Rhine; demand that the *emigrés* be dispersed. I might demand that they be given up to the country they insult, and to punishment. But no. If they have been greedy for our blood, let us not show ourselves greedy for theirs; their crime is having wished to destroy their country; let them be vagrants and wanderers on the face of the earth, and let their punishment be never to find a country. (Applause.) If the emperor delays to answer your demands, let all delay be deemed a refusal, and every refusal on his part to explain, a declaration of war. Attack whilst you yet may. If, in the Saxon wars, Frederic had temporized, the king of Prussia would at this moment be marquis of Brandenbourg, instead of disputing with Austria the balance of power in Germany which has escaped from your grasp.

"Up to this period you have only adopted half measures, and I may well apply to you the language which Demosthenes addressed to the Athenians, under similar circumstances: 'You act towards the Macedonians,' said he, 'like the barbarians, who combat in our games towards their adversaries; when they are struck on the arm they raise their hand to their arm; if struck on the head they raise their hand to their head; they never dream of defending themselves when they are wounded, nor of parrying the blows dealt them. Does Philip take up arms, you do the same; does he lay them down, you also lay down yours. If he attack one of your allies, you immediately dispatch a numerous army to the assistance of your ally. If he attack a city, you dispatch a numerous army to the relief of the city. Does he again lay down his arms, you do the same, without thinking of any means of forestalling his ambition; and placing yourself beyond the reach of his attacks. Thus you are at the orders of your enemy, and he it is who commands your army.'

"And I, I tell you the same of the *emigrés*. Do you hear that they are at Coblentz,—the citizens hasten to combat them; are they assembled on the banks of the Rhine,—two *corps d'armée* are dispatched thither; do foreign powers afford them shelter,—you propose to attack them; do you learn, on the contrary, that they have withdrawn to the north of Germany,—you lay down your arms; do they again offend you—your indignation is again aroused; do they make you specious promises,—you are again appeased. Thus, it is the *emigrés* and the cabinets that support them—who are your leaders, and who dispose of your counsels, your treasures, and your armies. (Applause.) It is for you to consider whether this humiliating part be worthy of a great nation. A thought flashes across my mind, and with that I will terminate. It appears to me, that the manes of past generations arise, to conjure you, in the name of all the evils that slavery has inflicted on them, to preserve from it future generations, whose destinies are in your hands; fulfil this prayer, and be for the future a second providence. Associate yourself with the eternal justice that protects the people. By meriting the title of benefactors of your country, you will also merit that of benefactors of the human race."

Loud and prolonged applause succeeded the different emotions that had been excited by this speech in every heart.

for Vergniaud, following the example of the ancient orators, instead of suffering his eloquence to grow cold in political combinations, heated it at the flame of his daring genius. The people comprehends only that which it feels; its sole orators are those who excite it, and emotion is the conviction of the populace. Vergniaud felt this, and knew how to communicate it. The knowledge that they labored for universal good, and the prospect of the gratitude of future ages, shed a halo—a noble pride around France, and of sanctity around liberty. It was one of the characteristics of this orator, that he almost invariably elevated the Revolution to the dignity of an apostleship, that he extended his humanity to all mankind, and that he only impassioned and worked upon the people by his virtues; such words produced an effect over all the empire, against which neither the king nor his ministers could strive.

XIV.

Moreover, as has been shown, Vergniaud and his party had friends in the council. M. de Narbonne and the Girondists met and concerted their plans at Madame de Stäel's, whose *salon*, in which some warlike measure was always being discussed, was called the camp of the Revolution: the Abbé Fauchet, the denouncer of M. de Lessart, here imbibed fresh ardor for the overthrow of this minister. M. de Lessart, by weakening as much as possible the threats of the court of Vienna and the anger of the Assembly, sought to gain time for better and wiser resolutions. His loyal attachment to Louis XVI., and his wise and prudent foresight, showed him that war would not restore, but shake the throne; and in this shock of Europe and France, the king would inevitably be crushed. The attachment of M. de Lessart to his master supplied the place of genius; he was the only obstacle in the path of the three parties who wished for war; it was necessary, at all risks, to remove him. He might have shielded himself by withdrawing from the contest, or by yielding to the impatience of the Assembly. But, though fully aware of the terrible responsibility that rested on him, and that this responsibility was death, he braved all, to afford the king a few days more for negotiation.—These days were numbered.

BOOK XII.

I.

Leopold, a pacific and philosophic prince, who, had he not been an emperor, would have been a revolutionist, had sought by every means in his power to adjourn the concussion between the two principles; he only demanded from France such concessions as would enable him to repress the ardor of Prussia, Germany, and Russia. The prince de Kaunitz, his minister, continually wrote to M. de Lessart in this strain; and the private communications which the king received from his ambassador at the court of Vienna, the Marquis de Noailles, breathed the same spirit of conciliation. Leopold only desired that guarantees should be given to the monarchical powers for the establishment of order in France, and that the constitution should be vigorously enforced by the executive power. But the last sittings of the Assembly, the armaments of M. de Narbonne, the accusations of Brissot, the fiery speeches of Vergniaud, and the applause he had gained, began to weary his patience; and the desire for war, so long repressed, now, in spite of himself, took possession of him. "The French wish for war," said he one day; "they shall have it—they shall see that the peaceful Leopold can be warlike when the interest of his people demands it."

The cabinet councils at Vienna became more frequent, in presence of the emperor. Russia had just concluded peace with the Ottoman empire, and was thus enabled to turn her eyes to France; Sweden fanned the flame of all the princes; Prussia yielded to the advice of Leopold; England observed, but pledged herself to nothing, for the struggle on the Continent would increase her importance. The armaments were decided upon, and on the 7th of February, 1792, the definitive treaty of alliance between Austria and Prussia was signed at Berlin. "Now," wrote Leopold to Frederic William, "it is France who menaces—who arms—who provokes: Europe must arm."

The party in favor of war in Germany triumphed. "It is very fortunate for you," said the elector of Mayence to the Marquis de Bouillé, "that the French were the aggressors; but for that we should never have had a war." War was resolved upon in the councils, yet Leopold still hoped. In an official note, which the Prince de Kaunitz transmitted to the Marquis de Noailles, for the king, Leopold yet showed himself willing to be reconciled. M. de Lessart replied confidentially to these last overtures, in a dispatch which he had the honesty to communicate to the diplomatic committee of the Assembly, composed of Girondists. In his reply the minister palliated the charges made against the Assembly by the emperor, and seemed rather to excuse France than justify. He acknowledged that there were some disturbances in the kingdom, some excesses in the clubs, some licence in the press; but he attributed these disorders to the excitement produced by the movements of the *emigrés*, and the inexperience of a people who essay their constitution and wound themselves with it.

" Indifference and contempt," said he, " are the fittest weapons with which to combat this pest. Could Europe stoop so low, as to quarrel with the French nation, because some few demagogues and madmen dwell amongst them, and would honor them so far as to reply to them by cannon balls?"

In a dispatch of the Prince de Kaunitz, addressed to all the European cabinets, was this phrase,—" Latest events give us cause to hope, for it is evident that the majority of the French nation, struck by the evils they are preparing for themselves, are returning to more moderate principles, and are inclined to restore to the throne the dignity and authority which form the bases of monarchical government." The Assembly remained silent from suspicion, and this suspicion was awakened whilst diplomatic notes and counter notes were exchanged between the cabinet of the Tuileries and the cabinet of Vienna. But no sooner had M. de Lessart descended from the tribune, and the Assembly closed the sitting, than the murmurs of mistrust were changed into loud and sullen exclamations of indignation.

II.

The Jacobins burst out into threats against the perfidious minister and the court, who united in a treasonable combination, called the Austrian Committee, concerted counter-revolutionary plans in the Tuileries, made signals to the enemies of the nation from the very foot of the throne, and secretly communicated with the court of Vienna, and dictated the language necessary to intimidate France. The Memoirs of Hardenberg, the Prussian minister, which have since been published, prove that these accusations were not entirely the dreams of the demagogues; and that in order to promote peace the two courts did all in their power to adopt the same tone with each other. It was resolved that M. de Lessart should be impeached, and Brissot, the leader of the diplomatic committee, the advocate of war, undertook to prove his pretended crimes.

The constitutional party abandoned M. de Lessart, without any defence, to the hatred of the Jacobins; this party had no suspicions, but vengeance to wreak upon M. de Lessart. The king had suddenly dismissed M. de Narbonne, the rival of this minister in the council. M. de Narbonne, feeling himself menaced, caused La Fayette to write a letter, in which he conjured him to remain at his post so long as the perils of his country rendered it necessary.

This step, of which M. de Narbonne was cognizant, appeared to the king an insolent act of oppression against his liberty and that of the constitution. The popularity of M. de Narbonne diminished proportionately as that of the Girondists became greater and inspired them with more audacity. The Assembly began to change its applause into murmurs, when he mounted the tribune, whence a short time before he had been shamefully forced to withdraw, becouse he had wounded the plebeian susceptibility by appealing to the *most distinguished* members of the Assembly. The aristocracy of his rank showed itself beneath his uniform, whilst the people wished for members of its own stamp in the councils; and thus between the offended king and the suspicious Girondists, M. de Narbonne fell. The king dismissed him, and he went to serve in the army he had organized. His friends did not conceal their resentment. Madame de Stäel lost in him her ambition and her ideal at the same time; but she did not abandon all hope of regaining for M. de Narbonne the confidence of the king, and of seeing him play a great political part. She had sought to render him a Mirabeau, she now dreamed of making him a Monk. From this day she conceived the idea of rescuing the king from the power of the Jacobins and Girondists—of carrying him off through the agency of M. de Narbonne and the constitutionalists—of re-seating him on the throne —of crushing the extreme parties, and establishing her ideal government—a liberal aristocracy. A woman of genius, her genius had the prejudices of her birth; a plebeian, who had found her way to court, it was necessary for her to have patricians between the throne and the people. The first blow at M. de Lessart was dealt by a man who frequented the *salon* of Madame de Stäel.

III.

But a more terrible and more unexpected blow fell on M. de Lessart: the very day on which he thus surrendered himself to his enemies, the unexpected death of the emperor Leopold was known at Paris, and with this prince expired the last faint hope of peace, for his wisdom died with him; and who could tell what new policy would arise from his tomb? The agitation that prevailed filled every one with terror, and this was soon changed into hatred against the unfortunate minister of Louis XVI. He had neither known, it was said, how to profit by the pacific disposition of Leopold whilst this prince yet lived, nor to forestall the hostile designs of those who succeeded him in the dominion of Germany. Everything furnished fresh accusation against him, even fatality and death.

At the moment of his decease all was ready for hostility. Two hundred thousand men formed a line from Bâle to the Scheldt. The duke of Brunswick, on whom rested every hope of the coalition, was at Berlin, giving his last advice to the king of Prussia, and receiving his final orders. Beschoffwerder, the general and confidant of the king of Prussia, arrived at Vienna to concert with the emperor the point and time of attack. On his arrival the Prince de Kaunitz hastily informed him of the sudden illness of the emperor. The 27th Leopold was in perfect health, and received the Turkish envoy; on the 28th he was in the agonies of death. His stomach swelled, and convulsive vomitings put him to intense torture. The doctors, alarmed at these symptoms, ordered copious bleeding, which appeared to allay his sufferings; but they enervated the vital force of the prince, who had weakened himself by debauchery. He fell asleep for a short time, and the doctors and ministers withdrew; but he soon awoke in fresh convulsions, and died in the presence of a valet de chambre, named Brunetti, in the arms of the empress, who had just arrived.

The intelligence of the death of the emperor, the more terrible as it was so unexpected, spread abroad instantly, and surprised Germany at the very moment of a crisis. Terror for the future destiny of Germany was joined to pity for the empress and her children: the palace was all confusion and despair; the ministers felt power snatched from their grasp; the grandees of the court, without waiting for their carriages, hurried to the court, in the disorder of astonishment, and grief and sobs were heard in the vestibules and staircases that led to the apartments of the empress. At this moment, this princess, without having time to assume black, appeared, bathed in tears, surrounded by her numerous children, and leading them to the new king of the Romans, the eldest son of Leopold, she threw herself at his feet, and implored his protection for these orphans. Francis I., mingling his tears with those of his mother and brothers, one of whom was only four years old, raised the empress, and embracing the children, vowed to be a second father to them.

IV.

This catastrophe was inexplicable to scientific men; politicians suspected some mystery; the people poison. These reports of poison, however, have neither been confirmed nor disproved by time. The most probable opinion is that this prince had made an immoderate use of drugs which he compounded himself, in order to recruit his constitution, shattered by debauchery and excess. Lagusius, his chief physician, who had assisted at the autopsy of the body, declared he discovered traces of poison. Who had administered it? The Jacobins and *emigrés* mutually accused each other, the one party to disembarrass themselves of the armed chief of the empire, and thus spread anarchy amongst the federation of Germany, of which the emperor was the bond that united them; the others had slain in Leopold the philosopher prince, who temporized with France, and who retarded the war. A female was spoken of who had attracted the notice of the emperor at the last *bal masqué* at the court, and it was said that this stranger, favored by her disguise, had given him poisoned sweetmeats, without its being possible to discover from whose hand they came. Others accused the beautiful Florentine, Donna Livia, his mistress, who, according to them, was the fanatical instrument of a few priests. These anecdotes are the mere chimeras of surprise and sorrow, for the people can never believe that the events which have had so vast an influence over their destiny are merely natural. But crimes, universally approved, are rare; opinion may desire, but never commits them. Crime, like ambition or vengeance, is personal: there was neither ambition nor vengeance around Leopold,—nought but a few female jealousies; and his attachments were too numerous and too fugitive to kindle in the heart of a mistress that love that arms the hand with poison or poniard. He loved at the same time Donna Livia, whom he had brought with him from Tuscany, and who was known in Europe as "La belle Florentine," Prokache, a young Polish girl, the charming countess of Walkenstein, and others of an inferior rank. The countess of Walkenstein had for some time past been his avowed mistress; he had given her a million (francs) in drafts on the bank of Vienna, and he had even presented her to the empress, who forgave him his weaknesses, on condition that he gave no one his political confidence, which up to that time he had confided to her alone. He was a devoted admirer of the fair sex, and it would be necessary to refer to the most shameful epochs of Roman history to find any emperor whose life was as scandalous as his own: his cabinet was found after his death to be filled with valuable stuffs, rings, fans, trinkets, and even a quantity of rouge. These traces of debauch made the empress blush when she visited them with the new emperor. "My son," said she, "you have before you the sad proof of your father's disorderly life, and of my long afflictions: remember nothing of them except my forgiveness and his virtues. Imitate his great qualities, but beware lest you fall into the same vices, in order that you may not, in your turn, put to the blush those who scrutinize your life."

The prince in Leopold was superior to the man: he had made trial of a philosophical government in Tuscany, and this happy country yet blesses his memory; but his genius was not suited for a more enlarged field. The struggle, forced on him by the French Revolution, compelled him to seize on the helm in Germany; but he did so without energy. He opposed the temporizing policy of diplomacy to the contagion of new ideas; he was the Fabius of kings. To afford the Revolution time was to insure it the victory. It could be only vanquished by surprise, and stifled in its own stronghold; the genius of the people was its negotiator and accomplice, and its increasing popularity was its army. Its ideas found new adherents in princes, people, and cabinets.

Leopold would have given it a share, but the share of the Revolution is the conquest of everything that opposes its principles. The principles of Leopold could conciliate the Revolution, but his power as the arbitrator of Germany could not conciliate the conquering power of France. His part was a double one, and his position false. He died at a right moment for his renown; he paralyzed Germany, and checked the impetus of France, and, by disappearing between the two, he left the two principles to clash together, and destiny to take its course.

V.

Opinion, already agitated by the death of Leopold, received another shock from the news of the tragical death of the king of Sweden, who was assassinated on the night of the 16th of March, 1792, at a masked ball. Death seemed to strike, one after another, all the enemies of France. The Jacobins saw its hand in all these catastrophes, and even boasted of them through their most audacious demagogues; but they proclaimed more crimes than they committed, and their wishes alone shared in these assassinations.

Gustavus, this hero of the counter-revolution, this chevalier of aristocracy, fell by the blows of his nobility. When he was ready to set forth on the expedition he projected against France, he had assembled his diet to insure the tranquillity of the kingdom during his absence. His vigorous measures had put down the malcontents; yet it was foretold to him, like Cæsar, that the ides of March would be a critical period of his destiny. A thousand traces revealed a plot, and his intended assassination was rumored over all Germany before the blow was struck. These rumors are the forerunners of projected crimes: some indication escapes the heart of the conspirator, and it is by this means that the vent is predicted before it happens.

The king of Sweden, warned by his numerous friends, who ntreated him to be upon his guard, replied, like Cæsar, that he stroke when once received was less painful than the perpetual dread of receiving it, and that if he listened to all these warnings, he could no longer drink a glass of water without trembling. He braved danger, and showed himself more than ever to the people. The conspirators had made several fruitless attempts during the Diet, but chance had preserved the king. Since his return to Stockholm, the king frequently went to pass the day alone at his château at Haga, a league from the capital. Three of the conspirators had approached the château, at five o'clock on a dark winter's evening, armed with carbines, and ready to fire on the king. The apartment he occupied was on the ground-floor, and the lighted candles in the library enabled them to see their victim. Gustavus, on his return from hunting, undressed, and fell asleep in an arm-chair, within a few feet of the assassins. Whether it was that they were alarmed by the sound of footsteps, or that the solemn contrast of the peaceful slumber of this prince with the death that threatened him, softened their hearts, they again abandoned their project, and only revealed this circumstance on their trial after the assassination, when the king acknowledged the truth and precision of their details. They were ready to renounce their intention, discouraged by a sort of divine intervention, and by the fatigue of having so long meditated this design in vain, when a fatal occasion tempted them too strongly, and made them resolve on the murder of the king.

VI.

A masked ball was given at the opera, which the king was to attend, and the conspirators resolved to take advantage of the mystery of the disguise and tumult of the fête to strike the blow, without allowing the hand to appear. A short time before the ball the king supped with a few of his most intimate courtiers. A letter was brought to him, which he opened, and reading it jestingly, then threw it on the table. The anonymous writer informed him that he was neither a friend to his person nor an approver of his policy, but that as a loyal enemy he desired to inform him of the death that menaced him. He counselled him not to go to the ball; or, if he persisted, he advised him to mistrust the crowd that might press around him, for that was the signal for the blow to be aimed at him. That the king might not doubt the warning thus given, he recalled to his memory his dress, gesture, and sleep in his apartment of Haga in the evening that he had believed himself quite alone. Such convincing proofs must have struck and intimidated the mind of the prince, but his intrepid soul made him brave, not only the warning, but death: he rose and went to the ball.

VII.

Scarcely had he reached the apartment, when he was surrounded, as he had been warned, by a group of masks, and separated, as if by preconcerted movement, from the body of officers who were in attendance. At this moment an invisible hand fired at his back a pistol loaded with slugs. The blow struck him in the left flank above the hip. Gustavus fell into the arms of Count d'Armsfeld, his favorite. The report of the fire-arm, the smell of powder, the cries of "*fire*," which resounded through the apartment, the confusion which followed the king's fall, the real or feigned anxiety of persons who hurried forward to save him, favored the escape of the assassins: the pistol had been dropped on the ground. Gustavus did not lose his presence of mind for a moment. He ordered the doors to be immediately closed, and desired all to unmask. Carried by his guards into an apartment in the opera-house, he was confided to his surgeons. He admitted some of the foreign ministers into his presence, and spoke to them with all the calmness of a strong mind. Even his pain did not inspire him with any feeling of vengeance. Generous even in death, he demanded anxiously if the assassin had been apprehended. He was told that he was unknown. "Oh God, grant," he said, "that he may not be discovered."

Whilst the king was receiving the first attentions, and being conveyed to the palace, the guards stationed at the doors of the ball-room compelled all to take off their masks, asked their names, and searched their persons: nothing suspicious was discovered. Four of the chief conspirators, men of the highest nobility in Stockholm, had succeeded in escaping from the apartment in the first confusion produced by the report of the pistol, and before the doors had been closed. Of nine confidants or accomplices in the crime, eight had already gone away without exciting any suspicion: only one was left in the apartment, who affected a slow step and calm demeanor as guarantees of his innocence.

He left the apartment last of all, raising his mask before the officer of police, and saying, as he looked steadfastly at him, "As for me, sir, I hope you do not suspect me." This man was the assassin.

They allowed him to pass; the crime had no other evidence than itself, a pistol, and a knife, sharpened as a poniard, found beneath the masks and flowers on the floor of the opera. The weapon revealed the hand. A gunsmith at Stockholm identified the pistol, and declared he had recently sold it to a Swedish gentleman, formerly an officer in the guards, named Ankastroem. They found Ankastroem at his house, neither thinking of exculpation nor of flight. He confessed the weapon and the crime. An unjust judgment, he averred, in which however the king spared his life, the wearisomeness of an existence which he had cherished to employ and make illustrious at its close for his country's advantage, the hope, if he succeeded, of a national recompense worthy of the deed, had, he declared, inspired this project; and he claimed to himself alone the glory or disgrace. He denied all plot and all accomplices. Beneath the fanatic he masked the conspirator.

He failed in his part, after a few days, beneath the truth and his remorse. He avowed the conspiracy, named the guilty, and the reward of his crime. It was a sum of money, that had been weighed, rix-dollar by rix-dollar, against the blood of Gustavus. The plot, planned six months before, had been thrice frustrated, by chance or destiny—at the diet of Jessen, at Stockholm, and at Haga. The king killed, all his favorites—all the instruments of his government—must be sacrificed to the vengeance of the senate and the restoration of the aristocracy. Their heads were to have been carried at the tops of pikes, in the streets of the capital, in imitation of the popular punishments of Paris. The duke of Sudermania, the king's brother, was to be sacrificed. The young monarch, handed over to the conspirators, was to serve as a passive instrument to re-establish the ancient constitution, and legitimate their crime. The principal conspirators belonged to the first families in Sweden; the shame of their lost power had debased their ambition, even to crime. They were the Count de Ribbing, Count de Horn, Baron d'Erensward, and Colonel Lilienhorn. Lilienhorn, commandant of the guards, drawn from misery and obscurity by the king's favor, promoted to the first rank in the army, and admitted to closest intimacy in the palace, confessed his ingratitude and his crime; seduced, he declared, by the ambition of commanding, during the trouble, the national guard of Stockholm. The part played by La Fayette in Paris seemed to him the ideal of the citizen and the soldier. He could not resist the fascination of the perspective; half-way in the conspiracy, he had endeavored to render it impossible, even whilst he meditated it. It was he who had written the anonymous letter to the king, in which the king was warned of the failure in the attempt at Haga, and that which threatened him at this fête; with one hand he thrust forward the assassin—with the other he held back the victim, as though he had thus prepared for himself an excuse for his remorse after the deed was done.

On the fatal day he had passed the evening in the king's apartments—had seen him read the letter—had followed him to the ball. Enigma of crime—a pitying assassin! the mind thus divided between the thirst for, and horror of, his benefactor's blood.

VIII.

Gustavus died slowly: he saw death approach and recede with the same indifference, or the same resignation; received his court, conversed with his friends, even reconciled himself to the opponents of his government, who did not conceal their opposition, but did not push their aristocratic resentment to assassination. "I am consoled," he said, to the Count de Brahé, one of the greatest of the nobility and chief of the malcontents, "since death enables me to recover an old friend in you."

He watched to the very last over his kingdom; nominated the Duke of Sudermania regent, instituted a council of regency, made his friend Armsfeld military governor of Stockholm, surrounded the young king, only thirteen years of age, with all that could strengthen his position during his minority. He prepared his passage from one world to another, awaiting his death, so that it should be an event to himself alone. "My son," he wrote, a few hours before he died, "will not come of age before he is eighteen, but I hope he will be king at sixteen;" thus predicting for his successor that precocity of courage and genius which had enabled him to reign and govern before the time. He said to his grand almoner, in confessing himself, "I do not think I shall take with me great merits before God, but at least I shall have the consciousness of never having willingly done harm to any person." Then, having requested a moment's repose to acquire strength, in order to embrace his family for the last time, he bade adieu, with a smile, to his friend Bergen stiern, and, falling asleep, never waked again.

The prince royal, proclaimed king, mounted the throne the same day. The people whom Gustavus had emancipated from the yoke of the senate, swore spontaneously to defend his institutions in his son. He had so well employed the day, which God had allowed him between assassination and death, that nothing perished but himself, and his shade seemed to continue to reign over Sweden.

This prince had nothing great but his soul, nor handsome but his eyes. Small in size, with broad shoulders, his haunches badly set on, his forehead singularly shaped, long nose, large mouth, the grace and animation of his countenance overcame every imperfection of figure, and rendered Gustavus one of the most attractive men in his dominions; intelligence, goodness, courage, beamed from his eyes, and pervaded his features. You felt the man, admired the king, appreciated the hero. There was heart in his genius, as there is in all really great men. Well informed, deeply read, eloquent, he applied all his endowments to the empire: those whom he had conquered by his courage, he vanquished by his generosity, and charmed by his language. His faults were display and pleasure; he liked the glory of those enjoyments and amours which are found and pardoned in heroes; his vices were those of Alexander, Cæsar, and Henri IV. The revenge of a disgraceful amour had something to do with the conspiracy which destroyed him; to resemble these great men, he only wanted their destiny.

When almost a child, he had rescued himself from the tutelage of the aristocracy; in emancipating the throne, he had emancipated the people. At the head of an army, recruited without money, and which he disciplined by its enthusiasm, he conquered Finland, and went on from victory to victory to St. Petersburgh. Checked in his greatness by a revolt of his officers, surrounded in his tent by his guards, he had escaped by flight, and had gone to the succor of another portion of his kingdom, invaded by the Danes. Again a victor against these deadly enemies of Sweden, the gratitude of the nation had restored to him his repentant army; and his sole vengeance was in again leading them to conquest.

He had subdued all without, tranquillized all within, and had only one ambition left—disinterested from every consideration but fame—to avenge the forsaken cause of Louis XVI., and to secure from her persecutors a queen whom he adored at a distance. This was the vision of a hero; it had but one mistake—his genius was vaster than his empire. Heroism with disproportioned means makes the great man resemble an adventurer, and transforms gigantic designs into follies. But history does not judge like fortune, and it is the heart rather than success that makes the hero. The romantic and adventurous character of Gustavus is still the greatness of a restless and struggling soul in the pettiness of its destiny. His death excited a shriek of joy amongst the Jacobins, who deified Ankastroem; but their burst of delight on learning the end of Gustavus, proved how insincere was their affected contempt for this enemy of the constitution.

IX.

These two obstacles removed, nothing now kept France and Europe on terms but the feeble cabinet of Louis XVI. The impatience of the nation, the ambition of the Girondists, and the resentment of the constitutionalists wounded through M. de Narbonne, united them to overthrow the cabinet. Brissot, Vergniaud, Guadet, Condorcet, Gensonné, Pétion, their friends in the Assembly, the council-chamber of Madame Roland, their Seids among the Jocobins balanced between two ambitions—equally open to their abilities—to destroy power or seize on it. Brissot counselled this latter measure. More conversant with politics than the young orators of the Gironde, he did not comprehend the Revolution without government; anarchy, in his opinion, did not destroy the monarchy more than it did liberty. The greater were events, the more necessary was the direction of them. Placed disarmed in the foremost rank of the Assembly and of opinion, power presented itself, and it was necessary to lay hands upon it. Once in their grasp, they would make of it, according to the dictates of fortune and the will of the people, a monarchy or a republic. Ready for anything that would allow them to reign in the name of the king or of the people, this counsel was pleasing to men who had scarcely emerged from obscurity, and who, seduced by the facility of their good fortune, seized on it at its first smile. Men who ascend quickly, easily become giddy.

Still a very profound line of policy was disclosed in the secret council of the Girondists, in the choice of the men whom they put forward, and whom they presented for ministers to the king.

Brissot in this gave evidence of the patience of consummate ambition. He inspired Vergniaud, Pétion, Guadet, Gensonné, as well as all the leading men of his party, with similar patience. He remained with them in the twilight close to power, but not included in the projected ministry, being desirous of feeling the pulse of popular opinion through secondary men, who could be disavowed or sacrificed at need, and keeping in reserve himself and the leaders of the Girondists, either to support or overthrow this weak and transitory ministry, if the nation should resolve upon more decisive measures. Brissot, and those who acted with him, were thus ready at all points, as well to direct as to replace power —they were masters without any responsibility. The doctrines of Machiavel were very perceptible in this tactic of statesmen. Besides, by abstaining from entering into the first cabinet, they would remain popular, and maintain, in the Assembly and Jacobins, those voices of power which would have been stifled in an administration. Popularity was requisite for their contest with Robespierre, who was treading so closely on their heels, and who would soon be at the head of opinion if they abandoned it to him. On entering upon their course they affected for this rival more con tempt than they really felt. Robespierre, single-handed, balanced their influence with the Jacobins. The vociferations of Billaud, Varennes, Danton, Collot d'Herbois, did not in the least alarm them. Robespierre's silence gave them considerable uneasiness. They had been successful in the question of war; but the stoical opposition of Robespierre, and the desire of the people for war, had not affected his reputation. This man had redoubled his power in his isolation. The inspiration of a mind alone and incorruptible was more powerful than the enthusiasm of a whole party. Those who did not approve, still admired him. He had stood aside to allow war to pass by him, but opinion always had its eyes on him, and it might have been said that a secret instinct revealed to the people that in this man was the destiny of the future. When he advanced, they followed him; when he did not move, they waited for him. The Girondists, therefore, were compelled, from prudential motives, to distrust this man, and to remain in the Assembly between their own course and him. These precautions taken, they looked about them for the men who were nullities by themselves, and yet, ingrafted on their party, of whom they could make ministers. They required instruments, and not masters,—Seids attached to their fortune, whom they could direct at will either against the king or against the Jacobins—could elevate without fear, or reject without compunction. They sought them in obscurity, and believed they had found them in Clavière, Roland, Dumouriez, Lacoste, and Duranton,—they made only one mistake: Dumouriez, under the guise of an adventurer, had talents equal to any emergency.*

X.

The party thus distributed, and Madame Roland informed of the proposed elevation of her husband, the Girondists attacked the ministry in the person of M. de Lessart, at the sitting of the 10th of March. Brissot read against this minister a bill of accusation, skilfully and perfidiously fabricated, in which the appearance presented by facts and the conjecture derived from proofs, cast on the negotiation of M. de Lessart all the odium and criminality of treason. He proposed that a decree of accusation should proceed against the minister for foreign affairs. The Assembly was silent or applauded. Some members, with a view of defending the minister, demanded time in order that the Assembly might reflect on the charge, and thus, at least, affect the impartiality of justice. "Hasten!" exclaimed Isnard; "whilst you are deliberating perhaps the traitor will flee." "I have been a long time judge," replied Boulanger, "and never did I decree capital punishment so lightly." Vergniaud, who saw the indecision of the Assembly, rushed twice into the tribune to combat the excuses and the delays of the right side. Becquet, whose coolness was equal to his courage, desirous of averting the peril, proposed that it should be sent to the diplomatic committee. Vergniaud began to fear that the moment would escape his party, and said, "No, no; we do not require actual proofs for a criminal accusation—presumptive proofs are sufficient. There is not one of us in whose minds the cowardice and perfidy which characterizes the acts of the minister have not produced the most lively indignation. Is it not he who has for two months kept in his portfolio the decree of the reunion of Avignon with France? and the blood spilled in that city, the mutilated carcasses of so many victims, do they not cry to us for vengeance against him? I see from this tribune the palace in which evil counsellors deceive the king whom the constitution gives to us, forge the fetters which enchain us, and

* This passage is somewhat obscure in the original: "*Dumouriez se trouva la génie d'une circonstance caché sous l'habit d'un aventurier.*" We trust we have caught its spirit."—H. T. R.

plot the stratagems which are to deliver us to the house of Austria. (Loud acclamations.) The day has arrived to put an end to such audacity and insolence, and to crush such conspirators. Dread and terror have frequently, in the ancient times, come forth from this palace in the name of despotism: let them return thither to-day in the name of the law (loud applauses); let them penetrate all hearts; let all those who inhabit it know that the constitution promises inviolability to the king alone; let them learn that the law will reach all the guilty, and that not one head convicted of criminality can escape its sword."

These allusions to the queen, who was accused of directing the Austrian committee, this threatening language, addressed to the king, went echoing into the king's cabinet, and forced his hand to sign the nomination of a Girondist ministry. This was a party manœuvre, executed beneath the appearance of sudden indignation in the tribune—it was more, it was the first signal made by the Girondists to the men of the 20th of June and the 10th of August. The act of accusation was carried, and De Lessart sent to the court of Orleans, which only yielded him up to the cut-throats of Versailles. He might have fled, but his flight would have been interpreted against the king. He placed himself generously between death and his master, innocent of every crime except his love for him.

The king felt that there was but one step between himself and abdication: that was, by taking his ministry from amongst his enemies, and giving them an interest in power, by placing it in their hands. He yielded to the times, embraced his minister, and requested the Girondists to supply him with another. The Girondists were already silently occupied in so doing. They had previously made, in the name of the party, overtures to Roland at the end of February.* "The court," they said to him, "is not very far off from taking Jacobin ministers: not from inclination, but through treachery. The confidence it will feign to bestow will be a snare. It requires violent men in order to impute to them the excesses of the people and the disorders of the kingdom: we must deceive its perfidious hopes, and give to it firm and sagacious patriots. We think of you."

XI.

Roland, whose ambition had soured in obscurity, had

smiled at the power which came to avenge his old age. Brissot, himself, had gone to Madame Roland on the 21st of the same month, and repeating the same words, had requested from her the formal consent of her husband. Madame Roland was ambitious, not of power but of fame. Fame lightens up the higher places only, and she ardently desired to see her husband elevated to this eminence. She spoke like a woman who had predicted the event, and whom fortune does not surprise. "The burden is heavy," she said to Brissot, "but Roland has a great consciousness of his own powers, and would derive fresh strength from the feeling of being useful to liberty and his country."

This choice being made, the Girondists cast their eyes on Lacoste, an active commissioner of the navy, a working man, his mind limited by his duties, but honest and upright; his very candor of nature preserving him from faction. Put into council to watch over his master, he naturally became his friend. Duranton, an advocate of Bordeaux, was called to the bureau of justice. The Girondists, who knew him, boasted of his honesty, and relied on his plasticity and weakness. Brissot intended for the finance department, Clavière, a Genevese economist, driven from his native land, a relation and friend of his own; used to intrigue; rival of Necker; brought up in the cabinet of Mirabeau, in order to bring forward a rival against this finance minister, so hateful to Mirabeau: a man without republican prejudices or monarchical principles, only seeking in the Revolution a part, and with whom the great aim and end was—to get on. His mind, indifferent to all scruples, was on a level with every situation, and at the height of all parties. The Girondists, new to state affairs, required men well conversant in the details of war and finance departments, and who yet were the mere tools of their government: Clavière was one of these. In the war office they had De Grave, by whom the king had replaced Narbonne. De Grave, who from the subaltern ranks of the army had been raised to the post of minister of war, had declared relations with the Girondists. The friends of Gensonné, Vergniaud, Guadet, Brissot, and even Danton, hoped, through their instrumentality, to save at the same time the constitution and the king. Devoted to both, he was the link by which he hoped to unite the Girondists to royalty. Young, he had the illusions of his age: constitutional, he had the sincerity of his conviction; but weak, in ill health, more ready to undertake than firm to execute, he was one of those men of the moment who help events to their accomplishment, and do not disturb them when they are accomplished.

The principal minister, however, he to whose hands was to be confided the fate of his country, and who was to comprise in himself all the policy of the Girondists, was the minister for foreign affairs, destined to replace the unfortunate De Lessart. The rupture with Europe was the most pressing matter with the party, and they required a man who would control the king, detect the secret intrigues of the court, cognizant of the mysteries of European cabinets, and who knew how, by his skill and resolution, at the same time to force our enemies into a war,—our dubious friends into neutrality,—our secret partisans to an alliance. They sought such a man: he was close at hand.

BOOK XIII.

I.

Dumouriez combined all the requisites of boldness, devotion to the cause, and talent, that the Girondists required, and yet, until then, a second-rate man, and almost unknown, had no fortune to hope for but as theirs culminated. His name would not give umbrage to their genius, and if he proved incompetent, or rebelled against their projects, they would remove him without fear, or crush him without pity. Brissot, the diplomatic oracle of the Gironde, was evidently to be the minister who was one day to control our foreign relations, and who *en attendant* was to govern for the moment under the name of Dumouriez.

The Girondists had discovered Dumouriez in the obscurity of an existence, until then very insignificant, through Gensonné, whose colleague Dumouriez had been in the mission which the Constituent Assembly had given him to visit and examine the position of the western departments, already agitated by the secret presentiment of civil war and the early religious troubles. During this inquiry, which lasted several months, the two commissioners had frequent opportunities for an interchange of their most private thoughts on the great events which at this moment agitated men's minds. They became much attached to each other. Gensonné detected with much tact in his colleague one of those intellects repressed by circumstances, and weighed down by the obscurity of their lot, which it is enough to expose to the open daylight of public action, in order to shine forth with all the brilliancy with which nature and study had endowed it: he had too found in this mind the spring of character strong enough to bear the movements of a revolution, and sufficiently elastic to bend to all the difficulties of affairs. In a word, Dumouriez had on the first contact exercised over Gensonné that influence, that ascendency, that empire which superiority, when it displays and humbles itself, never fails to acquire over minds to which it condescends to disclose itself.

This attractive power, the confidence of genius, was one of the characteristics of Dumouriez, and by that he subsequently made a conquest of the Girondists, the king, the queen, his army, the Jacobins, Danton,—Robespierre himself. It was what great men call their star,—a star which precedes them, and prepares their way. Dumouriez's star was fascination of manner; but this fascination was but the attraction of his just, rapid, quick ideas, into whose orbit the incredible activity of his mind carried away the mind of those who heard his thoughts or witnessed his actions. Gensonné, on his return from his mission, had desired to enrich his party with this unknown man, whose eminence he foresaw from afar. He presented Dumouriez to his friends of the Assembly, to Guadet, Vergniaud, Roland, Brissot, and De Grave: communicated to them his own astonishment at, and confidence in, the twofold faculties of Dumouriez as diplomatist and soldier. He spoke of him as of a concealed saviour, whom fate had reserved for liberty. He conjured them to attach to themselves a man whose greatness would enhance their own.

They had scarcely seen Dumouriez before they were convinced. His intellect was electrical: it struck before they had time to anatomize it. The Girondists presented him to De Grave, and De Grave to the king, who offered him the temporary management of foreign affairs, until M. de Lessart, sent before the *Haute Cour*, had proved his innocence to his judges, and could resume the place reserved for him in the council. Dumouriez refused the post of minister *pro tempore*, which would injure and weaken his position before all parties by rendering him suspected by all. The king yielded, and Dumouriez was appointed.

II.

History should pause a moment before this man, who, without having assumed the name of Dictator, concentrated in himself during two years all expiring France, and exercised over his country the most incontestible of dictatorships —that of genius. Dumouriez was of the number of men who are not to be painted by merely naming them, but of those whose previous life explains their nature; who have in the past the secret of their future; who have, like Mirabeau, their existence spread over two epochs; who have their roots in two soils, and are only known by the perusal of every detail.

Dumouriez, son of a commissioner in the war department, was born at Cambrai in 1739; and although his family lived in the north, his blood was southern by extraction. His family, originally from Aix, in Provence, evinced itself in the light, warmth, and sensibility of his nature; there was perceptible the same sky that had rendered so prolific the genius of Mirabeau. His father, a military and well-read man, educated him equally for war and literature. One of his uncles, employed in the foreign office, made him early a diplomatist. A mind equally powerful and subtle, he lent himself equally to all—as fitted for action as for thought, he passed from one to the other with facility, according to the phases of his destiny. There was in him the flexibility of the Greek mind in the stirring periods of the democracy in Athens. His deep study early directed his mind to history, that poem of men of action. Plutarch nourished him with his manly diet. He moulded on the antique figures drawn from life by the historian the ideal of his own life, only all the parts of every great man suited him alike: he assumed them by turns, realized them in his reveries, as suited to reproduce in him the voluptuary as the sage, the malcontent as the patriot; Aristippus as Themistocles; Scipio as Coriolanus. He mingled with his studies the exercises of a military life, formed his body to fatigue, at the same time that he fashioned his mind to lofty ideas; equally skilled in handling a sword, and daring in subduing a horse.

Demosthenes, by patience, formed a sonorous voice from a

stammering tongue. Dumouriez, with a weak and ailing constitution in his childhood, inured his body for war. The stirring ambition of his soul required that the frame which encased it should be of endurance.

III.

Opposing the desires of his father, who destined him for the war office, the pen was his abhorrence, and he obtained a sub-lieutenancy in the cavalry. As aide-de-camp of Marshal d'Armentières, he made the campaign of Hanover. In a retreat he seized the standard from the hands of a fugitive, rallied two hundred troopers round him, saved a battery of five pieces of cannon, and covered the passage of the army. Remaining almost alone in the rear, he made himself a rampart of his dead horse, and wounded three of the enemy's hussars. Wounded in many places by gun-shot and sabre wounds—his thigh entangled beneath a fallen horse—two fingers of his right hand severed—his forehead cut open—his eyes literally singed by a discharge of powder, he still fought, and only surrendered prisoner to the Baron de Beker, who saved his life, and conveyed him to the camp of the English.

His youth and good constitution restored him to health at the end of two months. Destined to form himself to victory by the example of defeats, and want of experience in our generals, he rejoined Marshal de Soubise and Marshal de Broglie; and was present at the routs which the French owe to their enmity and rivalry.

At the peace he went to rejoin his regiment in garrison at Saint Lô. Passing by Pont Audemer, he stopped at the house of his father's sister. A passionate love for one of his uncle's daughters kept him there. This love, shared by his cousin, and favored by his aunt, was opposed by his father. The young girl, in despair, took refuge in a convent. Dumouriez swore to take her thence, and went away. On his road, overcome by his grief, he bought some opium at Dieppe, shut himself up in his apartment, wrote his adieus to his beloved, a letter of reproaches to his father, and took the poison. Nature saved him, and repentance ensued—he went, and, throwing himself at his father's feet, they were reconciled.

At four and twenty years of age, after seven campaigns, he brought from the wars, only twenty-two wounds, a decoration, the rank of captain, a pension of 600 livres, debts contracted in the service, and a hopeless love, which preyed upon his mind. His ambition, spurred by his love, made him seek in politics that success which war had hitherto refused him.

There was then in Paris one of those enigmatic men who are at the same time intriguers and statesmen. Unknown and unconsidered, they play under some name parts hidden, but important in affairs. Men of police, as well as of politics, the governments that employ and despise them pay their services, not in appointments but in subsidies. Manœuvrers in politics, they are paid from day to day—they are urged onwards, compromised, and then disavowed, and sometimes even imprisoned. They suffer all, even captivity and dishonor, for money. Such men are things to buy and sell, and their talent and utility stamp their price. Of this class were Linguet, Brissot, even Mirabeau in his youth. Such at this period was one Favier.

This man, employed in turns by the Duc de Choiseul and M. d'Argenson, to draw up diplomatic memoranda, had an infinite knowledge of Europe; he was the vigilant spy of every cabinet, knew their back-games, guessed their intrigues, and kept them in play by counter-mines, of which the minister for foreign affairs did not always know the secret. Louis XV., a king of small ideas and petty resources, was not ashamed to take into his confidence Favier, as an instrument in the schemes he contemplated against his own ministers. Favier was the go-between in the political correspondence which this monarch kept up with the Count de Broglie, unknown to, and against the policy of, his own ministers. This confidence, suspected by, rather than known to, his ministers, talent as a very able writer, deep knowledge of national eras, of history, and diplomacy, gave Favier a credit with the administration, and an influence over affairs very much beyond his obscure position and dubious character; he was, in some sort, the minister of the intrigues of high life of his time.

IV.

Dumouriez seeing the high roads to fortune closed before him, resolved to cast himself into them by indirect ways; and with this view attached himself to Favier. Favier attached himself to him, and in this connection of his earlier years, Dumouriez acquired that character for adventure and audacity which gave, during all his life, something skilful as intrigue and as rash as a *coup de main* to his heroism and his policy. Favier initiated him into the secrets of courts, and engaged Louis XV. and the Duc de Choiseul to employ Dumouriez in diplomacy and war at the same time.

It was at this moment that the great Corsican patriot, Paoli, was making gigantic efforts to rescue his country from the tyranny of the republic of Genoa, and to assure to this people an independence, of which he by turns offered the patronage to England and to France. On reaching Genoa, Dumouriez undertook to deceive at the same time the Republic, England, and Paoli, united himself with Corsican adventurers, conspired against Paoli, made a descent upon the island, which he summoned to independence, and was partially successful. He threw himself into a felucca, to bring to the Duc de Choiseul information as to the new state of Corsica, and to implore the succor of France. Delayed by a tempest, tossed for several weeks on the coast of Africa, he reached Marseilles too late; the treaty between France and Genoa was signed. He hastened to Favier, his friend in Paris.

Favier informed him confidentially, that he was employed to draw up a memorial to prove to the king and his ministers the necessity of supporting the republic of Genoa against the independent Corsicans; that this memorial had been demanded of him secretly by the Genoese ambassador, and by a *femme de chambre* of the Duchesse de Grammont, favorite sister of the Duc de Choiseul, interested, like the brothers of the Du Barry*, in supplying the army: that 500 louis were the price of this memorial and the blood of the Corsicans; and he offered a portion of this intrigue and its profits to Dumouriez, who pretended to accept this, and then hastening to the Duc de Choiseul, revealed the manœuvre, was well received, believed he had convinced the minister, and was preparing to return, conveying to the Corsicans the subsidies and arms they expected. Next day, he found the minister changed, and was sent from the audience with harsh language. Dumouriez retired, and made his way unmolested to Spain. Aided by Favier, who was satisfied with

* Madame Du Barry was the favorite mistress of Louis XV., and her brother, as he was called, the Count Jean du Barry, had the king's patronage, and preyed on the public to a great extent, to supply his low habits and expensive tastes.—*Translator.*

having jockeyed him, and pitied his candor; assisted by the Duc de Choiseul, he conspired with the Spanish minister and French ambassador to effect the conquest of Portugal, whose topography he was empowered to study in a military point of view, as well as its means of defence. The Marquis de Pombal, first minister of Portugal, conceived suspicions as to Dumouriez's mission, and forced him to leave Lisbon. The young diplomatist returned to Madrid, learned that his cousin, over-persuaded by the priests, had abandoned him, and meant to take the veil. He then attached himself to another mistress, a young Frenchwoman, daughter of an architect established at Madrid, and for some years his activity reposed in the happiness of a participated love. An order of the Duc de Choiseul recalled him to Paris,—he hesitated: his beloved herself compelled him, and sacrificed him as if she had from afar anticipated his fame. He reached Paris, and was named quartermaster-general of the French army in Corsica, where, as everywhere else, he greatly distinguished himself, At the head of a detachment of volunteers, he seized on the Château de Corte, the last asylum and home of Paoli. He retained for himself the library of this unfortunate patriot. The choice of these books, and the notes with which they were covered in Paoli's hand, revealed one of those characters which seek their fellows in the finest models of antiquity. Dumouriez was worthy of this spoil, since he appreciated it above gold. The great Frederic called Paoli the first captain of Europe: Voltaire declared him the conqueror and lawgiver of his country. The French blushed at conquering him—fortune at forsaking him. If he did not emancipate his country, he deserved that his struggle should be immortalized. Too great a citizen for so small a people, he did not bear a reputation in proportion to his country, but to his virtues. Corsica remains in the ranks of conquered provinces; but Paoli must always be in the ranks of great men.

V.

After his return to Paris, Dumouriez passed a year in the society of the literary men and women of light fame who gave to the society of the period the spirit and the tone of a constant orgy. Forming an attachment with an old acquaintance of Madame Du Barry, he knew this *parvenue* courtezan, whom libertinism had elevated nearly to the throne. Devoted to the Duc de Choiseul, the enemy of this mistress of the king, and retaining that remnant of virtue which amongst the French is called honor, he did not prostitute his uniform to the court, and blushed to see the old monarch, at the reviews of Fontainebleau, walk on foot with his hat off before his army, beside a carriage in which this woman displayed her beauty and her empire. Madame Du Barry took offence at the forgetfulness of the young officer, and divined the cause of his absence. Dumouriez was sent to Poland on the same errand that had before dispatched him to Portugal. His mission, half diplomatic, half military, was, in consequence of a secret idea of the king, approved by his confidant, the Count de Broglie, and by Favier, the count's adviser.

It was at the moment when Poland, menaced and half-occupied by the Russians, devoured by Prussia, forsaken by Austria, was attempting some ill-considered movements, in order to repair its scattered limbs, and to dispute, at least, in fragments, its nationality with its oppressors—the last sigh of liberty which moved the corpse of a people. The king, who feared to come into collision with the Empress of Russia, Catherine, to give excuses to the hostilities of Frederic and umbrage to the court of Vienna, was still desirous of extending to expiring Poland the hand of France; but concealing that hand, and reserving to himself the power even to cut it off, if it became necessary. Dumouriez was the intermediary selected for this part; the secret minister of France, amongst the Polish confederates; a general, if necessary—but a general adventurer and disowned—to rally and direct their efforts.

The Duc de Choiseul, indignant at the debasement of France, was secretly preparing war against Prussia and England. This powerful diversion in Poland was necessary for his plan of campaign, and he gave his confidential instructions to Dumouriez; but, thrown out of the administration by the intrigues of Madame Du Barry and M. d'Argenson, the Duc de Choiseul was suddenly exiled to Versailles before Dumouriez reached Poland. The policy of France, changing with the minister, at once destroyed Dumouriez's plans. Still he followed them up with an ardor and perseverance worthy of better success. He found the Poles debased by misery, slavery, and the custom of bearing a foreign yoke. He found the Polish aristocrats corrupted by luxury, enervated by pleasures, employing in intrigues and language the warmth of their patriotism in the conferences and confederation of *Epéries.* A female of remarkable beauty, high rank, and eastern genius, the Countess of Mnizeck, stirred up, destroyed, or combined different parties, according to the taste of her ambition or her amours. Certain patriot orators caused the last accents of independence to resound again in vain. Certain princes and gentlemen formed meetings without any understanding with each other, who contended as partisans rather than as citizens, and who boasted of personal fame, without any reference to the safety of their country. Dumouriez availed himself of the ascendency of the countess, and endeavored to unite these isolated effects, formed an infantry, an artillery, seized upon two fortresses, threatened in all directions the Russians, scattered in small bodies over the wide plains of Poland, prepared for war, disciplined the insubordinate patriotism of the insurgents, and contended successfully against Souwarow, the Russian general, subsequently destined to threaten the republic so closely.

But Stanislaus, the king of Poland, the crowned creature of Catherine, saw the danger of a national insurrection, which, by drawing out the Russians, would endanger his throne; and he paralyzed it by offering to the federates to adhere, in his own person, to the confederation. One of them, Bohucz, the last great orator of Polish liberty, returned to the king, in a sublime oration, his perfidious succor, and then combined the unanimity of the conspirators into the last resource of the oppressed—insurrection. It burst forth. Dumouriez is its life and soul, flies from one camp to the other, giving a spirit of unity to the plan of attack. Cracovia was ready to fall into his hands; the Russians regain the frontier in disorder; but anarchy, that fatal genius of Poland, suddenly dissolves the union of the chiefs, and they surrender one another to the united efforts of the Russians. All desire to have the exclusive honor of delivering their country, and prefer to lose it rather than owe their success to a rival.

Sapieha, the principal leader, was massacred by his nobles. Pulauwski and Micksenski were delivered up, wounded, to the Russians; Zaremba, betrayed his country; Oginski, the last of these great patriots, roused Lithuania at the moment when lesser Poland had laid down its arms. Abandoned and fugitive, he escaped to Dantzig, and wandered for thirty years over Europe and America, carrying in his heart the memory of his country. The lovely Countess of Mnizeck languished and died of grief with Poland. Dumouriez wept for this heroine, adored in a country wherein he said the women are more men than the men. He brake his sword, despairing forever of this aristocracy without a people, bestowing on it, as he quitted it, the name of *Asiatic Nation of Europe.*

VI.

He returned to Paris. The king and M. d'Argenson, to save appearances with Russia and Prussia, threw him and Favier into the Bastille, and he there passed a year in cursing the ingratitude of courts and the weakness of kings, and recovered his natural energy in retreat and study. The king changed his prison into exile to the citadel of Caen; there Dumouriez found again, in a convent, the cousin he had loved. Free, and weary of a monastic life, she became softened on again beholding her former lover, and they were married. He was then appointed commandant of Cherbourg, and his indefatigable mind contended with the elements as if it were opposing men. He conceived the plan of fortifying this harbor, which was to imprison a stormy sea in a granite basin, and give the French navy a halting-place in the Channel. Here he passed fifteen years in domestic life, much troubled by the ill humor and ascetic devotion of his wife; in military studies constant, but without application, and in the dissipation of the philosophic and voluptuous society of his time.

The Revolution, which was drawing nigh, found him indifferent to its principles, and prepared for its vicissitudes. The justness of his penetration enabled him at a glance to measure the tendency of events. He soon comprehended that a revolution in ideas must undermine institutions unless institutions modelled themselves on the new ideas. He gave himself to the constitution without enthusiasm; he desired the maintenance of the throne, had no faith in a republic, foresaw a change in the dynasty; and was even accused of meditating it. The emigration, by decimating the upper ranks of the army, left space for him, and he was named general, by length of service. He preserved a firm and well-devised conduct, equi-distant from the throne and the people, from the counter-revolutionist and the malcontent, ready to go with the opinion of the court or of the nation, according as events might transpire. By turns he was in communication with all parties, as if to sound the growing power of Mirabeau and de Montmorin, the Duc d'Orleans and the Jacobins, La Fayette and the Girondists. In his various commands during these days of crises, he maintained discipline by his popularity, was on terms with the insurgent people, and placed himself at their head, in order to restrain them. The people believed him certainly on their side; the soldiery adored him; he detested anarchy, but flattered the demagogues. He applied very skilfully to his popularity those able tactics which Favier had taught him. He viewed the Revolution as an heroic intrigue. He manœuvred his patriotism as he would have manœuvred his battalions on the field of battle. He considered the coming war with much delight, knowing already all of a hero's part. He foresaw that the Revolution, deserted by the nobility, and assailed by all Europe, would require a general ready formed to direct the undisciplined efforts of the masses it had excited. He prepared hinself for that post. The long subordination of his genius fatigued him. At fifty-six years of age he had the fire of youth with all the coolness of age; his earnest desire was advancement; the yearning of his soul for fame was the more intense in proportion to the years he had already unavailingly passed. His frame, fortified by climates and voyages, lent itself, like a passive instrument, to his activity; all was young in him except his amount of years; they were expended, but not by energy. He had the youth of Cæsar, an impatient desire for fortune, and the certainty of acquiring it. With great men, to live is to rise in renown; he had not lived, because his reputation was not equivalent to his ambition.

VII.

Dumouriez was of that middle stature of the French soldier who wears his uniform gracefully, his haversack lightly, and his musket and sabre as if he did not feel their weight. Equally agile and compact, his body had the cast of those statues of warriors who repose on their expanded muscles, and yet seem ready to advance. His attitude was confident and proud; all his motions were as rapid as his mind. He vaulted into the saddle without touching the stirrup, holding the mane by his left hand. He sprung to the ground with one effort, and handled the bayonet of the soldier as vigorously as the sword of the general. His head, rather thrown backwards, rose well from his shoulders, and turned on his neck with ease and grace, like all elegant men. These haughty motions of his head made him look taller under the tricolored cockade. His brow was lofty, well-turned, flat at the temples, and well displayed; his muscles set in play by his reflection and resolution. The salient and well-defined angles announced sensibility of mind beneath delicacy of understanding and the most exquisite tact. His eyes were black, large, and full of fire; his long lids, beginning to turn gray, increased their brilliancy, though sometimes they were very soft; his nose, and the oval of his countenance, were of that aquiline type which reveals races ennobled by war and empire; his mouth, flexible and handsome, was almost always smiling; no tension of the lips betrayed the effort of this plastic mind—this master mind, which played with difficulties, overcame obstacles; his chin, turned and decided, bore his face, as it were, on a firm and square base, whilst the habitual expression of his countenance was calm and expansive cheerfulness. It was evident that no pressure of affairs was too heavy for him, and that he constantly preserved so much liberty of mind as enabled him to jest alike with good or bad fortune. He treated politics, war, and government with gayety. The tone of his voice was sonorous, manly, and vibrating, and was distinctly heard above the noise of the drum, and the clash of the bayonet. His oratory was straightforward, clever, striking; his words were effective in council, in confidence, and intimacy: they soothed and insinuated themselves like those of a woman. He was persuasive, for his soul, mobile and sensitive, had always in its accent the truth and impression of the moment. Devoted to the sex, and easily enamored, his experience with them had imbued him with one of their highest qualities—pity. He could not resist tears, and those of the queen would have made him a Seid of the throne; there was no position or opinion he would not have sacrificed to a generous impulse; his greatness of soul was not calculation, it was excessive feeling. He had no political principles; the Revolution was to him nothing more than a fine drama, which was to furnish a grand scene for his abilities, and a part for his genius. A great man for the service of events, if the Revolution had not beheld him as its general and preserver, he would equally have been the general and preserver of the Coalition. Dumouriez was not the hero of a principle, but of the occasion.

VIII.

The new ministers met at Madame Roland's, the soul of the Girondist ministry: Duranton, Lacoste, Cahier-Gerville received there, in all passiveness, their instructions from the men whose shadows only they were in the council. Dumouriez affected, like them, at first, a full compliance with the interests and will of the party, which, personified at Roland's by a young, lovely, and eloquent woman, must have had an additional attraction for the general. He hoped to rule by ruling the heart of this female. He employed with her all the plasticity of his character, all the graces of his nature, all the fascinations of his genius; but Madame Roland had a preservative against the warrior's seductions that Dumouriez had not been accustomed to find in the women he had loved—austere virtue and a strong will. There was but one means of captivating her admiration, and that was by surpassing her in patriotic devotion. These two characters could not meet without contrasting themselves, nor understand without despising each other. Very soon, therefore, Dumouriez considered Madame Roland as a stubborn bigot, and she estimated Dumouriez as a frivolous presuming man, finding in his look, smile, and tone of voice that audacity of success towards her sex which betrayed, according to her estimation, the free conduct of the females amongst whom he had lived, and which offended her decorum. There was more of the courtier than the patriot in Dumouriez. This French aristocracy of manners displeased the engraver's humble daughter; perhaps it reminded her of her lowly condition, and the humiliations of her childhood at Versailles. Her ideal was not the military, but the citizen; a republican mind alone could acquire her love. Besides, she saw at a glance that this man was too great to remain long on the level of her party; she suspected his genius in his politeness, and his ambition beneath his familiarity. "Have an eye to that man," she said to her husband after their first interview; "he may conceal a master beneath the colleague, and drive from the cabinet those who introduced him there."

IX.

Roland, too happy at being in power, did not foresee his disgrace, and encouraging his wife, trusted more and more to the admiration which Dumouriez feigned for him. He thought himself the statesman of the cabinet, and his gratified vanity lent itself credulously to the advances of Dumouriez, and even made him better disposed towards the king. On his entry to the ministry Roland had affected in his costume the bluntness of his principles, and in his manners the rudeness of his republicanism. He presented himself at the Tuileries in a black coat, with a round hat, and nailed shoes covered with dust. He wished to show in himself the man of the people, entering the palace in the plain garb of the citizen, and thus meeting the man of the throne. This tacit insolence he thought would flatter the nation and humiliate the king. The courtiers were indignant; the king groaned over it; Dumouriez laughed at it. "Ah, well then, really, gentlemen," he said to the courtiers, "since there is no more etiquette there is no more monarchy." This jocose mode of treating the thing had at once removed all the anger of the court, and all the effect of the Spartan pretensions of Roland.

The king no longer regarded the discourtesy, and treated Roland with that cordiality which unlocks men's hearts. The new ministers were astonished to feel themselves confiding and moved in the presence of the monarch. Having arrived suspicious and republican to their seats in the cabinet, they quitted it almost royalists.

"The king is not known," said Roland to his wife; "a weak prince, he is one of the best of men; he does not want good intentions, but good advice: he does not like the aristocracy, and has strong affection for the people: perhaps he was born to serve as the medium between republic and monarchy. By rendering the constitution easy to him we shall make him like it, and the popularity he will re-acquire by following our counsels will render government easy to ourselves. His nature is so great that the throne has been unable to corrupt it, and he is equally remote from the silly brute which has been held up to the laughter of the people as from the sensitive and highly accomplished man his courtiers pretend to adore in him; his mind, without being superior, is expansive and reflecting; in a humble position his abilities would have provided for him; he has a general and occasionally sound knowledge, knows the details of business, and acts towards men with that simple but persuasive ability which gives kings the precocious necessity of governing their impressions; his prodigious memory always recalls to him at the right time things, names, and faces; he likes work, and reads everything; he is never idle for a moment; a tender parent, a model of a husband: chaste in feeling, he has done away with all those scandals which disgraced the courts of his predecessors; he loves none but the queen, and his condescension, which is occasionally injurious to his politics, is at least a weakness 'which leans to virtue's side.' Had he been born two centuries earlier, his peaceable reign would have been counted amongst the number of happy years of the monarchy. Circumstances appear to have influenced his mind. The Revolution has convinced him of its necessity, and we must convince him of its possibility. In our hands, the king may better serve it than any other citizen in the kingdom; by enlightening this prince we may be faithful alike to his interests and those of the nation—the king and Revolution must be with us as one."

X.

Thus said Roland in the first dazzling of power; his wife listened with a smile of incredulity on her lips. Her keener glance had at the instant measured a career more vast and a termination more decisive than the timid and transitory compromise between a degraded royalty and an imperfect revolution. It would have cost her too much to renounce the ideal of her ardent soul; all her wishes tended to a republic; all her exertions, all her words, all her aspirations, were destined, unconsciously to herself, to urge thither her husband and his associates.

"Mistrust every man's perfidy, and more especially your own virtue," was her reply to the weak and vain Roland. "You see in this world but courts, where all is unreal, and where the most polished surfaces conceal the most sinister combinations. You are only an honest countryman wandering amongst a crowd of courtiers,—virtue in danger amidst a myriad of vices: they speak our language, and we do not know theirs. Would it be possible that they should not deceive us? Louis XVI., of a degenerate race, without elevation of mind, or energy of will, allowed himself to be enthralled early in life by religious prejudices, which have even lessened his intellect; fascinated by a giddy queen, who unites to Austrian insolence the enchantment of beauty and the highest rank, and who makes of her secret and corrupt court the sanctuary of her pleasures and the focus of her vices, this prince, blinded on the one hand by the priests, and on the other by love, holds at random the loose reins of an empire which is escaping from his grasp. France, exhausted of men, does not give to him, either in Maurepas, Necker, or Calonne, a minister capable of supporting him. The aristocracy is barren, and produces nothing but to its shame; the government must be renewed in the holier and deeper fount of the nation; the time for a democracy is here,—why delay it! You are its men, its virtues, its characters, its intelligence. The Revolution is behind you, it hails you, urges you onward, and would you surrender it to the first smile from the king because he has the condescension of a man of the people? No: Louis XVI., half dethroned by the nation, cannot love the nation that fetters him; he may feign to caress his chains, but all his thoughts are devoted to the idea of how he can spurn them. His only resource at this moment is to protest his attachment to the Revolution, and to lull the ministers whom the Revolution empowers to watch over his intrigues. But this pretence is the last and most dangerous of the conspiracies of the throne. The constitution is the forfeiture of Louis XVI., and the patriot ministers are his superintendents. Fallen greatness cannot love the cause of its decadence; no man likes his humiliation. Trust in human nature, Roland—that alone never deceives, and mistrust courts. Your virtue is too elevated to see the snares which courtiers spread beneath your feet."

XI.

Such language amazed Roland. Brissot, Condorcet, Vergniaud, Gensonné, Guadet, and especially Buzot, the friend and most intimate confidant of Madame Roland, strengthened at their evening meetings the mistrust of the minister. He armed himself with fresh distrust from their conversations, and entered the council with a more frowning brow and more resolute determination: the king's frankness disarmed him—Dumouriez discouraged him by his gayety—power softened him by its influence. He wavered between the two great difficulties of the moment, the double sanction required from the king for the decrees which were most repugnant to his heart and conscience, the decree against the emigrants, and the decree against the nonjuring priests; and he wavered as to war.

During this tergiversation of Roland and his colleagues, Dumouriez acquired the favor of the king and the people.

the secret of his conduct being comprised in what he had said a short time before to M. de Montmorin, in a secret conversation he had with that minister. "If I were king of France, I would disconcert all parties by placing myself at the head of the Revolution."

This sentence contained the sole line of policy capable of saving Louis XVI. In a time of revolution every king who is not revolutionary must be inevitably crushed between the two parties: a neutral king no longer reigns—a pardoned king degrades the throne—a king conquered by his own people has for refuge only exile or the scaffold. Dumouriez felt that his first step was to convince the king of his personal attachment, and take him into his confidence, or indeed make him his accomplice in the patriotic part he proposed to play; constitute himself the secret mediator between the will of the monarch and the exactions of the cabinet, to control the king by his influence over the Girondists, and the Girondists by his influence over the king; the part of the favorite of misfortune and protector of a persecuted queen pleased alike his ambition and his heart. A soldier, diplomatist, gentleman, there was in his soul a wholly different feeling for degraded royalty than the sentiment of satisfied jealousy which filled the minds of the Girondists. The *prestige* of the throne existed for Dumouriez; the *prestige* of liberty only existed for the Girondists. This feeling, revealed in his attitude, language, gestures, could not long escape the observation of Louis XVI. Kings have twofold tact, misfortune makes them more nice; the unfortunate perceive pity in a look; it is the only homage they are allowed to receive, and they are the more jealous of it. In a secret conversation the king and Dumouriez came to an understanding.

XII.

Dumouriez's restless conduct in his commands in Normandy, the friendship of Gensonné, the favor of the Jacobins for him, had prejudiced Louis XVI. against his new minister. The minister, on his side, expected to find in the king a spirit opposed to the constitution, a mind trammelled by routine, a violent temper, an abrupt manner, and using language imperious and offensive to all who approached him. Such was the caricature of this unfortunate prince. It was necessary to disfigure him in order to make the nation hate him.

Dumouriez found in him at this moment, and during the three months of his ministry, an upright mind, a heart open to every benevolent sentiment, unvarying politeness, endurance and patience which defied the calamities of his situation. Extreme timidity, the result of the long seclusion in which his youth had been passed, repressed the feelings of his heart, and gave to his language and his intercourse with men a stiffness and embarrassment which destroyed his better qualities of decided and calm courage; he frequently spoke to Dumouriez of his death as an event probable and doomed, the prospect of which did not affect his serenity nor preclude him from doing his duty to the last as a father and a king.

"Sire," said Dumouriez to him, with the chivalric sympathy which compassion adds to respect, and with that aspect in which the heart says more than language; "you have overcome your prejudices against myself; you have commanded me by M. de Laporte to accept the post he had refused." "Yes," replied the king. "Well, I come now to devote myself wholly to your service, to your protection. But the part of a minister is no longer what it was in former days: without ceasing to be the servant of the king, I am the man of the nation. I will speak to you always in the language of liberty and the constitution. Allow me then, in order to serve you better, that in public and in the council I appear in my character as a constitutionalist, and that I avoid everything that may at all reveal my personal attachment towards you. In this respect I must break through all etiquette, and avoid attending the court. In the council, I shall oppose your views, and shall propose as our representatives in foreign courts men devoted to the nation. When your repugnance to my choice shall be invincible and on good grounds, I shall comply; if this repugnance shall tend to compromise the safety of the country and yourself, I shall beg you to allow me to resign, and nominate my successor. Think of the terrible dangers which beset your throne—it must be consolidated by the confidence of the nation in your sincere attachment to the Revolution. It is a conquest which it depends on you to make. I have prepared four dispatches to ambassadors in this sense. In these I have used language to which they are unused from courts, the language of an offended and resolute nation. I shall read them this morning before the council; if you approve my labor, I shall continue to speak thus, and act in accordance with my language; if not, my carriage is ready, and, unable to serve you in the council, I shall depart whither my tastes and studies for thirty years call me, to serve my country in the field."

The king, astonished and much moved, said to him, "I like your frankness; I know you are attached to me, and I anticipate all from your services. They had created many prejudices against you, but this moment effaces them all. Go and do as your heart directs you, and according to the best interests of the nation, which are also mine." Dumouriez retired; but he knew that the queen, adored by her husband, clung to the policy of her husband with all the passion and excitement of her soul. He desired and feared at the same time an interview with this princess: one word from her would accomplish or destroy the bold enterprise he had dared to meditate, of reconciling the king with the people.

XIII.

The queen sent for the general into her most private apartments. Dumouriez found her alone, her cheeks flushed by the emotion of an internal struggle, and walking rapidly up and down the room, like a person whose agitated thoughts require corresponding activity of body. Dumouriez placed himself in silence near the fireplace, in the attitude of respect and sorrow, inspired by the presence of so august, so beautiful, and so miserable a princess. She advanced towards him with a mingled air of majesty and anger.

"Monsieur," said she, with that accent that reveals at once resentment against fortune, and contempt for fate; "you are all-powerful at this moment; but it is through popular favor, and that soon destroys its idols." She did not await his reply, but continued, "Your existence depends upon your conduct; it is said that you possess great talents, and you must imagine that neither the king nor myself can suffer all these innovations of the constitution. I tell you thus much frankly, so make your decision." "Madame," returned Dumouriez, "I am confounded by the dangerous disclosure your majesty has thought fit to make me; I will not betray your confidence, but I am placed between the king and the nation, and I belong to my country. Permit me," continued Dumouriez, with respectful earnestness, "to represent to you that the safety of the king—your own—and that of your children, and the very re-establishment of the royal authority—is bound up with the constitution. You are surrounded by enemies, who sacrifice you to their own interests. The constitution alone can, by strengthening itself, protect you and assure the happiness and glory of the king." "It cannot last long, beware of yourself," returned the queen, with a look of anger and menace. Dumouriez imagined that he saw in this look and speech an allusion to personal danger and an insinuation of alarm. "I am more than fifty years old, madame," replied he, in a low tone, in which the firmness of the soldier was mingled with the pity of the man; "I have braved many perils in my life; and when I accepted the ministry, I well knew that my responsibility was not the greatest of my dangers." "Ah," cried the queen, with a gesture of horror, "this calumny and disgrace was alone wanting! You appear to believe me capable of causing you to be assassinated." Tears of indignation checked her utterance. Dumouriez, equally moved with herself, disclaimed the injurious interpretation given to his reply. "Far be it from me, madame, to offer you so cruel an insult; your soul is great and noble, and the heroism you have displayed in so many circumstances, has forever attached me to you." She was appeased in a moment, and laid her hand on Dumouriez's arm, in token of reconciliation.

The minister profited by this return to serenity and confidence to give Marie Antoinette advice, of which the emotion of his features and voice sufficiently attested the sincerity. "Trust me, madame, I have no motive for deceiving you; I abhor anarchy and its crimes equally with yourself. But I have experience; I live in the centre of the different parties, and I take part in opinion. I am connected with the people, and I am better placed than your majesty for judging the extent and the direction of events. This is not, as you deem it, a popular movement; but the almost unanimous insurrection of a great nation against an old and decaying order of things. Mighty factions feed the flame, and in every one of them are scoundrels or madmen. I alone see in the Revolution the king and the nation, and that which tends to separate them, ruins them both. I seek to unite them, and it is for you to aid me. If I am an obstacle to your designs, and if you persist in them, tell me instantly, and I will retire, and mourn in obscurity the fate of my country and your own." The queen was touched and convinced; the frankness of Dumouriez at once pleased and won her. The heart of the soldier was a guarantee to her of the conduct of the statesman. Firm, brave, and heroic, she preferred to have the weight of his sword in the councils of his king, rather than those politicians, and specious orators, who, nevertheless, bent before every blast of opinion or sedition; and an intimate understanding soon existed between the queen and the general.

The queen was for some time faithful to her promises, but the repeated outrages of the people again moved her, in spite of herself, to anger and conspiracy. "See," said she to the king, before Dumouriez, one day, pointing to the tops of the trees in the Tuileries: "a prisoner in this palace, I do not venture to show myself at the windows that look on to the garden. The crowd collected there, and who watch even my tears, hoot me. Yesterday, to breathe the air, I showed myself at a window that looks at the court; an artillery-man on guard addressed the most revolting language to me. 'How I should like,' added he, 'to see your head on the point of my bayonet!' In this frightful garden I see on one side a man mounted on a chair, and vociferating the most odious insults against us, whilst he threatens, by his gestures, the inhabitants of the palace; on the other, the populace is dragging to the basin some priest or soldier, whom they overwhelm with blows and outrages, whilst, at the same time, and close to these terrible scenes, persons are playing at ball or walking about in the *allées*. What a residence—what a life—what a people!" Dumouriez could but lament with the royal family, and exhort them to be patient. But the endurance of the victims is exhausted sooner than the cruelty of the executioner. How could it be expected that a courageous and proud princess, who had been constantly surrounded by the adulation of the court, could love the Revolution that was the instrument of her humiliation and her torture? or see in this indifferent and cruel nation a people worthy of empire and of liberty?

XIV.

When all his measures with the court were concerted, Dumouriez no longer hesitated to leap over the space that divided the king and the extreme party, and to give the government the form of pure patriotism. He made overtures to the Jacobins, and boldly presented himself at their sitting the next day. The chamber was thronged, and the apparition of Dumouriez struck the tribunes with mute astonishment. His martial figure and the impetuosity of his conduct won for him at once the favor of the Assembly; for no one suspected that so much audacity concealed so much stratagem, and they saw in him only the minister who threw himself into the arms of the people, and every one hastened to receive him.

It was the moment when the *bonnet rouge*, the symbol of extreme opinion, a species of livery worn by the demagogues and flatterers of the people, had been almost unanimously adopted by the Jacobins. This emblem, like many similar ones received by the revolutions from the hand of chance, was a mystery even to those who wore it. It had been adopted for the first time on the day of the triumph of the soldiers of Châteauvieux. Some said it was the *coiffure* of the galley-slaves, once infamous, but glorious since it had covered the brows of these martyrs of the insurrection; and they added that the people wished to purify this head-dress from every stain by wearing it themselves. Others only saw in it the Phrygian bonnet, a symbol of freedom for slaves.

The *bonnet rouge* had from its first appearance been the subject of dispute and dissension amongst the Jacobins; the *exaltés* wore it, whilst the *modérés* yet abstained from adopting it. Dumouriez did not hesitate, but mounted the tribune, placed this sign of patriotism on his head, and at once assumed the emblem of the most prominent party, whilst this mute yet significant eloquence awakened a burst of enthusiasm on every side of the *Salle*. "Brothers and friends," said Dumouriez, "every instant of my life shall be devoted to carrying out the wishes of the people, and to justifying the king's choice. I will employ in all negotiation the force of a free people, and before long these negotiations will produce a lasting peace or a decisive war. (Applause.) If we have this war I will abandon my political post, and I will assume my rank in the army to triumph, or perish a free man with my brethren. A heavy weight presses on me, aid me to bear it; I require your counsels, transmit them to me through your journals. Tell me truth, even the most unpalatable; but repel calumny, and do not repulse a citizen whom you know to be sincere and intrepid, and who devotes himself to the cause of the Revolution and the nation."

The president replied to the minister that the society gloried in counting him amongst its brethren. These words occasioned some murmurs, which were stifled by the acclamations that followed Dumouriez to his place. It was proposed that the two speeches should be printed. Legendre opposed the motion from economical motives, but was hissed by the tribunes. "Why these unusual honors, and this reply of the president to the minister?" said Collot d'Herbois. "If he comes here as a minister, there is no reply to make him. If he comes here as an associate and a brother, he does no more than his duty; he only raises himself to the level of our opinions. There is but one answer to be made, —let him act as he has spoken." Dumouriez raised his hand, and gesticulated to Collot d'Herbois.

Robespierre rose, smiled sternly on Dumouriez, and said, "I am not one of those who believe it is utterly impossible for a minister to be a patriot, and I accept with pleasure the promises that M. Dumouriez has just given us. When he shall have verified these promises, when he has dissipated the foes armed against us by his predecessors, and by the conspirators who even now hold the reins of government, spite of the expulsion of several ministers, then, and then only, I shall be inclined to bestow on him the praises he will have merited, and I shall even in that case deem that every good citizen in this assembly is his equal. The people only is great, is worthy in my eyes; the toys of ministerial power fade into insignificance before it. It is out of respect for the people, for the minister himself, that I demand that his presence here be not marked by any of those homages that mark the decay of public feeling. He asks us to counsel the ministers; I promise him, on my part, to give him advice which will be useful to them and to the country at large. So long as M. Dumouriez shall prove by acts of pure patriotism, and by real services to his country, that he is the brother of all good citizens, and the defender of the people, he shall find none but supporters here. I do not dread the presence of any minister in this society, but I declare that the instant a minister possesses more ascendency here than a citizen, I will demand his ostracism. But this will never happen."

Robespierre left the tribune, and Dumouriez cast himself into his arms; the Assembly rose, and sealed by its applause their fraternal embrace, in which all saw the augury of the union of power and the people. The president Doppet read (the *bonnet rouge* on his head) a letter from Pétion to the society, on the subject of this new head-dress adopted by the patriots, and on which Pétion spoke against this superfluous mark of *civisme*.

"This sign," said he, "instead of increasing your popularity, alarms the public mind and affords a pretext for calumnies against you. The moment is serious, the demonstrations of patriotism should be as serious as the times. It is the enemies of the Revolution who urge it to these frivolities in order that they may have the right to accuse it of frivolity and thoughtlessness. They thus give patriotism the appearance of faction, and these emblems divide those they should rally. However great the vogue that counsels them to-day, they will never be universally adopted, for every man really devoted to the public welfare will be quite indifferent to a *bonnet rouge.* Liberty will neither be more majestic nor more glorious in this garb, but the very signs with which you adorn her will serve as a pretext for dissension amongst her children. A civil war, commencing in sarcasm and ending in bloodshed, may be caused by a ridiculous manifestation. I leave you to meditate on these ideas."

XV.

Whilst this letter was being read, the president, a timorous man, who perceived the agency of Robespierre in the advice of Pétion, had quietly removed from his head the repudiated *bonnet rouge,* and the members of the society, one after another, followed his example. Robespierre alone, who had never adopted this bauble of the fashion, and with whom Pétion had concerted this letter, mounted the tribune, and said, "I, in common with the mayor of Paris, respect everything that bears the image of liberty; but we have a sign which recalls to us constantly our oath to live and die free, and here is this sign. (He showed his cockade.) The citizens, who have adopted the *bonnet rouge* through a laudable patriotism, will lose nothing by laying it aside. The friends of the Revolution will continue to recognize each other by the sign of virtue and of reason. These emblems are ours alone; all those may be imitated by traitors and aristocrats. In the name of France I rally you again to the only standard that strikes terror into her foes. Let us alone retain the cockade and the banner, beneath which the constitution was born."

The *bonnet rouge* instantly disappeared in the Assembly; but even the voice of Robespierre, and the resolutions of the Jacobins, could not arrest the outbreak of enthusiasm that had placed the sign of *avenging equality* ("*l'égalité venge-*

resse") on every head; and the evening of the day on which it was repudiated at the Jacobins saw it inaugurated at all the theatres. The bust of Voltaire, the destroyer of prejudice, was adorned with the Phrygian cap of liberty, amidst the shouts of the spectators, whilst the cap and pike became the uniform and weapon of the citizen soldier. The Girondists, who had attacked this sign as long as it appeared to them the livery of Robespierre, began to excuse it as soon as Robespierre repulsed it. Brissot himself, in his report of what passed at this sitting, regrets this symbol, because, "adopted by the most indignant portion of the people, it humiliated the rich, and became the terror of the aristocracy." The breach between these two men became wider every day, and there was not sufficient space in the Jacobins, the Assembly, and the supreme power for these rival ambitions, which strove for the dictatorship of opinion.

The nomination of the ministers, which was entirely under the influence of Girondists, the councils held at Madame Roland's, the presence of Brissot, of Guadet, of Vergniaud at the deliberations of the ministers, the appointment of all their friends to the government offices, served as themes for the clamors of the *exaltés* of the Jacobins. These Jacobins were termed Montagnards, from the high benches occupied in the Assembly by the friends of Robespierre and Danton. "Remember," they said, "the almost prophetic sagacity of Robespierre, when, in answer to Brissot, who attacked the former minister De Lessart, he made this allusion to the Girondist leader, which has been so speedily justified,—'For me, who do not aim at the ministry either for myself or my friends.'" On their side the Girondist journals heaped opprobrium on this handful of calumniators and petty tyrants, who resembled Catiline in crimes if not in courage; thus war commenced by sarcasm.

The king, however, when the ministry was completed, wrote the Assembly a letter, more resembling an abdication into the hands of opinion than the constitutional act of a free power. Was this humiliating resignation an affectation of slavery, or a sign of restraint and degradation made from the throne to the armed powers, in order that they might comprehend that he was no longer free, and only see in him the crowned automaton of the Jacobins? The letter was in these terms:

"Profoundly touched by the disorders that afflict the French nation, and by the duty imposed on me by the constitution of watching over the maintenance of order and public tranquillity, I have not ceased to employ every means that it places at my disposal to execute the laws. I had selected as my prime agents men recommended by the purity of their principles and their opinions. They have quitted the ministry; and I have felt it my duty to replace them by men who hold a high position in public favor. You have so often repeated that this measure was the only means of insuring the re-establishment of order and the enforcement of the laws, that I have deemed it fitting to adopt it, that no pretext may be afforded for doubting my sincere desire to add to the prosperity and happiness of my country. I have appointed M. Clavière minister of the contributions, and M. Roland minister of the interior. The person whom I had chosen as the minister of justice has prayed me to make another choice: when I shall have again made it the Assembly shall be duly informed. (Signed) Louis."

The Assembly received this message with loud applause; for the king once in its power, it could employ him in the work of regeneration. The most perfect harmony appeared to reign in the council. The king astonished his new ministers by his assiduity and his aptitude for business. He conversed with every one on the subject that most interested him. He questioned Roland on his works, Dumouriez on his adventures, and Clavière on the finances, whilst he avoided the irritating topics of general policy. Madame Roland reproached her husband with these conversations, and besought him to make use of his time, to take abstracts of these conversations, and to keep an authentic register, which would one day cover his responsibility. The ministers agreed to dine four times a week together, in order to concert their acts and language in the king's presence. It was at these private meetings that Buzot, Guadet, Vergniaud, Gensonné, and Brissot infused into the ministers the feelings of their party, and reigned unseen over the Assembly and the king. Dumouriez soon became an object of suspicion to them—his mind escaped their dominion by its greatness, and his character escaped their fanaticism by its pliability. Madame Roland, seduced by his eloquence, yet experienced remorse for her admiration; she felt that the genius of this man was necessary to her party, but that genius without virtue would be fatal to the republic; and she infused distrust of Dumouriez into the mind of her allies. The king invariably adjourned the sanction which the Girondists demanded from him to the decree against the priests and *emigrés*. Foreseeing that they would be called upon, sooner or later, to give an account of their responsibility to the nation, Madame Roland wished to take precautionary measures. She persuaded her husband to write a confidential letter to the king, full of the most austere lessons of patriotism; to read it himself in council to this prince; and to keep a copy, which he would publish at the proper time as an accusation against Louis XVI. and a justification of himself. This treacherous precaution against the perfidy of the court was odious as a snare and cowardly as a denunciation. Passion only, which disturbs the sight of the soul, could blind a generous-minded woman as to the nature of such an act; but party feeling supplies the place of morality, justice, and even of virtue. This letter was a concealed weapon, with which Roland reserved to himself the power of mortally wounding the reputation of the king whilst he saved his own. This was his only crime, or rather the only error of his hate; and this was the only cause for remorse he felt at the foot of the scaffold.

XVI.

"Sire," said Roland in this celebrated letter, "things cannot remain in their present state; it is a state of crisis, and we must be extricated from it by some extreme measure (*une explosion quelconque*). France has given itself a constitution; the minority are undermining, the majority are defending, it. There arises a fierce internal struggle in which no person remains neuter. You enjoyed supreme power, and could not have laid it down without regret. The enemies of the Revolution took into calculation the sentiments they presume you entertain. Your secret favor is their strength. Ought you now ally yourself to the enemies or the friends of the constitution? Pronounce once for all. Royalty, clergy, nobility, aristocracy, must abhor these changes, which destroy them: on the other hand, the people see the triumph of their rights in the Revolution, and will not allow themselves to be despoiled. The declaration of rights has become their new Gospel: liberty is henceforth the religion of the people. In this shock of opposing interests, all sentiments have become extreme—opinions have assumed the accent of enthusiasm. The country is no longer an abstraction, but a real being, to which we are attached by the happiness it promises to us, and the sacrifices we have made for it. To what point will this patriotism be exalted at the moment now imminent, when the enemies' forces without are about to combine with the intrigues within to assail it? The rage of the nation will be terrible if it have not confidence in you. But this confidence is not to be acquired by words, but by acts. Give unquestionable proofs of your sincerity. For instance, two important decrees have been passed, both deeply important for the security of the state, and the delay of your sanction excites distrust. Be on your guard: distrust is not very wide from hatred, and hatred does not hesitate at crime. If you do not give satisfaction to the Revolution, it will be cemented by blood. Desperate measures which you may be advised to adopt to intimidate Paris, to control the Assembly, would only cause the development of that sullen energy, the mother of great devotions and great attempts (this was meant indirectly for Dumouriez, who had advised firm measures). You are deceived, Sire, when the nation is represented to you as hostile to the throne, and to yourself. Love, serve the Revolution, and the people will love it in you. Deposed priests are agitating the provinces: ratify the measures requisite to put down their fanaticism. Paris is uneasy as to its security: sanction the measures which summon a camp of citizens beneath its walls. Still more delays, and you will be considered as a conspirator and an accomplice. Just Heaven! hast thou stricken kings with blindess? I know that the language of truth is rarely welcomed at the foot of thrones: I know, too, that it is the withholding the truth from the councils of kings which renders revolutions so often necessary. As a citizen, and as a minister, I owe the truth to the king, and nothing shall prevent my making it reach his ear. I demand that we should have here a secretary of council to register our deliberations. Responsible ministers should have a witness of their opinions. If this witness existed, I should not now address your majesty in writing."

The threat was no less evident than the treachery of this letter; and the last sentence indicated, in equivocal terms, the odious use which Roland meant one day to make of it. The magnanimity of Vergniaud was excited against this step of the powerful Girondist minister: Dumouriez's military loyalty was roused by it: the king listened to the reading of it with the calmness of a man accustomed to put up with insult. The Girondists were informed of it in the secret councils at Madame Roland's, and Roland kept a copy to cover himself at the hour of his fall.

XVII.

At this moment secret understandings, unknown to Roland himself, were formed by the three Girondist chiefs, Vergniaud, Guadet, and Gensonné and the château, through Boze, the king's painter. A letter, intended for the monarch's perusal, was written by them. The iron chest guarded it for the day of accusation.

"You ask of us," runs this epistle, "what is our opinion as to the state of France, and the choice of measures fit to save the public weal. Questioned by you concerning such important interests, we do not hesitate to reply. The conduct of the executive power is the cause of all the evil. The king is deceived by persuading him that it is the clubs and factions which foment public agitation. This is placing the cause of the evil in its symptoms. If the people was reassured of the loyalty of the king, it would grow tranquil, and factions die a natural death. But so long as conspiracies, internal and external, appear favored by the king, troubles will perpetually spring up, and continually increase the mistrust of the citizens. The present tendency of things is evidently towards a crisis, all the chances of which are opposed to royalty. They are making of the chief of a free nation, the chief of a party. The opposite party ought to consider him, not as a king, but as an enemy. What is to be hoped from the success of manœuvres carried on with foreigners, in order to restore the authority of the throne? They will give to the king the appearance of a violent usurpation of the rights of the nation. The same force which would have served this violent restoration would be necessary to maintain it. It would produce a permanent civil war. Attached as we are to the interests of the nation, from which we shall never separate those of the king, we think that the sole means by which he can alleviate the evils that threaten the empire and the throne, is to identify himself with the nation. Renewed protestations are useless; we must have deeds. Let the king abandon every idea of increased power offered to him by the succor of foreigners. Let him obtain from cabinets hostile to the Revolution the withdrawal of the troops who press upon our frontiers. If that be impossible, let him arm the nation himself, and direct it against the enemies of the constitution. Let him choose his ministers amongst the leading men of the Revolution. Let him offer the muskets and horses of his own guard. Let him publish the documents connected with the civil list, and thus prove that the secret treasury is not the source of counter-revolutionary plots. Let him apply himself for a law respecting the education of the prince royal, and let him be brought up in the spirit of the constitution. Finally, let him withdraw from M. de La Fayette the command of the army. If the king shall adopt these determinations, and persist in them with firmness, the constitution is saved!"

This letter, conveyed to the king by Thierri, had not been sought by him. He was annoyed at the many plans of succor sent to him. "What do these men mean?" he inquired of Boze. "Have I not done all that they advise? Have I not chosen patriots for ministers? Have I not rejected succor from without? Have I not repudiated my brothers, and hindered, as far as in me lies, the coalition, and armed the frontiers? Have I not been, since my acceptance of the constitution, more faithful than the malcontents themselves to my oath?"

The Girondist leaders, still undecided between the republic and the monarchy, thus felt the pulse of power—sometimes of the Assembly, sometimes of the king; ready to seize it wherever they should find it; but discovering it on the side of the king, they judged that there was more certainty in sapping than in consolidating the throne, and they inclined more than ever to a factious policy.

XVIII.

Still, half-masters of the council through Roland, Claviere, and Servan, who had succeeded De Grave, they bore to a certain extent the responsibility of these three ministers. The Jacobins began to require from them an account of the acts of a ministry which was in their hands, and bore their name. Dumouriez, placed between the king and the Girondists, saw daily the increasing want of confidence between his colleagues and himself; they suspected his probity equally with his patriotism. He had profited by his popularity and ascendency over the Jacobins to demand of the Assembly a sum of 6,000,000 (240,000*l.*) of secret service money on his accession to the ministry. The apparent destination of this money was to bribe foreign cabinets, and to detach venal powers from the coalition, and to foment revolutionary symptoms in Belgium. Dumouriez alone knew the channels by which this money was to flow. His exhausted personal fortune, his costly tastes, his attachment to a seductive woman, Madame de Beauvert, sister to Rivarol; his intimacy with men of unprincipled character and irregular habits,—reports of extortion charged on his ministry, and falling, if not on him on those he trusted, tarnished his character in the eyes of Madame Roland and her husband. Probity is the virtue of democrats, for the people look first at the hands of those who govern them. The Girondists, pure as men of the ancient time, feared the shadow of a suspicion of this nature on their characters, and Dumouriez's carelessness on this point annoyed them. They complained. Gensonné and Brissot insinuated their feelings to him on this point at Roland's. Roland himself, authorized by his age and austerity of manners, took upon himself to remind Dumouriez that a public man owes respect to decorum and revolutionary manners. The warrior turned the remonstrance into pleasantry, replied to Roland that he owed his blood to the nation, but neither owed it the sacrifice of his tastes nor his amours; that he understood patriotism as a hero, and not as a puritan. The bitterness of his language left venom behind, and they separated with mutual ill-feeling.

From this day forth he no longer visited at Roland's evening meetings. Madame Roland, who understood the human heart by the superior instinct of her genius and her sex, was not deceived by the general's tactics. "The hour is come to destroy Dumouriez," she said boldly to her friends. "I know very well," she added, addressing Roland, "that you are incapable of descending either to intrigue or revenge; but remember that Dumouriez must conspire in his heart against those who have wounded him. When such daring remonstrances have been made to such a man, and uselessly made, it is necessary to strike the blow if we would not be struck ourselves." She felt truly, and spoke sagaciously. Dumouriez, whose rapid glance had seen behind the Girondists a party stronger and bolder than their own, began from this time to connect himself with the leaders of the Jacobins. He thought, and with reason, that party hatred would be more potent than patriotism, and that by flattering the rivalry of Robespierre and Danton against Brissot, Pétion, and Roland, he should find in the Jacobins themselves a support for the government. He liked the king, pitied the queen, and all his prejudices were in favor of the monarchy. He would have been as proud to restore the throne as to serve the republic. Skilful in handling men, every instrument was good that was available; to get rid of the Girondists, who, by oppressing the king, menaced himself, and to go and seek further off and lower than these rhetoricians, that popularity which was necessary to him when opposed to them, was a master-stroke of genius: he tried it, and succeeded. From this epoch may be dated his connection with Camille Desmoulins and Danton.

Danton and Dumouriez came to an understanding the sooner, because in their vices, like their good qualities, they closely resembled each other. Danton, like Dumouriez, only wanted the impulse of the Revolution. Principles were trifles with him; what suited his energy and his ambition was that tumultuous turmoil which cast down and elevated men, from the throne to nothing, from nothing to fortune and power. The intoxication of movement was to Danton, as to Dumouriez, the continual need of their disposition: the Revolution was to them a battle-field, whose whirl charmed and promoted them.

Yet any other revolution would have suited them as well, despotism or liberty, king or people. There are men whose atmosphere is the whirlwind of events—who only breathe easily in a storm of agitation. Moreover, if Dumouriez, had the vices or levities of courts, Danton had the vices and licentiousness of the mob. These vices, how different soever in form, are the same at bottom; they understand each other, they are a point of contact between the weaknesses of the great and the corruption of the small. Dumouriez understood Danton at the first glance, and Danton allowed himself to be approached and tamed by Dumouriez. Their connection, often suspected of bribery on the one hand, and venality on the other, subsisted secretly or publicly until the exile of Dumouriez and the death of Danton. Camille Desmoulins, freed of Danton and Robespierre, attached himself also to Dumouriez, and brought his name constantly forward in his pamphlets. The Orleans party, who held on with the Jacobins, by Sillery, Laclos, and Madame de Genlis, also sought the friendship of the new minister. As to Robespierre, whose policy was perpetual reserve with all parties, he affected neither liking nor dislike towards Dumouriez, but was secretly delighted at seeing him become a rival to his enemies. At least be never accused him. It is difficult r ng to hate the enemy of those whom we hate.

XIX.

The growing hatred of Robespierre and Brissot became daily more deadly. The sittings of the Jacobins and the newspapers were the continual theatre of the struggles and reconciliations of these two men. Equal in strength in the nation—equal in talent in the tribune—it was evident that they were afraid of each other in their attacks. They affected mutual respect, even when most offensive; but this repressed animosity only corroded their hearts more deeply, and it burst forth occasionally beneath the politeness of their language, like death beneath the glance of steel.

All these fermentations of division, rivalry, and resentment, boiled over in the April sittings. They were like a general review of two great parties who were about to destroy the empire in disputing their own ascendency. The Feuillants or moderate constitutionalists were the victims, that each of the two popular parties mutually immolated to the suspicions and rage of parties. Ræderer, a moderate Jacobin, was accused of having dined with the Feuillants, friends of La Fayette. "I do not only inculpate Ræderer," exclaimed Tallien, "I denounce Condorcet and Brissot. Let us drive from our society the ambitious and the Cromwellites."

"The moment for unmasking traitors will soon arrive," said Robespierre in his turn. "I do not desire to unmask them to-day. The blow when struck must be decisive. I wish that all France heard me now. I wish that the culpable chief of these factions, La Fayette, was here with all his army; I would say to his soldiers, whilst I presented my breast,—Strike! That moment would be the last of La Fayette and the *intrigants*" (this name had been invented by Robespierre for the Girondists.) Fauchet excused himself for having said that Guadet, Vergniaud, Gensonné, and Brissot might be, advantageously for the country, placed at the head of the government. The Girondists were accused of dreaming of a *protector*, the Jacobins a *tribune* of the people.

At last, Brissot rose to reply. "I am here to defend myself," he said. "What are my crimes? I am said to have made seven ministers—I keep up a connection with La Fayette—I desire to make a protector of him. Certainly great power is thus assigned to me by those who think that from my fourth story I have dictated laws to the Château of the Tuileries. But if it even were true that I had made ministers, how long has it been a crime to have confided the interests of the people to the hands of the people? This minister is about, it is said, to distribute all his favors to the Jacobins! Ah! would to heaven that all the places were filled by Jacobins!"

At these words Camille Desmoulins, Brissot's enemy, concealed in the chamber, bowing towards his neighbors, said aloud with a sneering laugh, "What a cunning rogue! Cicero and Demosthenes never uttered more eloquent insinuations." Cries of angry feeling burst from the ranks of Brissot's friends, who clamored for Camille Desmoulins' expulsion. A censor of the chamber declared that the remarks of the pamphleteer were disgraceful, and order was restored. Brissot proceeded. "Denunciation is the weapon of the people: I do not complain of this. Do you know who are its bitterest enemies? Those who prostitute denunciation. Yes; but where are the proofs? Treat with the deepest contempt him who denounces but does not prove. How long have a protector or a protectorate been talked of? Do you know why? Is it to accustom the ear to the name of tribuneship and tribune. They do not see that a tribuneship can never exist. Who would dare to dethrone the constitutional king? Who would dare to place the crown on his head? Who can imagine that the race of Brutus is extinct? And if there were no Brutus, where is the man who has ten times the ability of Cromwell? Do you believe that Cromwell himself would have succeeded in a revolution like ours? There were for him two easy roads to usurpation, which are to-day closed—ignorance and fanaticism. You think you see a Cromwell in a La Fayette. You neither know La Fayette nor your times. Cromwell had character—La Fayette has none. A man does not become protector without boldness and decision; and when he has both, this society comprises a crowd of friends of liberty, who would rather perish than support him. I first make the oath, that either equality shall reign, or I will die contending against protectors and tribunes. Tribunes! they are the worst enemies of the people. They flatter to enchain it. They spread suspicions of virtue, which will not debase itself. Remember who were Aristides and Phocion,—they did not always sit in the tribune."

Brissot, as he darted this sarcasm, looked towards Robespierre, for whom he meant it. Robespierre turned pale, and raised his head suddenly. "They did not always sit in the tribune," continued Brissot; "they were at their posts in the camp or at the tribunals (a sneering laugh came from the Girondist benches, accusing Robespierre of abandoning his post at the moment of danger). They did not disdain any charge, however humble it might be, when it was assigned them by the people: they spoke seldom; they did not flatter demagogues; they never denounced without proofs! The calumniators did not spare Phocion. He was the victim of an adulator of the people! Ah! this reminds me of the horrible calumny uttered against Condorcet! Who are you who dare to slander this great man? What have you done? What are your labors, your writings? Can you quote, as he can, so many assaults during three years by himself with Voltaire and D'Alembert against the throne, superstition, prejudices, and the aristocracy? Where would you be, where this tribune, were it not for these gentlemen? They are your masters; and you insult those who gain you the voices of the people. You assail Condorcet, as though his life had not been a series of sacrifices! A philosopher, he became a politician; academician, he became a newspaper writer; a courtier, he became one of the people; noble, he became a Jacobin! Beware! you are following the concealed impulses of the court. Ah, I will not imitate my adversaries, I would not repeat those rumors which assert they are paid by the civil list." (There was a report that Robespierre had been gained over to oppose the war.) "I shall not say a word of a secret committee which they frequent, and in which are concerted the means of influencing this society; but I will say that they follow in the track of the promoters of civil war. I will say, that without meaning it, they do more harm to the patriots than the court. And at what moment do they throw division amongst us? At the moment when we have a foreign war, and when an intestine war threatens us. Let us put an end to these disputes, and let us go to the order of the day, leaving our contempt for odious and injurious denunciations."

XX.

At this, Robespierre and Guadet, equally provoked, wished to enter the tribune. "It is forty-eight hours," said Guadet, "that the desire of justifying myself has weighed upon my heart; it is only a few minutes that this want has affected Robespierre. I request to be heard." Leave was accorded, and he briefly exculpated himself. "Be especially on your guard," he said, as he concluded, and pointed to Robespierre, "against empirical orators, who have incessantly in their mouths the words of liberty, tyranny, conspiracy—always mixing up their own praises with the deceit they impose upon the people. Do justice to such men!" "Order!" cried Fréron, Robespierre's friend; "this is insult and sarcasm." The tribune resounded with applause and hooting. The chamber itself was divided into two camps, separated by a wide space. Harsh names were exchanged, threatening gesticulations used, and hats were raised and shaken about on the tops of canes. "I am called a wretch," (*scelerat*) continued Guadet, "and yet I am not allowed to denounce a man who invariably thrusts his personal pride in advance of the public welfare. A man who, incessantly talking of patriotism, abandons the post to which he was called! Yes, I denounce to you a man who, either from ambition or misfortune, has become the idol of the people!" Here the tumult reached its height, and drowned the voice of Guadet.

Robespierre himself requested silence for his enemy. "Well," added Guadet, alarmed or softened by Robespierre's feigned generosity, "I denounce to you a man who, from love of the liberty of his country, ought perhaps to impose upon himself the law of ostracism: for to remove him from his own idolatry is to serve the people!" These words were smothered under peals of affected laughter. Robespierre ascended the steps of the tribune with studied calmness. His impassive brow involuntarily brightened at the smiles and applauses of the Jacobins. "This speech meets all my wishes," said he, looking towards Brissot and his friends: "it includes in itself all the inculpations which the enemies by whom I am surrounded have brought against me. In replying to M. Guadet, I shall reply to all. I am invited to have recourse to ostracism; there would, no doubt, be some excess of vanity in my condemning myself—that is the punishment of great men, and it is only for M. Brissot to class them. I am reproached for being so constantly in the tribune. Ah! let liberty be assured, let equality be confirmed; let the *intrigants* disappear, and you will see me as anxious to fly from this tribune, and even this place, as you now see me desirous to be in them. Thus, in effect, my dearest wishes will be accomplished. Happy in the public liberty, I shall pass my peaceful days in the delights of a sweet and obscure privacy."

Robespierre confined himself to these few words, frequently interrupted by the murmurs of fanatical enthusiasm, and then adjourned his answer to the following sittings, when Danton was seated in the arm-chair, and presided over this struggle between his enemies and his rival. Robespierre began by elevating his own cause to the height of a national one. He defended himself for having first provoked his adversaries. He quoted the accusations made, and the injurious things uttered against him, by the Brissot party. "Chief of a party, agitator of the people, secret agent of the Austrian committee," he said, "these are the names thrown in my teeth, and to which they urge me to reply! I shall not make the answer of Scipio or La Fayette, who, when accused in the tribune of the crime of *lèze-nation,* only replied by their silence. I shall reply by my life.

"A pupil of Jean Jacques Rousseau, his doctrines have inspired my soul for the people. The spectacles of the great assemblies in the first days of our Revolution have filled me with hope. I soon understood the difference that exists between those limited assemblies, composed of men of ambitious views, or egotists, and the nation itself. My voice was stifled there; but I preferred rather to excite the murmurs of the enemies of truth, than to obtain applauses that were disgraceful. I threw my glance beyond this limited circle, and my aim was to make myself heard by the nation and the whole human race. It is for this that I have so much frequented the tribune. I have done more than this—it was I who gave Brissot and Condorcet to France. These great philosophers have unquestionably ridiculed and opposed the priests; but they have not the less courted kings and grandees, out of whom they have made a pretty good thing. (Laughter.) You do not forget with what eagerness they persecuted the genius of liberty in the person of Jean Jacques Rousseau, the only philosopher who, in my opinion, has deserved the public honors lavished for a long time on so many political charlatans and so many contemptible heroes. Brissot, at least, should feel well inclined towards me. Where was he when I was defending this society from the Jacobins against the Constituent Assembly itself? But for what I did at this epoch, you would not have insulted me in this tribune; for it would not have existed. I the corrupter.

the agitator, the tribune of the people! I am none of these, I am the people myself. You reproach me for having quitted my place as public accuser. I did so when I saw that that place gave me no other right than that of accusing citizens for civil offences, and would deprive me of the right of accusing political enemies. And it is for this that the people love me; and yet you desire that I sentence myself to ostracism, in order to withdraw myself from its confidence. Exile! how can you dare to propose it to me? Whither would you have me retire? Amongst what people should I be received? Who is the tyrant who would give me asylum? Ah! we may abandon a happy, free, and triumphant country; but a country threatened, rent by convulsions, oppressed; we do not flee from that, we save, or perish with it! Heaven, which gave me a soul impassioned for liberty, and gave me birth in a land trampled on by tyrants—Heaven, which placed my life in the midst of the reign of factions and crimes, perhaps calls me to trace with my blood the road to happiness, and the liberty of my fellow men! Do you require from me any other sacrifice? If you would have my good name, I surrender it to you; I only wish for reputation in order to do good to my fellow-creatures. If to preserve it, it be necessary to betray by a cowardly silence the cause of the truth and of the people, take it, sully it,—I will no longer defend it. Now that I have defended myself, I may attack you. I will not do it; I offer you peace. I forget your injuries; I put up with your insults; but on one condition, that is, you join me in opposing the factions which distract our country, and, the most dangerous of all, that of La Fayette: this pseudo-hero of the two worlds, who, after having been present at the revolution of the New World, has only exerted himself here in arresting the progress of liberty in the old hemisphere. You, Brissot, did not you agree with me that this chief was the executioner and assassin of the people, that the massacre of the Champ-de-Mars had caused the Revolution to retrograde for twenty years? Is this man less redoubtable because he is at this time at the head of the army? No. Hasten then! Let the sword of the laws strike horizontally at the heads of great conspirators. The news which has arrived to us from the army is of threatening import. Already it sows division amongst the national guards and the troops of the line; already the blood of citizens has flowed at Metz; already the best patriots are incarcerated at Strasburg. I tell you, you are accused of all these evils; wipe out these suspicions by uniting with us, and let us be reconciled; but let it be for the sake of saving our common country."

BOOK XIV.

I.

Night was far advanced at the moment when Robespierre concluded his eloquent discourse in the midst of the enthusiasm of the Jacobins. The Jacobins and the Girondists then separated more exasperated than ever. They hesitated before this important severance, which, by weakening the patriotic party, might deliver the army over to La Fayette, and the Assembly to the Feuillants.* Pétion, friend of Robespierre and Brissot, at the same time closely allied to the Jacobins and with Madame Roland, kept his popularity in equilibrium for fear of losing half of it, if he decided positively for one side or the other. He tried next day to effect a general reconciliation. "On both sides," he said, with a tremulous voice, "I see my friends." There was an apparent truce; but Guadet and Brissot printed their speeches, with offensive additions, against Robespierre. They doggedly sapped his reputation by fresh calumnies. On the 30th of April another storm broke out.

It was proposed to interdict all denunciations unaccompanied by proofs. "Reflect on what is proposed to you," said Robespierre: "the majority here belongs to a faction, which desires by this means to calumniate us freely, and stifle our accusations by silence. If you decree that I am prohibited from defending myself from the libellers who conspire against me, I shall quit this place, and will bury myself in retreat." "We will follow you, Robespierre," exclaimed the women in the tribunes. "They have profited by the discourse of Pétion," he continued, "to disseminate infamous libels against me. Pétion himself is insulted. His

* The club of the Feuillants, of which La Fayette was the leading member, was formed after the 17th July, 1791. It consisted principally of Royalists, and was soon dissolved.—H. T. R.

heart beats in sympathy with mine; he groans over the insults with which I am assailed. Read Brissot's journal, and you will there see that I am invited not always to be apostrophizing the people in my discourses. Yes, it is to be forbidden to pronounce the name of the people under pain of passing for a malcontent,—a tribune. I am compared to the Gracchi: they are right so to compare me. What may be perhaps common between us is their tragical end. That is little: they make me responsible for a writing of Marat, who points me out as a tribune by preaching blood and slaughter. Have I ever professed such principles? Am I guilty of the extravagance of such an excited writer as Marat?"

At these words, Lasource, the friend of Brissot, wished to speak, and was refused. Merlin demanded if the peace sworn yesterday ought to bind only one of two parties, and to authorize the other to spread calumnies against Robespierre? The Assembly tumultuously insisted on the orators being silent. Legendre declared that the chamber was partial. Robespierre quitted the tribune, approached the president, and addressed him with menacing gestures, and in language impossible to be heard in the noise of the chamber, and the taunts and sneers profusely scattered by the opposing factions.

"Why do we see this ferocity among the *intrigants* against Robespierre?" exclaimed one of the partisans when tranquillity was re-established. "Because he is the only man capable of making head against their party, if they should succeed in forming it. Yes, in revolutions we require those men, who, full of self-denial, deliver themselves as voluntary victims to factions. The people should support them. You have found those men—Robespierre and Pétion. Will you abandon them to their enemies?" "No! no!" exclaimed a thousand voices, and a motion, proposed by the president (Danton), declaring that Brissot had calumniated Robespierre, was carried in the affirmative.

II.

The journals took part, according to their politics, in these intestine wars of the patriots. "Robespierre," said the *Revolution de Paris*, "how is it that this man, whom the people bore in triumph to his house when he left the Constituent Assembly, has now become a problem? For a long while you believed yourself the only column of French liberty. Your name was like the holy ark, no one could touch it without being struck with death. You sought to be the man of the people. You have neither the exterior of the orator, nor the genius which disposes of the will of men. You have stirred up the clubs with your language; the incense burnt in your honor has intoxicated you. The god of patriotism hath become a man. The apogee of your glory was on the 17th July, 1791. From that day your star declined. Robespierre, the patriots do not like that you should present such a spectacle to them. When the people press around the tribune to which you ascend, it is not to hear your self-eulogies, but to hear you enlighten popular opinion. You are incorruptible—true; but yet there are better citizens than you: there are those who are as good, and do not boast of it. Why have you not the simplicity which is ignorant of itself, and that right quality of the ancient times which you sometimes refer to as possessed by you?

"You are accused, Robespierre, of having been present at a secret conference, held some time since at the Princesse de Lamballe's, at which the queen, Marie Antoinette, was present. No mention is made of the terms of the bargain between you and these two women, who would corrupt you. Since then some changes have been seen in your domestic arrangements, and you have had the money requisite to start a newspaper. Could there have been such injurious suspicions against you in July, 1791? We believe nothing of these infamies: we do not think you the accomplice of Marat, who offers you the dictatorship. We do not accuse you of imitating Cæsar when Anthony presented to him the diadem. No: but be on your guard! Speak of yourself with less egotism. We have in our time warned both La Fayette and Mirabeau, and pointed out the Tarpeian rock for citizens who think themselves greater than their country."

III.

"The wretches," replied Marat, who was then sheltered beneath the patronage of Robespierre, "they cast a shade upon the purest virtues! His genius is offensive to them. They punish him for his sacrifices. His inclinations lead him to retirement. He only remained in the tumult of the Jacobins from devotion to his country; but men of mediocre understanding are not accustomed to the eulogiums of another, and the mob likes to change its hero.

"The faction of the La Fayettes, Guadets, Brissots circumvent him. They call him the leader of a party! Robespierre chief of a party! They show his hand in the disgraceful columns of the Civil List. They make the people's confidence in him a crime, as if a simple citizen without fortune and power had any other means of acquiring the love of his fellow-countrymen but from his deserts! as if a man who has only his isolated voice in the midst of a society of *intrigants*, hypocrites, and knaves, could ever be feared! But this incorruptible censor annoys them. They say he has an understanding with me to offer him the dictatorship. This is my affair, and I declare that Robespierre is so far from controlling my pen, that I never had the slightest connection with him. I have seen him but once, and the sole conversation has convinced me that he was not the man whom I sought for the supreme and energetic power demanded by the Revolution.

"The first word he addressed to me was a reproach for having dipped my pen in the blood of the enemies of liberty,—for always speaking of the cord, the axe, and the poniard; cruel words, which unquestionably my heart would disavow, and my principles discredit. I undeceived him, 'Learn,' I replied to him, 'that my credit with the people does not depend on my ideas, but on my audacity, the daring impetuosity of my mind, my cries of rage, despair, and fury against the wretches who impede the action of the Revolution. I know the anger, the just anger of the people, and that is why it listens to, and believes, in me. Those cries of alarm and fury, that you take for words in the air, are the most simple and sincere expression of the passions which devour my mind. Yes, if I had had in my hand the arms of the people after the decree against the garrison of Nancy, I would have decimated the deputies who confirmed it. After the information of the events of the 5th and 6th October, I would have immolated every judge on the pile; after the massacre of the Champ-de-Mars, had I but had 2000 men, animated with the same resentment as myself, I would have gone at their head to stab La Fayette in the midst of his battalion of brigands, burnt the king in his palace, and cut the throats of our atrocious representatives on their very seats!' Robespierre listened to me with affright, turned pale, and was for a long time silent. I left him. I had seen an honest man, but not a man of the state."

Thus the wretch had excited horror in the fanatic: Robespierre had obtained Marat's pity.

IV.

The first struggle between the Jacobins and the Girondists gave the skilful Dumouriez a double *point d'appui* for his policy. The enmity of Roland, Clavière, and Servan, no longer disturbed him in council. He balanced their influence by his alliance with their enemies. But the Jacobins demanded wages: he proffered them in war. Danton, as violent but more politic than Marat, did not cease to repeat that the revolutionists and the despots were irreconcilable, and that France had no safety to expect except from its audacity and despair. War, according to Danton, was the baptism or the martyrdom which liberty was to undergo, like a new religion. It was necessary to replunge France into the fire, in order to purify it from the stains and shame of its past.

Dumouriez, agreeing with La Fayette and the Feuillants, was also anxious for war; but it was as a soldier, to acquire glory, and thus crush faction. From the first day of his ministry he negotiated so as to obtain from Austria a decisive answer. He had removed nearly all the members of the diplomatic body; he had replaced them by energetic men. His dispatches had a martial accent, which sounded like the voice of an armed people. He summoned the princes of the Rhine, the emperor, the king of Prussia, the king of Sardinia, and Spain, to recognize or oppose the constitutional king of France. But whilst these official envoys demanded from the various courts prompt and categorical replies, the secret agents of Dumouriez insinuated themselves into the cabinets of princes, and compelled some states to detach themselves from the coalition that was forming. They pointed out to them the advantages of neutrality for their aggrandizement: they promised them the patronage of France after victory. Not daring to hope for allies, the minister at least contrived for France secret understanding: he corrupted by ambition the states that he could not move by terror: he benumbed the coalition, which he trusted subsequently to crush.

V.

The prince, on whose mind he operated most powerfully,

was the Duke of Brunswick, whom the emperor and the king of Prussia alike destined for the command of the combined armies against the French. This prince was in their hopes the Agamemnon of Germany.

Charles-Frederic-Ferdinand of Brunswick-Wolfenbuttel, bred in combats and in pleasures, had inspired in the camps of the great Frederic the genius of war, the spirit of the French philosophy, and the Machiavellianism of his master. He had accompanied this philosopher and soldier-king in all the campaigns of the seven years' war. At the peace he travelled in France and Italy. Received everywhere as the hero of Germany, and as the heir to the genius of Frederic, he had married a sister of George III., king of England. His capital, where his mistresses shone or philosophers harangued, united the epicurism of the court to the austerity of the camp. He reigned according to the precepts of sages; he lived after the example of the Sybarites. But his soldier's mind, which was but too easily given up to beauty, was not quenched in love; he only gave his heart to women, he reserved his head for glory, war, and the government of his states. Mirabeau, then a young man, had stayed at his court, on his way to Berlin, to catch the last glimpses of the shining genius of the great Frederic. The Duke of Brunswick had favorably received and appreciated Mirabeau. These two men, placed in such different ranks, resembled each other by their qualities and defects. They were two revolutionary spirits; but from their difference of situations and countries, the one was destined to create, and the other to oppose, a revolution.

Be this as it may, Mirabeau was seduced by the sovereign, whom he was sent to seduce.

"This prince's countenance," he writes in his secret correspondence, "betokens depth and finesse. He speaks with eloquence and precision: he is prodigiously well-informed, industrious, and clear-sighted: he has a vast correspondence, which he owes to his merit alone: he is even economical of his amours. His mistress, Madame de Hartfeld, is the most sensible woman of his court. A real Alcibiades, he loves pleasure, but never allows it to intrude on business. When acting as the Prussian general, no one so early, so active, so precisely exact as he. Under a calm aspect, which arises from the absolute control he has over his mind, his brilliant imagination and ambitious aspirations often carry him away; but the circumspection which he imposes on himself, and the satisfactory reflection of his fame, restrain him and lead him to doubts, which, perhaps, constitute his sole defect."

Mirabeau predicted to the Duke of Brunswick, from this moment, leading influence in the affairs of Germany after the death of the king of Prussia, whom Germany called the Great King.

The duke was then fifty years of age. He defended himself in his conversations with Mirabeau, from the charge of loving war. "Battles are games of chance," said he to the French traveller: "up to this time I have been fortunate. Who knows if to-day, although more lucky, I should be as well used by fortune?" A year after this remark he made the triumphant invasion of Holland, at the head of the troops of England. Some years later Germany nominated him generalissimo.

But war with France, however it might be grateful to his ambition as a soldier, was repugnant to his mind as a philosopher. He felt he should but ill carry out the ideas in which he had been educated. Mirabeau had made that profound remark, which prophesied the weaknesses and defects of a coalition guided by that prince: "This man is of a rare stamp, but he is too much of a sage to be feared by sages."

This phrase explains the offer of the crown of France made to the Duke of Brunswick by Custine, in the name of the monarchical portion of the Assembly. Free-masonry, that underground religion, into which nearly all the reigning princes of Germany had entered, concealed beneath its mysteries secret understandings between French philosophy and the sovereigns on the banks of the Rhine. Brothers in a religious conspiracy, they could not be very bitter enemies in politics. The Duke of Brunswick was in the depth of his heart more the citizen than the prince—more the Frenchman than the German. The offer of a throne at Paris had pleased his fancy. He fights not against a people, whose king he hopes to be, and against a cause, which he desires to conquer, but not to destroy. Such was the state of the Duke of Brunswick's mind;—consulted by the king of Prussia, he advised this monarch to turn his forces to the Polish frontier and conquer provinces there, instead of principles in France.

VI.

Dumouriez's plan was to separate, as much as possible, Prussia from Austria, in order to have but one enemy at a time to cope with; and the union of these two powers, natural and jealous rivals of each other, appeared to him so totally unnatural, that he flattered himself he could prevent or sever it. The instinctive hatred of despotism for liberty, however, overthrew all his schemes. Russia, through the ascendency of Catherine, forced Prussia and Austria to make common cause against the Revolution. At Vienna, the young Emperor Francis I. made far greater preparations for war than for negotiation. The Prince de Kaunitz, his principal minister, replied to the notes of Dumouriez in language that seemed a defiance of the Assembly. Dumouriez laid these documents before the Assembly, and forestalled the expressions of their just indignation, by bursting himself into patriotic anger. The *contre coup* of these scenes was felt even in the cabinet of the emperor at Vienna, where Francis I., pale and trembling with rage, censured the tardiness of his minister. He was present every day at the conferences held at the bedside of the veteran Prince de Kaunitz and the Prussian and Russian envoys charged by their sovereigns to foment the war. The king of Prussia demanded to have the whole direction of the war in his hands, and he proposed the sudden invasion of the French territory as the most efficacious means of preventing the effusion of blood, by striking terror into the Revolution, and causing a counter-revolution, with the hope of which the *emigrés* flattered him, to break out in France. An interview to concert the measures of Austria and Prussia, was fixed between the Duke of Brunswick and the Prince de Hohenlohe, general of the emperor's army. For form's sake, however, conferences were still carried on at Vienna between M. de Noailles, the French ambassador, and Count Philippe de Cobentzel, vice-chancellor of the court. These conferences, in which the liberty of the people and the absolute sovereignty of monarchs continually strove to conciliate two irreconcilable principles, ended invariably in mutual reproaches. A speech of M. de Cobentzel broke off all negotiations, and this speech, made public at Paris, caused the final declaration of war. Dumouriez proposed it at the council, and induced the king, as if by the hand of fatality, himself to propose the war to his people. "The people," said he, "will credit your attachment when they behold you embrace their cause, and combat kings in its defence."

The king, surrounded by his ministers, appeared unexpectedly at the Assembly on the 20th of April, at the conclusion of the council. A solemn silence reigned in the Assembly, for every one felt that the decisive word was now about to be pronounced—and they were not deceived. After a full report of the negotiations with the house of Austria had been read by Dumouriez, the king added in a low but firm voice, "You have just heard the report which has been made to my council; these conclusions have been unanimously adopted, and I myself have taken, the same resolution. I have exhausted every means of maintaining peace, and I now come, in conformity with the terms of the constitution, to propose to you, formally, war with the king of Hungary and Bohemia."

The king, after this speech, quitted the Assembly amidst cries and gestures of enthusiasm, which burst forth in the salle and the tribunes: the people followed their example. France felt certain of herself when she was the first to attack all Europe armed against her. It seemed to all good citizens that domestic troubles would cease before this mighty external excitement of a people who defend their frontiers. That the cause of liberty would be judged in a few hours on the field of battle, and that the constitution needed only a victory, in order to render the nation free at home, and triumphant abroad. The king himself re-entered his palace relieved from the cruel weight of irresolution which had so long oppressed him. War against his allies and his brothers had cost him many a pang. This sacrifice of his feelings to the constitution seemed to him to merit the gratitude of the Assembly, and by thus identifying himself with the cause of his country, he flattered himself that he should at least recover the good opinion and the love of his people. The Assembly separated without deliberating, and gave a few hours up to enthusiasm rather than to reflection.

VII.

At the sitting in the evening, Pastoret, one of the principal Feuillants, was the first to support the war. "We are reproached with having voted the effusion of human blood in a moment of enthusiasm; but is it to-day only that we are provoked? During four hundred years the house of Austria has violated every treaty with France. Such are our motives; let us no longer hesitate. Victory will adhere faithfully to the cause of liberty."

Becquet, a constitutional royalist, a profound and courageous orator, alone ventured to speak against the declaration of war. "In a free country," said he, "war is alone made to defend the constitution or the nation. Our constitution is but of yesterday, and it requires calm to take root. A state of crisis, such as war, opposes all regular movements of political bodies. If your armies combat abroad, who will repress faction at home? You are flattered with the belief that you have only Austria to cope against. You are promised that the other northern powers will not interfere; do not rely on this. Even England cannot remain neuter: if the exigencies of the war lead you to revolutionize Belgium, or to invade Holland, she will join Prussia to support the stadtholder against you. Doubtless England loves the liberty which is now taking root amongst you; but her life is commercial, she cannot abandon her trade in the Low Countries. Wait until you are attacked, and then the spirit of the people will fight in your cause. The justice of a cause is worth armies. But if you can be represented to other nations as a restless and conquering people, who can only exist in a vortex of turmoil and war, the nations will shun and dread you. Besides, is not war the hope of the enemies of the Revolution? Why give them cause to rejoice by offering it to them? The *émigrés*, now only despicable, will become dangerous on that day when foreign armies lend them their assistance."

This sensible and profound speech, interrupted repeatedly by the ironical laughter and the insults of the Assembly, was concluded amidst the outcries of the tribunes. It required no small degree of heroism to combat the proposed war in the French chambers. Bazire alone, the friend of Robespierre, ventured, like Becquet, the king's friend, to demand a few days' reflection, before giving a vote that would shed so much human gore. "If you decide upon war, do so in such a manner that treason cannot envelope it," said he. Feeble applause showed that the republican allusion of Bazire had been comprehended, and that above all, it was necessary to remove a king and generals whose fidelity was suspected. "No, no," returned Mailhe, "do not lose an hour in decreeing the liberty of the whole world." "Extinguish the torches of your disagreements in the blaze of your cannon, and the glitter of your bayonets," added Dubayet. "Let the report be made instantly," demanded Brissot. "Declare war against kings, and peace to all nations," cried Merlin. The war was voted.

Condorcet, who had been informed already of this by the Girondists of the council, read in the tribune a proposed manifesto to the nations. The following was its substance: "Every nation has the right of giving itself laws, and of altering them at pleasure. The French nation had every reason to believe that these simple truths would obtain the assent of all princes. This hope has not been fulfilled. A league has been formed against its independence; and never did the pride of thrones more audaciously insult the majesty of nations. The motives alleged by despots against France are but an outrage to her liberty. This insulting pride, far from intimidating her, serves only to excite her courage. It requires time to discipline the slaves of despotism; every man is a soldier when he combats against tyranny."

VIII.

But the principal orator of the Gironde mounted the tribune the last. "You owe it to the nation," said Vergniaud, "to employ every means to assure the success of the great and terrible determination by which you have signalized this memorable day. Remember the hour of that general federation when all Frenchmen devoted their life to the defence of liberty and the constitution. Remember the oath which you have taken on the 14th of January, to bury yourselves beneath the ruins of the temple rather than consent to a capitulation, or to the least modification in the constitution. Where is the icy heart that does not palpitate in these important moments—the grovelling soul that does not elevate itself (I venture to utter the words) to heaven amidst these acclamations of universal joy; the apathetic man who does not feel his whole being penetrated and his forces raised by a noble enthusiasm far above the common force of the human race? Give to France, to Europe, the imposing spectacle of these national fêtes. Reanimate that energy before which the Bastille fell. Let every part of the empire resound with these sublime words: '*To live free or die! The entire constitution, without any modification, or death!*' Let these cries reach even the thrones that have leagued against you; let them learn that it is useless to reckon upon our internal dissensions; that when our country is in danger, we are animated by one passion alone—that of saving her, or of perishing for her: in a word, should fortune prove false to so just a cause as ours, our enemies might insult our lifeless corses, but never shall one Frenchman wear their fetters."

IX.

These lyrical words of Vergniaud re-echoed at Berlin and at Vienna. "War has been declared against us," said the Prince de Kaunitz to the Russian ambassador, the Prince de Galitzin, "it is the same thing as if it had been declared against you." The command of the Prussian and Austrian forces was given to the Duke of Brunswick. The two princes by this act only ratified the choice of all Germany, for opinion had already nominated him. Germany moves but slowly; federations are but ill fitted for sudden wars. The campaign was opened by the French before Prussia and Austria had prepared their armaments.

Dumouriez had reckoned upon this sluggishness and inactivity of the two German monarchies. His skilful plan was to sever the coalition, and suddenly invade Belgium before Prussia could take the field. Had Dumouriez alone framed and carried out his own plan, the fate of Belgium and Holland was sealed; but La Fayette, who was charged to invade them at the head of 40,000 men, had neither the temerity nor the rapidity of this veteran soldier. A general of opinion rather than the general of an army, he was more accustomed to command citizens in the public square, than soldiers in a campaign. Personally brave, beloved by his troops, but more of a citizen than a soldier, he had, during the American war, headed small bodies of free men, but not undisciplined masses. Not to peril his soldiers; defend the frontiers with intrepidity; die bravely at a Thermopylæ; harangue the national guard; and excite his troops for or against opinions; such was the nature of La Fayette. The daring schemes of great wars, that risk much to save everything, and which expose the frontiers for a moment to strike at the heart of an empire, accorded but ill with his habits, much less with his situation.

By becoming a general, La Fayette had become the chief of a party; and whilst he was opposing foreign powers, his eyes were constantly turned towards the interior. Doubtless he needed glory to nourish his influence, and to regain the *rôle* of arbitrator of the Revolution, which now began to escape his grasp; but before everything, it was necessary that he should not compromise himself; one defeat would have ruined all, and he knew it. He who never risks a loss, will never gain a victory. La Fayette was the general of temporization; and to waste the time of the Revolution, was to destroy its force. The strength of undisciplined forces is their impetuosity, and everything that slackens that ruins them.

Dumouriez, impetuous as the volcano, instinctively felt this, and strove, in the conferences that preceded the nomination of the generals, to infuse some portion of his own fire into La Fayette. He placed him at the head of the principal *corps d'armeé*, destined to penetrate into Belgium, as the general most fitted to foment popular insurrection, and convert the war on the Belgian provinces into revolution; for to rouse Belgium in favor of French liberty, and to render its independence dependent on ours, was to wrest it from the power of Austria, and turn it against our foes. The Belgians, according to Dumouriez's plan, were to conquer Belgium for us; for the germs of revolt had been but imperfectly stifled in these provinces, and were destined to bud again at the step of the first French soldier.

X.

Belgium, which had been long dominated over by Spain, had contracted its jealous and superstitious Catholicism. The nation pertains to the priests, and the privileges of the priests appear to it the privileges of the people. Joseph II., a premature but an armed philosopher, sought to emancipate the people from sacerdotal despotism. Belgium had risen in arms against the liberty offered to her, and had sided with her oppressors. The fanaticism of the priests, and of the municipal privileges, united in a feeling of resistance to Joseph II,, had set all Belgium in a flame. The rebels had captured GHENT and BRUSSELS, and proclaimed the downfall of the house of Austria, and the sovereignty of the Pays Bas. Scarcely had they triumphed, than the Belgians became divided amongst themselves. The sacerdotal and aristocratic party demanded an oligarchical constitution, whilst the popular party demanded a democracy, modelled on the French Revolution.

VAN-DER-NOOT, an eloquent and cruel tribune, was the leader of the first party; VAN-DER-MERSH, a brave soldier, of the people. Civil war broke out amidst a struggle for independence. VAN-DER-MERSH, made prisoner by the aris tocratic party, was immured in a gloomy dungeon until Leopold, the successor of Joseph II., profited by these domestic feuds, again to subjugate Belgium. Weary of liberty, after having tasted it, she submitted without resistance. Van-der-noot took refuge in Holland. Van-der-Mersh, freed by the Austrians, was generously pardoned, and again became an obscure citizen.

All attempts at independence were repressed by strong Austrian garrisons, and could not fail to be awakened at the approach of the French armies. La Fayette appeared to comprehend and approve of this plan. It was agreed that the Maréchal de Rochambeau should be appointed commander-in-chief of the army that threatened Belgium, that La Fayette should have under his orders a considerable *corps* that would invade the country, and then La Fayette would command alone in the Netherlands. Rochambeau, old and worn out by inactivity, would thus only receive the honor due to his rank. La Fayette would in reality direct the whole of the campaign and of the armed propaganda of the Revolution. "This *rôle* suits him," said the old maréchal: "I do not understand this war of cities." To cause La Fayette to march on Namur, which was but ill defended, capture it, march from thence on Brussels and Liége, the two capitals of the Pays Bas, and the focus of Belgian independence—send General Biron forward at the head of ten thousand men on Mons, to oppose the Austrian General Beaulieu, whose force was only two or three thousand men—detach from the garrison at Lille another corps of three thousand men, who would occupy Tournay, and who, after having left a garrison in this town, would swell the corps of Biron—send twelve hundred men from Dunkirk to surprise Furnes, and then advance by converging into the heart of the Belgian provinces with these forty thousand men under the command of La Fayette—attack, on every side, in ten days an enemy ill prepared to resist—to rouse the populations to revolt, and then increase the attacking army to eighty thousand troops, and join to it the Belgian battalions raised in the name of freedom, to combat the emperor's army as it arrived from Germany:—such was Dumouriez's bold idea of the campaign. Nothing was wanting to insure its success but a man capable of executing it. Dumouriez disposed of the troops and the generals in conformity with this plan.

XI.

The impulse of France responded to the impulse of her genius.

On the other side of the Rhine the preparations were making with promptitude and energy. The emperor and the king of Prussia met at Frankfort, where they were joined by the Duke of Brunswick. The empress of Russia adhered to the aggression of the powers against France, and marched her troops into Poland, to repress the germs of the same principles that were to be combated at Paris. Germany yielded, in spite of herself, to the impulse of the three cabinets, and poured her masses towards the Rhine. The emperor preluded this war of thrones against people by his coronation at Frankfort. The head-quarters of the Duke of Brunswick were at Coblentz, the capital of the emigration. The generalissimo of the confederation had an interview there with the two brothers of Louis XVI., and promised to restore to them, ere long, their country and their rank, whilst they, in their turn, styled him the *Hero of the Rhine,* and the *Right arm of kings.*

Everything wore a military aspect. The two princes of Prussia, quartered in a village near Coblentz, had but one room, and slept on the floor. The king of Prussia was welcomed on every bank of the Rhine by the salvos of his artillery. In every town through which he passed the *emigrés,* the population, and the troops, proclaimed him beforehand the preserver of Germany. His name, written in letters of fire at the illuminations, was surrounded by this adulatory device, "*Vivat Villelmus, Francos deleat, jura regis restituat!*"—"*Long live William, the exterminator of the French, the restorer of royalty.*"

XII.

Coblentz, a town situated on the confluence of the Moselle and the Rhine, in the states of the Elector of Trèves, had become the capital of the French *emigrés.* A constantly increasing body of gentlemen, to the number of twenty-two thousand, assembled there, around the seven fugitive princes of the house of Bourbon. These princes were, the Comte de Provence and the Comte d'Artois, the king's brothers; the two sons of the Comte d'Artois, the Duc de Berri and the Duc d'Angoulême; the Prince de Condé, the king's cousin, the Duke de Bourbon, his son, and the Duc d'Enghien, his grandson. All the military noblesse of the kingdom, with the exception of the partisans of the constitution, had quitted their garrisons or their châteaus to join this crusade of kings against the French revolution. This movement—which now appears sacrilegious, since it armed citizens against their country, and led them to implore the assistance of foreign powers to combat France—did not at that time possess in the eyes of the French noblesse that parricidal character with which the more enlightened patriotism of the present age invests it. Culpable in the eyes of reason, it could at least explain itself before feeling. Infidelity to their country was termed fidelity to their king, and desertion, honor.

Allegiance to the throne was the religion of the French nobles; and the sovereignty of the people appeared to them an insolent dogma, against which it was imperative to take arms, unless they wished to be partakers of the crime. The noblesse had patiently supported the humiliation and the personal spoliation of title and fortune which the National Assembly had imposed on them by the destruction of the last vestiges of the feudal system; or rather, they had generously sacrificed them to their country on the night of the 6th of August. But these outrages on the king appeared more intolerable to them than those inflicted on themselves. To deliver him from his captivity—rescue him from impending danger—save the queen and her children—restore royalty—or perish fighting for this sacred cause, appeared to them the duty of their situation and their birth. On one side was honor, on the other their country: they had not hesitated, but had followed honor; and this was sanctified even more in their eyes by the magic word devotion. There was real devotion in the feeling that induced these young and these old men to abandon their rank in the army—their fortune—their country—their families, to rally around the white flag in a foreign land, to perform the duty of private soldiers, and brave eternal exile, the spoliation pronounced against them by the laws of their country, the fatigues of the camp, and death and danger on the battle-field. If the devotion of the patriots to the Revolution was sublime as hope, that of the emigrant nobles was generous as despair. In civil wars we should ever judge each party by its own ideas, for civil wars are almost invariably the expression of two duties in opposition to each other. The duty of the patriots was their country; of the *emigrés*, the throne: one of the two parties was deceived as to its duty, but each believed it fulfilled it.

XIII.

The emigration was composed of two entirely distinct parties—the politicians and the combatants. The politicians, who crowded round the Comte de Provence and the Comte d'Artois, and poured forth idle invectives against the truths of philosophy and the principles of democracy. They wrote books and supported papers, in which the French Revolution was represented to the foreign sovereigns as an infernal conspiracy of a few scoundrels against kings, and even against heaven. They formed the councils of an imaginary government—they sought to obtain missions—they formed plans—renewed intrigues—visited every court—stirred up the sovereigns and their ministers against France—disputed the favor of the French princes—devoured their subsidies—and transported to this foreign soil the ambitions, the rivalries, and the cupidity of a court.

The military men had brought nothing but the bravery, the *insouciance*, the recklessness, and the polish of their nation and profession. Coblentz became the camp of illusion and devotion. This handful of brave men deemed themselves a nation; and prepared, by accustoming themselves to the manœuvres and fatigues of war, to conquer in a few days a whole monarchy. The emigrants of every country and every age have presented this spectacle; for emigration, like the desert, has its mirage. The emigrants believe that they have borne away their country on the soles of their shoes, to employ the language of Danton, but they carry away nought but its shadow, accumulate nothing but its anger, and find nothing but its pity.

XIV.

Amongst the first *emigrés*, three factions corresponded to these different parties in the emigration itself.

The Comte de Provence, afterwards Louis XVIII., was a philosophic prince—a politician and a diplomatist somewhat inclined towards innovation; an enemy of the nobility, of the priesthood: favorable to the aristocracy; and who would have pardoned the Revolution, if the Revolution itself would have pardoned royalty. His early infirmities closing the career of arms to him, he became addicted to politics—he cultivated his mind—he studied history—he wrote well, and foreseeing the approaching downfall, he predicted the probable death of Louis XVI.—he believed in the vicissitudes of the Revolution, and prepared himself to become the pacificator of his country, and the conciliator of the throne and liberty. His heart possessed all the qualities and all the faults of a woman—he needed friendship, and he gave himself favorites; but he chose them rather for their elegance than their merit, and saw men and things only through books and the hearts of courtiers. Somewhat theatrical, he exhibited himself as a statue of right and misfortune to all Europe; studied his attitudes; spoke learnedly of his adversaries; and assumed the position of a victim and a sage: he was, however, unpopular with the army.

XV.

The Comte d'Artois, his junior, spoiled by nature, by the court, and by the fair sex, had taken on himself the *rôle* of a hero. He represented at Coblentz antique honor, chivalrous devotion, and the French character; he was adored by the court, whose grace, elegance, and pride were personified in him: his heart was good, his mind apt, but not well-informed, and of limited comprehension. A philosopher, through indolence and carelessness before the Revolution, superstitious afterwards, through weakness and *entrainment,* he threatened the Revolution with his sword from a distance. He appeared more fitted to irritate than to conquer, and at this early period he already manifested that unbridled rashness and that useless spirit of provocation which was one day to cost him a throne. But his personal beauty, his grace, and his cordiality, covered all these defects, and he seemed destined never to die. Old in years he was fated to reign, and die, eternally young. He was the prince of youth: at another epoch he would have been Francis I., in his own he was Charles X.

The Prince de Condé was a soldier by birth, inclination, and profession. He despised these two courts, transposed to the banks of the Rhine, for his court was his camp. His son, the Duc de Bourbon, served his first campaign under his orders, and his grandson, the Duc d'Enghien, in his seventeenth year, acted as his aide-de-camp. This young prince was the representative of manly grace in the camp of the *emigrés;* his bravery, his enthusiasm, his generosity, all seemed to promise another hero to the heroic race of Condé. He was worthy of conquering in a cause not doomed, of dying sword in hand on the battle field, and not to fall, some years later, in the fosse at Vincennes, by the "lantern dimly burning," with no other friend than his dog, by the balls of a platoon of soldiers, ordered out at dead of night, as if for an assassination.

XVI.

Louis XVI. trembled in his palace at the shock of this war which he himself had proclaimed, and which lowered on the frontiers. He did not conceal from himself that he was less the chief than the hostage of France, and that his head and that of his children would be forfeited to the nation on the first reverse or peril. Danger sees treason on every side, and the public journals and the clubs denounced more vehemently than ever the existence of the *comitié Autrichien,* of which the queen was the centre. This report was universally believed by the nation, and not only cost the queen her popularity during the peace, but during the war it might cost her her life. Thus, formerly accused of betraying the peace, this unfortunate family was now accused of betraying the war. In false positions everything is in danger; the king comprehended the extent of his perils, and hastened to avert the most impending.

He despatched a secret emissary to the king of Prussia and the emperor, to entreat them, as they valued his safety, to suspend hostilities, and to precede the invasion by a conciliating manifesto, which might allow France to retire from the contest without disgrace, and would place the life of the royal family under the safeguard of the nation. This secret agent was Mallet-Dupan, a young journalist of Geneva, established in France, and mixed up with the counter-revolutionary movement. Mallet-Dupan was attached to the monarchy by principle, and to the king by personal devotion. He left Paris under pretext of returning to Geneva, and from thence went to Germany, where he had an interview with the Maréchal de Castries, the foreign confidant of Louis XVI., and one of the leaders of the *emigrés.* Accredited by the Duc de Castries, he presented himself at Coblentz to the Duke of Brunswick, at Frankfort to the ministers of the king of Prussia and the emperor; they however refused to place any faith in his communications, unless he produced a letter in the king's own hand. On this the king transmitted him a slip of paper, about two inches long, on which was written: "*The person who will produce this note knows my intentions; implicit credence may be given to all he says in my name.*" This royal sign of recognition gave Mallet-Dupan access to the cabinets of the coalition.

Conferences were opened between the French negotiator, the Comte de Cobentzel, the Comte d'Haugwitz, and General Heyman, the plenipotentiaries of the emperor, and the king of Prussia. These ministers, after having examined the credentials of Mallet-Dupan, listened to his communications. They were to the effect that "the king alike prayed and exhorted the *emigrés* not to cause the approaching war to lose its appearance of power against power, by taking part in it, in the name of the re-establishment of the monarchy. Any other line of conduct would produce a civil war, endanger the lives of the king and queen, destroy the throne, and occasion a general massacre of the royalists. The king added, that he besought the sovereigns who had taken up arms in his cause, to separate, in their manifesto, the faction of the Jacobins from the nation, and the liberty of the people from the anarchy that convulsed them; to declare formally and energetically to the Assembly, the administrative and municipal bodies, that their lives should be answerable for all and every attempt against the sacred persons of the king, the queen, and their children; and to announce to the nation that no dismemberment would follow the war, that they would treat for peace with the king alone, and that in consequence the Assembly should hasten to give him the most perfect liberty, in order to enable him to negotiate in the name of his people with the allied powers."

Mallet-Dupan explained the sense of these instructions with that enlightened good sense, and that devoted attachment to the king that marked him; he painted in the most lively colors the interior of the Tuileries, and the terror to which the royal family was a prey.

The negotiators were moved almost to tears, and promised to communicate these impressions to their sovereigns, and gave Mallet-Dupan the assurance that the intentions of the king should be the measure of the language which the manifesto of the coalition would address to the French nation.

They did not however dissimulate their astonishment at the

fact that the language of the emigrant princes at Coblentz was so opposed to the views of the king at Paris. "They openly manifest," said they, "the intention of re-conquering the kingdom for the counter-revolution, of rendering themselves independent, of dethroning their brother, and proclaiming a regency." The confidant of Louis XVI. left for Geneva after this conference; whilst the emperor, the king of Prussia, the principal princes of the confederation, the ministers, the generals, and the Duke of Brunswick, went to Mayence. Mayence, where the fêtes were interrupted by the councils, became for some days the head-quarters of the monarchs, and there, at the instigation of the *emigrés*, extreme resolutions were adopted. It was resolved to combat a revolution that but increased in proportion as it received indulgence. The supplications of Louis XVI., and the warnings of Dupan were forgotten, and the plan of the campaign was fixed.

XVII.

The emperor was to have the supreme control of the war in Belgium, where his army was to be commanded by the Duke of Saxe-Teschen. Fifteen thousand men were to cover the right of the Prussians, and effect a junction with them at Longwy. Twenty thousand more of the emperor's troops, commanded by the Prince de Hohenlohe, were to establish themselves between the Rhine and the Moselle, cover the Prussian left, and operate upon Landau, Sarrelouis, and Thionville. A third corps, under Prince Esterhazy, and strengthened by five thousand *emigrés* under the Prince de Condé, would threaten the frontiers from Switzerland to Philipsbourg, and the king of Sardinia would have an army of observation on the Var and the Isère. These dispositions made, it was resolved to reply to terror by terror, and to publish in the name of the generalissimo the Duke of Brunswick, a manifesto, which would leave the French Revolution no other alternative than submission or death.

M. de Calonne proposed it, and the Marquis de Limon, formerly intendant des finances to the Duke of Orleans, first an ardent revolutionist like his master, then an *emigré* and an implacable royalist, wrote the manifesto and submitted it to the emperor, who in his turn submitted it to the king of Prussia. The king of Prussia sent it to the Duke of Brunswick, who murmured, and demanded a modification of some of the expressions, which was accorded. The Marquis de Limon, however, supported by the French princes, again restored the text. The Duke of Brunswick became indignant, and tore the manifesto to pieces, without however daring to disavow it, and the manifesto appeared, with all its insults and threats, to the French nation.

The emperor and the king of Prussia, informed of the secret leaning of the Duke of Brunswick to France, and of the offer of the crown made to him by the factions, caused him to undertake the responsibility of this proclamation either as a vengeance or a disavowal. This imperious defiance of the kings to freedom threatened with death every national guard taken with arms in his hand, protecting the independence of his country, and that in case the least outrage was offered by the factions to the king, Paris should be razed to the ground.

BOOK XV.

I.

WHILST a war to the death impended over the people, and menaced the king, discord continued to reign in the councils of the ministers. The minister of war, Servan, was accused by Dumouriez with obeying with servility, which resembled love rather than complaisance, the influence of Madame Roland, and of having wholly defeated the plans for the invasion of Belgium. The friends of Madame Roland, on their side, threatened Dumouriez that they would make the Assembly demand of him an account of the six millions of secret expenses, whose destination they suspected. Already Guadet and Vergniaud had prepared discourses and a project of a decree to demand a public reckoning for these sums. Dumouriez, who had bought friends and accomplices with this gold amongst the Jacobins and the Feuillants, revolted against the suspicion, refused, in the name of his outraged honor, to make any return of this expenditure, and boldly offered his resignation. Upon this a great number of members of the Assembly, Feuillants and Jacobins, Pétion himself, called at the residence of the insulted minister, and conjured him to return to his post. He consented, on condition that they would leave the disposal of these funds to his conscience alone. The Girondists themselves, intimidated by his retirement, and feeling that a man of his character was indispensable to their weakness, withdrew their motion, and passed a vote of public confidence in him. The people applauded him as he quitted the Assembly. These applauses sounded gloomily in the council-chamber of Madame Roland. The popularity of Dumouriez rendered her jealous. It was not in her eyes the popularity of virtue, and she coveted it all for her husband and her party. Roland and his Girondist colleagues, Servan, Clavière, redoubled their efforts to influence the mind of the king, and used threats in order to acquire it. To flatter the Assembly, court the people; irritate the Jacobins against the court; beset the king by the imperious demand of sacrifices which they knew were impossible; to injure him silently in opinion as the cause of all evil, or the obstacle to all good; to compel him, in fact, by insolence and outrage, to dismiss them, that they might afterwards accuse him of betraying in them the Revolution; such were their tactics, resulting from their weakness rather than from their ambition.

This feeling of backing the king, whose ministers they were, was the basis of a conspiracy of which Madame Roland was the origin. At Roland's there was nothing but ill humor; amongst his colleagues it was a rivalry of patriotism with Robespierre. At Madame Roland's it was that passion for a republic which was impatient of any remnant of a throne, and which smiled complacently at the factions ready to overturn the monarchy. When factions had arms no longer, Madame Roland and her friends hastened to lead them.

II.

We see a fatal example in the step of the minister of war, Servan. He, entirely controlled by Madame Roland, proposed to the National Assembly, without authority from the king, or the consent of the council, to assemble round Paris a camp of 20,000 troops. This army, composed of *fédérés* chosen from amongst the most enthusiastic persons of the provinces, would be, as the Girondists believed, a kind of central army of opinions devoted to the Assembly, counterbalancing the king's guard, repressing the national guard, and recalling to mind that army of the parliament which, under the orders of Cromwell, had conducted Charles I. to the scaffold.

The Assembly, with the exception of the constitutional party, seized on this idea as hatred seizes the arm which is offered to it. The king felt the blow; Dumouriez saw through the perfidy, and could not repress his choler against Servan in the council-chamber. His reproaches were those of a loyal defender of his king. The replies of Servan were evasive, but full of provocation. The two ministers laid their hands upon their swords, and but for the presence of the king, and the intervention of their colleagues, blood would have flowed in the council-chamber.

The king was desirous of refusing his sanction to the decree for the 20,000 men. "It is too late," said Dumouriez; "your refusal would display fears too well founded, but which we must take care not to betray to our enemies. Sanction the decree, I will undertake to neutralize the danger of the concentration." The king requested time for consideration.

Next day the Girondists called upon the king to sanction the decree against the nonjuring priests. They came into direct contact with the religious conscience of Louis XVI. Supported by that, this prince declared that he would rather die than sign the persecution of the church. Dumouriez insisted as much as the Girondists in obtaining this sanction. The king was inflexible. In vain did Dumouriez represent to him that by refusing legal measures against the nonjuring priests he exposed the priests to massacre, and thus made himself responsible for all the blood that might be shed. In vain did they represent to him that this refusal would render the ministry unpopular, and thus deprive them of all hope of saving the monarchy. In vain did they appeal to the queen, and implore her, by her feelings as a mother, to bend the king to their wishes. The queen herself was for a long time powerless. At last the king seemed to hesitate, and gave Dumouriez a private meeting in the evening. In this conversation he ordered Dumouriez to present to him three ministers, to succeed Roland, Clavière, and Servan. Dumouriez at once named Vergennes for finance, Naillac for foreign affairs, Mourgues for the interior. He reserved the war department for himself: dictatorial minister at the moment when France was becoming an army. Roland, Clavière, and Servan, stung to the quick at a dismissal they had provoked the more because they had not anticipated it, hastened to carry their complaints and accusations to the Assembly. They were received there as martyrs to their patriotism; they had filled the tribunes with their partisans.

III.

Roland, Clavière, and Servan were present, under pretence of rendering an account of the grounds of their dismissal. Roland laid before the Assembly the celebrated confidential letter dictated by his wife, and which he had read to the king in his cabinet. He affected to believe that the dismissal of ministers was the punishment of his own courage. The advice he gave to the king in this letter thus turned into accusations of this unfortunate prince. Louis XVI. had never received from the malcontents a more terrible blow than that now given by his minister. Passions trouble the conscience of the people, and there are days when treachery passes current for heroism. The Girondists made a hero of Roland. They had his letter printed, and circulated it in the eighty-three departments.

Roland left the chamber amidst loud applauses. Dumouriez entered it in the midst of uproar. He displayed in the tribune the same calmness as in the field of battle. He began by announcing to the Assembly the death of General Gouvion. "He is happy," he said, with sadness, "to have died fighting against the enemy, and not to have been the witness of the discords which rend us to pieces. I envy his death." The deep serenity of a powerful mind was felt in his every tone—a mind resolute to contend against factions unto death. He then read a memorial relating to the ministry of war. His exordium was an attack upon the Jacobins, and a claim for the respect due to the ministers of the executive power. "Do you hear Cromwell!" exclaimed Guadet, in a voice of thunder. "He thinks himself already so sure of empire, that he dares to inflict his commands upon us." "And why not?" retorted Dumouriez, proudly, and turning towards the Mountain. His daring imposed on the Assembly. The Feuillant deputies went out with him to the Tuileries. The king announced to him his intention to give his sanction to the decree for the 20,000 men. As to the decree of the priests, he repeated to the ministers that he had resolved, and begged them to take to the president of the Assembly a letter in his own writing, which contained the motives for his *veto*. The ministers bowed, and separated in consternation.

IV.

When Dumouriez reached his house, he learnt that there had been gatherings of the populace in the Faubourg St. Antoine, and he informed the king, who believing that he intended to alarm him, lost his confidence in Dumouriez, who instantly offered his resignation, which the king accepted. The portfolio of the ministry of foreign affairs was confided to Chambonas; that of war to Lajard, a soldier of La Fayette's party; that of the interior to M. de Monciel, a constitutional Feuillant and friend of the king. This was on the 17th of June. The Jacobins, the people incited by the Girondists, were already disturbing the capital: all announced a coming insurrection. These ministers, without any armed force, without popularity, without party, thus accepted the responsibility of the perils accumulated by their predecessors. The king saw Dumouriez once again—it was the last time. The farewell between the monarch and his minister was affecting.

"You are going to the army?" said the king. "Yes, sire," replied Dumouriez, "and I should leave with joy this fearful city, if I had not a feeling of the dangers impending over your majesty. Deign to listen to me, sire; I am never destined to see you again. I am fifty-three years of age, and have much experience. They abuse your conscience with respect to the decree against the priests, and are pushing you on to civil war. You are without strength, defenceless, and you will sink under it, whilst History, though full of commiseration for you, will accuse you of the misfortunes of your people."

The king was seated near a table where he had just signed the general's accounts. Dumouriez was standing beside him with clasped hands. The king took his hands in his own, and said to him, in a voice sorrowful but resigned, "God is my witness, that I only think of the happiness of France." "I never doubted it, sire," responded Dumouriez, deeply affected. "You owe an account to God, not only for the purity, but also for the enlightened use, of your intentions. You think to save religion: you destroy it. The priests will be massacred: your crown will be taken from you; perhaps even your queen and children——." He did not finish, but pressed his lips to the king's hand, who shed tears.

"I await—expect death," replied the king sorrowfully; "and I pardon my enemies already. I am grateful to you for your sensibility. You have served me well, and I esteem you. Adieu—be more happy than I am!" And on saying these words Louis XVI. went to a recess in a window at the end of the chamber, in order to conceal the trouble he felt. Dumouriez never saw him again. He shut himself up for several days in retirement, in a lonely quarter of Paris. Looking upon the army as the only refuge for a citizen still capable of serving his country, he set out for Douai, the head-quarters of Luckner.

V.

The Girondists remained a moment overwhelmed by the humiliation of their fall and the joy of their coming vengeance. "Here I am dismissed," was Roland's exclamation to his wife on his return home. "I have but one regret, and that is, that our delays have prevented us from taking the initiative." Madame Roland retired to a humble apartment, without losing any of her influence and without regretting power, since she carried with her into her retreat, her genius, her patriotism, and her friends. With her the conspiracy only changed place; from the ministry of the interior she passed at once into the small council which she gathered about her, and inspired with her own earnest enthusiasm.

This circle daily increased. The admiration for the woman mingled in the hearts of her friends with the attraction of liberty. They adored in her the future Republic. The love which these young men did not avow for her made, unknown to her, a portion of their politics. Ideas only become active and powerful when vivified by sentiment. She was the sentiment of her party.

This party was joined about this time by a man unconnected with the Gironde; but his youth, his remarkable beauty, and his energy naturally threw him into this faction of illusion and love, controlled by a woman. This young man was Barbaroux.

At this time he was only twenty-six years of age. Born at Marseilles, of a sea-faring family, who preserved in their manners and features something of the boldness of their life and the agitation of their element. The elegance of his stature, the poetic grace of his countenance, recalled the accomplished forms which antiquity adored in the statues of Antinous. The blood of that Asiatic Greece of which Marseilles is a colony revealed itself in the purity of the young Phocian's profile.* As richly endowed with the gifts of the mind as those of the body, Barbaroux early used himself to public oratory, that gift of the men of the south. He became a barrister and pleaded several causes with success; but the power and honesty of his mind revolted from that exercise of eloquence, so often mercenary, which simulates earnestness. He required a national cause, to which a man should give with language his soul and blood. The Revolution with which he was born offered this to him. He awaited with impatience the occasion and the hour to make use of it.

His youth still kept him away from the scene into which he ardently longed to cast himself. He passed his time near the village of Ollioules, on a small family estate, concealed beneath tall cork trees, which threw their slight shade over the calcined declivities of this valley. He there attended to the cultivated patches which the aridity of the soil and the burning sun dispute with the rocks. In his leisure he studied natural sciences, and kept up a correspondence with two Swiss, whose systems of physics then occupied the learned world—M. de Saussure and Marat. But science was not sufficient for his mind, which overflowed with sensitiveness, and which Barbaroux poured forth in elegiac poetry as burning as the noonday, and vague as the horizon of the sea beneath his view. There is felt that southern melancholy whose languor is closer allied to pleasure than weakness, and which resembles the songs of man seated in the broad sunshine, before or after labor. Mirabeau had thus begun his life. The most energetic lives frequently open in gloom, as if they had in their very germ presentiments of their contrary destiny. It would seem as though we read in the verses of this young man that through his tears he contemplated his faults, his expiation, and his scaffold.

VI.

After Mirabeau's election, and the agitations which fol-

* The Marseillais trace their origin to a colony of Phocians in the 1st year of the 43d Olympiad, 599 years B. C. It was the Massilia of the Romans, and called by Cicero the "mistress of Gaul," and by Pliny, the "mistress of education."—H. T. R.

lowed, Barbaroux was named secretary of the municipality of Marseilles. At the troubles of Arles he took arms, and marched at the head of the young Marseillais against the rulers of the Comtal. His martial figure, his gestures, his ardor, his voice, made him conspicuous everywhere: he fascinated all. Being deputed to Paris in order to give an account of the events of the south to the National Assembly, the Girondists, Vergniaud and Guadet, who were desirous of obtaining an amnesty for the crimes of Avignon, did all in their power to attach this young man to their party. Barbaroux, impetuous as he was, did not justify the butchers of Avignon; but detested the victims. He was a man requisite to the Girondists. Struck by his eloquence and his enthusiasm, they presented him to Madame Roland: no woman was more formed to seduce, no man more formed to be seduced. Madame Roland—in all the freshness of her youth, in all the brilliancy of her beauty, and also in all the fulness of sensibility, which all the purity of her life could not stifle in her unoccupied heart—speaks thus tenderly of Barbaroux: "I had read," she says, "in the cabinet of my husband, the letters of Barbaroux, full of sense and premature wisdom. When I saw him I was astonished at his youth. He attached himself to my husband. We saw more of him after we left the ministry; and it was then, that reasoning on the miserable state of things, and the fear of a triumph of despotism in the north of France, we formed the plan of a republic in the south. This will be our *pis aller*, said Barbaroux, with a smile; but the Marseillais army here will dispense with our attempting it."

VII.

Roland then lived in a gloomy house of the Rue St. Jaques, almost in the garrets: it was a philosopher's retreat, and his wife illumined it. Present at all the conversations of Roland, she witnessed the conferences between her husband and the young Marseillais. Barbaroux thus relates the interview in which the first idea of a republic was mooted: "That astonishing woman was there," said he. "Roland asked me what I thought the best means of saving France. I opened my heart to him: my confidence called for his. 'Liberty is gone,' he replied, 'if we do not speedily disconcert the plots of the court. La Fayette is meditating treason in the north: the army of the centre is systematically disorganized: in six weeks the Austrians will be at Paris. Have we then labored at the most glorious of revolutions for so many years to see it overthrown in a single day? If Liberty dies in France, it is lost forever to the rest of the world!—all the hopes of philosophy are deceived—prejudices and tyranny will again grasp the world. Let us prevent this misfortune, and if the north is subjected, let us take Liberty with us into the south, and there form a colony of free men.' His wife wept as she listened to him, and I myself wept as I looked at her. Oh! how much the outpourings of confidence console and fortify minds that are in desolation. I drew a rapid sketch of the resources and hopes of Liberty in the south. A serene expression of joy spread over Roland's brow: he squeezed my hand, and we traced on a map of France the limits of this empire of Liberty, which extended from the Doubs, the Ain, and the Rhone to La Dordogne, and from the inaccessible mountains of Auvergne to Durance and the sea. I wrote, by dictation of Roland, to request from Marseilles a battalion and two pieces of cannon. These preliminaries agreed upon, I left Roland with feelings of deep respect for himself and his wife. I have seen them subsequently, during their second ministry, as simple minded as in their humble retreat. Of all the men of modern times, Roland seems to me most to resemble Cato; but it must be owned that it is to his wife that his courage and talents are due."

Thus did the original idea of a federative republic arise in the first interview between Barbaroux and Madame Roland. What they dreamed of as a desperate measure of Liberty, was afterwards made a reproach to them for having conspired as a plot. This first sigh of patriotism of two young minds who met and understood each other, was their attraction and their crime.

VIII.

From this day the Girondists, disengaged from every obligation with the king and ministers, conspired secretly with Madame Roland, and publicly in the tribune, for the suppression of the monarchy. They appeared to envy the Jacobins the honor of giving the throne the most deadly blows. Robespierre as yet spoke only of the constitution, limiting himself within the law, and not going ahead of the people. The Girondists already spoke in the name of the republic, and motioned with gesture and eye the republican *coup* *d'état*, which every day drew nearer. The meetings at Roland's multiplied and enlarged: new men joined their ranks. Roland, Brissot, Vergniaud, Guadet, Gensonné, Condorcet, Pétion, Lanthenas, who in the hour of danger betrayed them; Valazé, Pache, who persecuted and decimated his friends; Grangeneuve, Louvet, who beneath levity of manners and gayety of mind veiled undaunted courage; Chamfort, the intimate of the great, a vivid intellect, heart full of venom, discouraged by the people before he had served it; Carra, the popular journalist, enthusiastic for a republic, mad with desire for liberty; Chénier,* the poet of the Revolution, destined to survive it, and preserving his worship of it until death, even under the tyranny of the empire; Dusaulx, who had beneath his gray hairs the enthusiasm of youth for philosophy—the Nestor of all the young men, whom he moderated by his sage exhortations; Mercier, who took all as a jest, even in the dungeon and death.

IX.

But of the men whom enthusiasm for the Revolution brought around her, he whom Madame Roland preferred to all was Buzot. More attached to this young female than to his party, Buzot was to her a friend, whilst the others were but tools or accomplices. She had quickly passed her judgment on Barbaroux, and this judgment, impressed with a certain bitterness, was like a repentance for the secret impression which the favorable exterior of this young man had at first inspired. She accuses herself with finding him so handsome, and seems to fortify her heart against the fascination of his looks. "Barbaroux is volatile," she said; "the adoration he receives from worthless women destroys the seriousness of his feelings. When I see such fine young men too conceited at the impression they make, like Barba-

* M. Lamartine does not here refer to André Chénier, an admirable lyric poet, from whom he has quoted at page 336; *he* was a Royalist, and as such condemned and guillotined in July 1794, in his thirty-second year. He had a brother, Joseph Chénier, his junior by two years, who was an enthusiastic republican, and wrote and brought out, from 1785 to 1795, a great many tragedies, viz. *Charles IX.*, *Calas*, *Henry VIII.*, *Timoleon*, *Tibère*, &c., and was elected member of the legislative assemblies from 1792 to 1802. He fell under Napoleon's displeasure, and he dismissed him from his appointment as inspector-general of public instruction, in 1803. The consul was becoming imperial in his aspirations. Joseph Chénier died in 1811, consistent to the last in his republican notions.—H. T. R.

roux and Hérault de Séchelles, I cannot help thinking that they adore themselves too much to have a great deal of adoration left for their country."

If we may lift the veil from the heart of this virtuous woman, who does not raise it herself for fear of developing a sentiment contrary to her duties, we must be convinced that her instinctive inclination had been one moment for Barbaroux, but her reflecting tenderness was for Buzot. It is neither given to duty nor liberty to fill completely the soul of a woman as lovely and impassioned as she: duty chills, politics deceive, virtue retains, love fills the heart. Madame Roland loved Buzot. He adored in her his inspiration and his idol. Perchance they never disclosed to each other in words a sentiment which would have been the less sacred to them from the hour in which it had become guilty. But what they concealed from one another they have involuntarily revealed at their death. There are in the last days and last hours of this man and this woman, sighs, gestures, and words, which allow the secret preserved during life to escape in the presence of death; but the secret thus disclosed keeps its mystery. Posterity may have the right to detect, but none to accuse, this sentiment.

Roland, an estimable but morose old man, had the exactions of weakness without having its gratitude or indulgence towards his partner. She remained faithful to him, more from respect to herself than from affection to him. They loved the same cause—Liberty; but Roland's fanaticism was as cold as pride, whilst his wife's was as glowing as love. She sacrificed herself daily at the shrine of her husband's reputation, and scarcely perceived her own self-devotion. He read in her heart that she bore the yoke with pride, and yet the yoke galled her. She paints Buzot with complacency, and as the ideal of domestic happiness. "Sensible, ardent, melancholy," she writes, "a passionate admirer of nature, he seems born to give and share happiness. This man would forget the universe in the sweetness of private virtues. Capable of sublime impulses and unvarying affections, the vulgar, who like to depreciate what it cannot equal, accuse him of being a dreamer. Of sweet countenance, elegant figure, there is always in his attire that care, neatness, and propriety, which announce the respect of self as well as of others. Whilst the dregs of the nation elevate the flatterers and corrupters of the people to station—whilst cutthroats swear, drink, and clothe themselves in rags, in order to fraternize with the populace, Buzot possesses the morality of Socrates, and maintains the decorum of Scipio: so they pull down his house and banish him, as they did Aristides. I am astonished they have not issued a decree that his name should be forgotten." The man of whom she speaks in such terms from the depths of her dungeon, on the evening before her death, exiled, wandering, concealed in the caves of St. Emilion, fell as though struck by lightning, and remained several days in a state of frenzy, on learning the death of Madame Roland.

Danton, whose name began to rise above the crowd, when his fame was but slight until now, sought at this period Madame Roland's acquaintance. All inquired what was the secret of the growing ascendency of this man? Where he came from? Who he was? Whither he was advancing? They sought his origin; his first appearance on the stage of the people; his first connection with the celebrated personages of his time. They sought in mysteries the cause of his prodigious popularity. It was pre-eminently in his nature.

X.

Danton was not merely one of those adventurers of demagoguism who rise, like *Masaniello*, or like Hébert,* from the boiling scum of the masses. He was one of the middle classes, the heart of the nation. His family, pure, honest, of property, and industrious, ancient in name, honorable in manners, was established at Arcis-sur-Aube, and possessed a rural domain in the environs of that small town. It was of the number of those modest but well-esteemed families, who have the soil for their basis, and agriculture as their main occupation, but who give their sons the most complete moral and literary education, and who thus prepare them for the liberal professions of society. Danton's father died young. His mother had married again to a manufacturer of Arcis-sur-Aube, who had (and himself managed) a small cotton mill. There is still to be seen near the river, without the city, in a pleasant spot, the house, half rustic half town built, and the garden on the banks of the Aube, where Danton's infancy was passed.

His step-father, M. Ricordin, attended to his education as he would have done that of his own child. He was of an open communicative disposition, and was beloved in

* Editor of the infamous Père Duchesne.--H. T. R.

spite of his ugliness and turbulence; for his ugliness was radiant with intellect, and his turbulence was calmed and repented of at the least caress of his mother. He pursued his studies at Troyes, the capital of Champagne. Rebellious against discipline, idle at study, beloved by his masters and fellow pupils, his rapid comprehension kept him on an equality with the most assiduous. His instinct sufficed without reflection. He learned nothing; he acquired all. His companions called him Catiline—he accepted the name, and sometimes played with them at getting up rebellions and riots, which he excited or calmed by his harangues—as if he were repeating at school the characters of his after life.

XI.

M. and Madame Ricordin, already advanced in years, gave him, after his education was finished, the small fortune of his father. He came to finish his studies in law at Paris, and bought a place in parliament as a barrister, where he practised little and without any notoriety. He despised chicanery; his mind and language had the proportions of the great causes of the people and the throne. The Constituent Assembly began to stir them. Danton, watchful and impassioned, was anxious to mingle with them: he sought the leading men, whose eloquence resounded throughout France. He attached himself to Mirabeau; became connected with Camille Desmoulins, Marat, Robespierre, Pétion, Brune (afterwards the marshal), Fabre d'Eglantine, the Duc d'Orleans, Laclos, Lacroix, and all the illustrious and second class orators who then "fulmined over" Paris. He passed his whole time in the tribunes of the Assembly, in the walks, and the coffee-houses, and his nights in the clubs. A few well-seasoned words, some brief harangues, some bursts of mysterious lightning: and above all, his hair like a horse's mane, his gigantic stature, and his powerful voice, made him universally remarked. Yet beneath the purely physical qualities of the orator men of intelligence remarked great good sense, and an instinctive knowledge of the human heart. Beneath the agitator they discerned the statesman. Danton, in truth, read history, studied the ancient orators, practised himself in real eloquence, that which enlightens in its passion, and beneath his actual part was preparing another much superior. He only asked the movement to raise him so high that he might subsequently control it.

He married Mademoiselle Charpentier, daughter of a lemonade-seller on the Quai de l'Ecole. This young lady controlled him by her affection, and insensibly reformed him from the disorders of his youth to more regular domestic habits. She extinguished the violence of his passions, but without being able to quench that which survived all others —ambition of a great destiny.

Danton lived in a small apartment in the Cour de Commerce, near his father-in-law, in rigid economy, receiving but a very few friends, who admired his talent and attached themselves to his fortunes. The most constant were Camille Desmoulins, Pétion, and Brune. From these meetings went forth signals of extensive sedition. The secret subsidies of the court came there to tempt the cupidity of the head of the young revolutionists. He did not reject them, but used them sometimes to excite and sometimes to control the agitations of opinion.

He had by this marriage two sons, whom his death left orphans in their cradle, and who succeeded to his small inheritance at Arcis-sur-Aube. These two sons of Danton, alarmed at the effects of their name, retired to their family domain, and cultivated it with their own hands, and in an honest and industrious obscurity limited to themselves all their father's notoriety. Like the son of Cromwell, they preferred the shade and silence the more, as their name had a too sinister reputation, and too wide an extension in the world. They remained unmarried, that the name might die with them.

At this moment Danton, whose ambitious instincts revealed the close return to fortune of the Girondists, sought to attach himself to this rising party, and give them the weight of his worth and importance. Madame Roland flattered him, but with fear and repugnance, as a woman would pat a lion.

XII.

Whilst the Girondists were exciting the anger of the people against the king, hostilities were beginning in Belgium, in consequence of reverses, which were attributed to treasons of the court: these were produced by three causes; the hesitation of the generals, who did not understand how to impart to their troops that ardor which impels the masses, and bears down resistance; the disorganization of the armies, which emigration had deprived of their ancient officers, and who had no confidence in the new; and finally, the want of discipline, that element of revolutions, which clubs and Jacobinism had spread amongst the troops. An army that discusses is like a hand which would think.

La Fayette, instead of advancing at once on Namur, according to Dumouriez's plan, lost a good deal of precious time in assembling and organizing at Givet, and the camp of Ransenne. Instead of giving the other generals in line with him, the example and the signal of invasion and victory, by at once occupying Namur, he moved about the country with 10,000 men, leaving the remainder of his forces encamped in France, and fell back at the first news of the checks sustained by the detachments of Biron and Théobald Dillon. These checks, though partial and slight, were disgraceful for our troops. It was the astonishment of an army unaccustomed to war, and fearful of entering the lists, but which, like a soldier at his first campaign, would soon grow used to battles.

The Duc de Lauzun commanded under La Fayette, and was called General Biron. He was a man of the court, who had gone over in all sincerity to the side of the people. Young, handsome, chivalrous, with that intrepid gayety which plays with death, he carried aristocratic honor into republican ranks. Loved by the soldiers, adored by the women, at his ease in camps, a roué in courts, he was of that school of sparkling vices of which the Marshal de Richelieu had been the type in France. It was said that the queen herself had been enamored of him, without being able to fix his inconstancy. Friend of the Duc d'Orleans, companion of his debaucheries, still he had never conspired with him. All treachery was abhorrent to him, all baseness of heart roused his utmost indignation. He adopted the Revolution as a noble idea, of which he was always ready to be the soldier, but never the accomplice. He did not betray the king, and always preserved a deep feeling of pity and sympathy for the queen; with an intense love for philosophy and liberty, instead of fomenting them by sedition, he defended them by war. He changed devotion to kings into devotion to his country. This noble cause, and the sorrows of the Revolution, gave to his character a more manly stamp, and made him fight and die with the conscience of a hero.

He was encamped at Quievrain with 10,000 men, and advanced against the Austrian general Beaulieu, who occupied the heights of Mons, with a very weak army. Two regiments of dragoons, who formed Biron's advanced guard, were seized with a sudden panic on beholding Beaulieu's troops. The soldiers cried out treachery, and in vain did their officers attempt to rally them; they turned bridle and scattered disorder and fear throughout the ranks. The entire army gave way and mechanically followed the current of flight. Biron and his aides-de-camp threw themselves into the centre of the troops to stay and to rally them. They struck at them with their swords, and fired at them. The camp of Quievrain, the military chest, the carriage of Biron himself, were plundered by the fugitives.

Whilst this defeat, without a battle, humiliated the French army, in its first step, at Quievrain, bloody assassinations stained our flag at Lille. General Dillon had left that city, the enemy showed itself on the plain to the number of nine hundred men. At its appearance only, the French cavalry uttered treacherous cries, and passing by the infantry, fled to Lille, without being followed, abandoning its artillery, carriages, and baggage. Dillon, hurried along by his squadrons to Lille, was there massacred by his own soldiers. His colonel of engineers, Berthois, fell beside his general, beneath the bayonets of the cowards who abandoned him. The dead bodies of these two victims of fear were hung up in the *Place d'Armes*, and then delivered up by the malcontents to the insults of the populace of Lille, who dragged their mutilated carcasses along the streets. Thus commenced in shame and crime those wars of the Revolution which were destined to produce, during twenty years, so much heroism, and so much military virtue. Anarchy had penetrated to the camps, honor was there no longer; order and honor are the two necessities of an army. In anarchy there is still a nation—without discipline there is no longer an army.

XIII.

Paris was in consternation at this news; the Assembly greatly troubled, the Girondists trembled, the Jacobins were vociferous in their imprecations against the traitors. Foreign courts and the emigrants had no doubt of an easy triumph in a few marches over a revolution which was afraid of its very shadow. La Fayette, without having been attacked, fell back, very prudently, on Givet. Rochambeau sent in his resignation as commandant of the army of the north.

Marshal Luckner was nominated in his place. La Fayette, much dissatisfied, kept the command of the central army.

Luckner was upwards of seventy years of age, but retained all the fire and activity of the warrior; he only required genius to have been a great general. He had a reputation for complaisance, which sufficed for everything. It is a great advantage for a general to be a stranger in the country in which he is serving. He has no one jealous of him: his superiority is pardoned, and presumed if it do not exist, in order to crush his rivals: such was old Luckner's position. He was a German,—pupil of the great Frederic, with whom he had served with *éclat* during the seven years' war, as commandant of the vanguard, at the moment when Frederic changed the war, and commenced its tactics. The Duc de Choiseul was desirous of depriving Prussia of a general of this great school, to teach the modern art of battles to French generals. He had attracted Luckner from his country by force of temptations, fortune, and honors. The National Assembly, from respect to the memory of the philosopher king, had preserved to Luckner the pension of 60,000 francs which had been paid to him during the Revolution. Luckner, indifferent to constitutions, believed himself a revolutionist from gratitude. He was almost the only one amongst the ancient general officers who had not emigrated. Surrounded by a brilliant staff of young officers of the party of La Fayette, Charles Lameth, du Jarri, Mathieu de Montmorency, he believed he had the opinions which they instilled into him. The king caressed, the Assembly flattered, the army respected, him. The nation saw in him the mysterious genius of the old war coming to give lessons of victory to the untried patriotism of the Revolution, and concealing its infinite resources under the bluntness of his exterior, and the obscure Germanism of his language. They addressed to him, from all sides, homage as though he were an unknown God. He did not deserve either this adoration, or the outrages with which he was soon after overwhelmed. He was a brave and coarse soldier, as misplaced in courts as in clubs. For some days he was an idol, then the plaything of the Jacobins, who, at last, threw him to the guillotine, without his being able to comprehend either his popularity or his crime.

XIV.

Berthier, who afterwards became Napoleon's right hand.

was then the head of Luckner's staff. The old general seized, with warlike instinct, on Dumouriez's bold plan. He had entered at the head of 22,000 men on the Austrian territory at Courtray and Menin. Biron and Valence, his two seconds in command, entreated him to remain there, and Dumouriez, in his letters, urged him in similar manner. On arriving at Lille, Dumouriez learnt that Luckner had suddenly retreated on Valenciennes, after having burnt the suburbs of Courtray; thus giving, on our frontier, the signal of hesitation and retreat.

The Belgian population, their impulses thus checked by the disasters or timidity of France, lost all hope, and bent beneath the Austrian yoke. General Montesquieu collected the army of the south with difficulty. The king of the Sardinians concentrated a large force on the Var. The advanced guard of La Fayette, posted at Gliswel, at a league from Maubeuge, was beaten by the Duke of Saxe-Teschen, at the head of 12,000 men. The great invasion of the Duke of Brunswick, in Champagne, was preparing. The emigration took off the officers, desertion diminished our soldiery. The clubs disseminated distrust against the commanders of our strong places.

The Girondists were urging on rebellion, the Jacobins were exciting the army to anarchy, the volunteers did not rise, the ministry was null, the Austrian committee of the Tuileries corresponded with various powers, not to deceive the nation, but to save the lives of the king and his family. A suspected government, hostile Assembly, seditious clubs, a national guard intimidated and deprived of its chief, incendiary journalism, dark conspiracies, factious municipality, a conspirator-mayor, people distrustful and starving, Robespierre and Brissot, Vergniaud and Danton, Girondists and Jacobins, face to face, having the same spoil to contend for —the monarchy, and struggling for pre-eminence in demagoguism in order to acquire the favor of the people; such was the state of France, within and without, at the moment when exterior war was pressing France on all sides, and causing it to burst forth with disasters and crimes. The Girondists and Jacobins united for a moment, suspended their personal animosity, as if to see which could best destroy the powerless constitution which separated them. The *bourgeoisie*, personified by the Feuillants, the national guard, and La Fayette, alone remained attached to the constitution. The Gironde, from the tribune itself, made that appeal to the people against the king which it was subsequently doomed to make in vain in favor of the king against the Jacobins. In order to control the city, Brissot, Roland, Pétion, excited the suburbs, those capitals of miseries and seditions. Every time that a people which has long crouched in slavery and ignorance is moved to its lowest depths, then appear monsters and heroes, prodigies of crime and prodigies of virtue; such were about to appear under the con spiring hand of the Girondists and demagogues.

BOOK XVI.

I.

In proportion as power snatched from the hands of the king by the Assembly disappeared, it passed into the commune of Paris. The municipality, that first element of nations which are forming themselves, is also the last asylum of authority when they are crumbling tô pieces. Before it falls quite to the people, power pauses for a moment in the council-chamber of the magistrates of the city. The Hôtel de Ville had become the Tuileries of the people; after La Fayette and Bailly, Pétion reigned there: this man was the king of Paris. The populace (which has always the instinct of position) called him *King Pétion.* He had purchased his popularity, first by his private virtues, which the people almost always confound with public virtues, and subsequently by his democratic speeches in the Constituent Assembly. The skilful balance which he preserved at the Jacobins, between the Girondists and Robespierre, had rendered him respectable and important. Friend of Roland, Robespierre, Danton, and Brissot, at the same time suspected of too close connection with Madame de Genlis and the Duc d'Orleans' party, he still always covered himself with the mantle of proper devotion to order and a superstitious reverence for the constitution. He had thus all the apparent titles to the esteem of honest men and the respect of factions; but the greatest of all was in his mediocrity. Mediocrity, it must be confessed, is almost always the brand of these idols of the people: either that the mob, mediocre itself, has only a taste for what resembles it; or that jealous cotemporaries can never elevate themselves sufficiently high towards great characters and great virtues; or that Providence, which distributes gifts and faculties in proportion, will not allow that one man should unite in himself, amidst a free people, these three irresistible powers, virtue, genius, and popularity; or rather, that the constant favor of the multitude is a thing of such a nature that its price is beyond its worth in the eyes of really virtuous men, and that it is necessary to stoop too low to pick it up, and become too weak to retain it. Pétion was only king of the people on condition of being complaisant to its excesses. His functions as mayor of Paris, in a time of trouble, placed him constantly between the king, the Assembly, and the revolts. He bearded the king, flattered the Assembly, and pardoned crime. Inviolable as the capital which he personified in his position of first magistrate of the commune, his unseen dictatorship had no other title than his inviolability, and he used it with respectful boldness towards the king, bowed before the Assembly, and knelt to the malcontents. To his official reproaches to the rioters, he always added an excuse for crime, a smile for the culprits, encouragement to the misled citizens. The people loved him as anarchy loves weakness; it knew it could do as it pleased with him. As mayor, he had the law in his hand; as a man, he had indulgence on his lips and connivance in his heart: he was just the magistrate required in times of the *coups d'état* of the faubourgs.

Pétion allowed them to make all their preparations without appearing to see them, and legalized them whenever they were completed.

II.

His early connection with Brissot had drawn him towards Madame Roland. The ministry of Roland, Clavière, and Servan obeyed him more than even the king; he was present at all their consultations, and although their fall did not involve him, it wrested the executive power from his grasp. The expelled Girondists had no need to infuse their thirst of vengeance into the mind of Pétion. Unable any longer to conspire legally against the king, with his ministers, he yet could conspire with the factions against the Tuileries. The national guards, the people, the Jacobins, the faubourgs, the whole city, were in his hands; thus he could give sedition to the Girondists to aid his party to regain the ministry; and he gave it them with all the hazards—all the crimes that sedition carries with it. Amongst these hazards was the assassination of the king and his family: this event was beforehand accepted by those who provoked the assembly of the populace, and their invasion of the king's palace. Girondists, Orleanists, Republicans, Anarchists, none of these parties perhaps actually meditated this crime, but they looked upon it as an eventuality of their fortune. Pétion, who doubtless did not desire it, at least risked it; and if his intention was innocent, his temerity was a murder. What distance was there between the steel of twenty thousand pikes and the heart of Louis XVI.? Pétion did not betray the lives of the king, the queen, and the children, but he placed them at stake. The constitutional guard of the king had been ignominiously disbanded by the Girondists; the Duc de Brissac, its commander, was sent to the high court of Orleans, for imaginary conspiracies,—his only conspiracy was his honor; and he had sworn to die bravely in defence of his master and his friend. He could have escaped, but though even the king advised him to fly, he refused. "If I fly," replied he, to the king's entreaties, "it will be said that I am guilty, and that you are my accomplice; my flight will accuse you: I prefer to die." He left Paris for the national court of Orleans: he was not tried, but massacred at Versailles, on the 6th of September, and his head with its white hairs was planted on one of the palisades of the palace gates, as if in atrocious mockery of that chivalrous honor that even in death guarded the gate of the residence of his king.

III.

The first insurrections of the Revolution were the spontaneous impulses of the people: on one side was the king, the court, and the nobility; on the other the nation. These two parties clashed by the mere impulse of conflicting ideas and interests. A word—a gesture—a chance—the assembling a body of troops—a day's scarcity—the vehement address of an orator in the Palais Royal, sufficed to excite the populace to revolt, or to march on Versailles. The spirit of sedition was confounded with the spirit of the Revolution. Every one was factious—every one was a sol dier—every one was a leader. Public passion gave the signal, and chance commanded.

Since the Revolution was accomplished, and the constitution had imposed on each party legal order, it was different. The insurrections of the people were no longer agitations. but plans. The organized factions had their partisans—their clubs—their assemblies—their army and their password. Amongst the citizens, anarchy had disciplined itself, and its disorder was only external, for a secret influence animated and directed it unknown even to itself. In the same manner as an army possesses chiefs on whose intelligence and courage they rely; so the *quartiers* and sections of Paris had leaders whose orders they obeyed. Secondary popularities, already rooted in the city and faubourgs, had been founded behind those mighty national popularities of Mirabeau, La Fayette, and Bailly. The people felt confidence in such a name, reliance in such an arm, favor for such a face; and when these men showed themselves, spoke, or moved, the multitude followed them without even knowing whither the current of the crowd would lead; it was sufficient for the chiefs to indicate a spot on which to assemble, to spread abroad a panic terror, infuse a sudden rage, or indicate a purpose, to cause the blind masses of the people to assemble on the appointed spot ready for action.

IV.

The spot chosen was most frequently the site of the Bastille, the Mons Aventinus of the people, the national camp where the place and the stones reminded them of their servitude and their strength. Of all the men who governed the agitators of the faubourgs, Danton was the most redoubtable. Camille Desmoulins, equally bold to plan, possessed less courage to execute. Nature, which had given this young man the restlessness of the leaders of the mob, had denied him the exterior and the power of voice necessary to captivate them; for the people do not comprehend intellectual force. A colossal stature and a sonorous voice are two indispensable requisites for the favorites of the people: Camille Desmoulins was small, thin, and had but a feeble voice that seemed to "pipe and whistle in the wind" after the tones of Danton, who possessed the roar of the populace.

Pétion enjoyed the highest esteem of the anarchists, but his official legality excused him from openly fomenting the disorder, which it was sufficient that he desired. Nothing could be done without him, and he was an accomplice.

After them came Santerre, the commander of the battalion of the faubourg St. Antoine. Santerre, son of a Flemish brewer, and himself a brewer, was one of those men that the people respect because they are of themselves, and whose large fortune is forgiven them on account of their familiarity. Well known to the workmen, of whom he employed great numbers in his brewery; and by the populace, who on Sundays frequented his wine and beer establishments—Santerre distributed large sums of money, as well as quantities of provisions, to the poor; and at a moment of famine, had distributed three hundred thousand francs' worth of bread (12,000*l.*) He purchased his popularity by his beneficence; he had conquered it by his courage, at the storming of the Bastille; and he increased it by his presence at every popular tumult. He was of the race of those Belgian brewers who intoxicated the people of Ghent to rouse them to revolt.

The butcher, Legendre, was to Danton what Danton was to Mirabeau, a step lower in the abyss of sedition. Legendre had been a sailor during ten years of his life, and had the rough and brutal manners of his two callings, a savage look, his arms covered with blood, his language merciless, yet his heart naturally good. Involved since '89 in all the Revolutionary movements, the waves of this agitation had elevated him to a certain degree of authority. He had founded, under Danton, the Cordeliers club, the club of *coups de main*, as the Jacobins was the club of radical theories; and he convulsed it to its very centre, by his eloquence untaught and unpolished. He compared himself to the peasant of the Danube. Always more ready to strike than to speak, Legendre's gesture crushed before he spoke. He was the mace of Danton. Huguenin, one of those men who roll from profession to profession, on the acclivity of troublous times, without the power to arrest his course; an advocate expelled from the body to which he belonged; then a soldier, and a clerk at the barrière; always disliked, aspiring for power to recover his fortune, and suspected of pillage. Alexandre, the commandant of the battalion of the Gobelins, the hero of the faubourg, the friend of Legendre. Marat, a living conspiracy, who had quitted his subterranean abode in the night; a living martyr of demagoguism, revelling in excitement, carrying his hatred of society to madness, exulting in it, and voluntarily playing the part of the fool of the people as so many others had played at the courts the part of the king's fool. Dubois Crancé, a brave and educated soldier. Brune, a sabre, at the service of all conspiracies. Mormoro, a printer, intoxicated with philosophy. Dubuisson, an obscure writer, whom the hisses of the theatre had forced to take refuge in intrigue. Fabre d'Eglantine, a comic poet, ambitious of another field for his powers. Chabot, a capuchin monk, embittered by the cloister, and eager to avenge himself on the superstition which had imprisoned him. Lareynie, a soldier-priest. Gonchon, Duquesnois, friends of Robespiere. Carra, a Girondist journalist. An Italian, named Rotondo. Henriot, Sillery, Louvet, Laclos, and Barbaroux, the emissary of Roland and Brissot, were the principal instigators of the *émeute* of the 20th of June.

V.

All these men met in an isolated house at Charenton, to concert in the stillness and secrecy of the night on the pretext, the plan, and the hour of the insurrection. The passions of these men were different, but their impatience was the same; some wished to terrify, others to strike, but all wished to act; when once the people were let loose, they would stop where destiny willed; there were no scruples at a meeting at which Danton presided; speeches were superfluous where but one feeling prevailed; propositions were sufficient, and a look was enough to convey all their meaning. A pressure of the hand, a glance, a significant gesture, are the eloquence of men of action. In a few words, Danton dictated the purpose, Santerre the means, Marat the atrocious energy, Camille Desmoulins the cynical gayety of the projected movement, and all decided on the resolution of urging the people to this act. A revolutionary map of Paris was laid on the table, and on it Danton traced the sources, the tributary streams, the course, and the meeting-place of these gatherings of the people.

The Place de la Bastille, an immense square into which opened, like the mouths of so many rivers, the numerous streets of the faubourg St. Antoine, which joins by the quartier de l'Arsenale and a bridge, the faubourg St. Marceau, and which, by the boulevard, opened before the ancient fortress, has a large opening to the centre of the city and the Tuileries, was the rendezvous assigned, and the place whence the columns were to depart. They were to be divided into three bodies, and a petition to present to the king and Assembly against the *veto* to the decree against the priests and the camp of 20,000 men, was the ostensible purpose of the movement; the recall of the patriot ministers, Roland, Servan, and Clavière, the countersign; and the terror of the people, disseminated in Paris and the château of the Tuileries, the effect of this day. Paris expected this visit of the faubourgs, for five hundred persons had dined together the previous day on the Champs Elysées.

The chief of the *fédérés* of Marseilles and the agitators of the central quarters had fraternized there with the Girondists. The actor Dugazon had sung verses, denunciatory of the inhabitants of the Château; and at his window in the Tuileries the king had heard the applause and these menacing strains, that reached even to his palace. As for the order of the march, the grotesque emblems, the strange weapons, the hideous costumes, the horrible banners, and the obscene language, destined to signal the apparition of this army of the faubourgs in the streets of the capital, the conspirators prescribed nothing, for disorder and horror formed a part of the programme, and they left all to the disordered imagination of the populace, and to that rivalry of cynicism which invariably takes place in such masses of men. Danton relied on this fact.

VI.

Although the presence of Panis and Sergent, two members of the municipality, gave a tacit sanction to the plan, the leaders undertook to recruit the sedition in silence, by small groups during the night, and to collect the fiercest *rassemblements* of the quartier Saint Marceau and the Jardin des Plantes, on the bank of the Arsenale, by means of a ferry, then the only means of communication between the two faubourgs. Lareynie was to arouse the faubourg St. Jacques and the market of the place Maubert, where the women of the lower classes came daily to make their household purchases. To sell and to buy is the life of the lower orders, and money and famine are their two leading passions. They are always ready for tumult in those places where these two passions concentrate, and nowhere is sedition more readily excited, or in greater masses of people.

The dyer Malard, the shoemaker Isambert, the tanner

Gibon, rich and influential artisans, were to pour from the sombre and fetid streets of the faubourg Saint Marceau their indigent population, who but rarely show themselves in the principal quartiers. Alexandre, the military tribune of this quarter of Paris, in which he commanded a battalion, was to place himself at its head on the place, before daybreak, to concentrate the people, and then give them the impulse that should lead them to the quays and the Tuileries. Varlet, Gonchon, Ronsin, and Siret, the lieutenants of Santerre, who had been employed in this system of tactics since the first agitations of '89, were charged with the execution of similar manœuvres in the faubourg St. Antoine. The streets of this quarter, full of manufactories and wine and beer shops, the abiding place of misery, toil, and sedition, which extend from the Bastille to la Roquette and Charenton, contained in themselves alone an army that could invade Paris.

VII.

This army had known its leaders for four years. They posted themselves at the openings of the principal streets, at the hour when the workmen leave the *ateliers;* they procured a chair and table from the nearest and best *cabaret,* and mounting on these wine-stained tribunes, they called by name some of the passers-by, who grouped round them; these stopped others, the street was blocked up by them, and this crowd was increased by all the men, women, and children, attracted by the noise. The orator addressed this motley assemblage, whilst wine or beer were gratuitously handed round. The cessation of work, the scarcity of money, the dearth of food, the manœuvres of the aristocrats to starve Paris, the treacheries of the king, the orgies of the queen, the necessity of the nation's defeating the plots of an Austrian court, were the usual themes of their addresses. When once the agitation rose to fever heat, the cry of "*Marchons*" was heard, and the mob set itself in motion down every street. A few hours afterwards masses of workmen from the quartiers Popincourt, Quinze-Vingts de la Grève, Port au Blé, and the Marché St. Jean, poured from the rues du Faubourg St. Antoine, and covered the Place de la Bastille. There the tumult of the meeting of all these tributaries of sedition for a moment stayed the progress of this living torrent; but the impulse soon carried them on, and the columns instinctively divided themselves, and plunged into the vast outlets and main streets of Paris. Some took the line of the boulevards, others marched along the quays to the Pont Neuf, there encountered the column of the Place Maubert, and poured, in constantly increasing masses, on the Palais Royal, and the gardens of the Tuileries.

Such were the plans ordered on the night of the 19th of June, to be executed by the agitators in the different quartiers, and who separated with a rallying word, which gave the movement of the morrow the excitement and uncertainty of hope, and which, without commanding the consummation of crime, yet authorized the last excesses, "*To make an end of the Château.*"

VIII.

Such was the meeting of Charenton, such were the unseen actors who were to set in motion a million of citizens. Did Laclos and Sillery, who were about to seek a throne for the Duc d'Orleans, their master, in the faubourgs, distribute his gold there? It has been asserted and believed, but never proved, and yet their presence at this meeting is suspicious. History has the right of suspecting without evidence, but never of accusing without proof. The assassination of the king would give the crown the next day to the Duc d'Orleans; Louis XVI. might be assassinated by the weapon of some drunken man—he was not. This is the only justification of the Orleans faction. Some of these men were disaffected, like Marat and Hébert; others, like Barbaroux, Sillery, Laclos, and Carra, were impatient malcontents; and others, like Santerre, were but citizens, whose love of liberty became fanaticism. The conspirators concerted together, and disciplined and organized the city. Individual and distorted passions kindled the mighty and virtuous love of the people for the triumph of democracy. It is thus that in a conflagration the most tainted substances oft light the fire; the combustible matter is foul, but the flames pure; the flame of the Revolution was liberty; the factious might dim, they could not stain, its brightness.

Whilst the conspirators of Charenton distributed their *rôles* and recruited their forces, the king trembled for his wife and children at the Tuileries. "Who knows," said he, to M. de Malesherbes, with a melancholy smile, "whether I shall behold the sun set to-morrow?"

Pétion, by ordering the municipal forces and the national

guards under his orders to résist, could have entirely put down the sedition. The directory of the department, presided over by the unfortunate Duc de la Rochefoucauld, summoned Pétion in the most energetic terms to perform his duty. Pétion smiled, took all on himself, and justified the legality of the proposed meetings and the petitions presented *en masse* to the Assembly.

Vergniaud in the tribune repelled the alarm felt by the constitutionalists, as calumnies against the innocence of the people. Condorcet laughed at the disquietude manifested by the ministers, and the demands for armed force they addressed to the Assembly. "Is it not amusing," said he, addressing his colleagues, "to see the executive power demanding the means of action from the legislators? let them save themselves, it is their trade." Thus derision was united to the plots against the unfortunate monarch; the legislators derided the power their hands had disarmed, and applauded the factious.

IX.

It was under these auspices that the 20th of June dawned. A second council, more secret and less numerous than the former, had assembled the men destined to put these designs into execution, and they only separated at midnight. Each of them went to his post, awoke his most trusty followers, and stationed them in small groups, to stop and assemble together the workmen, as they quitted their homes. Santerre answered for the neutrality of the national guard. "Do not fear," said he; "Pétion will be there." Pétion in reality had on the previous evening ordered the battalions of the national guard to get under arms, not to oppose the columns of the people, but to fraternize with the petitioners and swell the cortège of sedition. This equivocal measure at once saved the responsibility of Pétion to the department, and his complicity before the assembled people; to the one he said, I watch; to the other, I march with you.

At daybreak the battalions were assembled, and their arms piled on all the *grandes places*. Santerre harangued his on the Place de la Bastille, whilst around him flocked an immense throng, agitated, impatient, ready to rush upon the city at his signal. Uniforms and rags were blended, and detachments of invalides, gensd'armes, national guards, and volunteers, received the orders of Santerre, and repeated them to the crowd. An instinctive discipline prevailed amidst this disorder, and the half military half civil appearance of this camp of the people gave the assembly rather the character of a warlike expedition than an *émeute*. This throng recognized leaders, manœuvred at their command, followed their flags, obeyed their voice, and even controlled their impatience to await reinforcements and give detached bodies the appearance of a simultaneous movement. Santerre on horseback, surrounded by a staff of men of the faubourgs, issued his orders, fraternized with the citizens and insurgents, recommended the people to remain silent and dignified, and slowly formed the columns, ready for the signal to march.

X.

At eleven o'clock the people set out for the quartier of the Tuileries. The number of men who left the Place de la Bastille was estimated at twenty thousand: they were divided into three bodies; the first, composed of the battalions of the faubourg, armed with sabres and bayonets, obeyed Santerre; the second, composed of the lowest rabble, without arms, or only armed with pikes and sticks, was under the orders of the demagogue Saint-Huruge; the third, a confused mass of squalid men, women, and children, followed, in a disorderly march, a young and beautiful woman in male attire, a sabre in her hand, a musket on her shoulder, and seated on a cannon drawn by a number of workmen. This was Théroigne de Méricourt.

Santerre was well known: he was the king of the faubourgs. Saint-Huruge had been, since '89, the great agitator of the Palais Royal.

The Marquis de Saint-Huruge, born at Mâcon of a rich and noble family, was one of those men of tumult and disturbances who seem to personify the masses. Gifted by nature with a towering stature and a martial figure, his voice thundered above the roars of the crowd. He had his agitations, his fury, his moments of repentance, and sometimes even of cowardice; his heart was not cruel, but his brain was disturbed. Too aristocratic to be envious, too rich to be a spoliator, too frivolous to be a fanatic by principle, the Revolution turned his brain in the same manner as a rapidly flowing river carries with it the eye that in vain strives to gaze fixedly on it. His life seemed that of a maniac; he loved the Revolution when in motion because it was akin to madness. When yet very young he had sullied his name, ruined his fortune, and forfeited his honors by debauchery, women, and gaming. At the Palais Royal and the neighboring quartiers, the scene of every disorder, he possessed the infamous celebrity of scandal and shame. All the world had heard of him; his family had procured his incarceration in the Bastille, from which the 14th of July had freed him. He had sworn to be avenged, and he kept his oath; a voluntary and indefatigable accomplice of every faction, he had offered his unpaid services to the Duc d'Orleans, Mirabeau, Danton, Camille Desmoulins, the Girondists, and Robespierre: always an adherent of the party who went the greatest lengths; always a leader of those *émutes* that promised the most havoc and ruin. Awake before daybreak, present at every club, he hastened at the slightest noise to swell the crowd; at the smallest tumult to stir men up to more violence. He himself was consumed by the common passion, ere he comprehended its nature; and his voice, his gestures, the expression of his features communicated it to others. He vociferated tales of terror; he disseminated the fever; he electrified the wavering masses; he urged on the current; he was in himself a sedition.

XI.

After Saint-Huruge, marched Théroigne de Méricourt. Théroigne, or Lambertine de Méricourt, who commanded the third corps of the army of the faubourgs, was known among the people by the name of *La Belle Liégoise*. The French Revolution had drawn her to Paris, as the whirlwind attracts things of no weight. She was the impure Joan of Arc of the public streets. Outraged love had plunged her into disorder, and the vice, at which she herself blushed, only made her thirst for vengeance. In destroying the aristocrats she fancied she purified her honor, and washed out her shame in blood.

She was born at the village of Méricourt, near Liége, of a family of wealthy farmers, and had received a finished education. At the age of seventeen her singular loveliness had attracted the attention of a young *seigneur*, whose chateau was close to her residence. Beloved, seduced, and deserted, she had fled from her father's roof and taken refuge in England, from whence, after a residence of some months, she proceeded to France. Introduced to Mirabeau, she knew through him Siéyès, Joseph Chénier, Danton, Ronsin, Brissot, and Camille Desmoulins. Romme, a mystical republican, infused into her mind the German spirit of illuminatism. Youth, love, revenge, and the contact with this furnace of a revolution, had turned her head, and she lived in the intoxication of passions, ideas, and pleasures. Connected at first with the great innovators of '89, she had passed from their arms into those of rich voluptuaries, who purchased her charms dearly. Courtezan of opulence, she became the voluntary prostitute of the people; and like her celebrated prototypes of Egypt or of Rome, she lavished upon liberty the wealth she derived from vice.

On the first assemblage of the people she appeared in the streets, and devoted her beauty to serve as an ensign to the people. Dressed in a riding-habit of the color of blood, a plume of feathers in her hat, a sabre at her side, and two pistols in her belt, she hastened to join every insurrection. She was the first of those who burst open the gates of the Invalides and took the cannon from thence. She was also one of the first to attack the Bastille; and a sabre d'homme was voted her on the breach by the victors. On the days of October, she had led the women of Paris to Versailles, on horseback, by the side of the ferocious Jourdan, called "*the man with the long beard.*" She had brought back the king to Paris: she had followed, without emotion, the heads of the gardes du corps, stuck on pikes as trophies. Her language, although marked by a foreign accent, had yet the eloquence of tumult. She elevated her voice amidst the stormy meetings of the clubs, and from the galleries blamed their conduct. Sometimes she spoke at the Cordeliers. Camille Desmoulins mentions the enthusiasm which her harangues created. "Her similes," says he, "were drawn from the Bible and Pindar,—it was the eloquence of a Judith." She proposed to build the palace of the representative body on the site of the Bastille. "To found and embellish this edifice," said she, "let us strip ourselves of our ornaments, our gold, our jewels. I will be the first to set the example." And with these words she tore off her ornaments in the tribune. Her ascendency during the *émeutes* was so great, that with a single sign she condemned or acquitted a victim; and the royalists trembled to meet her.

During this period, by one of those chances that appear

like the premeditated vengeances of destiny, she recognized in Paris the young Belgian gentleman who had seduced and abandoned her. Her look told him how great was his danger, and he sought to avert it by imploring her pardon. "My pardon," said she; "at what price can you purchase it? My innocence gone—my family lost to me—my brothers and sisters pursued in their own country by the jeers and sarcasms of their kindred; the malediction of my father—my exile from my native land—my enrolment amongst the infamous caste of courtezans; the blood with which my days have been and will be stained; that imperishable curse attached to my name, instead of that immortality of virtue which you have taught me to doubt. It is for this that you would purchase my forgiveness? Do you know any price on earth capable of purchasing it?" The young man made no reply. Théroigne had not the generosity to forgive him, and he perished in the massacres of September. In proportion as the Revolution became more bloody, she plunged deeper into it. She could no longer exist without the feverish excitement of public emotion. However, her early leaning to the Girondist party again displayed itself, and she also wished to stay the progress of the Revolution. But there were women whose power was superior even to her own. These women, called the *furies* of the guillotine, stripped the belle Liégoise of her attire, and publicly flogged her on the terrace of the Tuileries, on the 31st of May. This punishment, more terrible than death, turned her brain, and she was conveyed to a mad-house, where she lived twenty years, which were but one long paroxysm of fury. Shameless and blood-thirsty in her delirium, she refused to wear any garments, as a souvenir of the outrage she had undergone. She dragged herself, only covered by her long white hair, along the flags of her cell, or clung with her wasted hands to the bars of the window, from whence she addressed an imaginary people, and demanded the blood of Suleau.

XII.

After Théroigne de Méricourt came other demagogues less widely known, but already celebrated in their own quartiers, such as Rossignol, the working goldsmith; Brière, a wine-seller; Gonor, the conqueror of the Bastille; Jourdan, surnamed *Coupe-tête;* the famous Polish Jacobin, Lozouski, afterwards buried by the people at the Carrousel;

and Henriot, afterwards the confidential general of the convention. As the columns penetrated into Paris, they were swelled by new groups, that poured forth from the crowded streets that open on the boulevards and the quays. At each influx of these new recruits, a shout of joy burst from the columns, the military bands struck up the air of the *Ça Ira*, the Marseillaise of assassins, whilst the insurgents sang the chorus, and brandished their arms threateningly at the windows of those suspected of being aristocrats.

These weapons did not resemble the arms of regular troops, which excite at once terror and admiration; they were strange and uncouth arms; caught up by the people in the first impulse of fury or defence.* Pikes, lances, spits, cutlasses, carpenters' axes, masons' hammers, shoemakers' knives, paviers' levers, saws, wedges, mattocks, crowbars, the commonest household utensils of the poor, and the rusty iron exposed for sale on the quays, were alike seized upon by the people; and these different weapons, rusted, black, hideous, each of which presented a different manner of inflicting a wound, seemed to increase the horror of death by displaying it in a thousand terrible and unwonted forms. The mixture of all sexes, ages, and conditions; the confusion of costumes and rags beside uniforms, old men beside young; even children, some carried in their mothers' arms, others holding their father's hand or his garments; common prostitutes, their silken dresses soiled and torn, indecency on their brow, and insult on their lips, hundreds of women of the lowest description, and from the dregs of the people, recruited to swell the cortège, and excite commiseration from the garrets of the faubourgs, clothed in tattered finery, pale, emaciated, their eyes hollow, and their cheeks sunken from misery, the personifications of want, in fact the people, in all the disorder, the confusion, the exposure of a city suddenly summoned from its houses, its workshops, its garrets, its scenes and haunts of debauch and infamy; such was the aspect of intimidation which the conspirators wished to give to this scene.

Here and there flags waved above the heads of the multitude. On one was written, *Sanction or death;* on another, *The recall of the patriot ministers;* on the third, *Tremble, tyrant, thine hour is come.* A man, his arms bared to the shoulders, bore a gibbet, from which hung the effigy of a

* Furor arma ministrat.—H. T. R.

crowned female, with the inscription, *Beware the lantern.* Farther on a group of hags raised a *guillotine*, with a card bearing the words, *National Justice on tyrants; death for Veto and his wife.* Amidst all this apparent disorder, a secret system of order was visible. Men in rags, yet whose white hands and shirts of the finest linen pointed them out as of superior rank, wore hats, on which signs of recognition were drawn with white chalk; the crowd regulated their march by them, and followed wherever they went.

The principal body thus marched by the Rue Saint Antoine, and the dark and central avenues of Paris, to the Rue Saint Honoré, the population of these quartiers swelling its numbers at each instant. The more this living torrent increased the more furious it became. Now a band of butchers joined it, each bearing a pike, on which was stuck the bleeding heart of a calf, with the words, *Cœur d'aristocrate.* Next came a band of chiffoniers dressed in rags, and displaying a lance, from which floated a tattered garment, with the inscription, *Tremble, tyrants, here are the sans culottes.* The insult which the aristocracy had cast at poverty, now, when adopted by the people, became the weapon of the nation against the rich.

This army defiled during three hours along the Rue Saint Honoré. Sometimes a terrible silence, only broken by the sound of thousands of feet on the pavement, oppressed the imagination, as the sign of concentrated rage of this multitude; then solitary voices, insulting speeches, and atrocious sarcasms, were mingled with the laughter of the crowd; then sudden and confused murmurs burst from this human sea, and rising to the roofs of the houses, left only the last syllables of their prolonged acclamations audible: *Long live the nation! Long live the sans culottes! Down with the veto!* This tumult reached the salle du Manège, where the Legislative Assembly was then sitting. The head of the cortège stopped at the doors, the columns inundated the court of the Feuillants, the court of the Manège, and all the openings of the salle. These courts, these avenues, these passages, which then masked the terrace of the garden, occupied the space which now extends between the garden of the Tuileries and the Rue Saint Honoré—that central artery of Paris. It was mid-day.

XIII.

Rœderer, the procureur syndic of the directory of the department, a post which in '92 corresponded with that of prefect de Paris, was at this moment at the bar of the Assembly. Rœderer, a partisan of the constitution, of the school of Mirabeau and Talleyrand, was a courageous enemy of anarchy. He found in the constitution the point of reconciliation between his fidelity to the people and his loyalty to the king; and he sought to defend this constitution with every weapon of the law which sedition had not broken in his grasp. "Armed mobs threaten to violate the constitution, the Chamber of Representatives, and the dwelling of the king," said Rœderer at the bar; "the reports of the night are alarming; the minister of the interior calls on us to march troops immediately to defend the château. The law forbids armed assemblies, and yet they advance—they demand admittance; but if you yourselves set an example by suffering them to enter, what will become of the force of the law in our hands? your indulgence will destroy all public force in the hands of the magistrates. We demand to be charged with the fulfilment of all our duties: let the responsibility also be ours, and let nothing diminish the obligation we are under of dying to preserve and defend public tranquillity." These words, worthy the chancellor L'Hôpital, or Mathieu Molé, were coldly listened to by the Assembly, and saluted by ironical laughter from the tribunes. Vergniaud affected to bow to them, and weakened their effect. "Yes, doubtless," said this orator, destined to be torn from the tribune, a year later, by an armed mob,—"doubtless, we should have done better never to have received armed men; for if to-day patriotism brings good citizens hither, aristocracy may to-morrow bring its janissaries. But the error we have committed authorizes that of the people. The assembly, formed up to the present time, appears sanctioned by the silence of the law. It is true that the magistrates demand force to put them down: but what should you do in such circumstances? I think that it would be an excess of severity to be inflexible to a fault, the origin of which is in your decrees: it would be an insult to the citizens to imagine they had any evil designs. It is said that this Assembly wishes to present an address at the château: I do not believe that the citizens who compose it will demand to be presented with arms in their hands to the king: I think that they will obey the laws, and that they will go unarmed, and like simple petitioners. I demand that these citizens be instantly permitted to defile before us." Dumolard and Raymond, indignant at the perfidy or the cowardice of these words, energetically opposed this weakness or complicity of the Assembly. "The best homage to pay the people of Paris," cried Raymond, "is to make them obey their own laws. I demand that before these citizens are introduced they lay down their arms." "Why," returned Guadet, "do you talk of disobedience to the law, when you have so often disobeyed it yourself? you would commit a revolting injustice; you would resemble that Roman emperor who, in order to find more guilty persons, caused the laws to be written in letters so obscure that no one could read them."

The deputation of the insurgents entered at these last words, amidst the bursts of applause and the indignant murmurs of the Assembly.

XIV.

The orator of the deputation, Huguenin, read the petition concerted at Charenton. He declared that the city had risen ready to employ every means of avenging the majesty of the people, whilst he deplored the necessity of staining their hands with the blood of the conspirators. "But," said he, with apparent resignation, "the hour has come; blood must be shed. The men of the 14th of July are not asleep, they had but appeared to be; their awakening is terrible: speak, and we will act. The people is there to judge its enemies: let them choose between Coblentz and ourselves; let them purge the land of their enemies—the tyrants; you know them. The king is not with you: we need no other proof of it than the dismissal of the patriot ministers and the inaction of the armies. Is not the head of the people worth that of kings? Must the blood of patriots flow with impunity to satisfy the pride and ambition of the perfidous château of the Tuileries? If the king does not act, suspend him from his functions: one man cannot fetter the will of twenty-five millions of men. If through respect we suffer him to retain the throne, it is on condition that he observe the constitution. If he depart from this he is no longer anything. And the high court of Orleans," continued Huguenin, "what is that doing?—where are the heads of those it should have doomed to death?" These sinister expressions threw the constitutionalists into alarm, and caused the Girondists to smile. The president, however, replied with a firmness which was not sustained by the attitude of his colleagues. It was decided that the people of the faubourgs should be allowed to defile before them under arms.

XV.

Immediately after this decree was voted, the doors, besieged by the multitude, opened, and admitted thirty thousand petitioners. During this long procession the band played the demagogical airs of the *Carmagnole* and the *Ça Ira*, those *pas de charge* of revolts. Females, armed with sabres, brandished them at the tribunes, who loudly applauded, and danced before a table of stone, on which were engraved the rights of man, like the Israelites before the Ark. The same flags and the same obscene inscriptions visible in the streets, disgraced the temple of the law. The tattered garments, hanging from their lances, the guillotine, and the *potence*, with the effigy of the queen suspended from it, traversed the Assembly with impunity. Some of the deputies applauded, others turned away their heads or hid their faces in their hands; some more courageous, forced the wretch who bore the *cœur saignant*, partly by entreaties, partly by threats, to retire with his emblem of assassination. Part of the people regarded with a respectful eye the salle they profaned; others addressed the representatives as they passed, and seemed to exult in their degradation. The rattling of the strange weapons of the crowd, the clatter of their nailed shoes and sabots on the pavement, the shrill shouts of the women, the voices of the children, the cries of *Vive la nation*, patriotic songs, and the sound of instruments, deafened the ear, whilst to the eye, these rags contrasted strangely with the marbles, the statues, and the decorations of the salle. The miasmas of this horde set in motion tainted the air, and stifled respiration. Three hours elapsed ere all the troop had defiled. The president hastened to adjourn the sitting, in the expectation of approaching excesses.

XVI.

But an imposing force was drawn up in the courts of the Tuileries and the garden, to defend the dwelling of the king against the invasion of the people. Three regiments of the line, two squadrons of gendarmes, several battalions of the national guard, and several pieces of cannon, composed the means of resistance; but the troops, undecided, and acted upon by sedition, were but an appearance of force. The cries of *Vive la nation*, the friendly gestures of the insurgents, the appearance of the women extending their arms towards the soldiers through the palisades, and the presence of the municipal officers, who displayed a disdainful neutrality towards the king, shook the feeling of resistance amongst the troops, who beheld on either side the uniform of the national guard; and between the population of Paris, in whose sentiments they participated, and the château, which was represented to them as full of treason, they no longer knew which it was their duty to obey. In vain did M. Rœderer, a firm organ of the constitution, and the superior officers of the national guard, such as MM. Acloque and De Romainvilliers, present the text of the law, ordering them to repel force by force. The Assembly set the example of complicity; and the mayor, Pétion, by his absence avoided responsibility. The king took refuge in his inviolability; and the troops, abandoned to themselves, could not fail to yield to threats or seduction.

In the interior of the palace, two hundred gentlemen, at the head of whom was the old Marshal De Mouchy, had hastened together at the first news of the king's danger. They were rather the voluntary victims of ancient French honor, than useful defenders of the monarchy. Fearing to excite the jealousy of the national guard and the troops, these gentlemen concealed themselves in the remote apartments of the palace, ready rather to die than to combat: they wore no uniform, and their arms were concealed under their coats—hence the name by which they were pointed out to the people of *Chevaliers du poignard*. Arriving secretly from their provinces to offer their services to the king unknown to each other; and only furnished with a card of entrance to the palace, they hastened thither whenever their was danger. They should have been ten thousand, and were but two hundred—the last reserve of fidelity; but they did their duty without counting their number, and avenged the French nobility for the faults and the desertion of the emigration.

XVII.

The mob, on quitting the Assembly, had marched in close columns to the Carrousel. Santerre and Alexandre, at the head of their battalions, directed the movement. A compact mass of the insurgents, followed by the Rue St. Honoré. The other branches of the populace, cut off from the main body, thronged the courts of the Manège and the Feuillants, and tried to make room for themselves by issuing violently by one of the avenues which communicated with the garden from these courts. A battalion of the national guard defended the approach to this iron gate. The weakness or complaisance of a municipal officer freed the passage, and the battalion fell back, and took up its ground beneath the windows of the Château. The crowd traversed the garden in an oblique direction, and passing before the battalions, saluted them with cries of *Vive la nation!* bidding them take their bayonets from their muskets. The bayonets were removed, and the mob then passed out by the entrance of the Port Royal, and fell back upon the gates of the Carrousel, which shut off this place from the Seine. The guards at these wickets again gave way, to allow a certain number of the malcontents to enter, and then shut the doors. These men, excited by their march, songs, the acclamations of the Assembly, and by intoxication, rushed with furious clamors into the courtyards of the Château. They ran to the principal doors, pressed upon the soldiers on guard, called their comrades without to come to them, and forced the hinges of the royal entrance gate. The municipal officer, Panis, gave orders that it should be opened. The Carrousel was forced, and the mob seemed for a moment to hesitate before the cannon pointed against them, and some squadrons of *gendarmerie*, drawn up in a line of battle. Saint Prix, who commanded the artillery, separated from his guns by a movement of the crowd, sent to the second in command an order to let them fall back in the door of the Château. He refused to obey: "*The Carrousel is forced,*" he said in a loud voice, "*and so must be the Château. Here, artillery men, here is the enemy!*" And he pointed to the king's windows, turned his guns, and levelled them at the palace. The troops following this desertion of the artillery, remained in line, but took the powder from the pans of their muskets in sight of the people, in sign of fraternity, and allowed a free passage to the malcontents.

At this movement of the soldiers, the commandant of the national guard, who witnessed it, called from the court to the grenadiers, whom he saw at the windows of the *Salle des Gardes*, to take their arms, and defend the staircase. The grenadiers, instead of obeying, left the palace by the gallery leading to the garden.

Santerre, Théroigne, and Saint-Huruge hastened by the gate of the palace. The boldest and stoutest of the men in the mob went under the vault which leads from the Carrousel to the garden, dashed the artillerymen on one side, and seizing one of the guns, unlimbered it, and carried it in their arms to the *Salle des Gardes*, on the top of the grand staircase. The crowd, emboldened by this feat of strength and audacity, poured into the apartment and spread like a torrent throughout the staircase and corridors of the Château. All the doors were burst in, or fell beneath the shoulders and axes of the multitude. They shouted loudly for the king; only one door separated them, and this door was already yielding beneath the efforts of levers and blows of pikes from the assailants.

XVIII.

The king, relying on Pétion's promises, and the number of troops with which the palace was surrounded, had seen the assemblage of the mob without uneasiness.

The assault suddenly made on his abode had surprised him in complete security. Retired with the queen, Madame Elizabeth, and his children to the interior apartments on the side of the garden, he had heard the distant thunder of the crowd without expecting that it was so soon to burst upon him. The voices of his frightened servants, flying in all directions, the noise of doors burst open and falling on the floors, the shouts of the people as they approached, threw alarm suddenly amongst the family party, which had met in the king's bedchamber. The prince, confiding, by his look, his wife, sister, and children to the officers and women of the household who surrounded them, went alone to the *Salle du Conseil*. He there found the faithful Marshal de Mouchy, who did not hesitate to offer the last days of his long life to his master; M. d'Hervilly, the commandant of the Constitutional Horse Guard, disbanded a few days previously; the governor Acloque, commandant of the battalion of the faubourg St. Marceau, at first a moderate republican, then overcome by the private virtues of Louis XVI., was his friend, and ready to die for him; three brave grenadiers of the battalion of the faubourg St. Martin, Lecrosnier, Bridau, and Gossé, who alone remained at their post of the interior on the general defection, and ready to protect the king with their bayonets, men of the people, strangers at court, rallied round him by the sole sentiment of duty and affection, only defending the man in the king.

At the moment the king entered this apartment, the doors of the adjacent room, called the *Salle des Nobles*, were dashed in by the blows of the assailants. The king rushed forward to meet the danger. The door-panels fell at his feet, lance heads, iron-shod sticks, spikes were thrust through the opening. Cries of fury, oaths, imprecations accompanied the blows of the axe. The king, in a firm voice, ordered two devoted *valets de chambre*, who accompanied him, Hue, and de Marchais, to open the doors. "What have I to fear in the midst of my people?" said the prince, boldly advancing towards the assailants.

These words, his advancing step, the serenity of his brow, the respect of so many ages for the sacred person of the king, suspended the impetuosity of the ringleaders, and they appeared to hesitate in crossing the threshold they had burst open. During this doubtful moment, the Marshal de Mouchy, Acloque, the three grenadiers and two servants made the king retreat a few paces, and then placed themselves between him and the populace. The grenadiers presented their bayonets, and for a moment kept the crowd at bay. But the increasing mob pushed forward the first ranks. The first who pressed in was a man in rags, with naked arms, haggard eyes, and foaming at the mouth. "Where is the *veto?*" he said, thrusting in the direction of the king's breast a long stick with an iron dart at the end. One of the grenadiers pressed down this stick with his bayonet, and thrust aside the arm of this infuriated creature. The brigand fell at the feet of the citizen, and this act of energy imposed on his companions, and they trampled upon the man as he lay. Pikes, hatchets, and knives were lowered or withdrawn. The majesty of royalty resumed its empire for a moment, and this mob restrained itself at a certain distance from the king, in an attitude rather of brutal curiosity than of ferocity.

XIX.

Several officers of the National Guard, roused by the report of the king's danger, had hastened to join the brave grenadiers, and made a space round Louis XVI. The king, who had but one thought, which was to keep the people away from the apartment in which he had left the queen, ordered the door of the *Salle de Conseil* to be closed behind him. He was followed by the multitude into the salon of the *Œil de Bœuf*, under pretence that this apartment, from its extent, would allow a greater quantity of citizens to see and speak with him. He reached the room surrounded by a vast and turbulent crowd, and was happy at finding that only himself was exposed to blows from weapons of all kinds, which thousands of hands brandished over his head; but as he turned his head he saw his sister, Madame Elizabeth, who extended her arms, and was anxious to rush towards him.

She had escaped from the women who retained the queen and children in the bedchamber. She adored her brother, and wished to die with him. Young, excessively beautiful, and deeply respected at court, for the piety of her life and her passionate devotion to the king, she had renounced all love from her intense affection for her family. Her dishevelled hair, her eyes swimming with tears, her arms extended towards the king, gave to her a despairing and sublime expression. "It is the queen!" exclaimed several women of the faubourgs. This name, at such a moment, was a sentence of death. Some miscreants rushed towards the king's sister with uplifted arms, and were about to strike her, when the officers of the palace undeceived them. The venerated name of Madame Elizabeth made them drop their arms. "Ah! what are you doing?" exclaimed the princess sorrowfully; "let them suppose I am the queen; dying in her place, I might perhaps have saved her." At these words an irresistible movement of the crowd thrust Madame Elizabeth violently from her brother, and drove her into the opening of one of the windows of the *salle*, where the crowd which hemmed her in still contemplated her with respect.

XX.

The king was in a deep recess of the centre window; Acloque, Vaunot, d'Hervilly, twenty volunteers and national guards, made him a rampart with their bodies. Some of the officers drew their swords. "Put your swords into their scabbards," said the king, calmly; "this multitude is more excited than guilty." He got upon a bench in the window, the grenadiers mounted beside him, the others in front of him; they thrust aside, parried, and lowered the sticks, scythes, and pikes lifted above the heads of the people. Ferocious vociferations now rose confusedly from this irritated mass. *"Down with the veto!—the camp of Paris! give us back our patriotic ministers! where is the Austrian woman?"* Some ringleaders advanced from the ranks every moment to utter louder threats and menaces of death to the king. Unable to reach him through the hedge of bayonets crossed in front of him, they waved beneath his eyes and over his head hideous flags, with sinister inscriptions, ragged breeches, the guillotine, the bleeding heart, the gibbet. One of them tried perpetually to reach the king with his lance in his hand; it was the same cutthroat, who, two years before, had washed with his own hands in a pail of water the heads of Berthier and Foulon, and carrying them by the hair to the Quai de la Ferraille, had thrown them amongst the people for symbols of carnage, and incentives to fresh murders.

A fair young man, elegantly dressed, with menacing gesture continually attacked the grenadiers, and cut his fingers with their bayonets in order to move them aside and make a clear passage. "Sire—Sire!" he shouted, "I summon you in the name of one hundred thousand souls who surround me, to sanction the decree against the priests: that is death!" Other persons in the crowd, although armed with drawn swords, pistols and pikes, made no violent gestures, and warded off every attempt on the life of the king. There were even seen expressions of respect and grief in the countenances of a great many. In this review of the Revolution, the people displayed themselves as very terrible, but did not identify themselves with assassins. A certain order began to establish itself in the staircases and apartments; the crowd, pressed by the crowd, after having seen the king, and uttered threats against him, wandered into other apartments, and went triumphantly over this *palace of despotism.*

Legendre the butcher drove before him, in order to find room, these hordes of women and children accustomed to tremble at his voice. He made signs that he desired to speak, and silence being established, the national guard separated a little in order to allow him to address the king "Monsieur!" he exclaimed, in a voice of thunder: the king at this word, which was a degradation, made a movement of offended dignity; "yes, sir," continued Legendre, with more emphasis on the word, "listen to us; you were made to listen to us! you are a traitor! you have deceived us always—you deceive us again; but beware! the measure is heaped up. The people are weary of being your plaything and your victim." Legendre, after these threatening words, read a petition in language as imperious, in which he demanded, in the name of the people, the restitution of the Girondist ministers and the immediate sanction of their decrees. The king replied with intrepid dignity, "I will do what the constitution orders me to do."

XXI.

Scarcely had one sea of people gone away, than another succeeded. At each new invasion of the mob, the strength of the king and the small number of his defenders was exhausted in the renewed struggles with a crowd which never wearied. The doors no longer sufficed to the impatient curiosity of these thousands of men assembled in this pillory of royalty; they entered by the roof, the windows, and the high balconies which open on to the terraces. Their climbing up amused the multitude of spectators crowded in the gardens. The clapping of hands, the cheers of laughter of this multitude without encouraged the assailants. Menacing dialogues in loud tones took place between the malcontents above and the impatient who were below. "Have they struck him?—is he dead?—throw us the heads!" they shouted. Members of the Assembly, Girondist journalists, political characters, Garat, Gorsas, Marat, mingled in this crowd, and uttered their jokes as to this martyrdom of shame to which the king was being subjected. There was for a moment a report of his assassination.

There was no cry of horror thereat among the populace, which raised its eyes towards the balcony, expecting to see the carcass. Still, in the very whirlwind of its passion, the multitude appeared to require reconciliation. One of the multitude handed a *bonnet rouge* to Louis XVI. at the end of a pike. "Let him put it on! let him put it on!" exclaimed the mob; "it is the sign of patriotism; if he puts it on we will believe in his good faith." The king made a signal to one of his grenadiers to hand him the *bonnet rouge*, and smiling, he put it on his head; and then arose shouts of

Vive le Roi! The people had crowned its chief with the symbol of liberty, the cap of democracy replaced the bandeau of Rheims. The people were conquerors, and felt appeased.

However, fresh orators, mounting on the shoulders of their comrades, demanded incessantly of the king, sometimes by entreaties, sometimes with threats, to promise the recall of Roland, and the sanction of the decrees. Louis XVI., invincible in his constitutional resistance, eluded, or refused to acquiesce in the injunctions of the malcontents. "Guardian of the prerogative of the executive power, I will not surrender to violence," he answered: "this is not the moment for deliberation, when it is impossible to deliberate freely." "Do not fear, sire," said a grenadier of the national guard to him. "My friend," was the king's reply, taking his hand, and placing it on his breast, "place your hand there, and see if my heart beats quicker than usual." This action, and the language of unshaken intrepidity, seen and heard in the crowd, had its effect on the rebels.

A fellow in tatters, holding a bottle in his hand, came towards the king, and said, "If you love the people, drink to their health!" Those who surrounded the prince, afraid of poison as much as the poniard, entreated the king not to drink. Louis XVI., extending his arm, took the bottle, raised it to his lips, and drank "to the nation!" This familiarity with the multitude, represented by a beggar, consummated the king's popularity. Renewed cries of *Vive le Roi!* burst from all tongues and reached even the staircases: these cries created consternation in the terrace of the garden amongst the groups who were expecting a victim, and thus learnt that his executioners were softened.

XXII.

Whilst the unfortunate prince thus contended alone against a whole people, the queen, in another apartment, was undergoing the same outrages and the same torments; more hated than the king, she ran more risks. Agitated nations require to have their hatreds personified as well as their love. Marie Antoinette represented in the eyes of the nation all the corruptions of courts, all the pride of despotism, and all the infamies of treason. Her beauty, her youthful inclination for pleasure, tenderness of heart provoked by calumny into excesses, the blood of the house of Austria, her pride, which she derived from her nature even more than from her blood, her close connection with the Comte D'Artois, her intrigues with the emigrants, her presumed complicity with the coalition, the scandalous or infamous libels disseminated against her for four years—made this princess the spied victim of public opinion. The women despised her as a guilty wife, the patriots detested her as a conspirator, political men feared her as the counsellor of the king. The name of *Autrichienne* which the people gave her, summed up all their alleged wrongs against her. She was the unpopularity of a throne of which she should have been the grace and forgiveness.

Marie Antoinette was aware of this hatred of the people to her person. She knew that her presence beside the king would be a provocation to assassination. This was the motive that restrained her to remain alone with her children in the bedchamber. The king hoped that she was forgotten. but it was the queen particularly the women of this mob sought and called for in terms the most offensive for a wife, a woman, and a queen.

The king was scarcely surrounded by the masses of people in the *Œil de Bœuf* than the doors of the sleeping apartment were beset with the same uproar and violence. But this party was principally composed of women. Their weaker arms were not so efficient against oaken panels and stout hinges. They called to their assistance the men who had carried the piece of ordinance into the *Salle des Gardes*, and they hastened to them. The queen was standing up, pressing her two children to her bosom, and listening with mortal anxiety to the vociferations at her door. She had near her no one but M. de Lajard, minister of war,—alone, powerless, but devoted; a few ladies of her suite, and the Princesse de Lamballe, that friend of her happy and unhappy hours. Daughter-in-law of the Duc de Penthièvre, and sister-in-law of the Duc d'Orleans, the Princesse de Lamballe had succeeded in the queen's heart to that deep affection which Marie Antoinette had long entertained for the Comtesse de Polignac. The friendship of Marie Antoinette was adoration. Chilled by the coldness of the king, who had the virtues only, and not the graces of a husband; detested by the people, weary of the throne, she gave vent in private predilections to the overflow of a heart equally desirous and void of sentiment. This favoritism was even accused; the queen was calumniated in her very friendships

The Princesse de Lamballe, a widow at eighteen, free from any suspicion of levity, above all ambition and every interest from her rank and fortune, loved the queen as a friend. The more adverse were the fortunes of Marie Antoinette, the more did her young favorite desire to share them with her. It was not greatness, but misfortune, that attracted her. *Surintendante* of the household, she lodged in the Tuileries, in an apartment adjacent to the queen, to share with her her tears and her dangers. She was sometimes obliged to be absent, in order to go to the Château de Vernon to watch over the old Duc de Penthièvre. The queen, who foresaw the coming storm, had written to her some days before the 20th of June a touching letter, entreating her not to return. This letter, found in the hair of the Princesse de Lamballe after her assassination, and *unknown until now*, discloses the tenderness of the one and the devotion of the other.

"Do not leave Vernon, my dear Lamballe, before you are perfectly recovered. The good Duc de Penthièvre would be sorry and distressed, and we must all take care of his advanced age, and respect his virtues. I have so often told you to take heed of yourself, that if you love me you must think of yourself; we shall require all our strength in the times in which we live. Oh, do not return, or return as late as possible. Your heart would be too deeply wounded; you would have too many tears to shed over my misfortunes, you who love me so tenderly. This race of tigers which infests the kingdom would cruelly enjoy itself if it knew all the sufferings we undergo. Adieu, my dear Lamballe; I am always thinking of you, and you know I never change."

Madame Lamballe, contrary to this advice, made all haste to return, and clung to the queen as though she sought to be struck with the same blow. By her side were also other courageous women,—the Princesse de Tarente, Latrémouille, Mesdames de Tourzel, de Mackau, de La Roche-Aymon.

M. de Lajard, a cool soldier, responsible to the king and himself for so many dear and sacred lives, collected in haste by the secret passages which communicated with the sleeping chamber and the interior of the palace, several officers and national guards wandering about in the tumult. He had the queen's children brought to her, in order that their presence and appearance, by softening the mob, might serve as a buckler to their mother. He himself opened the doors. He placed the queen and her ladies in the depth of the window. They wheeled in front of this the massive council-table, in order to interpose a barrier between the weapons of the malcontents and the lives of the royal family. Some national guards were around the table, on each side, and rather in advance of it. The queen, standing up, held by the hand her daughter, then fourteen years of age.

A child of noble beauty and precocious maturity, the anxieties of the family in the midst of whom she had grown up had already reflected their weight and sorrow in her features. Her blue eyes, her lofty brow, aquiline nose, light-brown hair, floating in long waves down her shoulders, recalled at the decline of the monarchy those young girls of the Gauls who graced the throne of the earlier races. The young daughter pressed closely against her mother's bosom, as though to shield her with her innocence. Born amidst the early tumults of the Revolution, dragged to Paris captive amidst the blood of the 6th of October, she only knew the people by its turbulence and rage. The dauphin, a child of seven years old, was seated on the table in front of the queen. His innocent face, radiant with all the beauty of the Bourbons, expressed more surprise than fear. He turned to his mother at every moment, raising his eyes towards her as though to read through her tears whether he should have confidence or alarm. It was thus that the mob found the queen as it entered and defiled triumphantly before her. The calming produced by the firmness and confidence of the king was already perceptible in the faces of the multitude. The most ferocious of the men were softened in the presence of weakness—beauty—childhood. A lovely woman, a queen, humiliated,—a young innocent girl,—a child, smiling at his father's enemies, could not fail to awaken sensibility even in hatred. The men of the suburbs moved on silent, and as if ashamed, before this group of humiliated greatness. Some of them the more cowardly made as they passed derisive or vulgar gestures, which were a dishonor to the insurrection. Their indignant accomplices checked them in their insolence, and made these dastards quit the room as speedily as possible. Some even addressed looks of sympathy and compassion, others smiles, and others a few familiar words to the dauphin. Conversations, half menacing, half respectful, were exchanged between the child and the throng. "If you love the nation," said a volunteer to the queen, "put the *bonnet rouge* on your son's head." The queen took the *bonnet rouge* from this man's hands, and placed it herself on the dauphin's head. The astonished child took these insults as play. The men applauded, but the women, more implacable towards a woman, never ceased their invectives. Obscene words, borrowed from the sinks of the fish-market, for the first time echoed in the vaults of the palace, and in the ears of these children. Their ignorance in not comprehending their meaning saved them from this horror. The queen, whilst she blushed to the eyes, did not allow her offended modesty to lessen her lofty dignity. It was evident that she blushed for the people, for her children, and not for herself. A young girl, of pleasing appearance and respectably attired, came forward and bitterly reviled in coarsest terms *l'Autrichienne.* The queen, struck by the contrast between the rage of this young girl and the gentleness of her face, said to her in a kind tone, "Why do you hate me? Have I ever unknowingly done you any injury or offence?" "No, not to me," replied the pretty patriot; "but it is you who cause the misery of the nation." "Poor child!" replied the queen; "some one has told you so, and deceived you. What interest can I have in making the people miserable? The wife of the king, mother of the dauphin, I am a Frenchwoman by all the feelings of my heart as a wife and mother. I shall never again see my own country. I can only be happy or unhappy in France. I was happy when you loved me."

This gentle reproach affected the heart of the young girl, and her anger was effaced in a flood of tears. She asked the queen's pardon, saying, "I did not know you, but I see that you are good." At this moment Santerre made his way through the crowd. Easily moved, and sensitive though coarse, Santerre had roughness, impetuosity, and feelings easily affected. The faubourgs opened before him and trembled at his voice. He made an imperious sign for them to leave the apartment, and thrust these men and women by the shoulders towards the door in front of the *Œil de Bœuf.* The current advanced by opposite issues of the palace, and the heat was suffocating. The dauphin's brow reeked with perspiration beneath the *bonnet rouge.* "Take the cap off the child," shouted Santerre; "don't you see he is half stifled." The queen darted a mother's glance at Santerre, who came towards her, and placing his hand on the table, he leaned towards Marie Antoinette and said, in an under tone, "You have some very awkward friends, madame; I know those who would serve you better!" The queen looked down, and was silent. It was from this moment that may be dated the secret understanding which she established with the agitators of the faubourgs. The leading malcontents received the queen's entreaties with complacency. Their pride was flattered in raising the woman whom they had degraded. Mirabeau, Barnave, Danton had in turns sold or offered to sell the influence of their popularity. Santerre merely offered his compassion.

XXIII.

The Assembly had again resumed its sitting on the news of the invasion of the Château. A deputation of twenty-four members was sent as a safeguard for the king. Arriving too late, these deputies wandered in the crowded courtyard, vestibules, and staircases of the palace. Although they felt repugnance at the idea of the last crime being committed on the person of the king, they were not very grievously afflicted in their hearts at this long-threatened insult to the court. Their steps were lost in the crowd, their words in the uproar. Vergniaud himself, from a top step of the grand staircase, vainly appealed to order, legality, and the constitution. The eloquence, so powerful to incite the masses, is powerless to check them. From time to time the royalist deputies, highly indignant, returned to the chamber, and, mounting the tribune, with their clothes all in disorder, reproached the Assembly with its indifference. Amongst these more conspicuously, Vaublanc, Ramond, Becquet, Girardin. Mathieu Dumas, La Fayette's friend, exclaimed, as he pointed to the windows of the Château, "I am just come from there; the king is in danger! I have this moment seen him, and can bear witness to the testimony of my colleagues MM. Isnard and Vergniaud, in their unavailing efforts to restrain the people. Yes, I have seen the hereditary representative of the nation, insulted, menaced, degraded! I have seen the *bonnet rouge* on his head. You are responsible for this to posterity!" They replied to him by ironical laughter and uproarious shouts. "Would you imply that the *bonnet* of patriots is a disgraceful mark for a king's brow?" said the Girondist, Lasource; "will it not be believed that we are uneasy as to the king's safety? Let us not insult the people by lending it sentiments which it does not possess. The people do not menace either the person of Louis XVI. or the prince royal. They will not commit excess or violence. Let us adopt measures of mildness and conciliation." This was the perfidious lulling of Pétion, and the Assembly was put to sleep by such language.

XXIV.

Pétion himself could not for any length of time feign ignorance of the gathering of 40,000 persons in Paris since the morning, and the entry of this armed mob into the Assembly and the Maison of the Tuileries. His prolonged absence recalled to mind the sleep of La Fayette on the 6th of October; but the one was an accomplice, and the other innocent. Night approached, and might conceal in its shades the disorders and attempts which would go even beyond the views of the Girondists. Pétion appeared in the courtyard, amidst shouts of *Vive Pétion!* They carried him in their arms to the lowest steps of the staircase, and he entered the apartment where for three hours Louis XVI. had been undergoing these outrages. "I have only just learned the situation of your majesty," said Pétion. "That is very astonishing," replied the king, in a tone of deep indignation, "for it is a long time that it has lasted."

Pétion, mounted on a chair, then made several addresses to the mob, without inducing it to move in the least. At length, being put on the shoulders of four grenadiers, he said, "Citizens, male and female, you have used with moderation and dignity your right of petition; you will finish this day as you began it. Hitherto your conduct has been in conformity with the law, and now in the name of the law I call upon you to follow my example and to retire."

The crowd obeyed Pétion, and moved off slowly through the long avenue of apartments of the château. Scarcely had the mass begun to grow perceptibly less, than the king, released by the grenadiers from the recess in which he had been imprisoned, went to his sister, who threw herself into his arms: he went out of the apartment with her by a side door, and hastened to join the queen in her apartment. Marie Antoinette, sustained until then by her pride against showing her tears, gave way to the excess of her tenderness and emotion, on again beholding the king. She threw herself at his feet, and clasping his knees, sobbed bitterly but not loudly. Madame Elizabeth and the children, locked in each other's arms, and all embraced by the king, who wept over them, rejoiced at finding each other as if after a shipwreck and their mute joy was raised to heaven with astonishment and gratitude for their safety. The faithful national guard, the generals attached to the king, Marshal de Mouchy, M. d'Aubier, Acloque, congratulated the king on the courage and presence of mind he had displayed. They mutually related the perils which they had escaped, the infamous remarks, gestures, looks, arms, costumes, and sudden repentance of this multitude. The king at this moment having accidentally passed a mirror, saw on his head the *bonnet rouge*, which had not been taken off; he turned very red, and threw it at his feet, then casting himself into an arm-chair, he raised his handkerchief to his eyes, and looking at the queen, exclaimed, "Ah, madame! why did I take you from your country to associate you with the ignominy of such a day?"

XXV.

It was eight o'clock in the evening. The agony of the royal family had lasted for five hours. The national guard of the neighboring quarters, assembling by themselves, arrived singly in order to lend their aid to the constitution. There were still heard from the king's apartment tumultuous footsteps, and the sinister cries of the columns of people, who were slowly filing off by the courts and garden. The constitutional deputies ran about in indignation, uttering imprecations against Pétion and the Gironde. A deputation of the Assembly went over the château, in order to take cognizance of the violence and disorder resulting from this visitation of the faubourgs. The queen pointed out to them the forced locks, the bursten hinges, the bludgeons, pike irons, panels, and the pieces of cannon loaded with small shot, placed on the threshold of the apartment. The disorder of the attire of the king, his sister, the children, the *bonnets rouges*, the cockades forcibly placed on their heads; the dishevelled hair of the queen, her pale features, the tremulousness of her lips, her eyes streaming with tears, were tokens more evident than these spoils left by the people on the battle ground of sedition. This spectacle moistened the eyes, and excited the indignation, even of the deputies most hostile to the court. The queen saw this: "You weep, sir?" she said to Merlin. "Yes, madame," replied the stoic deputy; "I weep over the misfortunes of the woman, the wife, and the mother; but my sympathy goes no further. I hate kings and queens!"

Such was the day of the 20th of June. The people dis

played discipline in disorder, and forbearance in violence: the king, heroic intrepidity in his resignation; and some of the Girondists, a cold brutality which gives to ambition the mask of patriotism.

XXVI.

Everything was preparing in the departments to send to Paris the 20,000 troops ordered by the Assembly. The Marseillais, summoned by Barbaroux at the instigation of Madame Roland, were approaching the capital. It was the fire of the soul in the south coming to rekindle the revolutionary hearth, which, as the Girondists believed, was failing in Paris. This body of twelve or fifteen hundred men was composed of Genoese, Ligurians, Corsicans, Piedmontese, banished from their country and recruited suddenly on the shores of the Mediterranean; the majority sailors or soldiers accustomed to warfare, and some bandits, hardened in crime. They were commanded by young men of Marseilles, friends of Barbaroux and Isnard. Rendered fanatic by the climate and the eloquence of the provincial clubs, they came on amidst the applauses of the population of central France, received, fêted, overcome by enthusiasm and wine at the patriotic banquets which hailed them in constant succession on their way. The pretext of their march was to fraternize, at the federation of the 14th of July,* with the other *fédérés* of the kingdom. The secret motive was to intimidate the Parisian national guard, to revive the energy of the faubourgs, and to be the vanguard of that camp of 20,00 men which the Girondists had made the Assembly vote, in order at the same time to control the Feuillants, the Jacobins, the king, and the Assembly itself, with an army from the departments wholly composed of their creatures. The sea of people was violently agitated on their approach. The national guard, the *fédérés*, the popular societies, children, women, all that portion of the population which lives on excitement of the streets, and runs after public spectacles, flew to meet the Marseillais. Their bronzed faces, martial appearance, eyes of fire, uniforms covered with the dust of their journey, their Phrygian head-dress, their strange weapons, the guns they dragged after them, the green branches which shaded their *bonnets rouges*, their strange language mingled with

* It was on the 30th July, 1792, that the Marseillais arrived in Paris —H. T. R.

oaths, and accentuated by savage gestures, all struck the imagination of the multitude with great force. The revolutionary idea appeared to have assumed the guise of a mortal, and to be marching under the aspect of this horde, to the assault of the last remnant of royalty. They entered the cities and villages beneath triumphal arches. They sang terrible songs as they progressed. Couplets, alternated by the regular noise of their feet on the road, and by the sound of drums, resembled chorusses of the country and war, answering at intervals to the clash of arms and weapons of death in a march to combat. This song is graven on the soul of France.

XXVII.

THE MARSEILLAISE.

I.

Allons, enfants de la patrie,
Le jour de gloire est arrivé !
Contre nous, de la tyrannie
L'étendart sanglant est levé.
Entendez vous dans ces campagnes
Mugir ces féroces soldats !
Ils viennent jusque dans vos bras
Egorger vos fils et vos compagnes !—
Aux armes, citoyens ! formez vos bataillons !
Marchons ! qu'un sang impur abreuve nos sillons !

II.

Que veut cette horde d'esclaves,
De traîtres, de rois conjurés ?
Pour qui ces ignobles entraves
Ces fers dès longtemps préparés ?
Français, pour vous, ah ! quel outrage,
Quels transports il doit exciter !
C'est vous qu'on ose méditer
De rendre à l'antique esclavage ;
Aux armes, &c.

III.

Quoi ! ces cohortes étrangères
Feraient la loi dans nos foyers ?
Quoi ! ces phalanges mercenaires
Terrasseraient nos pères guerriers ?
Grand Dieu ! par des mains enchainées,
Nos fronts sous le joug se ploieraient ;
De vils despotes deviendraient
Les maîtres de nos destineés !
Aux armes, &c.

IV.

Tremblez, tyrans! et vous, perfides,
L'opprobre de tous les partis!
Tremblez, vos projets parricides
Vont enfin recevoir leur prix!
Tout est soldat pour vous combattre:
S'ils tombent nos jeunes héros,
La France en produit les nouveaux,
Contre vous tout prêts à se battre.
Aux armes, &c.

V.

Français, en guerriers magnanimes,
Portez ou retenez vos coups;
Epargnes ces tristes victimes
A regret s'armant contre vous.
Mais ces despotes sanguinaires,
Mais les complices de Bouillé,
Tous ces tigres sans pitié
Déchirent le sein de leur mère.
Aux armes, &c.

VI

Amour sacré de la patrie,
Conduis, soutiens nos bras vengeurs!
Liberté, liberté chérie,
Combats avec tes défenseurs!
Sous nos drapeaux que la Victoire
Accoure à tes mâles accents;
Que tes ennemis expirants
Voient ton triomphe et notre gloire!
Aux armes, &c.

VERSE SUNG BY CHILDREN.

Nous entrerons dans la carrière,
Quand nos aînés n'y seront plus;
Nous y trouverons leur poussière,
Et la trace de leurs vertus!
Bien moins jaloux de leur survivre
Que de partager leur cercueil,
Nous aurons le sublime orgueil
De les venger ou de les suivre!
Aux armes, &c.*

---

* M. Lamartine has not in his work given the verses 3, 4, and 5; we have therefore supplied them, that "The Marseillaise" may be complete. The Marseillais ruffians entered Paris on the 30th July, 1792, by the Faubourg Saint-Antoine (the St. Giles's of Paris,) and headed by Santerre, went to the Champs Elysées, thus traversing the whole city from south to north,) where a banquet awaited them. Their arrival was marked by riots and bloodshed—Duhamel was murdered. This celebrated song was written by Rouget de Lisle, who also composed the air.

XXVIII.

These words were sung in notes alternately flat and sharp which seemed to come from the breast with sullen mutterings of national anger, and then with the joy of victory. They had something as solemn as death, but as serene as the undying confidence of patriotism. It seemed a recovered echo of Thermopylæ—it was heroism sung.

There was heard the regular footfall of thousands of men walking together to defend the frontiers over the resounding soil of their country, the plaintive notes of women, the wailing of children, the neighing of horses, the hissing of flames as they devoured palaces and huts; then gloomy strokes of vengeance, striking again and again with the hatchet, and immolating the enemies of the people, and the profaners of the soil. The notes of this air rustled like a flag dipped in gore, still reeking in the battle plain. It made one tremble —but it was the shudder of intrepidity which passed over the heart, and gave an impulse—redoubled strength—veiled death. It was the "fire-water" of the Revolution, which instilled into the senses and the soul of the people the intoxication of battle. There are times when all people find thus gushing into their national mind accents which no man hath written down, and which all the world feels. All the senses desire to present their tribute to patriotism, and eventually to encourage each other. The foot advances—gesture animates—the voice intoxicates the ear—the ear shakes the heart. The whole heart is inspired like an instrument of enthusiasm. Art becomes divine; dancing, heroic; music, martial; poetry, popular. The hymn which was at that moment in all mouths will never perish. It is not profaned on common occasions. Like those sacred banners suspended from the roofs of holy edifices, and which are only allowed to leave them on certain days, we keep the national song as an extreme arm for the great necessities of the country. Ours was illustrated by circumstances, whence issued a peculiar character, which made it at the same time

On the 18th Nivose, an. IV. (8th January, 1795,) an order of the Directory enjoined that at all theatres and sights the air of the "Marseillaise," and those of "Ca Ira,—Veillons au Salut de l'Empire," and "Le Chant du Depart," should be played. Louget de Lisle was an officer of engineers in 1790, and in spite of his republican opinions, incarcerated during the reign of terror, and only saved by the 9th Thermidor. He would assuredly have been accompanied to the guillotine by his own song.—H. T. R.

more solemn and more sinister: glory and crime, victory and death, seemed intertwined in its chorus. It was the song of patriotism, but it was also the imprecation of rage. It conducted our soldiers to the frontier, but it also accompanied our victims to the scaffold. The same blade defends the heart of the country in the hand of the soldier, and sacrifices victims in the hand of the executioner.

XXIX.

The *Marseillaise* preserves notes of the song of glory and the shriek of death: glorious as the one, funereal like the other, it assures the country, whilst it makes the citizen turn pale. This is its history.

There was then a young officer of artillery in garrison at Strasburg, named Rouget de Lisle. He was born at Lons-le-Saunier, in the *Jura*, that country of reverie and energy, as mountainous countries always are. This young man loved war like a soldier—the Revolution like a thinker. He charmed with his verses and music the slow dull garrison life. Much in request from his twofold talent as musician and poet, he visited the house of Dietrick, an Alsatian patriot (*maire of Strasbourg*), on intimate terms. Dietrick's wife and young daughters shared in his patriotic feelings, for the Revolution was advancing towards the frontiers, just as the affections of the body always commence at the extremities. They were very partial to the young officer, and inspired his heart, his poetry, and his music. They executed the first of his ideas hardly developed, confidantes of the earliest flights of his genius.

It was in the winter of 1792, and there was a scarcity in Strasburg. The house of Dietrick was poor, and the table humble; but there was always a welcome for Rouget de Lisle. This young officer was there from morning to night, like a son or brother of the family. One day, when there was only some coarse bread and slices of ham on the table, Dietrick, looking with calm sadness at De Lisle, said to him, "Plenty is not seen at our feasts; but what matter if enthusiasm is not wanting at our civic fêtes, and courage in our soldiers' hearts. I have still a bottle of wine left in my cellar. Bring it," he added, addressing one of his daughters, "and we will drink to liberty and our country. Strasburg is shortly to have a patriotic ceremony, and De Lisle must be inspired by these last drops to produce one of those hymns which convey to the soul of the people the enthusiasm which suggested it." The young girls applauded, fetched the wine, filled the glasses of their old father and the young officer until the wine was exhausted. It was midnight, and very cold. De Lisle was a dreamer; his heart was moved, his head heated. The cold seized on him, and he went staggering to his lonely chamber, endeavoring, by degrees, to find inspiration in the palpitations of his citizen heart; and on his small clavicord, now composing the air before the words, and now the words before the air, combined them so intimately in his mind, that he could never tell which was first produced, the air or the words, so impossible did he find it to separate the poetry from the music, and the feeling from the impression. He sung everything—wrote nothing.

XXX.

Overcome by this divine inspiration, his head fell sleeping on his instrument, and he did not awake until daylight. The song of the over night returned to his memory with difficulty, like the recollections of a dream. He wrote it down, and then ran to Dietrick. He found him in his garden. His wife and daughters had not yet risen. Dietrick aroused them, called together some friends as fond as himself of music, and capable of executing De Lisle's composition. Dietrick's eldest daughter accompanied them, Rouget sang. At the first verse all countenances turned pale, at the second tears flowed, at the last enthusiasm burst forth. The hymn of the country was found. Alas! it was also destined to be the hymn of terror. The unfortunate Dietrick went a few months afterwards to the scaffold to the sound of the notes produced at his own fireside, from the heart of his friend, and the voices of his daughters.

The new song, executed some days afterwards at Strasburg, flew from city to city, in every public orchestra. Marseilles adopted it to be sung at the opening and the close of the sittings of its clubs. The Marseillais spread it all over France, by singing it everywhere on their way. Whence the name of *Marseillaise.* De Lisle's old mother, a royalist and religious, alarmed at the effect of her son's voice, wrote to him: "What is this revolutionary hymn, sung by bands of brigands, who are traversing France, and with which our name is mingled?" De Lisle himself, proscribed as a royalist, heard it and shuddered, as it sounded on his ears, whilst escaping by some of the wild passes of the Alps. "What do they call that hymn?" he inquired of his guide. "The *Marseillaise*," replied the peasant. It was thus he learnt the name of his own work. The arm turned against the hand that forged it. The Revolution, insane, no longer recognized its own voice!

END OF THE FIRST VOLUME.

www.ingramcontent.com/pod-product-compliance
Lightning Source LLC
LaVergne TN
LVHW020915110826
845150LV00004B/682

* 9 7 8 1 4 2 5 5 5 5 9 9 3 *